ABOUT THE AUTHOR

Austin Buckley is Managing Director, Corporate Broking, Coyle Hamilton Ltd. in Cork. He has almost forty years of practical experience in the insurance industry, both in Ireland and London. In his current capacity, he is responsible for the servicing and development of major corporate accounts; he has also been involved in the settlement of some of the largest and most complicated claims in Ireland in recent times. He is a Chartered Insurance Practitioner, a fellow of the Chartered Insurance Institute and a member of the Society of Fellows of the Institute. He completed BCL (Hons) and LLM (Hons) degrees from University College, Cork.

Insurance Law in Ireland

Austin J. Buckley LLM FCII

Oak Tree Press
Dublin

Oak Tree Press
Merrion Building
Lower Merrion Street
Dublin 2, Ireland

A catalogue record of this book is
available from the British Library

ISBN 1-86076-066-X paperback
ISBN 1-86076-078-3 hardback

Printed in Ireland by Colour Books Ltd.

To Noreen

CONTENTS

FOREWORD

Since its introduction into our country, the insurance industry has had an indelible impact on Irish life — an impact which goes far beyond mere economic considerations. It has given a sense of safety and security to literally millions of people. These incalculable benefits can often be forgotten in the midst of public debate over premium levels or policy limitations. Insurance is something virtually every adult citizen has experience of, and few are without something to say on the matter.

However, while opinion on the state of the insurance industry in Ireland is not hard to find, expert opinion is another matter. This is particularly so in relation to the regulation of insurance matters by law. This is a vast and complex field, which affects the interests of a majority of citizens in this State; yet academic output to date has been minimal. One can imagine the relief, then, with which I, and my colleagues in every branch of the legal profession, greet this admirable new work on the subject. Not that its usefulness will be confined to the courtroom; for there is a clarity of presentation and lucidity of thought in this book which will benefit any interested party, whatever their prior knowledge of the topic.

Mr Buckley has nigh on four decades of practical experience in the insurance industry. He is thus uniquely qualified to pick out the areas in this vast field of particular interest to practitioners and the general public alike. To this experience he has added the academic qualifications in law which allow him to bridge the gap between the two disciplines and provide us, the readers, with a well-rounded account of this most important subject.

While the aim of the book is to outline the general principles governing the practice of insurance in Ireland, the author does not shy away from in-depth discussion of individual cases where required — as for example, the marathon case of *Superwood Holdings plc v Sun Alliance and London Insurance and Others* (Unreported Supreme

Court, 1995). While not afraid to explore the influence of English law and English court decisions on insurance in Ireland, he is to be especially commended for his dedication to finding and bringing to our notice existing Irish caselaw on the subject. A glance at the table of cases at the beginning of the book reveals the extent of his diligence. There are unreported High Court and Supreme Court decisions from as early as 1956 to as late as 1997; I noted also a reference to an unreported decision of the English Court of Appeal from 1977.

It is scholarship of this kind which leads to a book becoming the standard work in its field, and I confidently expect that the fruit of Mr Buckley's labours will be adopted by all and sundry as a readable, comprehensive and trustworthy guide to the intricacies of insurance law in Ireland.

Oak Tree Press is to be congratulated on providing a book which is relevant, learned and a welcome addition to Irish legal literature.

The Hon Mr Justice Liam Hamilton,
Chief Justice,
The Supreme Court.

PREFACE

*"Every area of trouble gives out a ray of hope, and the one un-
changeable certainty is that nothing is certain or unchange-
able." John F. Kennedy*

Insurance is one of a number of devices for handling risk. It manages
risk by substituting certainty for uncertainty. The theory is that the
equitably defined contributions of the many should make good the
losses of the few. In Ireland, insurance has become an emotive topic.
The increasing cost of the contributions to the fund, out of which the
losses of the few are met, and the cost of pursuing compensation
claims through the courts, have made insurance a live political issue.
Pressure from consumer and business interests led the Government,
in June 1995, to commission a report on the "Economic Evaluation of
Insurance Costs in Ireland", which was delivered by Deloitte &
Touche in October 1996. The recommendations in the report are currently "under consideration". I make no attempt in this book to address the political or emotive issues which surround insurance and
the law in Ireland. Neither do I attempt to deal with the law governing the regulation of insurance companies, life assurance, investment
intermediaries or the recent controversies surrounding such intermediaries. The law and practice of pensions in Ireland has already
been comprehensively covered in a work co-authored by a colleague.

What I am attempting to do in this book is to provide an insight
into the principles and practice of general insurance in Ireland and to
the law governing them. While I have attempted to avoid excessive
use of technical insurance jargon, I have tried to make the book sufficiently detailed to be of practical use and value to lawyers, practitioners and students of the subject. The topics and subjects covered in
this book are those which, on the basis of almost 40 years practical
experience, I believe are most relevant to practitioners of law and insurance.

I have made every effort to quote Irish authorities where possible. The reality, however, is that the majority of disputes concerning insurance contracts in Ireland, do not ever get to hearing in the courts. The arbitration clause in Irish insurance policies, unlike its English counterpart, requires all disputes under a policy to be referred to arbitration. Consequently, what judicial decisions there are cover but a small number of the basic insurance principles and the intricacies of the law relating to them. We therefore have to rely heavily on English authorities for an indication of how the law of insurance has been interpreted and developed there and how it might develop in this country. Our dependency on the law of insurance in England is, to an extent, due to the fact that the Irish insurance market originated as an extension of the British insurance market and for many years was dominated and controlled by insurers whose head offices were in Britain, and who endeavoured to apply the same principles, practices and law to the Irish market as applied in Britain. All that has now changed. The modern Irish insurance market is an expanding, independent market with Irish, American and European insurers all competing with the long established British insurers for a share of an increasing, if largely unprofitable, market. Alongside this development of the Irish insurance market, the Irish courts have begun to develop their own jurisprudence in insurance law, choosing to depart from precedent established in English courts, where they feel it necessary and desirable to reflect the differences and peculiarities of Irish society.

The Irish courts have, for instance, developed a different approach to the duty of disclosure, a fundamental principle of insurance, which was subjected to an exhaustive examination and re-appraisal in England, in the much publicised House of Lords decision in *Pan Atlantic*. The recent retrenchment, from expansion of the law of negligence, so evident in England, has not been followed by the Irish courts which are more inclined towards the protection of the individual.

Although competition and market pressures have resulted in some dilution of the principle of indemnity with the introduction of the concept of replacement on a "new for old" basis in relation to material damage insurance, the general principles of insurance remain largely unchanged. Pressure from consumers and Government has resulted in policies, increasingly, being written in "plain english" but, while such policies may be more readily intelligible, the law of contract, which has remained virtually unchanged, is still applicable to their interpretation. On more than one occasion, the Irish judiciary have expressed dislike for the manner in which insurers draft insurance policies, and they enthusiastically support the *contra preferens* rule. The wide scope of cover provided by the modern policy wordings is sometimes claimed to be responsible for the development of insurance fraud in Ireland. In *Superwood*, one of the longest running insurance law cases ever, the Supreme Court confirmed the very strict criteria which must be satisfied by insurers in any allegation of fraud on the part of the insured, and in so doing also delivered an extensive judgment on the ability of an insurer to repudiate liability for breach of a claims condition in a policy.

As a result of EU directives aimed at harmonising motor insurance legislation throughout the member states, motor insurance in Ireland has undergone some minor changes. In Ireland, there is no equivalent to the English Third Parties (Rights against Insurers) Act, 1930, although the Road Traffic Act, 1961 does give some protection to third parties injured in road accidents. The privity of contract rule, which denies third parties direct right of action against insurers, has been abrogated in most common law jurisdictions, and of all the EU member states, Ireland and England are the only ones which do not recognise third party rights in contract. The rule has been heavily criticised in England and the Law Commission there has recommended reform. The professional person in Ireland is now, more than ever before, exposed to legal action for professional negligence and is generally seen in the forefront of defendants in the event of project failure or commercial loss. A claims culture has developed in Ireland which expects and seeks legal remedies for every form of misfortune, irrespective of fault. New heads of damages and new causes of action have been and are being developed. The insurance industry has responded by making available appropriate forms of protection, but the industry is incapable, on its own, of stemming the tide of claims. The number, variety and cost of liability claims has continued to increase despite implementation of significant volumes of safety legislation.

The first printed work on Insurance, "Tractatus de Assecurationibus & Sponsionibus Mercatorum," published in 1552, was written by

Pedro Santarem, a Portuguese jurist. It was a study on the law of marine insurance, or a "most useful and everyday treatise on the assurances and promises of merchants". It laid down scientific foundations for insurance, distinguishing it from similar contracts and describing two fundamental insurance principles, Indemnity and Utmost Good Faith. Since then, numerous books have been written on insurance and the law of insurance in other jurisdictions, but apart from John Schutte's booklet, written for the National Insurance Broker's Association, no major work has been written on the law of insurance in Ireland. The Insurance Institute of Ireland has, in recent years, persuaded its parent examining body, the Chartered Insurance Institute, to include, in its examination syllabus, subjects specific to Ireland and excellent work has been done by members of the Irish Insurance Institute in adapting course textbooks to reflect the law and practice of insurance in Ireland. In 1995, Michael Corrigan and John Campbell made the first attempt to fill the void in Irish law literature by publishing their *Casebook of Irish Insurance Law* and in it they recognised the need for a book which would provide a comprehensive analysis of the law of insurance as it applies in Ireland. I do not claim that this book is the definitive work on the subject or even that it meets the aspirations of the authors of the casebook. I do, however, attempt to address all of the issues identified above and more. The book is intended as no more than a foundation, on which others, academics, jurists and practitioners, might find it possible to build.

I personally have long felt the need for a book which would be a practical aid in dealing with the many day-to-day problems which arise out of the very technical nature of insurance. Some years ago it was suggested to me that practising lawyers, as well as insurance practitioners, would welcome a source of legal materials, analysis and case law specifically related to insurance in Ireland. It was further suggested that my varied practical experience, coupled with recently acquired academic legal qualifications, would qualify me to attempt to meet the perceived need of both professions. The encouragement to undertake the task came from my family, who were at all times interested in the book's progress. Declan kindly agreed to read the draft and I am grateful to him for his constructive criticism and comments. Any errors or omissions are however mine and I accept responsibility for them. I am grateful also to the staff in the law library at University College Cork and in the library of the Chartered Insurance Institute London for the assistance so readily and willingly given in locating materials. Completion of the work would not however have been possible without the unstinting support, encouragement and forbearance of my wife, Noreen, not only over the years it has taken to complete the book, but throughout my entire career.

Austin Buckley,
September 1997

TABLE OF CASES

TABLE OF STATUTES

IRISH ACTS, POST-1922

UK ACTS, POST-1922

OTHER JURISDICTIONS

STATUTORY INSTRUMENTS

CHAPTER ONE

INSURANCE AND THE LAW

*"There is exhilaration in the study of insurance questions be-
cause there is a sense of elaborating new and increased powers
which have been devoted to the service of mankind."*[1]

Historical scholarship has failed to provide irrefutable evidence of the
origins of insurance. It has, however, confirmed beyond all doubt that
the origins are shrouded in obscurity.[2] Considerable classical and judicial controversy surrounds the existence in the ancient world of insurance as we know it today but there is general agreement[3] that
forms of contract resembling insurance were used by merchants and
businessmen from earliest times.[4] The Code of Hammurabi,[5] compiled
by the King of Babylon and discovered in 1902, clearly demonstrates
that the Babylonian civilisation which flourished some 3,000 years
BC used a commercial contract which later became known and used

---

[1] Sir Winston Churchill, Hansard, 25 May 1911.

[2] See Clayton (1971), p. 13.

[3] Raynes (1964); Trenerry (1926); Park (1842); Dover (1962).

[4] Professor Kimball, in his book *Insurance and Public Policy*, quotes "The Science
of Society" by Summer and Keller for the proposition that modern systems of
insurance are just elaborate and scientifically tested examples of a much wider
range of techniques by which man has, from the earliest times, tried to avert disaster, techniques which include, in the form of religious practices and rituals of
superstition, the payment of a premium in the form of some sacrifice or self denial.

[5] The Code, inscribed on a block of black diorite, consists of 282 clauses. It reveals
the business acumen of the Babylonians and that they had a very clear idea of
the value of money as a means of earning more through loans attracting simple
and compound interest.

the world over as "bottomry".[6] Whilst the expression refers only to marine contracts, the Babylonians evolved the principle so as to apply it to land trading, and the Phoenicians with whom they had significant trading relations adopted and adapted the commercial contract during the great Phoenician expansion of 1600 BC. With increasing domination of the Aegean Sea by Greek traders the contract was adopted and again adapted by the Greeks to such an extent that notable maritime lawyers of the nineteenth century claimed that contracts of "bottomry" in use in Greece and referred to by Demosthenes[7] were almost identical in nature to marine contracts issued in London in 1860. In or about 300 BC the "bottomry" contract was adopted by the Romans and again adapted. It is here that the controversy arises because some historians argue that it was the adoption and translation of the principles of bottomry by the Romans which first gave us insurance as we know it today.[8] It is not the function of this book to enter into or to try to resolve that controversy, merely to show that as long as man has been trading, there has been a recognised need for insurance in some form or other.[9] Whilst controversy also surrounds the date of issue and place of origin of the first marine insurance contract there is evidence that such contracts were common in Italy in

---

[6] Bottomry is a Flemish term derived from the figurative use of the bottom or keel of a ship to express the whole ship. A bottomry contract was a commercial contract whereby money (for goods) was advanced for trade purposes either as true loans at a certain fixed interest rate under which the lender had no right to any share of the proceeds of the trading venture, or as mixed loans and partnerships, which in addition to the payment of a fixed rate of interest to the lender, irrespective of the result of the trading, entitled him to receive a share of the profits if such profits exceeded a certain sum. This was on the understanding that the borrower should, in consideration of a high rate of interest (usually 100%) be freed from liability in the event of certain accidents occurring, e.g. failure of the goods to arrive at their intended destination. Should the goods arrive, however, the borrower would be liable for repayment of the loan plus interest.

[7] Demosthenes (born 384 BC), in his oration against Lacritus before the Athenian Court (*Demosthenes, Private Orations*, Loeb Classics Vol. 1, p. 283).

[8] Trenerry (1926), p. 107–22. The earliest documented reference to Marine Insurance is in Livy, (xxiii, 48 and 49) where he describes a guarantee given by the government in 215 BC; under the terms of the guarantee the government agreed in return for a premium to insure the safe arrival of certain shipments of supplies, shipped by private trading companies.

[9] Blackstock: "The contract of insurance is a derivative of expedients that in one form or another have subserved in primitive fashion the purpose of insurance from ancient times."

the early fourteenth century.[10] In a letter, written to one of his many agents, circa 1395, Francesco di Marco Datini wrote:

> With regard to your saying that the ship had reached Barcelona safely you were no prophet, and if some harm had come to her you would have regretted sending without insurance. For you have your orders never to send any merchandise of ours without insurance, and let this be said to you once and for all.[11]

Insurance underwriters then were no different to some of the underwriters of today. They were not always prepared to meet their contractual commitments and were sometimes unable to do so. Occasionally they stalled payment for a while or met only part of the loss insured against.[12] They lacked statistical knowledge and often underestimated the risk in setting premium rates.[13] There is some uncertainty as to when the first policy was issued in London. The Lombard merchants may have conducted insurance there in the fourteenth and fifteenth centuries but there is no record of insurance contracts predating the sixteenth. century. The earliest recorded policy[14] is one dated 1524 and the earliest policy still in existence is dated 1547.

---

[10] Pegalotti in a treatise dated 1350, refers to the insurance contract as a "rishio de mere c di genti".

[11] Datini was born in Tuscany about 1335 and, having had a brilliant commercial career in Avignon, moved to Prato, a town a few miles north of Florence. In Prato he became a merchant, a financier and in turn an underwriter. He ordered all his agents to preserve all their records and he did the same himself. As a result he was responsible for a unique collection of commercial documentation including some 400 insurance policies.

[12] In one of his letters to his wife in 1395 Datini says:
I dreamed last night of a house which had fallen to pieces and all my household were inside it. . . . And the meaning of this dream gives me much to ponder on, for there are no tidings of a galley which left Venice more than two months ago bound for Catalonia, and I had insured it for three hundred florins, as I did the other ship for Domenica and Cambia which perished the next day. . . . I am so vexed by many matters it is a wonder I am not out of my mind, for the more I seek the less I find. And God knows what will befall me.

[13] One of the accounts books preserved by Datini gave details of some of his insurance transactions. Written on the cover was: "This is the Book of Francesco of Prato and his partners living in Pisa, and we shall write in it all Insurances we make on behalf of others. May God grant us profit and protect us from dangers." Premium rates varied from 3.5 to 5 per cent whereas the market rate would have been in the region of 12 to 15 per cent.

[14] Records of the Court of Admiralty, London.

Whilst England may have been slower than most other European countries to adopt the practice of insurance it quickly caught up and the London Insurance market, with its origins in Edward Lloyds coffee house in 1687, soon became the insurance capital of the world. However, some 200 years before that the first law governing insurance had been passed in Spain and it was used as the model for the first marine insurance regulations adopted by Lloyds.[15]

Whatever controversy or uncertainty might exist in relation to the origins of insurance itself, there can be no dispute whatsoever as to its contribution to the Law's development. The early adoption and development of equitable rules as basic principles of insurance — e.g. indemnity, subrogation, contribution and utmost good faith — together with the funding of litigation to establish other general principles of law, greatly influenced the development of Contract, Tort and Maritime law.[16] The resolution of disputes concerning insurance was, for a long time, a matter for specially established Chambers of Insurance.[17] One such Chamber was established by statute in London in 1601, outside the normal legal system.[18] There are some legal cases dealing with insurance related disputes reported in the late seventeenth century but it is generally accepted that the Common Law Courts did not become actively involved in insurance related cases until the early eighteenth century[19] and that the appointment of Lord Mansfield as Chief Justice in 1756 was the beginning of the development of Insurance Law as a distinct jurisprudence.[20] By the time Lord

---

[15] In 1994, Banco Vitatico in Barcelona struck a medal to commemorate the 500th anniversary of the Libre del Consolat de Mar.

[16] Insurance related cases have also contributed to the definition of the criminal law.

[17] Birds (1993), p. 1–2.

[18] Ibid.

[19] *Lynch* v *Dalzell & Others* [1729] 4 Bro. Parl. Cas. 431 concerned the assignment of a fire policy. One of the earliest cases dealing with contribution was *Godin* v *London Assurance Co.* [1758] 1 Burr 489.

[20] *Carter* v *Boehm* [1766] 3 Burr 1905; *De Hahn* v *Hartley* [1786] 1 TR 343 et al.

Mansfield retired in 1788 the Common Law Courts had firmly established jurisdiction over insurance related disputes.[21]

The Irish Insurance market developed in the eighteenth century as an extension of the British market. The Sun Insurance Office, established in 1710, was the first insurance company authorised to transact business in Ireland but it did not in fact do so until 1811 when it appointed agents in the major cities and towns in Ireland. In 1720, the London Assurance was established, in London, and its Royal Charter extended to Ireland and "the rest of his Majesty's dominions". The London Assurance appointed its first agent in Ireland in 1721 and has been transacting business in Ireland ever since.[22] In the early 1830s, the total premium income of the Royal Exchange, which had opened an office in Dublin in 1722, was, after more than a century in business in Ireland, about £5,000, representing approximately 8 per cent of the company's total business. The gross written premium income of all companies transacting business in Ireland is now in excess of £3 billion.[23] Whilst the Irish insurance market might have been an extension of the British market, dominated by British insurers, it differs significantly from that market in the level of its unprofitability.[24] It has always been seen as a difficult market. As early as 1839, the Royal Exchange wrote to all its agents in Ireland, warning them against the acceptance of proposals from people who were "totally incompetent" to pay the premiums and who immediately assigned the policy to "those speculators by whose contrivances the assurances were made".[25] The agents were urged to make the most "rigid inquiries into the collateral circumstances of character

---

[21] n. 17 *supra*, and Park's *Law of Marine Insurance*, 1790:

> . . . the learned Judges . . . by adopting the true principles of commerce in their decision of the many intricate cases which have been brought before them, have added another pillar to that beautiful structure of rational jurisprudence, which has deservedly acquired the admiration of mankind.

[22] The London Assurance is now part of the Sun Alliance & London Insurance group recently merged with the Royal Insurance Company to form the Royal Sun Alliance Group.

[23] Irish Insurance Federation Fact file 1996.

[24] In each of the five years from 1990 the non-life sector made significant underwriting losses. The loss had reduced from £171m. in 1990 to £61m. in 1994 (Irish Insurance Federation Fact File 1995, p. 13).

[25] Pike (1991), p. 155.

and respectability of the referees and the life proposed" so that the agents' vigilance would increase "with their sense of the dangers with which assurance is fraught in Ireland".

The profitability of the non-life sector of any insurance market is determined by the amount of claims paid in relation to the premiums earned. Non-life insurers in Ireland have consistently failed to make profit on their underwriting activities because the cost of claims plus expenses has always exceeded the premiums earned.[26] Whilst a survey showed that, contrary to popular belief, Irish motorists claim less frequently than motorists in Britain,[27] claims when they are made tend to cost more. The fatal accident rate in Ireland has been shown to be two-and-a-half times that of the United Kingdom. Personal injury claims are four times more expensive to settle and damage claims are twice as expensive.[28] Personal injury claims constitute the greater proportion of all claims made in Ireland and independent surveys confirm that the generous system of compensation adopted here results in Ireland having the unenviable record of the highest average personal injury awards in Europe.[29] The development of a "claims culture" in Irish society has brought about a huge increase in personal injury actions with plaintiffs and their advisers exploring with ever-increasing success new causes of action such as post-traumatic stress disorder, chronic pain syndrome, repetitive strain injury, deafness, cancer and other latent diseases and conditions. Whilst most such actions are brought against nominal defendants they are in reality against the defendant's insurers whose defence of the action helps shape the law's development. Insurance and the law are inextricably linked in Ireland.

---

[26] see n. 24 *supra*.

[27] Coopers & Lybrand (1993)

[28] ibid.

[29] MacIntosh and Holmes (1994).

CHAPTER TWO

INSURANCE INTERMEDIARIES AND THE LAW

2.1 INTRODUCTION

In the eighteenth and early nineteenth centuries, insurance companies appointed an individual or firm as agent to receive and handle business in a particular town or area. The appointed agent might be a banker, solicitor, estate agent or other person likely to hear of people needing insurance. Such agents were not required to have any special knowledge of insurance. The principal agents in the district introduced business directly or through sub-agents, accepted offers of business subject to confirmation, arranged the investigation and settlement of claims and supervised the office fire engine. They had a plate on their door and were expected to represent one insurance company exclusively. Their sole allegiance was to that company. In the middle of the nineteenth century, general agents of this kind were replaced or supplemented by agents whose task was to introduce business for a commission. With the growth of insurance business, agents were appointed indiscriminately and the holding of multiple agencies became common.[1] A simple agency appointment letter defined the scope of the agent's authority. Towards the end of the nineteenth century insurance brokers entered the scene.[2] Demanding better commission terms than agents, they were viewed initially with suspicion by insurance companies who could not see why they should pay them more than their appointed agents whose sole allegiance was

---

[1] In 1786 the Sun Insurance office had only 123 agencies in Great Britain. By 1846 it had 677; by 1859 over 800 and by 1880, 1,213 (Dickson, 1960).

[2] The first insurance brokerage in Ireland was established by Alfred B. Coyle and Fred S. Myerscough in 1903 trading as Coyle & Co. from offices in Suffolk Street, Dublin.

to the insurance company which appointed them. Brokers were first and foremost the agent of the insured.[3] With the continued growth in the volume of business controlled by brokers, insurers appreciated the benefits of dealing with brokers and conceded differential terms to them. Whilst agency appointment letters were issued to brokers many brokers, refused to enter into agency agreements on the grounds that they were agents of the insured and not of the company. The enactment of the Insurance Act, 1989 forced insurers and brokers to re-think their traditional approach to agency agreements.

Whilst there are relatively few Irish cases where the insured, in the first instance, sued the broker, there has been an increasing tendency to join the broker in any action against the insurer where the insurer for one reason or another denies liability under a policy. To quote Buller J.:

> Time was, when no underwriter would have dreamed of making such an objection: if his solicitor had suggested a loophole by which he might escape he would have spurned the idea. He would have said "is it not a fair policy? Have I not received the premium? and shall I not now when the loss has happened pay the money?"[4]

That comment in 1798 was indicative of the way the insurance industry was to develop over the next two centuries and the law now contains numerous cases where insurers, responding to market and shareholders' pressures, repudiated liability under contracts of insurance, forcing the policyholder to seek redress against the broker.

2.2 INSURANCE ACT, 1989

The Act seeks to address defects in the system identified in the Final Report of the Committee of Inquiry into the Insurance Industry published in March 1976. The report listed six major defects as:

i)   the dual legal relationships of intermediaries

ii) the status of an intermediary in completing or helping to complete a proposal form

---

[3] *Rozanes* v *Bowen* [1928] 32 Lloyds Rep 98.

[4] *Woolff* v *Horncastle* [1798] 1 B&B 314 at 321.

iii) the absence of any qualification requirements for persons wishing to establish as insurance brokers

iv) the lack of a code of practice

v) the excessive rates of commission paid on life assurance policies to "introductory agents"

vi) irresponsible advertising in the life assurance area.

All of these defects have now been addressed and the Act makes a clear distinction between insurance agents and insurance brokers.

2.3 INSURANCE AGENTS

2.3.1 DEFINITION OF AN AGENT

Section 2(1) of the Insurance Act, 1989, defines an insurance agent as:

> any person who holds an appointment in writing from an insurer enabling him to place insurance business with that insurer but does not include an insurance broker, or an employee of the insurer when the employee is acting for that insurer.

Section 49(1) provides that no person shall act as an insurance agent or hold himself out to be an insurance agent unless:

a) he holds an appointment in writing from each insurer for which he is an agent;

b) he states on his letter headings and business forms that he is an insurance agent and specifies the name or names of the insurers for which he is an agent;

c) he informs any proposer for insurance that he is an insurance agent and the name of the insurer or insurers for which he acts.

Section 49(4) introduces the concept of a "tied agent" which is subsequently defined in Section 51(3) as

> any person who enters into an agreement or arrangement with an undertaking whereby that person undertakes to refer all proposals of insurance to the undertaking with whom he has made or entered into the agreement or arrangement, or any person who enters into an agreement or arrangement with an

undertaking which restricts in any way that person's freedom to refer proposals of insurance to an undertaking other than the undertaking with whom the agreement or arrangement has been made or entered into.

2.3.2 DUTIES OF AN AGENT

The duties of an insurance agent arise from the agency agreement, the nature of the agency relationship and the nature of the insurance business. In the relationship between the insurance agent and the insurer the duties and extent of the authority of the agent are generally expressed in the agency agreement. Because insurance agency is a fiduciary relationship and one of utmost good faith the law implies into the agreement a number of duties which must be fulfilled by the agent. These include the duty to:

- carry out the transaction which he is employed to do

- obey his instructions and act strictly in accordance with the terms of his authority

- act with reasonable and proper skill

- account for moneys received

- deal honestly with the principal.

2.3.3 AGENT OF INSURER OR INSURED?

It has long been a problem to determine at any given time in the negotiation of a contract of insurance whether an insurance agent is the agent of the insurer or the proposer.[5] The Insurance Act, 1989 goes some way to clarifying the position in a limited number of circumstances. Section 51(1) of the act says that an insurance agent shall be deemed to be acting as the agent of the insurer when he completes in his own hand or helps the proposer to complete a proposal for insurance with the insurer from whom the agent holds an appointment. In such circumstances only, the insurer shall be responsible for any er-

---

[5] The principles of agency law concerning the duties, authority and liability of agents are of crucial importance in determining the issue. See "Agency in Insurance Transactions" in Part VI of Ivamy (1986); also "The Role of Agents in Insurance Business", Chapter 6 of McGillivray and Parkington (1988). For the general principles of agency law see *Bowstead on Agency,* (1985); Forde (1990); *Fridman's Law of Agency* (1990).

rors or omission in the completion of the proposal. Section 51(2) stipulates that an insurer shall be responsible for any act or omission of its tied agent in respect of any matter pertaining to a contract of insurance offered or issued by that insurer, as if the tied agent was an employee of the insurer. Whilst the Act makes it clear that an insurer from whom a tied insurance agent holds an appointment is directly liable to the customer for the conduct of the tied agent, the Act exercises no control whatsoever over sub-agents appointed by tied agents under sub-agency agreements. No qualifications or conditions are laid down in the Act for such sub-agents but the Act does provide for payment of commission to them.[6] In circumstances other than specified in the Act the general law of agency applies to the relationships between the insurer and the insurance agent, between the insurer and third parties and between the insurance agent and third parties.

2.4 INSURANCE BROKERS

2.4.1 DEFINITION OF INSURANCE BROKER
The statutory definition of an Insurance Broker is contained in Section 2(1) of the Insurance Act, 1989:

> "Insurance Broker" means a person who, acting with the freedom of choice described in section 44(1)(b), brings together, with a view to the insurance of risks, persons seeking insurance and undertakings, and carries out work preparatory to the conclusion of contracts of insurance, but does not include an insurance agent or an employee of an insurer when the employee is acting for the insurer.[7]

2.4.2 STATUTORY REQUIREMENTS
The Act makes the distinction that a broker must be in a position to place business with at least five life insurance companies and five

---

[6] Section 46(3). Whilst the standard non-life tied agency agreement makes no reference to the appointment of sub-agents, the tied agency life agreement makes specific provision for their appointment subject to the insurers prior written consent.

[7] This definition of Insurance Broker is derived from EC Directive No. 77/92 EEC of December 1976. The freedom of choice referred to is the requirement that a broker have at least five life and five non-life agencies.

non-life insurance companies.[8] An ability to do so indicates that the individual or company is an insurance broker. The Act also requires that a broker must

> be a member of a representative body of insurance brokers which requires compliance with the provisions of this Act as a condition of membership, and that body is recognised as such by the Minister, and he otherwise complies with the provisions of this Act, or, not being a member of a recognised representative body, he complies with the provisions of this Act.[9]

For the purposes of this section of the Act the body recognised by the Minister is the Irish Brokers Association (IBA).

2.4.3 DUTIES OF AN INSURANCE BROKER

It has been held that the duties of an insurance broker are to ascertain the needs of the client, use reasonable skill and care to procure the cover the client asked for, either expressly or by implication and if he cannot obtain such cover to report back to the client and seek alternative instructions. However that is not the full extent of the broker's duties as Phillips J. explained:

> when a . . . broker accepts instruction from a client he undertakes to exercise reasonable skill and care in relation to his client's interests in accordance with . . . practice. The general duty will normally require the broker to perform a number of different activities on behalf of the client, but the performance of those activities constitute no more than the discharge of the duty to exercise reasonable skill and care. Failure to perform one of the activities will normally constitute a breach of that duty of care, not a breach of an absolute obligation. The breaches of duty for which I have found the brokers liable . . . all represent breaches of the general duty owed by the broker to exercise reasonable skill and care, not breaches of absolute obligations.[10]

---

[8] Section 44(1)(b). This had the effect of forcing brokers, who prior to the Act might have concentrated in either the non-life or life areas, to take up appointments in the other area to maintain their broker status.

[9] Section 44 (1)(a).

[10] *Youell v Bland Welch & Co.* [1990] 2 Lloyds Rep 431.

In the Supreme Court in *Chariot Inns Ltd.* v *Assicurazioni Generali & others* Kenny J. delivering a judgment, with which the other members of the court agreed, said:

> An insurance broker owes a contractual duty to his client to possess the skill and knowledge which he holds himself out to the public as having and to exercise this in doing the client's business.[11]

The plaintiffs had proposed to insure their licensed premises with the first named defendant and in answering questions on the proposal form, an employee of the second defendants, a firm of insurance brokers, was alleged to have advised the plaintiff that it would not be necessary to answer a question requiring the disclosure of a fire loss within the previous five years. The proposer had suffered fire damage to some furnishings stored at another location owned by an associated company. The broker, allegedly, advised the proposer not to disclose the loss, on the basis that the claim had been made by a company separate from the proposer and therefore not relevant to the proposal being completed. Following destruction of the licensed premises by fire, insurers repudiated liability on the grounds of non-disclosure. The trial judge at first instance held the non-disclosure was not material and dismissed the claim against the brokers. The decision was reversed on appeal.

The "professionalisation" of the broker's role probably means that the courts would now expect a broker to be proactive in determining the client's needs. It is unlikely that the courts would follow a previous High Court decision in *Curtis t/a Agencies Transport Ltd.* v *Cor-*

---

[11] *Chariot Inns Ltd. v Assicurazioni Generali SPA & others* [1981] IR 199 at 231.

coran Insurances Ltd.[12] that a broker, discussing Marine insurance in respect of a vehicle with his client, was under no duty to advise on Road Traffic Act cover unless he had been asked for advice.

2.5 CODE OF CONDUCT

The Code of Conduct imposed by the Irish Brokers Association on its members has been approved by the Minister under Section 56 of the Act. Prior to the introduction of the Insurance Act, 1989 anyone could call himself an "insurance broker" and thereby imply to the general public that he was a truly independent adviser on insurance matters capable of exercising considerable skill in advising clients on their insurance needs and the insurers most suitable for them. The Irish Brokers Association was formed out of the amalgamation of three professional bodies and a desire to ensure that the Government, in introducing legislation, would accept the concept of self-regulation. The code is very general in its requirements, providing useful guidelines as to the responsibilities expected of intermediaries, but it does not have the force of law and the policing of it is left to the insurers and the brokers association. The general principles of the code are:

- that brokers shall at all times conduct their business with the utmost good faith and integrity

- that they shall do everything possible to satisfy the insurance needs of their clients and place these requirements above all other considerations

- that brokers must avoid all misleading or exaggerated advertising of insurance products.

---

[12] In *Curtis t/a Agencies Transport Ltd.* v *Corcoran Insurances Ltd.* Unreported High Court 13 July 1973 Pringle J. said:
> . . . I am satisfied that the conversation which he had with the plaintiff . . . was concerned with Marine insurance and there was in my opinion no duty on him, either as a broker or consultant to advise the plaintiff on his Road Traffic Act cover on the vehicle unless he had been asked for advice. . . .

In *United Mills Agencies Ltd.* v *Harvey Bray & Co.* [1951] 2 Lloyds Rep 631, the marine policy arranged by the broker did not cover goods being packed prior to transit which were destroyed by fire. The court held that the broker in advising the client on the insurance required on the goods was entitled to expect that the client conducted their business in a prudent manner and that they had sufficient insurance on other risks associated with their business.

While the code does not have the force of law it can be an influential factor in determining the liability of an intermediary to his client. In the English case of *Harvest Trucking Co. Ltd.* v *Davis*[13] the judge in holding against the defendant intermediary pointed out that whilst the UK code was merely a voluntary code of practice, not binding on him, and that his decision could only be made on legal principles, the code was useful to the court in two ways. First it described the context in which an intermediary had to operate and secondly it was helpful to refer to the code to ensure that the standard of care which the court intends to apply is not considered to be unrealistic by the insurance industry. In deciding whether an insurance intermediary has been negligent a court must avoid adopting too high a standard of care. Reference to the Code of Conduct provides the court with an indication of the context within which intermediaries are generally expected to operate and thereby facilitates the application of a realistic standard.

2.6 DIFFERENCE BETWEEN AGENT AND BROKER

The Insurance Act clearly distinguishes between an insurance agent and an insurance broker in its requirement on the number of agencies held by each. It does not fully address the legal status of each in their dealings with the proposer or policyholder. The status of the tied agent is clear: he is to be regarded as an employee of the insurer from whom he holds his appointment.[14] An insurance agent is deemed to be the agent of the insurer when he completes in his own hand or helps the proposer to complete an insurance proposal.[15] It still leaves to be decided in respect of all other transactions or acts in the course of negotiating the contract whether the agent is the agent of the proposer or the insurer at any given time. It is a question which can only

---

[13] [1991] 2 Lloyds Rep 638. The plaintiff who was a haulage contractor had claimed that the defendant insurance agent had failed to negotiate the terms of the policy adequately or had failed to advise him of a restrictive condition on which insurers successfully relied in repudiating liability for one of his vehicles, stolen whilst unattended. The condition had previously been deleted in respect of one vehicle but had not been renegotiated in respect of the vehicle stolen and the insured was unaware of its application.

[14] Section 51(2).

[15] Section 51(1).

be determined on the precise facts of each case. Whilst the broker is undoubtedly the agent of the proposer for the purposes of arranging the insurance he may at other times be regarded as the agent of the insurer. The fact that he is generally remunerated by the insurer by payment of commission does not affect his position. All parties to the transaction are aware of the basis on which the broker is remunerated. The tendency of brokers to move away from commission to a fee-based system of remuneration affirms the broker's role as agent of the insured. Information disclosed to the broker as agent of the insured is not imputed to the insurer. In *Roberts* v *Plaisted*[16] the Court of Appeal strongly criticised that position saying:

> To persons unacquainted with the insurance industry it may seem a remarkable state of the law that a person who describes himself as a . . . broker who is remunerated by the insurance industry and who presents proposals and suggested policies on their behalf should not be the safe recipient of full disclosure; but it is undoubtedly the position in law as it stands at the moment.

2.7 DUTY OF CARE

Irrespective of whether the intermediary is classified as an agent or broker it is the function of the intermediary to exercise reasonable skill and care in meeting his client's insurance needs. In *Hedley Byrne*[17] Lord Pearse said:

> if persons holding themselves out in a calling or situation or profession take on a task within that calling, situation or profession, they have a duty of skill and care.

The law does not require "an extraordinary degree of skill . . . but only such a reasonable and ordinary degree as a person of average capacity and ordinary ability in his situation and profession might

---

[16] *Roberts* v *Plaisted* [1989] 2 Lloyds Rep 341. The Court of Appeal having found that the insured was not in breach of the duty of disclosure dealt with his alternative plea that information within the knowledge of the broker should be imputed to the insurer.

[17] *Hedley Byrne & Co. Ltd.* v *Heller & Partners* [1963] 1 Lloyds Rep 274; [1964] AC 465.

fairly be expected to exert".[18] Pringle J. in the High Court in *Curtis t/a Agencies Transport Ltd.* v *Corcoran Insurances Ltd.* said:

> The duty of an insurance broker to his client is in my opinion the same as that of any other agent, to his principal, that is to say he is under a legal duty to exercise reasonable care and skill in the performance of the duty that he undertakes under the particular circumstances. The question of whether reasonable skill and care has been exercised is a question of fact and the evidence of persons engaged in the same profession is admissible as to what would in the circumstances be reasonable care and skill.[19]

In litigation arising out of the problems associated with Lloyds in the early 1990s the English courts considered the standard of care required of insurance brokers.

In *Brown* v *KMR Services Ltd.* and *Sword-Daniels* v *Pitel*.[20] Gatehouse J. quoted Lord Diplock:

> No matter what profession it may be, the common law does not impose on those who practice it any liability for damages resulting from what in the event turns out to have been an error of judgment unless the error was such as no reasonably well informed and competent member of that profession could have made.[21]

This was accepted by Phillips J. in *Gooda Walker*[22] but qualified by him maintaining that it did not remove from the courts the duty of determining the standard of skill and care that ought properly to be demonstrated. He cited Jackson and Powell:

> It is for the court to decide what is meant by "reasonably competent members of the profession". They may or may not be equated with practitioners of average competence. . . . Suppose a profession adopts extremely lax standards in some aspects of

---

[18] *Harvest Trucking Co. Ltd.* v *Davies* [1991] 2 Lloyds Rep 638.

[19] *Curtis t/a Agencies Transport Ltd.* v *Corcoran Insurances Ltd.* Unreported High Court 13 July 1973. The plaintiff client instructed his brokers to substitute a new vehicle under a motor policy and the brokers failed to advise the client that the policy did not provide cover in respect of accidental damage to the vehicle.

[20] [1994] 4 All ER 385.

[21] In *Saif Ali* v *Sidney Mitchell & Co.* [1978] 3 All ER 1035 at 1041.

[22] *Gooda Walker, Feltrim and the Merrett Cases* [1994] 2 Lloyds Rep 468.

its work, the court does not regard itself as bound by those standards and will not acquit practitioners of negligence simply because they have complied with those standards.[23]

The standard of skill and care expected of professionals in Ireland is accepted as being that laid down in a medical negligence case by Finlay C. J.:

> The true test for establishing professional negligence . . . on the part of a . . . practitioner is whether he has proved to be guilty of such failure as no . . . practitioner of equal specialist or general status and skill would be guilty of in acting with ordinary care.[24]

In *Chariot Inns* v *Assicurazioni Generali & others*[25] the High Court accepted evidence of general practice in finding that the broker owed the plaintiff a duty to ensure that the necessary information was furnished to the insurers so as to protect the plaintiff against a possible repudiation of liability under the policy.

2.8 LIABILITY OF AN INSURANCE AGENT

The insurance agent can incur liability to the client for breach of his duty of care under any one of four main agency functions:

i)   failure to follow the client's instructions

ii) advising the client on his insurance needs

iii) completion or assistance in the completion of the proposal form

iv) compliance with correct procedures.

---

[23] Jackson and Powell (1987).

[24] *Dunne* v *National Maternity Hospital* [1989] IR 91.

[25] *Chariot Inns Ltd.* v *Assicurazioni Generali & Others* [1981] IR 199; [1981] ILRM 173.

2.8.1 INSTRUCTIONS

The agent may have a duty to effect or to maintain insurance on behalf of the client even in the absence of specific instructions.[26] In the
event of litigation between the parties the outcome will be determined by the way the court interprets the understanding between
them on the basis of the evidence before it. Even where an agent acts
gratuitously in arranging insurance he still owes a duty of care to his
principal.[27] However an agent's failure to follow the client's instructions exactly may not render him liable even though his failure
causes loss to either party to the contract.[28]

2.8.2 ADVICE

The power of an agent to bind insurers is usually limited by the terms
of the agency agreement. Difficulties arise when, in advising the client, the agent exceeds the authority given to him. Agents are expected to advise prospective insureds of the cover available under the
various insurance products of the insurers which the agent represents, the differences in cover and provide advice on the individual
needs of the prospective insured. If the prospective insured relies on
the advice given by the agent and that reliance was reasonable the

---

[26] *United Marketing Co.* v *Hasha Kara* [1963] 1 Lloyds Rep 331. The defendant
insurance agent had for a number of years arranged insurance for the plaintiff
shopkeeper with a particular insurer. The premiums were offset by the agent
against amounts owed by him to the plaintiff in respect of purchases. The plaintiff found himself uninsured after a fire due to non-payment of the premium to
the insurer. Defendant argued that he had no specific instructions to renew but
the court held for the plaintiff on the evidence.

[27] *Wilkinson* v *Coverdale* [1793] 1 Esp 74. The purchaser of property agreed with
the vendor that the policy in respect of the property should be assigned to him.
The vendor charged out the premium but failed to effect the assignment. The
court held that the fact that the vendor was acting without payment was no defence to the purchaser's claim against him.

[28] *Holland* v *Russell* [1863] 4 B&S 14. The defendant agent of a shipowner failed
to advise the plaintiff insurer of existing damage to the vessel to be insured. Insurers subsequently paid a loss and on learning of the previous damage sought to
recover the money from the agent. The court held that the non-disclosure was
neither fraudulent nor negligent but an honest mistake and as the insurers were
aware throughout the transaction that the agent was acting for the shipowner
they could not look to the agent for reimbursement of the moneys paid to him and
paid over by him to the shipowner.

insurer will be liable for the consequences.[29] If the agent is guilty of innocent misrepresentation the policyholder may rescind the contract.[30] However if the agent's advice is fraudulent he will be acting outside the scope of his authority and the insurer will not be bound to honour the policy but will be bound to return the premiums paid.[31] To establish negligence against the agent it is only necessary to prove that the agent acted in a way in which other competent agents would not have acted.[32]

2.8.3 PROPOSAL FORMS

Whereas prior to the Insurance Act, 1989 it was well established that the agent was the agent of the proposer when he completed or assisted in the completion of proposal forms, the Act now makes it absolutely clear that where an agent completes a proposal form in his own hand or helps the proposer to complete the proposal the agent shall in those circumstances be deemed the agent of the insurer and the insurer shall be responsible for any errors or omissions in the completed proposal. This provision does not apply to insurance brokers.

2.8.4 CORRECT PROCEDURES

The consequences for a policyholder of the failure of the agent to observe correct procedures will depend on the extent of the agent's authority under his agency agreement and the scope of his relationship with the insurer. The fact that an insurer debits an agent's account with a renewal premium is not confirmation of renewal where the agent is required to advise the insurer of non-payment of pre-

---

[29] *Fletcher* v *Manitoba Public Insurance Co.* [1990] 74 DLR (4th) 636. The plaintiff successfully sued the insurer for its employee's failure to advise him adequately about additional cover available.

[30] *Mutual Reserve Life Insurance Company Ltd.* v *Foster* [1904] 19 TLR 342. The House of Lords granted recission and return of premiums where insurer's agent had misrepresented a complex life policy to the plaintiff.

[31] *Hughes* v *Liverpool Victoria Legal Friendly Society* [1916–17] All ER 918; *Kettlewell* v *Refuge Assurance Soc. Ltd.* [1909] AC 243. Both cases arose from an agent's fraudulent advice and resulted in the court ordering refund of the premiums paid.

[32] *Rust* v *Abbey Life Assurance Co. Ltd.* [1979] 2 Lloyds Rep 386. Whilst the court found no negligence on the part of an agent alleged to have misrepresented the conditions surrounding a property bond the judge held that the agent in such transactions owed a duty more extensive than not to make misrepresentations.

mium within fifteen days of renewal date.[33] Where payment of premiums must be made by a certain method or payment by certain methods is prohibited then an agent cannot vary the procedures.[34] To the extent that an agent holds himself out as having special knowledge and skill in insurance matters, his liability for professional negligence will be that of an insurance broker.[35]

2.9 LIABILITY OF INSURANCE BROKER

2.9.1 PROFESSIONAL STATUS

Insurance brokers are regarded as professional persons in the eyes of the law.[36] The practical implication of possessing this professional status lies in the duty of care and the standard of skill which the law requires of them in their dealings with the client.[37] A professional

---

[33] *Acey* v *Fernie* [1840] 7 M&W 151. The agent had only limited powers in respect of the collection of premiums. He could receive premiums within 15 days of the due date but was obliged to give notice to insurers of non-payment.

[34] *London & Lancashire Life Assurance Co.* v *Fleming* [1897] AC 499. The agent accepted payment of premium by promissory note specifically against instructions. In *British Industry Life Assurance Co.* v *Ward* [1856] 17 CB 644, the agent was permitted by the terms of his appointment to accept premiums up to four weeks in arrears but he accepted payment eleven weeks after the due date.

[35] In *Harvest Trucking Co. Ltd.* v *Davis* [1991] 2 Lloyds Rep 638, the judge held that the defendant owed to the plaintiff client "a significant duty" to explain all of the essential terms of the cover as if the defendant had been a registered broker, on the basis that the defendant agent had fulfilled the same functions as a broker.

[36] The legal distinction of being recognised as a professional was once important. The original professions were the Church, the Army, and the Law. English common law provided that persons exercising a common calling were liable in damages independently of any contract for failure to exercise the degree of skill normally shown by persons of that calling. Such persons included common carriers, farriers, inn-keepers, blacksmiths, public officers and surgeons. The principle of liability in tort did not apply to those professional relationships which depended entirely on contract and had the following characteristics: vocations involving some branch of learning or science; a moral aspect (e.g. a high standard of ethical conduct expected of them); and membership of a professional body. See *IRC* v *Maxse* [1918] 12 Tax Cases 41 and McMahon and Binchy (1990), footnote p. 258.

[37] *Lanphier* v *Phiboss* [1838] ER 581:
> [The professional] does not undertake, if he is an attorney, that at all events you will gain your case, nor does a surgeon undertake that he will perform a cure; nor does he undertake to use the highest possible skill. There may be persons who have higher education and greater advantage than he has, but he undertakes to bring a fair reasonable and competent degree of skill.

such as an insurance broker has a duty to act with reasonable and proper care, skill and diligence. When a person employs an insurance broker the law does not imply a term into the contract that the broker will achieve the desired result, but only that he will use reasonable skill and care.[38]

2.9.2 STANDARD OF CARE

The standard, by which the duty is to be measured, is that of persons of like skill and experience in the profession.[39] Keane J. in *Chariot Inns* in considering the case against the second defendant, the plaintiff's broker, was clearly influenced by the evidence of other brokers, saying that:

> . . . the evidence of the various brokers in this case demonstrates that, even if a broker were satisfied that the . . . [information] was not material to the risk being insured, it would be normal practice to record the information and transmit it to the underwriters so that they could use their judgment about it.

However, the standard of care is not necessarily the standard which other members of the profession achieve, but the standard which, in the court's opinion, other insurance brokers ought to achieve. Where a broker advertises a special competence in a particular placing of risks, then the standards applicable would be those of a broker of similar status, i.e. that of a specialist in the same area as the defendant broker.[40] Exceptionally the professional standards may be higher

---

[38] *Smith* v *Cologon* [1788] 2 TR 188n.

[39] In *Bolam* v *Friern Barnet Hospital Managment Committee* [1957] 2 All ER 118, Mr J. McNair said:

> when you get situations which involve the use of some special skill or competence, then the test as to whether there has been negligence or not, is not the test of the man on the top of the Clapham omnibus, because he has not got that special skill. The test is the standard of the ordinary man exercising and professing to have that special skill. A man need not possess the highest expert skill; it is sufficient if he exercises the ordinary skill of an ordinary competent man exercising that particular art.

[40] *Duchess of Argyll* v *Beuselinck* [1972] 2 Lloyds Rep 173. Megarry J.:

> If the client employs a solicitor of high standing and great experience, will an action for negligence fail if it appears that the solicitor did not exercise the care and skill to be expected of him though he did not fall below the standards of a reasonably competent solicitor? If a client engages an expert and doubtless

than the law requires. In *United Mills Agencies Ltd.* v *Bray & Co.*[41] the court held that there was no legal duty on the defendant brokers to issue a cover note to the plaintiff client, immediately it was completed, even though there was evidence that it was accepted market practice of brokers to notify clients as soon as possible after cover had been placed. The practice was accepted by the court as good business management but the court held that failure to follow that practice did not involve the brokers in legal liability. The decision was followed by the Irish High Court in *Curtis t/a Agencies Transport Ltd.* v *Corcoran Insurances Ltd.*[42]

2.9.3 DUAL AGENCY STATUS

Insurance brokers differ from many other groups of professionals by reason of their dual agency status. Although the broker is regarded as the agent of the insured,[43] he is generally remunerated by commission paid by the insurer. This apparent anomaly is explained by the fact that the premium agreed between the broker and the insurer takes into account the commission to be paid and therefore in reality it is the insured who pays the broker for the services provided.[44] The broker's dual functions arise from (a) powers from the insurer either under a formal agency agreement or by custom and (b) authority from

---

expects to pay commensurate fees, is he not entitled to expect something more than the standard of the reasonably competent?

[41] *United Mills Agencies Ltd.* v *Bray & Co.* [1951] 2 Lloyds Rep 631 at 643 per McNair J.:

Evidence was called . . . that it is the practice of . . . insurance brokers . . . that when cover has been placed, the clients are notified as soon as possible. That seems to me to be good business and prudent office management, but on the evidence, I am completely unable to hold that it is part of the duty owed by the broker to the client to notify him, in the sense that failure so to notify would involve him in legal liability. . . . It seems to me to put quite an unreasonable burden on the broker to say that as a matter of law, apart from prudent practice, he is bound to forward the cover note as soon as possible.

[42] In the Irish High Court, Pringle J. quoted the above passage with approval in *Curtis t/a Agencies Transport Ltd.* v *Corcoran Insurances Ltd.* Unreported 13 July 1973.

[43] *Taylor* v *Yorkshire Insurance Co. Ltd.* [1913] 2 IR 1; *Sanderson* v *Cunningham* [1919] 2 IR 234; *Biggar* v *Rock Life Assurance Co.* [1902] 1 KB 516; *Searle* v *A.R. Hales & Co. Ltd.* [1996] LRLR 68

[44] *Bancroft* v *Heath* [1901] 17 TLR 425. This practice is well established and sanctioned by the courts: *Great Western Insurance Co. of New York* v *Cunliffe* [1869] LR 9 Ch. App. 525.

the client or policyholder to negotiate on their behalf in the purchase of insurance and the settlement of claims. The broker is charged with the responsibility of ensuring that the prospective insured meets the insurer's requirements for acceptance of the risk and at the same time ensuring on behalf of the client that they obtain adequate cover at reasonable and competitive terms. The fulfilment of this dual role is made more difficult when the broker is regarded as an expert and employed as such to advise the client on the types of cover available, including terms and cost, and the actual cover needed to meet the client's identified requirements. In addition the broker is often expected to give advice on a wide range of risk subjects, many of which are properly the province of other disciplines.

2.9.4 DUTY OF CARE

The duty of care imposed on all professionals has been extended by the courts in their desire to ensure that the consumer is adequately compensated for losses allegedly suffered at the hands of large institutions. This is particularly true of insurance in Ireland where the courts, when forced to hold in favour of an insurer, will invariably find negligence on the part of the insurance broker so that the policyholders can recover their loss from the broker and their professional liability insurer. This judicial approach, demonstrated in *Chariot Inns*[45] increases the duty of care imposed on insurance brokers, requiring a far higher degree of care than would otherwise exist. The duty of care is, in practice, more demanding than that expounded by Tindle C.J. in *Lanphier* v *Phiboss*:

> [The Professional] does not undertake, if he is an attorney, that at all events you will gain your case, nor does a surgeon undertake that he will perform a cure; nor does he undertake to use the highest possible skill. There may be persons who have higher education and greater advantage than he has, but

---

[45] *Chariot Inns Ltd.* v *Assicurazioni Generali SPA. and Others* [1981] IR 199; [1981] ILRM 173. Insurers repudiated liability for fire damage on the grounds of non-disclosure of an alleged material fact. Although the actual underwriter gave evidence that he would not have declined indemnity if he had not believed the insured responsible for the fire, the Supreme Court upheld the insurers repudiation. The court then found the brokers liable to the insured on the basis that they were aware of the facts not disclosed. The actual person in the brokers' organisation alleged to have had knowledge of the facts had died prior to the loss.

he undertakes to bring a fair, reasonable and competent degree of skill.[46]

The test in Ireland for establishing professional negligence is

whether [the professional] . . . has proved to be guilty of such failure as no . . . practitioner of equal specialist or general status and skill would be guilty of in acting with ordinary care.[47]

2.10 BROKER'S LIABILITY TO THE INSURER

Information conveyed to brokers holding a binding authority from insurers is imputed to those insurers who are liable to the policyholder but insurers are entitled to an indemnity, in respect of the loss, from the brokers.[48] The implied authority of a broker to issue a cover note on behalf of an insurer does not extend to entering into the complete policy of insurance which is substituted for the temporary cover note.[49] Whether a broker is acting for the insurer or not may be significant in law. The standard broker agency appointment agreement used in Ireland is silent on the matter of the broker's liability to the insurer. The IBA Code of Conduct only requires the broker to "observe the privileged nature of the relationship between insurer and intermediary". Whilst there is authority for the view that the broker owes no general duty towards an insurer,[50] an insurer who feels he has been misled by a broker, but nevertheless pays a claim, could have a claim against the broker in tort if not in contract. In the

---

[46] see n.37 supra.

[47] *Dunne* v *National Maternity Hospital* [1989] IR 91.

[48] *Woolcott* v *Excess Insurance Co. Ltd. and Others* [1979] 1 Lloyds Rep 231. Brokers holding a binding authority from insurers effected cover for the plaintiff who failed to disclose a criminal record. The brokers knew of the record and that knowledge was imputed to the insurers. The insurers were held liable to the plaintiff but entitled to an indemnity from the brokers.

[49] *Stockton* v *Mason* [1978] 2 Lloyds Rep 430. The Court of Appeal held that the brokers had implied authority to grant temporary cover on behalf of insurers who were liable under the terms of that cover in respect of losses occurring before any restrictions on the cover were conveyed to the insured.

[50] *Empress Assurance Corp.* Ltd. v *C.T. Bowring & Co. Ltd.* [1905] 11 Com. Cas. 107.

case of *The Zephyr*[51] it was held that the brokers did owe a duty of care to the insurers and that the earlier cases which suggested otherwise were no longer authoritative since the decision of the House of Lords in *Hedley Byrne*.[52]

2.11 BROKER'S LIABILITY TO THE CLIENT

The liability of the broker to the client arises out of the contract between the parties and in tort. It is not usual for the terms of the contract to be committed to writing and consequently problems arise in determining the extent of the contractual duty owed by the broker to the client. Whilst there was some judicial controversy as to whether a professional person whose relationship with their client was founded in contract could be exposed to a greater liability in negligence,[53] the House of Lords have expressed the opinion that a duty in negligence could arise concurrently with a duty in contract where the professional person assumed responsibility to provide services to another who in turn relied on those services. The fact that the parties originally came together under a contractual relationship was immaterial.[54] Where a concurrent liability exists in contract and in tort, the plaintiff may choose the most advantageous remedy available to him.[55] The main advantage of proceeding in negligence is the extended time limitation available. In Ireland this concept of concurrent

---

[51] *General Accident Fire & Life Assurance Corp. Ltd.* v *Tanter, "The Zephyr"* [1984] 1 Lloyds Rep 58; [1985] 2 Lloyds Rep 529.

[52] *Hedley Byrne & Co. Ltd.* v *Heller & Partners* [1963] 1 Lloyds Rep 274; [1964] AC 465.

[53] *Tai Hing Cotton Mill Ltd.* v *Liu Chong Hing Bank Ltd.* [1986] AC 80. Lord Scarman attacked the idea of concurrent liability saying:
> Lordships do not believe there is anything to the advantage of the law's development in searching for liability in tort where the parties are in a contractual relationship.

[54] *Henderson* v *Merrett Syndicates* and *Arbuttnott* v *Feltrim Underwriting Agencies* [1994] 3 All ER 506.

[55] see *Iron Trades Mutual Insurance Co.* v *J.K. Buckenham Ltd.* [1989] 2 Lloyds Rep 85 and *Islander Trucking Ltd.* v *Hogg, Robinson and Gardiner Mountain (Marine) Ltd.* [1990] 1 All ER 826.

liability has been accepted in *Finlay* v *Murtagh*[56] and in *Roche* v *Peilow*.[57] In *Chariot Inns* the defendant broker was found liable in tort and in breach of contract.[58] To succeed in negligence against a broker the client must establish that the broker owed him a duty of care, that the broker was in breach of that duty and that as a result he suffered loss of a reasonably foreseeable nature. In England it was generally the case that no duty was owed to a person whose loss was purely economic except where the loss arose out of negligent misstatement.[59] As a result of the decision in *Henderson* v *Merrett Syndicates*[60] negligent service by a broker can now, in certain circumstances, give rise to liability for economic loss. There must have been negligent service by a qualified person to or for an identifiable claimant; the relationship between the broker and the client must be one which the law characterises as one of proximity; and the circumstances must be such that the court considers it "fair, just and reasonable that the law should impose a duty".[61] In *Henderson* v *Merrett*[62] it was suggested that where a broker assumes responsibility to the client for certain services it is not necessary to enquire whether it is

---

[56] *Finlay* v *Murtagh* [1979] IR 249 Kenny J. said:

> The professional person, however, owes the client a general duty, which does not arise from contract but from the "proximity" principle to exercise reasonable skill and care in the performance of the work entrusted to him. . . . failure to have or to exercise reasonable skill and care is tortious or delictual in origin. So a plaintiff in such an action may successfully sue in contract or in tort or in both.

[57] *Roche* v *Peilow* [1985] IR 253.

[58] *Chariot Inns Ltd.* v *Assicurazioni Generali SPA & others* [1981] IR 199; [1981] ILRM 173; *Latham* v *Hibernian Insurance Co. Ltd. & Others* (No. 1) Unreported High Court, 22 March 1991. In *Vesta* v *Butcher* [1986] 2 Lloyds Rep 179, Hobhouse J. at first instance said:

> The plaintiff's case was that there were concurrent contractual and tortious obligations, breach of which could be put either as a claim in contract for breach of an implied term to exercise reasonable skill and care or as a claim in the tort of negligence. This was not in dispute before me as a correct analysis of the position. It is a status of professional relationship which is factually concurrent with a contractual relationship.

[59] *Hedley Byrne & Co. Ltd.* v *Heller & Partners* [1963] 1 Lloyds Rep 274; [1964] AC 465.

[60] [1994] 3 All ER 506.

[61] *Caparo Industries plc* v *Dickman* [1990] 2 AC 605 per Lord Bridge at 618.

[62] n. 60 *supra*.

"fair just and reasonable" to impose liability.[63] In Ireland, the courts have, on a number of occasions, stated that subject to considerations of public policy, there is no bar to recovery of economic loss in tort.[64]

Where there is concurrent liability in contract and in tort, the Courts had up to recently accepted that, where there is a contract, there is no advantage to the law's development in searching for liability in tort.[65] Even if tort was relevant, the parties rights and obligations in tort could not be any greater than those founded in contract. *Henderson v Merrett*[66] modified that approach in holding that managing agents at Lloyds owed duties in both contract and tort to the names. In endeavouring to establish rights in tort, the names sought to obtain the benefit of the more advantageous limitation period for bringing actions in tort as against contract. The House of Lords, while accepting that the names had no better rights in tort than in contract, distinguished between contractual rights which could not be exceeded and procedural advantages associated with tort actions. In a subsequent case, *Holt v Payne Skillington and de Groot Collis*,[67] the Court of Appeal distinguished *Tai Hing*[68] by holding that the contract between the parties limited the parties' rights, but only in respect of the rights covered by the contract. *Tai Hing*, on the other hand, had decided that if the parties have a contract, that contract determines the extent of their rights. In making the distinction in *Holt*, the court expressed the opinion that:

> there is no reason in principle why a . . . duty of care cannot arise in an overall set of circumstances where by reference to certain limited aspects of the circumstances, the same parties enter into a contractual relationship involving much more limited obligations than those imposed by the duty of care in

---

[63] ibid. per Lord Goff at 521.

[64] *Sweeney v Duggan* [1991] 1 IR 274; *McShane Wholesale Fruit & Vegetables Ltd. v Johnstone Haulage Ltd & Others* Unreported High Court, 19 January 1996; *Ward v McMaster* [1985] IR 29; *Dublin Port and Docks Board v Bank of Ireland* [1976] IR 118.

[65] *Tai Hing Cotton Mill Ltd. v Liu Chong Hing Bank Ltd.* [1986] AC 80; see n. 53 *supra*.

[66] *Henderson v Merrett Syndicates Ltd.* [1995] 2 AC 145.

[67] Unreported Court of Appeal, December 1995.

[68] n. 65 *supra*.

tort. In such circumstances, the duty of care in tort and the duties imposed by the contract will be concurrent but not co-extensive. The difference in scope between the two will reflect the more limited factual basis which gave rise to the contract and the absence of any term in that contract which precludes or restricts the wider duty of care in tort.

2.12 IMPLIED TERMS

In the absence of express terms the law imposes implied terms which are reasonable and necessary to give business efficacy to the transaction. The two most important terms which the courts have implied into the insurance broker's contract with the client are:

a) an implied term that the broker has authority to act. If loss results he will be strictly liable if he is in breach of this "warranty of authority". If for example a broker is authorised to issue cover notes on behalf of an insurer and without the broker's knowledge the insurer goes into liquidation, the broker is liable on the cover notes issued by them. The broker's lack of knowledge is no defence.[69]

b) an implied term that the broker should use reasonable and proper care skill and judgment to effect the insurance of his client.

2.13 BROKER'S DUTY TO FOLLOW INSTRUCTIONS

The broker must follow instructions promptly and accurately, although, unless he is told otherwise by the client, he is not obliged to treat his instructions as a matter of urgency.[70] If these instructions are ambiguous then he must obtain clarification of them.[71] Where a

---

[69] *Osman* v *Moss* [1970] 1 Lloyds Rep 313.

[70] In *Cok, Russell & Co.* v *Bray Gibb & Co.* [1920] 3 Lloyds Rep 72, the broker, instructed on a Friday afternoon to obtain cover on a cargo arriving in London the following Monday, failed to do so in time and was held not to be negligent. He did not know the date of arrival and hence the reason for the urgency, and was not bound to try to get cover before close of business on the Friday.

[71] In *Curtis t/a Agencies Transport Ltd* v *Corcoran Insurances Ltd.* Unreported High Court, 13 July 1973, Pringle J. said:
  if a client's instructions were not clear as to the type of insurance which he required, his [the broker's] duty would be to ask him what his requirements were.

broker had agreed to arrange insurance on a hotel against "all business risks" he was held liable when the hotel burnt down and there was no cover in force against loss of profits.[72] Where an horticulturist client indicated to his broker that he wanted "everything covered" the broker was held liable when the comprehensive policy arranged by him did not cover damage to plants by freezing caused by failure of a water pump.[73] The court held that where a client gave no specific instructions, the insurance broker was under a duty to plan the client's insurances. Where the broker does not know the actual facts he must make enquiries. If acting on incomplete or incorrect information the broker misrepresents the risk to the insurer he may be liable to the client for the losses sustained in the event of the insurer declining to indemnify the policyholder.[74] In *McNealy* v *The Penine Insurance Co. Ltd.*[75] Lord Denning M. R. said that

> It was clearly the duty of the broker to use all his reasonable care to see that the assured . . . was properly covered

and Waller J. said that

---

[72] *Beattie* v *Furness Houlder Insurance* [1976] SLT Nov. 5. The court held that there was no breach of contract but that the broker was negligent. Whilst the loss claimed was not proved the court felt the insurers might have made an "ex gratia" payment.

[73] *Fine Flowers Ltd.* v *General Accident Insurance Co. Ltd.* [1978] 81 DLR (3d) 139. The court held the broker liable on the grounds that the client had relied on him to ensure that he was adequately covered. Even if the cover was unobtainable there was an onus on the broker to advise the client so that he would appreciate the situation he was in.

[74] *Warren* v *Henry Sutton & Co.* [1976] 2 Lloyds Rep 276. Plaintiff asked the broker to cover an additional driver (aged 25) for a trip in a sports car to France. The plaintiff knew the driver had a bad record but did not tell the broker. The broker told the insurer that the driver had no accidents, convictions or disabilities. The majority of the Court of Appeal held that the positive mis-representation by the broker was due to his omission to make inquiries.

[75] *McNealy* v *The Penine Insurance Company Ltd.* [1978] 2 Lloyds Rep 18. The defendant brokers placed the plaintiff's motor insurance with an insurer who did not write insurance for part-time musicians. The broker had not asked the proposer if he was a part-time musician and he described himself on the proposal as a property repairer. The insurers claimed non-disclosure of a material fact and their repudiation of liability was upheld. The brokers were found liable to the client because they had a duty to ensure as far as possible that he was not within a category that the insurer found unacceptable.

> It was clearly his [the broker's] duty, in my view to make as
> certain as he reasonably could that the [assured] came within
> the categories acceptable to the [insurer].

The broker's obligations were extended further by Hobhouse J. in the
Zephyr[76] where he said that

> it is the broker's duty to do his best to see that the assured's
> obligations of disclosure and absence of misrepresentation are
> fulfilled. The broker's skill and expertise extends beyond
> merely giving advice and complying with his client's instruc-
> tions. He must make use of his knowledge of the market and
> use appropriate skills.

2.14 DUTY TO SATISFY CLIENT'S NEEDS

Whilst there was authority for the proposition that a broker instructed to obtain cover was under no duty to ensure that the client's
needs were fully satisfied by a standard policy,[77] such a proposition is
fundamentally out of step with practice. Indeed in *Youell* v *Bland
Welch & Co. Ltd.*[78] Phillips J. expressly stated that it is the initial
duty of an insurance broker to ascertain the client's needs. In the
celebrated *"Shergar* case"[79] Rattee J. adopted the dicta in *Youell* v
Bland Welch but noted that the client's express instructions are simply one source of the obligations imposed on the broker. The addi-

---

[76] *General Accident* v *Tanter*, *"The Zephyr"* [1984] 1 Lloyds Rep 58; 2 Lloyds Rep
529.

[77] *United Mills Agencies Ltd.* v *Bray* [1951] 2 Lloyds Rep 631. See n. 12 and n. 41
supra.

[78] *Youell* v *Bland Welch & Co. Ltd.* [1990] 2 Lloyds Rep 431.

[79] *O'Brien* v *Hughes Gibb & Co. Ltd.* [1995] LRLR 90. The case concerned the
mysterious disappearance of the racehorse "Shergar". Underwriters would have
regarded the loss as one of theft but the policy did not cover theft. Some years
prior to the loss the plaintiff had a block policy covering theft and mortality risks.
The policy had expired by the time cover was requested in respect of "Shergar".
Brokers had a binding authority providing mortality, transit and theft cover but
the binder did not permit cover on shares in a stud horse which was what was
required in this instance. Cover was therefore sought in the open market. The
plaintiff had never previously requested theft cover but had accepted it as part of
the standard terms and indeed was ignorant of its existence. The court was satisfied that if theft cover had been sought in respect of "Shergar" it would have
been provided at no additional premium. The court found the client's instructions
had been clear, there was no request for theft cover and there was no negligence
in carrying out the instructions.

tional cover necessary to have the loss met under the terms of the policy was, if not unusual, at least not a form of cover that was generally sought or given. The brokers were absolved of liability for the loss but the particular facts prevents the case being regarded as in any way narrowing the broker's responsibility to ascertain the client's needs.[80]

2.15 DUTY TO ADVISE THE CLIENT

The broker must protect the interests of the client, if necessary by advising him.[81] Whilst the broker may not be obliged to inform the client when the insurance has been effected the broker probably must give notice if the insurance has not been effected.[82] Market practice cannot take the broker outside his duty to protect his client's interests.[83] Two English cases demonstrate the extent of this duty. In *Fraser* v *B.N. Furman*[84] the plaintiff company asked the defendant brokers to take over the handling of its insurances. The brokers agreed and asked the company to send them the renewal notices when received from the existing insurers and also their insurance policies. An employee of the company was injured in an industrial accident and the company sought an indemnity from the brokers because there was no employer's liability insurance in place. In their defence the brokers pleaded that they were only concerned with the insurances for which the company had submitted renewal notices. The court rejected that argument and found the brokers in breach of contract and liable to the client. In *Strong* v *Allison*[85] a marine policy on a yacht arranged by the defendant brokers contained a "change of moorings" clause. The brokers failed to advise the client of the clause

---

[80] see para. 2.4.3 above.

[81] *Callander* v *Oelrichs & another* [1838] 5 Bing NC 58.

[82] *Smith* v *Lascelles* [1788] 2 TR 187. A merchant accustomed to arranging insurance on goods, the subject of transactions between him and another, was liable to that other for failing to advise him that he could not or would not arrange cover on a particular consignment.

[83] *North & South Trust* v *Berkeley* [1971] 1 All ER 980. Broker refused to disclose the contents of assessors report to his client.

[84] *Fraser* v *B.N. Furman* [1967] 2 Lloyds Rep 1.

[85] *Strong* v *Allison* [1926] 25 Lloyds Rep 504.

and when a loss occurred after a change of moorings the insurers denied liability. The brokers were held liable to the client.

2.16 DUTY TO DISCLOSE INFORMATION

Because a contract of insurance is *uberrimae fidei* then, as agent of the client, the broker must disclose all relevant information which the client provides to him.[86] The broker's duty to disclose has been extended by the Irish courts to include information of which the broker is aware from his own knowledge. The duty is owed to the client, not the insurer and in the event of the insurer successfully repudiating liability on the grounds of non-disclosure of the information then the broker can be held liable to the client for the loss sustained. In *Latham v Hibernian Insurance Company Limited and others*[87] the insurer successfully repudiated liability for fire damage to the insured premises, on the grounds that the insured failed to disclose at renewal the fact that he had been arrested and charged some months previously with receiving stolen goods. Blayney J. held that, while the fact that he was arrested and charged might not of itself be material, the fact that he admitted the offence and was guilty of the crime was undoubtedly material and should have been disclosed prior to renewal even though the criminal proceedings did not come to hearing until after renewal. The plaintiff, having failed against the insurer, pursued his action against his insurance broker who had arranged the policy on his behalf. He claimed that the broker had learned of the arrest and charge from casual conversation with his partner's sister-in-law. The judge accepted that the broker was aware of the arrest and charge and that once he had this information he was obliged to advise his client that it ought to be disclosed to insurers. The broker was held to have failed to exercise reasonable care in the handling of his client's affairs and liable to him in contract and in tort. Blayney J. said:

> the plaintiff's insurance broker owed the plaintiff a duty to exercise reasonable care in the handling of the plaintiff's affairs. And one of his duties in exercising such care would have been

---

[86] *Ogden & Co. Pty Ltd. v Reliance Fire Sprinkler Pty Ltd.* [1975] 1 Lloyds Rep 52.

[87] *Latham v Hibernian Insurance Co. Ltd. and Peter Sheridan & Co. Ltd.* (No. 1) Unreported High Court, 22 March 1991.

to advise the plaintiff as to the necessity of disclosing to the [insurer] that he had been arrested and charged with an offence of receiving stolen goods. His failure to do this was in my opinion a breach of his duty to the plaintiff. [The broker's] duty to the plaintiff was both a contractual duty and a common law duty in negligence.

In an English case, a broker who obtained certain information about his client, whilst dancing with a lady who subsequently became his client's wife, was found liable for failing to disclose that information to the insurers.[88]

2.17 DUTY TO KNOW THE LAW

The broker must be familiar with the general principles of insurance law and may in certain circumstances be under a duty to take legal advice.[89] A broker expressing an unqualified opinion without taking reasonable care to furnish himself with such information as would entitle him to give that opinion is guilty of negligence.[90]

---

[88] In the English case of *Woolcott* v *Excess Insurance Co. & Others* [1979] 1 Lloyds Rep 231 the broker who held a binding authority from insurers was held liable to indemnify the insurers in respect of a claim paid out under a policy issued under the binder and in respect of which the insurers failed to maintain a repudiation on grounds of alleged non-disclosure of the criminal record of the insured. The broker had learned of the record whilst dancing with a lady who subsequently became the insured's wife. The information given by her to the broker, despite being given in social circumstances was imputed to the insurers. The broker had not conveyed the material information to the insurers.

[89] *Park* v *Hammond* [1816] Taunt 495 — The defendant broker should have been aware of a rule of law that an insurance to commence from the loading of goods at a certain point would not attach to goods previously laden.

[90] *Sarginson Bros.* v *Keith Moulton & Co. Ltd.* [1942] 73 Lloyds Rep 104. Brokers asked to insure timber during the war advised the client that cover was not available due to wartime restrictions. That advice was incorrect and the brokers were liable to the client for the loss when the timber was destroyed. The court said:

> if people occupying a profession take it upon themselves to give advice upon a matter directly connected with their own profession then they are responsible for seeing that they are equipped with a reasonable degree of skill and a reasonable stock of information so to render it reasonably safe for them to give that particular piece of advice.

2.18 PROPOSAL FORMS

The IBA Code of Conduct requires the broker to "assist the client, where requested, in the completion of proposals, drawing his attention to the necessity of full disclosure of all relevant facts and explaining the consequences of non-disclosure". The general advice to brokers from their professional liability insurers is that they should not complete proposal forms for their clients. It is also recommended that the broker obtain a supplementary declaration, signed by the client, confirming that the client has read the completed form, that the answers are correct and, whether completed by the client or not, that the proposal is to be treated as if completed by the client. These "risk management" recommendations are intended to reduce the broker's exposure to claims of negligence from the client. Where a broker completes a proposal form or assists in its completion he does so as agent of the proposer and not as agent of the insurer. He may therefore be liable to the client for the consequences of any inaccuracies or false information contained in the form.[91] In the English case of *O'Connor* v *B.D.B. Kirby*,[92] the Court of Appeal absolved the broker of negligence where the broker, having obtained the correct information from the client, inserted the incorrect information on the proposal form. The case was, however, decided on its own particular facts and therefore of little general application.

2.19 CHOICE OF INSURER

A broker instructed by his client to insure with an unsuitable insurer is not obliged, unless asked, to tell the client of the insurer's unsuitability.[93] If, however, a client who is not well informed is advised by a broker to insure with a financially unsound company, the broker may

---

[91] *Chariot Inns Ltd.* v *Assicurazioni Generali SPA & Others* [1981] IR 199; [1981] ILRM 173; *Newsholme Bros.* v *Road Transport & General Insurance Co.* [1929] 2 KB 356.

[92] *O'Connor* v *B.D.B. Kirby & Co.* [1971] 2 All ER 1415. The client had been asked to read and check the proposal form before signing it but he failed to notice a material error. The court held that the duty of care did not extend to guaranteeing that every answer was correct. It is suggested that the court's decision was influenced by a suspicion of a conspiracy between the insured and the broker and that it believed the loss should lie with the insured.

[93] *Waterkeyn* v *Eagle Star & British Dominion Insurance Co. Ltd.* [1920] 5 Lloyds Rep 42.

be liable to the client for the consequences of the insurer's insolvency.[94] In the USA, a Federal District Court in New Jersey found that a broker's duty to use reasonable skill, care and diligence extends to selecting a financially secure insurer, and that a negligent broker may be liable for losses arising from the insurer's insolvency.[95] Despite the opening up of the Irish Insurance market under "Freedom of Services" directives, it is still necessary for insurers writing business in Ireland to be authorised under relevant legislation. Whilst there have been reported incidents of brokers placing business outside the country with insurers not authorised to write business in Ireland there has been no reported case of a client suing the broker arising out of their doing so. There are however a number of English cases which are relevant. In *Bedford Insurance Co. Ltd.* v *Instituto de Ressegures do Brazil*[96] the defendant reinsurers refused to pay claims under the reinsurance contract on the grounds that the contract was illegal because they were not authorised to write the insurance. The defence succeeded but there was no legal action taken against the plaintiff's broker. In the case of *Stewart* v *Oriental Fire and Marine Insurance Co. Ltd.*[97] it was held that the intention of the legislation was not to invalidate such contracts and thereby cause loss to the policyholder but rather to protect the innocent insured. These conflicting decisions were resolved by the Court of Appeal in *Phoenix General Insurance Co. of Greece* v *ADAS*[98] when the court confirmed the decision in *Bedford* that contracts made with unauthorised insurers are illegal and therefore void and unenforceable. It is likely that if a broker in Ireland placed insurance with an insurer, unauthorised to write business in Ireland, he would be liable to the client in negligence as he would be expected to know which companies were

---

[94] *Osman* v *Moss* [1970] 1 Lloyds Rep 313.

[95] *Carter Lincoln Mercury Inc.* v *Emar Group Inc.* 618a 2d 870 (NJ App. Div. 1993).

[96] [1985] QB 966; [1984] 1 Lloyds Rep 210; [1984] 3 All ER 766.

[97] [1985] 2 QB 988; [1984] 2 Lloyds Rep 109. There was no suggestion of negligence and the case was brought to test the correctness of the *Bedford* decision. In that case there had been collusion between the plaintiff and the brokers, whereas in the *Stewart* case the plaintiffs were unaware of the defendants lack of authorisation.

[98] [1986] 2 Lloyds Rep 552; [1987] 2 All ER 152 CA.

authorised.[99] In a more recent English case, *Re: Great Western Insurance Co. SA*[100] the Court of Appeal warned brokers of possible exposure to prosecution under the UK legislation saying:

> It must not be assumed that those with knowledge of the relevant facts can close their eyes to the possibility that criminal acts are involved and assume that they themselves are not also committing criminal offences. Agents acting in any respect for a company, domestic or overseas, which is carrying on business in this country without the requisite authorisation, must appreciate that they too may be committing criminal offences and subject to criminal and other sanctions.

2.20 USE OF SUB-BROKER

It is common practice for a broker, appointed by a client to arrange a particular form of cover, to use a sub-broker to gain access to a specialist niche market or to restricted underwriting facilities. As a matter of law, the client has a contract with the broker appointed by him and that broker has a contract with the sub-broker. There is however no contract between the client and the sub-broker. The appointed broker owes a duty of care, in both tort and contract, to his client, to ensure that the cover arranged and the policy wording meet the client's requirements. It has been unclear whether, in the absence of a contract between the parties, the sub-broker owes a duty of care to the client or whether the appointed broker is vicariously liable for the negligence of the sub-broker. The matter was considered in *Jones* v *Marsh McLennan* v *Crawley Colosso*,[101] where on the facts it was held that the insured's loss was caused by the combined negligence of the broker and sub-broker and liability was apportioned between them. The insured's brokers in the United States, Marsh McLennan, requested the defendant, London-based, brokers to arrange cover in London in respect of the development of a holiday resort on two un-

---

[99] *Bates* v *Barrow Ltd.* [1995] 1 Lloyds Rep 680. Defendant brokers had placed cover with a reputable but unauthorised insurer. The court held the broker was under a duty to ensure the policies complied with the legislation. However the loss was not foreseeable as given the reputation of the insurers the brokers would not have "contemplated such an eventuality as a real danger".

[100] Unreported Court of Appeal, 31 July 1996.

[101] Lloyds List, 1 August 1996.

inhabited islands in the Bahamas. The sub-brokers arranged the Contractors All Risks cover under three separate policies on the same terms and excluding liability for loss or damage to any part of the permanent works in respect of which a certificate of completion had been issued. Copies of the wording were submitted by the sub-broker to the appointed broker and they raised no objections to the exclusion. Part of the permanent works in respect of which a certificate of completion had been issued were seriously damaged by a hurricane. The leading insurer paid its portion of the loss but the following insurers declined to meet the claim, relying on the policy exclusion. The insured sued the sub-broker for breach of duty and assigned his rights to his appointed broker who then continued the action, maintaining that the sub-broker owed a duty of care to both parties. In their defence, the sub-brokers argued that, even if they did owe a duty of care, the brokers had been guilty of contributory negligence. The court agreed and apportioned liability two-thirds to the sub-broker and one-third to the producing broker. The court held that the producing broker had a duty to ensure that the policy wording provided the necessary cover and that the fact that the wording was provided by the sub-broker did not exempt the producing broker from checking it. The court also held that the sub-broker should have specifically drawn the exclusion to the broker's attention. The decision appears to establish that: a sub-broker owes a duty of care to the insured; it is insufficient for the sub-broker to send a wording to the appointed broker for approval; the sub-broker has a duty to draw the producing broker's attention to all relevant clauses and exclusions.

2.21 BROKER'S LIABILITY TO THIRD PARTIES

2.21.1 Whilst the broker's liability to the client arises primarily from the contract which exists between them, liability can also arise in tort. The broker can also be liable to the insurer and to certain third parties. *Hedley Byrne*[102] established the legal principle that negligent advice given to a third party, who is not in a contractual relationship with the defendant, may lead to liability on the part of the defendant if the third party relied upon the advice, and if the defendant knew or

---

[102] *Hedley Byrne & Co. Ltd.* v *Heller & Partners* [1963] 1 Lloyds Rep 485; [1964] AC 465.

should have known that the party would so rely. A broker may be liable for statements made before he is actually instructed by a client. Liability for damages could arise out of incorrect advice, given to a prospective client, as to the availability of insurance or the terms on which it might be available. A broker can be liable to a former client after his appointment has been terminated.[103]

2.21.2 The broker may owe a duty of care to third parties who were not previously involved with the brokers.[104] In conducting their business insurance brokers are required to use reasonable care. This duty of care is owed to any party who bears a relationship of proximity to them in terms of the "neighbour principle".[105] How far the courts will go in determining this duty of care remains to be seen but it is possible in an era of extreme consumer protectionism to speculate that an injured third party unable to obtain redress from a policyholder or the insurer might successfully sue the broker on the basis of the duty of care owed to them.[106]

---

[103] *Cherry Ltd.* v *Allied Insurance Brokers Ltd.* [1978] 1 Lloyds Rep 274. The defendant brokers were instructed to terminate all policies as the plaintiff client intended appointing new brokers. The defendant advised the client that insurers had refused to cancel mid-term, whereupon the client cancelled the new insurances he had arranged. The original insurers subsequently agreed to cancel and did so. The brokers omitted to advise the client and a loss occurred. The brokers were held liable for the former client's uninsured loss.

[104] *Bromley* v *Ellis* [1971] 1 Lloyds Rep 97. An uninsured motorist sued the brokers to the vendor of the car purchased by him when they failed to properly arrange transfer of the insurance or to advise him that cover had been withdrawn by the insurers.

[105] *Donoghue* v *Stevenson* [1932] AC 562:
> You must take reasonable care to avoid acts or omissions which you can reasonably foresee would be likely to injure your neighbour. Who, then, in law is my neighbour? The answer seems to be: persons who are so closely and directly affected by my act that I ought reasonably to have them in contemplation as being so affected when I am directing my mind to the acts or omissions which are called in question.

[106] In *Liberty National Life Insurance Company* v *Weldon* 267 Ala 171 [1958] an aunt insured the life of her niece despite having no insurable interest. She then murdered the niece. The parents of the niece successfully sued the insurers in negligence for creating the motive for murder by issuing the policy and they were awarded $75,000. The aunt was executed!

2.21.3 Whilst there are no decided Irish cases on the liability of brokers to third parties in respect of loss suffered by them, there have
been a number of cases in England and Ireland involving other professions which could be indicative of how the law might develop in
this area. In developing the law the courts are faced with a conflict
between the demands of consumerism and the consequences of establishing

> an indeterminate liability in an indeterminate amount for an
> indeterminate time to an indeterminate class.[107]

In *Hedley Byrne*[108] the House of Lords demanded the existence of a
special relationship between the parties, before imposing liability, but
subsequently Lord Denning M.R. seemed to dispense with that requirement when he said:

> Nowadays since *Hedley Byrne* . . . it is clear that a professional
> man who gives guidance to others owes a duty of care not only
> to the client who employs him but also to another who he
> knows is relying on his skill to save him from harm.[109]

In *Ross v Caunters,*[110] where a beneficiary under a will was disqualified, due to the negligence of solicitors, she recovered the legacy from
the solicitors, despite the absence of a contractual relationship between them, with the court holding that

> the solicitors owed a duty of care to the plaintiff since she was
> someone within their direct contemplation as a person so
> closely and directly affected by their acts and omissions in car-
> rying out their client's instructions to provide her with a share
> of his residue that they could reasonably foresee that she
> would be likely to be injured by their acts or omissions.

---

[107] Cardoza J. in *Ultramares Corporate* v *Touche* [1931] 255 NY 170.

[108] n. 102 *supra*.

[109] *Dalton* v *Bognor Regis United Building Co. Ltd.* [1972] 1 QB 373. Whilst the
actual decision was over-ruled in *Murphy* v *Brentwood District Council* [1990] 2
All ER 909 the quotation is still applicable.

[110] *Ross* v *Caunters* [1980] 1 Ch 297; [1979] 3 All ER 580.

2.21.4 The Irish Supreme Court, in *Wall* v *Hegarty*,[111] came to a similar conclusion in holding that a solicitor owed a duty of care to legatees, to draft a will with such reasonable care and skill, so as to ensure that the testator's wishes were not frustrated and the expectation of the legatee defeated through a lack of reasonable skill and care. The decision in *Ross* v *Caunters* was approved in *White* v *Jones*[112] with Lord Goff for the majority in the House of Lords giving an indication of the manner in which the law is prepared to respond to the demands of the consumer:

> it was open to the House to fashion a remedy to fill a lacuna in the law and so prevent an injustice which would otherwise occur on the facts of cases such as the present. . . . The House should in cases such as these extend to the intended beneficiary a remedy under the *Hedley Byrne* principle by holding that the assumption of responsibility by the solicitor towards his client should be held in law to extend to the intended beneficiary who, as the solicitor could reasonably foresee, might as a result of the solicitor's negligence be deprived of his intended legacy in circumstances in which neither the testator nor his estate would have a remedy against the solicitor.

Prior to *White* v *Jones,* the English Courts had adopted a restrictive approach to the extension of tortious duties owed to third parties requiring a proximity of relationship before finding the existence of a duty of care.[113] Given the inclinations of the Irish courts towards the

---

[111] *Wall* v *Hegarty* [1980] ILRM 124. The defendant solicitor failed to ensure the will was signed by two witnesses and the intended beneficiary was to the loss of £15,000.

[112] *White* v *Jones* [1993] 3 All ER 481 and *The Times* 17 February 1995, (House of Lords). The defendant solicitor failed to carry out the testator's instructions by not preparing a draft will within a reasonable time, and the testator died before he could execute a new will. The solicitor was held liable to the intended beneficiaries of the new will.

[113] In *Caparo Industries* v *Dickman* [1990] 2 AC 605 the House of Lords held that auditors owed a duty of care to the company which retained them but that shareholders had no individual right of action. In *Berg* v *Adams* [1992] BCC 661 Hobhouse J. said "it will only be in very clear and immediate circumstances that the creditor will be able to show the special relationship which gives rise to such a duty of care". In *Verderame & others* v *Commercial Union & Midland Bank Insurance Brokers Ltd.* [1992] BCLC 793 brokers retained by a limited company were held not to be liable to the individual shareholders for loss occasioned by their negligence. The company only had the right to bring the action. In *Pryke*

protection of the individual consumer it is not difficult to see the boundaries of the duty of care owed by insurance brokers being extended so as to fix the broker with liability where the intended beneficiary of an insurance policy is deprived of the benefit of the policy due to the negligence of the broker in arranging the insurance policy.

2.22 DEFENCES

The defence to be raised by an insurance broker to a claim of professional negligence will depend on the particular facts and circumstances surrounding the loss. The general defences available include:

2.22.1 NO LOSS SUFFERED

The broker may contend that even if the client's instructions had been carried out and the insurance placed with reasonable skill and care the insurers would not have accepted the risk or would in any event have repudiated liability.[114]

2.22.2 THE LOSS WAS TOO REMOTE

The brokers may claim that the alleged breach of duty was not the proximate cause of the loss. If, for instance, the insured was given the opportunity of checking the information on the proposal or other document the broker might claim that it was the failure of the in-

---

and the Excess v *Gibbs Hartley Cooper Ltd.* [1991] 1 Lloyds Rep 602 the brokers were found liable in tort to third parties for breach of a non-contractual undertaking. In *McCullagh* v *Lane Fox* [1994] *The Times* 25 January, an estate agent acting for a vendor was held to owe a duty of care to the purchaser. The judge applying the test for liability in negligence held that (a) damage to the purchaser was foreseeable, (b) the relationship between the parties was of sufficient proximity to give rise to a duty of care, and (c) it was just and fair in the circumstances that the law should impose a duty of care.

[114] In *Cheshire & Co.* v *Vaughan Bros. & Co.* [1917] 3 Lloyds Rep 213, the brokers were held not liable for failing to effect a policy deemed void under the Marine Insurance Act 1906. However, in *Fraser* v *B.N. Furman Ltd.* [1967] 2 Lloyds Rep 1, it was held the brokers could not avail themselves of the defence that the contract of insurance they failed to conclude would have been voidable at the election of the insurers.

sured to notice an error which was the cause of the loss. However, in *Dickson & Co.* v *Devitt*[115] it was held that

> when a broker is employed to effect an insurance, . . . the client is entitled to rely upon the broker carrying out his instructions, and is not bound to examine the documents . . . and see whether his instructions have in fact been carried out by the brokers.

2.22.3 CONTRIBUTORY NEGLIGENCE

When the circumstances are such that the broker's error was or should have been obvious the broker may allege contributory negligence on the part of the client. Whilst the courts have been prepared to discount the damages for a successful plea they are unlikely to absolve the broker of liability entirely. In *Reid* v *McCleave*,[116] the defendant received a cover note valid for thirty days from his insurance brokers, and after this expired, he received no further cover notes or insurance certificates. He did, however, receive verbal assurances from the broker that he was still insured to drive the motor vehicle and he accepted and relied on these assurances when it should have been obvious to him that the brokers may have made a mistake. The court rejected the submission that the insured was solely responsible for his own loss but allowed a discount of twenty-five per cent for contributory negligence.

2.22.4 EXCLUSION OR LIMITATION OF LIABILITY

It is unlikely that a broker could, in practice, exclude liability for his breach of duty or negligence. What client would have confidence in such a broker? However a broker could limit his exposure to his client by entering into a formal contract in the form of a "letter of engagement". Such a practice is becoming increasingly common in other jurisdictions. The letter sets out clearly the respective obligations and

---

[115] Mr. Justice Atkins in *Dickson & Co* v *Devitt* [1916] 86 LJKB 315. A broker instructed to insure against war risks cargo on a named steamer and/or steamers effected cover whilst on a named steamer only. It was held that although the client had opportunity to notice the error they were entitled to rely upon their instructions being carried out by the brokers.

[116] See also *Youell* v *Bland Welch* [1990] 2 Lloyds Rep 431 and *Vesta* v *Butcher* [1986] 2 Lloyds Rep 179; [1986] 2 All ER 488, [1988] 1 Lloyds Rep 19; [1988] 2 All ER 43; [1989] 1 Lloyds Rep 331; [1989] 1 All ER 402.

rights of the parties so that they both understand what is expected of them. The letter identifies and confirms the services which the broker undertakes to provide for the agreed remuneration and those services which can be provided on payment of additional fees. The broker's duty of care is no less in respect of those services which he is obliged to provide but he would have a defence in respect of any claim arising out of services consciously omitted from the terms of reference by the client.

2.22.5 TIME BAR

Generally, an action in tort or contract, not involving a claim for damages for personal injuries, cannot be brought after the expiration of six years from the date on which the cause of action accrued.[117] In an action in contract, the date of accrual of the cause of action is the date on which the contract is entered into.[118] In so far as actions in tort against insurance brokers are concerned the date of accrual of a right of action has been held to be the date when the broker procures the insurance contract which is voidable and that is when the client suffers financial loss. [119] The voidable contract affords the insured less contractual rights and is therefore less valuable than the contract the broker is instructed to obtain.[120] In *Johnston* v *Leslie & Godwin Financial Services Ltd.*[121] the plaintiff required documents in 1984 to enable him claim under a retrocession contract. The defendant brokers argued that as the documents had been mislaid by them some-

---

[117] Section 11(2)(a) Statute of Limitations 1957.

[118] see p. 619, Cheshire Fifoot & Furmston (1986).

[119] *Iron Trades Mutual Insurance Company Ltd.* v *J.K. Buckenham Ltd.* [1989] 2 Lloyds Rep 85; *Islander Trucking Ltd.* v *Hogg, Robinson, & Gardiner Mountain (Marine) Ltd.* [1990] 1 All ER 826; see also *Forster* v *Outred & Co.* [1982] 2 All ER 753.

[120] In *First National Commercial Bank plc* v *Humberts*, Unreported CA, 13 January 1995, the Court sought to distinguish previous cases involving insurance brokers *supra*, and other cases involving solicitors by saying:

> In all those cases, however, the court was able to conclude that the transaction then and there caused the claimant loss, on the basis that if the injured party had been put in the position he would have occupied but for the breach of duty, the transaction in question would have provided greater rights, or imposed lesser liabilities or obligations than was the case; and that the difference between these two states of affairs could be quantified in money terms at the date of the transaction.

[121] [1995] LRLR 472.

time in the early 1970s the plaintiff's claim was time barred. The court rejected the argument holding that the brokers were under a continuing duty to retain documentation necessary to the processing of the plaintiff's claims and the action was not therefore out of time.

2.23 DAMAGES

Where a broker is found to be in breach of contract or guilty of negligence he is required to put the plaintiffs, in money terms, in the position they would have been in if the broker had not been in breach of contract or guilty of negligence. Generally speaking the amount will be what the insurers would have paid out under the contract if it had not been void.[122] If the action arises out of the broker's failure to effect cover, but even if he had done so the contract would have been voidable, and the client, nevertheless, has suffered loss, the court will, in assessing damages, consider

> what were the chances that an insurance company of the highest repute and reputation . . . notwithstanding their strict legal rights, would, as a matter of business, have paid up under the policy.[123]

2.24 RETENTION OF RECORDS AND PRIVILEGE

The IBA Code of Conduct does not establish guidelines for brokers on the retention of records and there are no market standards. Lloyds Regulations require the retention of essential documentation for fifteen years in respect of personal lines business and eighty years in respect of commercial business.[124] In *Johnston* v *Leslie & Godwin Financial Services Ltd.*[125] it was held that a broker owes a continuing

---

[122] *Latham* v *Hibernian Insurance Company Ltd. & Others* (No. 2) Unreported High Court, 4 December 1991.

[123] *Fraser* v *Furman Productions Ltd.* [1967] 2 Lloyds Rep 1 per Diplock L. J.

[124] Lloyds Bylaws Part F 47.

[125] [1995] LRLR 472. The defendant brokers had placed retrocession contracts on behalf of the plaintiff in respect of claims occurring during 1956. With the notification of asbestosis claims from 1981 on, the plaintiff sought to claim under the contract in 1984. The defendant was unable to locate documentation which would have identified the retrocessionaires. The documentation had not been destroyed but mislaid. The judge held the broker in breach of contractual duty to exercise reasonable skill and care. The question of limitation or time bar did not arise as the brokers were found to be under a continuous contractual duty to maintain

duty of care in relation to the collection of claims and must retain sufficient information to enable a claim be made as long as a reasonable broker would regard a claim as possible. Where a dispute arises between a client and a broker, discovery will generally be sought by the plaintiff in respect of all relevant correspondence and documentation. Documentation prepared by the broker, for the purpose of obtaining professional advice, or arising out of a professional relationship, need not be disclosed and, to avail of this immunity, it is immaterial whether or not proceedings were contemplated at the time the documentation was prepared.[126] Where documentation comes into existence in anticipation of litigation, privilege can be claimed in respect of it and discovery refused.[127] It has also been held that

> where there is need for legal advice to be shared confidentially with parties with a community of interest, then the law should not be astute to find distinctions between, for instance . . . a reinsurer and his reinsured on the one hand, and an assured and his legal liability insurer on the other.[128]

---

records to enable them make a claim on behalf of the plaintiff.

[126] *Carrigan* v *Norwich Union* (No. 1) [1987] IR 618. O'Hanlon J. referring to his earlier judgment in *Silver Hill Duckling* v *Minister for Agriculture* [1987] IR 289 said:

> I adhere to the view expressed by me in the judgment in that case that privilege from disclosure may be claimed by a party to litigation in respect of a document which has come into existence prior to the commencement of proceedings, where it can be shown that the dominant purpose for the document coming into existence in the first place was the purpose of preparing for litigation then apprehended or threatened.

See also *Dunnes Stores Ltd.* v *Smith*, Unreported High Court, 24 July 1995.

[127] *Davis* v *St. Michael's House* Unreported High Court, 25 November 1993. The court upheld a claim to privilege by the insurer in respect of statements, report forms, notes and correspondence completed by the insured's staff shortly after the accident giving rise to the proceedings but a considerable time before the action was initiated.

[128] *Svenska Handelsbanken* v *Sun Alliance & London* [1995] 2 Lloyds Rep 84.

CHAPTER THREE

DUTY OF DISCLOSURE

"The Underwriter knows nothing and the man who comes to him to ask him to insure knows everything."[1]

3.1 INTRODUCTION

The ability of an insurance company to avoid a contract of insurance on grounds of misrepresentation or non-disclosure has been a matter of great debate and controversy among insurers, brokers, legal advisers and academics for many years. The law on the duty of disclosure is clear:

> The proposer for a policy of insurance has a duty to disclose all material facts which would influence the judgment of a prudent insurer in fixing the premium or determining whether he will take the risk.[2]

An insurance contract is the classic example of a contract *uberrimae fidei*.[3] Such contracts require disclosure by all parties to the contract of all facts and circumstances which might reasonably be thought to influence the other party in deciding whether to enter into a transaction and on what terms. This duty of disclosure was established in

---

[1] *Rozanes* v *Bowen* [1928] Lloyds Rep 98 per Scrutton L. J. at 102.

[2] Section 18(2), Marine Insurance Act, 1906.

[3] Insurance contracts are not the only contracts of this type. Whether a contract is one requiring *uberrima fides* or not must depend on its substantial character and how it came to be effected (*Seaton* v *Heath* [1899] 1 QB 782). These two reasons would account for the fact that contracts for family settlements, for the allotment of shares in companies, and, in some cases, contracts of suretyship and partnership, are *uberrimae fidei*. Anson's *Law of Contract* (1982), pp. 260–261.

common law, because often, in the restricted areas in which it applies, one side alone is in possession of vital details about the transaction contemplated, about which the other has to trust their word.
The first and most extended exposition of the doctrine, in so far as it
relates to insurance, is the oft quoted extract from the judgment of
Lord Mansfield:

> Men argue differently from natural phenomena and political
> appearances. They have different capacities, different degrees
> of knowledge and different intelligence. But the means of in-
> formation and judging are open to both. Each professes to act
> from his own skill and sagacity; and therefore neither needs to
> communicate to the other. The reason of the rule which obliges
> one party to disclose is to prevent fraud and encourage good
> faith. It is adapted to such facts as vary the nature of the con-
> tract; which one privately knows and the other is ignorant of
> and has no reason to suspect. The question, therefore, must
> always be whether there was under all the circumstance at the
> time the policy was underwritten a fair representation or a
> concealment; fraudulent if designed; or though not designed
> varying materially the object of the policy and changing the
> risque understood to be run.[4]

This duty of good faith propounded by Lord Mansfield over 200 years
ago represents the principle on which insurance law has developed
since then. It is now accepted as one of the central doctrines of insurance law. The rule was rigid, inflexible and strict when it first
emerged. As a result of statute and developing case law it became
stricter still. The English courts adhered rigidly to the policy underlying the rule even if they occasionally did so with expressed reluc-

---

[4] Lord Mansfield in *Carter* v *Boehm* [1766] 3 Burr 1905 at 1909/1911. In *Pan Atlantic* v *Pine Top Insurance Company Ltd.* [1994] WLR 677 Lord Mustill, at 699,
quoting from the above passage expressed the view that Lord Mansfield's judgment

> . . . not only contained the first and most extended exposition of the doctrine
> but was the starting point for the opinions of the notable scholars in England
> and the United States whose treatment of the subject had such a powerful in-
> fluence on the development of the law.

The American Jurist Vance writing at the turn of the century believed that when
Lord Mansfield became Chief Justice of the Kings Bench in 1756 it could "rightly
be considered as the date of the beginning of the development of the modern law
of insurance as part of the common law system" (Vance, 1909).

tance.[5] The Irish courts have, however, been less rigid in their application of the rule and to such an extent that it is now the main area of difference between the courts in the general area of insurance law. Whilst the English courts follow the original intention of the common law and statute in the protection of the insurer the Irish courts lean in favour of the insured.

3.2 MATERIALITY

3.2.1 STATUTORY BASIS

The Marine Insurance Act, 1906 codified the law in relation to marine insurance, confirmed that insurance contracts are contracts *uberrimae fidei*, defined what is material and deals generally with the duty of disclosure and the rights of the parties to the contract.[6] Section 18(2) of the Act says:

> Every circumstance is material which would influence the judgment of a prudent underwriter in fixing the premium or determining whether he will take the risk.

Since the enactment of the Act the courts have had significant difficulties in interpreting this definition and attempts have been made to substitute the "prudent proposer" for the "prudent underwriter" and to introduce a requirement that the actual underwriter's judgment should in fact be affected by the non-disclosure or misrepresentation.[7]

---

[5] *Lambert* v *Co-operative Insurance Society Ltd.* [1975] 2 Lloyds Rep 485, where at 491 MacKenna J. said: "The present case shows the unsatisfactory state of the law . . . the defendant company would act decently if they were to pay . . . it might be thought a heartless thing if they did not"; and at 492 Lawton J. said: "much as I sympathise with the point of view . . . I cannot accept that it can alter the law".

[6] The codifying Act was drafted by Sir MacKenzie Chalmers who also drafted other codifying legislation such as the Bills of Exchange Act, 1882 and the Sale of Goods Act, 1893, neither of which generated as many disputes as to what they meant as did the Marine Insurance Act.

[7] *Roselodge* v *Castle* [1966] 2 Lloyds Rep 113. In *Joel* v *Law Union and Crown Insurance* [1908] 2 KB 431, the Court of Appeal suggested that in some classes of personal insurance all that the law required was that the insured must disclose such facts as a reasonable man in his position would believe to be material. In the Law Commission Report 1980 No. 104 at para 10.9(c) it recommended that the duty should be modified so that

There was a large body of opinion in the 1950s which thought that the honest policyholder was put at a disadvantage by the duty to disclose all material facts when materiality was to be judged purely from the standpoint of the insurer, rather than the proposer, and in the context of the accumulated weight of decisions that had formed precedents over the last two centuries. In response to pressure the matter was referred on two occasions to the Law Reform Commission in England but no amending legislation was ever introduced despite the Commission's belief that:

> The state of the law is capable of leading to abuse in the sense that a variety of circumstances may entitle insurers after a loss has occurred, to repudiate liability as against an honest and at least careful insured.[8]

3.2.2 JUDICIAL INTERPRETATION

However, in response to the demand for a relaxation of the law the insurance industry did introduce Statements and Codes of Practice[9]

---

a fact should be disclosed to the insurer by an applicant if it is one which a reasonable man in the position of the applicant would disclose to his insurers, having regard to the nature and the extent of the insurance cover sought and the circumstances in which it is sought.

In *CTI* v *Oceanus* [1982] 2 Lloyds Rep 178 Lloyd J. at first instance, and *Berger and Light Diffusers Pty. Ltd.* v *Pollock* [1973] 2 Lloyds Rep 442 at 463 where Kerr J. said:

> It seems to me as a matter of principle that the court's task in deciding whether or not the insurer can avoid the policy for non-disclosure must be to determine as a question of fact whether, by applying the standard of the judgment of a prudent insurer, the insurer in question would have been influenced in fixing the premium or determining whether to take the risk if he had been informed of the undisclosed circumstance before entering into the contract. Otherwise one could in theory reach the absurd position where the court might be satisfied that the insurer in question would in fact not have been so influenced but that other prudent insurers would have been. It would then be a very odd result if the defendant insurer could nevertheless avoid the policy.

[8] [1957] Cmnd 62. para 11–14. The report confirmed that material was available to the committee which proved that such abuses had in fact occurred.

[9] In Ireland, Section 61 of the Insurance Act, 1989 enables the Minister for Industry and Commerce, where it is considered necessary in the public interest, to prescribe Codes of Conduct on the duty of disclosure and warranties following consultation with the insurance industry and consumer representatives. In anticipation of the legislation and in return for a promise not to enact the relevant provision, the Irish Insurance Federation introduced its own Codes of Practice and Statements of Insurance Practice on the lines of its English counterpart.

so that innocent non-disclosure or misrepresentation would not be penalised where the policy was effected by individual consumers. The then existing state of the law was however forcibly re-affirmed by the Court of Appeal in a landmark case in 1984 known as *CTI* v *Oceanus*.[10] At first instance, Lloyd J. interpreted the test for materiality as requiring some "difference of action" on the part of the underwriter so that he could only succeed on a defence of non-disclosure if he could satisfy the court that a prudent insurer, possessing the undisclosed information, would in fact have declined the risk or charged a higher premium.[11] This "new" test was unanimously rejected by the Court of Appeal which decided that the sole test for materiality was the "prudent insurer" test and that the phrase "would influence the judgment of a prudent insurer" meant that it was not necessary to show that a prudent insurer would have acted differently armed with the facts not disclosed. It was sufficient that a prudent insurer would have wished to have been made aware of that information. Kerr J. in delivering the main judgment said that the point at issue was not whether the undisclosed circumstances "would" in fact have influenced a prudent insurer to act otherwise but simply if the judgment to accept or reject the insurance proposal was affected:

> To prove the materiality of an undisclosed circumstance the insurer must satisfy the court on a balance of probability by evidence or from the nature of the undisclosed circumstance itself that the judgment in this sense of a prudent insurer would have been influenced if the circumstances in question had been disclosed. . . . The section [of the Act] is directed to what would

---

[10] *CTI International Inc. & Reliance Group Inc.* v *Oceanus Mutual Underwriting Association (Bermuda) Ltd.* [1984] 1 Lloyds Rep 476.

[11] [1982] 2 Lloyds Rep 178 at 187:
> . . . in general I would say that underwriters ought only to succeed on a defence of non-disclosure if they can satisfy the court by evidence or otherwise that a prudent insurer, if they had known the fact in question, would have declined the risk altogether or charged a higher premium. . . . some "difference of action" is required in order to establish materiality. The mind of the reasonable insurer must have been influenced so as to induce him to refuse the risk or alter the premium. . . . normally at any rate insurers must show that the result would have been affected.

have been the impact of the disclosure on the judgment of the risk formed by a hypothetical prudent insurer.[12]

This decision of the Court of Appeal, whilst questioned in subsequent High Court proceedings,[13] represented the law on the test for materiality in England until the House of Lords decision in *Pan Atlantic* delivered in July 1994.[14]

3.2.3 TEST FOR MATERIALITY IN ENGLAND

3.2.3.1 In the High Court in England, in *Pan Atlantic*, Waller J. said:

> It is accepted that I must take the law as laid down in *CTI* v *Oceanus*.[15] That case made clear that in considering Sections 18, 19, and 20 of the Marine Insurance Act, 1906 any circumstance is material, i.e. is one which would influence the judgment of a prudent insurer in fixing the premium or determining whether he will take the risk if it is a circumstance which would have had an impact on the formation of his opinion and on his decision-making process. . . . The case also made clear that the test in relation to non-disclosure or misrepresentation was influence on the judgment of a prudent insurer and that thus the right to avoid did not depend on whether the particular insurer was influenced as a fact in relation to determining the premium he charged or in his decision whether or not to take the risk.[16]

---

[12] In agreeing with this formulation Parker L. J. quoted from Mr. Justice Samuels' judgment in *Mayne Nickless Ltd.* v *Pegler* [1974] NSWLR 228:

> . . . I do not think it is generally open to examine what the insurer would in fact have done had he had the information not disclosed. The question is whether that information would have been relevant to the exercise of the insurer's option to accept or reject the insurance proposed. It seems to me that the test of materiality is this: a fact is material if it would have reasonably affected the mind of a prudent insurer in determining whether he will accept the insurance and if so at what premium and on what terms and conditions.

[13] *Highlands Insurance Co.* v *Continental Insurance* [1987] 1 Lloyds Rep 109, at 113.

[14] *Pan Atlantic* v *Pine Top Insurance Co. Ltd.* [1994] WLR 677. The House of Lords heard the appeal over six days and then took four months to consider their judgment.

[15] [1984] 1 Lloyds Rep 476.

[16] [1992] 1 Lloyds Rep 101.

Although he expressed some disquiet about finding that the failure to disclose additional losses should entitle the defendant insurer to avoid all liability[17] he did find that such non-disclosure was material and that he had no choice but to allow the contract be avoided.

3.2.3.2 On appeal of the *Pan Atlantic* decision to the Court of Appeal, the court saw fit to modify its own previous ruling in *CTI* v *Oceanus*. The court held that it was bound by the *CTI* ruling as to the irrelevance of the state of mind of the actual underwriter when faced with a misleading proposal and that a fact is material if it would cause a prudent insurer to appreciate that the risk was different from that actually presented to him. Applying that test to the facts before it the court affirmed the trial judge's ruling and the policy was held to be avoidable for breach of duty.[18] The ruling of the Court of Appeal was seen as authorising a fresh judicial approach to the whole question of non-disclosure and it was hoped that its practical operation might involve a more critical approach by judges to market evidence favouring a finding of materiality.

3.2.3.3 The matter was appealed to the House of Lords and by majority of three to two it held that the test of materiality remained the same as it was in *CTI*, namely that a fact is material if it would influence the decision-making process of a prudent insurer with regard to acceptance of the risk or the premium to be charged. However, their Lordships agreed unanimously that there was now to be implied into the Marine Insurance Act, 1906 a requirement that a material non-disclosure will only entitle the insurer to avoid the policy if it induced

---

[17] ibid. at 114.

[18] [1993] 1 Lloyds Rep 496. The leading judgment was given by Steyn L. J. with which Sir Donald Nicholls, Vice Chancellor and Farquarson L. J. agreed although he chose to add an interesting comment of his own at 508:

The issue of non-disclosure is decided by the objective standard of the prudent insurer. . . . that standard has to be applied even though . . . a prudent insurer would not have accepted the risk at the premium he (the actual underwriter) had quoted. Thus the result of setting aside this reinsurance treaty is that the reinsurer avoids all liability for his own bad bargain and moreover does so even though full disclosure would have resulted, not in his declining to take the risk but only in an increased premium. . . . Justice and fairness would suggest that, when an inadvertent non-disclosure came to light, what was required was an adjustment in premium or in perhaps the cover. . . . what is needed is a more sophisticated remedy, more appropriate, and in that sense more proportionate to the wrong suffered.

the making of the contract. Lord Mustill summarised the new two-part test as follows:

> A circumstance may be material even though a full and accurate disclosure of it would not in itself have a decisive effect on the prudent insurer's decision whether to accept the risk and if so at what premium.

> If the misrepresentation or the non-disclosure of a material fact did not in fact induce the making of the contract . . . the insurer is not entitled to rely on it as a ground for avoiding the contract.19

3.2.3.4 On that basis it appeared it would no longer be sufficient for the insurer to rely on the views of an independent expert insurer to establish that a misrepresented or non-disclosed circumstance was material. The actual underwriter would also have to give evidence to the court or arbitration tribunal that he was induced to underwrite the risk as a consequence of the matter being misrepresented or withheld from him.[20] The decision was the subject of intense analysis and comment in every insurance and every law journal at the time as it had been thought that the decision helped liberalise the law in favour of the insured. The subsequent decision of the Court of Appeal, in *St Paul Fire and Marine Co. (UK) Ltd.* v *McConnell Dowell Con-*

---

[19] In justifying the Lords decision to introduce a new test, Lord Mustill at 705 [1994] WLR 677 said:
> True, the inequalities of knowledge between assured and underwriter have led to the creation of a special duty to make accurate disclosure of sufficient facts to restore the balance and remedy the injustice of holding the underwriter to a speculation which he had been unable fairly to assess. But the consideration cannot in logic or justice require courts to go further and declare the contract to be vitiated when the underwriter having paid no attention to the matters not properly stated and disclosed has suffered no injustice thereby.

[20] The decision in *Pan Atlantic* was notable in that it was the first time since the Marine Insurance Act of 1906 was passed that the test of materiality had to be considered by the House of Lords. The comments of Lord Mustill at 714 [1994] WLR are of interest in the context of the power of the Lords to create law:
> If the Act, which did not set out to be a complete codification of existing law, will yield to qualification in one case, surely it must in common sense do so in another. If this requires the making of new law, so be it. There is no subversion here of established precedent. It is only in recent years that the problem has been squarely faced. Facing it now, I believe that a need for inducement can and should be implied into the Act.

structors Ltd.[21] that the "presumption of inducement" could be relied upon, where the particular underwriter did not give evidence, seemed to suggest that nothing may in fact have changed.

3.2.3.5 The "presumption of inducement" principle laid down in *Pan Atlantic* meant that insurers could successfully plead a breach of duty, if they could prove that the non-disclosed fact or misrepresentation was material, and that they were induced by it to enter into the contract, although proof of materiality gave rise to a presumption that the insurers were so induced and the onus would then be on the insured to prove otherwise. The principle was applied subsequently, in *Svenska Handelsbanken* v *Sun Alliance and London plc.*[22] when insurers, having shown that a misrepresentation was material, were allowed rely on the presumption that, as prudent insurers, they were induced to enter the contract. In *Marc Rich & Co. AG* v *Portman*[23] the court indicated that it is only in circumstances where the particular underwriter cannot give evidence that the presumption is relevant. Where evidence is given the court can of course decide the matter for itself. The reliance to be placed on the presumption is diminished where the underwriter is shown to be less than prudent and the underwriter must have very good reasons for failing to give evidence.

---

[21] Unreported judgment of the Court of Appeal, May 1995. It was accepted by the parties that, following *Pan Atlantic,* an insurer must prove that he was induced by the non-disclosure or misrepresentation to enter into the contract on terms which he would not have accepted if all the material facts had been made known to him. There were four relevant insurers involved and underwriters on behalf of three of them had given evidence at the trial of the action. It was clear from that evidence that, if they had been aware of the true facts, they would not have underwritten the risk at the same premium or the same terms. The court had no difficulty in finding proved the necessary inducement of those three underwriters. No evidence had been put forward on behalf of the fourth, but the court held there was a presumption on which the insurer could rely and that there was no evidence to rebut this presumption. The fourth insurer was held entitled to avoid the contract as were the other insurers even though the fourth insurer had tendered no evidence whatsoever. In the absence of an appeal to the House of Lords clarifying the position this decision of the Court of Appeal would seem to indicate that maybe nothing was changed by the *Pan Atlantic* decision.

[22] [1995] 2 Lloyds Rep 84.

[23] [1996] 1 Lloyds Rep 430. Much of the evidence in the case was heard prior to the decision in *Pan Atlantic* but the judgment was given after that ruling and before the decision in *St. Paul* (n. 21 *supra*).

Where evidence of inducement is not given the presumption is rebuttable.

3.2.4 THE IRISH TEST FOR MATERIALITY

3.2.4.1 The Irish test for materiality is:

> . . . Not what the person seeking insurance regards as material, nor is it what the insurance company regards as material. It is a matter of circumstance which would reasonably influence the judgment of a prudent insurer in deciding whether he would take the risk, and if so, in determining the premium which he would demand. The standard by which materiality is to be determined is objective and not subjective. In the last resort the matter has to be determined by the court: the parties to the litigation may call experts in insurance matters as witnesses to give evidence of what they would have regarded as material, but the question of materiality is not to be determined by such witnesses.

So stated Kenny J. in a Supreme Court judgment, with which Henchy J. and Griffen J. agreed, in the case of *Chariot Inns Ltd.* v *Assicurazioni Generali SPA and Others*.[24] The decision is generally accepted as the main authority relating to materiality and the duty of disclosure in Ireland. The plaintiffs in the action in proposing for insurance on a licensed premises had failed to disclose to the defendant insurer a previous loss by fire of furnishings stored at another location owned by an associated company. The insurer repudiated liability for a subsequent fire which destroyed the insured premises on the grounds of non-disclosure of the earlier fire and the plaintiffs sought a declaration in the High Court that the policy issued to them was valid. At first instance Keane J. held that the matters not disclosed had not been material to the risk underwritten and that accordingly the policy of insurance was a valid policy. Three expert witnesses gave it as their unanimous view that the matters not disclosed were material but the actual underwriter in evidence indicated that had the matters been disclosed to him it would not have affected his acceptance of the risk.

---

[24] [1981] IR 199 at 226.

3.2.4.2 At first instance, in holding for the plaintiff insured and against the expert evidence produced by insurers, Keane J. said that the fact that the particular insurer who seeks to avoid the contract would not have been affected by its disclosure in determining whether to accept the risk or in fixing the premium is not relevant. He then went on to quote Samuels J. in *Mayne Nickless Ltd.* v *Pegler*:[25]

> ... I do not think it is generally open to examine what the insurer would in fact have done had he had the information not disclosed. The question is whether that information would have been relevant to the exercise of the insurer's option to accept or reject the insurance proposed. It seems to me that the test of materiality is this: a fact is material if it would have reasonably affected the mind of a prudent insurer in determining whether he will accept the insurance and if so at what premium and on what terms.

3.2.4.3 On appeal, the Supreme Court reversed Keane J. but approved his quotation from *Mayne Nickless* v *Pegler*. In holding in favour of the defendant insurer the court did not regard the unanimous view of three independent experts as conclusive. The court held that the question whether any of the matters not disclosed were material was essentially an inference from facts established by the evidence. Counsel for the brokers (the second defendants) had strenuously argued that the insurers had to establish that the matter not disclosed did in fact affect the judgment of the particular underwriter. Kenny J. dismissed that argument with a quotation from McKinnon L. J.:

> What is material is that which would influence the mind of a prudent insurer in deciding whether to accept the risk or fix the premium and if this be proved it is not necessary further to prove that the mind of the actual insurer was so affected. In other words, the assured could not rebut the claim to avoid the

---

[25] [1974] 1 NSWLR 228. In emphasising that the test for determining materiality is an objective one, Keane J. quoted also from the opinion of the Judicial Committee in the case of *Mutual Life Insurance Company of New York* v *Ontario Metal Products Company* [1926] AC 344 at 351–2 where it stated:

> It is a question of fact in each case whether, if matters concealed or misrepresented had been truly disclosed, they would, on a fair consideration of the evidence, have influenced a reasonable insurer to decline the risk or to have stipulated for a higher premium.

policy because of a material misrepresentation by a plea that
the particular insurer concerned was so stupid, ignorant or
reckless that he could not exercise the judgment of a prudent
insurer and was in fact unaffected by anything the assured had
represented or concealed.[26]

The Supreme Court in finding in favour of the insurer gave judgment
to the plaintiff against the brokers for breach of contract and negligence.

3.2.4.4 An opportunity of reconsidering the doctrine of non-disclosure
and the test for materiality was presented to the Supreme Court in
the case of *Aro Road and Land Vehicles Ltd.* v *Insurance Corporation
of Ireland Ltd.*[27] This was an appeal from a judgment of Carroll J. in
the High Court. At issue was whether the defendant insurers were
entitled to repudiate liability under a policy on the ground that before
the policy was effected the Managing Director and main shareholder
in the insured company had not disclosed that some twenty years
previously he had been convicted on ten counts of receiving stolen
motor parts and sentenced to twenty-one months imprisonment. At
first instance Carroll J. was of the opinion that the conviction was not
material because the insurance (a Transit Policy) only operated
whilst the insured property was in the hands of a third party. The
defendant insurer produced expert witnesses who testified that had
they, as reasonable and prudent insurers, known of the conviction
they would never have issued a policy to the plaintiff insured and
that the conviction should most definitely have been disclosed. Carroll J. deferred to the expert testimony, although she did not accept
that the views expressed were reasonable, and found in favour of the
insurer. On appeal, McCarthy J. in the Supreme Court denounced

---

[26] *Zurich General Accident and Liability Insurance* v *Morrison* [1942] 2 KB 53 at
60. In *Svenska* (n. 22 *supra*), the judge found that the underwriter had not given
any serious attention to the scope of the cover requested and that he had been
prepared to accept the premium offered for the extension without asking what it
was intended to cover. Prior to *Pan Atlantic, supra*, the only question would have
been whether a prudent insurer would have regarded the facts as material. The
subjective test introduced by *Pan Atlantic* would seem to mean that if the insurer
in question did not regard the facts as material the insured is not in breach of the
duty of disclosure.

[27] [1986] IR 403. This case could not have arisen in the UK as it involved non-
disclosure of a criminal offence some twenty years previously and the Rehabilita-
tion of Offenders Act would have applied.

and criticised the approach of Carroll J. saying if a judge did not believe the views of expert witnesses to be reasonable then those views
should not be followed. He said "the insurance profession is not to be
permitted to dictate a binding definition of what is reasonable".[28] The
Court accepted that the test laid down in *Chariot Inns* was the correct test to be applied and followed.[29]

3.2.4.5 However McCarthy J. was also of the view that:

> . . . if the judgment of an insurer is such as to require disclo-
> sure of what he thinks is relevant but which a reasonable in-
> sured, if he thought of it at all, would not think relevant, then
> in the absence of a question directed towards the disclosure of
> such a fact the insurer, albeit prudent, cannot properly be held
> to be acting reasonably. . . . the insured is bound to disclose
> every matter which might reasonably be thought to be mate-
> rial to the risk against which he is seeking indemnity; that test
> of reasonableness is an objective one not to be determined by
> the opinion of underwriter, broker or insurance agent but by,
> and only by, the tribunal determining the issue.[30]

On the basis of that dicta it is possible to interpret McCarthy's judgment as amending the test for materiality to read

> every circumstance is material which would influence the
> judgment of what the courts would consider a reasonable and
> prudent insurer in fixing the premium or determining whether
> he will take the risk.

On another reading it would seem that McCarthy J. is advancing the
substitution of the reasonable proposer for the reasonable and prudent insurer. Towards the end of his judgment he said:

> If the determination of what is material were to lie with the
> insurer alone I do not know how the average citizen is to know

---

[28] ibid. at 411.

[29] At 408 Henchy J. in a concurring judgment accepted without question that:
it is a general principle of the law of insurance that a person seeking insurance
whether acting personally or through a limited company is bound to disclose
every circumstance within his knowledge which would have influenced the
judgment of a reasonable and prudent insurer in fixing the premium or in deciding whether to take on the risk.

[30] ibid. at 412.

what goes on in the insurer's mind unless the insurer asks him by way of questions in a proposal or otherwise. I do not accept that he must seek out the proposed insurer and question him as to his reasonableness, his prudence and what he considers material. . . . if the duty is one which requires disclosure by the insured of all material facts which are known to him then it may well require an impossible level of performance . . . how does one depart from a standard if reasonably and genuinely one does not consider some fact material.[31]

3.2.4.6 In a subsequent High Court case, *Kelleher* v *Irish Life Assurance Company Ltd.*,[32] Costelloe J. seemed to accept that there had been no change in the law when he said:

The general duty at common law is to disclose material facts, that is facts which would affect the mind of a prudent insurer either in deciding to underwrite the risk at all or in fixing the premiums.

Whilst later in his judgment he did make reference to the *Aro Road* case he did not deal with it in any great detail. He suggested that if the case laid down a new test there was no need for him to consider it as, on the facts, it would fail that test also. However, when the case went on appeal to the Supreme Court, Finlay J. seemed to accept that the test was that of the reasonable insured and not the reasonable insurer saying:

. . . the true and acid test must be as to whether a reasonable man reading the proposal form would conclude that the information over and above it which is in issue was not required.[33]

In the High Court case of *Latham* v *Hibernian Insurance Co. Ltd. & Others*, which was decided before the Supreme Court gave its judgment in *Kelleher* Blayney J. said:

As to whether a fact is material to be disclosed to the insurance company, the test is that laid down in Section 18(2) of the

---

[31] ibid. at 414. In *Pan Atlantic* much the same view was expressed by Lord Mustill when he asserted it would be "almost impossible" for a prospective insured or his broker to identify whether disclosure of a particular circumstance would produce a different decision by the hypothetical underwriter.

[32] Unreported High Court 16 December 1988.

[33] *Kelleher* v *Irish Life Assurance Co. Ltd.* [1993] ILRM 643 at 650.

Marine Insurance Act, 1906 which Kenny J. in *Chariot Inns* said is a correct guide to the law in insurance against damage to property or goods of all types.[34]

3.2.4.7 On the basis of the comments of the Supreme Court, it can be argued that the test for materiality in Ireland has moved from the traditional "prudent insurer" to the "reasonable proposer". The test for materiality, as applied in Ireland and in England, originates from the same statute and whilst the House of Lords in *Pan Atlantic* has now reinterpreted the intentions of the original drafters of the statute, and introduced a requirement of inducement, its decision is not binding on the Irish Courts, although it may be quoted as persuasive authority.[35] It is unlikely however, given the leniency shown by the Irish Supreme Court towards plaintiff insureds, that the House of Lords decision, which has since been interpreted in a manner favourable to the insurer, will be followed here. It is more likely that the Irish courts will adopt the view of Gavan Duffy J. in *Kirby* v *Burke & Holloway* that

> . . . the House of Lords established that memorable conclusion . . . by a majority of three to two. . . . where lawyers so learned disagreed an Irish judge could not assume . . . as a matter of course, that the view which prevailed must of necessity be true of the common law of Ireland. One voice in the House could have turned the scale.[36]

3.3 EXPERT EVIDENCE

3.3.1 ADMISSIBILITY

The law of evidence does not in general permit the admission of "opinion evidence". For witnesses to be allowed express their opinions on the matters in issue would amount to an usurpation of the function of the court. One of the exceptions to this rule is the court's acceptance of testimony from persons acknowledged as experts in their

---

[34] Unreported High Court 22 March 1991.

[35] Article 15.2 of the Irish Constitution provides that "the sole and exclusive power of making laws for the state is hereby vested in the Oireachtas. No other legislative authority has power to make laws for the state."

[36] [1944] IR 207. Gavan Duffy was referring to the decision in *Donoghue* v *Stevenson* [1932] AC 562.

particular field called for the express purpose of giving an opinion on the matter to be determined. The law recognises that, so far as matters calling for special knowledge or skill are concerned, judges are not necessarily properly equipped to draw the right inferences from facts stated by witnesses.[37]

> Their duty is to furnish the judge with the necessary scientific criteria for testing the accuracy of their conclusions, so as to enable the judge or jury to form their own independent judgment by the application of these criteria to the facts proved in evidence.[38]

3.3.2 RELIABILITY OF EXPERT WITNESSES

The practice in England and Ireland in insurance related court cases has been for the defendant insurer to call in aid evidence from experienced underwriters employed by competing insurers to give their opinion as to what their response would have been had the undisclosed or misrepresented facts been disclosed to them.[39] The purpose of calling such witnesses is to establish what the view of prudent insurers in general would be on the matter in issue. The view of the actual underwriter who accepted the risk has been held to be irrelevant.[40] The testimony of insurance experts may not be truly impartial for they are required to express opinions with the benefit of hindsight and free of the pressures of the marketplace. Expert testimony of insurers and brokers is freely admitted even though it could be argued that insurers if not brokers are to some extent judges in their own

---

[37] *Cross on Evidence* (1990), p. 489.

[38] Lord President Cooper in *Davie* v *Edinburgh Magistrates* [1953] SC 34 at 40.

[39] This practice has been permissible since an early date according to McGillivray and Parkington (1988) who quote *Chaurand* v *Angerstein* [1791] Peake 43; *Littledale* v *Dixon* [1805] 1 B&P (NR) 151; *Berthon* v *Loughman* [1817] 2 St 258.

[40] *CTI* v *Oceanus* [1984] 2 Lloyds Rep 476 where Kerr L. J. said:

> To prove materiality of an undisclosed circumstance, the insurer must satisfy the court on a balance of probability — by evidence or from the nature of the undisclosed circumstance itself — that the judgment, in this sense, of a prudent insurer would have been influenced if the circumstances in question had been disclosed. . . . The weight which the court would give to such evidence is then a matter for the court.

See also *Glasgow Assurance Corp. Ltd.* v *Symondson & Co.* [1911] 16 Com Cas 109; *Zurich General Accident & Liability Co. Ltd.* v *Morrison* [1942] 2 KB 53; and *Chariot Inns Ltd.* v *Assicurazioni Generali & others* [1981] IR 199.

cause.[41] The implication of the *Pan Atlantic* decision is that, in England, an insurer wishing to repudiate liability under a policy, on the ground of non-disclosure, will now have to call the actual underwriter to give evidence that the non-disclosed facts induced him to enter into the contract. It may be necessary for the underwriter to demonstrate a history of having considered matters of a similar nature when underwriting other similar risks, although at least one judge has indicated that it would be an unfortunate side effect of *Pan Atlantic* if every case involved evidence demonstrating past imprudence of the underwriter in support of a contention that he could not have been prudent in the particular case in question.[42] The *Pan Atlantic* decision, however, is unlikely to change the approach of the Irish Courts, so trenchantly expounded by Kenny J. in the Supreme Court, that

> . . . the parties to litigation may call experts in insurance matters as witnesses to give evidence of what they would have regarded as material, but the question of materiality is not to be determined by such witnesses.[43]

---

[41] In *Carter* v *Boehm* [1766] 3 Burr 1905, Lord Mansfield said of evidence of brokers, "it is mere opinion: which is not evidence. It is opinion without the least foundation from any previous precedent or usage." This view is no longer good law as expert testimony of brokers is now freely admissible. The reliance to be placed on the testimony of insurance underwriters was examined at length by McNair J. in *Roselodge* v *Castle* [1966] 2 Lloyds Rep 113 at 129:

> It has long been the practice in our courts to allow proof . . . by the evidence of underwriters. . . . In many cases the evidence of underwriters if fully accepted would work serious hardship to assureds. . . . The criticism against the objectivity of the [witnesses'] evidence is that when they came to give evidence they found themselves in the position that a heavy claim against a body of underwriters for whom they undertook responsibility had been made which they were not satisfied . . . was an honest claim. . . . they were anxious to defeat the claim if it could be legitimately defeated. . . . They were driven in cross examination to state such extreme views that I am unable to accept their evidence.

One of the expert witnesses had suggested a person who stole apples at the age of seventeen was more likely to steal jewellery at the age of sixty-seven and that had the theft of apples been disclosed to him he would have declined to insure the risk even though the insured had led a blameless life for fifty years!

[42] per Longmore J. in *Marc Rich* (n. 23 *supra*): "The question . . . is whether the underwriter abrogated his functions in relation to these risks, not in relation to numerous other risks written on different occasions."

[43] *Chariot Inns Ltd.* v *Assicurazioni Generali & others* [1981] IR 198 at 226; *Pan Atlantic* v *Pine Top* [1994] 1 WLR 677 at 720 where Lord Lloyd of Berwick said:

> Five experienced and prudent underwriters are just as likely — in my view more likely — to disagree about what they would want to know as about what

3.3.3 DETERMINATION BY THE COURT

This insistence by the Irish judiciary, that the courts and not expert witnesses should determine issues, was emphasised by Barron J. in *McMullen* v *Farrell*[44] when he quoted, with approval, an extract from the judgment of Oliver J. in *Midland Bank Trust* v *Hett, Stubbs & Kemp*.[45]

> I must say I doubt the value, or even the admissibility, of this sort of evidence, which seems to me to be becoming customary in cases of this type. The extent of the legal duty in any given situation must, I think, be a question of law for the court. Clearly, if there is some practice in a particular profession, some accepted standard of conduct, . . . evidence of that can be received. But evidence which really amounts to no more than an expression of opinion by a particular practitioner of what he thinks he would have done had he been placed, hypothetically and without the benefit of hindsight, in the position of the defendants, is of little assistance to the court . . . for that is the very question which it is the court's function to decide.

The materiality of facts and their influence on the judgment of the prudent insurer is clearly a matter for determination by the court, and whilst expert testimony may be admitted and might be useful to the court the party calling that evidence should not place too much reliance on it because "the judges are always free to test and revise any form of expert testimony".[46] Whilst it might seem odd that a

---

they would have done. If it were always possible to say what a prudent underwriter would or would not want to know . . . it is surprising that so many contested cases of non-disclosure have come before the courts since the *CTI* case was decided.

[44] Unreported High Court, 18 February 1992.

[45] [1978] 3 All ER 571.

[46] *Yorke* v *Yorkshire Insurance Company Ltd.* [1918] 1 KB 662:
The view of the courts as to expert evidence in insurance cases seems to have developed. In the days of Lord Mansfield such evidence was apparently regarded as irrelevant: see for example, *Carter* v *Boehm*. But the views of 150 years ago have been modified by the broader outlook of later judges and by a clearer realisation of the utility of expert testimony as an aid to the administration of justice. . . . Expert evidence may frequently afford great assistance to the court. . . . If excluded, it would deprive the court of ascertaining those considerations and views which a tribunal may well require to know, and the insurance witness would by a process of law be stricken with absolute silence upon matters of vital importance to him. Judges are always free to test and revise every form of expert testimony.

judge, as a lay person, should over-rule an expert, the judge in the context of materiality and disclosure determines whether the expert testimony supports an assertion which is contrary to common sense or the court's understanding of commercial fairness.[47]

3.4 DURATION OF THE DUTY

3.4.1 POSITION IN IRISH LAW

None of the reported decisions in Ireland on the duty of disclosure involved consideration of the duty continuing beyond formation of the contract, but the position would appear to be that the duty arises whenever the insurer is required to decide whether to accept the risk or the terms on which to do so. Such a decision has to be made on a proposal for new insurance, on renewal of an existing policy and in respect of a material change in an existing insurance contract of such a kind "as to substantially alter the nature of the bargain as affecting both sides".[48] In practice it is generally accepted that there is no duty of disclosure at any other time, but the duty of good faith, from which the duty of disclosure stems, is a continuing duty in other respects. Unless the contract stipulates otherwise there is no duty to notify changes in risk during the currency of the contract. If there is an extension or modification of the contract which affects the risk there is a limited duty of disclosure as regards the change in risk but the duty expires once the change is effected and only facts material to the change have to be disclosed.[49] If, as is common in Marine Insurance

---

[47] In *Aro Road & Land Vehicles Ltd.* v *Insurance Corporation of Ireland Ltd.* [1986] IR 403, Carroll J. accepted the testimony of expert insurance witnesses in support of the defendant insurer even though she did not believe their views were reasonable. She was subsequently rebuked by the Supreme Court with McCarthy J. saying "the insurance profession is not to be permitted to dictate a binding definition of what is reasonable".

[48] *Lishman* v *Northern Maritime* [1875] LR 10 Cp 179 at 181 per Bramwell B.

[49] *Lishman* (*supra*) p. 182 per Blackburn J.:

> If the alteration were such as to make the contract more burdensome to the underwriters, and a fact known at that time to the insured were concealed which was material to the alteration, I should say the policy would be vitiated. But if the fact were quite immaterial to the alteration, and only material to the underwriter as being a fact which shewd that he had made a bad bargain originally, and such as might tempt him, if it were possible, to get out of it, I should say there would be no obligation to disclose it.

contracts, cover is provided on "terms to be agreed" for risks, not part of the original cover, the policyholder wishing to take the benefit of the provision must act with the utmost good faith and disclose to insurers all relevant facts.[50]

3.4.2 ENGLISH LAW

It was generally assumed that on completion of the contract the only duty owed by the insured to the insurer during the term of the contract was not to provide false information or fail to disclose material facts when making a claim under the policy. In *Black King Shipping Co.* v *Massie*, ("The Litsion Pride")[51] the court, relying on Marine Insurance principles, held that there was a continuing duty of disclosure during the currency of the policy which applied to any situation in which the insured was required to provide information to the insurer. Where information was required the insured was under a duty to disclose any fact which might influence the insurer's actions under the contract. The court indicated that the duty was an implied term of the contract but in *Pan Atlantic*[52] it was made clear that the duty of utmost good faith is not dependent on any implied term. Prior to that, in *La Banque Financière* v *Westgate Insurance*,[53] it was stated that the continuing duty of utmost good faith was confined to the making of a claim under the policy. In *New Hampshire Insurance Co.* v *MGN Ltd.*[54] the insurers of a number of Fidelity Guarantee policies, relying on the *"Litsion Pride"*[55] decision claimed that the insured was under a continuing duty to disclose, at all times during the period of insurance, information which would influence a prudent insurer in deciding whether to exercise the right of cancellation under the policy. The Court of Appeal confirmed that a right of cancellation could not impose a continuing duty of disclosure and approved the statement of the trial judge that:

---

[50] *Liberian Insurance Agency Inc.* v *Mosse* [1977] 2 Lloyds Rep 560 per Donaldson J. at 568.

[51] [1985] 1 Lloyds Rep 437.

[52] [1994] 3 All ER 581.

[53] [1990] 1 All ER 947.

[54] *New Hampshire Insurance Co.* v *MGN Ltd.* Unreported Court of Appeal, September 1996.

[55] [1985] 1 Lloyds Rep 437.

the obligation of good faith . . . does not . . . apply so as to trigger positive obligations of disclosure of matters affecting the
risk during the currency of the cover except in relation to some
requirement, event or situation provided for in the policy to
which the duty of good faith attaches.

In *Hussain* v *Brown* (No. 2)[56] the insured's property had been damaged by fire within four months of cover being effected. The insured
had ceased to trade in the premises a number of weeks after effecting
cover and at the time of the loss the property had to all intents and
purposes been abandoned. The policy contained a cancellation clause
and a condition requiring the insured to give insurers notification of
any alteration likely to increase the risk. Insurers argued that these
two conditions constituted contractual requirements for the disclosure of information and that the duty of good faith applied throughout the duration of the contract. The court followed the decision in
MGN[57] in relation to the cancellation clause but having considered in
some detail the decision in *"The Litsion Pride"*[58] held that:

wherever there is a contractual requirement for the insured to
give the underwriter information which is material, in that it
would influence the judgment of a prudent underwriter in
making a decision under the contract for which the information is required, the continuing duty of good faith requires the
insured to make full disclosure of all material facts, whether or
not he realises their materiality, and not simply refrain from
dishonest, deliberate or culpable concealment.

The court accepted that the continuing duty of disclosure could be
modified by the terms of the contract between the parties and that, in
this particular case, the condition, requiring notification of any alteration likely to increase the risk, represented the extent of the insured's duty. If the insurers wished to make the contract subject to a
more extensive and continuing duty of utmost good faith it was necessary that they should do so by clear express terms in the policy. The
decision appears to accept that the insured is under a duty of good
faith at all times during the period of the policy but that the duty

---

[56] Unreported, November 1996.

[57] n. 54 *supra*.

[58] n. 55 *supra*.

may be modified by the express terms of the contract. The law on the matter was clarified by the Court of Appeal in *Manifest Shipping Co. Ltd. v Uni-Polaris Insurance Co. Ltd and Others ("The Star Sea")*.[59] The Court held that the duty of utmost good faith continues throughout an insurance contract but the degree of disclosure varies according to the stage of the parties' relationship. Where the policy is amended or extended, the pre-contract duty of disclosure is revived and the insured has a duty to disclose facts which are material to the amendment or extension. If, in such circumstances, there is non-disclosure of a material fact, the insurer is entitled to avoid the amendment or extension only and not the whole policy.

3.4.3 DUTY AT RENEWAL

Renewal of an existing policy is regarded in law as the making of a new contract of insurance and the insured is subject to a fresh or repeated duty of disclosure on each successive application for renewal of cover.[60] This has important practical consequences. Most lay people are not aware that such a duty exists and a heavy burden is placed on brokers to bring the duty to the attention of their clients prior to completion of renewal of the contract. Since the insured is not required to disclose facts which are known to the insurer,[61] he is only under a duty to disclose any material changes in circumstances that have occurred since the original application or the date of the last renewal as the case may be. A difficulty arises however, where the original application did not disclose a conviction within the previous five years as required by the proposal form but which on renewal is outside the five year period. It would seem that whilst the non-disclosure would have vitiated he original contract, the new (renewal) contract is unaffected by the non-disclosure.[62] The extent of the duty of disclosure at renewal was considered by the High Court in *Latham*

---

[59] [1995] 1 Lloyds Rep 651.

[60] *Lambert v Co-operative Insurance Society Ltd.* [1975] 2 Lloyds Rep 485.

[61] *Carter v Boehm* [1766] 3 Burr 1905 at 1911.

[62] *Whytes Estate v Dominion*, [1945] TPD 382 (South Africa). An argument could be made that the original non-disclosure is indicative of moral hazard and therefore should be disclosed but, given the pro-insured bias of the courts, that argument is unlikely to get much judicial support.

v *Hibernian Insurance Co. Ltd & Another*[63] where Blayney J. held that the fact that the insured had committed an offence prior to renewal, but had not at that stage been brought to trial, was a material fact which should have been disclosed at renewal. What had to be disclosed was the underlying fact that a crime had been committed. The court did not discuss whether a reasonable insured would have considered it reasonable to disclose that he had committed a crime even though at that stage he had not been tried or convicted. The court did, however, seem to be influenced by the fact that the insured had admitted the offence to investigating Gardai and had initially entered a plea of guilty to the charge.

3.4.4 INCREASE IN RISK

It is a general rule of insurance law that an insured is free, during the currency of the policy, to increase the risk underwritten by insurers, subject to a number of exceptions. The policy terms may restrict the actions of the insured; the insured may have had a pre-existing intention of increasing the risk, constituting a material fact which should be disclosed to insurers; the insured in completing the proposal for insurance may have warranted that the risk will not be increased; the insured is not entitled to materially change the risk.[64] Most insurance policies incorporate a condition requiring the insured to advise insurers of any alterations likely to increase the risk but it is generally accepted that such conditions do no more than restate the common law and emphasise the insured's duty which the law would otherwise imply into the contract. In *Hussain* v *Brown* (No. 2)[65] the court held that such a condition could be exhaustive of the insured's obligations and that if the insurers wished the clause to impose a continuing duty of utmost good faith then the terms of such a clause should expressly so provide. In a subsequent case, *Kauser* v *Eagle*

---

[63] Unreported High Court 22 March 1991. Blayney J. quoted in his support the English Court of Appeal decision in *Reynolds* v *Phoenix Assurance Co. Ltd. & Others* [1978] 2 Lloyds Rep 440. There was no discussion by the court of the implications of the Supreme Court judgment in *Aro Road* which seemed to substitute the "reasonable insured " for the reasonable "prudent insurer" in the test for materiality.

[64] *Exchange Theatre* v *Iron Trades Mutual* [1983] 1 Lloyds Rep 674.

[65] *Hussain* v *Brown* (No. 2) Unreported Court of Appeal, November 1996.

Star Insurance Co. Ltd.,[66] the Court of Appeal held that a mere increase in risk does not fall within the terms of a standard condition
wording. The case also emphasises the distinction between an increase in risk and a change in risk. The plaintiff had insured her
shop, which was let to a tenant, with the defendants and the policy
covered, among other risks, the risk of malicious damage. Post renewal, the insured discovered that an uninsured window in the shop
had been broken and the tenant threatened to sublet the premises
and to cause further damage to the property. The insurers repudiated
liability on the grounds that the threats from the tenant represented
an increase in risk which the insured was required to advise to insurers under a condition of the policy. The Court of Appeal confirmed
that an insured does not owe any duty of disclosure after an insurance contract has been entered into (subject to the exceptions above)
and that unless the risk is changed as opposed to being increased the
insurer is not relieved of liability. The insurer is liable for losses
originally in their contemplation, when the policy is effected, and the
condition applies only to increases in risk which could not be anticipated. The increased chance of an insured peril, such as the risk of
malicious damage increased during the period of the insurance, does
not, except in extreme cases, enable the insurer to rely on the condition to deny the insured's claim.

3.4.5 DUTY WHEN MAKING A CLAIM

The insured has a duty not to make a fraudulent claim and breach of
that duty entitles the insurer to avoid the policy. The duty of disclosure is, however, limited to not making a fraudulent claim and an
innocent misrepresentation or non-disclosure in respect of the claim
will not entitle insurers to decline liability. A claim by insurers that
the insured owed a broader duty of disclosure to insurers when making a claim under the policy was rejected by the Court of Appeal, in
"The Star Sea".[67]

---

[66] *Kauser* v *Eagle Star Insurance Co. Ltd.* [1996] Unreported Court of Appeal,
July 1996. The Court noted that the policy had been written in "plain English"
and that it was to be expected that such a policy would set out the insured's
common law position.

[67] *Manifest Shipping Co. Ltd.* v *Uni-Polaris Insurance Co. Ltd. and Others* unreported Court of Appeal, 20 December 1996.

3.5 MODIFICATION OF THE DUTY

3.5.1 BASIS OF CONTRACT CLAUSES

It is usual for insurers to modify the duty of disclosure by having the proposer for insurance sign a declaration at the bottom of the proposal form, warranting the truth and accuracy of the statements made and incorporating the warranty into the policy by making the information provided the basis of the contract. By doing so the insurers provide themselves with a potential defence, to an action on the policy, wider than that arising out of the duty of disclosure.[68] Generally no distinction is made between statements that are material and statements that are immaterial. The performance of the duty of disclosure is made a contractual obligation and if it is not performed the proposer is in breach of the contract rather than in breach of the duty of good faith and the contract is voidable. The use of such "basis of the contract clauses" has for long been the subject of judicial and extra-judicial criticism.[69] In *Provincial Insurance Co. Ltd.* v *Morgan and Foxon*,[70] Lord Wright set out the position clearly:

---

[68] Parke B. at 496 in *Anderson* v *Fitzgerald* [1853] 4 HL Cas 484 said: "The proviso is clearly a part of the express contract between the parties, and on the non-compliance with the condition stated in the proviso, the policy is unquestionably void." Lord Eldon C. at 262 in *Newcastle Fire Insurance Co.* v *MacMorran & Co.* [1815] 3 Dow 255 said:

> It is a first principle of the law of insurance, on all occasions: that where a representation is material, it must be complied with; if immaterial, that immateriality may be inquired into and shown; but if there is a warranty, it is part of the contract; that the matter is such as it is represented to be. Therefore the materiality or immateriality signifies nothing. The only question is as to the mere facts.

Viscount Haldane in *Dawsons Ltd.* v *Bonnin* [1922] 2 AC 413 at 423-424 said that when

> answers are declared to be the basis of the contract this can only mean that their truth is made a condition exact fulfilment of which is rendered by stipulation foundational to its enforceability.

[69] Hasson (1971); Law Commission Report No. 104 (1980) pp. 90–94; Corrigan, (1987); Ellis (1990).

For judicial criticism see: Fletcher Moulton L. J. in *Joel* v *Law Union and Crown Insurance Co.* [1908] 2 KB 863 at 885: "I wish I could adequately warn the public against such practices on the part of insurance offices."; Swift J. in *MacKay* v *London & General Assurance Co. Ltd.* [1935] 51 Lloyds Rep 201 at 202: "I think he [the insured] has been very badly treated — shockingly badly treated. They [the insurers] have taken his premium. They have not been in the least bit misled by the answers which he made."; Lord Wrenbury in *Glicksman* v *Lancashire &*

The policy is in a form which has in its general scheme long been in use by insurance companies, though the general scheme has exhibited many variations, some major and some minor, in detail. In that scheme there is a proposal form, signed by the assured, containing various particulars and answers to various questions, and a declaration that the answers are to be the basis of the contract and an agreement to accept the company's policy. The policy itself contains a recital incorporating the proposal and declaration, and it sets out the risks insured, certain exceptions and conditions, and a schedule embodying various particulars. Though this general scheme of policy has been, as it were sanctified by long usage, it has often been pointed out by judges that it must be very puzzling to assured, who may find it difficult to fit the disjointed parts together in such a way as to get a true and complete conspectus of what their rights and duties are and what acts on their part may involve the forfeiture of the insurance. An assured may easily find himself deprived of the benefits of the policy because he had done something quite innocently but in breach of a condition, ascertainable only by the dovetailing of scattered portions.

The questions asked by insurers in the proposal form may either enlarge or limit the proposer's duty of disclosure[71] but generally the fact that specific questions relating to the risk are asked does not relieve the proposer of the obligation to disclose all material facts.[72] The

---

General Assurance Co. Ltd. [1927] AC 139 at 144–145: "I think it a mean and contemptible policy on the part of an insurance company that it should take the premiums and then refuse to pay upon a ground which no one says was really material."

In *Zurich General Insurance Co.* v *Morrison* [1942] 2 KB 53 at 58, Lord Greene M. R. described such clauses as being traps for the insured and Lord St Leonards suggested if the courts were to give effect to such clauses "no prudent man (would) effect a policy of insurance with any company without having an attorney at his elbow to tell him what the true construction of the document is".

[70] [1932] 38 Com Cas 92 at 98.

[71] *Roselodge Ltd.* v *Castle* [1966] 2 Lloyds Rep 113 at 131.

[72] *Joel* v *Law Union* [1908] 2 KB 863 at 878, 892. However, see *McGillivray & Parkington on Insurance Law*, Eighth Edition, 1988, para 6.4.6 and in particular Finlay C. J. in *Kelleher* v *Irish Life Assurance Co. Ltd.* Unreported Supreme Court, 8 February 1993:

   I would also be satisfied that the true and acid test must be as to whether a
   reasonable man reading the proposal form would conclude that the information over and above it which is in issue was not required.

"basis of contract" clause first made its appearance in a reported case in 1834[73] and since then has been used frequently by insurers to avoid policies where the non-compliance with the warranty was totally immaterial to the risk or to the claim which they wished to decline. The case of *Dawsons Ltd.* v *Bonnin*[74] is a celebrated example. The insured had indicated on the proposal that the vehicle to be insured would usually be garaged at an address in Glasgow whereas it was in fact usually garaged at a farm on the outskirts of Glasgow. The inaccuracy was immaterial to acceptance of the proposal as the premium charged would have been the same and the risk was in fact lower outside Glasgow than in the centre of the city. However, when the vehicle was destroyed by fire the insurers refused to pay because of the mis-statement and the court upheld its repudiation of liability for the claim.

3.5.2 Breach of Warranty

The interpretation and application of "basis of contract" clauses in Irish law was considered at length in *Keenan* v *Shield Insurance Company Ltd.*[75] The plaintiff sought to set aside an arbitration award, in favour of the insurer, who had repudiated liability for a fire claim, on the grounds of misrepresentation of fact and non-disclosure of relevant information by the insured when making the proposal for insurance. The insured had stated, on the proposal, that he had never sustained loss or damage in respect of any of the risks or liabilities against which he wished to insure. This was incorrect as the previous year he had been paid £53 in respect of damage to a pump. The proposal form contained the usual declaration and warranty. Shortly after issue of the policy the insured sought to recover in respect of damage to his premises by fire. Blayney J. quoted from the Supreme Court judgment of Kenny J. in *Chariot Inns*[76] and other authorities in

---

[73] *Duckett* v *Williams* [1834] 2 C&M 348.

[74] [1922] 2 AC 413

[75] [1987] IR 113 High Court.

[76] [1981] IR 199 at 255 where it says:

A contract of insurance requires the highest standard of accuracy, good faith, candour and disclosure by the insured when making a proposal for insurance to an insurance company. It has become usual for an insurance company to whom a proposal for insurance is made to ask the proposer to answer a number of questions. Any misstatement in the answers given, when they relate to

support of the general common law position that any misstatements in the answers relating to material facts entitle the insurer to avoid the policy.[77] He held, however, that the common law does not apply where the proposer has warranted the truth and accuracy of the answers and that warranty is incorporated into the contract. Once that is done the materiality of the answers is irrelevant:

> [even if] the inaccuracy in the reply . . . was trivial, that would be no obstacle to the defendant repudiating the policy in view of the accuracy of the answers in the proposal having been warranted by the plaintiff.

In holding as he did, against the insured, Blayney J. was undoubtedly following precedent in the Irish and English courts but it is doubtful if the decision would be followed in today's consumer-friendly legal environment.

3.5.3 REQUIREMENT OF KNOWLEDGE

The Supreme Court, in *Keating* v *New Ireland Assurance Co.*,[78] had the opportunity of reconsidering the position a few years later, although the case concerned a life policy and the wording of the warranty and the basis of contract clause was different. The defendant insurer maintained that the deceased husband of the plaintiff had made false statements as to his state of health in completing the proposal form, but the evidence in the High Court did not establish that. In the Supreme Court, McCarthy J. in the leading judgment, with which all other members of the court agreed, conceded that people

---

a material matter affecting the insurance, entitles the insurance company to avoid the policy and repudiate liability if the event insured against happens. But the correct answering of any questions asked is not the entire obligation of the person seeking insurance: he is bound, in addition, to disclose to the insurance company every matter which is material to the risk against which he is seeking indemnity.

[77] *McGillivray and Parkington on Insurance Law* (7th edition) para 586 and 725. Blayney J. did not however refer to the judgment of McCarthy J. in the Supreme Court in *Aro Road and Land Vehicles Ltd.* v *Insurance Corporation of Ireland Ltd.* [1986] IR 403 which seemed to alter the common law position in Ireland. Although the case did not involve a proposal form McCarthy's views were of general application and suggest that insurers are under a strict obligation to ask specific questions in the proposal form and if they failed to ask such questions they could not later repudiate the claim because the material information had not been provided.

[78] [1990] 2 IR 383.

were always free to contract as they wished but was critical of the "basis of contract" clause. He repeated his support for the judgment of the reasonable proposer prevailing over that of the prudent insurer first expressed by him in *Aro Road*[79]:

> Such declarations and provisions are known as "basis of the contract" clauses. The contention is that their effect in law is that all answers in the proposal form are incorporated into the contract as warranties and that, if any one of them is inaccurate, the insurer may repudiate the contract for breach of warranty without regard to the materiality of the particular answer to the risk;[80] The corollary is that the fact that the insured may have answered the questions in good faith and to the best of his knowledge and belief is irrelevant if the answers are in fact inaccurate. . . . To read . . . the policy . . . as conveying a warranty that the proposer is accepting a contract on the basis that he had disclosed something of whose existence he was wholly ignorant is demonstrably an irrational interpretation. It is neither irrational nor inappropriate in seeking to find a reasonable interpretation of a commercial contract to pose the question as to how the casual onlooker or, indeed, the officious bystander, would react if told of the construction favoured by one party or another. . . . If the proposal were to contain a statement by the proposer that the statements and answers written in the proposal . . . shall form the basis of the proposed contract "even if they are untrue and incomplete for reasons of which I am wholly unaware" would there be any takers for such a policy?

The desire of the Supreme Court to protect the insured was emphasised by Walsh J. in his judgement in the same case, when he said:

> . . . but when insurers intend that there is to be a warranty of that sort they must make it perfectly plain that such is their intention and they must use unequivocal language, such as persons with ordinary intelligence may without any difficulty understand.

The decision would indicate that for an insurer, to rely on breach of the warranty introduced by the "basis of contract" clause, to avoid the policy it will have to prove that the insured had full knowledge of the

---

[79] [1986] IR 403.

[80] *Thomson* v *Weems* [1884] 9 App Cas 671 at 689.

implications and possible effects of the declaration and warranty that
he signed on the proposal form and that the breach was material to
the risk. Such knowledge has been held to be a necessary precondition for informed consent and essential to give the warranty its
intended effect[81] but this issue was not addressed by the High Court
in *Keenan*.

3.6 INSURER'S CODES OF PRACTICE

The need for reform of the duty of disclosure was recognised in the
Insurance Act, 1989.[82] Following discussions between the Irish Insurance Federation and the Minister for Industry and Commerce, and in
return for a promise by him not to implement the provisions of the
particular section of the Act, the Federation introduced its own voluntary Codes of Conduct and Statements of Insurance Practice.[83] These
generally follow the Statements of Insurance Practice introduced by
the insurance industry in England and like them have been subjected
to criticism.[84] The codes attempt to modify the rigours of the duty of
disclosure and the basis of contract clauses in so far as they apply to
individual insureds as distinct from those effecting policies in a commercial capacity. The Codes provide that:

---

[81] *Joel* v *Law Union and Crown Insurance Co.* [1908] 2 KB 863 where at 886
Moulton L. J. said:

> To make the accuracy of the answers a condition of the contract is a contrac-
> tual act, and if there is the slightest doubt that the insurers have failed to
> make clear to the man on whom they have exercised their right of requiring
> full information that he is consenting thus to contract, we ought to refuse to
> regard the correctness of the answers given as being a condition of the policy.

[82] Section 61 provides:

> Where the Minister considers it necessary in the public interest and following
> consultation with the insurance industry and consumer representatives, he
> may, by order, prescribe codes of conduct to be observed by undertakings in
> their dealings with proposers of policies of insurance and policyholders renew-
> ing policies of insurance in respect of the duty of disclosure and warranties.

[83] see Appendix for the full Codes of Conduct and Statements of Insurance Practice.

[84] see: "Insurers' Agreements not to Enforce Strict Legal Rights: Bargaining with
Government and in the Shadow of the Law", Richard Lewis, 1985 MLR Vol. 48 p.
275; "The Revised Statements of Insurance Practice", ADM Forte, 1986 MLR Vol.
49 p.754; "IIF's Codes of Practice and their Legal Implications", Michael Corrigan, *Irish Broker*, January and February 1993.

A statement should be included in the declaration or prominently displayed [on the proposal form], drawing attention to
the consequences of a failure to disclose all material facts that
an insurer would regard as likely to affect the assessment of a
proposal . . . there should be a warning that if the signatory is
in any doubt about whether certain facts are material they
should be disclosed. . . . Insurers should avoid asking questions
which would require knowledge beyond that which the signatory could reasonably be expected to possess. . . . Those matters which insurers have commonly found to be material
should as far as practical, be the subject of clear questions in
proposal forms.

In relation to the use of "basis of contract" clauses, Section 1(b) says:

Neither the proposal form nor the policy shall contain any general provision converting the statements as to past or present
facts into warranties about matters which are material to the
risk.

Section 3(a)(i) states that

an insurer will not repudiate liability to indemnify a policyholder on grounds of non-disclosure of a material fact which a
policyholder could not reasonably be expected to have disclosed.

The codes are probably an honest effort by insurers to reflect the
views of the Supreme Court in their interpretation of the duty of disclosure in dealings with individual consumers, but they have not been
sufficiently publicised or observed to have any major impact in rectifying the consumer's impression of the industry. It must also be emphasised that the codes are not legally binding and do not in any way
change the law on the duty of disclosure. It would require reforming
legislation to achieve that and there is no evidence to suggest that
such legislation is likely in the foreseeable future.[85]

---

[85] The Statements introduced in England were described as a mere "token ges-
ture to consumerism" effecting little change by Birds (1977) at 684. McGillivray
and Parkington (1988) at Para 705 say: "We do not regard these statements of
self-regulatory practice as a substitute for reform of the law." Ellis (1990), says:

It is not reasonable or even, perhaps, realistic to expect the judiciary to mod-
ernise such a complex area of law. For them to have to do so, as in the *Aro
Road* case, introduces an unnecessary element of uncertainty into the system.
Perhaps the short term answer would be to extend the scope of any Irish
Statement of Non-Life Insurance Practice to include "commercial" as well as

3.7 THE INSURANCE OMBUDSMAN

Although the Codes of Conduct and Statements of Insurance Practice do not have the force of law they have been of significant benefit to the Insurance Ombudsman in the adjudication of cases referred to her. The office of the Insurance Ombudsman was established at "arm's length" by the insurance industry to provide an objective, independent and impartial forum for the resolution of disputes between individual policyholders and insurers.[86] Successive Annual Reports issued by the Ombudsman confirm that by far the largest reason for complaints being referred to her was the repudiation of liability for claims by insurers on the grounds of non-disclosure.[87] In exercising her adjudicative functions the Ombudsman is not bound by strict legal principles. In relation to cases alleging non-disclosure she is not constrained by the "all or nothing" approach of the law but can and does apply the principle of proportionality, requiring both parties to the contract to play their part in demonstrating the utmost good faith.[88] The Ombudsman's decision whilst binding on insurers participating in the scheme is not binding on the complainant who may still have recourse to the courts.

"consumer" insurance contracts. In the long term, though, I think we should have more reform of insurance contract law, replacing any statements of practice with legislation.

[86] The first (1993) Annual Report quotes the Ombudsman's mission statement as follows:

> To achieve a simple, accessible, user-friendly system which will operate effectively in the interest of personal policyholders and will produce the resolution of disputes by way of mediation, conciliation or adjudication with results which are fair and reasonable in the circumstances.

[87] Annual Report 1993, p. 7; Annual Report 1994, p. 9.

[88] The 1994 report at p. 23 gives details of a case where the complainant's claim under a household policy was repudiated on grounds of non-disclosure of a previous loss. The Ombudsman found that the insurers' interpretation of the words "loss from the events you now wish to insure" was not appropriate on a true reading of the proposal form and as the complainant's failure to disclose information was innocent, she upheld the complaint and applied the proportionality principle, awarding the complainant 70 per cent of the claim.

CHAPTER FOUR

GENERAL PRINCIPLES OF INSURANCE

4.1 INDEMNITY

4.1.1 INTRODUCTION

The principle of indemnity is at the very foundation of insurance law. It is the bedrock on which the insurance industry has developed since the judgment of Brett L. J. in *Castellain* v *Preston*:

> The very foundation, in my opinion, of every rule which has been applied to insurance is this, namely that the contract of insurance contained in a marine or fire policy is a contract of indemnity only, and that this contract means that the assured, because of a loss against which the policy has been made, shall be fully indemnified but shall never be more than fully indemnified. That is the fundamental principle of insurance, and if ever a proposition is brought forward which is at variance with it, that is to say, which either will prevent the assured from obtaining a full indemnity, or which will give to the assured more than a full indemnity, that proposition must be wrong.[1]

4.1.2 REINSTATEMENT

The principle of indemnity has in recent years been eroded by insurers offering policies on a "new for old" or "reinstatement as new" basis, without any deduction for betterment or wear and tear, particularly in the areas of property damage and motor insurance.[2] No

---

[1] [1883] 11 QBD 380.

[2] It is common for a household policy to agree "to pay the full cost of repair or reinstatement as new of the damaged part of the building and to pay the full cost of replacement as new or repair the contents lost or damaged". Many motor poli-

problems arise where the reinstatement is carried out within a reasonable time after the loss. Difficulties do arise, however, where the property is in a poor state of repair or where the policyholder decides against reinstatement.[3] The application of the principle of indemnity in such circumstances can be difficult and can give rise to litigation.[4] A policy written on a "reinstatement as new" basis is subject to the principle of indemnity in that the insured cannot recover more than his loss. The sum insured in the policy is the maximum sum payable by insurers but not necessarily the amount paid. As Pennefather B. said in an early Irish case:

> while the insured may name any sum he likes as the sum for which he will pay a premium, he does not, by so proposing that sum, nor does the company by accepting the risk, conclude themselves as to the amount which the plaintiff is to recover in consequence of the loss.[5]

---

cies provide for replacement of an insured vehicle with a new one if the vehicle is written off within the first twelve months of purchase as new.

[3] Typical "reinstatement as new" conditions provide that the insurer will pay: the cost of reinstatement, being where the property is destroyed the cost of rebuilding or where the property is damaged the cost of repair to a condition substantially the same as but not better or more extensive than its condition when new. The insurer's liability shall be limited to payment of the value of the property at the time of its destruction or the amount of the damage if the work of reinstatement is not carried out as quickly as is reasonably practicable and until the cost of the reinstatement has actually been incurred.

[4] *St Albans Investment Co.* v *Sun Alliance & London Insurance Ltd.* [1983] IR 363; *Leppard* v *Excess Insurance Co. Ltd.* [1979] 2 Lloyds Rep 91.

[5] *Vance* v *Forster* [1841] Ir. Cir. Rep. 47:
You must not run away with the notion that a policy of insurance entitles a man to recover according to the amount represented as insured by the premium paid.

Cockburn C. J. addressing the jury in *Chapman* v *Pole* [1870] 22 Lt 306:
It is far too late to doubt that by common understanding of businessmen and lawyers alike the nature of such a policy controls its obligation implying conclusively that its statement of the amount the insurer promises to pay merely fixes the maximum amount which in any event he may have to pay and having as its sole purpose and therefore imposing as its only obligation the indemnification of the insured up to the amount of the insurance against loss from the accepted risk.

The joint judgment of the High Court of Australia in *British Traders Insurance Co. Ltd.* v *Monson* [1964] 111 CLR 86 at p. 92.

The insurer's liability to pay for reinstatement as new is generally restricted by policy provisions.[6] If the work of reinstatement is not carried out or is not carried out as quickly as is reasonably practicable the insurer is liable to pay the value of the property at the time of the loss. The assessment of that value is generally problematical and the courts are sometimes called on to establish the monetary value of the property, at the time of the loss, so that, in fulfilment of the principle of indemnity, the insured can be put in the position they would have been in, if the loss insured against had not occurred.[7] O'Connor L. J., in *Murphy* v *Wexford County Council*[8], identified the issues to be addressed:

> . . . you are not to enrich the party aggrieved; you are not to impoverish him; you are, so far as money can, to leave him in the same position as before. In dealing with buildings destroyed or injured, the following considerations suggest themselves: What sort of building was it? Had it a possibility of a different use, a potential use which an ordinary owner might be reasonably considered as likely to put it to hereafter? Would he for any reason that might appeal to an ordinary man in his position rebuild it if he got replacement damages or is his claim for such damages a mere pretence? And if he would rebuild, what sort of [building] would he put up? Would he re-

---

[6] see n. 3 *supra*.

[7] In *Dominion Mosaics and Tile Company Ltd.* v *Trafalgar Trucking Co. Ltd.* [1990] 2 All ER 246 it was held that whether indemnity was achieved by assessing the diminution in value of the damaged premises or the cost of reinstatement depended on the circumstances of the particular case. Because the plaintiff required premises to carry on the business it was a reasonable course to purchase new premises and the cost of those premises was the extent of indemnity. In *Reynolds* v *Phoenix Assurance Co. Ltd.* [1978] 2 Lloyds Rep 440 the plaintiffs had purchased a building for £18,000 which they insured for £550,000. Fire destroyed approximately 70 per cent of the building and the plaintiff claimed the cost of reinstatement. Insurers argued that the plaintiff was only entitled to the building's market value or the modern replacement value. They argued that reinstatement was inappropriate as no commercial person in their senses would contemplate spending so much on rebuilding obsolete premises if they were in a position to purchase a modern structure at a fraction of the cost. The court rejected the insurers arguments and accepted that the insured intended to reinstate. An award of £343,320 was made but the insured subsequently accepted £225,000 for a modern replacement structure.

[8] [1921] 2 IR 230 at 240. The case arose, not under a policy of insurance, but under statute giving compensation to persons whose property had suffered malicious damage.

build on the same scale or would he adopt something else equally suitable to his requirements having regard to modern conditions?

4.1.3 EXTENT OF INDEMNITY

Difficulties can arise in deciding whether a particular sum paid in respect of loss or destruction of an old building, or one in a poor state of repair, amounts to an enrichment or an impoverishment of the insured. Whilst the policy requires the insurer to pay the value of the property at the time of the loss or destruction it does not define what is meant by value or indicate how that value is to be calculated. In such circumstances, there are three possible bases for establishing the value of the building.

1. *Reinstatement Cost*: Where the policy contains "reinstatement as new" conditions the amount payable as indemnity is the cost of rebuilding to a condition substantially the same as but not better or more extensive than its condition when new. No deduction will be made for betterment or wear and tear.[9] The maximum amount payable is the sum insured in respect of the destroyed property. The policy conditions provide that this basis of valuation will not apply unless the reinstatement is carried out. Where the "reinstatement as new" conditions do not apply the insured can still seek to have the cost of reinstatement used as the basis of valuation in calculating the amount payable as indemnity.[10] However, the insured must show that he intends to reinstate the building, that reinstatement is not unreasonable or eccentric in the circumstances,[11] and that the proposed mode of reinstatement

---

[9] In *Harbutt's Plasticine Ltd.* v *Wayne Tank & Pump Co. Ltd.* [1970] 1 QB 447 at 473, Widgery L. J. suggested that a deduction for betterment "would be the equivalent of forcing the plaintiffs to invest in the modernising of their plant which might be highly inconvenient for them".

[10] In *Reynolds* v *Phoenix Assurance Co. Ltd.* [1978] 2 Lloyds Rep 440 at 450, Forbes J. said:

> I must reject . . . that the parties here contracted on the basis that indemnity was to be measured by the cost of reinstatement. But as the extent of indemnity still remains to be decided, the cost of reinstatement still remains a possible means of measuring it, even though prior agreement to that effect cannot be found in the contract.

[11] *Reynolds* (n. 10 *supra*) at 453.

is reasonable.[12] The amount recoverable will be subject to a deduction for betterment.[13] The cost of reinstatement is the maximum recoverable by the insured but there is nothing in the policy or by any legitimate inference which provides that the loss to be indemnified is to be the cost of reinstatement when that sum is greater than the actual loss.[14]

2. *The Cost of Equivalent Modern Replacement:* This method of arriving at a valuation of premises is sometimes used in difficult cases, involving old buildings, where no other suitable method of valuation is available. The rationale behind its use is that a building does not exist merely as a collection of bricks and mortar; it exists to be used for a purpose. If that purpose is established and agreed it should be possible to erect an alternative building to fulfil that purpose. The value of the building destroyed could therefore be said to be the cost of erecting the new building.[15]

3. *Market Value:* The market value of an old building may be difficult to determine if there is no ready market for buildings of its type. If the insured had no intention of selling the building immediately prior to its destruction it does not seem right to force acceptance of market value on him as the basis of indemnity. The proper calculation of indemnity value in such circumstances can only be de-

---

[12] Cantley J. in *Dodd Properties (Kent) Ltd.* v *Canterbury CC* [1979] 2 All ER 118 at 124:

> [the claimant is] not bound to accept a shoddy job or put up with an inferior building for the sake of saving the defendant's expense. But I do not consider they are entitled to insist on complete and meticulous restoration when a reasonable building owner would be content with less extensive work . . . and when there is also a vast difference in the cost of such work and the cost of meticulous restoration.

[13] *Harbutt's Plasticine Ltd.* v *Wayne Tank & Pump Co Ltd.* [1970] 1 QB 447 at 473.

[14] *Leppard* v *Excess Insurance Co. Ltd.* [1979] 1 WLR 512.

[15] In *Reynolds*, (n. 10 *supra*), Forbes J. considered that equivalent modern replacement was not a separate basis of assessment but a valuer's device to arrive at the market value of an old building.

termined by the facts in each particular case.[16] In *Leppard* v *Excess Insurance Company Ltd.*[17] the insured, who had bought a building for a nominal price, insured it for £14,000 which figure was intended to represent the full value of the building, i.e. what it would cost to replace the property in its existing form should it be totally destroyed. The insured had the property on the market with an asking price of £4,500 immediately before the fire which destroyed it. The insured claimed the cost of reinstatement, less an allowance for betterment, in the sum of £8,694. The insured, whilst not maintaining that he intended to reinstate the building, argued that since the sum insured by the policy was intended to represent full value he was entitled to an indemnity in the amount of that full value up to the sum insured under the policy in the event of a total loss. The Court of Appeal held that the insured was entitled to recover only his actual loss and since the insured was willing to sell the property for £4,500 immediately before the fire that was its real value and the insured's loss was £3,000 being the agreed value less the value of the site.

4.1.4 IRISH LAW

In the Irish case, *St. Albans Investment Co.* v *Sun Alliance & London Insurance Ltd. & Others*[18] the insured had purchased an old unoccupied warehouse for £15,000 and insured it for £300,000. The policy issued was in a standard form without reinstatement conditions. When the building was destroyed by fire, the insured sought a declaration from the High Court that the indemnity to which it was entitled under the policy should be measured on the basis of the cost of reinstating the building. The insured sought to justify its claim, ei-

---

[16] In *Phillips* v *Ward* [1956] 1 WLR 471 at 473, Denning L. J. (as he then was) said:

> It all depends on the circumstances of the case. . . . the general rule is that the injured person is to be fairly compensated for the damage he has sustained neither more nor less.

Henchy J. in *Munnelly* v *Calcon Ltd.* [1978] IR 387 at 399 said:

> In my view, the particular measure of damages allowed should be objectively chosen by the court as being that which is best calculated, in all the circumstances of the case, to put the plaintiff fairly and reasonably in the position in which he was before the damage occurred, so far as pecuniary award can do so.

[17] see n. 14 *supra*.

[18] [1983] IR 363.

ther on the ground that the contract of insurance contained a term requiring the indemnity to be calculated on a reinstatement basis, or on the ground that such an indemnity was appropriate, notwithstanding the absence of such contractual terms. The Supreme Court upheld the trial judge's finding that the contract between the parties did not contain terms which entitled the insured to an indemnity measured by the cost of reinstatement and that, in the absence of a proven firm intention to rebuild, the estimated market value was the correct basis for measuring the indemnity to which the insured was entitled. In arriving at its decision the Supreme Court considered the leading English authorities[19] and the different methods of valuation which might provide the insured with an indemnity.[20] Whilst deciding that market value was the appropriate basis, in the circumstances, the judgments indicate that in different circumstances an alternative basis might be applied.[21] It should be pointed out that in the case of partial loss, the insured under a standard fire policy is entitled to an indemnity, based on the cost of reinstatement of the damaged portion, less an allowance for betterment, provided the sum insured represents the full cost of reinstating the entire property at the date of the loss. If it does not, then the condition of average applies and the insured is only entitled to payment of the proportion of the actual loss

---

[19] *Harbutt's* v *Wayne Tank Co.* [1970] 1 QB 447; *Reynolds* v *Phoenix Assurance Co. Ltd.* [1978] 2 Lloyds Rep 440; *Hollebone* v *Midhurst & Fernhurst Builders* [1968] 1 Lloyds Rep 38; *Leppard* v *Excess Insurance Co. Ltd.* [1979] 1 WLR 512; *Castellain* v *Preston* [1883] 11 QBD 380; *British Traders Insurance Co. Ltd.* v *Monson* [1964] 111 CLR 86.

[20] If the insurer contends that market value is the measure of indemnity, the onus is on it to prove that there is a market for such a building and the level of value in that market. In *Pleasurama* v *Sun Alliance Insurance Ltd.* [1979] 1 Lloyds Rep 389, the court decided the reinstatement cost should be awarded since it was not possible to prove the value of a bingo hall which had been destroyed.

[21] O'Higgins C. J. came to the conclusion that the indemnity to which the plaintiff was entitled could only be secured by rebuilding on the site a suitable building with due allowance being made for betterment. In *Dominion Mosaics and Tile Co. Ltd.* v *Trafalgar Trucking Co. Ltd.* [1990] 2 All ER 246 the plaintiff's premises were business premises earning income, and the court held that the appropriate measure of loss was the cost of purchasing new premises which was less than the cost of rebuilding the old premises.

which the sum insured bears to the actual value of the property insured at the time of the loss.[22]

4.2 INSURABLE INTEREST

4.2.1 INTRODUCTION

The principle of indemnity is vitally linked with the principle of insurable interest. Indemnity is applicable when the insured suffers a loss and he can only suffer a loss if he has an insurable interest. To constitute insurable interest:

- There must be a person or a physical object exposed to loss or damage; or, alternatively, there must be some potential liability which may devolve on the insured;

- This person, object or liability must be the subject matter of the insurance; and

- The insured must bear some relationship thereto recognised by law in consequence of which he stands to benefit by the safety of the person or object or the absence of liability, or be prejudiced by loss sustained by the person or object or by the creation of the liability.[23]

Insurable interest may be defined, more concisely, as the necessary

---

[22] *Crowley* v *Cohen* [1832] 3 B&AD 478 at 486 per Lord Tenterden C. J.

[23] In *Lucena* v *Crauford* [1806] 2 B&P (NR) 269; [1806] 127 ER 630, insurable interest was defined as follows:

A man is interested in a thing to whom advantage may arise or prejudice happen from the circumstances which may attend it . . . and whom it importeth that its condition as to safety or other quality should continue; interest does not necessarily imply a right to the whole or a part of the thing, nor necessarily and exclusively that which may be the subject of privation, but the having some relation to, or concern in the subject of insurance, which relation or concern by the happening of the perils insured against may be so affected as to produce a damage, detriment, or prejudice to the person insuring; and where a man is so circumstanced with respect to matters exposed to certain risks or dangers, as to have a moral certainty of advantage or benefit, but for those risks or dangers, he may be said to be interested in the safety of the thing. To be interested in the preservation of a thing, is to be so circumstanced with respect to it as to have benefit from its existence, prejudice from its destruction. The property of a thing and the interest devisable from it may be very different; of the first the price is generally the measure, but by interest in a thing every benefit or advantage arising out of or depending on such thing may be considered as being comprehended.

relationship of the insured to the subject-matter of the insurance whereby he will be prejudiced by the event which constitutes a loss under the policy or he will benefit if such event does not arise.[24] The relationship must be capable of being expressed in monetary values.[25] It would be contrary to public policy for insurers to make payments under insurance contracts where no insurable interest existed. In such circumstances, the insured would have suffered no loss and the payments would constitute gain or profit and encourage gambling under the guise of insurance.[26] The availability of such contracts would be a temptation to fraud and the scientific basis of insurance would be undermined.[27]

4.2.2 STATUTORY PROVISIONS

The possibility of abuse was of such concern in England, in the very early days of life assurance, that the Life Assurance Act was introduced in 1774.[28] The Act forbade the making of any policy on:

> the life or lives of any person or persons, or on any other event or events whatsoever, wherein the person or persons for whose use, benefit, or on whose account such policy or policies shall

---

[24] In *Castellain* v *Preston* [1883] 11 QBD 380, it was stated: "What is it that is insured in a fire policy? Not the bricks and materials used in building the house, but the interest of the insured in the subject matter of the insurance."

[25] "The exposure to loss or the expectation of benefit must be one on which a pecuniary value can be set," per Lord Tenderden in *Halford* v *Kymer* [1830] 10 B&C 724, 728.

[26] The preamble to the Life Assurance Act, 1774 says: "It hath been found by experience, that the making of insurance on lives, or other events, wherein the insured shall have no interest, hath introduced a mischievous kind of gaming."

[27] See Harnett & Thornton (1948).

[28] In the United States, much the same reason was given for the requirement of insurable interest; see *Watson* v *Massachusetts Mutual Life Insurance Co.* 140 F 2d 673 and at 676 — in relation to life assurance it said:

> its purpose is intended not to take the gambling features out of each particular contract but to limit public opportunity to engage in speculative business of buying and selling insurance policies on the lives of others. Such a purpose can be accomplished by imposing two safeguards which limit the class of persons who can enforce such policies: (i) They must stand in a close family or financial relationship with the person whose life is the subject of the policy; (ii) They must acquire the insurance with the consent of such subject.

be made, shall have no interest, or by way of gaming or wagering.[29]

Some thirty years earlier, the Marine Insurance Act, 1745 had made
null and void all policies of insurance issued without the requirement
of an insurable interest.[30] It was therefore illegal to effect policies on
ships and goods laden on them and on lives where no insurable interest existed. Insurance on goods unconnected with ships seemed to be
exempt from the legislative provisions. The Marine Insurance Act of
1788 remedied this situation by requiring the existence of an insurable interest for all policies issued in respect of any ship "or any
goods, merchandises, effects or other property whatsoever".[31] The
legislation in this area had been confined to dealing with insurance
contracts but, by virtue of the Gaming Act, 1845 all contracts of
gambling or wagering were rendered null and void.[32] The Marine Insurance Act, 1906 repealed the Marine Insurance Act of 1745 and
those parts of the 1788 Act dealing with marine insurance. The Act
declares void any Marine insurance policy where no insurable inter-

---

[29] The essential features of the Act are: (i) insurances on the lives of people or on
any other event in which the person benefiting from the insurance has no interest
are null and void; (ii) no policies on lives or other events are lawful unless the
name of the person for whose benefit the policy is being effected is inserted in the
policy; (iii) no greater sum may be recovered than the amount of the interest of
the insured; (iv) the Act did not extend to insurances on ships, goods, or mer-
chandise.

[30] The Act forbade the issuing of policies of insurance which were made by
    any person or persons, bodies corporate or politic on any ship or ships belong-
    ing to his Majesty or any of his subjects or on any goods, merchandise or ef-
    fects, laden or to be laden, on board of any ship or ships, interest or no inter-
    est, or by way of gaming or wagering, or without benefit of salvage to the in-
    surer.

A practice had developed of attaching a clause to marine policies which stated
that possession of the policy was the only proof of interest required and hence the
reference to "interest or no interest or without further proof of interest".

[31] The Act also required the name of one person interested or concerned to be
inserted in the policy document.

[32] As a result all insurance contracts where no insurable interest existed were
rendered null and void, as such contracts were no more than wagers.

est exists at the time of the loss.[33] The Marine Insurance (Gambling Policies) Act, 1909 made it a criminal offence to effect a marine insurance policy where no insurable interest existed or where there was no *bona fide* expectation of there being such an interest.[34] The application of these statutes in Ireland has been a matter of some judicial disagreement. In *Keith* v *Protection Marine Insurance Co. of Paris*[35] it was held that the Marine Insurance Act of 1745 had no application here. The application of the Life Assurance Act, 1774 was extended to Ireland by the Life Assurance (Ireland) Act, 1886 but there was some doubt as to whether it applied to fire insurance.[36] Irrespective of statutory requirements the absence of insurable interest in a policy of indemnity renders the policy void. If the existence of an insurable interest is required by statute and such interest is missing then the policy is illegal and also null and void.[37] The requirements of the 1774 Act as applied in Ireland by the Life Assurance (Ireland) Act, 1886,

---

[33] The Act defines insurable interest as:

> In particular a person is interested in a marine insurance venture where he stands in any legal or equitable relation to the adventure or to any insurable property at risk therein, in consequence of which he may benefit by the safety or due arrival of insurable property, or may be prejudiced by its loss, or by damage thereto, or by the detention thereof, or may incur liability in respect thereof.

[34] Gaming and wagering contracts were unenforceable prior to this Act but were not illegal.

[35] *Keith* v *The Protection Marine Insurance Company of Paris* [1882] 10 LRI 51 where Fitzgerald B. said:

> However, the English ante-Union statute referred to, the Marine Insurance Act, 1745, [was] never expressly re-enacted by the Parliament of Ireland. . . . it would be necessary to show that the intention of the sovereign to bind Ireland was expressed, or could be collected by necessary implication. I confess it does not appear to me that any such intention can be collected from the language of the Marine Insurance Act, 1745.

[36] *Brady & Others* v *The Irish Land Commission* [1921] 1 IR 56 where O'Connor M. R. said: "We are not troubled in this case with any question arising under the Life Assurance Act, 1774, even assuming that this Act applies to fire insurance policies in Ireland, which is doubtful."

[37] The Irish Exchequer Chamber, in the case of *The British Commercial Insurance Company* v *Magee* [1834] Cooke & Al. 182, held that life policies devoid of an insurable interest were not void at common law but were void because of the requirements of the Life Assurance Act, 1774.

have been modified somewhat by the Assurance Companies Act, 1909 and the Insurance Act, 1936.[38]

4.2.3 ENGLISH LAW

In *Lucena* v *Crauford*[39] it was stated that an insurable interest exists wherever the insured stands in a legal or equitable relationship to property or otherwise stands to suffer loss as a result of its destruction. In *Macaura* v *Northern Assurance*,[40] the House of Lords interpreted the requirement of insurable interest narrowly, holding that a creditor does not have an insurable interest in the property of his debtor and that a shareholder does not have an insurable interest in the property of the company in which he holds shares. A legal or equitable interest in the property was held to be critical to establishing an insurable interest. In *Glengate-KG Properties Ltd.* v *Norwich Union Fire Insurance Society Ltd.*,[41] a recent case, turning on the interpretation to be given to the word "interest" in a material damage proviso in a consequential loss policy, the Court of Appeal divided 2:1 on the issue. The Court was required to decide whether the insured property developer had an insurable interest in plans and drawings, owned and used by the architects engaged in a development project for him. Insurers repudiated liability under a consequential loss policy for loss of revenue in respect of the period of delay caused when the plans were destroyed in a fire on the site of the development. Insurers relied on the absence of material damage insurance in respect of the plans and the operation of the policy proviso requiring the existence of material damage insurance "covering the interest of the in-

---

[38] As a result of these statutes the categories of persons who could be regarded as having an interest in the life of another have been extended to include almost all close relatives.

[39] [1806] 2 B&P 269.

[40] [1925] AC 619. The plaintiff insured had sold the timber on his estate to a company in which he was the sole shareholder. The timber was insured in the plaintiff's name rather than that of the company when it was destroyed by fire. The timber was the sole asset of the company. The House of Lords held that the plaintiff did not have an insurable interest in the timber with Lord Sumner saying:

> the fact that he was virtually the company's only creditor, while the timber is its only asset, seems to me to make no difference. . . . he was directly prejudiced by the paucity of the company's assets, not by the fire.

[41] [1996] 2 All ER 487 CA.

sured in the property". The insurers argued that the insured had an insurable interest in the plans and contrary to the provisions of the insurance policy had not insured the plans. The majority of the Court, in holding for the insured, distinguished the insured's personal interest dependent on ownership, or possession of the property from the insured's legal right to insure. The Court held that a person has a legal right to insure property, in which the insured has no direct right, if loss, damage or destruction would cause a loss to the insured. The "interest" referred to in the policy proviso was held to be "interest" dependent on ownership or possession and as the insured did not have such an interest in the plans he was not in breach of the proviso. The minority dissenting view was that the wide definition of insurable interest in *Lucena* v *Crauford*[42] meant that the insured had an interest in the plans and should have insured them. The position in English law would therefore appear to be that a person has an insurable interest in property if: (a) he owns the property or has a right to possession and enjoyment of the property; (b) he is exposed to loss if the property is lost, damaged, or destroyed; (c) the property is exposed to the risk of loss, damage or destruction by his activities.[43]

4.2.4 IRISH LAW

The uncompromising approach by the House of Lords in *Macaura*[44] has not been followed in other jurisdictions,[45] and in Ireland, in *Carrigan* v *Norwich Union Fire Society Ltd. & Others*,[46] the High Court,

---

[42] [1806] 2 B&P 269.

[43] *National Oilwell* v *Davy Offshore* [1993] 2 Lloyds Rep 583.

[44] [1925] AC 619.

[45] In Australia the *Macaura* decision was rejected as a technical rule which prevented the insured from recovering the loss actually suffered by him; para. 118 ff. Law Reform Commission Report No. 20, Insurance Contracts. In Canada, the Courts applied the decision until 1987 when the Supreme Court in *Constitution Insurance Company* v *Kosmopoulas* [1987] 1 SCR 2, involving circumstances very similar to *Macaura*, held the purpose of a rule requiring insurable interest could be sufficiently served by a rule based on economic interest alone and that the rule of indemnity was better served by a notional interest wider than that laid down in *Macaura*. In the United States, most States have based their insurable interest rule on economic interest alone since the decision in *Hayes* v *Milford Mutual Fire Insurance Co.* [1898] 49 NE 754.

[46] Unreported, High Court, 11 December 1987. A house, owned by the plaintiff company, was insured in the name of the individual plaintiff when it was seri-

on somewhat similar facts, had little difficulty in finding a beneficial ownership in the property, sufficient to give the insured shareholder an insurable interest. The Supreme Court, in *MIBI* v *PMPA Insurance Ltd.*[47] held that the Life Assurance Act, 1774 does not apply to "goods" and that the lack of insurable interest, at the time of entering into a contract for motor insurance, does not make that contract illegal. It is, however, void.[48] It should be noted that, generally, insurers will only raise the lack of insurable interest as a defence to a claim where they have reason to believe that the claim is fraudulent and other non-technical defences are also raised.[49]

4.3 SUBROGATION

4.3.1 HISTORICAL ORIGINS

Just as the requirement of insurable interest is linked to the principle of indemnity, so too is the doctrine of subrogation. The primary purpose of the doctrine is to prevent any infringement of the principle of indemnity by entitling insurers, after payment of a loss, to take the benefit of any rights the insured may possess whereby his loss may be extinguished or alleviated by recovery from other sources. In *Randall* v *Cockran*,[50] decided in 1748, it was held that the plaintiff insurers, after making satisfaction, stood in the place of the insured as to goods, salvage, and restitution in proportion for what they had paid.

---

ously damaged by fire. The Court found on the evidence that the individual plaintiff had a substantial beneficial interest through the company in the property damaged and consequently had an insurable interest.

[47] [1981] IR 142 per Henchy J.:

> Since an insurance of a motor vehicle is an insurance of "goods" within the meaning of the Life Assurance Act, 1774, and is therefore excluded from the requirement in that Act that the insured must have an insurable interest at the time of entering into the contract; the fact that Fr Mackin had no insurable interest . . . when he entered into the contract did not make the insurance illegal.

[48] *O'Leary* v *The Irish National Insurance Company Ltd.* [1958] Ir Jur Rep 1 HC.

[49] It is said that in *Macaura* v *Northern Assurance* [1925] AC 619, the House of Lords was influenced by unproved allegations of fraud (Keeton, 1971, p. 117). In *Carrigan* v *Norwich Union* (n. 46) the defendant insurers pleaded that in addition to the lack of insurable interest they were entitled to repudiate because the plaintiff or persons acting on his behalf had deliberately set fire to the insured premises.

[50] [1748] 1 Ves. Sen. 98.

The Lord Chancellor held that "the plaintiffs had the plainest equity that could be".[51] As a rule of equity, subrogation supports indemnity as the central principle of insurance law.[52] Apart from preserving the principle of indemnity it can also be justified on the grounds of general deterrence and as a tool of social engineering.[53] The Concise Oxford Dictionary defines subrogation as the substitution of one party for another, with a transfer of rights and duties. It was recognised by Lord Mansfield in 1782 when he said:

> Every day the insurer is put in the place of the insured. . . . The insurer uses the name of the insured. . . . I am satisfied that it is to be considered as if the insurer had not paid a farthing.[54]

Those words were uttered almost one hundred years before *Castellain* v *Preston*[55] was decided and Brett L. J. defined subrogation as follows:

> as between the underwriter and the assured the underwriter is entitled to every right of the assured, whether such right exists in contract, fulfilled or unfulfilled, or in remedy for tort, capable of being insisted upon, or in any other right, whether by condition or otherwise, legal or equitable, which can be, or has been exercised or has accrued, and whether such right could or could not be enforced by the insurer in the name of the assured by the exercise of or acquiring of which right or condition the

---

[51] Quoted by McCardie J. in *Edwards & Co. Ltd.* v *Motor Union Insurance Co. Ltd.* [1928] 2 KB 249 when outlining the historical development of the doctrine.

[52] In *Yorkshire Insurance Co.* v *Nisbet Shipping Co.* [1962] 2 QB 330, 339, per Diplock J.:
> Although often referred to as an "equity", [subrogation] is not an exclusively equitable doctrine. It was applied by the common law courts in insurance cases long before the fusion of law and equity, although the powers of the common law courts might in some cases require to be supplemented by those of the court of equity in order to give full effect to the doctrine; for example, by compelling an assured to allow his name to be used by the insurer for the purpose of enforcing the assured's remedies against third parties in respect of the subject matter of his loss.

[53] See Clarke (1994) pp. 832–835.

[54] *Mason* v *Sainsbury* [1782] 3 Doug. KB 61 at 64.

[55] *Castellain* v *Preston* [1883] 11 QBD 380.

loss against which the assured is insured, can be, or has been diminished.[56]

4.3.2 REQUIREMENTS

Before subrogation can arise there must be (a) a valid contract of indemnity; (b) a payment by insurers under the contract; and (c) a connection between the subject matter of insurance and the rights of the insured to which the insurers are subrogated. These rights can arise under contract, in tort, or under statute. Insurers generally modify the legal position by incorporating into the contract a condition which enables the insurers take over the insured's rights before the insurers actually indemnify the insured. The subrogation condition also provides for the insurer to pursue legal action in respect of those rights in the name of the insured thus enabling the insurer to maintain a cloak of anonymity. However, in two Irish cases, dealing with the principle of subrogation, the cloak was pulled aside by the defendant claiming that as the plaintiff had been indemnified under a policy of insurance he was not entitled to recover from the local authority under malicious injuries legislation.[57]

4.3.3 INSURERS' RIGHTS

The Irish Courts have vigorously upheld the insurers' right to subrogation, with the Supreme Court, in *Doyle v Wicklow County Council*[58] quoting Palles C. B. with approval:

> I am of the opinion that as held in *Mason v Sainsbury*[59] as regards England, so also in Ireland, although the hundred, barony, or county is not criminally responsible, it is for civil purposes put in the place of the wrongdoers, and the primary liability is on the hundred, barony or county, from which it follows that as between it and the person whose property is damaged his insurer and himself are one.[60]

---

[56] ibid., at 388.

[57] *Ballymagauran Co-op* v *County Councils of Cavan & Leitrim* [1915] 2 IR 85; *Doyle* v *Wicklow County Council* [1974] IR 55.

[58] see n. 57 *supra.*

[59] *Mason* v *Sainsbury* [1782] 3 Doug. KB 61.

[60] *Ballymagauran Co-op supra* at 100.

The right of insurers to subrogation may be limited by the terms of agreements between the insured and third parties. If the insured, as a party to a contract, undertakes to effect insurance against particular risks, that undertaking may be construed as relieving the other party of liability in respect of the loss to be insured. The most likely situation in which this arises is in relation to tenancy agreements. In *Mark Rowlands Ltd.* v *Berni Inns Ltd.*[61] it was held that the effect of insurance being taken out for the joint benefit of landlord and tenant was to substitute the fire insurance for the tenant's liability for fire damage. It followed that the landlord had no right of action against the tenant to which the insurer could subrogate. The decision imported into English Law a principle, referred to, in other jurisdictions, as the doctrine of the un-named co-insured. Where a policy effected by one party is intended to cover the interests of that party and another third party, that third party, does not become a party to the insurance contract, but is immune from subrogation by the insurer. It is not necessary to establish insurable interest on the part of the third party but only an implied agreement between the insured and the third party that the insured will look only to the insurers for payment of any loss giving rise to a claim under the policy.[62] Where the third party is included in the policy as a co-insured the insurers have no right of subrogation against the third party even if the loss is occasioned by that third party's negligence.[63] The insurer is obliged to indemnify the primary insured under the contract of insurance and if, having done so, the insurer seeks to exercise subrogation rights against the co-insured, in respect of his negligence, the insurer would in effect be denying him the benefit of the cover intended to be provided by the policy. There is therefore implied into every insurance contract a term that no subrogation rights can be exercised against a co-insured in respect of loss caused by a peril insured for his benefit under the policy. Subrogation is however possible if the policy provides the co-insured with coverage narrower than that provided to other co-insureds.[64]

---

[61] *Mark Rowlands Ltd.* v *Berni Inns Ltd* [1986] 1 QB 211, Court of Appeal.

[62] *National Oilwell (UK) Ltd.* v *Davy Offshore Ltd.* [1993] 2 Lloyds Rep 583.

[63] *Petrofina (UK) Ltd.* v *Magnaload Ltd.* [1984] 1 QB 127.

[64] n. 62 *supra*.

4.3.4 SUBROGATION WAIVER

It is common, particularly in relation to the construction industry, for insurers to be asked to waive subrogation rights against a particular potential defendant or class of defendant. Where a "waiver of subrogation" clause is inserted in a policy the insurer agrees with the insured that in the event of a loss insured under the policy the insurer, having indemnified the insured, will not pursue the party or parties named in the clause for recovery of the loss for which they may have been totally or partially responsible. The purpose of such an agreement is to reduce the cost of litigation between the parties in a joint venture or enterprise. The value of such agreements has recently been called into question in England.[65] The clause constitutes an agreement between the insured and the insurer and if the insurer sought to exercise subrogation against the named party or parties the insured could invoke the agreement. However, as the named third party is not a party to the insurance contract, privity of contract prevents him from invoking the agreement to waive subrogation rights and the clause is therefore of little benefit to him. In *National Oilwell*[66] it was held that a clause which waived subrogation against "any assured and any person, company or corporation whose interests are covered by this policy" was not a blanket abandonment of all rights against co-insureds under the policy and that the waiver operated only in respect of losses insured for the benefit of the co-insureds.[67] The judgment confirmed that the subrogation waiver clause could not be relied upon, by a person who is a partial party to an insurance contract, in respect of losses arising out of risks against which he is not insured under the policy.[68] The clause and the protection intended to be provided by it is clearly divisible between risks insured by the policy for the party named and those risks for which

---

[65] *National Oilwell* above and *Enimont Supply SA* v *Chesapeake Shipping Inc., "The Surf City"* [1995] 2 Lloyds Rep 242.

[66] n. 62 *supra.*

[67] ibid. at p. 603 where Coleman J. said:

> In my judgment the waiver of subrogation clause . . . confines the effect of the waiver to claims which are insured for the benefit of the party claimed against under the policy. In other words one does not qualify for the benefit of the waiver clause merely by being a party to the contract of insurance.

[68] Colman J. had decided this issue sometime previously in *Stone Vickers Ltd.* v *Appledore Ferguson Shipbuilders Ltd.* [1991] 2 Lloyds Rep 288.

no cover is provided. In the case of *Surf City*[69] it was conceded that a person covered by the waiver clause could rely upon it even though *National Oilwell* had decided otherwise. It was hoped that the confusion surrounding the value of these waiver clauses would have been resolved by the Court of Appeal when hearing the appeal against the *National Oilwell* decision but the case was settled before delivery of the Court's reserved judgment, having been at hearing for two weeks. The use of "waiver of subrogation clauses" is widespread in the construction industry in Ireland but as yet there has been no judicial pronouncement on their efficacy.

4.3.5 EQUITABLE BASIS OF DOCTRINE

Another aspect of the *Surf City* case worthy of comment is the trial judge's acceptance that it was "common ground that . . . it would not be equitable to allow the subrogated claim to proceed". The implication of this statement is that subrogation is an equitable doctrine which will not be implemented by the courts where implementation would produce results which would be inequitable. That view was previously expressed by Lord Denning M. R. in *Morris* v *Ford Motor Co. Ltd.*,[70] but it was a view with which the remainder of the Court of Appeal did not fully concur.[71] In that case the employers' liability insurers of the plaintiff's employer, having indemnified the defendant in respect of an award obtained against them by the plaintiff in respect of injuries sustained as a result of the misconduct of an em-

---

[69] n. 65 *supra*.

[70] *Morris* v *Ford Motor Co. Ltd* [1973] 1 QB 792.

[71] ibid. at 801 Denning said:
> . . . is it just and equitable that Fords should be compelled to sue, or to lend their name to sue, their own servant, . . . for damages, so as to make him personally liable? My answer to that is emphatic: it is not just and equitable.

Later at 807 Stamp L. J. said:
> He [Lord Denning] relying on the equitable nature of the right, takes the view that it ought not to be exercisable where its exercise would be inequitable. . . . I am not persuaded that the respondent might not be able to muster powerful and perhaps convincing arguments to the effect that the right of subrogation ought not to be cut down by consideration of what the court might think in any particular case would lead to an inequitable result.

James L. J. at 812 said:
> In my judgment the right of subrogation in contracts of insurance depends upon the essential element of the contract being one of indemnity. Where there is a contract of indemnity there is a right . . .

ployee of the defendant, sought to exercise subrogation rights against the employee responsible for the injuries sustained by the plaintiff. The Court of Appeal ruled, by a majority, that subrogation rights could not be exercised. If the two employees had been employed by the same employer there would not have been any question of the insurer attempting to exercise subrogation rights as insurers, in England, had entered into a "gentleman's agreement" not to enforce the strict legal rights accorded to them by the House of Lords ruling in *Lister* v *Romford Ice & Cold Storage Co. Ltd.*[72] No such agreement exists between insurers in Ireland. The right of an insurer to subrogate against an employee, whose negligence has caused an injury or loss in respect of which the insurer has indemnified the employer, was confirmed by the Supreme Court in *Zurich Insurance Co.* v *Shield Insurance Co. Ltd.*[73] Whilst the legal right exists, most employers' liability insurance policies issued in Ireland provide that the insurer will, at the request of the insured, indemnify an employee in

---

[72] [1957] AC 555. It was held that there was no implied term in a contract of employment that the employer would indemnify the employee in respect of their negligence and that the employer was entitled to recover damages which the employer had been obliged to pay to another employee injured by the employee's negligence. The decision caused considerable disquiet resulting in members of the British Insurance Association entering into an agreement that

> they will not institute a claim against the employee of an insured employer in respect of death of or injury to a fellow employee, unless the weight of evidence clearly indicates (1) collusion or (2) wilful misconduct, on the part of the employee against whom the claim is made.

In *Morris* v *Ford Motor Co. Ltd.*, above, Lord Denning, at 801, said that "*Lister* v *Romford* was an unfortunate decision".

[73] [1988] IR 174. In the High Court, Gannon J. had said at 181:

> If, and in so far as Quinnsworth might be held liable, vicariously, for injury to Martin Sinnott in respect of the negligent driving of their car by Edward Durning, Quinnsworth would be entitled to a full indemnity from Edward Durning whose liability would have to be discharged by the plaintiff under its policy. . . . The plaintiff . . . must indemnify Edward Durning, and in so far as it indemnifies Quinnsworth it is entitled by subrogation to have recourse to Edward Durning.

In the Supreme Court, McCarthy J. agreed with Gannon's conclusion (p. 183). See Section 4.4.4 below for facts.

respect of liability for injuries sustained by a fellow employee.[74] Whilst the right of an insurer to subrogate is well established in law, it is normal practice to insert into insurance policies of indemnity a subrogation condition which, in addition to affirming the insurer's legal rights, also deals with the conduct required of the insured, in the event of a claim under the policy.[75] The effect of the condition is to improve the insurer's legal position by enabling him to take over any rights the insured may have against a third party before the insurer actually indemnifies the insured. The insurer's right to bring a subrogated action against a third party does not arise until the insurer has paid the insured under the terms of the policy.[76]

4.4 CONTRIBUTION

4.4.1 INDEPENDENT EQUITABLE RIGHT

The principle of indemnity ensures that payment by an insurer of the full amount of an insured's loss will discharge the liability of any other insurer of the same insured in respect of the same risk.[77] The insurer who has paid the loss can however seek contribution from the

---

[74] A typical wording reads:
> Insurers will at the request of the Insured indemnify any Director, Partner or Employee of the Insured in respect of liability for which the Insured would have been entitled to indemnity under this policy if the claim had been made against the Insured.

Some insurers include employees in the policy definition of the Insured.

[75] A typical wording is as follows:
> Any claimant under this policy shall at the request and at the expense of the Company do and concur in doing and permit to be done all such acts and things as may be necessary or reasonably required by the Company for the purpose of enforcing any rights and remedies, or of obtaining relief or indemnity from other parties to which the Company shall be or would become entitled or subrogated upon its paying for or making good any destruction or damage under this policy, whether such acts and things shall be, or become necessary or required before or after his indemnification by the Company.

[76] *Dickenson* v *Jardine* [1868] LR 3 CP 639; *City Tailors Ltd.* v *Evans* [1922] 91 LJKB 379.

[77] In *Godin* v *London Assurance Co.* [1758] 1 Burr 489, per Lord Mansfield C. J. at p. 492:
> The second policy was effected on the same vessel, and in exactly the same sum, and upon the same terms; and in such case the payment by one insurer acts by way of satisfaction to the other.

other insurers on equitable principles.[78] The right to contribution
arises out of the fact that the insurers who have paid the loss in full
have paid out more than they ought equitably have paid, given the
existence of other insurance in respect of the same loss.[79] The right to
contribution is altogether different and distinct from the right of subrogation.[80] The principle of contribution is a wholly independent equitable doctrine not to be confused with subrogation, although in *Zurich Insurance Co. Ltd.* v *Shield Insurance Co. Ltd.*[81] the High Court
seemed to confuse the two. While subrogation ensures that the insured shall receive no more than an indemnity, contribution ensures
that insurers shall not indirectly suffer injustice *inter se* because of
that rule. A claim for subrogation must be brought in the name of the
insured whereas a claim for contribution must be brought in the
name of the insurer.[82]

---

[78] ibid. at 492 Lord Mansfield said:

> If the insured is to receive but one satisfaction, natural justice says that the
> several insurers shall all of them contribute *pro rata* to satisfy that loss
> against which they have all insured.

[79] ibid.:

> Where a man makes a double insurance on the same thing, in such a manner
> that he can clearly recover, against several insurers in distinct policies, a
> double satisfaction, the law certainly says that he ought not to recover doubly
> for the same loss, but be content with one single satisfaction for it. And if the
> same man really, and for his own proper account, insures the same goods
> doubly, though both insurances be not made in his own name, but one or both
> of them in the name of another person, yet that is just the same thing, for the
> same person is to have the benefit of both policies. And if the whole should be
> recovered from one, he ought to stand in the place of the insured, to receive
> contribution from the other who was equally liable to pay the whole.

[80] *Sickness and Accident Assurance Association* v *General Accident Assurance
Corp.* [1892] 19 IR 977 per Lord Low at p. 980:

> The claim of an underwriter, who has indemnified the insured, to claim con-
> tribution from the other underwriters cannot be founded on the doctrine of
> subrogation, because an assignee can have no higher right than his cedent,
> and a shipowner who has received a full indemnity from one underwriter can
> never make a claim against another underwriter. The answer, therefore, to
> the claim of an underwriter who had paid, if made only in the right and as an
> assignee of the insured, would be that the contract was one of indemnity and
> that the insured had already been indemnified.

[81] [1988] IR 174. Gannon J. referred to the plaintiff's claim for contribution being
based on the right to subrogation.

[82] *Austin* v *Zurich* [1945] 1 KB 250.

4.4.2 ESSENTIAL ELEMENTS

For the right of contribution to arise there are a number of conditions which must be fulfilled:

i) All of the insurance policies concerned must have a common subject matter. Each may cover a wider interest but the subject matter in respect of which the claim to contribution arises must be common to all policies. It is not necessary that the extent of cover should be the same in all policies but it is necessary that some portion of the property destroyed in respect of which the claim is made should be common to all.[83]

ii) All the policies must cover the peril which causes the loss.[84]

iii) All the policies must be effected by or on behalf of the same insured.[85]

iv) All the policies must be in force at the time of the loss and must be legally enforceable. A policy which is unenforceable for breach of a condition cannot give rise to a claim for contribution.[86]

4.4.3 POLICY CONDITION

All policies of indemnity include a contribution clause in one form or another.[87] The most common is a clause which provides that the insurer issuing the policy is not to be liable for more than its rateable proportion of a loss in the event of there being more than one policy

---

[83] *American Surety Co. of New York* v *Wrightson* [1910] 11 Comm. Cas. 37 at 56; *Godin* v *London Assurance Co.* [1758] 1 Burr 489 at 492.

[84] *North British & Mercantile Insurance Co.* v *London Liverpool & Globe Insurance Co.* [1877] 5 Ch. D. 569 at 581.

[85] ibid. at 577 per Jessel M. R.:

What is the meaning of the words "covering the same property"? They cannot mean the actual chattel; the most absurd consequences would follow if you read the words in that sense. I am satisfied that this condition was put in to apply to cases where it is the same property that is the subject matter of the insurance and the interests are the same.

[86] n. 79 *supra*, where the second policy had not attached as the premium had not been paid.

[87] Those in common use are "rateable proportion" and "co-existing insurance" clauses.

in force in respect of the loss.[88] A more onerous clause is one which relieves the insurer of all liability where the claimant is entitled to indemnity under another policy.[89] Where two policies covering the same loss contained the same exemption clause both insurers were held liable under their respective policies.[90] In the absence of a policy condition the insured could claim the full extent of the loss from one insurer leaving that insurer to seek contribution from all other insurers covering the same loss. The incorporation of a contribution condition relieves the insurer of being exposed to that situation and obliges the insured to claim from all insurers covering the loss to ensure that he is fully indemnified.

4.4.4 IRISH CASE LAW

The number of modern legal decisions on the principle of contribution is small and in Ireland there have been but a few.[91] In *Hibernian Insurance plc* v *Eagle Star Insurance plc & Others*[92] the court awarded the plaintiff insurer fifty per cent recovery against the defendant insurer in a motor insurance case but the decision was determined on the particular facts, without any discussion or consideration of the legal principles. In *Zurich Insurance Co.* v *Shield Insurance Co.*[93] the principles of subrogation and contribution were discussed in detail in

---

[88] A typical wording reads: "If at the time any claim arises under this policy there is any other insurance covering the same liability loss or damage the company shall not be liable to contribute more than its rateable proportion."

[89] "This policy does not insure against any loss damage or liability which at the time it arises is insured by or would but for the existence of this policy be insured by any other policy or policies except in respect of any excess beyond the amount which would have been payable under such policy or policies had this insurance not been effected."

[90] In *Gale* v *Motor Union Insurance Co. Ltd.* [1928] 1 KB 359, where two policies contained a clause excluding liability if the risk were covered by another policy it was held that the policies were not mutually exclusive and that a case of contribution arose.

[91] Probably because the basic legal principle is well established and insurers may have sharing agreements which determine the issue.

[92] Unreported High Court, 17 February 1987. On the evidence the court found that the second defendant's policy did not cover the circumstances of the loss but that the first defendant's policy did cover the same subject matter and that the cover was valid and in force.

[93] [1988] IR 174; see n. 73 *supra*.

both the High Court and the Supreme Court. An employee of Quinnsworth Ltd. was injured in a motor accident when travelling as a passenger in a car driven by a fellow employee. The driver had previously been held solely liable for the accident. Both employees were travelling in the course of their employment and Quinnsworth Ltd. was therefore vicariously liable to the injured passenger but entitled to a full indemnity from the driver. The plaintiff insurers, as insurers of the motor policy issued to Quinnsworth Ltd., indemnified the driver in respect of his liability to the passenger. The motor policy extended to provide an indemnity to any driver, driving with the authority of the insured and the driver was therefore an insured under the policy and could have enforced the policy against the insurers irrespective of Quinnsworth's right to do so in respect of their vicarious liability. Quinnsworth Ltd. had an employers' liability policy issued by the defendants indemnifying them against liability to pay compensation for illness or injury sustained by any employee arising out of and in the course of employment by Quinnsworth Ltd. Quinnsworth could therefore have claimed indemnity under that policy in respect of their vicarious liability to the injured passenger. The plaintiffs sought fifty per cent contribution from the defendant on the basis that there was double insurance. The High Court accepted the defendants' argument that neither the risk nor the insured interest were the same and held that as the interests insured and the risks covered were different the plaintiffs were not entitled to contribution. The decision was upheld in the Supreme Court where the equitable nature of the right to contribution was also recognised. McCarthy J. quoted extensively from English authorities in support of the application of the principle which according to him produced a decision "happily in accordance with common sense."[94] The requirement that the legal interests in the subject matter be the same was upheld in *Andrews & Others* v *Patriotic Assurance Co. of Ireland*[95] and more recently in *In Re: Kelly's Carpetdrome Ltd.*[96] It is clear from these decisions that it is not sufficient that the subject matter insured be the

---

[94] ibid. at 186; *North British and Mercantile Insurance Co.* v *London Liverpool & Globe Insurance Co.* [1877] 5 Ch. D. 569; *Castellain* v *Preston* [1883] 11 QBD 380.

[95] [1886] 18 LRI 355.

[96] Unreported High Court, 14 April 1985.

same; the legal interests insured must also be the same. In both cases the policies covered the different interests of landlord and tenant.

CHAPTER FIVE

GENERAL POLICY TERMS AND CONDITIONS

5.1 CLASSIFICATION OF TERMS

In the general law of contract a "condition" is a term which goes to the root of the agreement, and breach of which gives the victim a right to rescind the contract and to claim damages; a "warranty" is a term which affects only some minor part of the agreement and if broken gives the injured party a right to damages but no right to rescind the agreement. In Insurance Law a "warranty" is a term which if broken allows the insurers to repudiate the entire contract; a "condition" in an insurance contract may in effect be a warranty, or it may in fact be neither a warranty nor a condition. Insurance contracts are also subject to implied conditions that: (a) the insured has an insurable interest in the subject matter; (b) the insured will observe the utmost good faith; and (c) the subject matter exists at the inception of the policy.[1] In practice insurers insert in the policy express conditions which have the effect of those conditions which would otherwise be implied by law. Such express conditions may extend or restrict the scope of the implied conditions. Other terms in the policy may not amount to conditions and do not affect the validity of the policy or the liability of the insurers. The classification of the terms of an insurance policy is therefore more complex than the classification of terms in the general law of contract and the position is not helped by the manner in which insurers draft their policies,

---

[1] *Motor Insurers Bureau* v *PMPA Insurance* [1981] IR 142. The Supreme Court held that a policy of insurance being a contract of indemnity was subject to an implied term that the insurer would not be liable under the contract before the policyholder acquired an insurable interest.

placing warranties and conditions precedent to liability under the one heading of "general conditions".[2]

5.2 WARRANTIES

5.2.1 DEFINITIONS

A warranty in an insurance contract is a promise made by the insured relating to facts or to something which he agrees to do. The promise or warranty must be literally complied with.[3] Breach of a warranty entitles the insurer to repudiate liability and avoid the policy from the date of breach, even if the content of the warranty is not material to the risk or the breach material to the loss. The description given to a clause in the policy is not however conclusive proof of its effect but the place where the warranty is found may indicate the extent of its scope if that is in doubt.[4] No formal or technical language is necessary for the creation of a warranty and in determining whether a term is a warranty or a mere representation the court will take into consideration the substance of the promise or statement made to see if it is fundamental to the contract, bearing in mind its relation to the

---

[2] The position is further confused by the use of the word "warranty" to mean an exception, e.g. a "warranty" that a marine policy is free from particular average. Where an insurer relies on an exception to defeat a claim under a policy the insurance remains in force in respect of any other loss within the scope of the policy but where the insurer relies on breach of a warranty the insurance contract is avoided. The confusion even extends to the judiciary. Roskill J. at 236 in *Lane* v *Spratt* [1969] 2 Lloyds Rep 229:

> By a "condition" I mean a contractual term of the policy, any breach of which by the assured will in the event of a loss arising otherwise payable under the policy afford underwriters a defence to any claim irrespective of whether there is a causal connection between the breach of the contractual term and the loss. By a "warranty" I mean a contractual term of the policy a breach of which will not of itself afford a defence to the underwriters unless there is the necessary causal link between the breach and the loss which is the subject of the claim under the policy.

[3] *Anderson* v *Fitzgerald* [1853] 4 HL Cas 484, per Cranworth L. C.:

> Thus, if a person effecting a policy of insurance says . . . "I warrant such and such a thing, which is here stated, and that is part of the contract", then whether they are material or not is quite unimportant. The party must adhere to his warranty, whether material or immaterial.

[4] *Allan Peters* v *Brocks Alarms* [1968] 1 Lloyds Rep 387 at 391 where it was held that if a continuing warranty is attached by endorsement to the burglary section of a policy covering a jeweller's premises for various risks the warranty must be taken to apply to the burglary section only and not to the entire policy.

risk, its business purpose and whether it would be unfair to expose the insurer to a claim in the event of a breach of the term. The determining factor is however the intention of the parties and the use of the words "warranty" or "warranted" is good evidence of the intention to create a warranty. Provided the effect of the clause is made clear in the document the terminology is irrelevant.[5] In marine insurance there is a presumption that any statement of fact bearing upon the risk is to be construed as a warranty if it is written into the policy. In an early Irish case of *Sceales* v *Scanlan*[6] the Court of Exchequer Pleas was inclined to apply that particular feature of marine insurance law to a case concerning life assurance. In another Irish case, *Quin* v *National Assurance Co.*,[7] Joy C. B. thought that the description of the premises written into a fire policy must *ipso facto* be a warranty. If a proposer for insurance promises that something is true to the best of his knowledge and belief that is not a warranty of fact but a warranty of opinion. Insurers could not repudiate the contract unless they could prove that the statement was not made in good faith. It is not necessary for insurers to prove that a breach of warranty was material to the risk or the loss. Joy C. B. quoted with approval the following passage from Lord Eldon's judgment in *Newcastle Fire Insurance Co.* v *MacMorran & Co.*:[8]

> It is a first principle of the law of insurance on all occasions, that where a representation is material, it must be complied with; if immaterial, that immateriality may be enquired into

---

[5] A term of the insurance contract should not be construed as a warranty "except on very clear indications it was the intention of the contracting parties that it should have that effect", per Bramwell B. in *Wheelton* v *Hardisty* [1857] 8 El & Bl 232 at 300. Lord Blackburn adopting *Anderson* v *Fitzgerald* (above) said in *Thomson* v *Weems* [1884] 9 App Cas 671 at 682:
> Before a term is held to have the effect of a warranty it is necessary to see that the language is such as to show that the assured as well as the insurer meant it, and . . . the language in the policy being that of the insurers, if there is any ambiguity, it must be construed most strongly against them.

[6] [1843] 2 ILR 367

[7] *Quin* v *National Assurance Co.* [1839] Jo. & Car. 316.

[8] 3 Dow. PC 255; In *Thomson* v *Weems* (above) Lord Blackburn said:
> it is not of any importance whether the existence of that thing was or was not material; the parties would not have made it part of the contract if they had not thought it material, and they have a right to determine for themselves what they shall deem material.

and shewn, but if there is a warranty, it is part of the contract that the matter is such as it represented to be: therefore the materiality or immateriality signifies nothing, whether the misdescription arose from mistake, fraud or any other cause, it makes no difference. The only question is as to the mere fact, for in warranty it must be actually true.

Insurers relieve themselves of the burden of proving materiality, to either the risk or the loss, of statements made by the insured in the proposal form by having the proposer warrant the truth of the statements, by incorporating the proposal into the contract and making the information contained therein the "basis of the contract" between the parties.[9] When

> answers are declared to be the basis of the contract this can only mean that their truth is made a condition exact fulfilment of which is rendered by stipulation foundational to its enforceability.[10]

In the Irish case of *Anderson* v *Fitzgerald*, Lord Cranworth said:

> Nothing, therefore can be more reasonable than that the parties entering into the contract should determine for themselves what they think to be material, and, if they choose to do so, to stipulate that unless the assured shall answer a certain ques-

---

[9] In *Thomson* v *Weems* [1884] 9 App. Cas. 671 the policy provided that if anything declared to be true on the proposal "shall be untrue this policy shall be void". The court held that this had the effect of turning all statements made by the insured on the proposal form into warranties. In *Dawsons Ltd.* v *Bonnin* [1922] 2 AC 413 the proposer stated incorrectly the address at which the insured lorry was garaged in response to a question on the proposal form. The actual policy issued did not state that an untrue answer would render the policy void, but merely stated that the proposal would be the basis of the contract. The court held that this was sufficient to turn the statements on the proposal into warranties. In *Farrell* v *South East Lancashire Insurance Company Ltd.* [1933] IR 36, Kennedy C. J. in the Supreme Court upheld the decision of Hanna J. in favour of the insurer saying:

> The fact which he [the insured] undertook to be true was made the basis of the contract in the policy. The question of materiality of the fact warranted does not enter into the issue in these circumstances, the truth of the fact, whether material or immaterial, having been agreed to be the basis of the contract. . . . This is undoubtedly a very hard case. But the fact is that the plaintiff, no doubt innocently, warranted the truth of the statements inserted in the proposal. . . . The statement was not true and the contract fails.

[10] per Viscount Haldane at 425 in *Dawsons Ltd.* v *Bonnin* [1922] 2 AC 413.

tion accurately the policy or contract which they are entering into shall be void.[11]

5.2.2 BASIS OF CONTRACT CLAUSES

The all-important element in the declaration contained in the proposal form is the phrase which makes the declaration the "basis of the contract". In making the proposal the basis of the contract the proposer warrants the truth of his statements and in the event of a breach of the warranty the insurer can repudiate liability under the policy without reference to issues of materiality. Such "basis of contract" clauses have invariably been upheld by the courts on the grounds of maintaining the "sanctity of contract" but in doing so the courts have expressed their hostility to them.[12] In *Farrell* v *South East Lancashire Insurance Co. Ltd.*[13] the Supreme Court upheld a "basis of contract" clause where the proposer, on the proposal form, warranted the truth of the answers given. He had stated the purchase price of the vehicle to be insured as £800 whereas he had paid only £140 for it. In *O'Callaghan* v *Irish National Assurance Co. Ltd.*[14] the Circuit Court Judge believed he was entitled to disregard an untrue statement of age on a life proposal form provided he reduced the amount of the plaintiff's claim to that sum for which the defendant company would have insured the plaintiff's life if the correct age had been declared. The High Court rejected that contention holding that the plaintiff was bound by his signature on the proposal form warranting the truth of the statements contained in the form and since some of these were untrue the policy was void. The Irish Insurance Federation's Code of Practice for non-life insurance effectively prohibits insurers from converting questions in proposal forms into contractual warranties by the inclusion of a basis of contract clause in poli-

---

[11] [1853] 4 HL Cas 484 House of Lords.

[12] See Chapter Three para 3.5.

[13] [1933] IR 36.

[14] [1934] 68 ILTR 248; see also *Griffin* v *Royal Liver Friendly Society* [1942] 76 ILTR 82.

cies to which the Code applies.[15] In *Keating* v *New Ireland Assurance Co. Ltd.*, the most recent pronouncement of the Supreme Court on the matter, Walsh J. said:

> Insurers may stipulate for any warranty they please and if an insured undertakes that warranty, although it may be something not within his or her knowledge, he or she must abide the consequences.

However he went on to indicate that the Court would be more demanding of insurers by saying:

> But when insurers intend that there is to be a warranty of that sort they must make it perfectly plain that such is their intention and they must use unequivocal language, such as persons with ordinary intelligence may without any difficulty understand.[16]

The Court was extremely critical of the use, by insurers, of such "basis of contract" clauses, and its decision, in *Keating*, to refuse to find a breach of warranty indicates that the previous harsh decision of the High Court, in *Keenan* v *Shield Insurance Co. Ltd.*,[17] is unlikely to be followed. The insured gave an incorrect answer to a question on the proposal as to previous claims. The answer was untrue as he had previously sustained a minor trivial loss which was in no way material to the policy or the loss claimed for. Nevertheless, insurers were held entitled to repudiate liability under the policy.

---

[15] Para 1(b) of the code says:
> Neither the proposal form nor the policy shall contain any general provision converting the statements as to past or present fact in the proposal form into warranties. But insurers may require specific warranties about matters which are material to the risk.

The Code of Practice applies to non-life insurances of policyholders resident in the Republic of Ireland and insured in their private capacity.

[16] *Keating* v *New Ireland Assurance Company plc.* [1990] 2 IR 383. The insurers were unable to satisfy the court that these requirements had been met and the court found for the plaintiff.

[17] *Keenan* v *Shield Insurance Co. Ltd.* [1987] IR 113. The current Code of Practice for non-life insurance now provides that insurers will not repudiate liability to indemnify a policyholder "on grounds of a breach of warranty or condition where the circumstances of the loss are unconnected with the breach unless fraud is involved".

5.2.3 CONTINUING WARRANTIES

5.2.3.1 A warranty in a policy may apply not only to circumstances existing or statements made when the contract is arranged but also to circumstances arising during the currency of the contract. Such warranties are referred to as "continuing" or "promissory" warranties. The courts are slow to recognise such warranties as continuing for the period of cover and seek to limit them to the time of contracting.[18] Where it is reasonable to read an ambiguous term as either a present or continuing warranty the courts have been prepared to interpret it as a warranty relating to the position at inception of the contract. In *Woolfall & Rimmer* v *Moyle*[19] the court was asked to decide if a positive answer to a proposal form question, enquiring if the proposer's plant, machinery and ways were properly fenced and guarded, constituted a warranty that they would be so maintained during the term of the policy. The Court of Appeal held that the proposer's statement did not constitute a continuing warranty but related only to the situation when it was made with Lord Greene M.R. remarking that there was "not a particle of justification for reading into that perfectly simple question any element of futurity whatsoever."[20] That was followed, in Ireland, by the High Court, in *Sweeney* v *Kennedy*.[21] The assured had answered "no" to a question enquiring if any drivers were under twenty-one or had less than twelve months driving experience. He had also agreed that the declaration should be held "to be promissory and form the basis of the contract". The court held that while the use of the word "promissory" gave the answers the status of

---

[18] In *Re: Sweeney and Kennedy's Arbitration* [1950] IR 85, it was held that a reply in a proposal form warranted to be true only related to facts existing at the time the answer was given and not to facts existing during the term of the policy. Courts are influenced by whether the clause uses the future tense since it is so easy for the drafter to use that tense if it is the intention that the warranty should be a continuing warranty. See *Woolfall & Rimmer* v *Moyle* [1942] 1 KB 66 at 71. and Kingsmill Moore J in *Re: Sweeney* (above):

> Here, also, if the underwriters intended to refer to the future it is most unfortunate that a printed document . . . should not be so expressed. . . . had they intended that this question should carry the meaning which they now suggest, nothing would have been easier than to say so.

[19] [1942] 1 KB 66.

[20] ibid. at 71.

[21] *Sweeney* v *Kennedy* [1950] IR 85.

warranties the answer was confined to the facts as existing at the time the proposal was completed.

5.2.3.2 A warranty will be construed as continuing only if the words admit of no other construction or the warranty would have no purpose or function unless it continued for the duration of the contract. The continuing nature of the warranty may be found in the language used and insurers usually draft such clauses in the future tense. In determining whether a clause is a continuing warranty the courts are likely to consider: (a) does the clause have the appearance of a warranty; (b) is it clearly referable to a future situation; (c) is it a provision which would be of little or no value to the insurers if it related only to present facts; (d) does a breach of the clause permanently prejudice the insurers even if it is subsequently remedied? The Court of Appeal in *Hussain* v *Brown*[22] refused to accept that an affirmative answer to a question on a proposal form, enquiring as to the existence of an intruder alarm, constituted a continuing warranty that the premises were fitted with an alarm, that the alarm was operational and/or would be habitually set by the insured when the premises were unattended. Saville L. J. emphasised that a continuing warranty was a "draconian" term, breach of which automatically terminated cover even if the loss and the breach were unconnected. He said, in giving the unanimous decision of the Court:

> In my judgment . . . there is no special principle of insurance law requiring answers in proposal forms to be read, *prima facie* or otherwise, as importing promises as to the future. Whether or not they go depends on ordinary rules of construction, namely, consideration of the words the parties have used in the light of the context in which they have used them and . . . selection of that meaning which seems most closely to correspond with the presumed intention of the parties.[23]

In the case under consideration the question was posed in the present tense and sought no further information as to the insured's practice with regard to the setting of the alarm.

---

[22] [1996] 1 Lloyds Rep 627.

[23] at 629.

5.2.3.3 In *Transthene Packaging Co. Ltd.* v *Royal Insurance (UK) Ltd.*[24] the policy issued by the defendants, covering material damage and business interruption risks, contained a warranty that oily or greasy rags, not removed from the building, would be stored over- night in metal containers. Following a fire at the premises, insurers sought to avoid the policy on a number of grounds, including breach of the warranty. The court accepted the insurers argument that they were relieved of liability under the policy, once oily rags were stored in breach of the warranty. The court would not accept that the word- ing of the warranty allowed the warranty to be treated merely as a suspensory condition which would only relieve insurers of liability if it was not being complied with at the time of the fire.

5.3 CONDITIONS

5.3.1 EXPRESS CONDITIONS

There are certain conditions implied by law which affect the validity of every insurance policy unless the parties to the contract expressly agree to exclude them or modify their operation.[25] If it is intended to impose further obligations on the insured or make their fulfilment a condition of the contract the policy must contain an express state- ment to that effect.[26] In the Irish case of *Andrews* v *Patriotic Assur- ance Company* (No. 2) Palles C. B. said:

---

[24] [1996] LRLR 32.

[25] *Thomson* v *Weems* [1884] 9 App Cas 671 per Lord Blackburn at 683:
It is competent to the contracting parties, if both agree to it and sufficiently express their intention to agree, to make the actual existence of anything a condition precedent to the inception of the contract; and if they do so, the non- existence of that thing is a good defence. And it is not of any importance whether the existence of that thing was or was not material; the parties would not have made it a part of the contract if they had not thought it material, and they have a right to determine for themselves what they shall deem material.

[26] Lord Blackburn at 915 in *London Guarantee Co.* v *Fearnley* [1880] 5 AC 911:
It has long been the practice of companies insuring against fire for the purpose of their own security, to incorporate in the policies, by reference to their pro- posals, various stipulations for matters to be done by the assured making a claim before the company is to pay them and (as the remedy by action for not complying with the stipulation would not afford them any protection) to make the fulfilment of those conditions a condition precedent to their obligation to pay. . . . it has been settled law that this mode of protecting themselves is ef- fectual.

You would expect to find provisions relating to the conduct of the insured and those over whom he had control, provisions affecting or possibly making void the policy in case of fraud in its making or procurement, or in the event of circumstances which increase the actual risk above that which was contemplated and paid for and perhaps clauses . . . providing against anything more than a complete indemnity being recovered by the insured.[27]

The express conditions in the policy can be classified into:

(a) conditions precedent to the validity of the policy. Failure by the insured to fulfil these conditions renders the policy void *ab initio*.[28] Such conditions generally give expression to the conditions implied by law.[29]

(b) Conditions subsequent to the policy relating to matters arising after the formation of the contract and breach of which gives the insurer the right to avoid the policy from the date of the breach. Such conditions concern issues of assignment, alteration of risk, fraudulent claims, other insurance and warranties as described above.

(c) Conditions precedent to the liability of insurers relating to matters arising after a loss has occurred.

Failure to comply with these conditions entitles the insurer to repudiate liability for the loss but not to avoid the policy. Such conditions relate to premium payment, dispute resolution, loss notification, claims procedure and precautions to avoid loss.[30] Whether a term is a condition or not depends on the intention of the parties as expressed in the language used. It is a matter of construction to be determined

---

[27] *Andrews* v *Patriotic Insurance Co.* (No. 2) [1886] 18 LRI 355 at 361.

[28] *Thomson* v *Weems* [1884] 9 App Cas 671 at 683 per Lord Blackburn.

[29] See Section 5.1 above. Some policies include a clause stipulating that the "policy shall be voidable in the event of misrepresentation, misdescription or non-disclosure in any material particular".

[30] The English Law Reform Committee in their Report on "Conditions and Exceptions in Insurance Policies", 1957, Cmnd. 62, felt that the presence of such clauses was a very valuable protection to the insurers since their function was to facilitate prompt investigation of a loss, to ensure control by insurers of any litigation or negotiations with third parties, and generally to protect their interests in respect of salvage or subrogation.

according to the normal rules of construction. Policies often contain a general "Observance of Terms" clause stipulating that

> the due observance and fulfilment of the terms, conditions and memoranda of this policy in so far as they relate to anything to be done or complied with by the insured and the truth of the statements and answers contained in the proposal shall be conditions precedent to any liability of the Company to make any payment under this policy.

The purpose of this clause is to convert all stipulations in the policy into conditions precedent to liability[31] but in *Re: Bradley and Essex & Suffolk Accident Indemnity Society*[32] the majority of the Court of Appeal held that a stipulation in the policy requiring the insured to keep a proper wages book was not a condition precedent to liability, notwithstanding an express declaration that the due observance and fulfilment of the conditions of the policy was to be a condition precedent to liability of the insurers. In practice the stipulations of the policy are grouped together under the general heading of conditions but each stipulation is construed individually according to the wording used. Those intended to be conditions precedent are shown to be so intended either by the express language used or the subject matter to which they relate. Where a stipulation is expressed to be a condition precedent it will be construed as one.[33]

---

[31] A practice criticised by Farwell L. J. at 432 in *Re: Bradley & Essex and Suffolk Accident Indemnity Society* [1912] 1 KB 415 and by Humphreys J. in *Pictorial Machinery Ltd.* v *Nicholls* [1940] 164 LT 248 at 250.

[32] *Supra.*

[33] *London Guarantee Co.* v *Fearnley* [1880], 5 App Cas 911 per Lord Watson at 919:

> When the parties to a contract of insurance choose in express terms to declare that a certain condition of the policy shall be a condition precedent, that stipulation ought, in my opinion, to receive effect, unless it shall appear to be so capricious and unreasonable that a Court of Law ought not to enforce it, or to be *sua natura* incapable of being made a condition precedent.

In *Gamble* v *Accident Assurance Co.* [1869] IR 4 CL 204 per Pigot C. B. at 214:

> a most unreasonable condition . . . would still be binding, if its meaning was clear. If the words were capable of two constructions, we might adopt one which was reasonable and reject one which was not. But the language . . . is clear and unambiguous, and we cannot free either of the parties from a contract which they have both made for themselves, because we may think it was very unwise in one of the parties to engage in it.

5.4 REASONABLE PRECAUTIONS CONDITION

The condition found in most policies, requiring that "the insured shall at all times take reasonable precautions to prevent accidents loss or damage" is a good example of a continuing warranty and also of the confusion between policy conditions, warranties and exceptions.[34] If it is a term of a policy that the property insured be kept in a particular place, e.g. a safe, then cover ceases when it is removed from the safe. The term is generally an exception rather than a warranty. Cover is reinstated on the property once it is returned to the safe and if a loss subsequently occurs it is covered under the policy. This form of "reasonable precautions condition" has the effect of an exception more than of a warranty and is construed restrictively by the courts. Lord Diplock considered the effect of such a condition in a liability policy in *Fraser* v *Furman (Productions) Ltd.*[35]

> ... when one approaches the construction of the condition, one does so in [this] context, and applies the rule that one does not construe a condition as repugnant to the commercial purpose of the contract . . . it is the insured personally who must take reasonable precautions. . . . the obligation is to take precautions to prevent accidents. This means in my view to take measures to avert dangers which are likely to cause bodily injury. . . . "Reasonable" . . . means reasonable as between the insured and the insurer having regard to the commercial purpose of the contract. . . . What, in my view, is "reasonable" . . . is that the insured should not deliberately court a danger, the existence of which he recognises. . . . The purpose of the condition is to ensure that the insured will not, because he is cov-

---

[34] Whilst terminology is not decisive, per Scrutton L. J. in *Re: Morgan and Provincial Insurance Co.* [1932] 2 KB 70 at 79–80 the use of words such as "warranty" or "condition precedent" might suggest that the term is not an exception but a warranty, per Stirling L. J. in *Ellinger & Co.* v *Mutual Life Insurance Co.* [1905] 1 KB 31 at 38.

[35] [1967] 1 WLR 898. The interpretation of this condition was also considered in *British Food Freezers Ltd.* v *Industrial Estates Management for Scotland* [1977] Unreported Court of Appeal, where contractors using burning equipment had not taken any precautions to prevent fire damage. The court held the complete lack of fire precautions meant that the insured were in breach of the duty of care imposed on them and that the insurers were entitled to repudiate liability under the policy. In *Aluminium Wire & Cable Co. Ltd.* v *Allstate Insurance Co. Ltd.* [1985] 2 Lloyds Rep 280, it was held that insurers could only invoke the condition if they could prove that the insured had acted recklessly.

ered against loss by the policy, refrain from taking precautions which he knows ought to be taken.[36]

This approach by Diplock to the condition in a liability policy was adopted by O'Hanlon J. in *Brady* v *Irish National Insurance Co. Ltd.*[37] and applied by him to a case involving a marine insurance policy. The approach has been followed, in England, in relation to loss of property, with the Court of Appeal, in *Sofi* v *Prudential*[38] holding that, whatever the nature of the insurance, the obligation to take reasonable care meant no more than that the insured had to avoid recklessness in relation to the insured subject matter. The insured was held not to have acted recklessly in leaving jewellery locked out of sight in the glove compartment of his car whilst he went sightseeing. In *Glenmuir Ltd. and Fallstrom* v *Norwich Union*,[39] the High Court Judge, in interpreting *Sofi*, held that a claim is defeated by a reasonable care clause only where the insured has been reckless in a subjective sense, i.e. in recognising that a risk existed but in not caring whether or not there was exposure to that risk. The approach of Diplock was confirmed in *Devco* v *Legal and General*,[40] which extended the same principles to property insurance. Where the policy contains both property and liability sections and the reasonable care condition applies to both, the clause is to be construed for the purposes of both sections as implying only a requirement that the insured must avoid being reckless. The Irish Courts apply much the same criteria as applied in assessing the conduct of a person owing a duty of reasonable care in tort, in relation to the circumstances. The

---

[36] ibid. at 905. The court expressed the opinion that it was the insured personally who had to take reasonable precautions. Failure by an employee to do so, although it might render an employer liable in damages to anyone injured by the employee's negligence, would not be a breach of the policy condition. In an earlier case, *Woolfall and Rimmer Ltd.* v *Moyle* [1942] 1 KB 66, the Court of Appeal had held that the condition requiring the insured to take reasonable precautions to prevent accidents applied only to the personal acts of the insured himself and where those acts had been delegated to a trustworthy, and skilled, foreman the insured was not to be denied indemnity by the condition when the foreman's negligence caused an accident.

[37] [1986] ILRM 669.

[38] *Sofi* v *Prudential Assurance* [1993] 2 Lloyds Rep 559.

[39] Unreported High Court, December 1994.

[40] [1993] 2 Lloyds Rep 559.

likelihood of loss, the gravity of loss, the viability and expense of precautions against loss, and the importance of the activity being pursued when the loss occurred would all be relevant.[41]

5.5 ARBITRATION CONDITION

5.5.1 ARBITRATION AND LITIGATION
The main reason why there are so few judicial decisions on insurance law in Ireland is the inclusion in all insurance contracts of an arbitration condition requiring all disputes under a policy to be referred to arbitration.[42] The wording used in Irish policies differs from that used in England where the condition is concerned only with disputes as to the amount to be paid under the policy.[43] The purpose of the

---

[41] The 1995 Annual Report of the Insurance Ombudsman in Ireland (p. 31, case study 22) indicates that the onus of proving want of care rests with the insurer and that the condition requires something more than simple negligence. It indicates further that the Ombudsman will take into account, when evaluating the material behaviour, such factors as the value of the goods, the reasons for leaving them unattended, the precautions taken and the alternatives available. The issue has figured prominently in the annual reports of the Insurance Ombudsman Bureau in England. In 1995 the Bureau dealt with 109 cases alleging lack of reasonable care by the policyholder. The Winter 1995/6 Supplement to the 1995 Annual Report sets out in some detail the approach of the Ombudsman in applying the Diplock principles to the cases referred to the Bureau. Insurers have sought to overcome these principles by inserting in policies express wordings excluding loss in specific situations such as loss from unattended vehicles, or by excluding theft losses from vehicles unless the property is kept in a locked boot.

[42] A typical arbitration condition reads:
> All differences arising out of this Policy shall be referred to the decision of an Arbitrator to be appointed in writing by the parties in difference or if they cannot agree upon a single Arbitrator to the decision of two Arbitrators one to be appointed in writing by each of the parties within one calendar month after having been required in writing so to do by either of the parties or in the case of disagreement between the Arbitrators to the decision of an Umpire appointed in writing by the Arbitrators before entering upon the reference. The Umpire shall sit with the Arbitrators and preside at their meetings and the making of an award shall be a condition precedent to any right of action against the Company. After the expiration of one year after any destruction or damage or event the Company shall not be liable in respect of any claim thereof unless such claim shall in the meantime have been referred to arbitration.

[43] The English wording reads: "If any difference shall arise as to the amount to be paid under this Policy (liability being otherwise admitted) such difference shall be referred to . . . "

condition is to provide a quick, efficient, private and inexpensive means of dispute resolution without resort to litigation through the courts. In the *Bremer Vulkan* case,[44] Lord Diplock was of the opinion that there is:

> a fundamental difference between an action at law and arbitration. . . . As plaintiff and defendant in an action, the parties assume no contractual obligations to one another as to what each must do in the course of the proceedings; their respective obligations as to procedure are imposed upon them by the rules and practice of the court. In contrast to this, the submission of a dispute to arbitration under a private arbitration agreement is purely voluntary by both claimant and respondent. Where the arbitration agreement is in a clause forming part of a wider contract and provides for the reference to arbitration of all future disputes arising under or concerning the contract, neither party knows when the agreement is entered into whether he will be claimant or respondent in disputes to which the arbitration agreement will apply. . . . In an arbitration there is no fixed pattern of procedure; what steps are to be taken by each party in a particular arbitration and the timetable which each party must observe are matters to be determined by the arbitrator. . . . By appointing a sole arbitrator pursuant to a private arbitration agreement which does not specify expressly or by reference any particular procedural rules, the parties make the arbitrator the master of the procedure to be followed in the arbitration. Apart from a few statutory requirements . . . he has complete discretion to determine how an arbitration is to be conducted from the time of his appointment to the time of his award, so long as the procedure he adopts does not offend the rules of natural justice.

5.5.2 STATUTORY PROVISIONS

Arbitration is not a means of avoiding compliance with legal requirements. Arbitration is subject to statutory provisions and the normal rules of evidence and procedure apply. Until 1954 the submission to and enforcement of arbitration was governed by common law rules;

---

[44] *Bremer Vulkan Schiffbau und Maschinenfabrik* v *South India Shipping Corp. Ltd.* [1981] AC 909.

the Arbitration Act, 1889 did not apply to Ireland.[45] The Arbitration Act, 1954 was introduced "to make further and better provision in respect of arbitrations".[46] The intention of the Act was to provide a private and appropriate forum for the resolution of business disputes and this statutory intent is "particularly to be inferred" from Section 12 of the Act.[47] Section 12 was repealed and re-enacted in altered form by Section 4 of the Arbitration Act, 1980. Under Section 12 of the Act of 1954 the court had the power to stay proceedings when it was satisfied that there was not sufficient reason why the matter should not be referred in accordance with the agreement, but Section 5 of the Act of 1980 precludes the court from making an order staying proceedings:

> unless it is satisfied that the arbitration agreement is null and void, inoperative or incapable of being performed or that there is not in fact any dispute between the parties with regard to the matter agreed to be referred.

The 1980 Act gives effect to the Convention on the Recognition and Enforcement of Foreign Arbitral Awards signed at New York on 10 June 1958, and to certain provisions of the Convention on the Settlement of Investment Disputes between States and Nationals of other States opened for signature in Washington on 18 March 1965, and otherwise to amend the Arbitration Act, 1954. Arbitration proceedings are commenced by one party serving on the other a written notice requiring them to appoint or agree to the appointment of an arbitrator.[48] Where the arbitration clause so requires the notice must be

---

[45] The only relevant statutory provisions which related to the enforcement of arbitration was the statute of 1698 [an act for determining differences by arbitration] and the Common Law Procedure Amendment Act (Ireland), 1856. The procedural amendments were made necessary by the Supreme Court of Judicature Act (Ireland), 1877.

[46] In *Keenan v Shield Insurance Co. Ltd.* [1988] IR 89, per McCarthy J.:
The Act took as its model the English Acts of 1889 and of 1950 and was intended to provide a comprehensive scheme whereby matters commercial, such as in construction, insurance, financial services, shipping and kindred and other industries, might be resolved without recourse to the courts and, in many instances, by those best equipped for that purpose by training and experience in the particular field.

[47] ibid.

[48] Section 3(1), Arbitration Act, 1954.

given and proceedings commenced within the specified period.[49] However, Section 45 of the Act provides that where an agreement to refer disputes to arbitration limits the time in which arbitration may be commenced, the court, if it thinks undue hardship would otherwise be caused, may extend such time. In *Walsh* v *Shield Insurance Co. Ltd.*[50] Hamilton J. held that the insurance company having repudiated liability would not suffer prejudice if the grounds on which they repudiated were valid, whereas the plaintiff policyholder would be caused undue hardship if the court refused to extend the time limit, notwithstanding the inexcusable delay of the policyholder both in commencing arbitration and in applying to the court.[51] The statutes of limitation apply to an arbitration agreement in the same way as they apply to actions in the courts.[52] The authority of an arbitrator, appointed under an arbitration agreement, is irrevocable except by leave of the court.[53] If a party to the agreement commences proceedings in any court in respect of any matter agreed to be referred to arbitration, any party to the proceedings may at any time after an appearance has been entered, and before delivering any pleadings or taking any other steps in the proceedings, apply to the court to stay the proceedings.[54] The court, unless it is satisfied that the arbitration agreement is null and void, inoperative or incapable of being performed or that there is not in fact any dispute between the parties, shall make an order staying the proceedings. The High Court has a discretion under Section 39 of the Arbitration Act, 1954 to retain proceedings before a

---

[49] Usually twelve months.

[50] [1976–77] ILRM 218.

[51] The Court however ordered that the policyholder was to be liable for the costs of the application to the court and that he was not to be awarded the costs of the Arbitration if he was successful.

[52] Section 42, Arbitration Act 1954; Section 43 goes on to say that:
Notwithstanding any term in an arbitration agreement to the effect that no cause of action shall accrue in respect of any matter required by the agreement to be referred until an award is made under the agreement, a cause of action shall, for the purposes of the statutes of limitation (whether in their application to the arbitration or to other proceedings), be deemed to have accrued in respect of any such matter at the time when it would have accrued but for that term in the agreement.

[53] Section 9 of the Arbitration Act, 1954.

[54] Section 5(2) of the Act of 1980 which repealed Section 12 of the Act of 1954. see n. 45 above.

court and to refuse a request by one party for a stay to enable matters in dispute to be resolved at arbitration where the claims are of great magnitude and complexity involving difficult questions of law and allegations of fraud.[55]

5.5.3 APPOINTMENT OF ARBITRATOR

Unless the arbitration agreement provides otherwise there is an implied provision that the reference shall be to a single arbitrator.[56] However, where the agreement provides for reference to two arbitrators with one to be appointed by each party, and one of the appointed arbitrators refuses to act or is incapable of acting or dies, then the party who appointed that arbitrator may appoint a new arbitrator to act in their place.[57] Where the agreement provides for the appointment of two arbitrators and one party fails to make the necessary appointment within seven days of receipt of notice from the other party, then the party who has nominated an arbitrator may, unless the agreement provides otherwise, appoint that arbitrator to act as sole arbitrator and his award shall be binding on both parties. The court does however have power to set aside any appointment made in such circumstances.[58] There is an implied provision that where an agreement provides for the appointment of two arbitrators the two arbitrators so appointed shall appoint an umpire immediately after they are appointed.[59] The umpire normally sits with the arbitrators and hears

---

[55] *Winterthur Swiss Insurance Co. & others* v *Insurance Corporation of Ireland plc.* (under Administration) [1990] ILRM 159. The plaintiffs gave notice of their intention to apply for an order pursuant to Section 39 of the Arbitration Act, 1954 that the alleged arbitration agreement between the parties should cease to have effect and that the plaintiffs should be entitled to revoke the authority of the arbitrators allegedly appointed by or by virtue of that agreement. The defendant gave notice of its intention to apply to the court to stay the proceedings and the issues fell to be decided by the court. O'Hanlon J. in refusing to grant an order to stay the proceedings held that the High Court has the discretion to retain proceedings before a court and to refuse a request by one party for a stay to enable matters in dispute to be resolved by arbitration where the claims are of great magnitude and complexity. In such cases, a hearing before the High Court with a right of appeal on a point of law to the Supreme Court offered a better procedure than a hearing before arbitrators.

[56] Section 14 of the Arbitration Act, 1954.

[57] Section 15 of the Act.

[58] Section 15(2)(a) and (b) of the Act.

[59] Section 16(1) of the Act.

the evidence. If the arbitrators give notice to the umpire that they cannot agree then the umpire may enter upon the reference in lieu of the arbitrators.[60] At any time after the appointment of the umpire any of the parties to the agreement may apply to the court for an order requiring the umpire to enter upon the reference in lieu of the arbitrators as if he were the sole arbitrator.[61] Under Section 18 of the 1954 Act, the court has power to appoint an umpire or arbitrator, where the parties fail to agree on the appointment, or the appointed arbitrator refuses to act, or is incapable of acting, or dies.[62] The arbitration proceedings are conducted in the same way as a legal court action and the same rules and procedures apply to the taking of evidence, the attendance of witnesses and the production or discovery of documents.[63]

5.5.4 ARBITRATION AWARD

Unless the arbitration agreement provides otherwise, the arbitrator or umpire may make an award at any time and may, if he thinks fit, make an interim award.[64] An arbitrator who fails to use all reasonable dispatch in entering on and proceeding with the reference and the making of an award may be removed by the court on the application of any of the parties.[65] The award made by the arbitrator or umpire is

---

[60] Section 16(2) of the Act.

[61] Section 16(3) of the Act.

[62] Section 18.

[63] Sections 19, 20, 21, 22.

[64] Section 23 and Section 25.

[65] Section 24. In *Bremer Vulkan Schiffbau und Maschinenfabrik* v *South India Shipping Corporation* [1981] AC 909, the plaintiff claimed to be prejudiced by the delay of the defendant in prosecuting the arbitration and sought an injunction restraining continuance of the arbitration and a declaration that the arbitrator had power to strike out the defendant's claim for want of prosecution. The judge at first instance found that the delay was such that had the matter been the subject of litigation the court would have dismissed the case for want of prosecution. He granted the injunction on the grounds that the conduct constituted a breach of the agreement to submit the dispute to arbitration. On appeal, the Court of Appeal held that the parties to an arbitration agreement were under a duty not to deal with the presentation of the claim so as to frustrate the purpose of arbitration:

> the plaintiffs are entitled to treat the defendant's conduct as a repudiation of the arbitration agreement and as they had elected to rescind the court should grant the injunction.

final and binding on the parties,[66] even if it contains an error in law.[67] In *McStay* v *Assicurazioni Generali SPA and others*[68] the Supreme Court upheld the judgment of Carroll J. quoting with approval the *ratio decidendi* of her judgment:

> The arbitrator was given power to decide a specific question of law. . . . He decided that question. . . . The plaintiff could have asked for a special case to be stated for the High Court on the point. Having failed to do so he is bound by the arbitrator's decision on the point and it does not matter whether that decision was erroneous at law or not. Having decided that, it is not necessary for me to decide whether the decision was in fact erroneous.[69]

5.5.5 POWERS OF THE COURTS

Finlay C. J. in the Supreme Court reviewing the powers of the court in relation to arbitration proceedings referred to the finality of the decision of the arbitrator as "a fundamental ingredient of the concept of arbitration, as contained in the common law".[70] Even the possibility of an injustice could not permit him

> to reach a conclusion which would alter the legal consequences of the agreement to refer this precise point of law to the determination of the arbitrator. Those consequences undeniably

---

[66] Section 27 of the 1954 Act.

[67] *McStay* v *Assicurazioni Generali SPA* [1991] ILRM 237. However, O'Flaherty J. in a dissenting judgment said:

> I respectfully adopt and follow this reasoning and in my judgment the importance and central position of the arbitration agreement must always be kept in the forefront in determining the respective rights of the parties to it. . . . I agree with everything that has been urged that it is important that there should be finality in arbitrations; that indeed, is often the point of having arbitrations at all. . . . Nonetheless, I believe there was a fundamental misapprehension by both parties as to the effect of this agreement in this case. . . . I believe the justice of the case does call for the intervention of the court and that the matter should be remitted to the arbitrator with a direction that he is entitled to entertain an application for interest prior to the date of his award. I believe that this jurisdiction to remit is one that should be sparingly exercised but I believe it should be exercised in this case.

[68] [1991] ILRM 237.

[69] ibid. at 241.

[70] ibid. at 242.

are, as a matter of fundamental law, that the parties are bound by his decision.[71]

In *Winterthur Swiss Insurance Co. & Others* v *Insurance Corporation of Ireland plc.*[72] the defendant and the plaintiffs had entered into re-insurance contracts in relation to certain risks written by the defendant. The re-insurance contract contained an arbitration clause providing that any dispute, difference or question between the parties in respect of the construction, validity or performance of the contract should, as a condition precedent to any right of action, be referred to two arbitrators and an umpire. The plaintiffs sought to repudiate liability under the contract on the grounds of fraud, misrepresentation, non-disclosure and a breach of the duty of utmost good faith and issued proceedings accordingly. The defendant did not accept that the plaintiffs were entitled to issue proceedings and served notice of arbitration on Winterthur, nominating an arbitrator. Winterthur, having, without prejudice, nominated an arbitrator, applied for an order, pursuant to Section 39 of the Arbitration Act, 1954 to have the arbitration agreement set aside. The defendant then applied for an order to stay the proceedings and have the matter referred to arbitration. The High Court ruled that in exercising its discretion the court should have regard to all the salient features of the case, including the magnitude and complexity of the claim and the difficulty of the legal issues involved. It held that in cases of great magnitude and complexity, a hearing before the High Court, with a right of appeal to the Supreme Court, offered a better procedure than an arbitration, where the control exercisable by the arbitrators or umpire over the course of the proceedings was not as satisfactory as that which could be exercised by the court.

---

[71] ibid. at 243 Finlay C. J. quoted Lord Russell of Killowen in *Absalom Ltd.* v *Great Western (London) Garden Village Society* [1933] AC 592 at 607:

My Lords, it is, I think, essential to keep the case where disputes are referred to an arbitrator, in the decision of which a question of law becomes material, distinct from the case in which a specific question of law has been referred to him for decision. I am not sure that the Court of Appeal has done so. The authorities make a clear distinction between these two cases and as they appear to me, they decide that in the former case the court can interfere if and when any error of law appears on the face of the award, but that in the latter case no such interference is possible upon the ground that it so appears that the decision on the question of law is an erroneous one.

[72] [1990] ILRM 159.

5.5.6 CONDUCT OF THE ARBITRATOR

The arbitrator has the power to state any question of law, in the form of a special case, for the decision of the High Court, and the court has the power on the application of any of the parties, to direct the arbitrator to state such a case.[73] Such action can only be taken prior to the making of a final award. In *Keenan* v *Shield Insurance Co. Ltd.*,[74] in a judgment with which all members of the Supreme Court agreed, McCarthy J. said:

> In my view the operation of Section 35 ends once the arbitrator has made his award without any qualification. No request was made for the stating of any question of law or any part of the award in the form of a special case. It is now too late to do so. . . . Arbitration is a significant feature of modern commercial life; . . . it ill becomes the courts to show any readiness to interfere in such a process.

An arbitrator, who has misconducted himself or the proceedings, may be removed by the court.[75] Where an arbitrator has misconducted himself or the proceedings or an award has been improperly secured, the court may set the award aside.[76] In *Childers Heights Housing Ltd.* v *Molderings*[77] the defendants, being dissatisfied with the arbitrator's award, sought to have it set aside on the ground that the arbitrator was guilty of misconduct in that she (a) inspected the premises on her own, (b) did not allow sufficient time to the defendants to make their submissions and (c) did not answer all the questions put to her. Barron J. in allowing the plaintiff's claim for an order giving them liberty to enforce the award and making no order on the defendant's motion held that when the arbitrator indicated her desire to make the inspection on her own and no objection was made, it was not now open to either party to complain of the manner in which the inspection took place. The arbitrator is expected to act impartially and must not allow himself be compromised in situations where he could be accused of showing bias in favour of one of the parties to the dispute. In

---

[73] Section 35 of the Act of 1954.

[74] [1988] IR 89.

[75] Section 37 of the Act of 1954.

[76] Section 38 ibid.

[77] [1987] ILRM 47

Re: Bryan's Arbitration,[78] the arbitrator visited the property with one party "contrary to all principles of justice and fair play". In *State (Hegarty)* v *Winters*[79] it was alleged by the party whose property had been damaged that the arbitrator acted in bias against him in going to view the property accompanied by an engineer appointed by the party who had caused the damage. The Supreme Court held the action of the arbitrator might reasonably give rise in the mind of an unprejudiced onlooker to the suspicion that justice was not being done. The fundamental rule that justice must be seen to be done was broken and the award could not be allowed to stand. An award of an arbitrator may be enforced in the same manner as a judgment or order of a court.[80]

5.5.7 INSURERS' RELIANCE ON CONDITION

The arbitration condition in an insurance policy is a condition precedent to liability. However, an insurer cannot seek to rely on the arbitration clause if they have repudiated or avoided the policy. In *Ballasty* v *Army, Navy and General Assurance Association Ltd.*[81] the plaintiff brought proceedings to recover monies due to him under a motor insurance policy. The company had repudiated liability on the grounds that the insured was in breach of a condition which rendered the policy void. The insurers sought to stay the proceedings on the grounds that the policy contained an arbitration condition clause and that it was a condition precedent to liability that the claim be referred to arbitration. The court refused to grant a stay with Pim J. saying: "where one party says that the contract is gone and the premium forfeited, he cannot insist on going to arbitration under a contract which he says does not exist."[82] In another Irish case, *Furey* v *Eagle Star and British Dominions Insurance Ltd.*[83] the insurer repudiated the policy on the grounds that non-disclosure had rendered it null and void and sought to stay the action by the insured on the ground that

---

[78] [1910] 2 IR 84.

[79] [1956] IR 320.

[80] Section 41 Arbitration Act, 1954.

[81] [1916] 50 ILTR 114.

[82] ibid. at 116.

[83] [1922] 56 ILTR 23.

the policy contained an arbitration clause. The court again refused to grant a stay with Pim J. repeating what he said in *Ballasty*. Both these cases were followed in *Coen* v *The Employers' Liability Assurance Corp. Ltd.*[84] where the insurer denied the existence of the motor policy under which the plaintiff sought to claim and at the same time claimed to rely on a policy condition denying the plaintiff indemnity if his claim was not referred to arbitration within twelve months of the insurer repudiating liability.

In those Irish cases the courts were following the judgment of the House of Lords in *Jureidini* v *National British and Irish Millers Insurance Company Ltd.*[85] where Viscount Haldane L. C. said:

> when there is a repudiation which goes to the substance of the whole contract I do not see how the person setting up that repudiation can be entitled to insist on a subordinate term of the contract still being enforced.

In the Supreme Court, in *Superwood Holdings plc* v *Sun Alliance and London Insurance plc.*[86] Blayney J. referred to all of the above and applied the same reasoning to deny the defendants the right to rely on breach of a condition in the policy, requiring the insured to furnish books of account and other business records for the purpose of investigating or verifying the claim, when their repudiation of the policy on grounds of fraud had not been upheld.

5.6 FRAUD CONDITION

5.6.1 BREACH OF CONDITION
Most non-life policies contain a clause on the lines of the following:

---

[84] [1962] IR 314.

[85] [1915] AC 499.

[86] Unreported Supreme Court 27 June 1995. Denham J. delivering the main judgment of the court said:
> I am satisfied that the respondents having elected to repudiate the contract and thus refused to the Appellants the benefit of the contract, and further the fact that the ground of the repudiation was fraud and that this claim in this way denied the Appellants the right to arbitration on the issue, it would be, and was, entirely unfair to the Appellants to enable the Respondents at the same time to rely on the agreement. (p. 57).

> If the claim be in any respect fraudulent or if any fraudulent means or devices be used by the insured or anyone acting on behalf of the insured to obtain any benefit under this policy or if any damage be occasioned by the wilful act or with the connivance of the insured all benefit under this policy shall be forfeited.[87]

Insurers in Ireland, unlike insurers in England, have been slow to plead fraud to defeat claims, preferring instead to rely on technical grounds, such as non-disclosure, misrepresentation, breach of warranties or "basis of contract" clauses. The recent decisions of the Supreme Court on such issues[88] have made it more difficult for insurers to rely on a "technical breach" to defeat a claim they suspect of being fraudulent and they are now forced into pleading fraud where they feel the claim is fraudulent or so excessively exaggerated as to amount to fraud. In those cases where the insurer has pleaded fraud[89] the defence has more often than not been successful when the case has gone to hearing, but such cases represent only a small proportion of all cases contested, the majority of which would have been either withdrawn, compromised or settled. The main reason why there are so few reported cases of defences based on fraud within an increasing

---

[87] The problem of fraudulent claims is not unique to Ireland. In England it is estimated that fraud costs the insurance industry £585 million a year. The Report of the Joint Working Group of the Federation of Irish Insurers and the Department of Enterprise and Employment under the chairmanship of Prof. Dermot McAleese, published in March 1996 entitled "Growth and Development of the Irish Insurance Industry" concluded at p. 9 that "reducing the number and incidence of claims — and in particular spurious and fraudulent claims — is of critical importance to the future of the Insurance Industry in Ireland". At p. 51. para 3.2.4.4 it suggests:

> The elimination of fraudulent claims would be greatly assisted by disbarring claimants from pursuing some or all of their claim, where it is clearly shown to be fraudulent or exaggerated. It would also be desirable to create a new offence under general fraud legislation for the falsification of documents or attempts to obtain money through falsified or exaggerated insurance claims.

[88] *Aro Road & Land Vehicles Ltd.* v *Insurance Corporation of Ireland Ltd.* [1986] IR 403; *Keating* v *New Ireland Assurance Co. Plc.* [1990] ILRM 110; *Kelleher* v *Irish Life Assurance Co. Ltd.* [1993] ILRM 643.

[89] *Carrigan* v *Norwich Union*, Unreported High Court, 11 December 1987; *Fagan* v *General Accident*, Unreported High Court, 19 February 1993; *Superwood Holdings plc & Others* v *Sun Alliance & Others*, Unreported Supreme Court, 27 June 1995.

volume of insurance litigation is undoubtedly the heavy burden of proof required in such cases.

5.6.2 ONUS OF PROOF

Allegations of fraud can only come into play once a loss within the terms of the policy has been established and the burden of proving that loss rests with the insured. If the insurer believes the insured has been guilty of fraud in relation to the loss then the burden of proving that fraud rests with the insurer.[90] In England, the onus of proof on insurers alleging fraud against an insured, whilst not that of the criminal law standard of "beyond all reasonable doubt", is greater than the civil law standard of the "balance of probabilities". Lord Denning suggested:

> The more serious the allegation, the higher the degree of probability that is required, but it need not in a civil case reach the very high standard required of the criminal law.[91]

The Irish Supreme Court has been

> unable to discern, in principle or in practice, any rational or cogent reason why fraud in civil cases should require a higher

---

[90] The importance of separating these two distinct concepts was demonstrated in an Ontario Court of Appeal decision in *Shakur v Pilot Insurance Co.* 73 DLR (4th) 337 [1991]. The insured claimed in respect of a loss of jewellery and insurers pleaded that no robbery had in fact taken place. The trial judge held that, as fraud had been alleged, the burden of proving that there had been no robbery fell on the insurer. The Court of Appeal held that the trial judge had applied the wrong test. It further held that where a claim is made, it is the insured's duty to demonstrate on the balance of probabilities that a loss had taken place. If the insurer asserts that there has been no robbery, then while it is true that there is an allegation of fraud, that allegation does not have the effect of casting the burden of fraud on to the insurers and requiring them to demonstrate beyond reasonable doubt that there had been no robbery.

[91] *Hornal v Neuberger Products Ltd.* [1957] 1 QB 247 at 263:
> So, also in civil cases, the case may be proved by a preponderance of probability, but there may be degrees of probability within that standard; the degree depends on the subject matter. A civil court, when considering a charge of fraud, will naturally require for itself a higher degree of probability than that which it would require when asking if negligence is established. It does not adopt so high a degree as a criminal court, even when it is considering a charge of a criminal nature; but still it does require a degree of probability which is commensurate with the occasion.

degree of proof than is required for the proof of other issues in civil claims.[92]

This statement of the law was accepted as being correct and applied by Lynch J. in *Carrigan* v *Norwich Union*[93] and accepted also by Murphy J. in *Fagan* v *General Accident*.[94] O'Hanlon J. in the course of his judgment dealing specifically with the issue of fraud in *Superwood*[95] held that his findings of fact "lead on inexorably to a finding of fraud". His findings were comprehensively rejected by the Supreme Court on appeal with Denham J. holding: "The onus of proof is on the party who alleges fraud. There is a presumption that an insured making a claim is acting honestly." Having quoted Finlay C. J. in *Banco Ambrosiano*, she went on to say:

> Thus, the onus is on the respondents to prove the fraud on the balance of probabilities. However, here, as in the *Ambrosiano* case, the proof is largely a matter of inference and so it must not be drawn lightly or without due regard to all the circumstances including the consequences of a finding of fraud.

5.6.3 STANDARD OF PROOF
In practice the standard of proof applied in each particular case is determined by the facts of the case and the inferences to be drawn from those facts. As Henchy J. said in *Banco Ambrosiana* v *Ansbacher*:

> Proof of fraud is not so much a matter of establishing primary facts as of raising an inference from the facts admitted or proved. . . . if a court is satisfied on balancing the possible inferences open on the facts, that fraud is the rational and co-

---

[92] per Henchy J. in a judgment supported by the other members of the Supreme Court in *Banco Ambrosiano SPA* v *Ansbacher & Co. Ltd.* [1987] ILRM 669. The case was not insurance related but is regarded as the main authority in Ireland on fraud in general.

[93] *Carrigan & others* v *Norwich Union & Others* [1987] IR 618:
> I now come to the main defence to this action, namely that the whole claim is fraudulent. . . . the onus of proof on this issue rests with the defendants. The standard of proof is the balance of probabilities.

[94] *Fagan* v *General Accident Fire & Life Assurance Corp. plc,* unreported, High Court, February 1993, under appeal to the Supreme Court.

[95] *Superwood Holdings plc & others* v *Sun Alliance and London & others* (no. 2) unreported, High Court, 12 November 1991.

gent conclusion to be drawn it should so find; . . . and that conclusion is not to be shirked because it is not a conclusion of absolute certainty.[96]

However, Denham J., in a lengthy judgment in *Superwood*, seems to demand a higher standard of proof, including proof of fraudulent intent:

The High Court inferred fraud from circumstantial evidence. The nature of fraud is such that it is very difficult to prove dishonest intent directly; proof by way of circumstantial evidence is not uncommon. However, here this court is asked to make a double inference. First, to find that it was reasonable to infer a fraudulent intent from the circumstantial evidence; and secondly, such intent not being expressly found, then to infer that the necessary intent was found in the judgment of the High Court. This double inference is contrary to the fundamental rule of particularity necessary in fraud cases.[97]

5.6.4 DEFINITION OF FRAUD

Early English cases stated that, to be fraudulent, a claim must be "wilfully false in any substantial respect"[98] or known to be "false and unjust".[99] In *Derry v Peek*,[100] fraud was defined by Lord Herschell stating:

First, in order to sustain an action of deceit, there must be proof of fraud, and nothing short of that will suffice. Secondly, fraud is proved when it is shown that a false representation has been made (1) knowingly, or (2) without belief in its truth, or (3) recklessly, careless whether it is true or false. Although I have treated the second and third as distinct cases, I think the third is but an instance of the second for one who makes a

---

[96] *Banco Ambrosiano* v *Ansbacher & Co. Ltd.* [1987] ILRM 669.

[97] *Superwood Holdings plc & others* v *Sun Alliance and London Assurance plc & others* unreported, Supreme Court, 27 June 1995 at 52. The case was at hearing in the High Court for 116 days and the judgment of the trial judge covered 423 pages. The managing director of the insured company was in the witness box for a total of 35 days.

[98] *Goulstone* v *Royal Insurance Co. Ltd.* [1858] 1 F&F 276 at 279 per Pollock C. B.; *Britton* v *Royal Insurance Co. Ltd.* [1866] 4 F&F 905 at 908 per Willes J.

[99] *Chapman* v *Pole* [1870] 22 LT 306 at 307 per Cockburn C. J.

[100] [1889] 14 App Cas 337 at 374.

statement under such circumstances can have no real belief in
the truth of what he states. To prevent a false statement being
fraudulent, there must, I think, always be an honest belief in
its truth. And this probably covers the whole ground, for one
who knowingly alleges that which is false, has obviously no
such honest belief. Thirdly, if fraud be proved, the motive of
the person guilty of it is immaterial. It matters not that there
was no intention to cheat or injure the person to whom the
statement was made.

That definition was accepted by Denham J. in *Superwood* as a correct
analysis of the law.

5.6.5 EXAGGERATED CLAIMS

The English courts have accepted that advancing a claim that was
"preposterously extravagant" was not fraud but merely the adoption
of a bargaining position[101] and in the United States some degree of
claim inflation is accepted as a tactic in negotiating settlement of a
claim.[102] In the relatively recent Irish case of *Fagan* v *General Accident*[103] the insured house had been the subject of litigation arising out
of the insured's efforts to sell it. While unoccupied, it was extensively
damaged by fire and a large quantity of goods were removed from the
house by miscreants at the time of the fire. Insurers declined the
claim on the grounds that it was so grossly exaggerated as to amount
to fraud. Murphy J. in giving judgment for the insurer said:

> . . . if the insured had claimed for figures which were excessive
> in the sense that they represented an extremely optimistic
> view of the value of the items in question, that would not, in
> my view justify the Company in repudiating liability on foot of
> the policy. . . . it seems to me to have been established on the
> evidence as a whole that the insured, in breach of both his
> general and contractual obligations to the Company, claimed a
> loss under the policy based on figures which were deliberately

---

[101] *Ewer* v *National Employers Mutual Insurance Association Ltd.* [1937] 2 All ER
193 at 203 per McKinnon J.

[102] Emerson, University of Miami Law Review 907, 952 (1992).

[103] *Fagan* v *General Accident Fire & Life Assurance Corp. plc.* Unreported High
Court, February 1993. Insurers repudiated liability on the grounds that the items
alleged to have been destroyed in a fire were not in the building at the time of the
fire and also because the claim was so grossly exaggerated as to amount to fraud.

over-stated in the original claims and persisted in on the hearing of the action.

In the Supreme Court, in *Superwood*,[104] Blayney J. in over-ruling the trial judge held that exaggeration is not conclusive evidence of fraud. He quoted with approval Goddard J. in *London Assurance* v *Clare*[105]

> Mere exaggeration was not conclusive evidence of fraud, for a man might honestly have an exaggerated idea of the value of the stock, or suggest a high figure as a bargaining price.

5.6.6 EFFECT OF FRAUD

In *Fagan*[106] the insured had a perfectly valid policy which covered a substantial part of the loss but by virtue of the court's ruling he re-covered nothing. This principle which determines that if any part of the claim is fraudulent the whole claim fails did not have the full support of the Court of Appeal in *Orakpo* v *Barclays Insurance Services & Others*.[107] Whilst all three members of the Court were unanimous in dismissing the plaintiff insured's claim, Staughton L. J. expressed dissenting views on the effect of fraud on a claim. He said:

> Of course some people put forward inflated claims for the purpose of negotiation knowing that they will be cut down by an adjuster. If one examined a sample of insurance claims on

---

[104] *Superwood Holdings plc. & others* v *Sun Alliance and London Assurance plc. & others,* unreported, Supreme Court, 27 June 1995.

[105] [1937] 57 Lloyds Rep 254.

[106] *Fagan* v *General Accident Assurance Corp. plc.* unreported, High Court, February 1993. In Australia, Section 56 of the Insurance Contracts Act, 1984 provides:

> (1) Where a claim under a contract of insurance . . . is made fraudulently, the insurer may not avoid the contract but may refuse payment of the claim; (2) In any proceedings in relation to such a claim, the court may, if only a minimal or insignificant part of the claim is made fraudulently and non-payment of the remainder of the claim would be harsh and unfair, order the insurer to pay, in relation to the claim, such amount (if any) as is just and equitable in the circumstances.

[107] [1978] AC 78. The case arose out of repudiation by insurers of claims for damage and consequential loss allegedly suffered when flooding and storm gales were alleged to have damaged the insured building. Material misrepresentation in the completion of the proposal was one of two defences raised by insurers and on this part of the case the judges were unanimous in upholding the defence. The second defence was that the claim was fraudulently exaggerated.

household contents, I doubt if one would find many which stated the loss with absolute truth. From time to time claims are patently exaggerated; for example, by claiming the replacement cost of chattels, when only the depreciated value is insured. In such cases, it may perhaps be said that there is in truth no false representation, since the falsity of what is stated is apparent. I would not condone falsehood of any kind in an insurance claim. But in any event I consider that the gross exaggeration in this case went beyond what can be condoned or overlooked. . . . I do not know of any other corner of the law where the plaintiff who has made a fraudulent claim is deprived even of that which he is legally entitled to, be it a large or small amount. . . . I can readily accept that there is a duty not to make fraudulent claims; but I have doubts about the suggested punishment for the breach of that duty.

Lord Justice Hoffman and Sir Roger Parker both disagreed, with Hoffman L. J. quoting from Ivamy's *General Principles of Insurance Law*:

Since it is the duty of the assured to observe the utmost good faith in his dealings with the insurers throughout, the claim which he puts forward must be honestly made and if it is fraudulent he will forfeit all benefit under the policy whether there is a condition to that effect or not.

5.6.7 Duty of Disclosure

The continuing nature of the duty of good faith and in particular its application to claims was clearly accepted by Murphy J. in *Fagan* when he said, "the duty to exercise the utmost good faith continues throughout the relationship up to and including the making of a claim on foot of the policy"[108]. The duty of good faith undoubtedly requires the insured to make "full disclosure of the circumstances of the loss"[109] but the degree of disclosure required during the negotiation of

---

[108] Unreported High Court, February 1993.

[109] *Shepherd* v *Chowter* [1808] 1 Camp. 274 at 275 per Lord Ellenborough. In *Britton* v *Royal Insurance Co.* [1866], 4 F&F 905 at 909 per Wills J.:

The contract of insurance is one of perfect good faith on both sides, and it is most important that such good faith should be maintained. It is the common practice to insert in fire policies conditions that they shall be void in the event of a fraudulent claim. . . . But a condition is only in accordance with legal principle and sound policy. . . . if there is a wilful falsehood or fraud in the claim, the insured forfeits all claim whatever upon the policy.

the claim varies according to the relationship of the parties at the time. The level of disclosure appropriate to the making of a claim under the policy is different from that at the time when the contract is made. An innocent misrepresentation or non-disclosure in the claim does not defeat the claim; there must be fraud as described above. In the *Litsion Pride*[110] Hirst J. stated in relation to the common law in general that:

> . . . it must be right . . . to go so far as to hold that the duty in the claims sphere extends to culpable misrepresentation or non-disclosure. . . . I hold that any fraudulent statement which would influence a prudent underwriter's decision to accept, reject or compromise the claim is material.

Where the claim becomes the subject of negotiation between the parties, it is "doubtful whether in such circumstances the duty amounts to one of full disclosure of all material facts".[111] The point was taken further in the *Star Sea*[112] with Tuckey J. explaining:

> When the claim is presented there is obviously a duty, at least not to act fraudulently, and it may be that the duty is rather wider than this, so as at least to require the insured to be honest and open by disclosing the facts relevant to his claim which are unknown to the underwriters. . . . Once the claim has been declined, however, it must be assumed that the underwriters have good reasons for doing so and the parties then become adversaries. There is no reason why adversaries should be under a duty to provide ammunition to one another.

There is therefore no obligation on the insured to volunteer information which will assist the insurer in defeating a claim which is the subject of litigation. The insurer has a duty of disclosure towards the insured but the rules governing discovery and privilege as confirmed in *Carrigan* v *Norwich Union*[113] make it possible for an insurer to deny the insured access to investigative reports prior to the trial of

---

[110] *Black King Shipping Corp.* v *Massie* [1985] 1 Lloyds Rep 437.

[111] *Diggens* v *Sun Alliance & London Assurance plc.* Unreported, Court of Appeal, 29 July 1994, per Evans J.

[112] *Manifest Shipping Co. Ltd.* v *Uni-Polaris Insurance Co.* [1995] 1 Lloyds Rep 651.

[113] *Carrigan* v *Norwich Union* (No. 1) [1987] IR 618.

the action. [114]Because of the continuing duty on the insured to observe the utmost good faith in his dealings with the insurers any claim submitted under the policy must be honestly made. If it is fraudulent the insured "in accordance with legal principles and sound policy" forfeits all benefit under the policy even in the absence of a condition to that effect.[115] It is immaterial whether the whole claim is fraudulent or whether only part of the claim is so.[116] The rule that the presence of fraud in a claim defeats the claim and terminates the contract was accepted by Denham J. in *Superwood* in the Supreme Court when she confirmed that if fraud was proved the policy was void *ab initio*.[117] However, there are authorities in other jurisdictions[118] which suggest that earlier honest claims are not affected by the avoidance of the policy and that duties such as the duty to arbitrate earlier honest claims continue. It is clear from the judgments of both Blayney J. and Denham J. in the Supreme Court[119] that an insurer, having repudiated the policy on the grounds of alleged fraud, cannot then rely on the arbitration condition, or any other condition in the policy, in respect of the claim alleged to be fraudulent.

5.7 CLAIMS CO-OPERATION AND PROCEDURE

5.7.1 REQUIREMENTS

Insurance policies invariably contain a condition requiring the insured to give notice of loss and specifying the manner and the time

---

[114] ibid., where O'Hanlon J. held that:
> . . . privilege from disclosure may be claimed . . . in respect of a document which has come into existence prior to the commencement of proceedings, where it can be shown that the dominant purpose for the document coming into existence in the first place was the purpose of preparing for litigation then apprehended or threatened.

[115] n. 103 *supra*.

[116] ibid.

[117] Unreported, Supreme Court, 25 June 1995, at p. 51 of judgment, Denham J. said: "The effect of repudiation of the contract by the Respondents on the grounds of fraud was to render it void. The contract ceased to exist."

[118] *Lehmbecker's Earthmoving & Excavators (pty) Ltd.* v *Incorporated General Insurance Ltd.* [1983] 3 SA 513; *Gore Mutual Insurance Co.* v *Bifford* [1987] 45 DLR (4th) 763; *The Litsion Pride* [1985] 1 Lloyds Rep 437 at 515.

[119] n. 117 *supra*.

period within which the notice must be given.[120] Compliance with the requirements is generally a condition precedent to liability.[121] The usual claims condition requires the insured (a) to give notice of the loss to the company, (b) to do so immediately or within a stated period, (c) to notify the police where relevant, (d) to deliver a claim in writing within a stated period, (e) to provide such proof of loss as is required, (f) to take all reasonable steps to minimise the loss, and (g) to co-operate fully with the insurer in the investigation of the loss and make available all documentation, records and information required by the insurer.

5.7.2 NOTICE

Unless the condition stipulates otherwise the notice need not be in writing.[122] The notice must be given within the specified period or if no period is specified, within a reasonable time.[123] It has been held that time does not begin to run until it is clear that the insurers may be involved.[124] In *Layer Ltd* v *Lowe and Others*,[125] the policy written by the defendant Lloyds underwriters contained a requirement that the insured give "immediate notice in writing, with full particulars of a happening of any occurrence likely to give rise to a claim". A National Trust property in England sustained serious damage by fire in 1989 and, in order to facilitate the extensive repairs necessary, a temporary roof was erected which was subsequently blown off. The plaintiffs had supplied materials to the scaffolding contractors, including

---

[120] Insurers cannot impose further duties on the insured by inserting additional terms in the claim form. *Beeck* v *Yorkshire Insurance Co.* [1909] 11 WLR.

[121] In so far as motor insurance policies are concerned such conditions are of no effect in relation to third party claims compulsorily insurable under the Road Traffic Acts.

[122] *Prairie City Oil Co.* v *Standard Mutual Fire Insurance Co.* [1910] 19 Man R 720.

[123] *O'Flynn* v *Equitable Fire Insurance Co.* [1866] 1 Roscoe's Rep (cape) Sup. Ct. 372 where notice given two months after the fire was held not to have been given within a reasonable period.

> There is of course no such thing as a reasonable time in the abstract. . . . the only sound principle is that the "reasonable time" should depend on the circumstances which actually exist.

per Lord Herschell L. C. at 29 in *Hick* v *Raymond* [1893] AC 22.

[124] *Smellie* v *British General Insurance Co.* [1918] WC & Ins. Rep 233

[125] [1997] Unreported Court of Appeal, January 1997.

securing wedges. The National Trust brought an action against the contractor, two years later, in which the plaintiff was ultimately joined. The action was compromised, but only after significant legal costs had been incurred for which the plaintiff was liable under the terms of the compromise agreement, and for which they claimed indemnity under their policy with the defendant. The underwriters claimed breach of the claims notification clause in repudiating liability. The Court of Appeal held that as the clause required "immediate notice" it was relevant to consider the situation immediately after the occurrence. The plaintiffs had not designed the scaffolding or the temporary roof, but had merely supplied some materials, none of which was proven to have contributed to the failure of the roof. In a litigious age, it was possible that the National Trust or the contractor might claim against the insured but the wording of the policy used the term "likely" and not "possible". The Court held that "likely" implied at least, a fifty per cent chance that a claim would be made and that, immediately after the occurrence, a claim against the plaintiff would not have been deemed "likely".

5.7.3 COMPLIANCE WITH CONDITION

Notice may be given to the insurer's agent through whom the policy was negotiated as, in the absence of information to the contrary, the insured is entitled to assume that the insurer's agent has authority to accept notice and notice so given is binding on the insurer.[126] It has, however, been held, in an English case, that notice given to the insurance broker who negotiated the policy is not sufficient to comply with the policy condition.[127] If the policy requires that notice be given to the insurer personally or at the insurer's specified address then the requirement must be literally complied with.[128] If, in such circumstances, notice is given to the insurer's agent, the insured takes the risk of the agent failing to transmit the notice to the insurer and if that happens there is no valid notice within the terms of the policy.[129] If the notice condition has not been complied with the insurer may

---

[126] *Gale* v *Lewis* [1846] 9 QB 730.

[127] *Roche* v *Roberts* [1921] 9 Lloyds Rep 59.

[128] *Re: Williams and Lancashire & Yorkshire Accident Insurance Co.'s Arbitration* [1903] 19 TLR 82.

[129] ibid. and *Holwell Securities Ltd.* v *Hughes* [1974] 1 All ER 161.

repudiate liability under the policy. To sustain such a repudiation it is not necessary for insurers to prove that their interests have been prejudiced. In a case stated to the High Court, in an arbitration between *Gaelcrann Teoranta and Michael Payne and Others*,[130] it was held that unless non-compliance with the claims notification clause was trivial or had been waived expressly or implicitly by underwriters they were not obliged to show that they were prejudiced by non-compliance. An employee of the insured had been injured on two occasions in the course of his employment but underwriters were not advised until the issue of proceedings some two years later. In England, in *Pioneer Concrete*[131] Bingham J. held that proof of prejudice was not required and Moccata J. in *The Vainqueur Jose*[132] had said that if proof of prejudice was necessary "relatively little prejudice had to be shown". A notice of claim

> does not mean a precisely formulated claim with full details, but it must be such a notice as will enable the party to whom it is given to take steps to meet the claim by preparing and obtaining appropriate evidence for that purpose.[133]

5.7.4 PERIOD FOR SUBMISSION OF NOTICE

The wording of the condition, usually, requires the insured to submit particulars of the claim, in writing, within a specified period. Some policies require particulars to be submitted "immediately" or within "a reasonable time" after the happening of the loss. Where the submission of particulars within a specified time is a condition precedent, failure to submit particulars within the time specified relieves the insurer of liability[134] and a subsequent submission of the particulars does not entitle the insured to indemnity.[135] Where the insurer seeks to avoid liability under a policy, on grounds of failure to comply with a procedural condition, the onus of proving breach of the condition

---

[130] [1985] ILRM 109

[131] *Pioneer Concrete (UK) Ltd.* v *National Employers Mutual Insurance Association Ltd.* [1985] 2 All ER 395.

[132] [1979] 1 Lloyds Rep 557 at 566.

[133] *Rendal* v *Arcos Ltd.* [1937] 58 Lloyds Rep. 287 at 292, per Lord Wright.

[134] *Whyte* v *Western Assurance Co.* [1875] 22 LCJ 215 pc.

[135] n. 126 and n. 127 *supra*.

lies with the insurer. If a breach of condition is proved it is then a matter of determining whether compliance with the condition is a condition precedent to liability, or whether it is a condition, breach of which merely suspends liability for payment of the loss, until such time as the condition has been complied with. Determination of that issue is a matter of construction in accordance with the normal rules of construction. [136]

5.7.5 CO-OPERATION

In addition to providing notice and particulars of the loss the insured is required to protect his own and the insurer's position by doing or permitting to be done "all things which may be reasonably practicable" to minimise the loss.[137] Liability insurance policies, in addition to requiring the insured to co-operate in the investigation and defence of a third party claim, also prohibit the insured from making any admission of liability or offer to settle without the consent of the insurer.[138] The insured is released from his obligation where the insurer has wrongfully repudiated the policy. In *General Omnibus Co. Ltd.* v *London General Insurance Co. Ltd.*[139] it was stated to be settled law that it is no bar to indemnity that liability has been arrived at by agreement or compromise which was not improvident, unreasonable or *mala fide*. The right of the insurer to withhold consent to settlement by the insured

> must be exercised in good faith having regard to the interests
> of the insured as well as its own interests . . . and the insurer

---

[136] *Stoneham* v *Ocean, Railway & General Accident Insurance Co.* [1887] 19 QBD 237 per Mathew J.

[137] See wording quoted later in *Superwood*.

[138] A typical wording reads:
The insured shall not pay or offer or agree to pay any money or make any admission of liability without the previous consent of the insurer. The insurer shall be entitled in the name of and on behalf of the insured to take over and during such period as it thinks proper have absolute conduct and control of all negotiations and proceedings which may arise in respect of any claim and the settlement thereof and the insured shall give the company all necessary assistance for the purpose.

[139] [1936] IR 596.

must not have regard to considerations extraneous to the policy of indemnity.[140]

5.7.6 BREACH OF CONDITION

Breach of the duty of co-operation defeats the claim but the difficulty in proving such a breach in Ireland is graphically illustrated by the *Superwood* case.[141] The action arose out of a fire at the insured's premises following which the insured sought to recover under a policy providing indemnity for consequential loss. The insurers repudiated the policy on the grounds of fraud. Loss adjusters for the insurers had estimated the insured's loss at £131,465 whereas the insured had claimed an amount of approximately £2 million. In the High Court, O'Hanlon J., had determined the case, in favour of insurers, largely on breach of the claims co-operation condition in the policy[142] and, in response to a specific request addressed the issue of fraud in a separate judgment.[143] The trial judge had made findings of fact that

> there was a deliberate policy of non-co-operation, [that] all access to the books and records of Superwood were refused, [that] Superwood did their utmost to prevent the loss adjusters from uncovering the weaknesses inherent in the Group management, organisation and accounting systems, [and that] not merely obstruction, but actual deception, was practised on those who were inquiring into the claim on behalf of insurers.

On appeal to the Supreme Court, O'Hanlon's decision was comprehensively over-ruled by Denham J. in a lengthy judgment with which the other members of the Court agreed. Denham J. held that:

> the essence of the case is the issue of fraud and the repudiation of the contract of insurance by the respondents on the grounds of fraud. All else flowed from that. . . . while the trial judge wrote his judgment largely on Condition 4, that condition is of

---

[140] *Distillers Bio-Chemicals (Australia) Pty. Ltd.* v *Ajax Insurance Co. Ltd.* [1973] 130 CLR 1 at 26–27, per Stephen J.

[141] (No. 1) Unreported High Court, 13–15 August 1991; (No. 2) Unreported High Court, 12 November 1991; Unreported Supreme Court, 27 June 1995.

[142] Unreported High Court, August 1991.

[143] Unreported, High Court, November 1991.

secondary importance and the issue of fraud is the essential matter for determination in the case.[144]

She found that the trial judge had erred in deciding first the issue of breach of the claims co-operation condition and that he had further erred in making a generalised conclusion that his findings on that condition "lead on inexorably to a finding of fraud". Having expressed herself satisfied that a breach of the claims co-operation condition was not pleaded by the insurers and that no application had been made to amend the pleadings she went on to consider and make a determination on the condition "to prevent further possibly lengthy litigation".[145] She held that the insurers, having elected to repudiate the contract, denied the insured the right to arbitrate the dispute and that it would be, and was, entirely unfair to the insured to allow the insurers at the same time to rely on the claims co-operation condition of the contract.

5.7.7 CONDITION WORDING

The wording of the relevant condition was as follows:

> On the happening of any damage in consequence of which a claim is or may be made under this policy the insured shall forthwith give notice thereof in writing to the first named insurers and shall with due diligence do and concur in doing and permit to be done all things which may be reasonably practicable to minimise or check any interruption of or interference with the business or to avoid or diminish the loss and in the event of a claim being made under this policy shall not later than thirty days after the expiry of the indemnity period or within such further time as the insurers may in writing allow, at his own expense deliver to the insurers in writing a statement setting forth particulars of his claim together with details of other insurances covering the damage or any part of it or consequential loss of any kind resulting therefrom. The Insured shall at his own expense also produce and furnish to the Insurers such books of account and other business books, vouchers, invoices, balance sheets and other documents, proofs, information, explanation and other evidence as may reasonably be required by the Insurers for the purpose of investigating or verifying the claim together with (if demanded)

---

[144] at p. 11, Unreported Supreme Court, 27 June 1995.

[145] ibid. at p. 55.

a statutory declaration of the truth of the claim and of any matters connected therewith.

5.7.8 APPLICATION OF THE CONDITION

Insurers contended that the terms of the condition applied, in accordance with accepted practice, either from the time of the happening of the fire or from the time a claim was notified under the policy. The insured, on the other hand, contended that the condition was not applicable until a formal written statement of claim was submitted. Denham J., relying heavily on the last sentence of the condition wording quoted above, and on its location at the end of the condition, held that the condition applied to the submission of the statement of claim and not before. She held that the insurer is "entitled to make reasonable requests for documents supporting the claim so as to investigate or verify the claim after the statement of claim".[146] She held that the trial judge erred, in his interpretation of the condition, and that this had an effect on his analysis of the facts. He had applied the condition to the events following the fire rather "than considering the statement of claim". It would appear from the Supreme Court decision that the condition now must be regarded as applying to the submission of the statement of claim and the negotiations which take place after that and that it is not applicable to the investigation of the loss or the circumstances pertaining prior to the submission of the statement of claim. The judgment fails to distinguish between the notification of a claim under the policy and the submission of a statement of particulars in support of the claim. The decision would seem to deny the insurer the right to fully investigate the effect of the damage on the business in advance of a statement of claim being filed. This cannot be right.

5.7.9 INSURER'S OBLIGATIONS

The contract of insurance does not require the insurer to give notice to the insured of the claimed breach of the claims co-operation condition but the Supreme Court held that

> it is a fundamental tenet of constitutional law and fair procedures that if a person's position is to be detrimentally affected he should be placed on notice. Consequently, the appellants

---

[146] ibid. at p. 61.

would succeed on this ground alone in the absence of such notice.[147]

It would seem, therefore, that if insurers believe the insured has not
fully complied with the condition they are obliged to give notice and,
presumably, the opportunity to the insured to remedy the situation
before they repudiate liability. The issue of the continuing duty of
utmost good faith was not raised in the trial of the action. Given the
findings of fact by the High Court, it is unlikely the Supreme Court
could have overturned the decision, if it had been reached on the basis of a breach of the duty of utmost good faith, rather than on fraud
and a breach of the claims co-operation condition.

5.7.10 ENGLISH LAW

The avoidance of liability for fraudulent claims was discussed, recently in England, in *Transthene Packaging Co. Ltd.* v *Royal Insurance (UK) Ltd.*[148] The Policy at issue contained the standard fraud
condition providing that in the event that a claim was in any respect
fraudulent, the insured would forfeit all benefit under the policy.
Following a fire at the insured premises, the insured instructed loss
assessors to prepare a claim for submission to insurers. An informal
verbal claim was made by the insured's managing director. Insurers
appointed loss adjusters to investigate and report on the loss and
three weeks after the fire wrote to the insured seeking to avoid the
policy on a number of grounds, including non-disclosure, breach of
warranty, and breach of condition. A month after receipt of the letter,
the insured issued proceedings against insurers. The insurers entered
a defence against the proceedings, pleading arson by the managing
director, fraud in an understatement of salvage, gross exaggeration of
the claimed cost of reinstatement and a claim for loss of profits which
it was known could not have been earned, and finally breach of warranty. Subsequently the defence was amended to include a plea that
a fraudulent claim deprived the insured of all benefit under the policy
irrespective of any express fraud condition in the policy. The Court
held that any attempt at repudiation of the contract by the insurers
could only be effective if and when it was accepted by the insured. An

---

[147] ibid. at p. 82.

[148] [1996] LRLR 32.

insurer's claim to repudiation which could not be justified in law left the contract intact but amounted to a repudiation of the contract by the insurer. A repudiation by insurers gives the insured the right to accept the repudiation and bring the contract to an end, or to reject the repudiation and demand that insurers fulfil their obligations. On the evidence before the Court the judge could not determine that the insured had accepted the insurers repudiation of the contract and insurers were therefore entitled to rely on the terms of the contract. The judge was of the view that if the insured had accepted the repudiation, the insurers could not then rely on the policy conditions in respect of any subsequent breach of condition by the insured. The insurers, relying on the accepted principle of insurance contract law, that the insurer is in breach of contract and liable for damages once the peril insured against has occurred, advanced the argument that in those circumstances the insured's right of action arose on the happening of the insured peril and insurers could not then issue a repudiation of the contract, capable of acceptance by the insured. This argument was rejected and contrary to previous authorities, the judge ruled that on the basis of the actual contract between the parties the insurers had not accepted liability for the loss as of the date of the occurrence of the insured peril, were not in breach of contract on that date and that the letter issued three weeks after the occurrence did constitute a repudiation of the contract. The case is in many respects similar to *Superwood* but it is noticeable that the Irish Courts did not at any stage consider the possible effects of non-acceptance by the insured of the repudiation of the contract. The Supreme Court was adamant that once insurers repudiated the contract they could no longer rely on a subsequent breach of conditions by the insured or seek to enforce the arbitration clause.

5.8 CANCELLATION

5.8.1 INSURER'S RIGHT TO CANCEL
The insurer's right to cancel the insurance policy where there is an allegation of fraud, misrepresentation or non-disclosure arise from the contract being void *ab initio*.[149] The contract never attaches in

---

[149] See *Superwood* above.

such circumstances and the policy as evidence of the insurance contract is useless. Breach of condition may also affect the continuation of the policy. If the condition breached is a condition precedent of the policy, the effect is to entitle insurers to avoid the policy *ab initio* and no claim will be entertained under the policy even though the loss may have arisen prior to the insurer's decision to avoid the policy. Where the condition broken is a condition precedent to liability under the policy, the effect of the breach is to prevent the insured from enforcing a claim in respect of which there has been a breach of condition. The policy remains in force and the insured is entitled to recover in respect of subsequent losses provided there has been no further breach of condition in relation to them. Where the condition breached is a condition subsequent to the policy the effect of the breach is to entitle the insurers to terminate and avoid the policy from the date of the breach. The policy may cease to have effect where insurers fulfil their obligations under the policy on the happening of the event insured against.[150] The parties to the contract may at any time agree to cancellation either for the purpose of terminating the contract between them or for the purpose of replacing the policy with a policy on different terms. It is, however, usual for the rights of the parties in relation to cancellation to be stipulated in the policy. In most policies the right to cancel is reserved to the insurer[151] but some policies[152] specifically provide for cancellation by either party. The standard cancellation clause gives the insurer the right to cancel by sending notice by registered post to the insured's last known address. The period of notice given differs according to the practice of the insurers and the type of policy.[153]

5.8.2 REASONS FOR CANCELLATION

The courts will not enquire into the motives or the reasons of the insurers exercising their cancellation rights. In England, the Privy

---

[150] For example, on payment of the full sum insured in the event of loss or damage or the total loss of the item insured.

[151] Insurers will generally cancel at the request of the insured but may charge "short period" rates.

[152] Particularly home and private motor policies.

[153] The Road Traffic Acts require a minimum of seven days notice but it can be as much as ninety days in specially negotiated commercial contracts.

Council, in *Sun Fire* v *Hart*[154] in rejecting an argument that insurers could exercise their contractual rights to cancel the policy only on reasonable grounds, held that

> the sufficiency of the reasons moving them to desire the termination of the risk which they had undertaken is a matter of which the insurers are constituted the sole judges.

The issue was considered in Ireland, in the High Court, in *Carna Foods Ltd. & Edmund Mallon* v *Eagle Star Insurance Co. Ltd.*[155] Both plaintiffs held various policies with the defendant insurer. Shortly after a fire at the first plaintiff's premises the insurer notified both plaintiffs that it would not be inviting renewal of policies due for renewal later in the year and that in accordance with its contractual entitlement it was cancelling some other policies. The plaintiffs did not challenge the insurer's right to cancel the policies or their right to refuse to renew. They did, however, seek a declaration that the insurers were obliged to give reasons for their actions. The plaintiffs argued that the cancellation provision was an unfair and unjust contractual term and that the Court should imply a term into the contract requiring the insurer to give reasons. The Court did not accept these arguments and held that there were no principles of natural or constitutional justice which would extend the requirement to give reasons to the private contractual sphere.

> To decide otherwise would be a serious interference in the contractual position of parties in a commercial contract and with very wide-ranging consequences. [156]

---

[154] *Sun Fire Office* v *Hart* [1889] 14 App. Cas 98, 104–105 per Lord Watson. Nine fires destroyed over half the property insured. Prior to the ninth fire the insured received an anonymous letter threatening further fires which he disclosed to insurers. They promptly terminated cover and their decision was upheld by the Privy Council.

[155] Unreported High Court, 9 June 1995.

[156] ibid. The case is under appeal to the Supreme Court.

CHAPTER SIX

POLICY INTERPRETATION

"For when they insure it is sweet to them to take the monies but
when disaster comes it is otherwise and each man draws back
his rump and strives not to pay."[1]

6.1 INTRODUCTION

The insurance industry has developed for itself an unfortunate reputation for relying on small print in insurance policies[2] and for interpreting wordings in a way which defeats claims believed by policyholders to be legitimate. The manner in which insurance policies are
drafted has come in for severe judicial criticism. Chief Justice Kennedy in the Supreme Court referred to a policy in dispute as "an ill
drawn document, stupid and unintelligible in many parts, due perhaps to amendments made from time to time by unskilled drafts-
men".[3] and fifty years later Finlay C. J. felt obliged to comment that

> in so far as this combined document consists of what might be
> described as the ordinary policy of insurance it is wholly, com-

---

[1] Datini, a Tuscan cloth merchant, writing to his wife in the 1380s about his concern for a galley containing goods valued at 3,000 florins sailing from Venice to
Catalonia which, if it failed to arrive safely, exposed him to the loss of 500 florins.

[2] In so far as the courts are concerned the size of the print is immaterial.

[3] *General Omnibus Co. Ltd.* v *London General Insurance Co. Ltd.* [1936] IR 596.

pletely and absolutely inapplicable to the type of risk with
which either the insured or the insurer is concerned.[4]

In the United States some distinction is made between the interpretation of contracts and the construction of contracts[5] but in most
common law countries, and in Ireland in particular, no such distinction is made. Some policies include an interpretation clause to the
effect that:

> The Policy and Schedule shall be read together as one contract
> and any word or expression to which a specific meaning has
> been attached in any part of this Policy or of the Schedule shall
> bear such specific meaning wherever it may appear.

Such a clause is not really necessary as rules have been developed
which are of general application to commercial contracts and are used
by the courts to guide them in their interpretation or construction of
insurance policies.[6]

---

[4] *Brady* v *Irish National Insurance Co. Ltd.* [1986] ILRM 669; In *Re: Sweeney and
Kennedy's Arbitration* [1950] IR 85, Kingsmill Moore J. quoted, with approval, the
opinion of Lord Greene M. R. in *Woolfall & Rimmer Ltd.* v *Moyle* [1942] 1 KB 66
at 73 where he said
> There is no justification for underwriters, who are carrying on a widespread
> business and making use of printed forms, either failing to make up their
> minds what they mean, or, if they have made up their minds what they mean
> failing to express it in suitable language. Any competent draughtsman could
> carry out the intention which [counsel] imputes to this document, and, if that
> was what was really intended, it ought to have been done.

[5] In *McDonald Industries Inc.* v *INA*, 475 NW 2d 607, 618 the court said:
> Construction of an insurance policy — the process of determining its legal ef-
> fect — is a question of law for the court. Interpretation — the process of de-
> termining the meaning of words used — is also a question of law for the court
> unless it depends on extrinsic evidence or a choice among reasonable infer-
> ences to be drawn.

In 64 Columbia Law Review 833, 833–835 (1964), Patterson said that
> the process of interpretation often consists merely of the direct application of
> symbols [contract words etc.] used to the factual situation; [whereas construc-
> tion is] a legal process by which legal consequences are made to follow from
> the terms of the contract and its more or less immediate context, and from a
> legal policy or policies that are applicable to the situation.

[6] Lord Ellenborough C. J. in *Robertson* v *French* [1803] 4 East 130 said at 135:
> The same rule of construction which applies to all other instruments applies
> equally to this instrument of a policy of insurance, viz., that it is to be con-
> strued according to its sense and meaning, as collected from the terms used in
> it, which terms are themselves to be understood in their plain, ordinary and
> popular sense, unless they have generally in respect to the subject matter, as

6.2 GENERAL RULES

The general rules of interpretation applied by the courts are as follows:

(a) The intention of the parties must prevail;

(b) The intention must be sought in the words of the policy itself, the whole policy and not only a particular part of it must be considered;

(c) Printed and written portions must be construed together as far as possible, but, in case of any contradiction, the written portion, which applies more particularly to the special circumstances of the case must prevail over the printed portion which is of general application;

(d) The ordinary rules of grammar apply but these must give way if they are contrary to the obvious intention of the parties;

(e) Words must be taken in their ordinary and popular sense, unless it is clear that they are intended to have a special meaning;

(f) The meaning of a word may be limited by its context;

(g) The contract must be fairly construed between the parties and in the case of any ambiguity, the reasonable construction is to be preferred. Parol evidence is permitted to show the real intention of the parties. The onus of proof of an ambiguity rests with the party who seeks to vary the apparent meaning;

(h) Words in the policy emanating from the insurer will, in the event of ambiguity, be construed against the insurer, according to the legal maxim, *verba chartarum preferentem fortius accipiunter*.[7] The words will be construed in the way in which a reasonable insured would understand them.

---

by known usage of trade, or the like, acquired a peculiar sense distinct from the popular sense of the same words; or unless the context evidently points out that they must . . . be understood in some other special and peculiar sense.

[7] "The words of documents are construed against the grantor."

6.3 INTENTION OF THE PARTIES

The first task of any court required to interpret a policy of insurance is to ascertain the intention of the parties in relation to the facts in dispute. That intention must be gathered from the policy wording and any other documents incorporated with the policy.[8] In *Rohan Construction Ltd.* v *Insurance Corporation of Ireland Ltd.*,[9] Griffin J., in the Supreme Court, quoted with approval Ivamy's statement that:

> It is well settled that in construing the terms of a policy the cardinal rule is that the intention of the parties must prevail, but the intention is to be looked for on the face of the policy, including any documents incorporated therewith, in the words in which the parties themselves have chosen to express their meaning. The court must not speculate as to their intention, apart from their words, but may, if necessary, interpret the words by reference to the surrounding circumstances. The whole of the policy must be looked at, and not merely a particular clause.[10]

Later, in the same judgment, he quoted the statement of Lord Wilberforce that:

> When one speaks of the intention of the parties to the contract, one is speaking objectively — the parties cannot themselves give direct evidence of what their intention was — and what must be ascertained is what is to be taken as the intention which reasonable people would have had if placed in the situation of the parties. . . . What the court must do must be to

---

[8] In *Hutton v Watling* [1948] Ch. 398 at 403, per Greene M. R.:
   the true construction of a document means no more than that the court puts on it the true meaning, and the true meaning is the meaning which the party to whom the document was handed or who is relying on it would put on it as an ordinarily intelligent person construing the words in the proper way in the light of the relevant circumstances.

Where the policy itself is not sufficient to reveal the intention of the parties, reference may be made to such other documents as the proposal form. *South Staffordshire Tramways Co.* v *Accident Insurance Association* [1891] 1 QB 402.

[9] [1988] ILRM 373.

[10] *Ivamy on Insurance Law*, 5th Edition (1986) p. 333–334.

place itself in thought in the same factual matrix as that in which the parties were.[11]

The plaintiffs had contracted for the erection of a bulk molasses storage tank at Limerick docks but large quantities of water percolated into the tank rendering it useless. The plaintiffs were sued for very substantial damages for which they sought indemnity from the defendant under a professional indemnity policy or alternatively under a public liability policy also written by the defendants. The High Court held that the defendants were not liable to provide an indemnity under either of the policies but the Supreme Court decided that an indemnity should be provided under the professional indemnity policy.

6.4 LIBERAL INTERPRETATION

The wording of the policy must, if possible, be construed liberally, to give effect to the intention of the parties.[12] The extent to which an Irish court, in construing a policy of insurance, can take account of the reasonable or legitimate expectations of the insured has yet to be determined.

A large number of the complaints to the Irish Insurance Ombudsman arise out of the failure of insurance policies to meet the expectations of the policyholder. The Ombudsman's terms of reference, however, confine her to adjudicating disputes arising out of insurance policies purchased by individual consumers and she has no function in relation to insurance contracts negotiated commercially. In the United States the doctrine of legitimate or reasonable expectations

---

[11] *Rearden Smith Line Ltd.* v *Yngvar Hansen-Tangen* [1976] 3 All ER 570 at 574/575; Griffin J. went on to quote Lord Denning in *Staffordshire Area Health Authority* v *South Staffordshire Waterworks Co.* [1978] 3 All ER 769 at 775:
> We are to put ourselves in the same position as the parties were in at the time they drew up the instrument, to sit in their chairs with our minds endowed with the same facts as theirs were, and envisage the future with the same degree of foresight as they did. So placed we are to ask ourselves: what were the circumstances in which the contract was made?

[12] *Sheridan* v *Phoenix Life Assurance Co.* [1858] EB&E 156 per Pollock C. B. at 165: "If there be a doubt, we think of all instruments that come before us, none requires a more liberal construction than a life policy"; *Pelly* v *Royal Exchange Assurance Co.* [1757] 1 Burr 341; "It is certain that in construction of policies, the *strictum jus* or *apex juris* is not to be laid hold on; but they are to be construed largely for the benefit of trade, and for the assured."

has been applied enthusiastically to the construction of insurance policies.[13] The doctrine has been defined as a requirement that:

> the objectively reasonable expectations of applicants and intended beneficiaries regarding the terms of insurance contracts will be honoured even though painstaking study of the policy provisions would have negated those expectations.[14]

The doctrine also has support in Canada, with legislation on fire insurance permitting the court to condemn any exclusion, condition or warranty as "unjust or unreasonable".[15]

In England, equity and general principles of contract law, such as fundamental breach, rectification of unilateral mistake and estoppel, are used to produce a similar result. Clearly, if the insurer knew or should have known of the insured's expectations then in equity he should be responsible for fulfilling those expectations. The obligations on the insurer would be even greater if the insurer created or helped create the expectations. In such circumstances the doctrine of estoppel could apply.[16] The doctrine of legitimate or reasonable expectations is well established in Irish administrative law[17] but it is not clear how the Irish courts might view a claim for liberal interpretation of a contract based on the legitimate or reasonable expectations

---

[13] In *Kievet* v *Loyal Protective Life Insurance Co.* 170 A 2d 22 [1961] accident insurance was sold to a man aged 48, who later received a blow to his head which triggered latent Parkinson's disease. The insurer contested the claim under the policy, pleading an exception of "disability or other loss resulting from or contributed to by any disease or ailment". The court held that people would expect this kind of accident to be covered and that, if it were not covered, the insurance would be of little value to a man of 48.

[14] Keeton, 83 Harvard Law Review 961, 967 (1970). It is further suggested that policy clauses, which are contrary to the expectations of the insured, should not be enforced, even if the insured was aware of them.

[15] Baer, 22 Ottawa Law Review 389, 410 (1990).

[16] In *Smit Tak Offshore Services* v *Youell* [1992] 1 Lloyds Rep 154 at 159, Mustill J. observed that if

> English Law is moving in this direction it plainly has a long way to go, but if traces of such a doctrine can be discerned it is because . . . certain sorts of insurance are sold like any product and should be subject to the same rules of law. . . . Anything further from the present case is hard to imagine. This policy was not a commodity sold to lay consumers by sophisticated insurers, but a one-off contract placed at arm's length.

[17] *Webb* v *Ireland* [1988] IR 353; *Duggan* v *An Taoiseach* [1989] 1 ILRM 710; *Waterford Harbour Commissioners* v *British Railways Board* [1979] ILRM 296.

of a policyholder. A possible indication can be found in the application of the "officious bystander" test by McCarthy J. in the Supreme Court, in the case of *Keating* v *New Ireland Assurance Co. plc.*[18] and Finlay C. J. has expressed the view that the "doctrine of legitimate or reasonable expectations is but an aspect of the equitable concept of promissory estoppel".[19] An argument based on reasonable expectations would clearly have a greater chance of success in a case involving a personal lines type policy rather than a commercial type policy.

6.5 PRECEDENT

The ordinary rules of the doctrine of precedent apply to a court determining the proper construction to place on the words contained in an insurance policy.[20] Decisions on matters of interpretation in other jurisdictions are not binding on the Irish courts although they may be quoted as persuasive authority. However, significant differences between Irish insurance policy wordings and those of other jurisdictions mean that the judicial decisions on policy interpretation in other jurisdictions are of little relevance in Ireland. Such decisions will however command respect. Ronan L. J. in *Boggan* v *Motor Union Insurance Co. Ltd.*[21] in the Irish Court of Appeal said:

> American cases do not, of course, bind this court. If the view of the judges here does not agree with the American judgments, it is their duty not to follow them; but, at the same time, great respect must be paid to the decisions of distinguished American judges.

The point was made more forcibly, in England, by Scrutton L. J. when he said:

---

[18] [1990] 2 IR 383 at 395.

[19] *Webb* v *Ireland* [1988] IR 353. Plaintiffs were finders of treasure hoard which they handed over for safe-keeping to the National Museum, which assured them they would be honourably treated. Their claim for recovery of the treasure failed but they succeeded in a claim that they had a reasonable or legitimate expectation they would be honourably treated.

[20] Parke B. said in *Glen* v *Lewis*, [1846] 3 CB 437, at 470: "If a construction had already been put upon a clause precisely similar in any decided case we should defer to that authority."

[21] *Boggan* v *Motor Union Insurance Co.* [1922] 2 IR 184.

> I am not impressed by the fact that a different view has been
> taken by American Courts on American policies. Those courts
> frequently differ from ours on the construction of mercantile
> documents. English courts construe documents in the light of
> English decisions.[22]

Where the meaning of words used has previously been the subject of
judicial consideration and judgment, it will be inferred that the parties intended the words to have that meaning.[23] Those drafting insurance policy documents work to achieve certainty and standardisation
of terms and the courts are slow to interfere with the interpretation
given to well known documents in use for any considerable period of
time. Long standing clauses in policies are said to have "the great advantage of certainty".[24]

6.6 ORDINARY MEANING

6.6.1 POLICY CONSTRUCTION

"A policy of insurance . . . is to be construed according to its sense and
meaning as collected, in the first place, from the terms used in it,
which terms are themselves to be understood in their plain, ordinary
and popular sense."[25] This rule of construction is augmented by another general rule that the grammatical meaning of the words used
will be adopted.[26] However some policies are drafted in language
which make their construction according to strict grammar almost

---

[22] *Re: Hooley Hill Rubber and Royal Insurance Co.* [1920] KB 257, 272.

[23] *Clift* v *Schwabe* [1846] 3 CB 437, 470 per Parke B.

[24] per McCracken J. in *Carna Foods Ltd.* v *Eagle Star Insurance Co. (Ireland)
Ltd.* unreported High Court, 9 June 1995; "In commercial cases it is, I think, of
the highest importance that authority should not be disturbed," *Atlantic Shipping & Trading Co. Ltd.* v *Dreyfus & Co.* [1922] 2 AC 250, 257 per Lord Dunedin.

[25] *Robertson* v *French* [1803] 4 East 130 at 135 per Lord Ellenborough C. J.; "All I
have to do is to look at the words which (the parties) have used, and try to give
them their plain and common sense meaning," *Re: George & Goldsmiths and
General Burglary Association Ltd.* [1899] 1 QB 595 at 610 per Collins L. J.

[26] *Weir* v *Northern Counties of England Insurance Co.* [1879] 4 LR Ir. 689 at 693
per Lawson J.

impossible,[27] but where the intention of the parties is clear the grammatical construction must give way.[28] Whilst the policy wording must be construed according to the ordinary meaning of the language used, terms of art or technical words must be understood in their proper sense, unless the context controls or alters their meaning.[29] Technical legal words must be given their strict technical meaning.

6.6.2 "RIOT OR CIVIL COMMOTION"

For example, it was held in *Boggan* v *Motor Union Insurance Co. Ltd.*[30] that the word "riot" as used in insurance policies is used in the technical sense of criminal law rather than in the popular sense. The

---

[27] In particular Marine Insurance policies, in respect of which Lord Esher, M. R. said:

> Now to say that the language of these Lloyds policies can be construed according to strict grammar is, as has often been observed, next to impossible. The phraseology used in them is in many respects regardless of grammar, but the meaning of it has been understood for many years among shipowners and mercantile men in a certain sense. Still, one must examine the language of this memorandum or warranty, and construe it, having regard, as far as possible, to ordinary rules of grammar.

Price & Co. v *AI Ships Small Damage Insurance Association* [1889] 22 QBD 580 at 584.

[28] In another Marine Insurance case Lawrence J. said:

> It is wonderful, considering how much property is at stake upon instruments of this description, that they should be drawn up with so much laxity as they are, and that those who are interested should not apply to some man whose habits of life and professional skill will enable him to adapt the words of the policy to the intention professed by the parties. In construing these instruments we must always look for what was the intention of the parties without confining ourselves to a strict grammatical construction; for it is impossible in many instances to construe them, without departing widely from the object intended. Thus we find a policy meant to cover a risk of goods only, will have words relating for the most part to an insurance on ship, to which it would extend but for some loose memorandum.

Marsden v *Reid* [1803] 3 East 572 at 579. An obvious grammatical error may be corrected in order to restore the intention of the parties; *Glen's Trustees* v *Lancashire & Yorkshire Insurance Co.* [1906] 8 F 915.

[29] *Clift* v *Schwabe* [1846] 3 CB 437 at 469 per Parke B. In *Borradaile* v *Hunter* [1843] 5 M&G 639, the words "die by his own hand" were interpreted as meaning any form of suicide, whether involving the use of hands or not and as not including unintentional self-destruction.

[30] In *Boggan* v *Motor Union Insurance Co.* [1922] 2 IR 184; [1923] 130 LT 588. The High Court of Appeal for Ireland in considering similar facts held in favour of the insurers in *Cooper* v *General Accident Fire & Life Assurance Corp. Ltd.* [1922] 2 IR 38.

Court of Appeal in Ireland held that the theft of a motor car by four armed men in 1920 did not constitute "loss or damage arising during or in consequence of . . . riot or civil commotion" under a motor policy covering loss by theft. However the House of Lords held that the loss fell within the exception. In a recent House of Lords decision[31] the majority held that the word "theft" was to be given its pure technical meaning. It held that in the particular case there was no coincidence of the *actus reus* and the *mens rea* of the crime and that therefore the policy which covered theft did not apply. In the same judgment it found that the word "persons" in the insuring clause of the policy was intended to apply only to "real live persons" and not to companies.

6.6.3 "LEFT UNATTENDED"

The difficulty of establishing the ordinary meaning is demonstrated in the English courts by the number of cases hinging on the interpretation of the phrase "left unattended". In *Starfire Diamond Rings* v *Angel*,[32] an employee left his car locked while he went forty yards to relieve himself. The car was broken into and jewellery stolen. The court held that the jewellery had been left unattended on the ordinary and clear meaning of the words. Upjohn L. J. said: "I deprecate any attempt to expound the meaning or further to define words such as these which are common words in every day use, having a perfectly ordinary and clear meaning." In *Langford* v *Legal and General*[33] the insured drove her car on to her driveway, took out some of the jewellery, locked the car, activated the alarm and deposited the jewellery in her house. While she was doing so the car was broken into and she was assaulted when she tried to prevent the theft. The court distinguished *Starfire* and found in favour of the insured. In *O'Donoghue* v *Harding*,[34] an employee, when filling his car with petrol, chose the pump nearest the cash desk and attempted to keep an eye on his locked vehicle. The car was broken into and jewellery stolen. The court held in favour of the insured that the vehicle had not been left unattended.

---

[31] *Deutsche Genossenschaftsbank* v *Burnhope* [1995] 4 All ER 717.

[32] [1962] 2 Lloyds Rep 217.

[33] [1986] 2 Lloyds Rep 104.

[34] [1988] 2 Lloyds Rep 281.

6.6.4 CONTEXT

The ordinary meaning of a word is determined by the context in which it is used. Context can comprise the phrase, the sentence, the paragraph, the section of the policy, past dealings between the parties, trade usage and the purposes of the policy. All these facets of context must be considered until the meaning intended by the parties is found,[35] In *Curtis & Sons* v *Mathews*,[36] the court was required to consider a fire policy exclusion, of damage caused by "war, bombardment, military or usurped power," and Roche J. said:

> The Dublin rising was not merely felonious, but it was treasonable. Further it had distinct connection with the war in which this country was engaged against the Central Powers. The Provisional Government in their proclamation claimed to be "supported by gallant allies in Europe" — that is to say, by Germans. . . . It is true that the rising was in fact as hopeless as the proclamations of its leaders were vainglorious, but I am satisfied that Easter week in Dublin was a week not of mere riot but of civil strife amounting to warfare waged between military and usurped powers and involving bombardment.

Express definitions in the policy of particular words will of course prevail.

6.7 CONTRA PREFERENS RULE

Where the wording is ambiguous and one reading produces a fairer result than the other, the reasonable interpretation must be adopted. In the early Irish case of *Jameson* v *Royal Insurance Company*,[37] Fitzgerald J. stated the rule quite clearly:

> The language of this instrument is capable of two constructions; but, in as much as it is the language of the Defendants for the purpose of ensuring their own protection, I think we should give it the construction most favourable to the insured, — especially too, as it happens to be the more grammatical.

As the language used in insurance policies is generally that of the insurers any ambiguity in the language will be construed against the

---

[35] *Gamble* v *Accident Insurance Co. Ltd.* [1989] IR 4 CL 204, 214.

[36] [1918] 2 KB 825; [1919] 1 KB 425.

[37] [1873] IR 7 CL 126.

insurers. In *Rohan Construction Ltd.* v *Insurance Corporation of Ireland Ltd.*[38] Keane J. said:

> It is clear that policies of insurance, such as those under consideration in the present case, are to be construed like other written instruments. In the present case, the primary task of the court is to ascertain their meaning by adopting the ordinary rule of construction. It is also clear that, if there is any ambiguity in the language used, it is to be construed more strongly against the party who prepared it, i.e. in most cases against the insurer.

This rule of construction, known as the *contra preferens* rule, has for many years been used by the courts to strike down ambiguity in favour of the insured, because the courts feel

> it is extremely important with reference to insurance, that there should be a tendency rather to hold for the insured than for the company, where any ambiguity arises on the face of the policy.[39]

The rule was affirmed by Hanna J. in the High Court in *General Omnibus Co. Ltd.* v *London General Insurance Co. Ltd.*[40] when he said:

> The law is that the insurance company must bring their case clearly and unambiguously within the exception under which they claim benefit, and, if there is any ambiguity, it must be given against them on the principle *contra preferentes*.

The rule will not be applied by the courts to justify an unreasonable construction in favour of the insured. "Extreme literalism" supporting an interpretation of words "beyond the limits of reasonable interpre-

---

[38] [1986] ILRM 419. In *Re: Sweeney and Kennedy's Arbitration* [1950] IR 85, Kingsmill Moore J. cited with approval the opinion of Lord Greene M. R. in *Woolfall & Rimmer Ltd.* v *Moyle*, [1942] 1 KB 66 at 73 where he said:

> . . . if underwriters wish to limit by some qualification a risk which, *prima facie*, they are undertaking in plain terms, they should make it perfectly clear what that qualification is. They should, with the aid of competent advice, make up their minds as to the qualifications they wish to impose and should express their intention in language appropriate for achieving the result desired.

See also n. 4 *supra*.

[39] *Fitton* v *Accidental Insurance Co.* [1864] 17 CBNS 122, 134, 135.

[40] [1936] IR 596.

tation" will not be accepted.[41] The whole of the policy must be considered and not merely a particular phrase or clause[42] and the policy must be read in the way in which a person of ordinary intelligence would read it.[43]

6.8 PAROL EVIDENCE

6.8.1 ADMISSIBILITY

In considering the interpretation of contracts expressed in writing the courts will not generally admit parol evidence, either oral or written,

---

[41] *Condogianis* v *Guardian Assurance Co. Ltd.* [1921] 2 AC 125 at 131 per Lord Shaw. In *Sangster's Trustees* v *General Accident Assurance Corp.* [1896] 24 R 56, a personal accident policy excluded the risk of "wilful exposure to unnecessary danger" and it was pointed out that many of the normal and everyday actions of life possess a remote element of danger and that most such actions could be regarded as wilful and unnecessary. The court held that a strict literal interpretation was not justified where the result would be to destroy the purpose of the insurance. In *Cornish* v *Accident Insurance Co.* [1889] 23 QBD 453, the court was asked to consider the exception of "exposure of the insured to obvious risk of injury" and held

> . . . the words are very general. . . . to ascertain the true meaning of the exception the whole document must be studied, and the object of the parties to it steadily borne in mind. The object of the contract is to insure against accidental death and injuries, and the contract must not be construed so as to defeat that object nor so as to render it practically illusory. A man who crosses the road is exposed to obvious risk of injury; and if the words in question are construed literally the defendants would not be liable in the event of the insured being killed or injured in so crossing, even if he was taking reasonable care of himself. Such a result is so manifestly contrary to the real intention of the parties that a construction that leads to it ought to be rejected.

[42] *Boggan* v *Motor Union Insurance Co.* [1922] 2 IR 184, per Dodd J. in the Court of Appeal in Southern Ireland:

> The contract must be construed as a whole, and on the facts of this particular case I am of the opinion that what occurred was not within the contemplation of the parties a "riot"; or, if it can be brought within the word, the loss did not arise "during" or "in consequence of" the riot, nor was it "occasioned" thereby. . . . I have been influenced by the consideration that if the insured owners are not protected against risk such as this the premiums have been flung away.

See also *Braunstein* v *Accidental Death Insurance Co.* [1861] 1 B&S 782, Blackburn J at 799.

[43] "The policy must be read in a way in which a person of ordinary intelligence would read it, and in construing this particular clause we must not confine our attention to that clause, but must look to the whole of the policy." per Atkin L. J. in *Hamlyn* v *Crown Accidental Insurance Co. Ltd.* [1893] 1 QB 750, at 754.

to explain or vary the terms of the written document, but in relation to insurance contracts the courts will, in a limited number of circumstances, admit parol evidence to:

- identify the subject matter of the insurance;

- supplement the terms of the policy, provided that the supplementary terms are in harmony with the policy itself;

- interpret the meaning of a word used where the word is not clearly understandable without some indication of the meaning intended by the parties, or where the word has a special local, technical or trade meaning;

- show that the policy contract was intended to be conditional on some external arrangement between the parties;

- show that the terms of the policy are not in accordance with the terms of the contract agreed;

- show that the policy is void for want of good faith.

6.8.2 INTERPRETATION

In *Dillon* v *McGovern*[44] the court was required to determine the meaning of "failure to pass the routine brucellosis test" in an insurance policy and Geoghegan J. said:

> It has been forcibly argued . . . that the words . . . are quite clear and are open only to one meaning. If [that] was right, it would not be permissible to adduce parol evidence to explain or vary the clause. This is a general principle of the law of contract . . . but with reference to insurance contracts . . . the parol evidence, however, would at any rate be admissible to show the circumstances under which the parties contracted and the general context within which the contract was entered into. . . . I am satisfied . . . as a matter of law I am entitled to have regard to the parol evidence only for the purpose of helping me to construe the written words in the light of the intention of the parties and the general context and not for the purpose of varying the written agreement.

---

[44] Unreported High Court, 16 March 1993.

6.8.3 CONTEXT

A contract does not have to be considered in a vacuum. The words used must be considered in the light of the circumstances in which the contract was made. Whether this can mean the rejection of the literal meaning of the words in favour of an interpretation in line with the business purpose of the contract was the point at issue in *Charter Re-insurance Co. Ltd.* v *Fagan*.[45] The plaintiff sought to recover from its reinsurers sums for which it was liable but which, because it was insolvent, it had not actually paid to the insured. The court of first instance was asked to construe words commonly used in reinsurance contracts that reinsurers were "only liable if and when the Ultimate Nett Loss sustained" by the reinsured exceeded a specified figure. The policy defined Ultimate Nett Loss as "the sum actually paid by the reinsured in settlement of losses or liability". The reinsurers argued that the ordinary and primary meaning of these words meant that they were not liable to the reinsured until the reinsured had made actual payment but this argument was rejected by the judge holding that policy construction should never be a "wholly abstract or literal exercise divorced from any consideration of context or practical implications" and viewed in that light the words did not require actual payment as a precondition of liability of reinsurers. That decision was affirmed by the Court of Appeal and the appeal to the House of Lords was dismissed with all of the law lords, except Nourse L. J., agreeing that, on the ordinary meaning of the words, the reinsurers were not obliged to pay the reinsured until the reinsured had paid the insured. The judges read the words in a wider context, which took them outside the ordinary meaning, and which required consideration of the purpose of reinsurance. They accepted that the purpose was to relieve the reinsured from a portion of the risk previously undertaken by them and to protect them from exposures which could otherwise imperil their solvency or profitability. In a judgment, with which all the other Law Lords agreed, Lord Mustill held that the words "actually paid" did not have the narrow and literal meaning argued for them by the reinsurers. He was of the opinion that, "set in the landscape of the instrument as a whole" from which the true "shape of the policy" became clear, the words were

---

[45] [1995] CLC 1345; [1996] 2 WLR 726; [1996] 1 Lloyds Rep 261; [1996] 2 Lloyds Rep 113 (HL).

concerned with the amount of the payment rather than the timing of it.[46]

6.9 EXCEPTIONS

An insurance policy is generally written in a form whereby the positive contractual promise which it evidences is cut down by a number of negative terms in the form of exceptions. "It is the very function of exceptions to limit the extent of the general undertaking given in the first instance."[47] These exceptions are equivalent to a class of stipulations, but instead of imposing obligations on the insured as do ordinary policy conditions, they merely restrict the cover provided by the policy. Exceptions either limit the subject matter of the insurance by excluding certain classes of persons or property, or limit the perils against which the policy provides protection. Policy exceptions may be expressed or implied. Express exceptions are written into the policy and are terms of the contract. Implied exceptions usually limit the extent of cover provided.[48] The operation of an exception suspends cover under the policy but once the exception ceases to operate, cover is automatically reinstated.[49] Any claim arising out of a loss which occurs whilst the exception operates will not be admitted but the policy continues in force and will, subject to its terms, cover subsequent losses. To that extent an exception can be distinguished from a warranty, breach of which entitles the insurer to avoid the policy.[50] Because the insurance contract is drafted by the insurer any ambiguity in an exception will be construed against the insurer.[51]

---

[46] For a full analysis of the decision see "Insurance Contracts: Construction of the policy and the policy of construction", R. Halson, LMCQ, 1996.

[47] per Branson J. in *Concrete Ltd.* v *Attenborough* [1940] 65 Lloyds Rep 174 at 179.

[48] For instance explosion is an implied exception of a policy covering fire risks only, as also is inevitable deterioration under an All Risks policy.

[49] If it is a term of a policy that the insured property be kept in a specified place, e.g. a bank vault, then cover is suspended when the property is removed from the vault. However, should a loss occur when the property is returned to the vault the loss would be covered.

[50] see chapter 5 *supra*.

[51] see Contra Preferens Rule above; *General Omnibus Co. Ltd.* v *London General Insurance Co. Ltd.* [1936] IR 596.

6.10 PROXIMATE CAUSE OF LOSS

6.10.1 CAUSE AND EFFECT

The doctrine of proximate causes is a general legal principle and not one peculiarly applicable to insurance law.[52] In so far as insurance is concerned the doctrine requires that between the operation of the peril insured against and the loss caused thereby there should be a direct relationship equivalent to that between cause and effect. Lord Sumner, in *Motor Oil Hellas (Corinth) Refineries SA* v *Shipping Corporation of India*[53] said:

> There is no mystery about it. Cause and effect are the same for underwriters as for other people. Proximate cause is not a desire to avoid the trouble of discovering the real cause or the "common sense" cause, and though it has been and always should be rigorously applied in insurance cases, it helps one side no oftener than the other. I believe it to be nothing more or less than the real meaning of the parties to a contract of insurance. . . . I dare say few assured have any distinct view of their own on this point, and might not even see it if it were explained to them: but what they intend individually does not depend on what they understand individually. If it is implied in the nature of the bargain, then they intend it in law, just as much as if they said it in words. I think that it is so implied. Indemnity involves it apart from decisions. In effect it is the act of the parties.

The doctrine, common to all classes of insurance, is based on the presumed intention of the parties as expressed in the contract and must be applied to give effect to that intention and not to defeat it.[54] The loss must be such as was within the contemplation of the parties.[55]

---

[52] In his "Maxims of the Law", Lord Bacon says: "It were infinite for the law to consider the causes of causes, and their impulsions one of the other; therefore it contenteth itself with the immediate cause." In *Lawrence* v *Accident Insurance Co. Ltd.* [1881] 7 QBD 216, Watkin Williams J. quoted Bacon and said: ". . . according to the true principles of law, we must look at only the immediate and proximate cause."

[53] *"The Kanchenunga"* [1990] 1 Lloyds Rep 391. The carrier had waived his right not to take his ship into an unsafe port.

[54] *Fitton* v *Accidental Death Insurance Co.* [1864] 17 CBNS 122.

[55] *Taylor* v *Dewar* [1864] 5 B&S 58, where it was held that a "collision liability" clause in a marine policy did not protect the shipowner against loss of life.

The doctrine is incorporated in the Marine Insurance Act 1906, Section 55(1) of which provides:

> Subject to the provisions of this Act, and unless the policy otherwise provides, the insurer is liable for any loss proximately caused by a peril insured against, but, subject as aforesaid, he is not liable for any loss which is not proximately caused by a peril insured against.

In *Gray* v *Barr*,[56] Lord Denning said:

> it has been settled in insurance law that the "cause" is that which is the effective or dominant cause of the occurrence, or, as it is sometimes put, what is in substance the cause, even though it is more remote in point of time, such cause to be determined by common sense.[57]

One of the issues to be resolved was whether, when Gray shot Barr in the course of a struggle, his injuries could be said to be "bodily injury caused by accident" and an accidental event leading inevitably to loss. Denning M. R. was of the view that the act which caused the loss was the threatening and deliberate approach by Gray holding a gun. In so far as the proximate cause was concerned, he found that this non-accidental conduct of Gray was the dominant cause which led inexorably to the loss.

---

[56] [1971] 2 Lloyds Rep 1.

[57] Lord Denning was referring to the case of *Leyland Shipping Co. Ltd.* v *Norwich Union Fire Insurance Society* [1918] AC 350 where Lord Shaw had said, at 369:
> To treat *proxima causa* as the cause which is nearest in time is out of the question. Causes are spoken of as if they were distinct from one another as beads in a row or links in a chain, but if this metaphysical logic has to be referred to, it is not wholly so, the chain of causation is a handy expression, but the figure is inadequate. Causation is not a chain, but a net. At each point influences, forces, events, precedent and simultaneous, meet; and the radiation from each point extends indefinitely. At the point where these various influences meet it is for the judgment as upon a matter of fact to declare which of the causes thus joined at the point of effect was the proximate and which was the remote cause. . . . The cause which is truly proximate is that which is proximate in efficiency. That efficiency may have been preserved although other causes may meantime have sprung up which have not yet destroyed, or truly conquered it, and it may culminate in a result of which it still remains the real efficient cause to which the event can be ascribed.

6.10.2 SUCCESSIVE CAUSES

Whilst common sense might dictate that an insurance policy should respond to cover any loss which can fairly be attributed to the operation of an insured peril, the doctrine does raise the question whether the loss was caused by the peril insured against or whether the peril was brought into operation by an excepted cause. The question becomes difficult to answer where there are a number of successive possible causes of the loss. In such circumstances the doctrine is applied to determine if the loss was caused by an insured peril. It was the rule that, where there are a number of successive causes, the last cause in time was held to be the cause of the loss,[58] but the House of Lords put an end to that rule, in *Leyland Shipping Co. Ltd.* v *Norwich Union Fire Insurance Society Ltd.*[59] A ship, torpedoed in the First World War, was towed to a quay in the outer harbour at Le Havre. The port authorities, fearing she might sink there and obstruct the quay ordered her out and she soon sank, having been unable to withstand being buffeted by heavy seas. The shipowners argued that the loss was caused by perils of the sea and therefore insured but the insurers contended that loss was the consequences of the hostilities and therefore excluded under the policy. The House of Lords held that the proximate cause of the loss was the torpedo.

6.10.3 POLICY WORDING

The words used in the policy will determine whether the proximate cause of the loss is an insured or uninsured peril. Clearly the use of words such as "caused by" or "arising from" is unambiguous. Such words have been interpreted as relating to the proximate cause.[60] Other relevant words interpreted include "direct cause",[61] "dominant cause",[62] "effective cause",[63] "immediate cause".[64] Where the policy cov-

---

[58] *Trew* v *Railway Passengers' Assurance Co.* [1861] 6 H&N 839.

[59] [1918] AC 350.

[60] *Coxe* v *Employers' Liability Assurance Corp.* [1916] 2 KB 629; *Motor Union Insurance Co. Ltd* v *Boggan* [1924] 130 Lt 588; *Bell* v *Lothiansure Ltd.* (Inner Court of Session) unreported, 1 February 1991.

[61] *Coxe* v *Employers Liability Assurance Corp.* [1916] 2 KB 629; *Oei* v *Foster* [1982] 2 Lloyds Rep 170.

[62] *Lloyd (J.J.)* v *Northern Star Insurance Co.* ("*Miss Jay Jay*") [1987] 1 Lloyds Rep 32.

ers or excludes loss or damage occasioned by specified perils or causes
it has been held that the act causing the loss or damage must be attributable to one of the specified perils or causes but nothing more. In
Cooper v *General Accident Fire & Life Assurance Co.*[65] insurers repudiated liability, relying on a policy exception of "loss or damage occasioned through Riot or Civil Commotion occurring within the land
limits of Ireland". The insured motor vehicle was taken one evening
from the insured's garage in Cork by at least two persons, who
threatened the insured when he tried to intervene. The theft was neither riot nor civil commotion but the House of Lords held that the
exception applied. There was civil commotion in Cork at the time, and
it was probable that the vehicle was taken for some purpose connected with the civil commotion.

6.10.4 LOSS ARISING "DIRECTLY OR INDIRECTLY"

Where the policy refers to loss "directly or indirectly" caused by a
peril or circumstance, the direct cause is obviously the proximate
cause but "indirectly" implies something less than proximate. Where
a rented house was damaged by fire, when the occupant inadvertently failed to turn off the heat under a deep-fat fryer, the Court in
Oei v *Foster*,[66] held that the damage arose indirectly from the occupation of the house so as to bring the damage within the exception of
"damage arising directly or indirectly from . . . ownership or occupation of any land or building". The judge held that the preparation of
meals is a necessary and inevitable incident of the occupation of a
house.

6.10.5 FINAL CAUSE

Where the last cause is not a peril insured against but a preceding
cause is an insured peril, it is then necessary to consider whether the
last cause is so intimately connected with the preceding cause that
the loss is the effect of the preceding cause and therefore insured.
Where each cause in the sequence from the insured peril to the last

---

[63] *"Miss Jay Jay"* at 37.

[64] *Shera* v *Ocean Accident and Guarantee Corp. Ltd.* [1900] 32 Ont. R 411.

[65] [1923] 128 ILT 481.

[66] [1982] 2 Lloyds Rep 170.

cause, is the reasonable and probable consequence, resulting directly and naturally in the ordinary course of events from the cause which precedes it, the peril insured against is held to be the cause of the loss within the meaning of the policy.[67] Any loss resulting from a necessary and bona fide effort to put out a fire, such as the spoiling of goods by water or the destruction of adjoining property by explosion to check the fire, would be loss proximately caused by fire and within the policy cover. It is immaterial how many causes operate between the insured peril and the final cause of loss[68] so long as there is no break in the chain of causation between the insured peril and the loss. Where, however, the sequence of causes or the chain of causation is broken by the intervention of an independent cause, the loss is held to be caused not by the insured peril but by the intervening cause.[69] The fact that the insured peril may have rendered the subject matter of the insurance policy more susceptible to loss by the intervening cause is immaterial.[70]

---

[67] *Stanley* v *Western Insurance Co.* [1868] LR 3 Exch 71 per Kelly C. B., at 74:

> Any loss resulting from an apparently necessary and bona fide effort to put out a fire, whether it be by spoiling the goods by water, or throwing articles of furniture out of the window, or even the destroying of a neighbour's house by an explosion for the purpose of checking the progress of the flames, in a word, every loss that clearly and proximately results, whether directly or indirectly from the fire, is within the policy.

In *Isitt* v *Railway Passengers' Assurance Co.* [1889] 22 QBD 504, the assured confined to bed as a result of an accident, developed pneumonia and died. His death was held to be the result of the injuries sustained in the accident and therefore covered by the policy.

[68] *Mardorf* v *Accident Insurance Co.* [1903] 1 KB 584, where a scratch produced septicaemia, which developed into septic-pneumonia resulting in death, which was held to be caused by the scratch.

[69] *Clan Line Steamers Ltd.* v *Board of Trade* [1928] 2 KB 557, where Scrutton L. J. said at 371:

> Suppose an Insurance policy is effected against consequences of railway operations, and a misguided person commits suicide by jumping in front of a train. Would that be a consequence of railway operations within the meaning of the policy? To me it seems the proximate cause of death is the man's own act.

[70] A person weakened by a railway accident, run over by a bus, which owing to his weakened state he is unable to avoid, is deemed to have died as a result of the street accident and not the railway accident, per Wiles J. at 512 in *Isitt* v *Railway Passenger's Assurance Co.* [1889] 22 QBD 504.

6.10.6 EXCEPTED CAUSES

Difficulties arise where an insured peril and an excepted cause operate and the consequences of each cannot readily be identified with accuracy. The doctrine of Proximate Cause must be applied in such circumstances to determine if the loss comes within the cover provided by the policy. It has been held that if the peril insured against is the reasonable and probable consequence, directly and naturally resulting in the ordinary course of events from the excepted cause, the excepted cause is the cause of the loss.[71] It is not necessary that the excepted cause should continue to operate right up to the moment of loss; it is sufficient that it should have started the chain of causation leading to the loss.[72] On the other hand, where the sequence is broken, and an insured peril is an independent cause whose connection with the excepted cause is accidental and not causal, the insured peril is deemed to be the cause of the loss. In *Lawrence* v *Accident Insurance Co.*[73] the insured, in the course of a fit, fell from a railway platform, and was killed by a passing train. He was deemed to have been accidentally killed and the fit was not the proximate cause of his death. If the excepted cause is the reasonable and probable consequence of an insured peril and there is a causal connection between the insured peril and the loss, the excepted cause is regarded as merely a link in the chain of causation and the loss is deemed to be caused by the insured peril.[74]

6.10.7 CONCURRENT CAUSES

If the loss is caused by two independent causes operating concurrently but independently, and one cause is an excepted cause and the

---

[71] *Letts* v *Excess Insurance Co.* [1916] 32 TLR 361.

[72] *Mair* v *Railway Passengers' Assurance Co. Ltd.* [1877] 37 LT 356. The policy had an exception of death or injury to the insured person whilst under the influence of intoxicating liquor. It was held sufficient that the insured was under the influence at the time the injury which resulted in death was sustained.

[73] *Lawrence* v *Accident Insurance Co.* [1881] 7 QBD 216. A shop window damaged by a mob attracted by a fire in adjacent premises, was held to be damaged by the actions of the mob and not the result of the fire; *Marsden* v *City and County Assurance Co.* [1866] LR 1 CP 232.

[74] *Fitton* v *Accidental Death Insurance Co.* [1864] 17 CBNS 122 where hernia caused by an accidental fall was held not to come within an exception against hernia.

other an insured peril, the loss is said to be attributable as much to one cause as the other and the loss does not come within the policy cover.[75] In *Jason* v *British Traders Insurance Co. Ltd.*[76] the insured had effected a personal accident policy against "accidental bodily injury resulting in and being — independently of all other causes — the exclusive, direct, and immediate cause of the injury or disablement". No benefit was payable in respect of "death, injury, or disablement directly or indirectly caused by or arising or resulting from or traceable to . . . any physical defect or infirmity which existed prior to an accident". The insured suffered a coronary thrombosis caused by stress when involved in a motor accident, a clot forming and occluding the coronary artery already narrowed by a pre-existing disease. The insured's claim in respect of the injury received failed, it being held that the bodily injury was not "independently of all other causes the exclusive cause of the disablement". There were two concurrent causes, the pre-existing disease and the formation of the clot. These two causes were independent of each other, and the thrombosis would not have occurred unless both had operated.

6.10.8 MODIFIED WORDING

The doctrine may be modified by the use of clear words in the policy wording.[77] In *Coxe* v *Employers' Liability Assurance Corp.*[78] it was said that:

> The words "directly or indirectly" . . . could not be reconciled with the maxim that the proximate cause only was to be regarded, and their effect was to throw them back to something behind the proximate cause.

The use of words such as "in consequence of" or "originating from" do not however prevent the operation of the doctrine.[79] A requirement that the cause of loss must be "accidental or external" will however

---

[75] *Saqui and Lawrence* v *Stearns* [1911] 1 KB 426.

[76] [1969] 1 Lloyds Rep 281.

[77] *Oei* v *Foster* [1982] 2 Lloyds Rep 170.

[78] [1916] 2 KB 629.

[79] *Ionides* v *Universal Marine Insurance Co.* [1863] 14 CB 259; *Marsden* v *City and County Insurance Co.* [1865] LR 1 CP 232.

qualify the doctrine. In *"Miss Jay Jay"*[80] a yacht, insured against damage "directly caused by accidental external means" was damaged in bad weather. the Court of Appeal held that as the weather conditions were markedly worse than average, such conditions had contributed to the damage and that damage was caused by means which were both accidental and external.

---

[80] *"Miss Jay Jay"* [1987] 1 Lloyds Rep 32.

CHAPTER SEVEN

THIRD PARTY RIGHTS AGAINST INSURERS

7.1 PRIVITY OF CONTRACT

A person who is not party to the contract of insurance between the insurer and the insured has, in general, no rights at common law against the insurer. Such a person is caught by the privity of contract rule which says that no one may enforce all or part of a contract, to which they are not a party.[1] There are, of course, exceptions to the

---

[1] *Dunlop Pneumatic Tyre Co. Ltd.* v *Selfridge & Co. Ltd.* [1915] AC 847. The appellants brought an action for breach of a contract made between the respondents and a third party which contained terms as to the re-sale of goods of the appellant's manufacture. It was held that the contract was unenforceable at the suit of the appellants. "In the law of England" said Viscount Haldane L. C. at 853,

certain principles are fundamental. One is that only a person who is party to a contract can sue on it. Our law knows nothing of a *jus quaesitum tertio* arising by way of contract. Such a right may be conferred by way of property as, for example, under a trust, but it cannot be conferred on a stranger to a contract as a right to enforce the contract *in personam*.

This traditional rule was challenged in the Australian Courts in *Trident General Insurance Co. Ltd.* v *McNeice Bros. Pty Ltd.* [1988] 62 ALJ 508 where a liability insurance, in respect of a limestone crushing plant, was held intended to extend to the plant and all contractors and sub-contractors engaged in construction work at the plant. The main contractor, although not a party to the policy, sought to enforce it. The Court of Appeal found in favour of the contractor on the basis that at common law the beneficiary of an insurance contract can sue on the contract even though not a party to it or providing consideration. An appeal to the High Court of Australia was dismissed. The House of Lords has declined on a number of occasions to abandon the traditional rule; see, for example, *Silicones Ltd.* v *Scruttons Ltd.* [1962] AC 446, *Beswick* v *Beswick* [1968] AC 58, *Woodar Investment Development Ltd.* v *Wimpey Construction UK Ltd.* [1980] 1 All ER 571.

rule.[2] These exceptions arise through the use of trusts and under statute. In England, the Law Reform Commission has recently recommended reform of the rule, arguing that, in its present form, it is not only unjust to third parties, but it operates to defeat the intention of the contracting parties.[3] In the United States,[4] New Zealand,[5] parts of Australia[6] and in most common law jurisdictions, the rule has been abrogated. The legal systems of most member states of the European Union allow third parties to enforce contracts. The rule has been subjected to significant judicial[7] and academic[8] criticism. Those arguing in favour of change in the rule generally maintain that:

- the rule prevents effect being given to the intentions of the contracting parties

- a third party who has suffered loss cannot sue while a person who has suffered no loss has a right of action

- the exceptions to the rule render the law complex and uncertain

- the rule causes difficulty in commercial life.[9]

Even though third parties have less rights in Irish law than in English law, there has been no demand for reform.

---

[2] Apart from the exceptions, a person wishing to extend the benefit of an insurance contract to a third party may contract not only on his own behalf but as agent for the third party, so that the latter becomes a party to the contract and ceases to be a third party.

[3] *Privity of Contract: Contracts for the Benefit of Third Parties*, Law Com. No. 242, published 31 July 1996.

[4] Restatement (Second) of Contracts (1981), Section 302.

[5] Contracts (Privity) Act, 1982.

[6] Western Australia Property Law Act, 1969, Section 11; Queensland Property Law Act, 1974, Section 55.

[7] See "Reforming Privity of Contract", A. Burrows, LMCLQ, 1996.

[8] *Beswick* v *Beswick* [1968] AC 58 at 72; *Woodar Investment Developments Ltd.* v *Wimpey Construction UK Ltd.* [1980] 1 WLR 277 at 300; *Swain* v *Law Society* [1983] 1 AC 598; *"The Pioneer Container"* [1994] 2 AC 324; *White* v *Jones* [1995] 2 AC 207; *Darlington Borough Council* v *Wiltshire Northern Ltd.* [1995] 1 WLR 68.

[9] Corbin (1930); Dowrick (1956); Furmston (1960); Beatson (1992); Wilson (1996).

7.2 THIRD PARTY RIGHTS UNDER A TRUST

7.2.1 LIFE ASSURANCE

Whilst, in principle, a trust may be used in relation to any kind of insurance it is, in practice, most frequently used in relation to life assurance. To create an express trust under a life policy there must be (a) trust property in the form of the benefit of the policy, (b) identified beneficiaries of the trust, (c) a clear purpose for the trust and (d) a clear intention to create a trust. In the creation of a trust in favour of a third party it is essential that clear and unambiguous words are used,[10] but it is not necessary to use technical language to create a trust, since "equity regards the intention rather than the form".[11] It is not uncommon for an assured to assign a life policy to trustees to hold on trust for a specified party and it is now becoming increasingly popular for life policies to be purchased from assureds by third parties who then continue to pay the premiums and benefit from a resulting trust.

7.2.2 RIGHTS OF EMPLOYEES

7.2.2.1 The existence of a trust giving a beneficiary the right to proceed against the insurer is frequently claimed in relation to group insurance schemes such as those arranged by employers for the benefit of employees. In *Bowskill* v *Dawson*,[12] a company established

---

[10] Halsbury, Vol. 48, nos. 542 ff. In *Re: Schebsmann* [1944] CH 83 at 104, Du Parcq L. J. said:

> It is true, that by the use of possibly unguarded language, a person may create a trust, as Monsieur Jourdain talked prose without knowing it, but unless an intention to create a trust is clearly to be collected from the language used and the circumstances of the case, I think that the court should not be astute to discover indications of such an intention.

[11] No difficulty arises where the policy is expressed to be "held in trust for" or "upon trust to pay" the third party, but it has been held in *Re: Burgess's Policy* [1915] 113 LT 443, that it is not enough that the policy be expressed "for the benefit of" the third party.

> . . . the mere fact that A takes out a policy that is expressed to be for the benefit of B or on behalf of B does not constitute a trust for B; and . . . the mere fact that the policy provides moneys are to be payable to B does not create a trust in favour of B.

per Plowman J. in *Re: Foster's Policy* [1966] 1 WLR 222 at 225, relying on *In Re: Webb* [1941] CH 225.

[12] [1955] 1 QB 13.

an employee benefit scheme whereby trustees effected group life cover on behalf of the company's employees. One of the insured employees was killed in a road accident and insurers paid over the sum assured to the trustees. In assessing an award of damages to the employee's personal representatives, the trial judge took into account the moneys paid under the group life policy and reduced the award accordingly. The Court of Appeal, having considered the terms on which the scheme had been set up, concluded that the employees:

> may be regarded as beneficiaries under a voluntary trust for their benefit. . . . they had more than mere expectancies. . . . they had rights which the courts would recognise and enforce. . . . Indeed, it may well be that, had the insurance company refused to pay, and the trustees declined to sue, the employees themselves could have sued the insurance company, adding the trustees as defendants.[13]

7.2.2.2 In *Green* v *Russell*,[14] a group personal accident policy, effected by the employer, covering specified employees as the "insured persons", stated that the insured employer was "the absolute owner of the policy and shall not be bound to recognise any equitable or other claim or interest in the policy". The employees were aware of the existence of the policy, but it formed no part of their terms of employment. The Court of Appeal, pointing out that "there was nothing to prevent the employer at any time, had he chosen to do so, from surrendering the policy and receiving back a proportionate part of the premium he had paid",[15] held that an insured employee had no legal right to the policy proceeds. However, a life policy, effected "on the life of and for the benefit of" the insured's daughter, under the terms of which the beneficial interest would lie solely with the daughter on reaching the age of 25, was held, on a true construction of the policy, to constitute a trust in favour of the daughter, with the court adding that:

> If, according to the terms of the policy, a time comes when the grantee of the policy ceases to have any beneficial interest in

---

[13] ibid at p. 28 per Romer L. J.

[14] *Green* v *Russell, McCarthy (third party)* [1959] 2 QB 226.

[15] ibid at p. 241.

it, it is not difficult to imply a trust for the person for whose benefit the policy is expressed to have been taken out.[16]

7.2.2.3 In *Re: Irish Board Mills Ltd. (in Receivership)*,[17] the High Court was asked to determine whether moneys payable under a group accident policy effected by the employer on a number of specified employees should be treated, by the receiver, as assets of the company or whether they were to be treated as the property of the personal representatives of a deceased employee, whose accidental death had caused the moneys to become payable. The policy document, on the face of it, clearly indicated that the benefits were payable to the employer for the employer's sole benefit, but the company had executed an assignment of the policy to trustees as a perquisite of office of the insured employees. Barrington J., in approving and following *Green* v *Russell*,[18] held that the onus of proving that the policy proceeds properly belonged to someone other than the employer rested with the person so alleging but that the onus was not discharged merely by proving a "reasonable expectation".[19] He admitted and accepted a considerable body of evidence, including affidavits from directors of the company, which confirmed the traditional practice and intention of the company in relation to such policies, finding in favour of the personal representatives of the deceased employee, on the grounds that the company, in assigning the policy to trustees, were not dealing with assets of the company but assets held on trust.

7.2.2.4 The High Court, in *McManus* v *Cable Management (Ireland) Ltd.*,[20] refused to accept that an employer, in effecting an Employers' Liability policy, does so in the capacity of a trustee for his employees, and that the employees are beneficiaries under the policy and as such entitled to sue the insurer in respect of injuries or disease sustained in the course of employment. Morris J. held that, whilst the employer

---

[16] In *Re: Foster's Policy* [1966] 1 WLR 222 at 227 per Romer L. J.

[17] In the matter of *Irish Board Mills Ltd. (in Receivership)*; *McCann* v *Irish Board Mills Ltd. and Others* [1980] ILRM 216.

[18] n. 14 *supra*.

[19] [1980] ILRM 216 at 217.

[20] *McManus* v *Cable Management (Ireland) Ltd., Radford Communications Ltd. and Hibernian Insurance Co. plc.* Unreported High Court, 8 July 1994.

could be said to have entered into the policy as trustee of the employee in so far as it provided an indemnity to the employee in the event of him injuring a third party, the policy conferred no rights on the employee in respect of the injuries which he had sustained.[21]

7.3 THIRD PARTY RIGHTS BASED ON ESTOPPEL

The Supreme Court, in *Boyce* v *McBride*[22] and in *Doran* v *Thompson*,[23] refused to invoke the doctrine of estoppel to enable plaintiff third parties join insurers in an action against negligent policyholders. In *Boyce* v *McBride*, Kenny J. held that even if the factual basis for the estoppel existed and had been made out, it would have been fruitless to grant an order joining the insurers as defendants because the action was one founded on an allegation of negligence:

> The liability of insurers (if any) arises as a matter of contract under the policy of insurance. A third party cannot claim against insurers under the policy save where that is specially allowed by Statute.[24]

7.4 THIRD PARTY RIGHTS UNDER PROPERTY INSURANCE

7.4.1 CONTRACTUAL PROVISION

Where the contract provides insurance against loss of or damage to property, a third party might wish to claim for losses sustained by

---

[21] The policy in question, as with most Employers' Liability policies, included in the definition of insured, "if the policyholder so requires, . . . any person employed by the insured under a contract of service or apprenticeship". Morris J. relied on *Bradley* v *Eagle Star Insurance Co. Ltd.* [1989] 1 All ER 961, and quoted Denning M. R. in *Post Office* v *Norwich Union* [1967] 1 All ER 577: ". . . the right to sue for these moneys does not arise until the liability is established and the amount ascertained".

[22] *Joseph Boyce* v *Peter McBride* [1987] ILRM 95.

[23] *Kevin Doran* v *Thomas Thomson & Sons Ltd.* [1978] IR 223, the plaintiff injured in an accident at work, claimed that the defendant was estopped by the acts and representations of the defendant's insurers from pleading that the plaintiff's action was statute barred. The Supreme Court held that any misapprehension in the mind of the plaintiff or his solicitor had not been induced by any representation of the defendant or his insurer.

[24] per Henchy J. (with Finlay C. J. and Griffin J. concurring) [1987] ILRM 95, at 97/98.

him or might wish to avoid the possibility of insurers exercising subrogation rights against him where he has been responsible for the
loss or damage. In the first instance, the third party will need to
prove that he is in some way a party to the contract and that there is
a contractual relationship between him and the insurer. If, in the second instance, he can prove that he is a party to the contract, he will
be immune to subrogation. Where it is necessary to do so, third party
interests in property insurance contracts are generally protected either by assignment of the policy,[25] inclusion of the third party as a co-
insured, or notation of the third party interest. However, whilst the
noting of interests is a widespread and common practice, it does not
make the third party a party to the contract, nor does it provide an
immunity against subrogation. Likewise the inclusion of a subrogation waiver clause in the policy, whereby the insurer agrees not to
exercise subrogation rights against the named third party, is worthless, for if the third party is not a party to the contract he cannot rely
on it. If he is a party to the contract then he has immunity anyway.

7.4.2 Loss Payee Clause

Even if the third party interest is not noted on the policy, the third
party may be immune to subrogation, if, as in *Rowlands* v *Berni Inns
Ltd.*,[26] he can prove that he is the true beneficiary of the policy and
has paid the premium. Where the interest of the third party is protected by the inclusion of a loss payee clause, under which the insurer
agrees to make payment to the third party in the event of a loss, it is
doubtful that the protection is of any value as the third party cannot
enforce it against the insurer.[27] However, in a recent decision of the

---

[25] Two recent decisions of the Privy Council clarify the rights of third party as-
signees; *Colonial Mutual General Insurance Co. Ltd.* v *ANZ Banking Group (New
Zealand) Ltd.* [1995] Unreported Privy Council, and *Colonia Vershicerung AG* v
Amoco Oil Co. [1995] 1 Lloyds Rep 570.

[26] *Mark Rowlands* v *Berni Inns Ltd.* [1986] 1 QB 211.

[27] "Such a clause gives no rights to the loss payee unless it also constitutes or
evidences an assignment of the assured's rights under the policy or evidences the
fact that the designated person is an original insured," per Donaldson J. in *"The
Angel Bell", Iraqi Ministry of Defence* v *Arcepey Shipping Co. SA* [1979] 2 Lloyds
Rep 491 at 497.

Privy Council,[28] it was held that the noting of a bank's interest on a policy is sufficient to ensure that the bank is entitled to be paid in the event of a loss where it has lent money by way of mortgage on the insured property and the mortgagor covenants to insure. The noting of the bank's interest was held to be notice of assignment to it of the benefit of the policy.

7.4.3 INTENTION OF THE PRIMARY INSURED

The intention of the primary insured is critical. In *National Oilwell (UK) Ltd.* v *Davy Offshore Ltd.*,[29] it was held that a policy may cover the interests of an unnamed party provided the party effecting the insurance had the intention, at the time of arranging the insurance, of covering the third party's interests. In the High Court, in the Matter of the Arbitration Act, 1954 between *Church and General Insurance Company and Patrick Connolly and Others*,[30] Costello J. upheld an arbitrator's finding that the defendant, as tenant at will, had an insurable interest in the property destroyed, and that they were entitled to be indemnified under a policy of insurance effected by them. The insureds did not own the property, but were using it with permission for the purposes of a youth club. It was held that they should be indemnified not only in respect of the loss and damage they suffered to their limited interest but also in respect of the loss and damage to the owners in fee of the property, despite the fact that the owner's interest was not noted on the policy. The fact that a policy is noted as covering the interests of a named third party does not auto-

---

[28] *Colonial Mutual General Insurance Co. Ltd.* v *ANZ Banking Group (New Zealand) Ltd.* [1995] Unreported.

[29] [1993] 2 Lloyds Rep 582.

[30] Unreported, 7 May 1981; Costello J. said at p. 11:
> The law permits a person with a limited interest in a property to insure not only his interest but the interest which others may have in the same property and what the arbitrator has found in this case is that the defendants have done what the law permits them to do.

matically make that party a co-insured under the policy unless the policyholder intends to do so.[31]

7.5 THIRD PARTY RIGHTS UNDER LIABILITY INSURANCE

A liability insurance policy constitutes a promise by the insurer to indemnify the insured against such sums as the insured becomes legally liable to pay in respect of property damage or personal injury. If the insurer does not honour its promise, the insured has a claim against the insurer for breach of contract, but the party to whom the sums are payable does not at common law have any rights exercisable against the insurer.[32] The right to be indemnified by the insurer is one personal to the insured and the third party to whom the sums are payable has no interest in either equity or at law in the proceeds of the policy either before or after payment to the insured. The insurer's promise to indemnify the insured does not constitute a debt owed by the insurer to the insured and so cannot be the subject of garnishee proceedings. A claim upon an insurance policy is classified as a claim for unliquidated damages. If the promise is not honoured, the insured has a claim for breach of contract but since there is no debt due there

---

[31] In *D.G. Finance* v *Eagle Star*, Unreported 1995, the Court of Appeal ruled that the plaintiff finance company, which had advanced finance in respect of a trailer, could not sue insurers when the trailer was stolen and the insured went bankrupt. The court ruled that whilst the insured was under an obligation to compensate the finance company if insurers indemnified him, that did not entitle the finance company to sue the insurers directly.

[32] *Firma C. Trade* v *Newcastle Protection and Indemnity Association, "The Fanti"* and *Socony Mobil Oil Co. Inc. and Others* v *West Of England Ship Owners Mutual Insurance Assoc. (London) Ltd.*, *"The Padre Island"* [1990] 2 All ER 705; at p. 517, Lord Goff of Chievely said:

> I am unable to accept . . . that a condition of prior payment is at common law, implicit in a contract of indemnity. I accept that, at common law, a contract of indemnity gives rise to an action for unliquidated damages, arising from the failure of the indemnifier to prevent the indemnified person from suffering damage, for example by having to pay a third party. I also accept that at common law, the cause of action does not (unless the contract provides otherwise) arise until the indemnified person can show actual loss: see *Collinge* v *Heywood* [1839] 9 Ad & El 633; 112 ER 1352. . . . As a general rule, "Indemnity requires that the party to be indemnified shall never be called upon to pay" (see *Re: Richardson, ex parte Governors of St. Thomas's Hospital* [1911] 2 KB 705 at 706 per Buckley L. J.); and it is to give effect to that underlying purpose of the contract that equity intervenes, the common law remedies being incapable of achieving that result.

is nothing in the hands of insurers which can be garnished. The insurer can discharge his obligation to the insured by satisfying the insured's liability to the third party.[33]

7.5.1 POSITION IN UNITED KINGDOM

7.5.1.1 Prior to the introduction of the Third Party (Rights against Insurers) Act, 1930, if an insured in England became bankrupt or, being a company, went into liquidation, the money payable by insurers under a liability insurance policy became part of the general assets of the insured, available for distribution among the creditors of the insured. Unless the third party to whom the moneys were owed had previously managed to obtain a judgment and enforced it against the insured, he was obliged to prove the debt in the bankruptcy or liquidation with all other creditors.[34] The Act was passed to correct this obvious injustice.[35] In effect the Act constituted a statutory as-

---

[33] *Israelson* v *Dawson* [1933] 1 KB 301.

[34] Section 5 of the Workmen's Compensation Act, 1906 provided that if the employer of an injured workman were wound up the rights of the employer against its insurer should vest in the workman. This section was re-enacted as Section 7 of the Workmen's Compensation Act, 1925, but its field of application was not extended. In *Re: Harrington Motor Co. Ltd.*, [1927] 29 Lloyds Rep 102; [1928] CH 105, a pedestrian was injured by the negligent driving of a company vehicle. He sued the company and obtained judgment. A winding up order was then made against the company and a liquidator appointed. The company's insurers paid the sum of the pedestrian's claim and costs to the liquidator and the pedestrian sought to recover that payment in full from the liquidator. It was held that the payment formed part of the general assets of the company available for distribution among its creditors of whom the pedestrian was only one. Both Lord Hansworth M. R. (at pp. 105, 116) and Lord Justice Atkin (at pp. 105 and 108, 117 and 123–124) regarded the law as unsatisfactory. The ratio of the decision was applied in *Hood's Trustees* v *Southern Union General Insurance Co. of Australasia Ltd.* [1928] 31 Lloyds Rep 237. The Third Party (Rights Against Insurers) Act, 1930, was introduced to remedy the potential injustice highlighted by *Re: Harrington*.

[35] "An Act to confer on third parties rights against insurers of third party risks in the event of the insured becoming insolvent, and in certain other events," 20 & 21 Geo 5 C 25. In *Bradley* v *Eagle Star Insurance Co. Ltd.* [1989] 2 WLR 568, Lord Brandon of Oakbrook at 574/575 referring to *Re: Harrington Motor Co. Ltd., Ex parte Chaplin* [1928] 1 CH 105 and *Hoods Trustees* v *Southern Union General Insurance Company of Australasia Ltd.* [1928] 1 CH 783, said:

> These two decisions showed that, even where an injured person obtained a judgment for damages against a wrongdoer, if the wrongdoer being a company went into liquidation, or being an individual became bankrupt, and the judgment had not by then been enforced by execution, the moneys payable by way

signment[36] of the insured's rights under a policy of insurance to the injured party providing that party with a direct right of action against the insurer, and removing the insured's claim to indemnity from the bankruptcy or liquidation proceedings and transferring it to the third party.[37] Section 1 of the 1930 Act provides that where, under any contract of insurance, a person is insured[38] against liability which he may incur to third parties, then if he becomes bankrupt or makes a composition with his creditors, or if (the insured being a company) a winding-up order is made, or a resolution for voluntary winding-up is passed,[39] or a receiver or manager is appointed or possession taken by or on behalf of debenture holders, the rights of the insured against the insurer in respect of any such liability incurred before or after such event shall be transferred to the third party to whom the liability was incurred.[40] Section 1(6) provides that the Act does not apply to a company that is wound up voluntarily merely for the purposes of reconstruction and the Act does not apply in any case to a company which has been completely wound up if in that case there is no longer any means by which the existence and amount of liability can be es-

---

of indemnity under any policy of insurance by which the wrongdoer was insured against liability to third parties, did not go solely to benefit the injured person but were payable to the liquidator or the trustee in bankruptcy of the wrongdoer for distribution *pari passu* among all the unsecured creditors. This was recognised to be plainly unjust, and the Act of 1930 was passed to remedy that injustice.

[36] per Lord Alness in *Greenlees* v *Port of Manchester Insurance Co. Ltd.* [1933] SC 383 at 400.

[37] *Re: Compania Marbello San Nicholas SA* [1973] CH 75, per Megarry J. at 90/91.

[38] If a term of a contract of insurance states that there is no cover for a particular head of liability unless the insurers shall otherwise determine in their discretion, the insured is not a person who "is insured" in respect of that liability for purposes of the 1930 Act: *"The Vainqueur Jose"* [1979] 1 Lloyds Rep 557, 580 per Mocatta J.

[39] The Act does not apply to a voluntary winding-up merely for the purposes of reconstruction or amalgamation (Section 1(6)) nor where a company has been dissolved as a result of being struck off the register under Section 353 of the Companies Act 1948; *Re: Harvest Lane Motor Bodies Ltd.* [1969] 1 CH 457. The provisions of the Act apply where there is an order for the administration in bankruptcy of a deceased debtor (Section 1(3)).

[40] Actions under the 1930 Act are brought by claimants in their own names on the basis of what Harman L. J. called a "statutory assignment of rights" in *Post Office* v *Norwich Union Fire Insurance Society Ltd.* [1967] 2 QB 367, at 376.

tablished.[41] The third party has no right to prevent a settlement between the insured and the insurer for an amount that is inadequate to cover the liability of the insured to the third party, even though the practical effect of the settlement is that the insured becomes insolvent.[42]

7.5.1.2 To derive the benefit of the Act it is not sufficient for the third party to have a claim against the insured; he must have established his claim in proceedings against the insured.

> If there is an unascertained claim for damages in tort, it cannot be proved in the bankruptcy nor in the liquidation of the company. But nevertheless the injured person can bring an action against the wrongdoer. In the case of a company he must get the leave of the court. No doubt leave would automatically be given. The insurance company can fight an action in the name of the wrongdoer. In that way liability can be established and the loss ascertained. Then the injured person can go against the insurance company.[43]

It is also necessary that there should be liability cover in force. The Act does not apply if the liability comes within a policy exception. The third party can have no better right than the insured. In the words of the courts, "the third party steps into the shoes of the insured,[44] but

> it is not all the rights and liabilities of the insured under the insurance contract which are transferred to the third party,

---

[41] *Bradley* v *Eagle Star Insurance Co. Ltd.* [1989] 1 All ER 961.

[42] *Normid Housing Association Ltd.* v *Ralphs* [1989] 1 Lloyds Rep 265; *Bradley* v *Eagle Star Insurance Co. Ltd.* [1989] AC 957 at 960 per Lord Brandon.

[43] *Post Office* v *Norwich Union Fire Insurance Society Ltd.* [1967] 2 QB 363 per Lord Denning M. R. at 375. Contractors working on a highway damaged a cable belonging to the Post Office, who claimed for the damage. The contractors denied liability, claiming the engineer engaged by the Post Office had not correctly indicated the route of the cable. The contractor then went into liquidation before the issue of liability could be determined and the Post Office sued the insurers, relying on the provisions of the 1930 Act. The action failed because the contractor's liability had not been established, the extent of the liability had not been quantified and if the contractor had admitted liability he would have been in breach of policy conditions.

[44] *"The Padre Island"* [1987] 2 Lloyds Rep 408, per Leggatt J. at 414.

only the particular rights in respect of the liability incurred by
the insured to the third party.[45]

7.5.1.3 The determination of the third party's rights involves the
application of all the terms of the contract and the consideration of all
the defences available to the insurer. If there is an arbitration clause
in the policy, then the third party will be bound to arbitrate.[46] If the
insurer has a right to repudiate or avoid the policy or accepts a repudiation of the policy from the insured, then the third party cannot
recover under the Act.[47] A policy requirement that the insured make
no admission of liability is equally binding on the third party,[48] as is a
condition precedent to liability that any writ or notice of proceedings
be forwarded to insurers.[49] A provision limiting the insurer's liability *made*
is also binding on the third party.[50] If the insurance was vitiated by a *invalid*
misrepresentation,[51] non-disclosure or breach of warranty by the insured, then the insurer can deny cover to the third party.[52] The rights
transferred are transferred subject to any conditions or qualifications
affecting those rights.[53] The House of Lords, in *"The Padre Island"*,[54]

---

[45] *Murray* v *Legal & General Assurance Society Ltd.* [1970] 2 QB 495, per Cum-
ming-Bruce L. J. at 503.

[46] *Freshwater* v *Western Australia Assurance Co. Ltd.* [1933] 1 KB 515; *Smith* v
Pearl Assurance Co. Ltd. [1939] 1 All ER 95; *"The Padre Island"* [1990] 2 Lloyds
Rep 408 (see n. 32 *supra*).

[47] *Greenlees* v *Port of Manchester Insurance Co.* [1933] SC 383; *Cleland* v *London
General Insurance Co.* [1935] 51 Lloyds Rep 156.

[48] *Post Office* v *Norwich Union Fire Insurance Society Ltd.* [1967] 2 QB 363.

[49] *Hassett* v *Legal & General Assurance Society Ltd.* [1939] 63 Lloyds Rep 278;
Pioneer Concrete (UK) Ltd. v *National Employers Mutual General Insurance Association* [1985] 1 Lloyds Rep 274.

[50] *Avandero* v *National Transit Insurance Co. Ltd.* [1984] 2 Lloyds Rep 613.

[51] *McCormick* v *National Motor & Accident Union Ltd.* [1934] 40 Com Cas 76;
Greenlees v *Port of Manchester* [1933] SC 383.

[52] *Cleland* v *London General Insurance Co. Ltd.* [1935] 51 Lloyds Rep 156.

[53] However, in the case of compulsory motor insurance the Road Traffic Acts limit
the defences available to the insurers, and in relation to time limitations, the
limitation period runs not from the time when the insured becomes bankrupt or
insolvent but from the time when the insured's cause of action against the insurer first arose. *Lefevre* v *White* [1990] 1 Lloyds Rep 569; *Post Office* v *Norwich
Union* [1967] 2 QB 363.

upheld a contract condition requiring an insured to discharge his liability to a third party before he could recover from the insurer, with the result that, where an insured has not discharged his liability and such a condition applies and the insured is wound up before payment, no cause of action has accrued to the insured against the insurer and no right of indemnity can be transferred to the third party claimant. The House of Lords also decided that such a condition in a contract of insurance was not contrary to Section 1(3) of the Act designed to prevent parties to the contract of insurance from contracting out of the Act.

7.5.1.4 Employers in the UK, unlike here in Ireland, are obliged by statute[55] to insure their liability to employees for death, illness or disease sustained in the course of their employment, but if an employer fails to insure, an injured employee has no right of action in respect of that failure.[56] If an uninsured employer went into liquidation before payment of damages, the injured employee to whom the damages were payable ranked as a creditor in the liquidation prior to the Third Parties (Rights against Insurers) Act, 1930. Now, because of the Act, the injured employee can proceed against the insurer of the employer, if the employer is insured in respect of his liability. However, the injured employee's right to proceed against the insurer depends on liability being established in proceedings against the insured employer.

---

[54] *Firma C. Trade SA* v *Newcastle Protection & Indemnity Association*, *"The Fanti"; Socony Mobil Oil Co. Inc. and Others* v *West of England Ship Owners Mutual Insurance Association (London) Ltd.*, *"The Padre Island"* [1990] 2 All ER 705. Lord Goff of Chieveley at 713, said:

> The central question is one which has troubled maritime lawyers in the City of London and in the Temple ever since the enactment of the Third Parties (Rights against Insurers) Act, 1930. It is whether the Act confers on a third party, who has a claim against an insolvent shipowner [whose ship is insured] an effective right to proceed directly [against the insurer] for the loss or damage suffered by him despite the presence of a condition of prior payment. . . . What is transferred to and vested in the third party is the member's right against the [insurer]. That right is, at best, a contingent right to indemnity, the right being expressed to be conditional on the [insured] having in fact paid the relevant claim or expense. If that condition is not fulfilled the [insured] has no right to be indemnified . . . and the statutory transfer of his right to the third party cannot put the third party in any better position than the insured. It is as simple as that.

[55] Employers' Liability (Compulsory Insurance) Act, 1969.

[56] *Richardson* v *Pitt Stanley & Others* [1995] 2 WLR 568.

Where the employer was a company which is no longer in existence —
and it is not therefore possible to establish a claim in proceedings
against the company — the injured employee would have no right of
action against the insurer.[57] In an era of gradually developing industrial diseases it was considered unreasonable that an injured employee should be denied compensation because a company for which
he worked was no longer technically in existence. Consequently, Section 141 of the Companies Act, 1989 was introduced to enable a company be restored to the register of companies, i.e. "to bring it back to
life", within a period of twenty years after it has been dissolved, to
enable an injured employee pursue an action for damages against it
and its insurers. The employee must be able to establish negligence
or breach of statutory duty against the employer and he receives no
greater rights to indemnity than those of the insured against the insurer.

7.5.1.5 The general purpose of the Third Parties (Rights against Insurers) Act, 1930, is to allow the victim of a negligent person, whose
negligence is insured, to obtain priority over the proceeds of the insurance policy, by providing that, in the event of the insured becoming insolvent, the insured's right of action against the insurer is
transferred to the injured party. The Law Commission's Working Paper on Privity of Contract, issued in 1995, regarded the Act as unsatisfactory in operation, and in January 1997, prepared a consultation
paper outlining the problems and suggesting possible reforms. Six
major reforms were put forward for consideration:

1) Permit the injured third party join the insurer in the proceedings
   against the insured wrongdoer at any time after the insolvency of
   the insured;

---

[57] *Bradley* v *Eagle Star Insurance Co. Ltd.* [1989] 2 WLR 26, per Lord Brandon of
Oakbrook at 33:

> [The Act] was not passed to remedy any injustices arising from other matters;
> in particular, it was not passed to remedy any injustice which might arise as a
> result of the dissolution of a company making it impossible to establish the
> existence and the amount of the liability of such company to a third party.
> That kind of situation was not, in my view, contemplated by the legislature at
> all.

2) Allow the injured third party proceed against the insurer alone, i.e. make the insurer the sole defendant;

3) Allow the injured third party make application to the court for leave to bring proceedings against the insurer when the insured wrongdoer is not insolvent but where the injured third party is not likely for other reasons to obtain compensation from the insured wrongdoer;

4) Provide the injured third party with a general right to proceed directly against the insurer;

5) Remove the injured third party's right of direct action against the insurer, but allow his claim to have priority over the insurance proceeds;

6) Where there are multiple claims against limited insurance proceeds, apportion them *pro rata* between the claimants.

It is expected that the Law Commission will issue a full Consultative Document at the end of 1997.

7.5.2 POSITION IN IRELAND

7.5.2.1 In Ireland there is no equivalent statute to the Third Parties (Rights against Insurers) Act, 1930. Apart from the provisions in Section 76 of the Road Traffic Act, 1961, the only statutory reference of relevance is Section 62 of the Civil Liability Act, 1961.[58] That section provides that where a person or company insured under a liability insurance policy dies, becomes bankrupt, or is wound up, moneys payable under the policy shall be applied, only to discharging in full all valid claims against the insured in respect of which those moneys are payable, and the moneys shall not be regarded as assets of the insured, or used for payment of the debts of the insured other than for payment of those claims. It is sometimes suggested that Section 62 of the Civil Liability Act, 1961 is the Irish equivalent of the Third

---

[58] The constitutionality of the Act was challenged in the Supreme Court in *Gaspari v Iarnrod Eireann*, Unreported, 16 July 1996. The case arose out of a collision between a pilgrimage train and a herd of cattle owned and driven by a Mr Diskin in September 1989. In the action determining the substantive issue of liability, Diskin was found 70 per cent liable but the injured party, Gaspari, deemed him to be a person "without any significant means" and opted under the 1961 Act to recover in full from Iarnrod Eireann.

Parties (Rights against Insurers) Act, 1930,[59] and constitutes a statutory exception to the privity of contract rule. This belief is apparently based on an interpretation of the Supreme Court Judgment, in *Dunne v P.J. White Construction Co. Ltd. (in Liquidation) and Michael Payne and others*.[60] In that case, the plaintiff employee had obtained judgment in default of defence against his employer, the first defendant in respect of an injury sustained by him in the course of his employment. The employer went into liquidation prior to the judgment being obtained and the plaintiff sought to enforce the judgment against the second defendant, who were the insurers of the employer under an employers' liability insurance policy, on the grounds that they were liable under the provisions of the policy between them and the insured employer. The insurers maintained that they were entitled to repudiate liability to the insured due to breach of policy conditions. In the High Court, Murphy J. held, as a matter of law, that the onus was on the plaintiff, not only of establishing that a policy of insurance existed and was issued by the insurers to the first defendants, which covered the risk of an accident such as the accident in respect of which the plaintiff had received damages, but that there was also on the plaintiff the onus of proving as a negative that a right asserted or alleged by the defendants to rescind or repudiate the policy of insurance had not arisen. The High Court held that the plaintiff had failed to discharge the onus on him and the plaintiff appealed the decision to the Supreme Court, relying on section 62 of the Civil Liability Act, 1961 to ground his action.

7.5.2.2 In the Supreme Court, Finlay C. J. in a judgment with which the other four members all concurred, identified the net issue before the court as being whether the trial judge was correct in his view of the onus which the law placed on the plaintiff.[61] The Court suggested that in order to properly implement the protection which Section 62 of the Civil Liability Act, 1961 afforded to persons in the precise position of the plaintiff, and in accordance with established rules in relation to the onus of proof, it was necessary that the onus of proof

---

[59] Corrigan and Campbell, *Casebook of Irish Insurance Law*, p. 519, 520.

[60] [1989] ILRM 803.

[61] ibid at 804.

should be on the insurance company to prove what it alleged. The Court directed a new trial but the matter was compromised before it came for further hearing. In the course of his judgment, Finlay C. J. had said:

> Section 62 of the Act of 1961 is specifically designed to protect an injured plaintiff in the precise position of Mr Dunne in this action so as to ensure that moneys payable on a policy of insurance to an insured who is dead, bankrupt, and, in the case of a corporate body, who is gone into liquidation, will not be eaten up by other creditors, but will go to satisfy his compensation, and with that purpose in mind the section must, it seems to me, give to the plaintiff a right to have that right enforced and protected by the courts and that means that he has got a right to sue as he has sued in this action.[62]

These comments of the Chief Justice were however *obiter* and not part of the decision itself. The judgment was given *ex tempore* and was not reserved. The case before the Supreme Court was, according to the Court itself,[63] concerned with establishing the onus of proof and nothing else. The alleged right of the plaintiff to sue the insurers under the policy was not argued before the High Court or raised in the pleadings and consequently, because it went unchallenged, the Supreme Court was obliged to assume that such a right existed.[64] However, Finlay C. J. was, as always, careful in his choice of words. In saying that Section 62 of the 1961 Act gave injured plaintiffs a right of action against insurers he qualified the statement by referring to plaintiffs in the precise position of the plaintiff in that action. That plaintiff had obtained judgment against the insured employer and was seeking a declaration that the defendant insurers were, by virtue of Section 62, obliged to pay the damages and costs awarded to the plaintiff.

7.5.2.3 There can be no doubt but that a plaintiff who has obtained judgment against an insured, who subsequently fails to meet that judgment because of death, bankruptcy, or liquidation has, by virtue of Section 62 of the Act, a right to proceed against insurers for pay-

---

[62] ibid at 805.

[63] n. 61 *supra*.

[64] per Finlay C. J. at 805.

ment of the moneys due under a policy of insurance, covering the insured's liability to the plaintiff, and to prevent the moneys being included in the assets of the insured and "eaten up by other creditors". But that is as far as the Act goes. It does not, as does the UK Act, transfer to the plaintiff the rights of the insured under the policy. It does not give the plaintiff the right to sue for specific performance of the contract. It does not give the plaintiff third party the right to arbitrate under the policy if the policy contains an arbitration clause. It does not in any way attempt to interfere with the privity of contract rule. The UK Act on the other hand, in statutorily assigning the policy rights of an insolvent insured to an injured third party plaintiff, gives the third party all the benefits of the policy in so far as they relate to their particular claim against the insured. If the policy contains an arbitration clause, then the third party must proceed under the terms of that clause as if they were the insured.[65] Section 62 of the Irish Act applies only to moneys "payable" under a policy of insurance and it must first be established that the moneys are payable before the third party can claim to have them applied to satisfaction of a judgment obtained against the insured. If the insurer had successfully repudiated liability under the policy, Section 62 does not give any rights to the third party to challenge that repudiation. Any such challenge would have to be made by the representatives of the insured or the liquidator of the insured company.

7.5.2.4 Section 62 of the 1961 Act repealed Section 76(4) of the Road Traffic Act, 1961 and is identical, almost word for word, with the repealed section. By virtue of Section 76(1) of the Road Traffic Act, 1961, an injured party is given a direct right of action against the insurer of the vehicle which occasioned the injury and such right of action arises immediately the injury is sustained and is not dependent on establishing the liability of the vehicle owner or user or the liability of the insurer under the policy issued in respect of the vehicle oc-

---

[65] *Freshwater* v *Western Australia Assurance Co. Ltd.* [1933] 1 KB 515; "*The Padre Island*" [1987] 2 Lloyds Rep 408.

casioning the injury.[66] The repealed Section 76(4) was intended to protect persons, injured in circumstances to which the Road Traffic Acts applied, against the possibility of moneys payable by insurers being used to offset debts of a deceased or insolvent insured. By repealing the Section and incorporating it into the Civil Liability Act, the legislature were simply extending the protection it afforded to other persons injured in circumstances to which the Road Traffic Acts do not apply and liability for which is not compulsorily insurable. If it was intended to give persons injured in circumstances not compulsorily insurable direct right of action against insurers, the legislature would, it is suggested, have included the same specific provisions in the Civil Liability Act as existed in Section 76(1) of the Road Traffic Act. Both Acts were passed in the same year and it is safe to assume that the drafters and the legislature were conscious of what they were doing.[67] Direct right of action against insurers is of course desirable and justifiable where injuries are sustained in circumstances where the wrongdoers are obliged to insure their liability. However, the law as it stands does not extend direct right of action against insurers to circumstances where liability for injury to third parties is not compulsorily insurable.

7.5.2.5 If the Supreme Court judgment in *Dunne* v *White* was to be interpreted as providing injured employees with a direct right of action against the insurers of the company, at the time of the injured employee's employment out of which the injury or disease arose, without the necessity of first establishing liability against the employer, such employee plaintiffs would need only to prove the insurer's involvement with the insured company and it would then be

---

[66] "Where a person . . . claims to be entitled to recover from the owner of a mechanically propelled vehicle or from a person . . . using a mechanically propelled vehicle . . . or has in any court of justice (in proceedings of which the vehicle insurer . . . had prior notification) recovered judgment against the owner for a sum . . . for which the owner or user is insured by an approved policy of insurance, . . . the claimant may serve by registered post on the vehicle insurer . . . a notice in writing of the claim or the judgment for the sum."

[67] In bringing forward the Civil Liability Act, which came into force on 17 August 1961, the Government were advised by the eminent academic lawyer, Glanville Williams. The original Bill was accompanied by a comprehensive explanatory memorandum with the stated purpose of attempting to remedy to some extent the lack of textbooks on Irish law.

up to the insurer to disprove liability. This could not be right. Even the English 1930 Act does not go that far,[68] and Section 141 of the English Companies Act, 1989, while restoring the employer company to life, does not alter or mitigate the need for the employee plaintiff to establish negligence or breach of statutory duty, and to have the resuscitated company's liability quantified by way of an award, before the plaintiff can proceed against the insurer concerned. The plaintiff employee receives no greater rights than those of the insured employer under the policy and has to prove the existence, validity and applicability of the policy to the injuries or disease allegedly sustained. Insurers have available to them all of the normal defences they would have had against the insured had the claim been made prior to the dissolution of the insured company.

7.5.2.6 Under the Irish Companies Acts, any amounts due by a company in liquidation in respect of damages payable to an employee injured in an accident in the course of their employment rank as a preferential debt to the extent that the company is not effectively indemnified by insurers.[69] Where an indemnity is being provided by an insurer, Section 62 of the 1961 Civil Liability Act entitles an injured employee to apply to have the moneys due under a policy of insurance paid directly to him as compensation, in priority to ordinary creditors provided (a) he has already established or can establish before winding up of the company that the company is liable to him for the injury sustained and the financial extent of that liability and (b) the assets of the company are sufficient to meet the liability of the company to all preferential creditors. Where the assets are insufficient, all preferential creditors' claims are abated in equal proportions.[70] In most

---

[68] per Lord Brandon, *Bradley* v *Eagle Star Insurance Co. Ltd.* [1989] 2 WLR 26; see n. 57 *supra*.

[69] Section 285(2)(g) provides that in a winding up there shall be paid in priority to all other debts:

> . . . unless the company is being wound up voluntarily merely for the purpose of reconstruction or of amalgamation with another company, all amounts due from the company in respect of damages and costs, payable to a person employed by it in connection with an accident occurring before the relevant date and in the course of his employment with the company, to the extent that the company is not effectively indemnified by insurers against such damages and costs.

[70] Section 285(7) Companies Act, 1963.

liquidations the assets available for distribution are insufficient to meet all creditors' claims and the claims of injured employees against uninsured companies are unlikely to be met in full, if at all. There is no provision in the Irish Companies Acts similar to Section 141 of the English Companies Act of 1989, allowing companies to be brought back to life to enable former employees pursue actions for compensation in respect of injury or disease sustained during the course of employment by the company.[71] This defect in Irish company law may present problems for employees seeking compensation for illness or disease manifesting itself many years after the company has been wound up.

7.6 THIRD PARTY RIGHTS UNDER MOTOR INSURANCE

7.6.1 ROAD TRAFFIC ACTS
In the context of insurance in Ireland the only statutory exception to the privity of contract rule is contained in the Road Traffic Act, 1961 where Section 76(1) provides:

> Where a person . . . claims to be entitled to recover from the owner of a mechanically propelled vehicle or from a person . . . using a mechanically propelled vehicle . . . or has in any court of justice (in proceedings of which the vehicle insurer . . . had prior notification) recovered judgment against the owner or user for a sum . . . for which the owner or user is insured by an approved policy of insurance . . . the claimant may serve by registered post, on the vehicle insurer . . . a notice in writing of the claim or judgment for the sum. . . .

Section 76(1)(d) provides that:

---

[71] Section 310(1) of the Companies Act, 1963, does provide that:
> where a company has been dissolved, the court may at any time within two years of the date of dissolution, on an application being made for the purpose by the liquidator of the company or by any other person who appears to the court to be interested, make an order, upon such terms as the court thinks fit, declaring the dissolution to have been void, and thereupon such proceedings may be taken as might have been taken if the company had not been dissolved.

This Section is not the equivalent of Section 141 of the English Companies Act of 1989 and does not have the same purpose.

> where the claimant has not so recovered judgment for the sum,
> the claimant may apply to any court of competent jurisdiction
> in which he might institute proceedings for recovery of the sum
> from the owner or user for leave to institute and prosecute
> those proceedings against the insurer . . . in lieu of the owner
> or user . . . and the court may grant the application and there-
> upon the claimant shall be entitled to institute and prosecute
> those proceedings against the insurer . . . and to recover
> therein from the insurer . . . any sum which he would be enti-
> tled to recover from the owner or user and the payment of
> which the insurer . . . has insured.[72]

The 1961 Act repealed, and re-enacted, Section 78 of the Road Traffic
Act, 1933, which according to Budd J., in *O'Leary* v *Irish National
Insurance Co. Ltd.*[73] "undoubtedly altered the law by allowing an injured third party to proceed directly against the insurers or indemni-
fiers of the owner or driver of a motor car liable to the third party".
The Section applies only to liability in respect of which the owner or
user of the vehicle is insured. In *Brady* v *Brady*,[74] the High Court refused an application under Section 78(1) of the Road Traffic Act,
1933, where the vehicle was being driven by the policyholder's son,
with his consent and in the knowledge that, by reason of his age, he
was not entitled to hold a licence. In refusing the application, the
court upheld a policy exception relieving the insurers of liability if the
vehicle was being driven by a person who to the knowledge of the
policyholder did not hold a licence to drive. The onus of proof lies on
the third party plaintiff to establish that the defendant's vehicle was,
at the time of the accident causing the injury, insured within the

---

[72] In *McGee* v *London Assurance Company* [1943] 77 ILTR 133, Sheehy J. said of
Section 78:

> I have no doubt as to its meaning. It appears to have two objects. On the one
> hand it is to protect a person injured — a third party — through the negli-
> gence of an insured driver in the event of such insured person proving to be
> without assets. That is the principal purpose of the section. It provides, where
> a person has a claim for damages for negligence against an insured person,
> that if he gives notice of such action to the insurance company, then the insur-
> ance company is rendered liable jointly with the insured person. On the other
> hand, it is a protection for the company. It is quite clear that notice of proceed-
> ings against the insured person must be given to the insurance company.

[73] [1958] IR Jurist Rep 1.

[74] [1938] IR 103.

terms of the policy.[75] In *Whelan* v *Dixon*,[76] the first case under the provisions of the Section to come before the Supreme Court, Lavery J., whilst agreeing that the onus was on the third party, suggested that the onus might not be as great as that which the insured might ordinarily have:

> It must be remembered that the decisions on claims by an insured person against insurers depend entirely on the terms of the contract which the policy represents and may not be applicable in applications under Section 78 where the claimant is an outsider to the contract seeking to enforce the statutory right conferred by the Section. It is clear of course that this right is governed by the terms of the contract but it may be that this burden of proof falling on him may not be the same as that which falls on an insured person claiming against his insurers.[77]

The plaintiff had recovered judgment for damages in an action for personal injuries caused by the negligence of the defendant's agent or servant in the driving of a car in Dublin. The judgment remained unsatisfied and the plaintiff applied for leave to execute the judgment against the insurers who had repudiated liability on the ground that at the time of the accident the vehicle was being used for a purpose other than those covered by the policy. The Supreme Court upheld the judgment of the trial judge that the onus was on the plaintiff to prove that the vehicle was being used within the limitations as to use contained in the policy. For the section to avail a third party, a valid policy of insurance covering the liability claimed must exist,[78] and the

---

[75] per Murnaghan J., following *O'Reilly* v *Hennessy*, Unreported High Court, 17 June 1949, in *Whelan* v *Dixon* [1963] ILTR 195.

[76] [1963] ILTR 195.

[77] ibid.

[78] *O'Leary* v *Irish National Insurance Company Ltd.*, [1958] IR Jurist Rep 1, per Budd J.:

> Section 78 of the Road Traffic Act, 1933, has undoubtedly altered the law by allowing an injured third party to proceed directly against the insurers or indemnifiers of the owner or driver of a motor car liable to the third party. Moreover, the insurer is not to plead any invalidity of the policy arising out of the fraud, misrepresentation or false statement to which the claimant was not party or privy. . . . It is also apparent from the wording of the Section that the third party, therein referred to as the claimant, can only recover, as one would in all common sense suppose, against a person bound to indemnify the owner or driver respectively against whom the claim in the first instance arises.

liability must be one which is compulsorily insurable under the Road Traffic Acts. In *Stanbridge* v *Healy*[79] Hamilton J. in confirming that the Section applies only to "claims against the liability for which an approved policy of insurance is required,"[80] held that a roadway, in the grounds of a country house, where the accident occurred, did not constitute a "public place" to which the Road Traffic Acts applied and consequently the plaintiff was not entitled to proceed against insurers under the Section. In *Bus Eireann* v *Insurance Corporation of Ireland*,[81] the High Court held that the Section did not create a new cause of action in respect of which a separate limitation period would be applicable. "All the Section does is to enable an injured party to substitute for a . . . defendant, the insurance company holding cover at the time."[82]

7.6.2 MOTOR INSURERS BUREAU OF IRELAND

Under an agreement between the insurers licensed to underwrite motor insurance in Ireland (MIBI) and the Irish Government, the MIBI undertakes to compensate third parties injured in accidents caused by the negligent use of a mechanically propelled vehicle in or on a public place where there is no valid policy of insurance covering the use of the vehicle, provided the vehicle was not owned by the state or an exempted person.[83] Whilst the original agreement was concerned primarily with the compensation of persons sustaining personal injuries in road traffic accidents, the current agreement now covers property damage arising out of accidents occurring on or after the 31 De-

---

[79] *Stanbridge* v *Healy and Ensign Motor Policies at Lloyds* [1985] ILRM 290.

[80] Section 76(3), Road Traffic Act, 1961.

[81] Unreported High Court, 10 May 1994.

[82] ibid per Morris J.

[83] Agreement dated 21 December 1988, replacing earlier agreements, made as part of the implementation of the Second EC Directive on Motor Insurance — Directive EC 84/5/EEC of 30 December 1983.

cember 1992.[84] Because the agreement is between the insurers and the Irish Government, the insurers could invoke the "privity of contract rule" to prevent an injured party seeking specific performance of the agreement. However, the MIBI have given an undertaking to the Government that they will never use the "privity of contract" defence to defeat a claim coming within the terms of the agreement.[85] In England, where a similar agreement operates, the courts have not questioned the need for consideration in the contract before allowing a third party to the contract enforce the benefits of the agreement,[86] and the Motor Insurers Bureau there has not raised the point. In *Hardy* v *MIB*[87] Diplock L. J. suggested the MIB could not raise the point without being in breach of the Agreement, and in a subsequent case,[88] he held that the court was entitled to proceed on the assumption that the MIB had for good consideration contracted with the plaintiff to perform its obligations under the Agreement, or was estopped for some good reason from invoking the defence of privity of contract. The House of Lords, whilst critical of the practice of ignoring the strict legal position of the plaintiff,[89] has nevertheless accepted the situation.[90]

---

[84] European Communities (Road Traffic) (Compulsory Insurance) (Amendment) Regulations, 1995, (S.I. No. 353) made under the European Communities Act, 1972 (No. 27) Section 3, give effect to Council Directives 72/166/EEC, 84/5/EEC and 90/232/EEC; increase the statutory minimum coverage for property damage arising out of one accident to £90,000 and revise the geographic coverage of motor insurance policies to take account of new members of the European Community; operative from 1 January 1996.

[85] See Chapter Eight, "Motor Insurance", for full details of the Agreement.

[86] *Gurtner* v *Circuit* [1968] 1 All ER 328; *Albert* v *MIB* [1971] 2 All ER 1345; *Gardner* v *Moore & others* [1984] 1 All ER 1102; *Hardy* v *MIB* [1964] 2 QB 745, where Lord Denning expressed the hope that the point would never be raised.

[87] *Hardy* v *MIB* [1964] 2 QB 745 at 766.

[88] *Gurtner* v *Circuit* [1968] 2 QB 587 at 589.

[89] *Albert* v *MIB* [1971] 2 All ER 1345 per Lord Viscount Dilhorne at 1354.

[90] idem at 1347, 1348 per Lord Donovan; *MIB* v *Meanen* [1971] 2 All ER 1372; *Gardner* v *Moore* [1984] AC 548.

CHAPTER EIGHT

MOTOR INSURANCE

*"We must not allow ourselves to be warped by any prejudice
against motor cars, and so to strain the law against them."*[1]

8.1 STATUTORY DEFINITION

Motor Insurance business is defined in the Insurance Act, 1936 as:
"The business of effecting contracts of insurance against loss of or
damage to or arising out of or in connection with the use of mechanically propelled vehicles including third party risks".[2]

8.2 STATUTORY REQUIREMENTS

8.2.1 COMPULSORY INSURANCE

Prior to 1933, most, if not all, vehicle owners in Ireland insured
against liability for claims arising out of the negligent driving or use
of their vehicles. The Road Traffic Act, 1933, introduced for the first

---

[1] *Bastable* v *Little* [1907] 1 KB 59 at 62 per Lord Alverstone C. J.

[2] Section 3 of Part 1 of Insurance Act 1936. In 1995 the gross written premiums of
the members of the Irish Insurance Federation amounted to £650.4 million of
which an underwriting loss of £40 million was recorded. There were 145,692 new
claims in that year, costing £568.2 million, according to IIF newsletter no. 43,
July 1996. According to the Dept. of Enterprise and Employment, on 1 October
1996 there were 25 insurers authorised to write motor insurance business in
Ireland. The 1996 Report of the MIBI claimed that between 4 per cent and 6 per
cent of drivers were uninsured and confirmed that claims for uninsured drivers
totalled £30 million in that year, bringing the total outstanding liability of the
MIBI to £117 million.

time into Ireland the concept of compulsory insurance.[3] The 1933 Act was subsequently repealed by the Road Traffic Act, 1961, but its provisions in relation to insurance were carried on and extended.[4] Section 56(1) of the Act provides that:

> A person . . . shall not use in a public place a mechanically propelled vehicle unless either a vehicle insurer, a vehicle guarantor or an exempted person would be liable for injury caused by the negligent use of the vehicle by him at that time or there is in force at that time:
>
> a) an approved policy of insurance whereby the user or some other person who would be liable for injury caused by the negligent use of the vehicle at that time by the user, is insured against all sums without limit (save as is hereinafter otherwise provided) which the user or his personal representative shall become liable to pay to any person (exclusive of the excepted persons) by way of damages or costs on account of injury to person or property caused by the negligent use of the vehicle at that time by the user. . .

Section 56(1)(b) provided for an approved guarantee instead of an approved policy of insurance, but that option was removed by section 53 of the Road Traffic Act, 1968.

8.2.2 COUNCIL OF EUROPE DIRECTIVES

The statutory requirements have been significantly amended to comply with directives emanating from the Council of Europe aimed

---

[3] The Act resulted from the recommendations in the report of the Interdepartmental Committee on the control and regulation of Road Traffic, 1928. The Act made it compulsory, subject to specified limited exceptions, to have a specified minimum level of cover in respect of the driving of all classes of vehicles and took account of the insurance practices which had developed. It was:

> An Act to amend and consolidate the law relating to mechanically propelled vehicles, the regulation and control of road traffic, and the use of mechanically propelled vehicles for the carriage of passengers, to make provision for compulsory insurance against liabilities arising from negligent driving of mechanically propelled vehicles and to make provision for other matters connected with the matters aforesaid.

[4] Notably the compulsory insurance provisions referred to "use" of the vehicle as distinct from "driving" in the 1933 Act and provided for the extension of compulsory insurance to passengers in the classes of vehicles to be specified by the Minister in subsequent regulations, e.g. Road Traffic Act (Compulsory Insurance) Regulations, 1962, SI no. 14 of 1962.

at harmonising the level of compulsory insurance in each member state and ensuring that insurance cover applies to all vehicles being used within the Community, irrespective of the member state in which it is based or in which it is being used.[5] The directives generally focus the need for insurance on to the vehicle rather than the driver and try to guarantee a high level of protection for the victims of accidents, involving motor vehicles, as well as those responsible for them. [6]

The First Council Directive on Motor Insurance[7] sought to bring about a situation where the national law of each member state would provide for the "compulsory insurance of vehicles against civil liability" and that such insurance would be valid throughout the entire Community.[8] The directive did not attempt to lay down minimum levels of cover, but the Second Directive did.[9] That Directive made liability for property damage as well as personal injury compulsorily insurable.[10] It also prohibited clauses or provisions which excluded from insurance the use or driving of vehicles by persons driving with-

---

[5] 72/166/EEC; 4/5/EEC; 0/232/EEC.

[6] The effectiveness of the directives was demonstrated in the decision *"Bernaldez"*, handed down by the European Court of Justice in March 1996. Bernaldez had caused an accident by driving whilst intoxicated. He was prosecuted by the Spanish authorities and an order made against him in respect of the damage he had caused to third party property. The Spanish Courts upheld his insurers' refusal to provide him with an indemnity on the grounds that a 1986 Spanish Act exempted them from liability "where the driver was intoxicated".On appeal a reference was made to the Court of Justice for a ruling on whether such a form of exclusion was permitted by the Directives. The court ruled that Spain had failed to implement the directives correctly and that the directives did not permit the exclusion of losses caused by an intoxicated driver from the scope of compulsory insurance. Whilst the insurers might retain a right of recovery against the driver, they were obliged to indemnify the injured party.

[7] 72/166/EEC.

[8] Article 3.1 ibid.

[9] 84/5/EEC. Article 1.2 specified minimum limits of 350,000 ECU for personal injury where there is only one victim; where more than one victim is involved the amount specified is multiplied by the number involved. In the case of damage to property the limit was 100,000 ECU, irrespective of the number of claimants. Alternatively, member states were permitted to provide for a minimum amount of 500,000 ECU for personal injury where more than one victim was involved or a combined limit of 600,000 ECU for personal injury and property damage whatever the number of victims or the nature of the damage.

[10] Article 1.1 ibid.

out consent, unlicensed drivers or persons in breach of statutory requirements concerning the condition and safety of the vehicle concerned.[11] Any such provision is deemed void in respect of claims by
third parties who have been victims of an accident involving a mechanically propelled vehicle. The Directive required each member
state to set up or authorise a body with the task of providing compensation for damage to property or personal injuries caused by an unidentified vehicle or a vehicle for which the insurance obligations outlined were not satisfied, and member states were given the option, in
the case of vehicles stolen or obtained by violence, of providing for the
payment of compensation by the body referred to rather than by insurers. As a result of the Directive a new agreement between the
Minister and the Motor Insurers Bureau of Ireland was entered into
on 21 December 1988 and it replaced the agreement existing since
1964. SI no. 321 of 1987, which implemented the Directive, provides
that a third party victim of a road accident, where the driver of an
insured vehicle did not have the consent of a named person, or the
driver did not hold a valid driver's licence, would be able to recover
from the motor insurers, but could not do so where the claim arose
out of the negligent use in a public place of a vehicle which had been
stolen or obtained by violence or taken and used without lawful
authority.[12] Such claims will be recoverable from the Motor Insurers
Bureau, subject to certain conditions. Ireland obtained derogation
from the directive until the 31 December 1992 in so far as it related to
compulsory insurance for property damage.

8.2.3 PROPOSED DIRECTIVES

The stated objectives of all directives emanating from the European
Commission is to achieve harmonisation of the law throughout all
member states. The traditional view of motor insurance in Ireland
and the UK has been that insurance attaches to the driver rather
than the vehicle. This contrasts with the European view that it is the
vehicle rather than the driver which is insured. The European
Commission has been working on proposals to extend the protection
afforded to victims of motor accidents and is concerned with the

---

[11] Article 2.1 ibid.

[12] Article 4 of SI no. 321 of 1987.

problems facing an EU national involved in an accident in another member state required to bring proceedings in that state. There is no harmonisation of the procedures to be completed to sustain an action against insurers in such circumstances. Most, but not all, member states require the injured party to obtain a judgment against the driver of the vehicle causing the injury and for that judgment to remain unsatisfied for seven days before the insurer becomes liable. The European Commission is of the view that this requirement imposes a substantial and unnecessary obstacle on the EU national visiting another member state. The solution proposed by the Commission is to remove the need for a judgment to be obtained and the introduction of direct action against the insurers. The proposed directive will also provide for the appointment by insurers of a claims representative in every member state in which the insurer does not have an establishment, and who will be empowered to collect all the necessary information from the victim and settle the claim in the victim's home state. The appointment of such claims representatives will not entitle the victim to proceed against the insurer in the victim's home state. Any necessary proceedings must be taken in the state where the accident occurred.

8.2.4 EXTENSION OF COMPULSORY INSURANCE

The Third Council Directive on Motor Insurance required all member states to pass implementing legislation extending compulsory insurance to all passengers, other than the driver, arising out of the use of a vehicle[13] and to ensure that all compulsory insurance policies cover, on the basis of a single premium, the entire territory of the Community.[14] Ireland obtained derogation until 1996 in respect of the extension of cover to the entire Community and until 1998 in respect of compulsory insurance of pillion passengers on motor cycles.[15]

---

[13] 90/232/EEC, Article 1, implemented in Ireland by SI no. 346 of 1992.

[14] Article 2 ibid.

[15] Article 6.2 ibid.

8.3 EXTENT OF COMPULSORY INSURANCE

8.3.1 CONDITIONS

The full extent of insurance cover required by the Act of 1961 is not specified completely in the Act but is set out in secondary legislation.[16] Section 56 of the Act requires the existence of "an approved policy of insurance" covering the liabilities specified, and Section 62(1) provides that a policy of insurance shall be an "approved policy of insurance" if it complies with the following conditions:

a) it is issued by a vehicle insurer to a named person;

b) the insurer by whom it is issued binds himself by it to insure the named person (the Insured) against all sums without limit which the insured or his personal representatives shall become liable to pay to any person (exclusive of excepted persons) whether by way of damages or costs on account of injury to person or property caused by the negligent use of a mechanically propelled vehicle to which the policy applies;

c) the liability of the insurer under the policy is not subject to any condition, restriction or limitation prescribed as not to be inserted in an approved policy of insurance and

d) the period of cover is not capable of being terminated before its expiration by effluxion of time by the insurer except with the consent of the insured or after seven days notice in writing to the insured.[17]

8.3.2 LIMITATION OF LIABILITY

Section 62(2) permits the insertion of provisions additional to and not inconsistent with the specified conditions for an "approved policy". Section 62(3) permits the limitation of liability for injury to property to £1,000 in respect of any one act of negligence and the exclusion of liability in excess of common law or statutory liability undertaken by the insured under contract. The limit of £1,000 in respect of damage

---

[16] Principally SI no. 14 of 1962 and those statutory instruments enacted implementing the EU Directives.

[17] Similar conditions applied to approved guarantees but the acceptability of such guarantees was abolished by Section 53 of the 1968 Act.

to property has now been increased to £90,000 by The European Communities (Road Traffic) (Compulsory Insurance) (Amendment) Regulations, 1995.[18]

8.3.3 EXCEPTED PERSONS

The excepted persons referred to in (b) above are defined in Section 65 of the Act. The definition includes:

a) persons claiming in respect of injuries sustained whilst in or on a mechanically propelled vehicle of a class specified by the Minister;

b) persons claiming in respect of damage to property conveyed in the vehicle;

c) persons claiming in respect of damage to property while the property was owned by or was in the possession, custody or control of the insured;

d) persons claiming in respect of damage to weigh bridges or any road or anything in or below the surface of the road due to the weight of or vibration caused by the mechanically propelled vehicle;

e) persons claiming in respect of damage to property due to explosion of a boiler forming part of the vehicle or due to sparks or ashes proceeding from the vehicle;

f) persons claiming in respect of personal injury sustained and caused by or arising out of their employment by the insured.

8.3.4 LIABILITY TO PASSENGERS

The class of vehicle, in respect of which liability to passengers was permitted to be excluded by the Act, was specified in the Road Traffic (Compulsory Insurance) Regulations, 1962 as:

a) public service vehicles;

---

[18] SI no. 353 of 1995, Section 3(2)(a). In practice insurers in Ireland did not apply the original limit to approved private motor policies. Unlimited Indemnity was and is provided for personal injury and property damage. In the case of commercial vehicle or special type policies a limit of £10,000 was specified in the Act but this has now been increased to £90,000. Most Insurers provide indemnity for much higher limits as part of their standard cover.

b) vehicles constructed primarily for the carriage of one or more pas-
    sengers;

c) station wagons, estate cars and other similar vehicles constructed
    or adapted for alternative purposes which are fitted with seats.[19]

The Road Traffic (Compulsory Insurance) (Amendment) Regulations,
1992[20] which implemented the provisions of the Third Council Directive[21] extend cover to the remaining principal category of passengers
not covered by compulsory insurance, i.e. those carried on commercial
vehicles and motor cycles designed and constructed with seating accommodation for passengers.[22]

8.3.5 DEFINITION OF "IN OR ON"

Section 65 of the Act contains a special definition clause, Subsection
2, which provides that reference to injury sustained while "in or on a
vehicle" includes "injury while entering, getting onto, being put into
or on, alighting from, or being taken out of or off, the vehicle, and injury caused by being thrown out of or off the vehicle". In *Kenny v Motor Insurers Bureau of Ireland*[23] Costello J. held injuries sustained
when the wheels of a vehicle rolled over a boy, thrown off the vehicle,
constituted injuries sustained "by being thrown off" a vehicle and so
constituted injuries sustained whilst "in or on" a vehicle within the
meaning of Section 65. The boy had been travelling in the rear of an
open flat-bodied truck and was an "excepted person" within the
meaning of the Act, at the time, and in respect of whom there was no
obligation to insure. However, an appeal to the Supreme Court[24] overturned the High Court decision and ruled that the plaintiff was not

---

[19] Section 6.1 of SI no. 14 of 1962. In *Cunningham* v *Thornton*, Unreported High
Court, 21 July 1972, it was held that where there are two constructions that
could be put on the words "constructed primarily for", that in favour of the plaintiff should succeed.

[20] SI no. 346 of 1962.

[21] 90/232/EEC of 14 May 1990.

[22] The Regulations became effective 31 December 1995 in respect of passengers in
commercial type vehicles and 31 December 1998 for passengers on pillion seats or
in sidecars of motor cycles.

[23] *Kenny* v *MIBI* [1991] IR 441.

[24] Unreported SC, 3 April 1995.

an "excepted person" when he sustained the injuries. The court accepted that when the plaintiff was thrown from the truck, he was an excepted person, but that he ceased to be so once he fell to the ground, and was not an "excepted person" when the wheels of the truck went over him and caused his injuries.

8.3.6 "HIRE OR REWARD"

Prior to the passing of the 1961 Act it was not compulsory to insure in respect of liability to passengers unless they were carried for hire and reward or by reason of or in pursuit of a contract of employment.[25] The words "hire or reward" were not defined and caused some difficulty in relation to car sharing arrangements between employees travelling to and from their place of employment. In *Albert* v *Motor Insurers Bureau*,[26] the House of Lords decided that the words should be given a narrow meaning and only apply where the passengers were being carried under some form of legally binding and enforceable contract. The policy issued in respect of a private car will normally exclude use for hire or reward and to overcome the difficulties in relation to the common practice of car-sharing, most insurance companies now endorse their private car policies to the effect that:

> the receipt of contributions as part of a car-sharing arrangement for social or other similar purposes in respect of the carriage of passengers on a journey in the insured vehicle will not be regarded as constituting the carriage of passengers for hire or reward or the use of the vehicle for hiring provided that (a) the vehicle is not constructed or adapted to carry more than eight passengers excluding the driver; (b) the passengers are not being carried in the course of a business of carrying passengers; (c) the total contributions received for the journey relate solely to the cost of fuel and do not involve an element of profit.

8.3.7 CONTRIBUTORY NEGLIGENCE

The extension of compulsory insurance to all passengers in or on mechanically propelled vehicles, other than vehicles not generally designed or constructed to carry passengers, does not however provide

---

[25] Section 66(1), Road Traffic Act, 1933.

[26] [1972] AC 301.

complete protection in all circumstances. The defence of contributory negligence remains available to the driver and his insurers and where for instance the passenger has failed to wear a safety belt, the courts have had no hesitation in reducing the damages payable.[27] It is also possible that public policy may prevent a passenger from proceeding against the driver or the insurer in circumstances where both the driver and the passenger are engaged in a common illegal purpose.[28] In *Pitts* v *Hunt*,[29] the plaintiff and the defendant spent an evening drinking at a disco before going home on the defendant's motor-cycle with the plaintiff travelling as pillion passenger. The plaintiff knew that the defendant was neither licensed nor insured to drive the motor-cycle. The defendant, encouraged by the plaintiff, drove in a fast and reckless manner deliberately intending to frighten members of the public. The motor-cycle collided with a motor car, the plaintiff was seriously injured and his friend was killed. The plaintiff brought an action against the defendant's estate which was dismissed, at first instance, on the grounds *ex turpi causa non oritur actio*, i.e. a court will not lend its aid to a person whose cause of action is founded on an illegal or immoral act. The Court of Appeal held that if a driver and passenger of a motor vehicle jointly commit an offence or series of offences so serious that the driver is precluded on grounds of public policy from claiming indemnity under a policy of insurance, required to be effected by the Road Traffic Acts, the same public policy would preclude the passenger from claiming compensation if he is jointly guilty of that offence. Since the plaintiff had played a full and active part in encouraging the driver to commit offences, which amounted to a dangerous act, the plaintiff ought not to be permitted to recover for the injuries he had sustained and public policy precluded the court from finding that the driver owed any duty of care to the plaintiff.

---

[27] *Sinnott* v *Quinnsworth Ltd.* [1984] ILRM 522; *Conley* v *Strain* [1988] IR 628.

[28] In *Ashton* v *Turner* [1981] QB 137, the court refused to allow the passenger in a "getaway car" to sue the driver and fellow participant in a bank raid, for negligent driving while trying to escape from the police.

[29] [1990] 3 All ER 344.

8.3.8 INJURY TO EMPLOYEES

A further consequence of the extension of cover to all passengers is that liability for injury to employees arising from the use of motor vehicles is now transferred from the Employers' Liability policy to the Motor policy of the employer, provided the employee passenger is conveyed on fixed seating.[30] The regulations provide that for purposes of Section 65(2) of the Act "seating accommodation for passengers" means, in the case of a vehicle, a fixed or folding seat permanently and securely installed in or on the vehicle. Motor insurance policies are now endorsed to the effect that insurers shall not be liable except so far as is necessary to meet the requirements of the Road Traffic Acts in respect of injury to persons in the employment of the insured or of any person claiming to be indemnified under the policy when such injury arises out of and in the course of such employment.

8.4 STATUTORY DEFINITIONS

Section 3 of the Road Traffic Act, 1961 and the various regulations made under the Act contain many definitions, only some of which are relevant here.

8.4.1 USE

8.4.1.1 "Use", in relation to a vehicle, includes park, and cognate words shall be construed accordingly.[31] "Park" means keep or leave stationary.[32] "Use" means "to have the use of" and the owner of a bro-

---

[30] Employers' Liability policies now contain a standard exclusion to the effect that the policy does "not apply to liability for which compulsory insurance is required under any Road Traffic Act legislation". Motor policies generally excluded liability "in respect of death of or bodily injury to any person arising out of or in the course of such person's employment by the person claiming to be indemnified". In the Supreme Court, in *Zurich* v *Shield* [1988] IR 174 McCarthy J. at 185 expressed the view that such a clause was "clearly in breach of the prohibited conditions provisions of the RTA 1961" even though its effect was avoided by the policy provision requiring the insured to reimburse the insurer any amounts paid by the insurer by virtue of the provisions of the RTA and which it would not otherwise have had to pay.

[31] Section 3(1) Road Traffic Act, 1961. "Use" is the verb used throughout the Act whereas the 1933 Act referred to "drive".

[32] ibid.

ken down car left on the street may therefore be deemed to "use" it,[33] but an unlicensed car, parked on the public highway was not proof of "use" and its mere presence was not proof that it was a mechanically propelled vehicle.[34] A vehicle towed and steered is also in "use",[35] as is a vehicle stationary on the road for the purposes of loading or unloading.[36] The Court of Appeal in *Dunthorne* v *Bentley*,[37] recently decided that an insurance policy covering a woman against liability "caused by or arising out of use" of her vehicle, should provide indemnity, when her estate and her insurers were sued by the driver of a vehicle seriously injured when she ran into the path of his car, when dashing across the road to talk to a colleague. Her car had run out of petrol ten minutes earlier on a major road. The insurers contended that as the woman had parked her car safely and properly sometime before the accident it could not be said that the accident had arisen out of her use of the car. The Court of Appeal, however, held that the doctrine of causation did not apply and that motive was a relevant factor. The question was whether the woman was on the road for a reason arising out of her use of the car.[38] Some motor insurance policies issued in Ireland have the exact same wording although some policies refer to "injury or damage arising out of an accident caused by or in connection with the insured vehicle". The decision of the Court of Appeal would probably have been the same even if the alternative wording had applied, as the woman's decision to cross the road was

---

[33] *Elliott* v *Gray* [1960] 1 QB 367. "Use" means "have the use of " and the owner of a broken down car left in the street may therefore "use" it, per Lord Parker at 372. In *Williams* v *Jones* [1975] RTR 433, a vehicle jacked up with its wheels and battery removed was held to be "in use" as a mechanically propelled vehicle and liable to be insured, but in *Thomas* v *Hooper* [1986] RTR 1 it was held that the user must have some control, management or operation of the vehicle as a vehicle and that there is no "use" of a totally immovable vehicle whose wheels will not turn.

[34] *A-G (O'Gara)* v *Cunningham* [1949] 84 ILTR 76.

[35] *Milstead* v *Sexton* [1964] Crim LR 474.

[36] *Andrews* v *Kershaw* [1951] 2 All ER 765.

[37] *Dunthorne* v *Bentley* [1996] *The Times*, 11 March 1996.

[38] In the Australian Case of *Dickinson* v *Motor Vehicle Insurance Trust* [1987] 163 CLR 500 the driver left his two children in his car whilst he went into a shop. The children, playing with some matches which they found in the car, set fire to it, causing them to receive serious burn injuries. It was held that the loss arose out of the use of the car even though it had not been caused by the use of the car.

undoubtedly "connected" with her vehicle. The decision, if followed in Ireland, would seem to extend the liability of motor insurers beyond that which they might previously have understood it to be.[39]

8.4.2 CONSENT

8.4.2.1 At common law, the owner of a motor vehicle is liable for the negligence of the person driving it if that person is the servant acting in the course of his employment by the owner, or if that person is his agent. The driver is regarded as the owner's agent when the driver, with the owner's consent, is driving the vehicle on the owner's business or for the owner's purposes. Mere consent by the owner of the vehicle to another person driving does not make the driver the servant or agent of the owner.[40] In Ireland, the law was changed when insurance against negligence in the driving of a motor vehicle was made compulsory in 1933 and now a vehicle owner may be held liable for injury or damage to property caused through the negligent use of the vehicle by someone other than himself.[41] Section 118 of the Road Traffic Act, 1961 states:

> Where a person (in this section referred to as the user) uses a mechanically propelled vehicle with the consent of the owner of the vehicle, the user shall, for the purpose of determining the liability or non-liability of the owner for injury caused by the negligent use of the vehicle by the user, and for the purposes of determining the liability or non-liability of any other person for injury to the vehicle or persons or property therein caused by negligence occurring while the vehicle is being used by the user, be deemed to use the vehicle as the servant of the owner,

---

[39] Would insurers be expected to indemnify the driver of a vehicle who accidentally injures another customer whilst in the forecourt shop of a filling station paying for petrol?

[40] *Hewitt* v *Bonnin* [194] 1 KB 188; *Ormrodd* v *Crossville Motor Services Ltd.* [1953] 1 WLR 1120.

[41] In England, a claim of liability in such circumstances would be based on the common law principles of vicarious liability arising out of the relationship of master and servant or principal and agent.

but only in so far as the user acts in accordance with the terms of such consent.[42]

However, a limited liability company as owner of a vehicle cannot incur liability as user of the vehicle except on the principle of vicarious liability for the driver and the owner whose liability is vicarious only would be entitled in all cases of negligent driving to full indemnity from the driver.[43]

8.4.2.2 Critical to the operation of the Section is the requirement that the vehicle be used with the consent of the owner. Unlike Section 172 of the 1933 Act which it replaced, the Section does not specify if expressed or implied consent is necessary, but the Supreme Court, in *Buckley* v *Musgrave Brook Bond Ltd.*,[44] stated that the omission from the Section was of no significance as "the consent referred to . . . may be either an express consent or a consent to be implied from the circumstances".[45] A lorry driver, employed by an associate company of the defendants, borrowed a vehicle from the defendants to enable him travel home from Dublin to Cork one Saturday. He undertook to return the vehicle to Dublin by Monday morning at the latest. The vehicle was involved in an accident in Cork on the Sunday evening. The driver was killed and the plaintiff who was a passenger in the vehicle was seriously injured. At the hearing of the action, the defendants successfully applied to have the case withdrawn from the jury on the grounds that there was no proof of consent to use by the driver, at the time of the accident. The Supreme Court allowed the plaintiff's appeal and directed a new trial.

8.4.2.3 Consent of the owner obtained by false pretences is vitiated by the fraud of the driver and the owner is not liable for the negli-

---

[42] This statutory extension of the principle of vicarious liability is clearly intended to widen the protection afforded to victims of road accidents. The Section differs significantly from Section 172 of the Road Traffic Act, 1933 which it replaced and which referred to "driving" as distinct from "use".

[43] *Zurich Insurance Co. Ltd.* v *Shield Insurance Co. Ltd.* [1988] IR 174 at 179, 180.

[44] [1969] IR 440.

[45] ibid at 448 per O'Dalaigh C. J.

gence of the driver.[46] Consent can be implied depending on the relevant circumstances,[47] and where the owner has refused consent a waiver of prohibition may also be implied by the circumstances.[48] Where, however, consent has in the past been adamantly refused, consent is unlikely to be implied,[49] even if the borrowing is for a purpose of benefit to the owner.[50] In other circumstances, use for a purpose of benefit to the owner may result in consent being implied even where such use is not the primary object of the borrowing.[51] Where the principal object of the borrowing is a use for a purpose of benefit to the owner it is possible to justify an implied consent,[52] but the statutory provision does not require that the driver's purpose should benefit the owner; it is enough that the driving or use has been consented to. Any withdrawal of consent must be shown to have been effectively communicated before the owner can rely on it.[53]

8.4.2.4 Where consent is given subject to terms which limit the use or the particular purpose, use for any other purpose is outside the terms of the consent.[54] In the Supreme Court, in *Homan* v *Kiernan & Lombard & Ulster Banking Ltd.*[55] it was held that the failure of the lessee to insure the vehicle, as required by the terms of the leasing agreement, did not vitiate the consent of the lessor, given to the lessee to drive the vehicle, and the lessor was liable to the plaintiff for

---

[46] *Kelly* v *Lombard Motor Company Ltd.* [1974] IR 142. In a criminal case, *Whittaker* v *Campbell* [1983] 3 All ER 582, the High Court quashed a conviction under the Theft Act 1968, Section 12(1) where the appellant, who did not hold a licence, hired a vehicle on the strength of a licence he had found. The Court held the hirer had given his consent to the hiring even though the consent had been obtained by fraudulent misrepresentation and that therefore no crime had been committed.

[47] *Beechinor* v *O'Connor* [1939] Ir Jur Rep 5.

[48] *Coogan* v *Dublin Motor Co.* [1915] 49 ILTR 24; *Maher* v *Great Northern Railway Co. and Warren* [1942] IR 206.

[49] *Gibson* v *Keeney* [1928] NI 66 CA; a car was borrowed against the wishes of an adamant mother.

[50] *Kiernan* v *Ingram* [1931] IR 119.

[51] *Dowling* v *Robinson* [1909] 43 ILTR 210.

[52] *Thompson* v *Reynolds* [1926] NI 131.

[53] *O'Connor* v *Minister for Finance and Mullen* [1945] Ir Jur Rep 18.

[54] *Mulligan* v *Daly* [1939] 73 ILTR 34.

[55] Unreported Supreme Court, 22 November 1996.

injuries sustained by the negligent use of the uninsured vehicle by the lessee. Consent can be given limited in time, or geographically, or as to purpose.[56] In *Browning* v *Phoenix Assurance Co. Ltd.*[57] a car owner left his car into a garage for some maintenance work to be carried out on it and authorised the mechanic to use it for his social and domestic purposes prior to carrying out the work, as such use would facilitate the work necessary. The mechanic had an accident whilst using the vehicle for social purposes after the work had been completed, and the court held that his use of the vehicle was outside the terms of his consent so that the insurers were not liable.

8.4.2.5 Difficulties can arise in establishing compliance with the terms of consent governing the use of company vehicles in the custody or control of employees[58] unless very precisely formulated rules govern the times and occasions when the vehicle may be used, the purposes for which it may be used and by whom it may be used. In *Kiely* v *McCrea*,[59] a commercial traveller, provided with a company car which was not to be used for private purposes, was involved in an accident whilst using the car to drive fellow employees to a social function. His terms of employment required him to "use his best endeavours to effect the sale of the company's goods". The Circuit Court Judge accepted the submission that his presence at the function was calculated to promote the sale of the goods of the company and that he was acting in the best interests of the company and for the legitimate purposes of the company's business. The High Court disagreed, with Hanna J. stating he "could not possibly accept the submission that he was on his firm's business. In essence, it was a private journey . . . upon which he took his friends." Where someone other than the owner gives consent to the use of the vehicle, the owner will not be liable unless it can be proved that the person giving the consent

---

[56] *Singh* v *Rathour* [1988] All ER 16.

[57] [1960] 2 Lloyds Rep 360.

[58] *Buckley* v *Musgrave Brook Bond Ltd.* [1969] IR 440.

[59] [1940] Ir Jur Rep 1.

was at the time acting as the agent of the owner and had authority to give consent.[60]

8.4.3 PUBLIC PLACE
8.4.3.1 Irish Law

"Public place" means any street, road or other place to which the public have access with vehicles whether as of right or by permission and whether subject to or free of charge.[61] In *Stanbridge* v *Healy*[62] the grounds of a country house were held not to be a public place on the basis that the words "the public" mean the public generally and not the special class of members of the public who had occasion for business or social purposes to traverse a private roadway leading to the house.[63] Grafton Street in Dublin was held not to be a public place when pedestrianised and closed to traffic during certain times of the day.[64] "Whether a place is a 'public place' or not largely depends on the facts of any particular case."[65] In *Lynch* v *New PMPA Insurance Co. Ltd.*[66] Costello J. held that a car park at the factory where the plaintiff was employed was a public place within the meaning of the Act. The car park was used by employees of the factory as well as by suppliers to the factory and customers of the factory who included not just persons with whom the factory had contracts to supply meat products but also members of the public who drove in to buy the factory's products. In addition, the factory was situated near a football ground and on a regular basis used by members of the public attending matches there. Farmers attending the local mart also used the car park. At the time of the accident there were no boundary walls between the factory and the roadway and there were no gates at the

---

[60] *Kett* v *Shannon* [1987] ILRM 364; *Armagas Ltd.* v *Mandogas SA* [1985] 3 All ER 795.

[61] Section 31, Road Traffic Act, 1961. Section 22 of the Air Navigation and Transport Act, 1950 declares a state aerodrome as being a public place for the purpose of any enactment.

[62] [1985] ILRM 290.

[63] ibid per Murphy J.

[64] *DPP* v *Molloy* [1993] Unreported High Court, 3 March 1993.

[65] per Costello J. in *Lynch* v *New PMPA Insurance Co. Ltd.* [1995] Unreported High Court, 13 October 1995.

[66] ibid.

entrance to the metalled roadway leading to the factory carpark. There were no notices restricting entry and no gatemen employed. In the circumstances, Costello J. had no difficulty in holding that the carpark was a public place.[67] In a recent *ex tempore* judgment in the Supreme Court, in *Richards* v *Dublin Corporation and the MIBI*,[68] a park used by cyclists, with the permission of the Corporation, was held to be a public place for the purposes of the RTA. The plaintiff, while cycling through the park was injured by a motor-cyclist who disappeared without trace. The MIBI objected to being joined in the action claiming that the park was not a public place. The Court held that pedal cyclists were unquestionably using the park with the permission of the Corporation, and as the Corporation had failed to pass bye-laws or put up notices prohibiting motorcyclists from the park, there was a form of implied permission allowing motorcyclists to have access to the park. The park was therefore a public place.

8.4.3.2 English Law

The situation is different in England, where Section 196(1) of the Road Traffic Act, 1988 defines a "road" as "any highway and any other road to which the public has access and including bridges over which a road passes". A car park to which the public has access without charge had been held not to be a road,[69] and likewise a school driveway.[70] The criteria applied in that jurisdiction had been the existence of a definable route between two points and whether the public had access to it.[71] However, the definition has been the subject of two

---

[67] A second issue arising in the case was whether the plaintiff, who had parked the vehicle and walked away from it shortly before being injured by it, was "the person driving or in charge for the purpose of driving" within the terms of the insurance policy. The plaintiff had been lent the vehicle by her father and whilst she was therefore, as the borrower, in charge of the vehicle in the general sense, Costello J. interpreted the policy wording as intended to exclude liability to a person claiming in respect of injury sustained while physically driving the vehicle at the time of the accident or who was in charge physically of the vehicle for the purpose of driving it when the accident occurred. A person who had left the vehicle was no longer physically in charge of it for the purpose of driving it.

[68] Supreme Court, 12 June 1996.

[69] *Griffin* v *Squires* [1958] 1 WLR 1106

[70] *Randal* v *MIB* [1968] 1 WLR 1200; *Buchanan* v *MIB* [1955] 1 WLR 488.

[71] *Oxford* v *Austin* [1981] RTR 416; *McGurk and Dale* v *Coster* [1995] 10 CL 521; *Severn Trent Water Authority* v *Williams* [1955] 10 CL 638.

recent decisions by the Court of Appeal. In *Clarke* v *Kato*,[72] the plaintiff had been walking through a car park when she was struck by a car driven by the defendant. The defendant was uninsured and the plaintiff issued proceedings against the driver and the Motor Insurers Bureau. To succeed against the MIB it was necessary to establish that the accident had occurred on a "road". Within the car park, there was a pedestrian walkway, and the plaintiff was on that walkway when the accident occurred. The Court of Appeal was of the view that the question to be decided was whether all or any of the car park was to be considered a "road". The court held that the evidence proved that the walkway was regularly used by members of the public and that it was a definable route for pedestrian traffic. The walkway was therefore a "road" and the MIB were liable to indemnify the plaintiff. The Court did not determine that the car park as a whole was a "road", only that a public walkway through a car park is a "road". In *Cutter* v *Eagle Star*,[73] the plaintiff had been a passenger in a car parked in a multi-storey car park. While the car was parked, a container of lighter fuel, in the car, had been leaking inflammable gas. On re-entering the car the driver lit a cigarette and the plaintiff was seriously injured by the ensuing ignition. The plaintiff had obtained a judgment against the driver but the judgment remained unsatisfied. He then sought to have the judgment enforced against insurers of the vehicle. Insurers argued that the accident had not occurred on a "road" and that they were therefore not liable as the policy covered statutory liability only. The Court held that the question to be addressed was whether within the car park there was a roadway marked out for the passage of vehicles, and if there was, the fact that the roadway was used to obtain access to a parking place rather than to some destination could not prevent it from being a "road" within the meaning of the Act.

8.4.4 MECHANICALLY PROPELLED VEHICLE

8.4.4.1 Section 3(1) of the 1961 Act defines a mechanically propelled vehicle as a vehicle intended or adapted for propulsion by mechanical (including electrical or partly electrical) means, including:

---

[72] Unreported, 10 December 1996.

[73] Unreported, 2 December 1996.

a) a bicycle or tricycle with an attachment for propelling it by mechanical power, whether or not the attachment is being used;

b) a vehicle the means for propulsion of which is electrical or partly electrical and partly mechanical, but not including a tram car or other vehicle running on permanent rails.

8.4.4.2 "Vehicle" is not defined in the Acts, but "pedestrian controlled vehicle", "public service vehicles" and "street service vehicles" are defined in terms related to their use. In *Fallon* v *Ferns*[74] it was held that there was no doubt that "vehicle" includes a motor vehicle. A vehicle substantially disabled (by accident, breakdown or the removal of the engine or vital part) so that it is no longer capable of being propelled mechanically is exempt from being a "mechanically propelled vehicle" by Section 3(1) of the Act. If there is no reasonable prospect of it being made mobile again it is no longer a mechanically propelled vehicle,[75] but a vehicle without its propulsive unit may be a mechanically propelled vehicle within the Act if there is a reasonable prospect of it being made mobile again.[76] A vehicle with no engine or gear box is not a mechanically propelled vehicle,[77] but a car with a flat battery is.[78] A moped is a mechanically propelled vehicle, even if being pedalled,[79] but not if vital parts have been removed.[80] In *Symington* v *McMaster*[81] a motorised tricycle, known as a "fun bike", intended for sport or amusement over rough terrain, and not suitable for use on the road, as it lacked a horn and traffic indicators, was held not to come within

---

[74] Unreported High Court, 13 July 1962. It was held that there is no doubt that "vehicle" includes motor vehicle; it is not necessary to define every important word in a statute and in the absence of such definition, the word must be read in accordance with the usual canons of interpretation.

[75] *Smart* v *Allen* [1963] 1 QB 289. In *Bink* v *Dept. of the Environment* [1975] RTR 318, it was stated that the test to be followed was whether the vehicle had reached a stage that it could be said that there was no reasonable prospect of it ever being mobile again.

[76] *Newberry* v *Simmonds* [1961] 2 QB 345.

[77] *Reader* v *Bunyard* [1987] 85 Crim App Rep 185.

[78] *R* v *Paul* [1952] NI 61.

[79] *Floyd* v *Brush* [1953] 1 All ER 265.

[80] *Lawrence* v *Howlett* [1952] 2 All ER 74.

[81] [1985] NI 293.

the statutory definition, as there was no evidence which could justify the conclusion that the bike was intended by anyone or adapted in any sense of the word for use on the road. "Adapted" has been held to mean some amount of alteration to the original construction, either initially or later,[82] but the fitting of rails to a vehicle to accommodate the carriage of goods in such a way as permitted the carriage of passengers when goods were not being carried did not amount to adaptation.[83]

8.4.4.3 Trailers

The European Communities (Road Traffic) (Compulsory Insurance) (Amendment) Regulations, 1992 amended Subsection 9 of Section 56 of the Act so that the definition of mechanically propelled vehicle was extended to include "a semi-trailer or trailer (whether coupled or uncoupled to a mechanically propelled vehicle) used in a public place".[84] As a result of the amendment all trailers (including semi-trailers and caravans) used in a public place, e.g. a car park, or public road, must be covered by third party insurance. The cover must apply to the trailer whilst it is being towed by a mechanically propelled vehicle and when it is uncoupled and parked in a public place. Whilst most private car policies automatically include cover in respect of a trailer whilst being towed it is now necessary to have such policies extended to provide cover whilst the trailer is uncoupled and parked in a public place.[85] The Directive did not define "Trailer" but the Department of the Environment has chosen to interpret the word in its widest sense. The requirement of compulsory insurance now applies to all types of trailers, from articulated heavy industrial trailers to the small two-wheel car trailer, and cover previously provided by non-motor policies is no longer operative. A recently negotiated agreement between in-

---

[82] *Madden* v *Starer* [1962] 1 All ER 831.

[83] *Taylor* v *Meade* [1961] All ER 426.

[84] Article 5(1) of SI no. 347 of 1972. The instrument came into effect on 1 January 1993 but it was sometime before the insurance industry or the Department of the Environment appreciated its implications in so far as its provisions relating to trailers were concerned.

[85] It has always been necessary to make special provision for insurance of trailers under commercial vehicle policies but insurance cover is not compulsory in respect of the detached risk in respect of all trailers parked in a public place.

surers and intermediaries now provides that all private car policies issued by members of the Irish Insurers Federation will automatically provide indemnity for liability in respect of trailers detached from the towing vehicle without the necessity of notifying insurers. The agreement applies in respect of any single-axle trailer up to one-half tonne unladen weight excluding caravans, mobile homes, trailer tents, boat trailers and any trailer which incorporates machinery or other equipment. Trailers used with commercial vehicles will need to be notified to insurers before cover will operate.

8.4.5 VEHICLE INSURER

8.4.5.1 Section 58 of the 1961 Act defined "vehicle insurer" but the definition has been amended by the European Communities (Road Traffic) (Compulsory Insurance) (Amendment) Regulations, 1992[86] so that it now means:

a) an undertaking within the meaning of Article 2(1) of the EC (Non-life Insurance) Regulations, 1976[87] as amended by Article 4 of The European Communities (Non-life Insurance) (Amendment) (No. 2) Regulations, 1991[88] which carries on a class 10 mechanically propelled vehicle insurance business in the State; or

b) a syndicate, within the meaning of Section 3 of the Companies Act of 1963 carrying on that business in the State.

8.4.5.2 Article 9 of Statutory Instrument no. 347 of 1992 replaces Section 78 of the 1961 Act and provides that a person "shall not carry on a class 10 mechanically propelled vehicle insurance business in the State unless he is a member of the Bureau" (the Bureau meaning the Motor Insurers Bureau of Ireland).

8.4.5.3 Exempted Persons

There is provision, under the Acts, to exempt certain persons from the compulsory insurance requirements. Such exempted persons were defined in Section 60 and referred to in Sections 61 and 78 of the

---

[86] Article 6 of SI no. 347 of 1992.

[87] SI no. 115 of 1976.

[88] SI no. 142 of 1991.

1961 Act. Sections 54 and 55 of the Road Traffic Act, 1968 amended[89] the requirements to be met in order to become an "exempt person" so that in effect only "State Sponsored Bodies" may now be exempted persons under the Acts. To qualify as an exempt person the body must:

a) be either:

    (i)   a board or other body established by an act of the Oireachtas; or

    (ii) a State sponsored body or company within the meaning of Section 2 of the Companies Act, 1963; or

    (iii) a company within the meaning of Section 2 of the Companies Act, 1963 in which the majority of shares are held by a State sponsored body or company;

    in respect of which the Minister has issued a certificate that it is an exempt person for the purposes of the Road Traffic Acts;

b) pay a deposit to the account of the High Court where required by the Minister;

c) give to the Motor Insurers Bureau of Ireland an undertaking to deal with third party claims in respect of its vehicles on terms similar to those agreed between the Minister and the Bureau.

Some "exempted persons" covered for specific agreements are: Coras Iompair Éireann, Bus Atha Cliath, Bus Éireann, Iarnrod Éireann, Telecom Éireann and Coillte Teoranta.

8.4.5.4 Exempted Vehicles

As well as providing for "exempted persons", the Acts also exempt certain vehicles. Section 4(2) of the 1961 Act provides that the compulsory insurance provisions of the Acts do not apply to:

---

[89] The 1968 Act inserted new Sections 60 and 61 into the 1961 Act which were brought into operation on 26 October 1970 by SI no. 244 of 1970.

a) a vehicle owned by the State, or a person using such a vehicle in the course of his employment;[90]

b) a vehicle seized by a State servant in the course of his duty or used in the course of his employment[91]

c) a Garda or officer of any Minister using a vehicle for the purposes of tests, removal, or disposition under the Road Traffic Acts or regulations thereunder.

8.4.6 "IN FORCE"

There is no definition in the Acts of what is meant by "in force" and difficulties can arise in determining whether a policy issued by a motor insurer is operative at the material time. In *O'Leary* v *Irish National Insurance Co. Ltd.*[92] the injured third party was not allowed proceed against the insurer as it was held that a valid policy did not exist. Budd J. held that

> if a person purports to effect a policy of insurance in respect of a motor vehicle of which he is not the owner, it being represented to or understood by the insurers that he is in fact the owner, no valid contract of insurance comes into operation. The absence of a valid contract of insurance between the proposer and the insurer enables the insurer to rely upon the invalidity of the policy in order to escape liability thereon, notwithstanding the provisions of the Road Traffic Acts.

---

[90] An employee of the Government who uses a State-owned vehicle for purposes other than the public service without insurance is guilty of an offence under the Act; *Salt* v *McKnight* [1947] SC (J) 99. Section 59 of the Civil Liability Act, 1961 repealed and replaced section 118 of the 1961 Road Traffic Act and makes the State liable for the negligent use of its vehicles.

[91] A policeman driving his car without insurance while on police duty was successful in the appeal against his conviction; *Jones* v *County Council of Bedfordshire* [1978] Crim LR 502.

[92] *O'Leary* v *Irish National Insurance Co. Ltd.* [1958] Ir Jur Rep 1. The plaintiff had been injured in an accident with a motor car insured with the defendant insurer under a policy effected by the father of the driver. The vehicle was at all times the property of the son but the father in effecting cover had declared that the vehicle belonged to him. The policy of insurance indemnified anyone driving with the insured's permission provided he held a licence to drive. As the policyholder did not own the vehicle he could not give permission to anyone to drive the vehicle. The policyholder had no insurable interest in the vehicle and the policy was therefore invalid.

When the vehicle which is the subject matter of the policy is sold, the owner's rights in respect of it cease and the policy is at an end. Cover does not extend to a vehicle being used instead of the insured vehicle.[93] Where the insured parts with the car, the subject of the insurance policy, he ceases to have the benefit of an extension indemnifying him whilst driving another car not owned by him despite the fact that he may not have cancelled the policy on parting with the original car.[94]

8.4.7 "APPROVED POLICY OF INSURANCE"

8.4.7.1 One of the requirements[95] to qualify as an "approved policy of insurance" under Section 62 of the 1961 Act, as amended,[96] is that the policy must not contain any condition, restriction or limitation prohibited by Ministerial regulations. The terms and conditions which are prohibited are set out in the First Schedule of the Road Traffic

---

[93] Per Lord Buckmaster in *Rogerson* v *Scottish Automobile and General Insurance Co. Ltd.* [1931] 146 LT 26. In that case the policy provided that the insurance should cover the liability of the insured in respect of the use by him of any motor car being used instead of the insured car. The insured traded in the insured car and purchased a new car in which he had an accident. He made no arrangements to transfer cover to the new car but in court claimed that he was covered by the policy extending cover to "any car being used instead of the insured car". Lord Buckmaster disagreed saying: "To me this policy depends on the hypothesis that there is in fact an insured car. When once the car which is the subject matter of this policy is sold, the owner's rights in respect of it cease and the policy so far as the car is concerned is at an end."

[94] *Tattersall* v *Drysdale* [1935] 2 KB 174 also dealt with the same issue on somewhat similar facts. Goddard J. (as he then was) interpreted the House of Lords decision in n. 92 *supra* as confirming that the subject matter of a motor insurance policy is the insured vehicle and once the insured has parted with that vehicle he is no longer interested in the policy of insurance.

> The policy insures the assured in respect of the ownership and user of a particular car. . . . It gives the assured by the extension clause a privilege or further protection while using another car temporarily but it is the scheduled car which is always the subject of the insurance. . . . The clause I am considering is expressly stated to be an extension clause, that is, extending the benefits of the policy and accordingly if the insured ceases to be interested in the subject matter of the insurance the extension falls with the rest of the policy.

See also *Peters* v *General Accident Fire and Life Assurance Corp. Ltd.* [1937] 4 All ER 628.

[95] The other requirements are detailed in para. 8.3.1 above.

[96] Amended by SI no. 178 of 1975, and SI no. 332 of 1987.

(Compulsory Insurance) Regulations, 1962[97] as amended by the 1964,[98] 1977[99] and 1987[100] regulations. The original regulations were challenged as being *ultra vires* the Minister's powers in *Greaney* v *Scully*[101] but the Supreme Court held that in drafting the regulations the Minister had acted *intra vires* his delegated powers under the 1961 Act. The reason for prohibiting the specified conditions in motor insurance policies is that to allow such conditions to be inserted in policies would adversely affect the rights of injured third parties and diminish the effectiveness of the compulsory insurance requirements.

8.4.7.2 A prohibited condition is defined as:

> every condition, restriction or limitation on the liability of the insurer under an approved policy of insurance which comes within any of the classes specified in the First Schedule to these regulations or any other condition, restriction or limitation which has substantially the same effect as a condition, restriction or limitation which is so specified.[102]

8.4.7.3 The conditions set out in the First Schedule of the regulations can be categorised as follows:

a) Conditions which depend on something being done or omitted to be done after an accident caused by the negligent use of the vehicle where such use was covered by the policy.[103]

---

[97] SI no. 14 of 1962.

[98] SI no. 58 of 1964.

[99] SI no. 359 of 1977.

[100] SI no. 321 of 1987.

[101] [1981] ILRM 340. The defendant was convicted of driving without insurance under Section 56 of the 1961 Act. There was a policy of insurance in force in respect of the vehicle, but it restricted cover to the defendant's father only. The defendant claimed that the Minister had exceeded his powers in drafting the regulations but the Supreme Court held that the regulations were not *ultra vires*.

[102] Article 5.1 of SI no. 14 of 1962 as amended.

[103] *McCarthy* v *Murphy* [1938] IR 737. The policy of insurance was a "Motor Trade" type policy and contained a condition precedent to liability that "before each and every departure of a motor vehicle from the insured's premises there shall be recorded . . . the date and time of departure of such vehicle". The plaintiff had been awarded damages against the defendants arising out of an accident which occurred when the condition precedent had not been complied with. The insurers had denied indemnity to the insured and the plaintiff had obtained lib-

b) Conditions which limit or restrict the persons or classes of persons or the physical or mental conditions of persons whose driving of the vehicle is covered by the policy except conditions which limit the persons so covered in any one or more of the following ways:

(i)   by specifying by name the persons to be covered;

(ii)   by specifying by name the persons not to be so covered;

(iii)   by specifying by name persons whose employees are to be covered;

(iv)   by requiring persons so covered to be accompanied by a named person or an employee of a named person;

(v)   by requiring persons so covered to have the consent of a named person to such driving;

(vi)   by limiting cover to cases where the person driving either holds a licence to drive the vehicle or having held a licence has not been disqualified from holding one;

(vii) by limiting the cover to cases where the person driving holds a licence to drive a public service vehicle or having held one has not been disqualified from holding it;

(viii) by specifying the maximum or minimum ages of persons to be so covered;

(ix)   by specifying that the vehicle must not have been stolen or obtained by violence or taken without the consent of the owner or other lawful authority.

c) any condition under which the existence or liability of the insurer depends on:

(i)   the weight, construction, equipment, maintenance or state of repair of a vehicle the use of which is covered;

(ii)   the speed at which the vehicle is to be driven;

---

erty from the court to execute the judgment against the insurers and the insurers appealed. The High Court held that the condition could properly be complied with by entering the necessary details after the accident had occurred and consequently was a condition "under which the liability of the insurer depends on some specified thing being done or omitted to be done after a negligent driving" and therefore a prohibited condition under the regulations.

(iii)   the keeping or carrying of anything on the vehicle;

(iv)   the times at which or the areas within which the vehicle is to be used;

(v)   the number of persons to be carried on the vehicle (except where the vehicle insured is a cycle);

(vi)   the weight or physical characteristics of the goods to be carried on the vehicle.

d) any condition requiring the existence or amount of liability to be determined by arbitration.

e) any condition under which the liability of the insurer depends on the existence or otherwise of any insurance other than the approved policy of insurance.

f) any condition which would have the effect of extending the rights of the insurer under Section 76(1)(e) of the Act to refuse payment to a claimant or to defend proceedings by a claimant on the ground that the approved policy of insurance was obtained by fraud, misrepresentation or false statement.

8.4.7.4 Conditions in a policy, relieving insurers of liability by reason of some act or omission by the insured after the happening of the event giving rise to the claim, are, by virtue of (a) above, of no effect against third parties in respect of liabilities compulsorily insurable under the Act but a policy term requiring the insured to repay to the insurers sums which they have become liable to pay, or have paid, in satisfaction of such claims is valid.[104]

8.4.7.5 The legality of (b)(i) above was the point at issue in the case stated to the Supreme Court in *Greaney* v *Scully*.[105] The defendant had been convicted in the District Court of driving without insurance. There was a policy of insurance in force but it confined cover to the defendant's father. The defendant appealed to the Circuit Court where the judge was of the opinion that whilst the restriction of cover

---

[104] *Jones* v *Birch Bros Ltd.* [1933] 2 KB 597 per Scrutton L. J. at 613.

[105] [1981] ILRM 340.

to the defendant's father was permitted by the regulations, the regulations exceeded the minister's powers and were *ultra vires*:

> The courts, it seems to me, must endeavour to safeguard the position of third parties irrespective of any contractual arrangements made between the insurers or the insured or any liability over which may exist in favour of an insurer against the user of a vehicle the subject of an approved policy of insurance.[106]

Henchy J. did not agree, saying that the scheme of compulsory insurance contained in Part VI of the Road Traffic Acts imposed no such duty on the courts and that the Minister had not exceeded the powers delegated to him under the Acts.

8.4.7.6 The limitations or restrictions permitted by (b)(iv) to (b)(vii) do not apply with respect to claims by injured parties against insurers under Section 76 of the 1961 Act.[107] A policy condition requiring the insured to use only steady and sober drivers was held not to be a condition which limited or restricted the persons or classes of persons or the physical or mental condition of the persons whose driving of the vehicle is covered by the policy.[108] The Supreme Court, in *A-G* v *Daniel Reilly*,[109] held that a clause in a policy which restricted driving to a person holding "a licence to drive or having held one is not disqualified . . ." was not more restrictive than was permitted by the regulations. The Supreme Court in reversing the High Court confirmed that such a wording allowed driving by a person holding a provisional licence. In *A-G* v *Wren*,[110] the High Court held that a provisional licence holder, who had previously driven whilst accompanied, but who was unaccompanied at the material time, was covered under a policy which covered the insured and any person driving with his consent who held a licence to drive "such a vehicle" or who having

---

[106] idem at 343 per Henchy J. quoting the Circuit Court judge.

[107] SI no. 321 of 1987, Road Traffic Act (Compulsory Insurance) Amendment Regulations, 1987.

[108] *National Farmers* v *Dawson* [1941] 2 KB 424.

[109] Unreported Supreme Court, 17 November 1966.

[110] *A-G (Wren)* v *O'Brien*, Unreported High Court, 16 July 1965. See *Rendelsham* v *Dunne* [1964] 1 Lloyds Rep 192, where cover was upheld even though the driver was in breach of the conditions attaching to his provisional driving licence.

previously held a licence was not disqualified from holding one. A licence obtained through the making of a false statement is inoperative and a driver holding such a licence and relying on it was not covered under the terms of a policy which excluded vehicles driven by "persons who to the knowledge of the insured does not hold a licence to drive such a vehicle unless such person has held and is not disqualified from holding such a licence".[111] Exception (b)(ix) was inserted by Statutory Instrument no. 321 of 1987 and effectively transferred liability for compensating the victims of "joy riding" and others to the Motor Insurers Bureau of Ireland under the new 1988 agreement.

8.4.7.7 A condition in a motor cycle policy excluding use of the motor cycle while carrying a passenger, unless a sidecar was attached, was upheld, with the court finding that a sidecar could not be deemed "equipment" under the regulations.[112] A policy exception applying while the vehicle carried a load in excess of that for which it was designed could only apply in cases where a weight load was specified for the particular vehicle, be it a lorry or a van, and could not be relied upon where a car designed to carry four passengers was carrying five.[113] A clause excluding liability if the insured vehicle is used other than for "social domestic and pleasure purposes" or in connection with a specified business, is not invalidated as being a condition related to the physical characteristics of the goods carried.[114]

8.4.7.8 The prohibition on the insertion of an arbitration clause is applicable only in relation to third party claims and such a clause is valid as between the insured and the insurers.[115] Section 76(1)(e) of the 1961 Act referred to in (f) above prevents an insurer from raising as a defence against third party claims the fraud, misrepresentation or false statements of the insured unless these have been the subject

---

[111] *Brady* v *Brady* [1938] IR 103. The driver had obtained a licence by misrepresenting his age on the application and the court held the licence issued to him was of "no force or effect".

[112] *Higgins* v *Feeney* [1953] IR 45.

[113] *Haughton* v *Trafalgar Insurance Co.* [1954] 1 QB 247.

[114] *Jones* v *Welsh Insurance Corp. Ltd.* [1937] 4 All ER 149

[115] *O'Donnell* v *Yorkshire Insurance Co. Ltd.* [1949] IR 187 per Dixon J.

of a criminal conviction. The regulations do not prohibit a condition operative against the insured, nor a condition requiring the insured to be responsible for a deductible under the policy in respect of each and every claim, nor a clause restricting cover to specified classes of use of the vehicle.

8.4.8 THIRD PARTY RIGHTS AGAINST INSURERS

8.4.8.1 Where an injured party claims to be entitled to recover from the owner or user of a mechanically propelled vehicle, or has obtained a court judgment against the owner or user for a sum against the liability for which the owner or user is insured by an approved policy of insurance, and in respect of which proceedings the insurers had prior notice, the injured party may serve a notice in writing of the claim or the judgment and on the service of such notice the following statutory provisions apply:[116]

a) the insurer shall not pay to the owner or user any greater amount than the amount, if any, which the owner or user has actually paid to the injured third party claimant;

b) where the claimant has obtained judgment for a sum (whether damages or costs) or, after service of notice on the insurers, obtains judgment, the insurers must pay so much of such sum as is covered under the policy of insurance and such payment by insurers, shall as against the insured be a valid payment under the policy;

c) where the amount of the judgment is not recovered from the owner or user or insurer the claimant may apply to the court in which he obtained the judgment for leave to execute the judgment against the insurer and the court may, if it thinks proper, grant the application in respect of the whole of the amount or part of it;

d) where the claimant has failed to recover the judgment, he may apply to any Court of competent jurisdiction for leave to institute or prosecute proceedings against the insurer in lieu of the owner or user, and the Court, if satisfied that the owner or user is not in the State, or cannot be found or cannot be served with the process

---

[116] Section 76(1) of Road Traffic Act, 1961.

of the Court, or that it is for any other reason just and equitable, may grant the application;

e) the insurer cannot, as a ground for refusing payment, or as a defence to proceedings by the claimant, rely on or plead any invalidity of the policy of insurance arising from the fraud or any misrepresentation or false statement to which the claimant was not a party or privy and which was not the subject of a prosecution and conviction.

8.4.8.2 The above provisions apply only to claims against the liability for which it is compulsory to insure under the Act. In *Stanbridge* v *Healy*,[117] the defendant insurers, against whom an application was brought under Section 76 of the Act, were able to convince the High Court that the accident giving rise to the proceedings had not occurred in a public place and that there was not therefore any obligation on the owner or user to have in force a valid policy of insurance. According to Judge Sheehy, in *McGee* v *London Assurance Company*:[118]

> the principal purpose of the provisions is to protect a person injured through the negligence of an insured driver in the event of such person proving to be without assets. . . . if he gives notice . . . to the Insurance Company, then the Insurance Company is rendered liable jointly with the insured person.

The burden of proof is on the claimant to show that the claim, or the judgment, is for a sum against the liability for which the owner or user is insured under a valid policy.[119] The High Court, in *Hayes* v *Legal Insurance Co. Ltd.*[120] held it was "just and equitable" to grant leave to prosecute proceedings against the insurer where consequent on a collision between two vehicles the driver of one of the vehicles

---

[117] [1985] ILRM 290.

[118] [1943] 77 ILTR 133. This was a case taken under Section 78 of the 1933 Act, which was re-enacted as Section 76 of the 1961 Act.

[119] *Whelan* v *Dixon* [1963] ILTR 195. The Supreme Court held that the onus was on the claimant to prove that the judgment was for a sum against the liability for which the owner or driver of the vehicle is insured. Where the policy of insurance limits use of the vehicle to social, domestic and pleasure purposes the claimant has to establish that the use came within the policy terms.

[120] *Hayes* v *Legal Insurance Co. Ltd.* [1941] Ir Jur Rep 49.

died, and, more than four months later, representation to his estate not having been taken out, the owner of the other vehicle applied for leave to institute proceedings in negligence against the insurer of the first vehicle.

8.4.8.3 The provisions require prior notice of proceedings be given to insurers because, as Lawton J. explained:

> Insurers may have repudiated liability as against their insured but they may have their own reasons for taking control of any litigation there may be. It may well be that if the facts are gone into, for example, a plaintiff may have no grounds of claim at all and unless the insurers have notice of the commencement of proceedings, they are not in a position to intervene. It is important from the insurers' point of view, too, that they should have notice . . . because of the danger of judgment in default of appearance being given against the defendant insured.[121]

Notice to insurers may come from anyone although in practice it will usually come from the third party claimant.[122] It is likely that the requirement of prior notification of proceedings would be satisfied by a firm expression of intention to commence proceedings even though details of the proceedings may not be capable of being given.[123] However, notification that a claim may be made is not notification of proceedings.[124] Notice may be given to the agent of the insurers, but such notice must be reasonably informative and certain.[125]

---

[121] *McGoona* v *MIB* [1969] 2 Lloyds Rep 34 at 47.

[122] *Harrington* v *Pinkey* [1989] 2 Lloyds Rep 310 at 316.

[123] idem at 315 and *Ceylon Motor Insurance Association Ltd.* v *Thumbugala* [1953] AC 584.

[124] n. 106 *supra*.

[125] *Herbert* v *Railway Passengers Insurance Co.* [1938] 1 All ER 650.

8.5 MOTOR INSURANCE POLICY TERMS AND CONDITIONS

8.5.1 POLICY DESIGN

There is not now any standard form of policy document in use by insurers.[126] The modern motor insurance policy covers a variety of risks and competition between insurers for different sectors of the motor insurance market has resulted in policies being designed for different gender, age and occupational groups which provide a wide range of different benefits. However, all motor policies must provide cover which complies with the statutory requirements, to qualify as an approved policy, and in this regard the policy terms and conditions tend to be the same. The terms and conditions which are standard generally relate to the persons whose liability is insured, the vehicles insured, the use to which the vehicle may be put, the condition of the vehicle and the obligations on the insured in the event of an accident giving rise to a claim under the policy.

8.5.2 PERSONS WHOSE LIABILITY IS COVERED

8.5.2.1 The Insured

Insurers will indemnify the insured in respect of any legal liability they incur in respect of the death of or bodily injury to any person, or accidental damage to property arising out of the use of or caused by the insured vehicle. In the case of private car policies issued to individuals most policies will, in addition, cover the insured's liability arising out of the use or driving of any other private type car, provided that the vehicle is not owned by the insured, or hired to him under a hire purchase agreement, or leased to him under a lease hire contract agreement. Indemnity will not be provided to the insured unless the insured holds a licence to drive the vehicle or has held and is not disqualified from holding or obtaining such a licence. Generally, insurers will, in addition, pay in respect of any event which may be the subject of indemnity under the policy:

a) solicitor's fees for representation at any coroner's inquest or legal inquiry of a court of summary jurisdiction;

b) costs and expenses incurred with insurers' written consent;

---

[126] At one time the majority of insurers operating in Ireland belonged to the Accident Offices Association which agreed common basic premium rates and policy wordings for use by members of the Association.

c) the costs of defence against a charge of manslaughter or causing death by careless or dangerous driving.

8.5.2.2 Persons Driving with the Insured's Consent

Unless the motor policy specifically restricts driving to the insured, it is usual for the policy to extend cover to persons driving with the permission of the insured. Such an extension indemnifies such persons for sums which they might personally become legally liable to pay and the policy does not merely indemnify the insured as owner.[127] In *Zurich* v *Shield*,[128] Gannon J. in the High Court expressed the view that the extension of cover to persons other than the insured driving the insured vehicle was intended to indemnify the driver against all claims arising out of the negligent driving of the vehicle and would, if necessary, provide an indemnity against a claim by the owner for indemnity against the owner's vicarious liability to an injured third party. Whether permission has been granted or whether it has been granted subject to terms is generally a matter of fact but if a person is permitted to drive for a particular purpose, insurers will not be liable if the vehicle is used for a different purpose.[129] An agent of the insured, acting within the scope of his authority, may grant permission to other persons to drive.[130] The extension of cover to persons, other than the insured, driving on the order of or with the permission of the insured, is generally subject to the qualification that the person driving should hold a licence to drive such a vehicle or having held a licence is not disqualified from holding one. "Disqualified" means disqualified by order of a court or by reason of age.[131] The extension of cover to such persons has no effect once the insured has disposed of his interest in the vehicle insured under the policy and the purchaser of the vehicle has no right to an indemnity under the policy as purchaser or assignee of the policy unless insurers have agreed to the

---

[127] *Williams* v *Baltic Insurance Association of London Ltd.* [1924] 2 KB 282.

[128] [1988] IR 174 at 180.

[129] *Browning* v *Phoenix Assurance Co. Ltd.* [1960] 2 Lloyds Rep 360.

[130] see para 8.4.1.3 above; *Pailor* v *Co-Operative Insurance Society Ltd.* [1930] 38 Lloyds Rep 237.

[131] "Disqualified" does not mean prohibited from holding a licence by reason of mental or physical disability; *Edwards* v *Griffiths* [1953] 1 WLR 199; *Mumford* v *Hardy* [1956] 1 WLR 163.

assignment.[132] The extension of cover to persons other than the insured is subject to a requirement that the person relying on the extension for indemnity "shall as though he were the insured, observe, fulfil and be subject to the terms, limitations, exceptions and conditions of the policy in so far as they can apply". Policy conditions relating to actions required of the insured following an accident are therefore binding on the person driving with the insured's permission and relying on the extension.[133] In the event of injury to the insured, whilst a passenger in their own vehicle, driven by another person within the terms of the policy extension, the insured in effect becomes a third party under the policy and indemnity is provided in respect of any liability of the driver to the insured in respect of the personal injuries sustained by them.[134]

8.5.2.3 Dual Indemnity

Most policies provide that the indemnity provided to persons other than the insured will not operate if that person is entitled to indemnity under any other policy. It is possible for dual indemnity to operate where a driver, whose policy covers him whilst driving a vehicle other than his own, is driving a friend's car or his employer's car with their permission within the terms of the policy on that vehicle. In

---

[132] *Peters* v *General Accident Fire and Life Assurance Corp. Ltd.* [1937] 4 All ER 628. The plaintiff had been injured by a recently purchased vehicle driven by the purchaser who was relying for insurance cover on the policy in force by the vendor before the sale and given to him by the vendor when handing over the vehicle. The policy contained an extension clause whereby insurers agreed to treat as the policy holder any person driving the vehicle with the policy holder's permission. The plaintiff brought the action against insurers under the terms of the Road Traffic Act as the judgment obtained against the driver remained unsatisfied. Goddard J., in holding for the insurers, confirmed his decision in *Tattersall* v *Drysdale* [1935] 2 KB 174, saying that it could not by any stretch of the imagination be said that the driver, having purchased the vehicle was then driving with the consent of the vendor as he had disposed of his interest in the vehicle and could not therefore give permission to anyone. The decision and Goddard's comments were quoted with approval by Budd J. in the High Court in *O'Leary* v *Irish National Insurance Co. Ltd.* [1958] Ir Jur Rep 1.

[133] *Austin* v *Zurich General Accident and Liability Insurance Co. Ltd.* [1945] 1 KB 250.

[134] *Digby* v *General Accident Assurance Corp. Ltd.* [1943] AC 121. The actress Merle Oberon was injured whilst a passenger in her own vehicle driven by her chauffeur. The House of Lords in awarding damages to her held that insurers were liable to indemnify the chauffeur under the extension clause.

normal circumstances this would result in any claim being shared by the two insurers.[135] In an effort to address this problem, members of the Irish Insurance Federation entered into a Dual Indemnity Undertaking in 1988 which provided that, in the event of dual indemnity operating, the driver's insurers would meet any third party claims arising.[136] This gave rise to some unforeseen difficulties. Under the terms of the Dual Indemnity Undertaking, where an employee, driving his employer's car for social and domestic purposes, with the permission of the employer, was involved in an accident, occasioning injury or damage to a third party, the resulting claim would be dealt with, not under the employer's policy but under the employee's private car policy, if that policy provided a "driving other cars" extension. The consequences for the employee were that his no claim discount could be disallowed and his premium loaded whilst the employer's insurers who had received premium for the risk would not be required to pay anything towards the cost of the claim. Following strong representations from the broking profession, the Undertaking was revised in 1991 so that now all claims made against insured drivers of vehicles owned by any company, business or firm will be met in full by the insurers of the vehicle and not by the insurers of the driver.

8.5.2.4 Passengers' Liability

Even though passengers in a vehicle, over the driving of which they have no control, are not deemed to be using the vehicle under the

---

[135] With consequent loss of both "no claims bonuses" by both insureds.

[136] Dual Indemnity Undertaking:

Where a policy issued by the insurers of a motor vehicle provides Third Party Indemnity to a driver who is also entitled to Third Party Indemnity under another policy, no contribution or indemnity will be sought from the insurers of such vehicle by the insurers of the driver, provided that both policies have been issued in the Republic of Ireland. This undertaking shall apply notwithstanding any limitation restricting either indemnity where other insurance exists against liability for damage or injury. Where the loss is paid by another signatory to this Undertaking the purposes of this Undertaking shall be effected by reimbursement between the signatories subject to the limits of the policies issued by such signatories. This Undertaking shall operate: (a) in respect of accidents occurring in Member States of the European Communities, the Isle of Man and the Channel Islands on or after 1 January 1988; (b) in priority to Loss Settlement Agreements between signatories which existed before 1 January 1988.

terms of the Act,[137] and their liability for death, injury or property damage is not therefore compulsorily insurable, most motor policies now extend indemnity to passengers in private cars, provided they are travelling in or on the vehicle or getting into or out of the vehicle, with the permission of the insured, and the vehicle is not being driven by a driver, who to their knowledge, does not hold a licence to drive the vehicle, unless such person having held a licence is not disqualified from holding or obtaining such a licence.

8.5.2.5 Persons Using the Vehicle

Insurers will usually indemnify under the terms of the policy persons "using" but not driving the insured vehicle for social, domestic and pleasure purposes, provided the vehicle is being used with the permission of the insured and is not being driven by a person who to the knowledge of the person using it does not hold a licence to drive such a vehicle unless the person driving, having held such a licence is not disqualified from holding or obtaining such a licence. The extension of cover to such persons "using" the vehicle requires a distinction between "driving" and "using". Section 3 of the Act states that "driving" includes "managing" or "controlling". A person closing the door of a vehicle is not managing the vehicle within the statutory definition.[138] In *R v McDonagh*,[139] it was stated that the essence of driving is the use of the driver's controls in order to direct the movement, however that movement is produced.[140] A passenger, leaning across, with both hands on the steering wheel and steering the car was held to be driving, as was the person in the driver's seat controlling the propulsion.[141] The distinction was well illustrated in *Samuelson* v *NIGG*

---

[137] *Brown* v *Roberts* [1965] 1 QB 1.

[138] *Neill* v *Minister for Finance* [1948] IR 88.

[139] [1974] RTR 372. The pushing of a vehicle whilst steering it with one hand was held not to be "driving".

[140] In *R* v *Kitson* [1955] 39 CAR 66, a person drunk and asleep in a car previously driven by someone else woke up to find the vehicle moving with no-one in the driver's seat and no keys in the ignition. He steered the vehicle downhill to safety and was held to be driving the vehicle.

[141] *Tyler* v *Whitmore* [1976] RTR 83. The degree of control in that case was confirmed as amounting to driving in the ordinary sense in *Jones* v *Pratt* [1983] RTR 54.

Ltd.,[142] which also dealt with the definition of a person "in charge for the purpose of driving". The High Court, in *Lynch* v *New PMPA Insurance Co. Ltd.* held that a person who was injured by the vehicle she had parked and moved away from was no longer physically in charge of the vehicle for the purpose of driving it and the insurer could not rely on an exception in the policy which relieved them of liability for the death of, or bodily injury to the person driving or in charge for the purpose of driving the insured vehicle.[143]

8.5.3 USE OF THE INSURED VEHICLE

8.5.3.1 Policies generally contain a clause relieving insurers of liability if the vehicle insured is being used with the consent of the insured other than in accordance with the limitations as to use written into the policy. All private car policies and most commercial vehicle policies cover use of the vehicle for "social domestic and pleasure purposes". In *Wood* v *General Accident Fire and Life Assurance Corp. Ltd.*[144] the insured's policy covered such use only, and an accident occurred when the vehicle was being used on a journey to negotiate a contract in connection with the insured's motor trade business. The insured maintained that the use of the car was more pleasurable than the use of a commercial vehicle and that as the journey differed only from a pleasure trip in that there was a business purpose at the end of it, the policy should operate. The Court disagreed, holding that the words "use for social, domestic and pleasure purposes" had a well-established meaning, and that a business trip could not be brought within that meaning merely because it was a more pleasurable means of travel. Carrying tools or timber for use in the garden comes within the definition,[145] and "social purposes" has been held to include social

---

[142] [1984] 3 All ER 107; [1985] 2 Lloyds Rep 541.

[143] per Costello J., Unreported High Court, 13 October 1995.

[144] [1948] 88 Lloyds Law Rep 77.

[145] *Piddington* v *Co-Operative Insurance Co. Ltd.* [1934] 2 KB 236.

activities of a local authority of which the insured was a member.[146] If an insured driving for social purposes gives a lift out of kindness, courtesy or charity to someone travelling on business of their own, it would not cause the vehicle to be used other than for social purposes.[147] The position would be otherwise if the primary purpose of the journey was to accommodate the passenger's business.[148]

8.5.3.2 If the vehicle is used for a dual purpose, neither being predominant, and one purpose is a permitted use under the policy and the other excluded, the vehicle is not being used solely for the permitted use and the policy does not therefore operate.[149] In *Kelleher* v *Christopherson*[150] the plaintiff was insured under a policy covering use for "social domestic and pleasure purposes and the use by him personally in his business". His business was described as a builder's labourer. He carried on pig farming in a small way. He used the vehicle to travel to and from his place of work every day and from there he carried home swill from the canteen to feed the pigs. An accident occurred when he was returning home from work and carrying swill. Insurers repudiated liability on the grounds that the vehicle was being used outside the limitations of use in the policy. The Court held that the carrying of swill made no difference to the insurance position, refusing to accept the proposition that by carrying the swill he converted a journey that was covered by insurance into a journey that was not. Unless specifically provided for, policies generally exclude use for "hire or reward". The distinction between hire and reward was

---

[146] *D.H.R. Moody (Chemists) Ltd.* v *Iron Trades Mutual Insurance Co.* [1971] 1 Lloyds Rep 386. The "description of use clause" in the policy restricted cover to use for "social domestic and pleasure purposes and use for the business of the insured including carriage of goods (namely the business of pharmacists and no other . . .)" An employee of the insured was a member of the local Urban District Council and obtained the loan of the insured's vehicle to take some foreign visitors to the council back to the airport. The vehicle was driven by an employee of the council but it was nevertheless held that the vehicle was being used for social purposes and not for the purposes of the driver's employment.

[147] *Passmore* v *Vulcan Boiler and General Insurance Co.* [1936] 54 Lloyds Law Rep 92, per DuParc J. at 94.

[148] *Seddon* v *Binnions* [1978] 1 Lloyds Law Rep 581.

[149] idem. *Browning* v *Phoenix Assurance Co.* [1960] 2 Lloyds Law Rep 360 and n. 147 *supra. McGoona* v *MIB* [1969] 2 Lloyds Rep 34.

[150] [1957] 91 ILTR 191.

made in *Bonham* v *Zurich Insurance Co. Ltd.*[151] where the court held that "hire" took place when there was an obligation to pay, but a vehicle was used for reward when there was no obligation to pay.

8.5.4 POLICY CONDITIONS

8.5.4.1 Standard Conditions

All motor policies contain conditions which are standard to insurance policies generally, such as conditions dealing with the obligation of the insured to observe the terms of the policy, basis of contract, claims notification, subrogation, cancellation, and contribution. It is to be hoped that Irish insurers, in applying these conditions, would never place an insured in the position of an American policyholder whose automobile insurer insisted on fighting a third party claim in court, rather than settling it for the policy limit of $50,000. The third party was awarded $253,000 and the insured's home and other assets were put at risk in endeavouring to meet the award. He sued the State Farm Mutual and the court found that the insurer had acted unreasonably. The jury awarded the insured $2.6 million compensatory damages and $145 million punitive damages. The insurers are appealing![152]

8.5.4.2 Maintenance

Motor policies require the insured to maintain the vehicle insured in an efficient and roadworthy condition and to take all reasonable steps to safeguard it from loss or damage. Insurers cannot, however, rely on breach of this condition to defeat a claim for property damage or personal injury compulsorily insurable under the Act,[153] but the term is enforceable as against the insured. In determining the meaning of "roadworthy condition", the courts were originally influenced by marine insurance decisions on "unseaworthiness". In *Barrett* v *London General Insurance Co.*[154] the court felt that in order for the insurer to rely on breach of the condition, the insurer would have to prove that the vehicle was unroadworthy when it commenced the journey and

---

[151] [1945] KB 292.

[152] *Campbell* v *State Farm Mutual*, Lloyds List, 13 August 1996.

[153] Article 5(1) of SI no. 14 of 1962, Condition 3(a).

[154] [1935] 1 KB 238 per Goddard J.

not merely that the vehicle was unroadworthy at the time of the accident. That reasoning was subsequently disapproved of by the Privy Council which held that insurers were relieved of liability if the vehicle was in an unsafe condition at the time of the accident and that insurers did not have to prove that the insured was aware of the defect.[155] The attitude of the courts to policy conditions requiring the insured to "take reasonable care" has changed in favour of the insured[156] so that breach of such a condition now requires negligence on the part of the insured. If there has been a complete failure by the insured to maintain the vehicle, the insured is clearly in breach of the condition, but if the insured has had the vehicle serviced regularly and a fault develops which could not reasonably have been discovered by the insured there is no breach of the condition.[157] In a recent English case, *Amey Properties Ltd.* v *Cornhill*[158] it was decided that the object of the "efficient and road worthy condition" clause is:

> to ensure that the insurer does not face liability, where liability arose due to the insured's negligent maintenance of the vehicle. In the case of vehicles owned by a company or firm, the obligation is imposed on the employer and not on individual employees, so that insurers can only avoid liability if it can be shown that the failure to maintain was that of an officer of the company.

The carriage of more passengers than the vehicle is designed to carry has been held to make the vehicle unroadworthy even though the vehicle may have been properly designed, manufactured and maintained.[159] The faulty loading of a commercial vehicle does not, of itself, make the vehicle itself unsafe.[160] "Efficient condition" has been held to mean the taking of reasonable steps to make or to keep the vehicle

---

[155] *Tricket* v *Queensland Insurance Co.* [1936] AC 159.

[156] see Chapter Five para 5.4.

[157] *Conn* v *Westminister Motor Insurance Association Ltd.* [1966] 1 Lloyds Rep 407.

[158] per Mr Justice Tucker in *Amey Properties Ltd.* v *Cornhill Insurance plc.* [1996] Lloyds List, 19 March 1996.

[159] *Clarke* v *National Insurance and Guarantee Corp. Ltd.* [1964] 1 QB 199.

[160] *AP Salmon Contractors* v *Monksfield* [1970] 1 Lloyds Rep 287. A load of timber inadequately secured fell off the vehicle and injured pedestrians. The vehicle was held not to have been driven in "an unsafe condition".

roadworthy.[161] The case of *Amey* above would seem to suggest that where the observance and fulfilment of the terms and conditions of the policy is a condition precedent to liability, and the policy contains a clause requiring the insured to take all reasonable steps to maintain the vehicle in an efficient condition, it may be sufficient for insurers to escape liability, if they can show that the vehicle has not been so maintained, without having to prove that the inefficient condition caused, or contributed to, the accident giving rise to the claim. In *Amey*[162] the insured had failed to maintain the tyres of the vehicle and the court found in favour of the insurer without considering whether the defective tyres had contributed to or caused the accident. A policy condition requiring the insured to take reasonable precautions to safeguard the vehicle insured and keep it in a good state of repair imposes on the insured an obligation to have an adequate system of routine maintenance and repair in respect of the vehicle insured.[163]

8.5.4.3 Arbitration

The usual arbitration clause provides for all differences under the policy to be referred to arbitration in accordance with the statutory provisions in force and that the making of an award shall be a condition precedent to any right of action against the insurers. It further provides that any claim for which the insurer disclaims liability and which has not, within a year of such disclaimer, been referred to arbitration shall be deemed to have been abandoned. The arbitration clause constitutes a "prohibited condition" under section 62 of the Act but is not illegal[164] and is valid as between the insurers and the insured.[165] A repudiation of liability as between the insurers and the insured, in respect of a particular event giving rise to a claim, is a

---

[161] per Sellors J. in *Brown* v *Zurich General Accident & Liability Insurance Co. Ltd.* [1954] 2 Lloyds Rep 243 at 246 and repeated by him in *Conn* v *Westminister*, n. 157 above, and approved by the Court of Appeal, per Wilmer J. [1966] 1 Lloyds Rep 407 at 409.

[162] n. 157 *supra*.

[163] *Liverpool Corporation* v *T. & H.R. Roberts* [1965] 1 WLR 938.

[164] *Scott* v *Avery* 5 HLC 811; *General Omnibus Co. Ltd.* v *London General Insurance Co. Ltd.* [1936] IR 596.

[165] *O'Donnell* v *Yorkshire Insurance Co. Ltd.* [1949] IR 187.

difference under the policy and subject to the arbitration clause.[166] The time limit for submitting the difference to arbitration commences at the date of the original disclaimer of liability.[167] Insurers are not disentitled from relying on the arbitration clause simply because they do not bring it to the insured's attention when repudiating liability.[168]

8.5.4.4 Insurer's Right of Recovery

The Act imposes very onerous obligations on insurers towards third parties and it is usual for insurers to insert into all motor policies a condition requiring the insured to repay to insurers all sums paid by them under the policy which they would not have paid but for the requirement of the Act, if the insurers would not otherwise have been liable for such sums under the terms of the policy. The effect of the condition is to enable insurers who have settled a claim, or satisfied a judgment, against the insured or any other person covered by the policy, to recover the amount paid if they would not have been liable to provide indemnity but for the statutory provisions.

8.6 MOTOR INSURERS BUREAU OF IRELAND

8.6.1 AGREEMENT WITH MINISTER FOR THE ENVIRONMENT

A motor insurer operating in the State must, by virtue of Section 78 of the 1961 Act, as amended, be a member of the Motor Insurers Bureau of Ireland or have given an approved form of undertaking to deal with claims arising out of the use of vehicles insured by him. "Exempted persons" are required to give similar undertakings. The Bureau (MIBI) is a body established by the insurance industry to provide a source of compensation where the obligations of the user or owner of a vehicle to insure have not been fulfilled. The MIBI have entered into an agreement with the Minister for the Environment which sets out the rules and conditions governing the administration of the compensation scheme.[169] The MIBI is incorporated as a com-

---

[166] *Heyman* v *Darwins Ltd.* [1942] 1 All ER 337; quoted by Dixon J. in n. 158 *supra*.

[167] per Dixon J. n. 158 *supra*.

[168] idem.

[169] see Appendix.

pany limited by guarantee under the Companies Act, 1963 and it can sue and be sued in its own name. The agreement with the Minister may be terminated by him at any time and by the MIBI on giving two years notice.[170]

8.6.2 SCOPE OF THE AGREEMENT

The Agreement, dated 21 December 1988, between the Minister of the Environment and the Motor Insurers Bureau of Ireland, extends, with effect from the dates specified therein, the scope of the Bureau's liability, with certain exceptions, for the compensation of victims of road accidents involving uninsured or stolen vehicles and unidentified or untraced drivers to the full range of compulsory insurance in respect of injury to person and damage to property under the Road Traffic Act, 1961. The Agreement is supplemental to the Principal Agreement of 10 March 1955, which was determined by an Agreement in 1964 and that Agreement was in turn determined by the 1988 Agreement. The 1988 Agreement does not apply to accidents which may have occurred prior to 31 December 1988. Such accidents and the claims arising from them are subject to the 1964 Agreement, which was similar to but more restrictive than the new Agreement. It did not, for instance, give claimants the right to sue the MIBI or to apply directly to it for compensation. It did not cover claims in respect of damage to property, or claims for personal injuries from persons injured by unidentified or untraced drivers. It also excluded claims for personal injury from certain passengers in stolen vehicles or vehicles used without lawful authority. To qualify for compensation under the Agreement, the claimant must be the innocent third party victim of an accident in a "public place" caused by or arising out of the use of a mechanically propelled vehicle where:

a) there is not an approved policy of insurance in force in respect of the use of the vehicle, e.g. no policy effected in respect of the vehicle or the policy unenforceable for lack of insurable interest;[171] or

---

[170] Clause 8 of the Agreement. Should the MIBI give such notice it will continue to be liable for claims arising within the terms of the Agreement up to the date of termination.

[171] *Stanbridge* v *Healy* [1985] ILRM 290; *Lynch* v *New PMPA*, Unreported High Court, 13 October 1995.

b) there is a policy in force but it is ineffective in respect of the particular accident, e.g. vehicle being used outside the limitations as to use or being driven by a person not a permitted driver under the policy; or

c) the vehicle had been stolen or was being used without lawful authority; or

d) the driver of the vehicle was untraceable or unidentifiable.

The Agreement only applies to accidents occurring in circumstances where the compulsory insurance requirements of the Road Traffic Act operate. It does not apply to accidents occurring in places other than a "public place" as defined in the Act[172] or to accidents involving machinery or equipment other than mechanically propelled vehicles as defined. If the accident giving rise to the claimant's injuries was occasioned solely by the negligence of the claimant then the MIBI have no liability under the Agreement, but if there was contributory negligence the MIBI will be liable to the extent of the uninsured driver's negligence.

8.6.3 ENFORCEMENT OF THE AGREEMENT

A person who qualifies as a claimant under the Agreement may seek to enforce the Agreement by:

(1) submitting a claim directly to the MIBI who may settle the claim with or without an admission of liability; or

(2) joining the MIBI as co-defendants in proceedings against the owner or user of the vehicle giving rise to the claim where the owner or user of the vehicle can be identified, or

(3) seeking a court order for performance of the Agreement by the MIBI provided a claim for compensation has first been made against the MIBI under (1) above and such claim has been declined or the compensation offered by the MIBI is considered inadequate by the claimant.[173]

---

[172] *O'Leary* v *Irish National Insurance Co. Ltd.*, [1958] Ir Jur Rep 1; *Flynn* v *Mackin* [1974] IR 101.

[173] In *Kinsella* v *MIBI*, Unreported Supreme Court 2 April 1993. The claimant having had his claim for compensation refused by the MIBI then issued proceedings against it.

8.6.4 CONDITIONS PRECEDENT

Clause 3 of the Agreement stipulates that before the MIBI will accept liability the following conditions must be complied with:

(i) the claimant must have given notice in writing by registered post of his intention to seek compensation and such notice must, in the case of personal injuries have been given not later than three years from the date of the accident giving rise to the claim and in the case of property damage not later than one year from the date of the accident;

(ii) the claimant must provide the MIBI with all material information reasonably required by it in relation to the processing of the claim for compensation including details of the accident, the injuries sustained including medical treatment, property damage and costs and expenses incurred;

(iii) copies of all documentation relating to the accident giving rise to the claim and any legal proceedings arising therefrom together with copies of all correspondence, statements and pleadings must be provided to the MIBI;

(iv) the claimant must endeavour to establish if an approved policy of insurance covering the vehicle involved in the accident exists by demanding the necessary details from the user or owner of the vehicle in accordance with Section 73 of the Act;

(v) the claimant must provide the MIBI with details of any claim of which he is aware in respect of damage to property arising from the accident under any insurance policy or otherwise and of any report or notice given to any person of which he is aware in respect of the damage or the use of the vehicle, as the MIBI may reasonably require;

(vi) notice of proceedings must be given by registered post in advance of the commencement of proceedings to the insurer where there was in force at the time of the accident an approved policy of insurance covering the use of the vehicle and the existence of which was known to the claimant before the commencement of the proceedings and in all other cases to the MIBI;

(vii) the claimant must, if required by the MIBI and subject to an indemnity from them in respect of reasonable costs, take or have taken all reasonable steps against any person against whom the claimant might have a remedy in respect of the personal injuries or damage to property. Any dispute as to reasonableness of a requirement of the MIBI shall be referred to the Minister whose decision shall be final;

(viii) all judgments obtained under (vii) above must be assigned to the MIBI;

(ix) the MIBI must be give credit for any amounts received by the claimant from the tortfeasor in respect of the liability for injury or property damage.

8.6.5 DOMESTIC AGREEMENT

In cases where there is an ineffective policy in force, the MIBI will normally arrange for the insurer who issued the policy, the "insurer concerned", to handle the claim on behalf of the MIBI. If there is no policy in existence, the MIBI will usually assign the handling of the claim to one of the member insurers. An agreement known as the "Domestic Agreement", entered into by the MIBI and the member insurers, sets out conditions and provisions for the operation of the MIBI and in particular defines the "insurer concerned" as the insurer who, at the time of the accident which gave rise to the Road Traffic Liability, was providing any insurance against such liability in respect of the vehicle involved. An insurer may be the "insurer concerned" notwithstanding that:

(i) the insurance was obtained by fraud misrepresentation non-disclosure of material facts or mistake;

(ii) some term, description, limitation, exception or condition of the insurance excludes the insurer's liability;

(iii) the person against whom judgment was obtained was in unauthorised possession of the vehicle.

The insurer ceases to be the insurer concerned where

(i) a public policy issued for a term of twelve months or more lapses by provision of the policy or by notice in writing by either party;

(ii) a policy issued for a term of twelve months or less expires;

(iii) before the date of the accident, a policy has been cancelled by agreement of the parties or by provisions of the policy

(iv) the interest in the vehicle has been transferred

(v) before the date of the accident, there had been a prosecution and conviction which would entitle insurers to refuse payment under Section 78(1)(e) of the Act.

8.6.6 PROCEDURES

Section 73 of the 1961 Act provides that where a person, against whom a claim is made in respect of liability compulsorily insurable, receives a demand in writing, by registered post, he must:

a) state whether the liability was so covered, and give the name and address of the insurers together with the relevant details of the policy,

b) give the same information, if the liability would have been covered but for the policy having been avoided, cancelled or otherwise terminated;

c) if he is an "exempt person" or vehicle insurer state the fact and provide the particulars referred to in Section 68 of the Act;

d) if none of the foregoing apply state the fact.

In most cases involving personal injuries, the Gardai will be involved and will demand the necessary insurance details. These can subsequently be obtained on request by an injured party or his legal advisors. Difficulties previously experienced in this regard have, to a large extent, been eliminated by the statutory requirement to display an insurance disc on the vehicle.

8.6.7 SATISFACTION OF JUDGMENTS

The MIBI undertake to satisfy any judgment, in respect of liability required to be covered under an approved policy of insurance, if such judgment is not satisfied within twenty-eight days from the date when the person obtaining it becomes entitled to enforce it. The undertaking applies whether or not the person against whom the judgment is obtained is covered by insurance and covers taxed costs or such portion of the costs as is attributable to the relevant liability.

Any benefit or compensation obtained from another source in respect of damage to property will be deducted from the amount otherwise payable together with the amounts specified in Clause 7 of the Agreement. Where judgment has not been obtained and the claimant applies to the MIBI for compensation, the MIBI undertake to give a decision together with reasons for the decision as soon as is reasonably practicable. Where the application for compensation is granted and the amount agreed the MIBI undertake to pay such amount within twenty-eight days.

8.6.8 EXCLUSIONS

8.6.8.1 Clause 5(1) of the Agreement excludes from the Agreement claims for compensation in respect of the death of, or personal injury to, or damage to property of, any person, in a stolen vehicle or a vehicle taken without the consent of the owner or other lawful authority, who stole or took the vehicle or was in collusion with the persons who did steal or take the vehicle.

8.6.8.2 Clause 5(2) excludes claims in respect of injury or damage to property where the injured party claiming knew, or ought reasonably to have known, that there was not in force an approved policy in respect of the use of the vehicle and claims from persons travelling in or on a vehicle, by consent, where the person knew, or ought reasonably to have known, that there was not in force an approved policy of insurance. In *Kinsella* v *MIBI*[174] the plaintiff had obtained judgment against the driver of the vehicle in which he had been travelling, as a passenger, and which had been involved in an accident, causing him serious personal injuries. The car had been insured on an "owner only driving" basis, and when the judgment remained unsatisfied for twenty-eight days, the plaintiff sought satisfaction of the High Court award from the MIBI, who declined to admit the claim on the grounds that the plaintiff ought reasonably to have known that there was no insurance cover in force covering the driving of the particular driver at the time of the accident and they were not therefore liable under the terms of the Agreement. In the Supreme Court the defendants did not suggest that the plaintiff knew the vehicle was uninsured but that he should reasonably have known so. Finlay C. J. de-

---

[174] Unreported Supreme Court, 2 April 1993.

clared that the onus was on the defence to prove that the plaintiff either knew or should reasonably have known that the use of the vehicle on the occasion was not covered by insurance. In considering the interpretation of the clause in the Agreement he said:

> the question as to whether or not a claimant "should reasonably have known" of the absence of insurance is essentially a subjective question. The issue is not: "would a reasonable person have known?" but rather: "should the particular individual, having regard to all the circumstances, have known?"

In allowing the plaintiff's appeal, he placed significant regard on the fact that on the evidence before the trial judge it was uncontested that the plaintiff had a bona fide belief, although an incorrect one, that the driver of the vehicle was covered by insurance. He also expressed the opinion that the clause could not be relied upon to defeat a claim from a person with defective reasoning or mental powers, or a young child.

8.6.8.3 In *Curran* v *Mary Gallagher, Joseph Gallagher and the MIBI*,[175] the Supreme Court considered the judgment of Finlay C. J. in *Kinsella*,[176] and reaffirmed that the test to be applied was a subjective one. The court has to consider whether the plaintiff, having regard to all the circumstances, knew or should have known that the use of the vehicle was not covered. It is also for the court to consider whether the attitude and conduct of the plaintiff at the time was blameworthy insofar as the actions of the plaintiff condoned the commission of an offence. The onus of proving that the plaintiff knew or should have known that the driver had no insurance rests with the MIBI. The plaintiff and the first defendant had been travelling as passengers in a car driven by the first defendant's boyfriend when it broke down. The first defendant then went to where her mother's car (owned by the second defendant) was parked and removed the keys from under the mat of the unlocked car. The plaintiff sat into the car with the first defendant and they drove towards their original intended destination, subsequently colliding with a wall. The plaintiff recovered judgment in default against the first and second defen-

---

[175] Unreported Supreme Court, 17 May 1997.

[176] *supra*

dants. By virtue of Section 118 of the Road Traffic Act, 1961, in the absence of a denial by the second defendant, the first defendant was deemed to have been driving with the consent of the second defendant. The third defendant denied that it was obliged to satisfy the judgment obtained by the plaintiff on the grounds that the plaintiff knew or should have known that the driving by the first defendant was not covered by an approved policy of insurance. The trial judge, Carroll J., held against the plaintiff because she found she had invented a story that the first defendant's mother handed the keys of the car to the first defendant. In the Supreme Court, Lynch J. allowed the plaintiff's appeal, holding that the conclusions of the learned trial judge were not supported by the evidence, and that the MIBI had failed to discharge the onus of proof as to the state of knowledge of the plaintiff. In a dissenting judgment, Murphy J. was of the opinion that the trial judge was entitled to infer that the plaintiff was prepared to travel in the car when he knew or should have known that the first defendant was not entitled to drive.[177]

8.6.8.4 Where two vehicles are involved in an accident and both are uninsured, the MIBI will not be liable under the Agreement for any judgment or claim in respect of injury, death or damage to the property of the user of either vehicle. Whilst this is in keeping with the intention of the Agreement not to compensate persons who are responsible for accidents, or for knowingly using, or allowing themselves be conveyed in, vehicles in circumstances where there is no insurance in force, this exclusion could deny compensation to an innocent driver of an uninsured vehicle, which the driver reasonably and honestly believes to be insured, who is injured in collision with an unidentified vehicle or untraceable driver.

8.7 THE IRISH VISITING MOTORISTS BUREAU

This bureau was set up as a sister bureau to the MIBI in 1952 and under the current agreement between bureaux in all member states,

---

[177] See also *Cranny v Kelly and Another*, Unreported High Court, 5 April 1996. The plaintiff was the husband of the deceased, and the case was concerned with whether the deceased had had knowledge that the first named defendant was not insured to drive the vehicle. The court, applying the principle in *Kinsella*, held that the deceased must have reasonably known that the vehicle was not insured.

effective from January 1991, provides a system of compensation to victims of accidents occasioned by foreign registered vehicles in Ireland similar to that provided by the MIBI. The bureau is deemed to be the insurer of any foreign registered vehicle normally based in another member state.[178] Victims of accidents involving vehicles registered in countries not party to the international agreement can proceed against the MIBI. Arising out of the First EC Motor Insurance Directive,[179] participating bureaux agreed in 1975 that each national bureau would guarantee compensation as required by local legislation in respect of accidents occurring within its territory and occasioned by foreign vehicles whether such vehicles were insured or not. Motor Insurance policies issued in Ireland now automatically extend to provide the minimum cover required to comply with the laws relating compulsory insurance of vehicles in any country which is a member of the European Union, and any other country in respect of which the Commission of the European Union is satisfied that arrangements have been made to meet the requirements of Article 7(2) of the First Directive.[180]

---

[178] Article 13 of the Mechanically Propelled Vehicles (International Circulation) Order, 1961, implemented by SI no. 269 of 1961.

[179] EC 72/166, implemented by SI no. 178 of 1975.

[180] EC 72/166.

CHAPTER NINE

LIABILITY INSURANCE

"Woe unto you also, ye lawyers! for ye lade men with burdens grievous to be borne, and ye yourselves touch not the burdens with one of your fingers."[1]

9.1 INTRODUCTION

Liability insurance was developed to provide an indemnity to insured persons in respect of legal liability for death, injury, damage to property, financial or other loss sustained by third parties arising out of the activities or actions of the insured.[2] As a form of insurance it is of much more recent origin than marine, life, or fire insurance.[3] The late development of liability insurance is due to a once commonly held view that the provision of such insurance was contrary to "public policy". In the litigious society in which we live today, no individual or corporate body could afford not to have insurance protection against the ever-increasing range of legal liabilities. Insurance has kept pace with that development and there are few legitimate risks which cannot be covered by a liability insurance policy.

---

[1] St. Luke 11:46.

[2] Liability insurance is "any insurance protection which indemnifies liability to third parties". *Quinlan* v *Liberty Bank Co.* 575 So 2 d 336, 339. Section 11(7) of the Insurance Contracts Act, 1984 in Australia says it is a "contract of general insurance that provides cover in respect of the insured's liability for loss or damage to another person".

[3] The pioneering insurer was the London and Provincial Carriage Insurance Co. Ltd. who, in 1875, issued a third party liability policy in relation to horse-drawn vehicles. The first third party lift insurance was issued in 1888 and Property Owner's liability policies were offered by the Northern Accident Insurance Co., Ltd. in 1897; see Batten and Dinsdale (1960).

9.2 PUBLIC POLICY

9.2.1 INTENTIONAL ACT

The law will not assist a person to profit from, or be indemnified in respect of, his own deliberate unlawful act. It is a rule of insurance law that a person cannot recover under a policy of insurance where he has intentionally brought about the circumstances or the event insured against.[4] This rule is not based on the principle of "public policy" but on the interpretation or construction of the insurance contract and the intention of the parties to that contract. It is presumed that the insurance contract is intended to cover fortuitous events and not those brought about by the deliberate intentional actions of the party insured.[5] The insured is not, however, prevented from recovering under the policy where his deliberate, but lawful, act contributed to but was not the proximate or immediate cause of the loss.[6] He will be held to have caused the loss through his deliberate act if he engages in a course of conduct in which there is the risk of the loss occurring, even if he has no intention of causing the loss.[7] Public policy dictates that no insurance policy should indemnify a person in respect of a loss intentionally caused by his own criminal or wrongful act.[8] More than two hundred years ago Lord Mansfield said:

> No court will lend its aid to a man who founds his action upon an immoral or illegal act. If, from the plaintiff's own stating or otherwise, the cause of the action appears to arise *ex turpi*

---

[4] *Bell* v *Carstairs* [1811] 14 East 374; *Britton* v *The Royal Insurance Co.* [1866] 4 F&F 905.

[5] *Beresford* v *Royal Insurance Co.* [1938] AC 586, 595; *Gray* v *Barr* [1971] 2 QB 554, 587.

[6] *Aubert* v *Gray* [1861] 3 B&S 169, 171.

[7] *Gray* v *Barr* [1971] 2 QB 554.

[8] *Beresford* v *Royal Insurance Co. Ltd.* [1938] AC 586; *Hardy* v *MIB* [1964] 2 QB 745; *Cleaver* v *Mutual Reserve Fund Life Assoc.* [1892] 1 QB 147. A murderer cannot recover under a policy effected by him on the life of the person murdered; *Prince of Wales Assurance* v *Palmer* [1858] 28 Beave. 605. A murderer cannot benefit under the will of the person murdered by him — *In the Estate of Crippen* [1911] 104 LT 224 at 108.

causa (from a base cause) or the transgression of the law of the country, then the court says he has no right to be assisted.[9]

9.2.2 UNINTENDED LOSS

Difficulties arise, however, where the insured intentionally commits a crime which indirectly causes a loss under the policy although the loss may not have been intended. If the loss is the natural or probable result of the insured's criminal act then it can be said to have been caused by the intentional criminal act of the insured. The principle is well illustrated by the case of *Gray* v *Barr*.[10] The defendant's wife had been having an affair with his neighbour Gray and suspecting that she was in the neighbour's house he took his gun and went there to confront her, On entering the house he encountered Gray at the top of the stairs. Gray denied that Barr's wife was in the house but Barr did not believe him. Barr started up the stairs to check for himself, firing a shot into the ceiling to frighten Gray, who, fearing for his life, struggled with Barr and fell down the stairs. The gun went off in the course of the struggle and Gray was shot dead. Barr was charged with, but acquitted of, manslaughter, it being accepted at his trial that he never intended to fire the shot or to kill Gray. The administrators of Gray's estate then sued Barr in negligence. The defendant held a policy to "indemnify him in respect of all sums which he should become legally liable to pay as damages in respect of bodily injury to any person caused by accidents". Barr joined the insurers in the action but the Court of Appeal held that his claim failed because the injuries were not caused by an accident and that public policy made the claim unenforceable. The effective and dominant cause of death was the deliberate act of Barr in threatening Gray with a loaded gun and firing a warning shot into the ceiling, since the sequence of events which followed were the foreseeable and probable result of that conduct.[11] The Court was also of the opinion that the defendant's conduct amounted to unlawful assault with violence and the defendant could not be indemnified in respect of the consequences of his

---

[9] *Holman* v *Johnson* [1775] 1 Cowp. 341.

[10] [1971] 2 QB 554.

[11] ibid. per Lord Denning M. R. and Phillimore L. J. at 567 and 587.

crime.[12] Lord Denning believed that "public policy" was "rightly regarded as an unruly steed which should be cautiously ridden," and
that the principle undoubtedly required that no-one threatening unlawful violence with a loaded weapon should be allowed to enforce a
claim for indemnity, against any liability that might be incurred
through having so acted. His Lordship added that he did "not intend
to lay down any wider proposition".[13] The Court's decision confirmed
that an insured who deliberately engages in a course of conduct
which is criminal and likely to occasion a loss under the policy as a
foreseeable and probable result of that conduct will not, on grounds of
public policy, be indemnified for that loss, even though it was not intended. The conduct of many motorists on the roads regularly comes
within the description of conduct laid down by the Court but insurers
do not deny coverage on the grounds of public policy even where the
motorist is convicted of manslaughter or causing death by dangerous
driving. In this context, Diplock L. J. has said:

> The liability of the insured, and thus the rights of the third
> party against the insurers, can only arise out of some wrongful
> (tortious) act of the insured. I can see no reason in public policy
> for drawing a distinction between one kind of wrongful act, of
> which the third party is the innocent victim, and another kind
> of wrongful act; between wrongful acts which are crimes on the
> part of the perpetrator and wrongful acts which are not crimes,
> or between wrongful acts which are crimes of carelessness and
> wrongful acts which are intentional crimes. It seems to me to
> be slightly unrealistic to suggest that a person who is not de-
> terred by the risk of a possible sentence of life imprisonment
> from using a vehicle with intent to commit grievous bodily
> harm would be deterred by the fear that his civil liability to his

---

[12] ibid. p. 581. In *Hardy* v *MIB* [1964] 2 QB 745, the plaintiff security officer was
injured when the driver of a van being questioned by him drove off while he was
holding on to the vehicle. The driver was subsequently convicted of maliciously
causing grievous bodily harm with intent and the MIB raised in defence the argument that the plaintiff's injury was caused by an intentional criminal act. The
Court of Appeal, whilst agreeing that the injuries were intentionally caused, held
that the MIB were obliged to indemnify the injured plaintiff. The House of Lords
approved *Hardy* in *Gardner* v *Moore* [1984] AC 548, holding that the MIB is
bound to pay even though the driver intentionally causes the injury. In *Gardner*,
the plaintiff was injured by a car deliberately and criminally driven at him by an
uninsured driver.

[13] [1971] 2 QB 554 at 567.

victim would not be discharged by his insurers. I do not, myself, feel that, by dismissing this appeal, we shall add significantly to the statistics of crime.[14]

9.2.3 INSURANCE FOR WRONGFUL ACTS

This apparent contradictory interpretation of public policy is explained by the overwhelming requirement of public policy that the innocent victims of accidents be compensated for their injuries and that policies of insurance which provide for such compensation should be effective. The courts, in developing and following that interpretation, have relied on a life assurance precedent set by Lord Justice Fry, who said that: "The rule of public policy should be applied so as to exclude from benefit the criminal and all claiming under her but not so as to exclude alternative or independent rights."[15] The Road Traffic Acts confer such rights, in certain circumstances, on the victims injured in motor accidents. Motor insurance policies are required by law to cover liability arising from any use, even an intentionally criminal one, of a vehicle in a public place. Whilst the motor policy may preclude the perpetrator of the criminal act from being indemnified under it, the injured plaintiff is not prevented from recovering compensation.[16] Similarly, it is desirable that those engaged in industrial activities which are potentially dangerous, but socially and commercially beneficial, should be able to insure against the consequences of their negligence or breach of statutory duties even if their actions constitute an offence punishable by the criminal courts. Accordingly, it is now accepted that there is no rule of public policy which prevents a person from insuring the consequences of their own

---

[14] *Hardy* v *MIB* [1964] 2 All ER 742 at 752.

[15] *Cleaver* v *Mutual Reserve Fund Life Assoc.* [1892] 1 QB 147.

[16] In *Pitts* v *Hunt* [1990] 3 All ER 344, it was held that if a driver and a passenger of a motor vehicle jointly committed an offence or series of offences so serious that the driver was precluded on the grounds of public policy from claiming indemnity under a policy of insurance required to be effected under the Road Traffic Acts, the same public policy would preclude the passenger from claiming compensation. On the facts found by the court the plaintiff passenger was playing a full and active part in encouraging the driver to commit offences which if they had resulted in the death of a third party would have amounted to manslaughter. The plaintiff had been injured and the defendant killed in a collision between a motor cycle driven by the defendant and a motor car. Both the driver and the passenger were drunk at the time.

negligence. It is therefore possible for a person to insure their liability for wrongful acts committed innocently, or through carelessness without deliberate intention to do wrong, and whilst they cannot recover an indemnity in respect of the consequences of their own intentional criminal acts they can recover in respect of liability accidentally and unintentionally incurred in the course of committing the criminal offence.

9.3 INSURANCE AND THE LAW OF TORT

9.3.1 THE PRINCIPLE OF TORT

Liability insurance provides indemnity in respect of "liability at law" and is dependent on the law of tort.

> . . . the general purpose of the law of torts is to secure a man indemnity against certain forms of harm to person, reputation, or estate, at the hands of his neighbours, not because they are wrong but because they are harms. The true explanation of the reference of liability to a moral standard . . . is not that it is for the purpose of improving men's hearts, but that it is to give a man a fair chance to avoid doing harm before he is held responsible for it. It is intended to reconcile the policy of letting accidents lie where they fall, and the reasonable freedom of others with the protection of the individual from injury.[17]

The relationship between insurance and the law of torts, and the influence of each on the development of the other, has long been the subject of academic controversy.[18] The formulation and application of tort law represented society's attempt to reduce accidents, to compensate for loss and to implement a particular pattern of wealth distribution.[19] The concepts of punishment, admonition and deterrence are now of less practical relevance than the compensation of the victim and the distribution of the loss on the basis of the fault principle. "Tort liability exists primarily to compensate the person injured by

---

[17] "The Common Law" by O.W. Holmes. p. 144.

[18] See "The Impact of Liability Insurance" (1948); Atiyah (1993) Ch. 10; James and Thornton (1950).

[19] Prosser (1971), pp. 14–15.

compelling the wrongdoer to pay for the damage he has done."[20] The law of torts, concerned as it is with the allocation of losses and the compensation of injuries sustained by persons, arising out of the actions or activities of other members of society, must allocate those losses in the interests of the public good. Initially concerned with protection against bodily injury and damage to property, the law of torts is increasingly called upon to protect against less palpable injuries such as post-traumatic stress disorders, gradually developing diseases, emotional distress, and injury to reputation by defamation. In the commercial world the law is now used to provide a remedy against deceit, unfair competition, passing off, interference with profitable commercial relationships and infringement of copyright.

9.3.2 INFLUENCE OF LIABILITY INSURANCE ON TORT

The availability of liability insurance has greatly influenced the trend of loss distribution in tort law.[21] Although it has been held that ". . . in determining the rights *inter se* of A and B the fact that one of them is insured is to be disregarded",[22] Lord Denning has said: "We assume that the defendant in an action in tort is insured unless the contrary appears."[23] In reality the person named as the defendant in a tort action is only a nominal party to the litigation which is conducted by the insurers concerned, and the existence of insurance cover eliminates the admonitory and deterring effect of the judicial decision on the offending conduct. There is no evidence, however, that the availability of insurance encourages irresponsible behaviour; on the contrary, it is frequently a prerequisite to insurance that the insured should have undertaken or agreed to undertake measures intended to

---

[20] Fleming (1977).

[21] Hepple and Mathews (1985), pp. 768–769. The authors suggest that the "legal rules have been invisibly affected by the existence of insurance" and quote by way of example the development of the manufacturers' duty (*Donoghue* v *Stevenson* [1932] All ER Rep 1); the raising of the standard of care for learner drivers (*Nettleship* v *Weston* [1971] 3 All ER 581); the conversion from "fault" to "negligence without fault" through the *res ipsa loquitur* doctrine (*Scott* v *St. Katherine Docks Co.* [1861–73] All ER 246); the imposition of strict liability for dangerous escapes (*Rylands* v *Fletcher* [1861–73] All ER 1).

[22] Viscount Simmonds in *Lister* v *Romford Ice & Cold Storage Co. Ltd.* [1957] 1 All ER 125 at 133.

[23] *Post Office* v *Norwich Union* [1967] 2 QB 363 at 375.

manage the risk and eliminate potential hazards. While there is a widespread social consensus in favour of deterring wrongdoing and compensating accident victims, there is a view[24] that tort law does not currently serve these goals and that the concepts of deterrence and compensation should be separated. The tort system is perceived as unjust in the way it unequally distributes the funds held largely by insurers, and as incomplete in that many people who suffer similar illnesses and injuries are excluded from its scope.[25] It is suggested that victims should be compensated through an expanded social security system and deterrence effected through regulatory safety agencies, the market, self-protection and private morality.[26] Whilst the present system is undoubtedly unpredictable, expensive to administer, slow and difficult for the victim to understand, it is doubtful if it will be changed in this or the adjoining jurisdictions where it is embedded into the life, culture and economy of society. A system of compensation regardless of fault would offer no solution to the problems facing the insurance industry and the law in Ireland.

9.4 COMPENSATION IN IRELAND

9.4.1 COMPENSATION LEVELS

The last thirty years has seen an unprecedented increase in the number of personal injury actions in Ireland and in the amounts of the awards.[27] The cost of liability insurance rose accordingly and to such an extent that it was claimed to affect the competitiveness of Irish business. In 1994, the Government introduced proposals for legislation which would set maximum levels of awards for personal injuries,

---

[24] "Doing away with Tort Law", Sugarman, California Law Review, vol. 17 (1985); "Economic Analysis of Tort Law," Shavell.

[25] "Liability Insurance and Compensation", CII Advance Study Group No. 225 Sept. 1994, Insurance Institute of London.

[26] n. 24 *supra*.

[27] In 1995 liability Insurers in Ireland incurred underwriting losses of £40 million on premium income of £230.3 million. Gross incurred claims amounted to £225.9 million, according to the Irish Insurance Federation, Insurance Update No. 43, July 1996.

quoting in support of the idea the experience in the United States.[28] The proposal was abandoned, however, following objections from the legal profession and lobbies claiming that it was unconstitutional.[29] It was conceded that the underlying premise of the proposals might not be valid, and an economic evaluation of the impact of liability insurance costs on the competitiveness of Irish business was commissioned.[30] The subsequent report recommended that, subject to detailed examination, a Personal Injuries Tribunal be established to reduce settlement costs in personal injury cases where the amount at issue is small, liability is not in dispute and both sides are in agreement to place their case before it.[31] The report also recommended that the Irish judiciary be requested to establish a specialist panel to draw up guidelines for general damages awards in personal injury actions which would be appropriate in the context of Irish tradition and case law. In making that recommendation, the authors of the report were obviously influenced by the experience in the UK where the judiciary produced guidelines for the assessment of general damages in personal injury cases, classifying the types and severity of injuries and recommending ranges of awards for each classification.[32]

In Ireland, in the case of severe personal injuries, the courts have generally been consistent in the level of the awards made for general damages following the principles set down by the Supreme Court in

---

[28] In the United States concern had arisen in relation to the high level of damages being awarded, particularly in respect of medical negligence, and various states introduced capping in relation to general damages and punitive damages. The capping of awards has, however, given rise to a number of constitutional and legal problems, with the Supreme Court overturning the legislation passed by a number of States. There is as yet no conclusive evidence available that capping is an effective way of controlling insurance costs.

[29] It was believed the proposal would be open to challenge as an invasion of the personal rights guaranteed under the constitution.

[30] "Report on the Economic Evaluation of Insurance Costs in Ireland", October, 1966, prepared by Deloitte & Touche.

[31] ibid. p. 10. par 2.2.2. In response the Minister set up a Committee to investigate and advise him on the setting up of the proposed tribunal.

[32] The guidelines are produced and updated by the UK Judicial Studies Board and are guidelines only. Whilst a judge may accept or reject the guidelines in individual cases, they do represent a consensus on the levels of awards considered appropriate and are designed to promote consistency.

Sinnott v *Quinnsworth.*[33] In that case, the High Court, sitting with a jury, had assessed general damages at a total sum of £800,000 for the plaintiff, who had become a quadriplegic as a result of injuries sustained in a road traffic accident. The defendants appealed to the Supreme Court on the amount of the award, and there O'Higgins C. J. said:

> To talk of compensating for such a terrible transformation is to talk of assaying the impossible. Nevertheless, it is this impossible task which the court must attempt in endeavouring to determine in terms of money, compensation for such an injury. The danger is that in doing so all sense of reality may be lost. . . . In my view a limit must exist, and should be sought and recognised, having regard to the facts of each case and the social conditions which exist in our society. . . . What is to be provided . . . in the way of general damages is a sum, over and above those other sums, which is to be compensation, and only compensation. In assessing such a sum, the objective must be to determine a figure which is fair and reasonable. To this end, it seems to me that some regard should be had to the ordinary living standards of the country, to the general level of incomes, and to the things on which the plaintiff might reasonably be expected to spend money. It may be that in addition, on the facts of a particular case, other matters may arise for consideration in assessing what, in the circumstances, should be considered as reasonable. However, a yardstick of a reasonable nature must be applied if reality is to be retained in the assessment of such compensation. In this case the jury assessed general damages at a total sum of £800,000. In my view, such an assessment lacks all sense of reality. . . . In my view, unless there are particular circumstances which suggest otherwise, general damages in cases of this nature should not exceed a sum in the region of £150,000. I express that view having regard to the contemporary standards and money values and I am conscious that there may be changes and alterations in the future, as there have been in the past.[34]

---

[33] [1984] ILRM 523. See also *Reddy* v *Bates* [1984] ILRM 197, where a limit of £120,000 was put on general damages.

[34] ibid. at 532.

9.4.2 IRISH AND UK COMPARISONS

That cap, on general damages, was generally applied but there were exceptions. In 1988 in *Conley* v *Strain*[35] Lynch J. awarded £170,000 for past and future pain and suffering and in *Crilly* v *T. & J. Farrington Ltd. and Another*,[36] Denham J., gave an award of £60,000 for general damages to the date of hearing and a further amount of £150,000 for future general damages. In 1996, in *Connolly* v *Bus Eireann & Others*.[37] Barr J. held that as it had been eleven years since the Supreme Court had determined the limit of general damages to be awarded, the true limit should now be £200,000. The Supreme Court recently approved the new maximum of £200,000 for general damages in *Allen* v *Ó Súilleabháin and the Mid-Western Health Board*.[38] By comparison, the UK Judicial Guidelines for Personal Injuries recommend an upper limit of stg£125,000 for catastrophic injuries and the highest ever awarded in the English Courts was stg£130,000.[39] However, a recent comparison of High Court awards with the UK Guidelines found that 85 per cent of the Irish High Court awards examined fell within the range of the UK guidelines.[40] The problem in Ireland is not so much the level of awards in the case of serious injury, but rather the frequency of claims and the relatively high cost of settling claims. It is estimated that Irish insurers deal with approximately 24,300 liability claims per annum[41] at a cost of £225.9 million

---

[35] *Conley* v *Strain* [1988] IR 628.

[36] *Crilly* v *T. & J. Farrington Ltd.* [1992] Unreported High Court, 26 August 1992.

[37] *Connolly* v *Bus Eireann & Others* [1996] Unreported, High Court, 29 January 1996; An amount of £220,000 was awarded by Carney J., in *Hughes* v *O'Flaherty & Another*, Unreported High Court, January 1996.

[38] Unreported, 11 March 1997; see also *Coppinger* v *Waterford County Council & Others* [1996] 2 ILRM 427.

[39] *Whiteside* v *Howes* [1994], per UK Law Commission Consultative Paper No. 140, "Damages for Personal Injury Non-Pecuniary Loss", 1995. A feature of the English system not applicable in Ireland is the facility available to a plaintiff, following the service of a writ on the defendant, to apply to the Court for an interim payment. This provides the plaintiff who has been severely injured with financial assistance at an early stage and facilitates the setting up, before the trial of the action, of care and therapy arrangements which can be properly costed and evaluated.

[40] "Report on the Economic Evaluation of Insurance Costs in Ireland", 1996, Deloitte & Touche, p. 7.

[41] ibid. pp. 24, 27.

and that average claims costs in the UK are between 40 per cent and 50 per cent of the Irish average. The average claims cost per employee in the UK in 1994 was £32 compared to £116 in Ireland.[42]

9.4.3 INTERIM AWARDS

It is not unusual for total damages awarded to an injured person to exceed £1 million and there have been calls for the introduction of interim awards and structured settlements. The Law Reform Commission, in its recent report on "Personal Injuries: Period Payments, Structured Settlements"[43] was of the view that a plaintiff who obtains an award of damages for injury, pain and suffering and economic loss to date should be entitled to receive that sum immediately, rather than have it made part of a structured settlement. It suggests that the structured settlement process should only apply to future injury and loss. It recommends that provision should be made for the interim award of damages, but that such awards should not be based on need. The resources of the defendant should not be relevant and any such award should be conditional on an admission of liability.

9.5 INDEMNITY AND LIABILITY INSURANCE

9.5.1 RIGHT TO BE INDEMNIFIED

Liability insurance policies, just like property insurance policies, are contracts of indemnity.[44] At common law there was no obligation on an insurer to pay a liability claim until the insured had suffered a

---

[42] ibid. p. 26. In England in 1994 there were 130,000 Employers' Liability claims costing £689 million; see *Post* Magazine 7 November 1996.

[43] Delivered to the Attorney General, 16 December 1996.

[44] *Lancashire Insurance Co.* v *Inland Revenue Commissioners* [1899] 1 QB 353; Bruce J. at 359 said:

> It seems to me . . . that the liability of the insured to compensate his workmen lies at the very root of the contract; it is the cardinal event upon which the liability of the insurer to pay the money under the policy depends. It is in truth and substance a contract of indemnity.

British Cash and Parcel Conveyors Ltd. v *Lamson Store Service Co. Ltd.* [1908] 1 KB 1006 at 1014, per Fletcher Moulton L. J.:

> Contracts of indemnity . . . are well known to the law. They are of the most varied kinds. . . . Frequently the insurance is against claims which may be made by third parties. . . . the courts have never shown any disapprobation of such contracts or any disinclination to enforce them.

loss[45] and nothing less than payment of damages to the third party would suffice as proof of loss.[46] Equity intervened, however, and it is now accepted that a loss is suffered once the insured's liability and the extent of the liability is ascertained in legal proceedings or otherwise.[47] The right of an insured to be indemnified, under a liability insurance policy, arises when the insured's liability to the third party has been determined by agreement, award or court judgment and not when the incident or occurrence giving rise to the liability takes place. According to Lord Denning,

> The insured only acquires a right to sue [the insurer] for the money when his liability to the injured person has been established so as to give rise to a right to indemnity . . . either by the judgment of the court or by an award in arbitration or by agreement.[48]

A liability insurance policy indemnifies the insured in respect of sums which the insured becomes legally liable to pay as damages or compensation and will, generally, in addition pay costs and expenses recovered by the claimant against the insured and costs and expenses incurred in the defence of the action by the insured with the permission of the insurer.

9.5.2 EXTENT OF INDEMNITY

Generally there is no problem in establishing the extent of indemnity to be provided to the insured in so far as the amount for which they are liable to the third party plaintiff is established by a court, an arbitrator or by agreement and the insurer is generally involved in any such proceedings to determine liability and quantum. However,

---

[45] per Lord Denning M. R. in *Post Office* v *Norwich Union* [1967] 2 QB 363 at 374, 378, approving Devlin J in *West Wake Price & Co.* v *Ching* [1957] 1 WLR 45.

[46] In *Re: Richardson ex parte Governors of St. Thomas's Hospital* [1911] 2 KB 705; *McGillivray* v *Hope* [1935] AC 1.

[47] Marine policies have a "pay to be paid" clause which in effect restores the common law rule. In *"The Fanti"* and *"The Padre Island"* [1990] 2 Lloyds Rep 191, the House of Lords held that such a clause in a policy was effective to relieve the insurers of liability to indemnify the insured until the insured had discharged his liability to the cargo owners for their losses.

[48] *Post Office* v *Norwich Union* [1967] 2 QB 363; confirmed in *Bradley* v *Eagle Star* [1989] AC 957, per Lord Brandon at 966. This could be of importance in circumstances where the Statute of Limitations is relevant.

where the damages awarded include an element of punitive or exemplary damages, it is unclear whether a liability policy does or should respond to indemnify the insured in respect of that element. Some policies make the position clear by specifically excluding punitive or exemplary damages, but some insurers have relied on the accepted definition of "compensation" and public policy arguments to avoid liability for such damages. In the development of tort law the principles of punishment and compensation competed for primacy,[49] but it is now generally accepted[50] that compensation of the victim is the principal purpose of an award of damages in a tort action. Whilst in cases of unconstitutional or wanton interference with a plaintiff's rights the courts have accepted that punitive or exemplary damages could be awarded,[51] O'Higgins C.J. in the Supreme Court in *Sinnott* v *Quinnsworth*[52] said that money could not possibly compensate for severe injuries but

> [It] would be a ground for legitimate complaint if the sum awarded were so high as to constitute a punishment for the infliction of the injury rather than a reasonable, if imperfect, attempt to compensate the injured.

9.5.3 EXEMPLARY DAMAGES

In *Rookes* v *Barnard*,[53] the House of Lords accepted that an award might take into account the motives and conduct of the defendant where they aggravate the injury done to the plaintiff,[54] but held that exemplary damages might be awarded only where:

1) the injury is the result of "oppressive, arbitrary or unconstitutional action by the servants of the Government";

---

[49] See McGregor (1965).

[50] See: Friedman (1970); McGregor (1971); White (1987).

[51] *Kennedy* v *Ireland*, [1988] ILRM 472; *Noblett* v *Leitrim County Council* [1920] 2 IR; *Worthington* v *Tipperary County Council* [1920] 2 IR 233; *Sligo Corporation* v *Gilbride* [1929] 1 IR 342; *Melling* v *O'Mathgamhna* [1962] 1 IR 1.

[52] [1984] ILRM 522.

[53] [1964] AC 1129.

[54] ibid. 1221.

2) "the defendant's conduct has been calculated by him to make a profit for himself which may well exceed the compensation payable to the Plaintiff";

3) "exemplary damages are expressly authorised by statute."[55]

9.5.4 IRISH LAW

9.5.4.1 It is not clear from the Irish decisions[56] if the Irish Courts fully subscribe to these principles. It had been suggested that there was a distinction between "punitive" and "exemplary" damages,[57] although other common law jurisdictions accept the words as being interchangeable, but the Supreme Court has now said that the words

---

[55] ibid. at 1226 per Lord Devlin. In *Broome* v *Cassell & Co.* [1971] 2 QB 354 the Court of Appeal made a trenchant criticism of Lord Devlin's speech in *Rookes* v *Bernard* [1964] AC 1129 on the question of exemplary damages and that what they called this "new doctrine" about exemplary damages was arrived at *per incuriam* and that they were not bound by it. The House of Lords on appeal held that the decision in *Rookes* v *Bernard* was not arrived at *per incuriam* and was binding on the Court of Appeal. The speech of Lord Devlin was subjected to devastating criticism in *Uren* v *John Fairfax & Sons Pty. Ltd.* [1967] ALR 25 by the High Court of Australia which refused to follow it. Courts in Canada and New Zealand have also refused to follow it and it has found no favour in the United States of America. In *Australia Consolidated Press Ltd.* v *Uren* [1969] 1 AC 590, the Privy Council found it impossible to say that the High Court in Australia were wrong in being unconvinced that a changed approach in Australia was desirable in the light of the decision in *Rookes* v *Bernard*.

[56] *Dillon* v *Dunnes Stores Ltd.* [1968] Unreported Supreme Court, 20 December; *McDonald* v *Galvin* [1976] Unreported High Court, 23 February; *Whelan* v *Madigan* [1978] ILRM 136; *Garvey* v *Ireland* [1981] ILRM 266; *Kearney* v *Minister for Justice* [1986] IR 116; *Kennedy* v *Ireland* [1988] ILRM 472; *Conway* v *Ireland*. [1988] Unreported High Court, 2 November; *McIntyre* v *Lewis, Dolan, Ireland and the Attorney General* [1990] 1 IR 121; *Conway* v *Irish National Teachers Organisation* [1991] 2 IR 305.

[57] per Hamilton P. in *Kennedy* v *Ireland* [1988] ILRM 472:
   . . . damages may be compensatory, aggravated, exemplary or punitive . . . [and] it was quite clear from a consideration of the Civil Liability Act, 1961, and in particular Sections 7(2) and 14(4) thereof that Irish Law recognises a distinction as between "punitive damages" and "exemplary damages".

are synonymous.[58] In *Whelan* v *Madigan*[59] the High Court awarded aggravated, not exemplary damages, with Kenny J. quoting the remark of Lord Devlin that "aggravated damages in this type of case do most, if not all, of the work that could be done by exemplary damages".[60] A case has been made[61] for a doctrine of exemplary damages, to be recognised by the Irish courts, wider than that laid down by Lord Devlin in *Rookes* v *Bernard*.[62] It was suggested that liability for exemplary damages should arise where the defendant intentionally and recklessly injured the plaintiff or his property in circumstances where the misconduct was so gross as to warrant punishment over and above compensatory damages, (with "recklessness" meaning the conscious taking of an unjustifiable risk of injury).

9.5.4.2 The Supreme Court was presented with an opportunity to clarify the position, in *McIntyre* v *Lewis, Dolan, Ireland and the Attorney General*,[63] when hearing an appeal against an award of com-

---

[58] In *McIntyre* above at 139 O'Flaherty J. stated that while the words "exemplary damages" were referred to in Section 7(2) of the Civil Liability Act, 1961 and the words "punitive damages" were used in Section 14(4) of the Act, the terms were synonymous. He believed this to be so because it is impossible to articulate separate concepts of "exemplary" and "punitive" damages. He referred to the interchange of the words in older cases and quoted a passage from Moloney C. J. in *Worthington* v *Tipperary County Council* [1920] 2 IR 233 at 245: "punitive or vindictive damages stand upon an entirely different footing, and are given not merely to repay the plaintiff for temporal loss, but to punish the defendant in an exemplary manner." In *Conway* v *Irish National Teachers Organisation* [1991] 2 IR 305, Finlay C. J. at 318 said:

> I do not consider, notwithstanding the provisions of the Civil Liability Act, 1961, that it is possible to maintain any real distinction between punitive and exemplary damages. As a matter of the ordinary use of words and as a matter of common sense it is almost impossible to award damages for the purpose of making an example of a person without, to some extent, at least, punishing that person. It is equally impossible to award damages for the purpose of punishing a person without, to some extent, making an example of him. . . . Without attempting to give a reason for the statutory use of these two separate terms I am satisfied that they must be considered as eventually meaning the same thing.

[59] Unreported High Court 18 July 1978.

[60] [1964] AC 1129 at 1230.

[61] White (1987).

[62] [1964] AC 1129.

[63] *McIntyre* v *Lewis, Dolan, Ireland and the Attorney General* [1990] 1 IR 121.

pensatory damages for assault and false imprisonment, and exemplary damages for malicious prosecution. The court (Hederman, McCarthy, O'Flaherty JJ.) was less than definitive in its view of the basis or circumstances for the award of exemplary damages. Hederman J. expressed the view that exemplary damages could be awarded in cases where there was an abuse of power by employees of the State but did not give consideration to or express any opinion on whether exemplary damages could be awarded in any other circumstances. He did say that where exemplary damages are awarded, they should bear some relation to the compensatory damages and that exemplary damages were one of the ways of vindicating the rights of citizens subjected to oppressive conduct by employees of the State.[64] McCarthy J. recognised the need for consideration of the circumstances where exemplary damages might be awarded but, reserving such consideration for a more appropriate time, he confined himself to saying that "it was inconsistent with the dynamism that characterises the common law to delimit in any restrictive way the nature of its development as was suggested in *Rookes* v *Bernard*".[65] O'Flaherty J. was in no doubt that exemplary damages could be awarded in the circumstances of the case and went on to distinguish the different categories of damages, citing a passage from *Salmond and Heuston on the Law of Torts*:

> Compensatory damages are awarded as compensation for and are measured by the material loss suffered by the plaintiff. A distinct category is that of aggravated damages which may be awarded when the motives and conduct of the defendant aggravate the injury to the plaintiff. Insulted and injured feelings are a proper subject for compensation, . . . yet another distinct category is that of exemplary damages, which reflect the jury's view of the defendant's outrageous conduct. Aggravated damages are given for conduct which shocks the plaintiff, exemplary damages are given for conduct which shocks the jury.[66]

9.5.4.3 O'Flaherty J. added that aggravated damages were meant to compensate the plaintiff whereas exemplary damages were not compensatory at all. He declined to decide whether or not exemplary

---

[64] ibid. at 141.

[65] ibid. at 138.

[66] Salmond and Heuston (1987), p. 594.

damages could only be awarded along the lines of the categories referred to in *Rookes* v *Bernard*[67] but he adopted the three considerations of Lord Devlin as always requiring to be borne in mind when awards of exemplary damages were being considered. He summarised these as follows:

1) the plaintiff cannot recover exemplary damages unless he is the victim of punishable behaviour;

2) the power to award exemplary damages constitutes a weapon that, while it can be used in defence of liberty, could also be used against liberty. There is a need for restraint in the amount of damages that should be awarded;

3) the means of the parties are material in the assessment of exemplary damages. Everything which aggravates or mitigates the defendant's conduct is relevant.[68]

He agreed with Hederman J. that a reasonable proportion had to be kept between the award of exemplary damages and compensatory damages but went further and suggested that awards of exemplary damages, which be should rarely made, should be kept on a tight rein.[69]

9.5.4.4 While the judgment in *McIntyre* was being delivered, a differently constituted Supreme Court (Finlay C. J., Griffin, McCarthy JJ.) was considering arguments in relation to exemplary damages in the case of *Conway* v *Irish National Teachers Organisation*.[70] The reserved judgment, when delivered two months later, confirmed the absence of unanimity in the Supreme Court on the issue. The Chief Justice concluded that the three headings under which damages might be awarded in Irish Law in respect of tort or breach of constitutional right are:

1) Ordinary compensatory damages, being sums calculated to recompense a wronged plaintiff for physical injury, mental

---

[67] [1964] AC 1129 at 1230.

[68] [1990] 1 IR 121 at 140, 141.

[69] ibid. 141.

[70] *Conway* v *Irish National Teachers' Organisation and Others* [1991] 2 IR 305.

distress, anxiety, deprivation of convenience, or other harmful effects of a wrongful act and/or for moneys lost or to be lost and/or expenses incurred or to be incurred by reason of the commission of the wrongful act.

2) Aggravated damages, being compensatory damages increased by reason of:

a) the manner in which the wrong was committed, involving such elements as oppressiveness, arrogance or outrage, or

b) the conduct of the wrongdoer after the commission of the wrong, such as a refusal to apologise or to ameliorate the harm done or the making of threats to repeat the wrong, or

c) conduct of the wrongdoer and/or his representatives in the defence of the claim of the wronged plaintiff, up to and including the trial of the action.

3) Punitive or exemplary damages arising from the nature of the wrong which has been committed and/or the manner of its commission which are intended to mark the court's particular disapproval of the defendant's conduct in all the circumstances of the case and its decision that it should publicly be seen to have punished the defendant for such conduct by awarding such damages, quite apart from its obligation, where it may exist in the same case, to compensate the plaintiff for the damage he or she has suffered. I have purposely used the above phrase "punitive or exemplary damages" because I am forced to the conclusion that, notwithstanding relatively cogent reasons to the contrary, in our law punitive and exemplary damages must be recognised as constituting the same element.[71]

9.5.4.5 Finlay C. J. went on to say that bearing in mind the reasons for the existence of a right to award exemplary damages and the pur-

---

[71] ibid. at 317, the Chief Justice adding that:

such a list of the circumstances which may aggravate compensatory damages until they can properly be classified as aggravated damages is not intended to be in any way finite or complete. Furthermore, the circumstances which may properly form an aggravating feature in the measurement of compensatory damages must, in many instances, be in part a recognition of the added hurt or insult to the plaintiff who has been wronged, and in part also a recognition of the cavalier or outrageous conduct of the defendant.

poses which in his opinion a court must be seeking to achieve in making an award of exemplary damages,

> as a general principle they should not be awarded if, in the opinion of the court, the amount necessarily payable by the wrongdoer in the form of compensatory damages constituted a sufficient public disapproval of and punishment for the particular form of his wrongdoing.[72]

Griffin J. agreeing with the judgment of the Chief Justice added his own views on the question of exemplary damages saying that:

> such damages may be awarded where there has been, on the part of the defendant, wilful and conscious wrongdoing in contumelious disregard of another's rights. The object of awarding exemplary damages is to punish the wrongdoer for his outrageous conduct, to deter him and others from such conduct in the future, and to mark the court's . . . detestation and disapproval of that conduct. Such damages are to be awarded even though the plaintiff who recovers them obtains the benefit of what has been described in the case law as a fortunate windfall.[73]

9.5.4.6 Griffin J. accepted that the three considerations summarised by O'Flaherty J. in *McIntyre* should be borne in mind in awarding exemplary damages but he could see no valid reason, in logic or common sense, for limiting the right to recover exemplary damages for oppressive, arbitrary or unconstitutional action to the acts of servants of the executive.[74] McCarthy J. declined the opportunity to engage in a detailed consideration of the issue and simply rejected that the

---

[72] ibid. at 321, 322.

[73] ibid. at 323.

[74] Griffin J. at 324 quoted a passage from the judgment of Salmon J. in the Court of Appeal in *Broome* v *Cassell & Co.* [1971] 2 QB 354 at 356:
> Why should exemplary damages be recoverable only for outrageous conduct by servants of the crown? The public equally requires protection against such conduct if it is perpetrated by local authorities, nationalised industries, the police, trade unions, large corporations and indeed by anyone, especially if in a position of power.

Griffin J. said that the passage is, in his view,
> not only sound common sense but would also appear to be in line with the law on the question of exemplary damages as applied in all common law countries with the exception of England and Wales.

categories for the award of exemplary damages are as limited as set out in the speech of Lord Devlin in *Rookes* v *Bernard*.[75] The judgments of the Supreme Court, while not completely definitive, nevertheless confirm that an award of exemplary damages is not intended to be compensatory. Such an award would not therefore be deemed "compensation" within the terms of a liability insurance policy providing "indemnity in respect of liability for sums which the insured shall become legally liable to pay as compensation".

9.5.4.7 English Law

The Court of Appeal in England recently took the opposite view in *Lancashire County Council* v *Municipal Mutual Insurance*.[76] The plaintiff local authority held a liability insurance policy providing indemnity in respect of "all sums which the insured shall become legally liable to pay as compensation". The plaintiff had been held vicariously liable for damages awarded against police officers for wrongful arrest, malicious prosecution and false imprisonment. The damages included an element for exemplary damages.[77] Insurers admitted the claim for indemnity in so far as it related to the damages awarded for loss suffered by the victims of the police officers' actions, but declined to meet the liability for exemplary damages. The plaintiff applied to the High Court for a declaration that the defendant insurers were liable for the full amount of the award. The Court found in favour of the insured. It found that as a matter of policy construction the word "compensation" covered both compensatory and

---

[75] at 326 McCarthy J said:

 Rookes v *Bernard* [1964] AC 1129 [has] been the subject of significant comment in other common law jurisdictions and the relevant principles set out in the case have been expressly rejected. . . . Members of the Court of Appeal in England have described the categories for exemplary or punitive damages in *Rookes* v *Bernard* as "hopelessly illogical and inconsistent" or as coming from an "unworkable" decision. . . . The condemnation of *Rookes* v *Bernard* was rejected by a majority of four Law Lords to three. It is sufficient . . . to state that I do not accept that the categories for the award of exemplary damages are as limited as set out in the speech of Lord Devlin in *Rookes* v *Bernard* [1964] AC 1129.

[76] *Lancashire County Council* v *Municipal Mutual Insurance* [1996] Unreported Court of Appeal, April 1996.

[77] In an earlier case of *Threadway* v *Chief Constable of West Midlands* [1994] *The Times* 24 October, a man injured during questioning by police was awarded £10,000 compensatory damages and £40,000 exemplary damages.

exemplary damages. It also held that there was no reason in public policy for excluding exemplary damages and, in the absence of clear authority holding that public policy objected to the provision of indemnity in respect of such damages, the court was unwilling to hold that it was so.

9.5.4.8 The insurers had argued that it would be contrary to public policy to indemnify an insured in respect of an award of exemplary damages. The Court of Appeal, in upholding the High Court's finding in relation to the proper construction of the policy, recognised that the word "compensation" was ambiguous but agreed that it should be construed as including exemplary damages.[78] In the leading judgment, given by Brown L. J., it was accepted that the ordinary meaning of "compensation" in the context of legal liability to pay damages was one that excluded any element of exemplary damages, but this meaning was not wholly clear and unambiguous.[79] It was, he believed, very much a literal lawyer's understanding of the term which would not command universal acceptance. The Court further held that whilst it was not permissible for a person to insure himself against the consequences of a crime, whether or not it was one of deliberate violence, public policy did not prevent recovery under a liability insurance policy, in respect of vicarious liability, even where the primary wrongdoer had been guilty of criminal conduct. Brown L. J. declared that, in the absence of criminality, English Law should not rule that there can be no recovery under an insurance policy for an award of exemplary damages. He did not believe that public policy would be best served by a prohibition of indemnity for exemplary damages and that it would be inappropriate for the common law at

---

[78] An endorsement on the policy provided pollution cover but specifically excluded punitive damages and the court held it was reasonable therefore to hold that the word "compensation" as used in the body of the policy covered exemplary damages. Furthermore the principle of *contra preferentum* required that the wording be construed in favour of the plaintiff.

[79] To support his contention, he cited a passage from the judgment of Stephenson, L. J. in *Riches* v *News Group Newspapers Ltd.* [1986] 12 QB 256 in which the word "compensation" was used four times; the second time to refer to exemplary damages. Since the word was capable of being used in the sense of either including or excluding exemplary damages, he concluded that the question was what meaning it was intended to bear in the policy under consideration. There seemed to him to be only one possible answer: that it included exemplary damages.

this stage to invent new public policy rules when Parliament had not done so.[80]

9.5.4.9 In a subsequent case, *Hsu* v *Commissioner of Police for the Metropolis*,[81] the plaintiff had successfully sued for wrongful arrest, assault and false imprisonment, and had been awarded damages of £220,000. The Court of Appeal did not interfere with the compensation award of £20,000 but reduced the exemplary damages from £200,000 to £15,000. In so doing, the Court stressed that aggravated damages could be awarded if there were aggravating features about the case which would mean that the plaintiff did not get sufficient compensation for the injury suffered if the award was restricted to a basic one. However, it held that the total figure for basic and aggravated damages should not exceed what could be considered fair compensation for the injury suffered. If exemplary damages were awarded, such damages, although compensatory and not intended to punish, would contain a penal element as far as the defendant was concerned.

9.5.4.10 Some insurers endeavour to limit their exposure to claims for exemplary damages by the inclusion of a clause in the policy excluding liability

> in respect of any occurrence which results from a deliberate or intentional act or omission of the insured and which could reasonably have been expected by the insured having regard to the nature and circumstances of the such act or omission,

---

[80] In support of his argument, Brown L. J. cited the following considerations: (a) by allowing an insured to recover an award of exemplary damages, the prospects of the victim recovering the full award were enhanced, and this outweighed the deterrent and punitive value of an award of exemplary damages; (b) an award of exemplary damages even if recovered from insurers still had a deterrent and punitive effect in that insurers might increase the premium in the future or impose a higher level of deductible under the policy; (c) public policy required that parties be held to their contracts; (d) the imposition on insurers of liability for exemplary damages awarded against their policyholders might increase premiums for policyholders generally but if liability was not imposed and local authorities were rendered liable for such losses the burden would be cast on local council tax payers.

[81] Unreported Court of Appeal, 19 February 1997.

but this would not necessarily save them in circumstances where the insured is vicariously liable. In the Supreme Court, McCarthy J. made a point of saying that if the liability for damages was vicarious, as the employer of the primary tortfeasor, then the liability was for the entire amount of the damages.[82] It remains to be seen how the courts and insurers in Ireland react to the English decision.

9.5.5 CLAIMANT'S COSTS

Most liability insurance policies incorporate a clause whereby insurers agree that:

> In respect of a claim for damages to which the indemnity expressed in this policy applies the Company will also indemnify the insured against
>
> a) all costs of litigation recovered by any claimant from the insured,
>
> b) all costs and expenses incurred with the written consent of the Company.

Unless there is provision to the contrary, such costs are payable in addition to the amount of damages awarded against the insured. Costs incurred by the insured in pursuing a counter claim against the third party would not be covered as such a claim would not be a claim "to which the indemnity expressed in the policy applies",[83] but the fact that the insurer has agreed to indemnify the insured in respect of his costs does not preclude him from recovering his costs from an unsuccessful third party claiming against him.[84] In the absence of specific reference to indemnity in respect of costs, sums expended by the insured in defending a third party claim are a proper matter for indemnity, provided they are reasonable and subject otherwise to the policy terms and conditions.[85] A policy which provided that "the Company will indemnify the insured against all sums for which the insured shall become legally liable to pay as compensation" was held to

---

[82] *McIntyre* v *Lewis and Others* [1991] IR 121 at 139.

[83] *Cross* v *British Oak Insurance* [1938] 2 KB 167.

[84] *Cornish* v *Lynch* [1910] 3 BWCC 343.

[85] *Forney* v *Dominion Insurance Co. Ltd.* [1969] 1 WLR 928, per Donaldson J. at 935; *Capel-Cure Myers Capital Management Ltd.* v *McCarthy* [1995] LRLR 498.

refer to damages only and not to include third party costs.[86] This, it is suggested, is a very narrow interpretation and most insurers using such a wording now add after "compensation", "and claimants' costs and expenses". Where the consent of the insurer is required it will be implied that such consent is not to be unreasonably withheld.[87]

9.5.6 DEFENCE COSTS

Most liability insurance policies also extend to cover the payment of solicitors' fees, incurred with the written consent of the insurer, for representation of the insured, at proceedings in any Court of Summary Jurisdiction, arising out of an alleged breach of statutory duty, resulting in an event or occurrence which may be the subject of indemnity under the policy, or at any Coroner's Inquest or Fatal Accident Inquiry in respect of such an occurrence. Sometimes the reference to any Court of Summary Jurisdiction is amended to apply to any Court so that costs incurred in an appeal would be covered. The purpose of the extension is to ensure that insurers are not prejudiced by inadequate representation at inquests or fatal accident inquiries. Breach of statutory duty can often result in a criminal prosecution and insurers have a common interest with the insured in defending such a prosecution, as a conviction makes more difficult the successful defence of a civil action for damages. The indemnity provided does not extend to any fines or penalties imposed on the insured by the court. It is also usual now for liability policies to cover legal costs and other expenses incurred with the written consent of the insurer and the costs of a prosecution awarded against the insured arising out of any prosecution of the insured for a breach or alleged breach of the Safety (Health and Welfare at Work) Act, 1989 as a result of an occurrence likely to give rise to claim under the policy.

9.5.7 LIMIT OF INDEMNITY

Liability policies generally contain a stated sum in respect of the limit of the liability of the insurer for all compensation payable to any claimant or number of claimants. The limit does not generally apply

---

[86] *Aluminium Wire & Cable* v *All State Insurance Co.* [1985] 2 Lloyds Rep 280.

[87] *Hulton & Co. Ltd.* v *Mountain* [1921] 8 Lloyds Rep 249.

to costs which are payable in addition.[88] Sometimes the limit is stated to apply to "any one accident" or "any one occurrence or series of occurrence arising out of one original cause" or may be the aggregate limit in respect of any one period of insurance. It is usual for the policy to provide that the insurer may pay to the insured the maximum sum payable under the policy in respect of any one occurrence or any lesser sum for which the claim or claims can be settled, and the insurer will not then be under any further liability in respect of that occurrence except for the payment of costs and expenses of litigation incurred prior to payment of the amount by the insurer.

9.5.8 OCCURRENCE VERSUS CLAIMS MADE

Most liability policies issued in Ireland provide cover on an "occurrence" basis.[89] Such policies provide cover in respect of loss injury or damage arising out of an event or accident occurring during the period of the policy even though the negligent act or omission may have occurred outside the period. "Claims made" policies, on the other hand, provide cover in respect of claims made during the period of the policy, regardless of when the injury or activity giving rise to the claim occurred. Such policies are illegal in Belgium and in the US, where they originated. Insurers and reinsurers who negotiated the change from "occurrence" to "claims made" wordings were said by the Supreme Court to be guilty of unlawful collusion.[90]

9.6 LEGAL LIABILITY

Liability insurance policies provide indemnity in respect of the insured's legal liability only. No indemnity is provided in respect of social or moral obligations. Legal liability can arise in tort, contract or under statute. Liability policies generally cover liability in tort or arising out of breach of statutory duty, but do not cover liability for breach of contract. Liability for bodily injury or damage to property assumed under agreement may be covered subject to limitations.

---

[88] It is common in respect of policies covering products liability risks in the US or pollution liability for policies to have a limit of liability which is inclusive of costs.

[89] Professional Indemnity policies and policies covering products liability in the USA would normally be on a "claims made" basis.

[90] *Hartford Fire Insurance Co.* v *California* [1993] 113 S Ct 2891.

Statutory liability generally arises in the areas of property,[91] products[92] and safety legislation.[93] By far the greatest number of third party claims are founded in negligence, but wherever possible breach of statutory duty will also be pleaded.[94] In order to establish negligence the injured third party must prove that the insured owed him a duty of care, that the insured was in breach of that duty, that there was a causal connection between the insured's conduct and the injury sustained, and that the resultant damage was not too remote.

9.6.1 DUTY OF CARE

It has been said that, of all the judicial developments of the twentieth century, the greatest has been the in the law of negligence.[95] Prior to 1932 it was accepted that no one could sue a contracting party except the person who had made the contract with that party.[96] A person, not a party to the contract, but injured by the carelessness of a contracting party carrying out the contract, had no right of redress against the person responsible for the injury. The courts had begun to develop a category of dangerous things[97] before the Master of the Rolls, Brett (later Lord Esher), tried in *Heaven* v *Pender*[98] to establish a

---

[91] Occupiers Liability Act, 1995.

[92] Defective Products Act, 1991.

[93] Factories Act, 1955; Safety (Health and Welfare at Work) Act, 1989.

[94] All claims by employees against their employers will invariably allege breach of statutory duty.

[95] Denning (1979), *The Discipline of the Law*, London: Butterworths, p. 227.

[96] *Earl* v *Lubbock* [1905] 1 KB 253.

[97] *Dixon* v *Bell* [1816] 105 ER 1023; *Langridge* v *Levy* [1837] 150 ER 863 (guns); *Winterbottom* v *Wright* [1842] 152 ER 402 (coach); *Longmeid* v *Holliday* [1851] 155 ER 752 (lamp); *George* v *Skivington* [1869] LR 5 Ex 1 (hairwash); *Parry* v *Smith* [1879] 4 CPD 325; and *Dominion Natural Gas Co. Ltd.* v *Colling & Perking* [1909] AC 640 (gas appliances).

[98] [1883] 11 QBD 503. The plaintiff, a workman in the employment of a firm engaged to paint a ship in the defendant's dry dock, was injured when the scaffolding collapsed. Brett M. R. attempted to formulate a comprehensive general rule:
> The proposition . . . is that whenever one person is by circumstances placed in such a position with regard to another that everyone of ordinary sense who did think would at once recognise that if he did not use ordinary care and skill in his own conduct with regard to those circumstances he would cause danger of injury to the person or property of the other, a duty arises to use ordinary care

wide formulation of the duty of care. His efforts did not find favour with his judicial colleagues and he recanted his views somewhat in *Le Lievre* v *Gould*[99] ten years later. From then to 1932 the common law seemed to prefer to continue to develop a category of dangerous things and particular duties of care rather than accept broad conceptual principles. However, eventually in that year, in *Donoghue* v *Stevenson*,[100] Lord Atkin called on Brett's judgment in *Le Lievre* v *Gould* to support his establishment of proximity, foreseeability and the "neighbour principle" as concepts of the duty of care in negligence. The case arose out of a snail in a bottle of ginger beer consumed by a person other than the person who had bought it. According to the law as it stood, she had no claim against the manufacturers. The case was a Scottish appeal to the House of Lords who had to determine whether the appellant had a cause of action. By a bare majority of 3:2 they found in her favour. In the course of his now famous judgment Lord Atkin said:

> In English law there must be, and is, some general conception of relations giving rise to a duty of care. . . . But acts or omissions which any moral code would censure cannot in a practical world be treated so as to give a right to every person injured by them to demand relief. . . . The rule that you are to love your neighbour becomes in law, you must not injure your neighbour; and the lawyer's question, "Who is my neighbour?" receives a restricted reply. You must take reasonable care to avoid acts or omissions which you can reasonably foresee would be likely to injure your neighbour. Who then in law is my neighbour? The answer seems to be — persons who are so closely and directly affected by my act that I ought reasonably have them in contemplation as being so affected when I am directing my mind to the acts or omissions which are called into question.[101]

9.6.1.1 Since that landmark decision, the law of negligence has been expanded in a manner which the majority of their lordships could not

---

and skill to avoid such danger. . . . this proposition includes, I think, all the recognised cases of liability.

[99] [1893] 1 QB 491. It was held that there was no liability for negligent misstatement.

[100] [1932] AC 562.

[101] ibid. 578.

possibly have anticipated. The concepts of proximity, foreseeability and the neighbour principle were expanded in *Hedley Byrne*,[102] to create liability for negligent misstatement, in *Dorset Yacht Co.*,[103] to establish that public authorities owe duties of care alongside their statutory duties, in *Junior Books*,[104] and *Anns*[105] to hold that economic loss was recoverable without damage or injury being incurred, in *McLoughlin* v *O'Brien*[106] to determine that nervous shock was a recoverable form of loss, and in *Wall* v *Hegarty*[107] and *Ross* v *Caunters*[108] to establish that professional people owed a duty of care not only to their clients but also to persons who might be adversely affected by their negligent conduct or advice. This expansion of the law of negligence was driven by the demands of consumer protection and the application of what the courts regarded as policy considerations.[109] Denning M. R. in *Spartan Steel & Alloys Ltd.*[110] said:

> The more I think about these cases, the more difficult I find it to put care into its proper pigeon hole. Sometimes I say: "There was no duty." In others I say: "The damage was too remote." So

---

[102] *Hedley Byrne & Co. Ltd.* v *Heller & Partners* [1964] AC 465.

[103] *Dorset Yacht Co.* v *Home Office* [1970] AC 1026.

[104] *Junior Books Ltd.* v *Veitchi & Co.* [1982] 2 All ER 201.

[105] *Anns* v *Merton Borough Council* [1978] AC 728.

[106] *McLoughlin* v *O'Brien* [1982] 2 All ER 298.

[107] *Wall* v *Hegarty* [1980] ILRM 124.

[108] *Ross* v *Caunters* [1979] 3 All ER 580.

[109] In *Dorset Yacht Co.* v *Home Office* [1970] AC 1026, Lord Reid said he detected: a steady trend towards regarding the law of negligence as depending on principle so that when a new point of import emerges one should ask not whether it is covered by authority but whether recognised principles apply to it. Atkin's statement should be regarded as a statement of principle not treated as a statutory definition.

In *Dutton* v *Bognor Regis Urban District Council* [1972] 1 QB 373, Lord Denning M.R. said:
It seems to me that it is a question of policy which we, as judges, have to decide. The time has come when, in cases of new import, we should decide them according to the reason of the thing. In previous times, when faced with a new problem, the judges have not openly asked themselves the question: what is the best policy for the law to adopt? But the question has always been in the background. It has been concealed behind such questions as: Was the defendant under any duty to the plaintiff. . . . In short, we look to the relationship of the parties, and then say, as a matter of policy, on whom the loss should fall.

[110] *Spartan Steel & Alloys Ltd.* v *Martin & Co. (Contractors) Ltd.* [1973] 1 QB 27.

much so that I think the time has come to discard those tests which have proved so elusive. It seems to me better to consider the particular relationship in hand, and see whether or not, as a matter of policy, economic loss should be recoverable.

9.6.1.2 In *Anns v Merton Borough Council*,[111] Lord Wilberforce had attempted to redefine the boundaries of the concept of a duty of care and introduce a two-stage test. He suggested that the test of whether a duty of care existed rested solely on whether: (a) there was a "sufficient relationship of proximity or neighbourhood such that, in the reasonable contemplation of the alleged wrongdoer, carelessness on his part may be likely to cause damage" to the other party; and (b) whether there "are any considerations which ought to negative, or to reduce or limit the scope of the duty or the class of person to whom it is owed or the damages to which a breach of it may give rise".[112] The proposition, whilst widely criticised,[113] was followed in the subsequent House of Lords decision in *Junior Books*[114] but subsequently unanimously rejected by the House of Lords in *Murphy v Brentwood District Council*.[115]

9.6.1.3 In Ireland, the courts had placed a heavy emphasis on proximity as the basis of the duty of care long before the House of Lords

---

[111] *Anns v Merton Borough Council* [1978] AC 728 decided that a defect in a foundation which subsequently threatened damage to the superstructure was physical damage and not economic loss and that damages were recoverable for the costs incurred in rectifying the superstructure and the defects in the foundations if imminent danger of injury or damage existed.

[112] ibid. at 751.

[113] The test had been openly criticised in a number of cases: *Governors of the Peabody Donation Fund v Sir Lindsay Parkinson & Co. Ltd.* [1985] AC 210; *Leigh and Sullivan Ltd v Alkiamon Shipping Co. Ltd.* [1986] AC 785; *Curran v Northern Ireland Housing Co-Ownership Assoc. Ltd.* [1987] AC 724.

[114] *Junior Books v Veitchi & Co.* [1982] 2 All ER 201.

[115] [1990] 2 All ER 909. The House of Lords held that *Anns* had been wrongly decided and that it and all subsequent cases which had been based on it should be over-ruled. In an earlier case *Yuen Kun-Yeu v A-G. for Hong Kong* [1987] 2 All ER 705 the Privy Council had said that Lord Wilberforce's two-stage test had been elevated to a degree of importance greater than its merits and greater than perhaps its author had intended. Foreseeability of harm is a necessary ingredient of the relationship referred to in *Donoghue v Stevenson* but it is not the only ingredient.

had called a halt to the expansion of negligence.[116] The retrenchment from *Anns* found support in the Irish High Court[117] but the Supreme Court took a different view, with McCarthy J. in *Ward* v *McMaster and Louth County Council* preferring "not . . . to dilute the words of Lord Wilberforce". He believed "the duty of care arose from the proximity of the parties, the foreseeability of the damage and the absence of any compelling exemption based upon public policy".[118] The plaintiff had bought a house from the first defendant with the help of a loan from the County Council. The house contained both dangerous and non-dangerous defects which made it uninhabitable. He sued the Council in negligence. The Council had engaged an auctioneer rather than an engineer or surveyor to carry out a valuation and the auctioneer had failed to discover the defects. The Council were found guilty of negligence on the basis that:

> there was a sufficient relationship of proximity or neighbour-hood between the plaintiff and the Council such that in the reasonable contemplation of the Council carelessness on their part in the carrying out of the valuation of the bungalow . . . might be likely to cause him damage.[119]

In *McComiskey* v *McDermott*[120] the Supreme Court was divided as to whether the concept of the duty of care was to be determined on objective criteria or by reference to the particular circumstances. The case arose out of an accident as a result of which the plaintiff, acting as a navigator in a motor rally, was injured when the defendant drove the car into a ditch and overturned it while trying to avoid an

---

[116] *Purtill* v *Athlone UDC* [1968] IR 205; *McNamara* v *ESB* [1975] IR 1.

[117] *Ward* v *McMaster* [1985] IR 29; *McMahon* v *Ireland* [1988] ILRM 610.

[118] *Ward* v *McMaster, Louth County Council & Others* [1988] IR 337. The county council had lent money to the plaintiff to purchase a house built by McMaster and on foot of a valuation by valuers, appointed by the council, certifying it as structurally sound, which it was not. The builder was not a mark so the plaintiff sued the council in negligence for not hiring a person sufficiently qualified to do an adequate structural survey as distinct from a valuation. The valuers appointed did not hold themselves out as qualified to do a structural survey. In the High Court Costello J. followed *Yuen Kun-Yeu* v *A-G. for Hong Kong* [1987] 2 All ER 705. In the Supreme Court, on appeal, the council were also found liable but on the application of Lord Wilberforce's test.

[119] pp. 21, 22 of Supreme Court judgment.

[120] [1974] IR 75.

obstacle. The jury in the High Court had found that the driver was not guilty of negligence. Walsh J., dissenting, was of the view that:

> The duty which the defendant owed to all persons . . . was the same. To hold otherwise would lead to rather absurd results. . . it could not be seriously contemplated that the liability . . . to each of the injured parties would be governed by different standards of duty.[121]

However, Henchy J., for the majority, held that:

> While the duty owed . . . to other[s] . . . is the objective one of showing due and reasonable care, the duty becomes particularised and personalised in the circumstances of the case. . . . Therefore it is necessary in each case to consider who is the person claiming to be owed the duty of care, who is the person it is claimed against, and what are the circumstances.[122]

9.6.2 CAUSATION

9.6.2.1 An insured cannot be held liable to a third party unless by their act or omission they caused the injury alleged. The third party must establish a causal connection between the act or omission constituting the breach of duty and the injury. If such a connection is established the insured may be liable. In the law of tort the question of causation "has plagued the courts and scholars more than any other".[123] Establishing causation is primarily a matter of fact, of cause and effect. In endeavouring to establish the proximate cause of injury the courts have developed the "but for" test which requires the third party to prove on the balance of probabilities that he would not have suffered the injury "but for" the insured's negligence. In *Barnett* v *Chelsea and Kensington Hospital Management Committee*,[124] three fellow night-watchmen presented themselves at the casualty department of the hospital, complaining that they had become ill having drunk some tea. The nurse on duty, having consulted the medical casualty officer, told them to go home to bed and call in their own doctors. The men left and some hours later one of them died from poi-

---

[121] ibid. at 82.

[122] ibid. at 88.

[123] Fleming, *The Law of Torts*, p. 172.

[124] [1969] 1 QB 428.

soning by arsenic which had been in the tea. The court dismissed an action by his widow claiming that his death was caused by the negligence of the defendant in not diagnosing or treating his condition. The court, whilst holding that the hospital owed a duty to exercise skill and care, and that the medical officer had been negligent in not examining the deceased, held that the hospital were not liable as the man would have died of the poisoning even if he had been admitted and treated. The plaintiff had failed to prove that the defendant's negligence had caused the death. In the Irish case of *Kenny* v *O'Rourke*[125] the plaintiff who was employed by the defendant fell from a ladder which was shown to be defective. The ladder was supplied by the main contractors who had engaged the defendant employers who owed a duty of care to provide proper and safe equipment. In admitting the ladder was dangerous the defendant adduced evidence to show that the cause of the plaintiff's fall was not the defect in the ladder but was "due to his having, unnecessarily, leaned over too far and thus overbalanced".[126]

9.6.2.2 The insured will be liable in negligence if his breach of duty causes or materially contributes to the injury suffered, notwithstanding that there are other factors for which the insured is not responsible, which also contribute to the injury.[127] Where the insured's breach of duty materially contributes to the risk of injury, the courts will, in the absence of positive proof to the contrary, find that the breach of

---

[125] [1972] IR 339.

[126] ibid. at 341 per O'Dalaigh C. J.; see also *Meehan* v *Reid & Murphy* [1985] Unreported High Court, 5 March; *Kearney* v *Paul & Vincent Ltd.* Unreported High Court, 30 July 1985; *Berkery* v *Flynn* Unreported High Court, 10 June 1982.

[127] *McGhee* v *National Coal Board* [1972] 3 All ER 1008.

duty materially contributed to the actual injury.[128] Where the injury is attributable to a number of possible causes, one of which is the insured's negligence, the combination of a breach of duty of care and the injury do not give rise to a presumption that the injury was caused by the insured. The third party must prove on the balance of probabilities that a causal link exists. In *Wilsher* v *Essex Area Health Authority*,[129] the infant plaintiff was born prematurely suffering from various illnesses including oxygen deficiency. While in a special baby unit in the hospital where he was born a catheter was twice inserted into a vein rather than an artery and on both occasions the plaintiff was given excess oxygen. The plaintiff was later discovered to be suffering from an incurable condition of the retina resulting in near blindness. The plaintiff's retina condition could have been caused by excess oxygen but it also occurred in premature babies who were not given oxygen but who suffered from five other conditions common in premature babies and all of which had afflicted the plaintiff. The plaintiff sued the hospital in negligence alleging the excess oxygen had caused his retinal condition. The House of Lords, in reversing the Court of Appeal, held that the burden remained on the plaintiff to prove the causative link between the defendant's negligence and his injury, although that link could legitimately be inferred from the evidence. Since the plaintiff's retinal condition could have been caused by any one of a number of different agents and it had not been proved that it was caused by the failure to prevent excess oxygen being given to him the plaintiff had not discharged the burden of proof as to causation.

---

[128] ibid. The plaintiff was required by his employers to clean out brick kilns where he was exposed to clouds of abrasive brick dust. Despite the dirty working conditions the employer provided no adequate washing facilities. Medical evidence showed that dermatitis had been caused by the working conditions in the brick kilns and that the fact that the plaintiff had to cycle home after work with brick dust adhering to his skin had added materially to the risk that he might develop the disease. On appeal to the House of Lords it was held that the defendant employer was liable in negligence to the plaintiff if the defendant's breach of duty had caused, or materially contributed to, the injury suffered by the plaintiff notwithstanding that there were other factors, for which the defendant was not responsible, which had contributed to the injury.

[129] *Wilsher* v *Essex Area Health Authority* [1988] 1 All ER 871.

9.6.2.3 In *Hotson* v *East Berkshire Area Health Authority*,[130] the plaintiff was injured in a fall in school grounds and sustained an acute fracture of the hip which was not immediately diagnosed by the defendant's hospital staff. Five days later he was brought back to hospital and the injury was correctly diagnosed and treated. He subsequently developed a medical condition which lead to a permanent disability. He sued the Health Authority in negligence. The Authority admitted that the delay in diagnosis when the plaintiff was first examined amounted to a breach of duty but denied that the resulting treatment had adversely affected the plaintiff's long-term condition. The House of Lords held that the crucial question which had to be determined was whether the cause of the plaintiff's injury was his fall or the Health Authority's negligence in making a correct diagnosis and delaying treatment, since if the fall had caused the injury the negligence of the Authority was irrelevant in regard to the plaintiff's disability. That question was to be decided on the balance of probabilities and since the trial judge had held that on the balance of probabilities, given the plaintiff's condition when he arrived at the hospital, even correct diagnosis and treatment would not have prevented the disability from occurring, it followed that the plaintiff had failed on the issue of causation.

9.6.2.4 The causal link between the insured's breach of duty and the third party's injury is sometimes broken by an intervening act which is of such a kind that it is deemed to be the sole or new cause of the injury — *novus actus interveniens*. The intervening act or omission may be that of another party, an independent physical event,[131] or a voluntary act of the injured third party. In *Crowley* v *AIB and Others*,[132] the plaintiff was seriously injured when he fell from the flat roof of the bank's branch office in Bandon, County Cork. The architects were joined as defendants on the grounds that in designing the premises they had failed to specify the need for a railing around the roof of the building. In the High Court, the architects were found to

---

[130] *Hotson* v *East Berkshire Area Health Authority* [1987] 2 All ER 907

[131] *Ashworth* v *General Accident* [1955] IR 268.

[132] *Crowley* v *AIB and O'Flynn, Green, Buchan and Partners* [1978] ILRM 225. The plaintiff, although permanently disabled and confined to a wheelchair, went on to become an elected member of the European Parliament.

be 30 per cent liable but the Supreme Court reversed the decision holding that there was no nexus between the negligence of the architects and the plaintiff's injury. The link between the injury and the architects' negligence was broken by the fact that the bank knew that boys regularly played on the unprotected flat roof and did not attempt to prohibit or prevent them from doing so. The failure of the bank to act constituted a *novus actus interveniens* which relieved the architects of liability.

9.6.2.5 In *Conole* v *Redbank Oyster Co.*[133] the defendants had taken delivery of a newly built boat which following trials they knew was unseaworthy and unsafe. Despite the known defects and in contravention of an order to tie up the boat the captain took fifty children out in the boat. The boat capsized and the plaintiff's daughter and nine other children were drowned. The defendants sought to recover contribution towards the damages awarded against them from the builders of the boat but the Supreme Court refused on the grounds that the sole cause of the accident was the defendants' negligence through the reckless act of the captain. The negligence of the boat builder did not cause the accident.

> The proximate cause of the accident was the decision of the defendants . . . to put to sea with passengers when they had a clear warning that the boat was unfit for the task. The defendants were the sole initiators of the causative negligence.[134]

9.6.2.6 In *Connolly* v *South of Ireland Asphalt Co. Ltd.*,[135] a motorcyclist skidded on ice outside the premises of the South of Ireland Asphalt Co. Ltd., and was struck and killed by a motor car driven by the plaintiff, Connolly. The motor cyclist's widow successfully sued Connolly and was awarded damages. Connolly then sought to recover a contribution from the South of Ireland Asphalt Co. Ltd on the grounds that it had been negligent and had created a public nuisance in allowing the road area outside their premises to deteriorate and fill with water which had frozen and caused the motor cyclist to fall in

---

[133] *Conole* v *Redbank Oyster Co.* [1976] IR 191.

[134] per Henchy J. at 196, 197.

[135] *Connolly* v *South of Ireland Asphalt Co. Ltd.* [1977] IR 99.

the first instance. Although Connolly had been guilty of gross negligence, the Supreme Court held that gross negligence did not constitute a *novus actus* negating the negligence of the company in failing to maintain the road. The type of harm which in fact occurred was a foreseeable consequence of the company's original negligence and it was irrelevant that the precise manner in which the harm happened was unforeseeable. Gross negligence of the intervening actor was insufficient to break the chain of causation. The principle of *novus actus interveniens* did not release from liability a builder who had negligently constructed a screen wall at Croke Park which, many years later, collapsed and injured a number of people during the All Ireland Hurling Final of 1985. The High Court held that the GAA, in the light of a number of UK and European disasters, had a duty to have an expert examination of the stadium carried out and found them guilty of negligence, apportioning 20 per cent of the blame to them and 80 per cent to the builder.[136] The intervening act will not be considered voluntary so as to relieve the original tortfeasor or wrongdoer if it is a reflex action,[137] or if it is performed by way of a moral or legal duty.[138]

9.6.2.7 Whilst the third party need only prove the causal connection on the lower standard of the balance of probabilities this may sometimes be difficult. In *Hanrahan* v *Merck Sharp and Dohme (Irl) Ltd.*[139] the scientific proof and technical evidence required of the plaintiff was extremely demanding. The plaintiffs, in proceedings based primarily in nuisance, claimed that emissions from the defendant's fac-

---

[136] *Cowan* v *Freaghaile, De Spainne, Cumann Luthchleas Gael Teo. and Thos. McInerney and Sons Ltd.* [1991] Unreported High Court, 24 January.

[137] *Scott* v *Shephard* [1773] 96 ER 525. The defendant threw a lighted squib into a market place, where it fell near a stallholder who, from natural instinct of self-preservation picked it up and threw it at random at another man's stall. That man threw it further and it exploded in the face of the plaintiff injuring his sight. The defendant had neither thrown the squib at the plaintiff nor intended bodily injury to anyone, but nevertheless the proximate cause of the injury to the plaintiff was the original act of the defendant and not the intervening acts of the stallholders. Accordingly he was held liable.

[138] *Haynes* v *Harwood* [1935] 1 KB 146; *Baker* v *T.E. Hopkins & Sons Ltd.* [1959] 1 WLR 966.

[139] [1988] ILRM 629.

tory caused damage to the health of the plaintiffs and their livestock. In the Supreme Court, Henchy J. said:

> The ordinary rule is that a person who alleges a particular tort must, in order to succeed, prove . . . all the necessary ingredients of that tort and it is not for the defendant to disprove anything. . . . What the plaintiffs have to prove in support of their claim . . . is that they suffered some or all of the mischief complained of and that it was caused by the . . . defendants. . . . To hold that it is for the defendants to disprove either or both of these matters would be contrary to authority and not be demanded by the requirements of justice. There are of course difficulties facing the plaintiffs in regard to proof of those matters, particularly as to the question of causation, but mere difficulty of proof does not call for a shifting of the onus of proof.[140]

In contrast, in *Kielthy* v *Ascon Ltd.*,[141] the Supreme Court held that, although there was no direct evidence as to how the deceased fell, there was sufficient evidence to find that the fall was caused by the defendant's failure to provide a safe system of access and that there was no contributory negligence on the part of the deceased. The workman had been found dead at the bottom of a wall on a building site and it was shown in evidence that a recognised route to the defendant's office at the site was along the nine-inch wide wall in question, although this was not the safest or indeed the only route.

9.6.3 RES IPSA LOQUITUR

9.6.3.1 In cases where there is no explanation of what actually occurred the courts will sometimes apply the principle of *res ipsa loquitur* (the facts speak for themselves). The principle is a rule of evidence and not a rule of substantive law. It is used where the facts which the plaintiff can prove are of themselves inadequate to prove the case but are sufficient to raise an inference that the injury is more likely to have occurred as a result of the defendant's negligence than through any other cause. The Supreme Court in *Mullen* v *Quinnsworth Ltd.*[142] approved the statement of principle of Erle C. J. in 1865 when he said:

---

[140] ibid. at 635.

[141] [1970] IR 122.

[142] [1990] 1 IR 59 per Griffin J. at p. 62, 63.

There must be reasonable evidence of negligence. But where the thing is shown to be under the management of the defendant or his servants, and the accident is such as in the ordinary circumstances does not happen if those who have the management use proper care, it affords reasonable evidence, in the absence of explanation by the defendants, that the accident arose from want of care.[143]

9.6.3.2 Before the plaintiff can set up the maxim of *res ipsa loquitur*, he must satisfy the court on two preconditions: (a) the thing that caused the injury or damage was under the direct control of the defendant, his servants or agents; and (b) the accident must be such that in the ordinary course of things it could not have occurred without negligence. The doctrine does not have to be pleaded before a plaintiff can rely on it. If the facts pleaded and the facts proved show that the doctrine is applicable to the case that is sufficient.[144] The application of the principle in Ireland has been clouded by the statement of Henchy J., in the Supreme Court case of *Hanrahan*, that "*res ipsa loquitur* applies where damage has been caused to the plaintiff in circumstances in which such damage would not usually be caused without negligence on the part of the defendant".[145] This approach by Henchy J. seems to merge the separate elements of the principle and was questioned in the Supreme Court, by Keane J. In a judgment, with which the Chief Justice agreed, in *O'Shea* v *Tilman Anhold and Horse Holiday Farm Ltd.*,[146] Keane J. called for reconsideration of the doctrine but the Chief Justice preferred to reserve his judgment on that. The plaintiff had recovered damages in the High Court in respect of a collision between a horse, owned by the defendants, and the plaintiff's car, while being driven by him on the public road. The evidence indicated that the horse, when last tended by the defendants shortly before the accident, was in a field adequately fenced and with a securely locked gate. No evidence was advanced by the plaintiff

---

[143] *Scott* v *London & St. Katherine Docks Co.* [1865] 159 ER 665 at 667. A customs officer was passing in front of a warehouse when six bags of sugar fell on him. It was held that the facts were sufficient in themselves to set up an inference of negligence.

[144] per Griffin J. in *Mullen* above, with Finlay C. J. concurring and applying *Bennett* v *Chemical Construction (GB) Ltd.* [1971] 1 WLR 1572.

[145] *Hanrahan* v *Merck Sharp & Dohme* [1988] ILRM 629.

[146] Unreported Supreme Court, 23 October 1996.

which proved that the collision had been caused by the negligence of
the defendants. The trial judge, Costello J., determined the case by
concluding that:

> The situation was that either the fencing on the laneway or
> field was inadequate or someone had opened the gate, let out
> one horse and closed the gate again. On balance the first pos-
> sibility was much more likely than the second. The problem of
> fencing is a difficult one and the defendant was unable to dis-
> charge the onus of proof on it. The plaintiff had shown a breach
> of duty. There was no contributory negligence on the part of
> the plaintiff.

9.6.3.3 In the Supreme Court, O'Flaherty J. disagreed with the reasoning of Costello J., saying that the defendants had disproved any
negligence on their part, through the evidence of expert witnesses
that the fencing was adequate, and that testimony had not been con-
tradicted by the plaintiff. The defendants were not required to take
the further step of proving how the horse came to be on the road. The
most that was required of a defendant in this situation, where the
onus of proof rested on him, was to disprove any negligence. In a
separate judgment, also allowing the appeal, Keane J. referred to the
legal principles governing liability for animals[147] and the change effected by the Animals Act, 1985. He said that, in the present case, it

---

[147] The common law rules were summarised by Lord Du Parcq, in *Searle* v *Wall-
bank* [1947] AC 341:

> the truth is that, at least on country roads and in market towns, users of the
> highway, including cyclists and motorists, must be prepared to meet from time
> to time a stray horse or cow, just as they must expect to encounter a herd of
> cattle in the care of a drover . . . an underlying principle of the law of the
> highway was that all those lawfully using the highway, or land adjacent to it,
> must show mutual respect and forbearance; the motorist must put up with the
> farmer's cattle and the farmer must endure the motorist.

The position as recounted by Du Parcq also represented the law in Ireland until
changed by the Animals Act, 1985, Section 2(1) of which provides that so much of
the rules of the common law, relating to liability for negligence, as excludes or
restricts the duty which a person might owe to others, to take such care as is
reasonable to see that damage is not caused by an animal straying on to the public road, was abolished. Prior to that Act, owners of animals which strayed on to
the public road were not liable for damage caused by the animals. While the Act
abolished that immunity to the ordinary rules of negligence it did not impose any
form of strict or absolute liability. It does impose a burden or onus on the owner
to show that he has taken reasonable care.

was accepted that the horse which collided with the plaintiff's car was the property of the second named defendant and had escaped, in some fashion from the first named defendant's land on to the highway. On those facts being established, the onus shifted to the defendants to prove, on the balance of probabilities, that they had taken such care as was reasonable to see that damage was not caused by horses escaping from the land on to the public road. It was a case in which the principle of *res ipsa loquitur* clearly applied. He preferred the "classic formulation of the doctrine", quoted by Erle J. above, to the "recent restatement of the doctrine" by the Supreme Court in *Hanrahan* v *Merck Sharpe & Dohme (Ireland) Ltd.*[148] which "has been criticised and may need to be reconsidered at some stage". He explained that in the instant case, the first element of the *res ipsa loquitur* doctrine was clearly present in that the defendants were the persons who had brought the horse into the field adjoining the highway and had provided such fences and gates as were there. The second requirement was satisfied by the fact that the accident was such as in the ordinary circumstances did not happen if those who had the management used proper care. A horse would not normally escape from lands on to the public road if adequate fencing is provided and any gates are kept in a closed position. While there was reasonable evidence, in the absence of explanation by the defendants, that the accident arose from their want of care, the defendants had produced an explanation supported by expert evidence. The explanation was that someone had opened the gate and allowed the horse to get on to the road. To hold that the defendants should be liable, where the admitted evidence was that they had taken all the precautions which a reasonable person would take to prevent the particular animals from straying on to the road, would be to impose a higher duty than the duty "to take such care as is reasonable" which the law required.

9.6.3.4 In a more recent decision, *Merriman* v *Greenhill Foods Ltd.*,[149] the Supreme Court held that it was not unfair to require a defendant to explain why a part of a motor vehicle fractured, resulting in an accident, since liability could be avoided, even where no explanation

---

[148] [1988] ILRM 629.

[149] Unreported Supreme Court, 28 June 1996.

could be provided, if the defendant proved all reasonable care had been taken in ensuring the plaintiff's safety. The plaintiff was employed as a truck driver and was driving the defendant's vehicle when it suddenly turned off the road and struck a ditch. The High Court dismissed the plaintiff's action, finding that there was no evidence of a defect in the truck, that the accident occurred because of a fracture in a leaf of a spring, that the maintenance of the truck was of a reasonable standard and that the principle of *res ipsa loquitur* did not apply. In allowing the appeal, the Supreme Court held that, as the defendant had not provided any explanation as to why the leaf of the spring had broke, the case came within the principle that in such circumstances reasonable evidence was thereby afforded that the accident arose from the want of care on the part of the defendant. The explanation proffered by the defendant did not go far enough because it did not explain why the leaf had broken. All the plaintiff knew was that the leaf of the spring broke. The doctrine of *res ipsa loquitur* should apply so as to throw the onus on the defendant to prove no negligence.

9.6.4 REMOTENESS
In determining the liability of an insured to a third party, the court will not concern itself with a rigorous analysis of cause and effect. The trial of an action for damages is "not a scientific inquest into a mixed sequence of phenomena, or an historical investigation of the chapter of events. . . . it is a practical enquiry".[150] To a large extent each case turns on its own individual facts but, according to Bacon,

> it were infinite for the law to consider the causes of causes, and their impulsions one on the other: Therefore it contenteth itself with the immediate cause and judges acts by that without looking to any further degree.[151]

The courts, in deciding to what extent a person should be liable for the consequences of their negligent act or omission, have had to consider whether the tortfeasor should be liable for all the natural consequences of their act or whether they should be liable only for the reasonably foreseeable consequences. The direct consequences rule

---

[150] *Weld-Blundell* v *Stephens* [1920] AC 956 per Lord Sumner.

[151] Bacon (1630).

had been established in *Re: Polemis*[152] in 1921 and applied by the courts until 1961 when the Privy Council[153] decided that foreseeabilty was the sole test to be applied. In *Re: Polemis*, workmen engaged by the charterer in unloading a ship dropped a plank into the hold of the ship causing an explosion and setting the ship on fire and destroying it. In an action against the charterers by the shipowners, the charterers maintained that the damage was too remote and that they should only be liable for the direct consequences of their actions. The court found the charterers liable for all the direct consequences including the burning of the ship as it was clear that negligence in knocking the plank into the hold might cause some injury.

> To determine whether an act is negligent, it is relevant to determine whether any reasonable person would foresee that the act would cause damage; if it would not, the act is not negligent. But if the act would or might probably cause damage, the fact that the damage it in fact causes is not the exact kind of damage one would expect is immaterial, so long as the damage is in fact directly traceable to the negligent act.[154]

In the *"Wagon Mound"* (No. 1)[155] the plaintiffs were the owners of a wharf in Sydney Harbour and the defendants who had chartered the vessel, *"The Wagon Mound"* carelessly allowed oil from the vessel to leak into the water. Employees of the plaintiff working on the wharf at the time with welding equipment stopped work on seeing the oil. Having enquired as to the possibility of the oil catching fire work was resumed and some days later molten metal fell into the water causing the oil to ignite and destroy the wharf. In the resulting action the defendants admitted negligence in allowing the oil to leak but disputed the extent of their liability. They argued against the application of the *Re: Polemis* test on the basis that it was unfair and imposed an excessive burden on a defendant who was merely negligent. The Judicial Committee decided that in resolving the remoteness issue it was illogical and unjust to use two different standards. Reasonable

---

[152] *Re: Polemis and Furness Withy & Co.* [1921] 3 KB 560.

[153] *Overseas Tankship (UK) Ltd.* v *Morts Dock and Engineering Co. Ltd.* *("The Wagon Mound")* (No.1) [1961] AC 388.

[154] per Scrutton L. J. [1921] 3 KB 560 at 577.

[155] n. 153 *supra.*

foreseeability was to be the sole standard to be applied. Although damage to the wharf was foreseeable and damage did occur, the damage which was foreseeable was fouling by oil whereas the damage which occurred was damage by fire. The decision has been approved in a number of cases in Ireland[156] with Barrington J. accepting:

> . . . that in determining liability for the consequences of a tortious act of negligence the test to be applied is whether the damage is of such a kind as a reasonable man should have foreseen. I also accept that if the damage is of such a kind that a reasonable man should have foreseen, it is quite irrelevant that no one foresaw the actual extent of the damage.[157]

9.7 LIABILITY POLICY TERMS AND CONDITIONS

9.7.1 CONTRIBUTION

Legal liability for personal injury or loss of or damage to property can arise out of a wide range of activities, and indemnity in respect of that liability can be provided under a number of different forms of liability insurance. There is a serious chance of policies over-lapping[158] and it is usual for such policies to contain a "contribution" clause or a "non-contribution" clause.[159] A common form of clause provides that:

> if at the time of any claim arising under this policy there may be other insurance covering the same risk or part thereof, the Company shall not be liable for more than its rateable proportion thereof.

The right to contribution does not depend on the inclusion of a clause in the policy as it is an equitable right[160] which arises where:

---

[156] *Riordan's Travel & Riordan's Shipping Ltd.* v *Acres & Co. Ltd.* (No. 2) [1979] ILRM 3; *Irish Shipping* v *Dublin Port & Docks Board* [1965] 101 ILTR 182; *Burke* v *John Paul & Co. Ltd.* [1967] IR 277; *Condon* v *CIE and Others* [1984] Unreported High Court, 16 November.

[157] n. 153 *supra*, citing *Burke* v *John Paul & Co. Ltd.* [1967] IR 277; and *"The Wagon Mound"* (No. 1).

[158] Motor, Engineering and Public Liability insurance policies for example.

[159] Sometimes referred to as "co-insurance" or "other insurance" clauses.

[160] *Newby* v *Reed* [1763] 1 Wm. Bl. 416; *Godin* v *London Assurance Co.* [1758] 1 Burr. 489 per Lord Mansfield at 492: "If the insured is to receive but one satisfaction, natural justice says that the several insurers shall all contribute *pro rata* to satisfy that loss against which all of them have insured."

- all the policies concerned comprise the same subject matter;

- all policies provide cover against the same peril;

- all policies are effected by or on behalf of the same insured;

- all policies are in force at the time of the loss giving rise to the claim;

- all policies are legal contracts of insurance;

- no policy contains a clause excluding it from contribution.

9.7.1.1 The right of contribution is altogether different and distinct from the right of subrogation,[161] although the High Court, in *Zurich Insurance Co.* v *Shield Insurance Co.*[162] appears to have confused the two principles. The plaintiff insurer was liable under a motor insurance policy to indemnify Quinnsworth against liability in respect of the negligent driving of Quinnsworth's cars, and furthermore was liable to indemnify the driver of any such car driving with the permission of Quinnsworth. The defendant insurer had issued an employer's liability policy under which it was obliged to indemnify Quinnsworth against liability to pay compensation for injury, accident or disease sustained by any employee of Quinnsworth arising out of and in the course of his employment with Quinnsworth. An employee of Quinnsworth was seriously injured whilst travelling in a motor car owned by Quinnsworth and driven by another employee of Quinnsworth. Both employees were at the time travelling in the course of their employment. In proceedings brought by the injured employee against Quinnsworth and the driver the injured passenger was awarded substantial damages which the plaintiff insurer paid on behalf of Quinnsworth. However, Quinnsworth had been held entitled to indemnity from the employee who was driving as he had been found totally liable for the accident. The plaintiff sought 50 per cent contribution from the defendant on the grounds that Quinnsworth had enjoyed a double indemnity against its liability to the injured employee. Gannon J. in the High Court said:

---

[161] *Sickness and Accident Assurance Association* v *General Accident Fire & Life Assurance Corp.* [1892] 19 IR 977.

[162] [1988] IR 174.

It is an accepted principle of law that a claimant who has recovered full satisfaction in damages from one party cannot also
recover the same or any part of that claim from another party
equally liable for the same damage. A corollary of this principle is that as between those persons who are liable in damages
to compensate the same claimant upon the same cause of action, the one who discharges the liability in full is entitled in
equity by subrogation to recover from the others a contribution
of the proportions of what he has paid commensurate with the
liability of such others to the same claimant. The basis for the
claim by the plaintiff herein against the defendant is the right
of subrogation which the plaintiff claims to have to enable it
recover from the defendant on foot of Quinnsworth's policy
with the defendant a contribution of a proportionate part,
namely 50 per cent of the amount paid by the plaintiff on behalf of Quinnsworth to [the injured employee] on foot of
Quinnsworth's policy with the plaintiff.[163]

Although, Gannon J. quoted extensively from English authorities on
contribution and subrogation, it is suggested, with respect, that he
confused the two principles. He stated the principles quite clearly:

In the circumstances of double insurance the insurer by whom
the claim is discharged in full has an equitable right to require
contribution from the other insurers so that the payment is
borne fairly by all.[164]

He then sought to distinguish contribution from subrogation, saying:

But an insurer who has made payment to the insured under
the policy of indemnity is entitled to the benefit of all the
rights of the insured in respect of the loss for which the indemnity was provided, including the right of action against the
tortfeasor who has caused the loss. Thus, by subrogation the
insurer may in the name of the insured recover from the tortfeasor the loss of the insured for which the insurer provided
indemnity under the policy.[165]

---

[163] ibid. p. 177.

[164] ibid. p. 178 quoting *North British & Mercantile Insurance Co.* v *London Liverpool & Globe Insurance Co.* [1877] 5 CH D 569.

[165] ibid.

9.7.1.2 The plaintiffs' claim was for a declaration that they were entitled to a contribution from the defendants on the basis that there was a dual indemnity available to Quinnsworth under the policies issued by the two insurers. The plaintiffs did not base their claim on the principle of subrogation as suggested in the above extract. The court found that the two policies did not cover the same interests or risks and that the plaintiffs were not entitled to contribution. Unfortunately, the confusion was not resolved in the Supreme Court. McCarthy J., in a judgment with which all four other members[166] of the court agreed, restated the principle of contribution and whilst he omitted reference to the "basis for the claim . . . [being] the right to subrogation" he did not endeavour to resolve the confusion apparent in the judgment of the High Court. The appeal was dismissed; a result "happily in accordance with common sense".[167] The unfortunate confusion of the two principles in the High Court ignored the critical differences between the principles. Contribution arises only where there is more than one policy in force covering the same risk, the same interest, and the same perils. Subrogation requires the existence of but one policy. The right to contribution is a right of the insurer who has paid the loss in full and is exercisable by the insurer in its own name against all other insurers covering the loss. The right to subrogation, whilst a right of the insurer, can only be exercised in the name of the insured against third parties who have a liability to the insured for the loss. The insured's legal remedies are enforced for the benefit of the insurers.

9.7.1.3 Where an insurer seeks to invoke the contribution clause, it is necessary for the insurer to prove "not only that there is another policy in existence but that there is one under which the insurers can be called upon to pay the loss".[168] The right to contribution is not lost because one policy extends to a far greater variety of risks than another, so long as both policies cover the risk arising out of which the

---

[166] Finlay C.J., Henchy J., Griffin J., and Hederman J.

[167] ibid. p. 186.

[168] *Jenkins* v *Deane* [1933] 47 Lloyds Rep 342 per Goddard J. at 346: "'other contract of insurance' means a binding contract of insurance, hence one which is in force at the relevant time."

claim has been made.[169] If two or more liability policies are in force covering the same risk and interest, and each contains a contribution clause in the form quoted above, each insurer will be liable under its policy for its rateable proportion of the loss. Difficulties can, however, arise where the policies provide for different limits of indemnity. In *Commercial Union* v *Hayden*,[170] two liability policies were in force covering the same interest but with different indemnity limits. One provided indemnity up to a limit of £100,000 in respect of any one accident and the other had a limit of £10,000 in respect of any one accident. A third party claim was settled for £4,425. Both policies contained rateable contribution clauses. The High Court decided that the policies should contribute on the basis of the respective maximum limits of indemnity so that the insurer whose limit was £100,000 was held liable for 10/11ths and the other insurer for the balance. The Court of Appeal reversed the decision, holding that the contribution clause should be applied on the basis of "independent liability" and not the maximum indemnity limits of the policies. Claims up to the lower limit of £10,000 should be shared equally and claims over that amount apportioned on the basis of the independent liability of each insurer. It should first be ascertained what would have been each insurer's liability, if it had been the only insurer, and that the total liability to the insured should be divided in proportion to those liabilities. On a claim for £40,000 the plaintiff's independent liability would be £40,000 and the defendant's £10,000. On that basis, the apportionment would be in the ratio of 4:1. The plaintiff would pay £32,000 and the defendant £8,000.

9.7.1.4 Some liability policies contain a "non-contribution" clause which provides that

> if at the time of any occurrence or claim there is or but for the existence of this policy would be any other policy of indemnity or insurance in favour of or effected by or on behalf of the insured applicable to such occurrence or claim the Company shall not be liable under this policy to indemnify the Insured in respect of such occurrence or claim except so far as concerns any excess beyond the amount which would be payable under

---

[169] per McCarthy J. [1988] IR 174 at 185.

[170] *Commercial Union* v *Hayden* [1977] 2 QB 804.

such other indemnity or insurance had this policy not been effected.

The effect of such a clause is, in the event of dual insurance, to convert the policy into an "excess of loss" contract[171] covering a different layer of risk from other policies in respect of the same risk and so prevent the principle of contribution from operating. If all policies covering the same risk contain "non-contribution" clauses, then none of the policies would operate to provide an indemnity in respect of the loss[172] resulting in the

> absurdity and injustice of holding that a person who has paid premium for cover by two [or more] insurers [is] left without insurance cover because each insurer has excluded liability for the risk against which the other[s] has indemnified him.[173]

To avoid such a ridiculous situation it has been held that each policy should be examined independently and if each policy would be liable for the loss, but for the existence of another policy, the "non-contribution" clauses should be treated as cancelling each other out and all insurers are liable for their rateable proportion of the loss.[174] Where one policy contains a "contribution" clause and another policy contains a "non-contribution" clause and both cover the same risk and interest, any claims will be paid under the policy with the contribution clause up to the policy limit.

---

[171] Such policies were explained by Leggat J. in *Irish National Insurance Co. Ltd.* v *Oman* [1983] 2 Lloyds Rep 453 at 460, 461; he said: "I accept that the principal means of identifying Excess of Loss insurance is to see whether or not the policy concerned is in excess of another insurance policy."

[172] *National Employers Mutual General Insurance Association Ltd.* v *Haydon* [1972] 2 Lloyds Rep 235 at 238 per Lloyd J.

[173] *NEM* v *Haydon* [1980] 2 Lloyds Rep 149 at 152, per Stephenson L. J.

[174] Rowlatt J. at 567, 568 said:
> The reasonable construction is to exclude from the category of co-existing cover any cover which is expressed to be itself cancelled by such co-existence. . . In other words [the insured] is not "entitled to indemnity under any other policy" within the meaning of [the first policy] when the other policy negatives liability when there are two policies. At that point the process must cease. If one proceeds to apply the same argument to the other policy and lets that react upon the policy under construction, one would reach the absurd result that whichever policy one looks at it is always the other one which is effective.

The decision was applied in *Austin* v *Zurich* [1944] 77 Lloyds Rep 409.

9.7.2 SUBROGATION

9.7.2.1 The right of an insurer to subrogate against a third party exists independently of any policy condition and enables ultimate liability for providing an indemnity to be fixed on the party responsible for the loss. Sometimes the circumstances of the loss mean that an insured is entitled to recover the amount of the loss, or part of it, from a third party as well as from his insurer. If he claims indemnity from his insurer, his rights against the third party vest in the insurer to the extent of the indemnity it has provided. Liability policies do not generally have a policy condition entitled "subrogation" but do have a condition giving insurers control of claims and the right to "prosecute at its own expense and for its own benefit any claim for indemnity or damages against any other persons". The condition extends the common law principle by enabling the insurer to take over any rights which the insured may have against third parties before the insurer actually indemnifies the insured,[175] but the right to bring an action against a third party cannot be enforced until the insured has been indemnified under the terms of the insurance policy.[176] The insured's rights to which the insurer can subrogate may arise in tort or in contract. If the rights arise in the tort of negligence, the rights of the insurer, being no greater than those of the insured, will be limited by any contributory negligence on the part of the insured.[177] If the rights arise in contract and the insured has agreed that the liability of the

---

[175] In *Orakpo v Manson Investments Ltd.* [1978] AC 95 Lord Diplock at 104, suggested:

> [Subrogation] embraces more than a single concept in English law. It is a convenient way of describing a transfer of rights from one person to another, without assignment or assent by the person from whom the rights are transferred and which takes place by operation of law in a whole variety of widely different circumstances. Some rights by subrogation are contractual in their origin, as in the case of contracts of insurance. Others . . . are in no way based on contract and appear to defeat classification except as an empirical remedy to prevent a particular kind of unjust enrichment.

In *Napier and Ettrick v Hunter* [1993] 1 All ER 385, the House of Lords confirmed that the right of subrogation was a proprietary right in equity, casting some doubt on the view of Lord Diplock.

[176] *Dickenson v Jardine* [1868] LR 3 CP 639; *City Tailors Ltd. v Evans* [1922] 91 LJKB 379; *AGF Insurances Ltd. v City of Brighton* [1972] CLR 655.

[177] *Thames & Mersey Marine Insurance Co. v British & Chilean Steamship Co.* [1916] 1 KB 30; *Goole & Hall Steam Towing Co. Ltd. v Ocean Marine Insurance Co. Ltd.* [1928] 1 KB 589.

third party shall be excluded or limited, the rights of the insurer enforceable in subrogation are limited to the same extent.[178] However, if the insured in any way prejudices his rights so as to deprive his insurers of the benefit of subrogation, he incurs a personal liability to insurers to the extent of the prejudice caused.[179] As a general rule the rights to which the insurers are subrogated must be enforced in the name of the insured,[180] and the insurers are not entitled to sue in their own names.[181] The entitlement to sue does not amount to an assignment of the right of action and the insurer has no right at law to make use of the insured's name. If the insured does not consent to the use of his name the insurer may have to go to court to compel him to allow it.[182] An assignment by an insured to his insurer of the insured's rights against a third party is enforceable by the insurer in the insurer's own name.[183]

9.7.2.2 The requirement that actions be brought in the insured's name does undoubtedly suit insurers in most cases, in that it provides them with a cloak of anonymity so that the true parties to the action are seldom made public. However, the requirement does not

---

[178] *Lister* v *Romford Ice & Cold Storage Ltd.* [1957] AC 555 per Lord Somervell at 600.

[179] *Commercial Union* v *Lister* [1874] LR 9 CH 483; *Boag* v *Standard Marine* [1937] 2 KB 113; *"The Gold Sky"* [1972] 2 Lloyds Rep 187; *"The Vasso"* [1993] 2 Lloyds Rep 309.

[180] *Mason* v *Sainsbury* [1782] 3 Doug. KB 61; *London Assurance Co.* v *Sainsbury* [1783] 3 Doug KB 245; *Esso Petroleum Co. Ltd.* v *Hall Russell & Co. Ltd.* ("*The Esso Bernicia*") [1989] AC 643.

[181] *London Assurance Co.* v *Sainsbury* [1783] 3 Doug KB 245 per Lord Mansfield C. J. at 253:

The relation of the plaintiffs is by the insurance which is a contract of indemnity. It follows that in respect of salvage the insurer stands in the place of the insured and vice versa as to damage. I take it to be maxim, that as against the person sued, the action cannot be transferred. As between the parties themselves the law has long supported it for the benefit of commerce, but the assignee must sue in the name of the assignor, by which the defence is not varied.

[182] *Morris* v *Ford Motor Co.* [1973] 1 QB 792, per Denning M. R. at p. 800.

[183] *Compania Colombiania de Seguros* v *Pacific Steam & Navigation Co.* [1964] 1 All ER 216 per Roskill J. at 230; *King* v *Victoria Insurance Company* [1986] AC 250; Insurers are generally reluctant to take an assignment of an insured's action, as they believe their chances of recovery in litigation are reduced if they appear as the party prosecuting the action.

always act to the benefit of the insurer, as for an action to proceed the insured must exist and have legal personality. A problem can arise for insurers if, having indemnified the insured under the policy of insurance, the insured then goes bankrupt and is wound up before the insurer can proceed against the third party responsible for the loss in respect of which the insurer has provided indemnity. In such circumstances, the Court of Appeal in England has decided that the full technicalities of the law will be applied to deny the insurer recovery. In *M.H. Smith (Plant Hire) Ltd.* v *Mainwaring t/a Inshore*,[184] the judge at first instance decided in the insurer's favour saying that it did not matter what form the action took. The plaintiff had hired a barge from the defendants to transport a dumper. When it sank insurers paid the claim under the policy and began an action in the name of the insured plaintiff claiming that the sinking had been caused by the negligence of the defendant. On discovering that the plaintiff company had been wound up an application was made to have the insurer's name substituted for that of the plaintiff. On appeal the court held that the insurers were only entitled to bring an action in the name of the insured if the company actually existed. A non-existent party could not be involved in an action and there was nothing in the law of subrogation which could save the insurers. The Court of Appeal recognised that the insurers could have taken an assignment of the right of action from the insured at some time before the winding up and the action would then have become the insurers' alone and would not have been affected by the subsequent demise of the insured company. There is nothing in the limited number of Irish cases on subrogation to indicate that Irish courts might not take the same approach.[185]

---

[184] [1986] BCLC 342.

[185] In *Ballymagauran Co-operative Agricultural and Dairy Society Ltd.* v *The County Councils of Cavan and Leitrim* [1915] 2 IR 85, the Court of Appeal decided that a third party against whom a possible right of action exists cannot avoid liability on the ground that the insured has or will be indemnified by insurers. The Supreme Court endorsed that decision in *Doyle* v *Wicklow County Council* [1974] IR 55, holding that a claim for malicious injury was not to be reduced by any sums already recovered by the applicant from his insurers. See also *In re: Driscoll, Deceased* [1918] 1 IR 152; *Andrews and Others* v *The Patriotic Assurance Co. of Ireland* [1886] 18 LRI 355.

9.7.2.3 The Irish Courts have recognised the right of liability insurers to subrogate against an employee whose negligence has occasioned injury to a fellow employee of an insured in respect of which the insurers have been obliged to indemnify the insured.[186] The right was established in England by the House of Lords decision in *Lister* v *Romford Ice and Cold Storage Co. Ltd.*,[187] In that case an employee of the company employed to drive a motor vehicle injured his father whom he had taken as his mate in the vehicle. The father recovered damages from the company on the ground of his son's negligent driving of the vehicle. The company then sued the driver as a joint tortfeasor against whom the company was entitled to contribution and on the ground that the company was entitled to damages for breach of an implied term that he would exercise reasonable care in the performance of his duties as servant. It was held that there was no implied term in the contract of employment that the employers would indemnify the servant (whether the company was insured against the servant's negligence or was required by statute to be insured against that risk or ought, as a reasonably prudent employer, to have taken out a policy of insurance against that risk) and that the company was entitled to recover damages from the driver, their servant. The decision came in for considerable criticism[188] but its ill effects were avoided by the members of the British Insurance Association entering into an agreement not to enforce it.[189] The Irish case of

---

[186] *Zurich Insurance Co.* v *Shield Insurance Co. Ltd.* [1988] IR 174.

[187] *Lister* v *Romford Ice and Cold Storage Co. Ltd.* [1957] AC 555.

[188] "To make the servant personally liable would not only lead to a strike. It would be positively unjust. . . . it was an unfortunate decision," per Lord Denning M. R., *Morris* v *Ford Motor Co.* [1973] 1 QB 792 at 801. Denning invoked an equitable discretion to deny insurers the right to take over the insured's right of action against the insured's negligent employee on the grounds that the insured did not wish to pursue the employee in the interests of good industrial relations. The decision is inconsistent with *Lister* v *Romford Ice & Cold Storage Co.* [1957] AC 555, and it is doubtful if a court would refuse subrogation to an insurer on equitable grounds simply because the insured would prefer not to sue the third party. The dissenting minority in the Court of Appeal and in the House of Lords in *Lister* favoured the withholding of subrogation from insurers, but on the grounds that there was an implied term in the negligent employee's contract of employment with the insured, that the employee should have the benefit of the insurance policy effected by the employer.

[189] The Minister of Labour appointed an interdepartmental committee to study the implications of the decision. In the Committee's report in 1959 (36-244) it did

Zurich Insurance Co. v *Shield Insurance Co. Ltd.*[190] arose out of an earlier personal injuries action, *Sinnott* v *Quinnsworth.*[191] Sinnott, an employee of Quinnsworth Ltd., was injured when the motor car in which he was travelling as a passenger — which was owned by Quinnsworth and driven by Edward Durning, who was also an employee of Quinnsworth — collided with a bus. At the time of the accident both Sinnott and Durning were travelling in the course of their employment with Quinnsworth. In proceedings brought against Quinnsworth and Durning for damages, Sinnott was awarded a substantial sum and Quinnsworth was held to be entitled to an indemnity from Durning for the full amount of the award. The Zurich Insurance Co., having paid the compensation in full to Sinnott under the Motor insurance policy it had issued to Quinnsworth then sought to recover 50 per cent from Shield Insurance Co. Ltd. who had issued an employers' liability policy to Quinnsworth. In the High Court, Gannon J. held that

> If Quinnsworth had called upon the defendant to indemnify it against its liability to Martin Sinnott, the defendant would be entitled to claim by subrogation in Quinnsworth's name from Edward Durning the amount for which Quinnsworth might be held liable to Martin Sinnott.[192]

---

not recommend legislation to reverse the decision because it felt insurers would not abuse it:

> The decision . . . shows that employers and their insurers have rights against employees which, if exploited unreasonably would endanger good industrial relations. We think employers and their insurers, if only in their own interests, will not so exploit their rights.

The members of the British Insurance Association and Lloyds Underwriters entered into an agreement which stated:

> Employers' Liability Insurers . . . will not institute a claim against the employee of an insured employer in respect of the death of or injury to a fellow employee unless the weight of the evidence clearly indicates (i) collusion or (ii) wilful misconduct on the part of the employee against whom a claim is made.

See G. Gardiner, Comment (1959) 22 MLR 652. Insurers in Australia are denied the right to subrogation in such circumstances by The Insurance Contracts Act, 1984 unless the negligence of the employee amounts "serious or wilful misconduct".

[190] [1988] IR 174.

[191] [1984] ILRM 538.

[192] [1988] IR 174 at 181.

In the Supreme Court McCarthy J. delivered a unanimous judgment on behalf of the Court rejecting the appeal and in the course of which he said:

> The defendant's [employers' liability] policy provided for indemnity by it of Quinnsworth in respect of any liability to pay compensation for injury by accident arising out of and in the course of his employment by the insured to any employee in the immediate service of the insured. Martin Sinnott was in the immediate service of the insured and was found by the judge to have sustained personal injury by accident arising out of and in the course of his employment by the insured; that insured [Quinnsworth] was liable to pay compensation for such injury and, therefore, entitled to be indemnified by the defendant in respect of such compensation. . . . Accepting as I do, the principles enunciated by Brett L. J. in *Castellain* v *Preston*[193] cited by Gannon J.[194] in his judgment, the pursuit of the subrogation claim by the plaintiff through Quinnsworth against Durning inexorably leads to Durning's liability to satisfy all claims without the benefit of any indemnity directly from Quinnsworth. Durning enjoys no benefit from the defendant's cover given to Quinnsworth.[195]

In the event, Durning's liability was held to be covered by the motor insurance policy issued by the plaintiff insurer, but in determining the issues between insurers the Supreme Court did at least recognise the right of an insurer to exercise subrogation against an employee of the insured where the negligence of the employee has incurred liability on the insured as employer and for which the insurer provides indemnity. Most liability policies issued in Ireland will provide indemnity, at the request of the insured, to "any person employed by the insured under a contract of service or apprenticeship". The right of subrogation is therefore seldom, if ever, exercised in Ireland against an employee, although insurers do retain the legal right to do so, and probably would do so where the liability was incurred in circumstances indicating collusion or wilful misconduct on the part of the employee.

---

[193] [1883] 11 QBD 380.

[194] [1988] IR 174 at 178, 179.

[195] ibid. at 184, 185.

9.7.3 REASONABLE PRECAUTIONS CONDITION

9.7.3.1 Liability insurance policies generally include a condition requiring the insured to take all reasonable precautions to prevent occurrences or activities which might give rise to liability under the policy and to maintain premises, works, machinery and plant in a sound and safe condition. There is no agreed standard wording for the condition, but a form of wording commonly in use is:

> The insured at his own expense shall (a) take all reasonable precautions to prevent or diminish loss destruction or damage or any occurrence or cease any activity which may give rise to liability under this policy and to maintain all buildings furnishings ways works machinery and plant in sound condition, (b) exercise care in the selection and supervision of employees and (c) as soon as possible after discovery cause and defect or danger to be made good or remedied and in the meantime shall cause such additional precautions to be taken as the circumstances may require.

9.7.3.2 The inclusion of such a condition in a liability insurance policy seems on the face of it contradictory in that the condition requires the insured to avoid being negligent when the policy is intended to provide an indemnity against the consequences of the insured's negligence. It is well settled however that insurers cannot rely on a breach of the condition to avoid liability under the policy except where the insured's behaviour is wilful or reckless. Application of the condition is dependent on the definition of what is "reasonable" in the circumstances of the loss. In *Fraser* v *B.N. Furman (Productions) Ltd.*[196] Diplock L.J. explained the condition:

> The condition cannot mean that the insured must take measures to avert dangers which he does not himself foresee, although the hypothetical reasonably careful insured would have foreseen them. That would be repugnant to the commercial purpose of the contract, for the failure to foresee dangers is one of the commonest grounds of liability in negligence. What, in my judgment, is reasonable as between the insured and the insurer, without being repugnant to the commercial purpose of the contract is that the insured, where he does recognise a

---

[196] [1967] 3 All ER 57. The interpretation to be applied to the condition was also considered in *British Food Freezers Ltd* v *Industrial Estates Management for Scotland* [1977] Unreported Court of Appeal.

danger, should not deliberately court it by taking measures which he himself knows are inadequate to avert it. In other words, it is not enough that the employer's omission to take any particular precautions to avoid accidents should be negligent; it must be at least reckless, that is to say, made with actual recognition by the insured himself that a danger exists, and not caring whether or not it is averted. The purpose of the condition is to ensure that the insured will not, because he is covered against loss by the policy, refrain from taking precautions which he knows ought to be taken.

9.7.3.3 The effect of the condition is to impose a personal obligation on the insured to act in an ordinarily prudent manner and not in a way which knowingly increases the risk of accidents. Failure by a servant or employee of the insured, to take reasonable precautions does not constitute breach of the condition by the insured even though the insured is vicariously liable for the consequences of the failure. In *Woolfall & Rimmer Ltd.* v *Moyle,*[197] the insured was held to have complied with a condition requiring him "to take reasonable precautions to prevent accidents and to comply with all statutory regulations" when he delegated to a competent foreman the task of providing suitable and safe materials for scaffolding. In *Aluminium Wire & Cable Co. Ltd.* v *All State Insurance Co. Ltd.*[198] it was held that insurers could only invoke the condition if they could show that the insured had acted recklessly. The plaintiff engineering company had engaged contractors, insured by the defendants, to carry out work on their premises. During the course of the work involving the use of oxy-acetylene equipment the premises were damaged by fire. The contractor went into liquidation before the plaintiff could recover in respect of the damage and pursued the action against the insurers of the contractor under the Third Party (Rights Against Insurers) Act, 1930. The insurers pleaded that the insured contractor had been in breach of a policy condition requiring that "the insured shall exercise reasonable care to prevent accidents" and that the due observance of the condition was a condition precedent to liability. The court held that the contractors' conduct, although negligent fell far short of conduct which showed that failure to take precautions was done reck-

---

[197] [1942] 1 KB 66.

[198] [1985] 2 Lloyds Rep 280.

lessly, that is, with actual recognition of the danger and not caring whether or not that danger was averted. In *British Food Freezers Ltd. v Industrial Estates Management for Scotland*,[199] the failure of contractors to take any precautions to prevent damage when working with oxy-acetylene equipment was held to be a clear breach of the duty imposed by the condition.

9.7.3.4 The wording of the condition quoted above makes it clear that any costs incurred by the insured in complying with the requirements of the condition are to be borne by the insured. In that respect, liability policies differ from marine insurance policies where "suing and labouring" clauses require the insured to take all reasonable steps to prevent a loss, and to mitigate the loss if one occurs, but require the insurers to indemnify the insured for the costs involved.[200] An unsuccessful attempt was made to imply a similar provision into a liability policy in the case of *Yorkshire Water v Sun Alliance & London Insurance Ltd.*[201] The plaintiffs were owners and operators of a waste tip situated close to the banks of a river. Following the collapse of an embankment a large quantity of sludge from the tip entered the river and affected a number of businesses, one of which initiated proceedings against the plaintiff. Claims were anticipated from the other businesses affected and the plaintiff effected flood alleviation works costing £4.6 million in an effort to prevent further damage and to reduce the danger of other claims. The plaintiff claimed against its liability insurers in respect of its legal liability to the affected businesses and the costs of the remedial work undertaken. The Court was asked to decide if the policy expressly provided for recovery by the insured of the costs incurred, and if not could a term permitting recovery be implied into the policy. There was no doubt but that the

---

[199] *British Food Freezers Ltd. v Industrial Estates Management for Scotland* [1977] Unreported.

[200] Under standard marines wordings as adopted by the Marine Insurance Act, 1906, Section 78, the suing and labouring clause is regarded as distinct from the policy itself, so that insurers are liable for losses under the policy and for any suing and labouring costs incurred. Insurers may also face suing and labouring costs where there has been no loss or where the insured has taken reasonable but unsuccessful steps to avoid or mitigate a loss.

[201] *Yorkshire Water v Sun Alliance & London Insurance Ltd.* [1996] Unreported Court of Appeal.

policy provided indemnity in respect of the insured plaintiff's liability for damage to and interference with the property of the affected businesses but the Court of Appeal rejected the plaintiff's arguments that indemnity should be provided in respect of the consequences of the event causing the insured to incur the costs of remedial works following an event giving rise to a loss and which might give rise to future losses in the absence of remedial works. The policy had a condition which required the insured to take reasonable precautions, at his own expense, to prevent circumstances which might give rise to liability under the policy and the Court held that this made it clear that the insured was to be liable for the costs of any preventative measures. The Court found it impossible to imply any term into the contract which would relieve the insured of that liability as such an implied term would be inconsistent with the express provision of the policy requiring the insured to bear the costs of preventative measures.

9.7.4 CLAIMS NOTIFICATION

9.7.4.1 Liability policies contain a condition, said to be a condition precedent to insurers' liability, requiring the insured to give notice to insurers within a particular time of any incident or occurrence likely to give rise to a claim under the policy. The purpose of such a clause is to give insurers the opportunity to complete their investigations as soon as possible, to control the proceedings and to take whatever steps are necessary to mitigate the cost of the loss to them.[202] Failure by the insured to comply with the terms of the condition gives insurers the right to repudiate liability under the policy. The condition will be construed strictly so that if a condition requires notice of "any ac-

---

[202] A common wording in use reads as follows:

(a) The insured shall give notice to the company as soon as possible after the occurrence of any accident with full particulars thereof. Every letter claim writ summons and/or process shall be notified or forwarded to the Company immediately on receipt. Notice shall also be given to the Company immediately after the insured shall have knowledge of any incident prosecution or inquest in connection with any accident for which there may be a claim under this policy. (b) No admission, repudiation, offer, payment or indemnity shall be made or given on behalf of the insured without the written consent of the Company which shall be entitled if it so desires to take over and conduct in the name of the Insured the defence or settlement of any claim or to prosecute in the name of the Insured for its own benefit any claim for indemnity or damages or otherwise and shall have full discretion in the conduct of any proceedings and in the settlement of any claim and the Insured shall give all such information and assistance as the Company may require.

cident or claim or proceedings" and the insured gives notice of proceedings only, they will be in breach of the condition.[203] The use of the
word "or" in the wording of the condition has, in two Irish cases, been
held to be used in the disjunctive, and not the conjunctive, sense so as
to impose on the insured the obligation of giving notice of all three
matters.[204] The High Court determined in *Gaelcrann Teo* v *Michael
Payne*[205] that:

> In every instance in which to the knowledge of the insured an
> occurrence happens which he recognises could give rise to a
> claim under the policy, the insured must give to insurers im-
> mediate notice in writing of the happening of such occurrence,
> or alternatively give them the like immediate notice of his re-
> ceipt of the claim if such be made; in the event of a claim being
> made or received which arises from no identifiable occurrence
> as a happening, or of the happening of which the insured was
> unaware, . . . he must give immediate notice in writing of his

---

[203] *Pioneer Concrete (UK) Ltd.* v *National Employers Mutual General Insurance
Association* [1985] 1 Lloyds Rep 274; see also *Farrell* v *Federated Employers Insurance Association Ltd.* [1970] 2 Lloyds Rep 170 — an insured who gave notice
of proceedings only and not of the occurrence which gave rise to them was held to
be in breach of a condition requiring written notice of "any accident or claim or
proceedings" so that insurers were relieved of liability to indemnify the insured.

[204] In the Matter of the Arbitration Act 1954, and of an Arbitration between *Gaelcrann Teoranta and Michael Payne and Others, Underwriters at Lloyds* [1985]
ILRM 109; *Capemel Ltd. t/a Oakline Kitchens* v *Lister* [1989] IR 319.

[205] *Gaelcrann* v *Payne* above. The case arose out of a case stated by the Arbitrator
in a dispute between the Underwriters and the insured employer under an employers' liability policy. An employee of the insured allegedly sustained injuries
on two separate occasions in 1975 and issued proceedings against the insured in
respect of both accidents in 1977. The insured notified the insurers of the claims
on receipt of the plenary summonses but had not given previous notice of the
accidents giving rise to the claims. Insurers denied liability under the policy alleging breach of the claims notification condition in the policy which was stated in
the policy to be a condition precedent to liability. The case stated by the Arbitrator sought the opinion of the High Court on (a) the interpretation of the claims
notification condition and whether the insured had been in breach of it; (b)
whether the condition was a condition precedent to liability; (c) whether the insurers would be entitled to avoid liability if it were found as a fact that they had
suffered no prejudice by reason of the failure of the insured to give notice to them
in writing of the happening or an occurrence which could give rise to a claim under the policy. The Court found in favour of the insurers on all three issue.

receipt of such claim; in every case he must give . . . immediate
notice in writing of the institution of proceedings.[206]

In the same case, Gannon J. accepted that a distinction must be made
between a condition expressed in a policy to be a condition precedent
and one which is not so described in the policy. He agreed that non-
compliance with a condition stated to be a condition precedent prevents the party in default enforcing the contract.[207] He went on to
consider whether in the event of a trifling default it was necessary for
the insurer to show that its position had been prejudiced by the default before the insurer could rely on it to avoid liability.[208] The position in English law had been confused by some remarks of Lord Justice Denning M. R. in *Barratt Bros. (Taxis) Ltd. v Davies*[209] to the effect that insurers could not rely on breach of the policy condition to

---

[206] ibid. per Gannon J. at 114.

[207] In the course of a well-reasoned judgment Gannon J. referred to the decision
in *Re: Coleman's Depositories* [1907] 2 KB 798 which he accepted as authority for
the proposition that an insured in default of a condition stated to be a condition
precedent to liability cannot enforce the contract against insurers. However, he
quoted with apparent approval the comments of Fletcher Moulton L. J. at 807:

> The courts have not always considered that they are bound to interpret provi-
> sions of this kind with unreasonable strictness, and although the word
> "immediate" is no doubt a strong epithet I think that it might fairly be con-
> strued as meaning with all reasonable speed considering the circumstances of
> the case.

[208] [1985] ILRM 109 at 115, 116.

[209] Also reported as *Lickiss v Milestone Motor Policies at Lloyds* [1966] 2 All ER
972. The insured motor-cyclist failed to notify immediately his insurers of an intended prosecution, contrary to the provisions of the policy. The Court of Appeal
held that insurers had waived the breach of condition in subsequent correspondence, but towards the end of his judgment at p. 976 Denning M. R. said:

> [The] Condition was inserted in the policy so as to afford a protection to the in-
> surers so that they should know in good time about the accident and any pro-
> ceedings consequent on it. If they obtain all material information from another
> source so that they are not prejudiced at all by the failure of the insured him-
> self to tell them, then they cannot rely on the condition to defeat the claim.

These remarks were submitted as authority for the contention that there could be
no breach of a condition entitling insurers to repudiate liability unless the breach
had caused actual prejudice to the insurers in *Farrell v Federated Employers
Insurance Association Ltd.* [1970] 1 All ER 360, but rejected by McKenna J. at
364 when he distinguished *Lickiss v Milestone* above. The remarks were subsequently regarded *obiter dicta*; *"The Vainqueur José"* [1979] 1 Lloyds Rep 557;
*Pioneer Concrete (UK) Ltd. v National Employers Mutual General Insurance As-
sociation Ltd.* [1985] 1 Lloyds Rep 274, 281.

defeat an insured's claim unless they were prejudiced by it. Gannon J. refused to adopt Denning's remarks as a statement of the law and held that unless the non-compliance with the condition is trivial or has been waived expressly or implicitly by the insurers, they are not obliged to show that they are prejudiced by the non-compliance. The decision was applied subsequently by Costello J. in *Capemel Ltd.* v *Lister.*[210]

9.7.4.2 The claims notification condition generally provides that the insurer shall be entitled to defend any action and to settle any claim within its absolute discretion[211] but does not give the insured a right to be defended or impose on the insurer a duty to defend the insured. However, it is normal practice in third party proceedings for the insurer to support the defendant insured in the defence of an action so as to protect the insurer against the insured's claim for indemnity.[212] If, having received proper notice of a claim from the insured, the insurers refuse to take over the defence of the claim, they will be precluded from subsequently contesting the amount of the settlement, but the insured will still be required to establish that he had a liability and that the settlement was not improvident, unreasonable, or *mala fide.*[213] The insured is not required to go to litigation in such cir-

---

[210] *Capemel Ltd.* v *Lister* [1989] IR 319, 321.

[211] See n. 200 *supra.*

[212] *Brice* v *Wackerbath (Australasia) Pty. Ltd.* [1974] 2 Lloyds Rep 274 per Roskill J. at 277.

[213] *General Omnibus Co. Ltd.* v *London General Insurance Co. Ltd.* [1936] IR 596. Hanna J. in the High Court said: "it is settled law that it is no bar to an indemnity that the liability has been arrived at by agreement or compromise which was not improvident, unreasonable, or mala fide." The judgment was unanimously endorsed in the Supreme Court. In the case of *Smith* v *Compton*, 3 B. & Ad. 407 and in the Irish case *Caldbeck* v *Boon* IR 7 CL 32, it was decided that it was open to show that such a compromise was not unreasonable. The same principle was established in *Lord Newborough* v *Schroeder*, 7 CB 342.

cumstances. In *Rohan* v *Insurance Corporation of Ireland*,[214] the High Court had no difficulty in being satisfied that the settlement entered into by the insured was reasonable and prudent in the circumstances and that:

> it would have been folly in the extreme [for the insured] to have rejected the advice of their lawyers and committed themselves and the defendants whom they were hoping would indemnify them, to litigation which would be protracted, expensive and, from their point of view, at best uncertain in its outcome.

9.7.4.3 The insured will be unable to establish liability if he has not conducted the defence in an adequate and proper manner.[215] If the insurers choose to defend the claim, they must do so properly and can decide the manner in which the claim is handled provided they do so in the common interest of the insurers and the insured.[216] The insurer will, in practice, generally wish to choose the solicitor to conduct the defence, and may be entitled to do so by the terms of the policy, but if the insured faces criminal prosecution or if there is a conflict of interest between the insured and the insurer, the insured may insist on a solicitor of their own choice.[217] Whether the solicitor is appointed by the insurer or the insured, they owe a duty of care to the insured, but the duty is not the same as that which arises in the ordinary client–solicitor relationship where the client requires the solicitor to act in accordance with their instructions. The purpose of the policy condition would be defeated if the insured were entitled to interfere with the conduct of the defence of the claim and the insured is not:

---

[214] *Rohan Construction Ltd. and Rohan Group Plc.* v *Insurance Corporation of Ireland Plc.* [1988] ILRM 373. The plaintiffs were employed as main subcontractors under a contract for the construction of a storage tank. The employer took an action against the plaintiffs alleging negligence in the performance of the work and the plaintiffs were also sued together with a sub-contractor for negligence and breach of contract. The actions were settled for £750,000 plus costs, with the plaintiffs paying £150,000 and a proportionate amount of the costs. The defendants had refused the plaintiff's claim for indemnity under a professional indemnity and a public liability policy.

[215] *Liberian Insurance Agency Inc.* v *Mosse* [1977] 2 Lloyds Rep 560.

[216] *Groome* v *Crocker* [1939] 1 KB 194 per Sir Wilfred Greene at 203.

[217] *Barratt Bros. (Taxis) Ltd.* v *Davies* [1966] 2 Lloyds Rep 1.

entitled to complain of anything done by solicitors upon the instructions, express or implied, of the insurers, provided that it falls within the class of things which the insurers are . . . entitled to do under the terms of the policy.[218]

The solicitor must, however, keep the insured informed of developments and must inform them of any possible conflict of interest arising between the insured and the insurer.[219] Generally a solicitor will not be appointed until the insurer has fully investigated the circumstances giving rise to the claim and satisfied itself that the claim is one in respect of which they are obliged to provide an indemnity under the policy. The Supreme Court endorsed the comments of Johnson J. that:

> . . . insurance companies should conduct their investigations in as thoroughgoing a manner as possible prior to instructing solicitors to act, rather than . . . instructing solicitors to act, then undertaking their investigations.[220]

Where insurers continue the defence of a claim, having discovered a breach of condition or warranty or other grounds for avoiding liability under the policy, their conduct may be regarded as a waiver of their right to avoid payment under the policy.[221]

9.7.5 PREMIUM ADJUSTMENT

Liability policies generally contain a condition which provides that if the premium for the policy has been calculated on any estimates given by the insured, the insured shall keep an accurate record con-

---

[218] *Groome* v *Crocker* [1939] 1 KB 194 at 202, 203.

[219] ibid. pp. 222 and 227.

[220] *O'Fearail* v *McManus* [1994] ILRM 81, per O'Flaherty J. (Egan and Denham JJ. concurring). The case arose out of an incident between the parties when the defendant was alleged to have committed a wrongful assault and battery on the plaintiff as a result of which the plaintiff sued for damages. The motor insurers for the defendant instructed solicitors to take up the matter on their behalf and he entered a defence. Subsequently the insurers decided that the event was not covered by their policy and withdrew their instructions from solicitors. The solicitors then applied to the court for permission to come off record and the application was granted on appeal to the Supreme Court. Costs of all parties to the application were awarded against the insurers.

[221] *Barratt Bros. (Taxis) Ltd.* v *Davies* [1966] 2 Lloyds Rep 1; *Fraser* v *B.N. Furman (Productions) Ltd.* [1967] 1 WLR 898; *Evans* v *Employers Mutual Insurance Association* [1936] 1 KB 505.

taining all relevant particulars and shall at any reasonable time allow insurers to inspect such record. The insured is further required,
following the expiry of each period of insurance, to supply to insurers
a statement or declaration, and if requested by insurers to have such
statement or declaration certified by auditors, so that the premium
for the period of insurance may be calculated and any difference paid
to the insurers or allowed to the insured as the case may be. The
right of the insurer to repudiate liability under a policy in the event
of a mis-statement of wages or salaries was upheld in *W.H. Ryan Ltd.
v MacMillan & Others.*[222]

9.7.6 ARBITRATION

All liability policies issued in Ireland contain an Arbitration condition
requiring any dispute under the policy between the insured and insurers in respect of a claim, liability or the amount to be paid to be
referred to Arbitration within twelve months of the dispute arising.
Most disputes arise out of an insurer's repudiation of liability because
of an alleged breach of condition or warranty or misrepresentation or
concealment of material information. The application of the Arbitration condition in a liability policy has been fully considered by the
Irish courts, with Budd J. in *Coen* v *Employers' Liability Assurance
Corporation Ltd.*[223] conducting an exhaustive review of the Irish and

---

[222] Unreported High Court, 20 December 1978, and *Carey* v *Ryan & Another*
[1982] ILRM 121 SC.

[223] [1962] IR 314. The plaintiff held a motor insurance policy issued by the defendants which contained an Arbitration condition. A passenger in the plaintiff's car
recovered judgment against the plaintiff for damages in respect of personal injuries suffered as a result of an accident involving the plaintiff's car. Insurers dis-
claimed liability on the grounds that injury to passengers was not covered under
the policy and that the insured did not have an insurable interest in the insured
car. The plaintiff did not refer the dispute to arbitration but instituted High
Court proceedings seeking a declaration that insurers were liable to indemnify
him under the contract of insurance.

English case law.[224] It is clear that an insurer cannot rely on grounds of repudiation of liability which challenge the validity of the insurance contract and at the same time seek to rely on the Arbitration condition. The Supreme Court has expressed support for the Arbitration process in commercial life and the desirability of making Arbitration awards final.[225] The courts are reluctant to interfere unless the award "shows on its face an error of law so fundamental that the courts cannot stand aside and allow it to remain unchallenged".[226]

---

[224] *Ballasty* v *Army Navy and General Assurance Association Ltd.* [1916] 50 ILTR 114; *Furey* v *Eagle Star and British Dominions Insurance Co. Ltd.* [1922] 56 ILTR 23; *Jureidini* v *National British and Irish Insurance Co. Ltd.* [1915] AC 499; *Kennedy* v *London Express Newspapers* [1931] IR 532; *Toller* v *Law Accident Insurance Society* [1936] 2 All ER 952; *Stevens & Sons* v *Timber and General Mutual Accident Insurance Association Ltd.* 102 LJKB 337; *Heyman* v *Darwins Ltd.* [1942] AC 356; *Gaw* v *British Law Life Insurance Co.* [1908] 1 IR 245; *Scott* v *Avery* 5 HL Cas. 811.

[225] *Keenan* v *Shield Insurance Co. Ltd.* [1988] IR 89.

[226] ibid. per McCarthy J. (Finlay C. J., Walsh, Griffin, Hederman JJ. all concurring). In *McStay* v *Assicurazioni Generali SPA and Maguire* [1991] ILRM 237 at 242, Finlay C. J. expressed the view that:

> A fundamental ingredient of the concept of arbitration, as contained in the common law, is the finality of the decision of the arbitrator, subject, of course, to certain qualifications and precautions. Broadly speaking, however, as one might expect, the law appears to acknowledge that where two parties agree to refer a particular question which is in dispute between them to the decision of a particular individual by way of arbitration, they are taken to have abandoned their right to litigate that precise question.

CHAPTER TEN

PUBLIC LIABILITY INSURANCE

10.1 PUBLIC LIABILITY POLICIES

Unlike motor insurance there is no compulsory requirement in respect of the insurance of public liability risks. Individuals and commercial concerns are therefore free to decide whether or not to insure liability to members of the public in respect of injury or damage to property caused by their negligence. There is no standard wording in use, but the general public liability policy is intended to insure the risk of accidental personal injury and physical damage to material property. Whilst it is possible to include the risks of nuisance, trespass, obstruction, wrongful arrest and defamation in a general public liability policy, it is necessary to arrange separate and specific policies in respect of the risks of infringement of copyright, patent, trademarks, indirect economic loss, and professional liability. The indemnity provided by a general public liability policy relates only to legal liability arising out of an accident event or occurrence which results in personal injury, illness, disease, loss of or damage to property of third parties.

10.2 SCOPE OF COVER

10.2.1 INDEMNITY

A general public liability policy provides that the insurer will, subject to the terms, exceptions, limits, and conditions of the policy, indemnify the insured against:

1) All sums which the insured becomes legally liable to pay as damages in respect of (a) accidental bodily injury to or illness of any person, (b) accidental loss of or damage to property, occurring

within the territorial limits during the period of insurance and happening in connection with the business.

2) All costs and expenses (a) recovered by any claimant against the insured, (b) incurred with the written consent of the insurer, in respect of a claim against the insured for damages to which the indemnity expressed in the policy applies.

10.2.2 ACCIDENTAL INJURY/DAMAGE

Some policies do not refer to "accidental" injury or damage but emphasise the intention of the policy to cover only unexpected and unintended events or occurrences by excluding liability in respect of any occurrence which results from a deliberate act or omission of the insured and which could reasonably have been expected by the insured, having regard to the nature and circumstances of such act or omission.[1] In *Gray* v *Barr*[2] the Court of Appeal decided that a loss was not accidental if it had resulted from reckless conduct of the insured even if the loss had not been intended by them. In *University of Western Ontario* v *Yanush*,[3] the Ontario High Court accepted that the consequences of a defendant's conduct which amounted to gross negligence constituted an "accident" for which insurers should provide an indemnity under a public liability policy. The defendant, a student at the university, returned to his rooms at the university late at night having consumed a considerable quantity of alcohol. In an attempt to wake a friend he covered the friend's bed with toilet paper and set fire to it. The resulting fire caused extensive property damage and personal injury. The insurers of the university, having settled the claims sought to exercise subrogation rights against the defendant who claimed indemnity from the insurers of a liability policy issued to his parents on the ground that what had happened was an "accident". The court agreed that the loss had been caused by "accident", noting that the defendant had "never thought of himself as negligent, nor did he realise the dangers of his actions, nor did he deliberately as-

---

[1] The Supreme Court acknowledged the necessity for an "accidental" occurrence to trigger cover under a public liability policy in *Rohan Construction Ltd. and Rohan Group Plc.* v *Insurance Corporation of Ireland Ltd.* [1986] ILRM 373.

[2] [1971] 2 QB 554.

[3] [1988] 56 DLR (4th) 552.

sume the risk of it". The court stressed that negligence concepts were immaterial to the issue and the question whether or not the loss was accidental was not the same question as whether or not the loss was reasonably foreseeable. The case can be distinguished from *Gray* v *Barr*[4] in so far as the defendant was intoxicated and unable to appreciate the consequences of his actions, but in both cases the defendants had acted deliberately in creating a dangerous situation without the intention of causing any actual loss.[5]

10.2.3 DEFINITION OF "ACCIDENT" BY CUSTOM

A precise definition of the word "accident" is critical to an understanding of the principle of public liability insurance. In *Trim Joint District School Board of Management* v *Kelly*,[6] Lord Loreburn said:

> A good deal was said about the word "accident". Etymologically, the word means something which happens — a rendering which is not very helpful. We are to construe it in the popular sense, as plain people would understand it; but we are also to construe it in its setting, in the context, and in the light of the purpose which appears from the Act itself [Workman's Compensation Act, 1906 (repealed)]. Now there is no single rigid meaning in the common use of the word. Mankind has taken the liberty of using it, as they use so many other words, not in any exact sense but in a somewhat confused way, or rather in a variety of ways. We say that someone met a friend in the street quite by accident, as opposed to appointment, or omitted to mention something by accident, as opposed to intention, or that he is disabled by an accident, as opposed to disease, or made a discovery by accident, as opposed to research or reasoned experiment. When people use this word they are usually thinking of some definite event which is unexpected, but it is not so always, for you might say of a person that he is foolish as a rule and wise only by accident. Again, the same thing, when occurring to a man in one kind of employment, would not be called accidental, but would be so described if it occurred to another not similarly employed. A sol-

---

[4] n. 2 *supra*.

[5] In Canada the terms of insurance contracts are closely regulated by legislation. The decisions of the Canadian Courts are not of course binding in Ireland but the case is of interest in that it was decided on the basis of the common law and not local legislation.

[6] [1914] AC 667.

dier shot in battle is not killed by accident, in common par-
lance. An inhabitant trying to escape from the field might be
shot by accident. It makes all the difference that the occupation of the two was different. In short, the common meaning of
this word is ruled neither by logic or etymology, but in custom,
and no formula will precisely express its usage for all cases.

10.2.4 DIFFICULTY OF DEFINITION

The difficulty in defining the word was recognised by Paull J. in *Mills*
v *Smith*,[7] when he said:

> one judge very many years ago said the word was undefinable.
> The dictionary definition is . . . "Anything that happens with-
> out foresight or expectation or is an unusual effect of a known
> cause." The application of that definition depends almost en-
> tirely on the point of view from which the particular matter is
> approached. If, quite unexpectedly, someone coming up to me,
> hits me in the face and gives me a black eye, the event, so far
> as I am concerned, is quite unexpected, yet I would not say
> that I got the black eye by accident; I would say that I got it by
> an unprovoked assault. Nor would it be an accident so far as
> the attacker is concerned. Yet, under the . . . Act, an injury by

---

[7] [1963] 2 All ER 1078 at 1079; *McCollum (R.D.) Ltd.* v *Economical Mutual Insurance Co.* [1962] QB 850, per Lancheville P. at 858:

> In common parlance, when one hears someone relate that there has been an
> accident it . . . does not follow that there has been no negligence involved at
> all. For the word "accident" has in commonplace the significance of being op-
> posed to a wilful and deliberate act, or, short of this, one which is so obviously
> gross negligence (as to be) the obvious and natural result of a most imprudent
> and unreasonable act.

In *Makin (F & F) Ltd.* v *London & North Eastern Railway Co.* [1943] 1 KB 467,
Lord Greene M. R. said at 474:

> When Parliament in 1794 refers to an accidental flowing of water (The Peak
> Forest Canal Act, 1794), did it intend to exclude from that category of flowing
> of water caused by an event which to the ordinary person would be described
> as accidental, but which to the more technical mind of a lawyer might have to
> be put for certain purposes under the special label of "Act of God"? In my
> opinion, that is a refinement which is not justified by anything in this section.
> It seems to me that, if Parliament meant damage caused by the accidental
> flowing of water or the accidental breach of the reservoir, those words are wide
> enough in their natural meaning to cover something caused by an "Act of God".
> It is to be observed that the language here does not deal with the cause of the
> breach, nor does it deal with the cause of the water flowing or of the other
> matters. . . . In any event in ordinary language the word "accident" seems to
> me without doubt to cover an "Act of God".

an unprovoked attack has been decided to be an injury by accident for the purpose of the Act.

10.2.5 RELEVANCE TO PUBLIC LIABILITY

The Supreme Court, in *Rohan Construction Ltd* v *Insurance Corporation of Ireland Ltd.*,[8] in the course of determining the intention of a public liability policy, accepted the statement of Lord Lindley in *Fenton* v *Thorley & Co. Ltd.*[9] that:

> The word "accident" is not a technical legal term with a clearly defined meaning. Speaking generally, but with reference to legal liabilities, an accident means an unintended and unexpected occurrence which produces hurt or loss. But it is often used to denote any unintended and unexpected loss or hurt apart from its cause; and if the cause is not known, the loss or hurt itself would certainly be called an accident. The word "accident" is also often used to denote both the cause and the effect, no attempt being made to discriminate between them. The great majority of what are called accidents are occasioned by carelessness; but for legal purposes it is often important to distinguish carelessness from other unintended and unexpected events.

10.2.6 INTERPRETATION

Policies generally refer to "bodily injury" rather than personal injury as the latter could be interpreted as including libel, slander or wrongful arrest. Likewise "property" can be interpreted as including intangibles such as copyright, patents, design rights, trademarks, trade names and any estate, right or interest in property, loss of or damage to which could involve the owner in financial loss. For that reason general public liability policies either exclude liability for such losses

---

[8] *Rohan* v *ICI* above. The plaintiffs had been contracted to construct a storage tank in part of a dry dock in Limerick. During the course of the work a decision was made to change the original specifications and when the work was completed there was a massive leak in the piping and water penetrated the membrane of the tank. It transpired that the pipes had not been properly joined with the result that ingress of surrounding concrete had occurred and a significant part of the pipe was blocked. There were also other defects in the workmanship and some of the materials used were below specification. The plaintiffs agreed to contribute towards the compromise of the claims brought against them and other parties and then sought indemnity from the defendants under a public liability policy or a professional indemnity policy.

[9] [1903] AC 443 at 448 and 453.

or refer to "loss of or physical damage to physical property". The loss of third party property as distinct from damage to the property is covered. In *Stansbie v Troman*[10] a painting contractor working in a house left it unoccupied and unlocked whilst he went to collect materials. He was absent for about two hours during which time the house was entered and jewellery stolen. The contractor was held liable for the loss.

10.3 NUISANCE, TRESPASS AND OBSTRUCTION

Whilst the general public liability policy is intended primarily to provide indemnity in respect of the tort of negligence, some policies go further and extend cover to loss arising from trespass, nuisance or interference with any easement of air, light, water, or way.[11] This extension of cover is of particular relevance to construction contractors and property developers.

10.3.1 NUISANCE

> The term nuisance contemplates an act or omission which amounts to an unreasonable interference with, disturbance of, or annoyance to another person in the exercise of his rights. If the rights so interfered with belong to the person as a member of the public, the act or omission is a public nuisance. If these rights relate to the ownership or occupation of land, or of some easement, profit, or other right enjoyed in connection with land, then the acts or omissions amount to a private nuisance.[12]

10.3.2 PUBLIC NUISANCE

Public nuisance is a crime occasioning injury to the reasonable convenience of the public or a section of the public. Unless a person has suffered particular or special damage over that suffered by other members of the public, it is only the Attorney General who may bring

---

[10] *Stansbie v Troman* [1948] 1 All ER 599.

[11] For a detailed treatment of these torts see McMahon and Binchy (1990), *Irish Law of Torts*, Chapters 23 and 24, 2nd edition, Butterworths; Winfield, "Nuisance as a Tort", 4 Camb LJ 189 (1931); Newark, "The Boundaries of Nuisance", 65 LQ Rev 480 (1949); Ekelaar, "Nuisance and Strict Liability", 8 Ir. Jur. (1973).

[12] *Connolly v South of Ireland Asphalt Co.* [1977] IR 99 per O'Higgins C. J. at 103.

civil proceedings.[13] The unauthorised opening of a trench on the public road is a public nuisance as is the failure to refill a trench lawfully opened or to restore the surface of the highway to make it fit for traffic.[14] While generally speaking any obstruction of the highway could be said to constitute a public nuisance,[15] the courts have recognised that some obstruction is unavoidable in modern day life.[16] The Supreme Court, in *Convery (Grace)* v *Dublin County Council*,[17] confirmed that a public nuisance consisted of an act or omission which caused injury to or materially affected the reasonable comfort and convenience of the public, or a section of the public. It was, however, only actionable at the suit of an individual if they had suffered particular damage over and above that suffered by other members of the public. The case arose out of the construction of The Square Town Centre, Tallaght, and the consequent increase in traffic in the area. The High Court had held that a County Council could be sued for public nuisance if it arose due to the negligence of the Council in the exercise of its statutory duty and that the failure of the defendants to take any concrete steps to alleviate the problem amounted to negligence. The Supreme Court over-ruled that decision, holding that the traffic in question had not originated in any premises owned or occupied by the Council and was not generated as a result of any activities carried on by them on land in the area. To treat the council as the legal author of a public nuisance would, in the circumstances of the case, have been entirely contrary to principle and wholly unsupported by authority.

10.3.3 PRIVATE NUISANCE

Private nuisance is the unreasonable interference with the reasonable use and enjoyment of land.[18] The test of liability in nuisance is akin to that in negligence and is the doing or permitting of something

---

[13] *Smith* v *Wilson* [1903] 21 IR 45; *A-G* v *Mayo County Council* [1902] 1 IR 13.

[14] *Wall* v *Morrissey* [1969] IR 10 at 21.

[15] *Cunningham* v *McGrath Bros.* [1964] IR 209, per Kingsmill Moore J. at 213.

[16] *McKenna* v *Stephens and Alexander E. Hall & Co.* [1923] 2 IR 112 per Moloney C. J. at 122.

[17] Unreported Supreme Court, 12 November 1996.

[18] See Gearty, "The Place of Private Nuisance in a Modern Law of Torts", [1989] Camb. LJ 214.

of which the natural and probable consequence is the creation of a nuisance.[19] An occupier of land is entitled to the comfortable and healthy enjoyment of the land to the degree that would be expected by an ordinary person whose requirements are objectively reasonable in all the particular circumstances.[20] The interference must be substantial and not just trifling inconvenience[21] and actual damage must be proved, i.e. physical injury to land, substantial interference with the enjoyment of land or interference with servitudes.[22] There must be a causal link between the damage alleged and the activity complained of.[23]

10.3.3.1 Tree Roots

Physical injury to land caused by the encroachment of trees or tree roots can ground an action in nuisance.[24] The Court of Appeal, in *Solloway v Hampshire County Council*,[25] emphasised that a person responsible for a tree would only be under the duty arising from the nuisance it caused if they knew or ought to have known of the existence of that nuisance and of the danger caused by it. The duty extends to taking reasonable steps to prevent or minimise the known danger of damage, bearing in mind the expense and practicality of the remedial measures. In *Davey v Harrow Corporation*,[26] the plaintiff had bought a house eight metres from the pavement on which stood a 60 foot tree. Following a hot summer, subsidence occurred,

---

[19] per McWilliam J. in *Gillick v O'Reilly* [1984] ILRM 402, applying the dictum of Kingsmill-Moore J. in *Cunningham v McGrath Bros.* [1964] IR 209.

[20] *Hanrahan v Merck Sharp & Dohme (Ireland) Ltd.* [1988] ILRM 629 per Henchy J. at 634.

[21] *St Helen's Smelting Ltd. v Tipping* [1865] 11 ER 1483.

[22] *Scott v Goulding Properties Ltd.* [1973] IR 200; *Gannon v Hughes* [1937] IR 284; *Smyth v Dublin Theatre Co. Ltd.* [1936] IR 692.

[23] *Hanrahan v Merck Sharp & Dohme (Ireland) Ltd.* [1988] ILRM 629. The House of Lords re-affirmed the need for the plaintiff to establish causation in all circumstances, in *Wilsher v Essex Area Health Authority* [1988] 2 WLR 557.

[24] *Middleton v Humphries* [1912] 47 ILTR 160; *Butler v Standard Telephone & Cables Ltd.* [1940] 1 KB 29; see also "Roots of Trees: Liability for Injury Caused to Neighbour's Premises", 6 Ir. Jur. 20 (1940); "Injuries Caused by Growing Trees", 25 Ir. Jur. 20 (1959).

[25] *Solloway v Hampshire County Council* [1981] LGR 449.

[26] [1958] 1 QB 60. Decision analysed in 25 Ir. Jur. 20 (1959) per V. T. Delaney.

but the council were not liable for the cost of repair as the risk was considered too remote and the expense of practical prevention too great. The encroachment of trees or tree roots entitles the injured party to apply for an injunction or to seek damages,[27] but they can also protect themselves by cutting the roots or branches as soon as they encroach into their property without waiting for damage to be done to it.[28]

10.3.3.2 Trees

In *Lynch* v *Hetherton*[29] the High Court held that landowners having on their lands a tree or trees adjoining the highway or their neighbour's land is bound to take such care as a reasonable and prudent landowner would take to guard against the danger of damage being done by a falling tree, and if they fail to exercise this degree of care and damage results from such failure on their part, a cause of action will result against them.[30] For the plaintiff to succeed in an action of this kind it is necessary for them to establish as a matter of probability that the landowner was aware, or should have been aware, of the dangerous condition of the tree.[31] Section 70(2)(a) of the Roads Act, 1993 obliges the owner or occupier of any land to take all reasonable steps to ensure that a tree, shrub, hedge or other vegetation on the land is not a hazard to persons using the public road and that it does not interfere with the safe use of the public road. Section 76(5) of the Act contains provisions requiring owners or occupiers of land adjacent to a public road to take all reasonable steps to ensure that water is not prevented, obstructed or impeded from draining onto the land from the public road, and to prevent water, soil or other material from flowing or falling on to a public road from their land.

---

[27] *Middleton* v *Humphries* [1912] 47 ILTR 160; *Davey* v *Harrow Corporation* [1958] 1 QB 60.

[28] *Lemmon* v *Webb* [1894] 3 CH 1 at 24; [1895] AC 1.

[29] *Lynch* v *Hetherton* [1991] IR 405.

[30] ibid. per O'Hanlon J. relying on principles laid down in English cases: *Noble* v *Harrison* [1926] 2 KB 332; *Cunliffe* v *Bankes* [1945] 1 All ER 459; *Brown* v *Harrison* [1947] WN 191; *Caminer* v *Northern Investment Trust Ltd.* [1951] AC 88; *Quinn* v *Scott* [1965] 1 WLR 1004, and following *Gillen* v *Fair* [1959] 90 ILTR 119.

[31] ibid. n. 25.

10.3.3.3 Pollution

Actions in nuisance can also arise from the presence of cattle on the public road,[32] noise,[33] dust,[34] blasting,[35] fumes,[36] smoke,[37] vibrations,[38] sewage,[39] emission of toxic substances.[40] Private nuisance actions are an important and effective weapon in the war against pollution of the environment in that the remedies which they demand, injunctions and damages, are the strongest the courts can provide. However, plaintiffs face major obstacles in the form of legal costs, the burden of proving causation and the establishment of *locus standi*.[41] The law on the matter dates from the nineteenth century Industrial Revolution

---

[32] *Gillick* v *O'Reilly* [1984] ILRM 402. The plaintiff was injured when his motorcar collided, at night on a main road, with a bullock owned by the defendant. The animal was one of a herd that had strayed on to the road through an open gate. On the facts the plaintiff failed to establish that there was any breach of duty by the defendant.

[33] *O'Kane* v *Cambell* [1985] IR 115; *Mullin* v *Hynes*, Unreported Supreme Court, 13 November 1972; *Stafford* v *Roadstone Ltd.* [1980] ILRM 1; *Dewar* v *City and Suburban Racecourse Co.* [1899] 1 IR 345.

[34] *Leech* v *Reilly*, Unreported High Court, 26 April 1983; *Malone* v *Clogrennane Lime & Trading Co. Ltd.* Unreported High Court, 14 April 1978.

[35] *Malone supra*; *Buckley* v *Healy* [1965] IR 637; *Halpin* v *Tara Mines Ltd.* Unreported High Court, 16 February 1976; *Patterson* v *Murphy* [1978] ILRM 85; *Stafford* v *Roadstone Ltd.* [1980] ILRM 1.

[36] *St. Helen's Smelting Co.* v *Tipping* [1865] 11 ER 1483.

[37] *Hatch* v *Pye* [1983] 59 NDR (2d) 170.

[38] *Bellew* v *Cement Ltd.* [1948] IR 61. The conflict between the social utility of the defendant's conduct and the plaintiff's legal right was determined in the plaintiff's favour with Murnaghan C. J. saying at p. 64, 65:

> I am afraid that I cannot attach very much importance to the effect of this injunction upon the public convenience. It is a dispute between parties and concerned only with the rights of those parties. . . . I do not think that we are entitled to deprive Mr Bellew of his legal rights on some idea of public convenience.

Halpin v *Tara Mines Ltd.* Unreported High Court, 16 February 1976; *Patterson* v *Murphy* [1978] ILRM 85; *Goldfarb* v *Williams & Co.* [1945] IR 433.

[39] *Wallace* v *McCartan* [1917] IR 397; *Gibbings* v *Hungerford* [1904] 1 IR 211.

[40] *Hanrahan* v *Merck Sharpe & Dohme (Ireland) Ltd.* [1988] ILRM 629.

[41] It is believed that the Supreme Court in *Hanrahan*, whilst restating the legal rules, applied them in a very liberal way so as to assist an individual plaintiff in a battle with a major international Corporation: Gearty (1989), "The Place of Private Nuisance in a Modern Law of Torts", Camb LJ 214 at 216 ff. 26.

and consequently is biased in favour of the defendant industrialist and against the individual plaintiff, who faces an almost impossible burden in proving causation.

10.3.3.4 Onus of Proof

These difficulties were graphically illustrated in *Hanrahan* v *Merck Sharp & Dohme (Ireland) Ltd*.[42] The plaintiff operated a thriving dairy farm of some 264 acres in a quiet rural area which, up to 1976, was virtually free from industrialisation. In that year, the defendants opened a factory for the manufacture or processing of pharmaceutical products in a nearby townland, approximately one mile from the plaintiff's farm. The operation of the factory necessarily involved the storage and use of large quantities of toxic substances and the keeping and disposal of toxic and dangerous chemical waste. The plaintiffs complained that as a result of the emission of toxic and dangerous gases, dusts, liquids and other substances, they suffered ill health and inconvenience. The plaintiffs formulated their claim in nuisance, negligence and breach of the rule in *Rylands* v *Fletcher*,[43] but in the High Court and in the Supreme Court the claim was dealt with as essentially one of nuisance. The case ran in the High Court for 47 days and in a reserved judgment Keane J. found that the plaintiffs

---

[42] [1988] ILRM 629.

[43] [1868] LR 3 HL 330. The plaintiff in the original action was Fletcher, a colliery owner. The defendant, Rylands, owned a nearby mill. The defendant created a dam on his own land to run the mill and in the course of so doing discovered some old mine shafts which unknown to him connected through adjoining third party property to the plaintiff's (Fletcher's) colliery. The dam burst and flooded the colliery. In the resulting action by Fletcher in the Court of Exchequer, Rylands was found not liable because (a) he did not have the requisite knowledge of the connection to the colliery and (b) he had employed contractors to carry out the work and for whom he was not liable. Fletcher appealed successfully and Rylands then appealed to the House of Lords. The Law Lords were of the opinion that there was no cause of action in negligence or nuisance because it was a once-off event but developed liability on the basis of a new rule: (1) the defendant can use the land for any purpose which can be described as ordinary user of land; (2) if in the course of this user an accumulation of water passed naturally on to the adjoining land there would be no cause of action; (3) where the defendant engaged in non-natural user of land in the course of which water escapes, then the defendant is engaged in the non-natural user at his peril; (4) if water or any dangerous thing escapes in such circumstances then the defendant is strictly liable for resulting damage. Anything brought onto land is dangerous if it is likely to do mischief if it escapes and the defendant is strictly liable if it does escape.

had not proved that the personal injuries, loss and damage complained of had resulted from any act or default of the defendant. In the Supreme Court, Henchy J., in a lengthy detailed judgment said that:

> To provide a basis for the award of damages for the private nuisance relied on, the plaintiffs have to show that they have been interfered with, over a substantial period of time, in the use and enjoyment of their farm, as a result of the way the defendants conducted their operations in the factory. The plaintiffs do not have to prove want of reasonable care on the part of the defendants. It is sufficient if it is shown as a matter of probability that what they complain of was suffered by them as occupiers of their farm in consequence of the way the defendants ran their factory.[44]

In allowing the appeal, he rejected the trial judge's finding, saying that:

> it would be to allow scientific theorising to dethrone fact to dispose of this claim by saying, as was said in the judgment under appeal, that there was "virtually no evidence in this case of injury to human beings or animals which has been scientifically linked to any chemicals emanating from the defendant's factory".[45]

The claim was remitted to the High Court for the assessment of damages and subsequently was compromised for an undisclosed sum.[46] A general public liability policy, in the usual form, would not respond to provide indemnity in respect of the substantial damages and costs awarded in a case such as *Hanrahan*. All such policies contain an exclusion in respect of pollution or contamination other than that caused by a sudden identifiable and unexpected incident which takes place in its entirety at a specific time and place during the period of

---

[44] [1988] ILRM 629, at 631.

[45] ibid.

[46] The amount of the agreed settlement was believed to be in the region of £2.3 million, *Irish Times*, 15 December 1990.

the policy.[47] Even if the exclusion did not apply, the insured would have difficulty in establishing that the liability arose out of an accidental occurrence so as to bring liability within the terms of the policy.[48]

10.3.3.5 Dust

Dust arising from construction or demolition operations is frequently the source of claims grounded in nuisance. The Court of Appeal in England has held that in such circumstances no duty in either negligence or nuisance could arise in relation to any discomfort and annoyance suffered and that there could be liability only if physical injury could be demonstrated. In *Hunter* v *Canary Wharf Ltd.*[49] residents in East London brought two separate actions in respect of disturbance suffered by them. The first action related to the erection of the Canary Wharf Tower which, it was alleged, interfered with the television reception in the area occupied by the residents. The second action related to the construction of the Limehouse Link Road which caused abnormal amounts of dust to be deposited on nearby properties. The Court of Appeal was asked to determine preliminary issues of law. The action in relation to the interference with the televison reception was brought in nuisance and the Court held that in so far as private nuisance was concerned the interference was not of itself sufficient to ground an action as it was the mere presence of the building which was the cause of the problem. The action in respect of the dust was also brought in nuisance and the Court found that while the residents would have a cause of action if they could show that more than a normal level of dust had been created, it was not sufficient to show that the plaintiffs' enjoyment of their property had been restricted. It was necessary to prove that the dust had caused actual physical injury and damage.

---

[47] For the purpose of the exclusion "pollution or contamination" is generally taken to mean pollution or contamination of buildings or other structures or of water land or atmosphere and all loss or damage or injury directly or indirectly caused by such pollution or contamination.

[48] A small number of insurers specialise in underwriting Environmental Impairment Liability risks and the cover provided, in addition to covering the legal liability of the insured, will also cover the clean up costs.

[49] [1995] *The Times*, 13 October.

10.3.4 TRESPASS TO THE PERSON

The essence of the tort of trespass is that wrongful conduct should cause a direct injury to the plaintiff but an action for trespass to the person does not lie if the injury to the plaintiff, although the direct consequence of the wrongful act of the defendant, was caused unintentionally and without negligence.[50] The general rubric of trespass to the person covers the distinct torts of Assault, Battery, Intentional Infliction of Mental Distress, False Imprisonment and Malicious Prosecution which may all be pleaded separately or together where a particular set of facts give rise to an action for more than one species of the more general tort. All of these distinct torts involve a deliberate act on the part of the perpetrator and, public policy considerations apart, would therefore fall outside the scope of cover provided by a general public liability policy. It is, however, possible for an insured to be unwittingly involved in the false imprisonment of another and subjected to an action for malicious prosecution. Some insurers are therefore prepared to extend a general public liability policy to provide limited indemnity against liability for such torts.[51] The high incidence of theft and assault in society generally and the necessity for the use of security personnel by all businesses expose all commercial concerns to allegations of trespass to the person in all its forms. Some of these torts are uninsurable but nevertheless are worthy of consideration here as the factual circumstances may also involve negli-

---

[50] *Fowler* v *Lanning* [1959] 1 All ER 290, per Diplock L. J. at 297. For the distinction between an action in negligence and in trespass generally, see also *Letang* v *Cooper* [1964] 2 All ER 929.

[51] Where insurers are prepared to provide the cover it is usually on the lines of the following wording:

> The Company will indemnify the insured in respect of all sums which the insured shall become legally liable to pay in respect of damages and/or costs and/or expenses awarded against the insured as a result of charges of wrongful arrest or malicious prosecution, libel and slander being made against the insured arising out of any allegation of shop lifting or other improper conduct by any customer or customers or by any other person or persons (other than an employee of the insured) during the currency of the policy.

gence,[52] and where allegations of trespass to the person are made, people will automatically look to their insurers for protection and indemnity.

10.3.4.1 Assault

An assault is an act which places another person in reasonable apprehension of an immediate battery being committed upon him.[53] Mere words, no matter how harsh, lying, insulting, or provocative, can never amount in law to assault,[54] but words can negative what otherwise might have amounted to an assault.[55] The tort consists of a touching of the mind not the body.[56] Apprehension, not fear, is the test and the tort is committed where the apprehension is reasonable although mistaken, e.g. a threat with an unloaded gun. The apprehension must be immediate so that where a person is stabbed in the back it is likely that a charge of assault would not be made out as the

---

[52] *Letang* v *Cooper* [1964] 2 All ER 929. The plaintiff was sunbathing near a car park when the defendant drove his motor car drove over her legs, injuring her. She brought an action in negligence and for unintentional trespass. The action in negligence was statute barred and the court was asked to determine if the action for unintentional trespass was likewise barred. Diplock L. J. was of the view that "an action for unintentional trespass is treated as if it were negligence" but Denning M. R. thought that ". . . causes of action in modern law are divided as to intentional or unintentional. . . . if the conduct is intentional there is an action in trespass, if it is unintentional there is no cause of action in trespass — the only cause of action is in negligence and that is statute barred."

[53] *Dullaghen* v *Hillen* [1957] Ir. Jur. 10. The defendant, a customs officer, responded to verbal abuse from the plaintiff by breaking his nose and falsely imprisoning him. The plaintiff claimed the defendant had committed a battery on him and the defendant pleaded that his actions were merely a defence to the provocative words of the plaintiff which he alleged constituted an assault.

[54] ibid. at 14 per Fawsitt J. reminding the defendant of:
   . . . the commonplace but trite couplet which runs: "sticks and stones may break your bones but words will never hurt you," and in which there is a definition of the law of assault, namely that mere words, no matter how harsh, lying, insulting and provocative they may be, can never in law amount to an assault.

[55] *Tubberville* v *Savage* [1669] 1 Mod 3. The parties had an argument on the street and the plaintiff put his hand on his sword and said: "If it was not assize time I would not take such language from you." Words can negate what otherwise might amount to an assault.

[56] *Kline* v *Kline* [1902] 64 NE 9.

injured party would not have had any apprehension of the injury. There must be means of carrying out the threat.[57]

10.3.4.2 Battery

The definition of assault outlined above necessitates a definition of battery. In essence it involves the direct application of physical contact upon the person of another without their consent, express or implied.[58] Passive obstruction does not constitute battery.[59] The physical contact only must be intended and not necessarily the consequences of the contact,[60] and unless self-evident from the act itself, the plaintiff must plead the facts which show the contact to be hostile. The true test is not whether there was hostile intent on the part of the defendant but whether an absence of consent on the part of the plaintiff can be inferred.[61] Most of the ordinary day-to-day physical contacts between people in modern life are not actionable because they are impliedly consented to by all who move in society.[62] The real test of whether physical contact is battery is whether the touching is hostile but hostile may not mean malevolent.[63]

---

[57] *Stephens* v *Myers* [1830] 170 ER 735.

[58] *Dullaghen* v *Hillen* [1957] Ir Jur. 10; *Donoghue* v *Coyle* [1953–54] Ir Jur Rep 30.

[59] *Innes* v *Wylie* [1884] 174 ER 800. The plaintiff had been a member of a society but barred from attending its meetings. He attempted to attend the annual dinner but was obstructed by a policeman acting as agent of the defendant. The case hinged on whether the policeman was entirely passive merely preventing entry or whether he took active steps to prevent entry. If the policeman was entirely passive then the plaintiff was not put in a position of apprehending a battery but if the policeman had taken active steps then the case of assault would be made out.

[60] *Wilson* v *Pringle* [1986] 2 All ER 440.

[61] ibid.

[62] *Collins* v *Willcock* [1984] 3 All ER 374. A policewoman, questioning the plaintiff on the street, touched her when she went to move away and the plaintiff then scratched the policewoman. The plaintiff was convicted of assaulting the policewoman but on appeal it was held that the policewoman had exceeded her authority in touching the plaintiff, with Gough L. J. stating that ". . . it is a fundamental principle that everyone's body is inviolate and any touching can therefore be a battery".

[63] ibid. per Croom-Johnston. J.

10.3.4.3 False Imprisonment

False imprisonment is the unlawful and total restraint of the personal liberty of another whether by constraining him or compelling him to go to a particular place or confining him in prison or police station or private place or by detaining him against his will in a public place. The essential element of the offence is the unlawful detention of the person, or the unlawful restraint on his liberty. The fact that a person is not actually aware that he is being imprisoned does not amount to evidence that he is not imprisoned, it being possible for a person to be imprisoned in law, without his being conscious of the fact and appreciating the position in which he is being placed, laying hands on the person of the party imprisoned not being essential. There may be an effectual imprisonment without walls of any kind. The detainer must be such as to limit the party's freedom of motion in all directions. In effect, imprisonment is a total restraint of the liberty of the person. The offence is committed by mere detention without violence.[64]

To constitute the offence, the imprisonment must be a total restraint of the liberty of the plaintiff and not merely partial obstruction of the will.[65] Where an employee was restrained and questioned in relation to the theft of property from his place of employment, Atkin L. J. was of the opinion that

. . . knowledge of the restraint does not have to be proved. . . . the only question is whether there is evidence on which the

---

[64] *Dullaghen* v *Hillen* [1957] Ir Jur 10 at 15 per Fawsitt. J.

[65] *Birds* v *Jones* [1845] 7 QB 742. The plaintiff was walking over a bridge when the defendant obstructed his way with seats and fencing. The plaintiff ignored the obstruction and climbed over the fence. The defendant tried to stop him by pulling at his coat but the plaintiff did get into the fenced-off area where he was stopped by two policemen. The plaintiff hit the defendant and was then imprisoned overnight. The plaintiff claimed false imprisonment and the defendant justified his actions on the grounds of assault. The plaintiff claimed he was falsely imprisoned when confined within the fenced-off area. The majority of the court, stating that imprisonment meant the total restraint of liberty and not merely partial obstruction of will, found that the plaintiff had not been imprisoned because he had been given the opportunity of exiting from the area even though it was not his choice of exit. The dissenting judgment held that an opportunity for exit must be reasonable and that on the facts the court was not convinced the plaintiff would have been allowed out through any other exit. See also: *Robinson* v *Balmain Ferry Co. Ltd.* [1910] AC 295; *Philips* v *G.N. Railway Co. Ltd.* [1903] 4 NIJR 154.

jury could find that the plaintiff was imprisoned so that his liberty was restrained regardless of his knowledge.[66]

The Supreme Court has held that overt surveillance of a suspected person does not constitute detention or restraint provided the person is permitted to go where they wish.[67] Detention in prison is not necessary as the courts have found false imprisonment to have occurred in such places as retail stores,[68] railway stations,[69] cars,[70] lavatories,[71] and polling booths.[72]

10.3.4.4 Malicious Prosecution

To succeed in an action for malicious prosecution a plaintiff must prove (a) that the criminal proceedings terminated in his favour; (b) that the defendant initiated or participated in the proceedings maliciously; (c) that there was no reasonable or probable cause for the proceedings; (d) that the plaintiff suffered damage.[73] False imprisonment and assault will sometimes lead to a charge of malicious prosecution and the difference between the torts was referred to by Gannon J. in the High Court in *McIntyre* v *The Attorney General and Others*:

> . . . false imprisonment and assault relate to each other in the nature of the action and what happened. But malicious prose-

---

[66] *Meering* v *Graham White Aviation* [1920] 122 LT 46. The plaintiff and a friend both worked for the defendant company and shared a house. Property, missing from the company's premises was found in the house following a search and the plaintiff's friend was arrested. The plaintiff was taken by security personnel to the company's offices and in response to his enquiry as to why he was being brought there he was told he was being questioned with a view to giving evidence against his friend. Duke L. J. held there had been no false imprisonment as the plaintiff did not have the "slightest suspicion his liberty was being restrained," but the majority of the court found for the plaintiff.

[67] *Kane* v *Governor of Mountjoy Prison* [1988] ILRM 724.

[68] *Dillon* v *Dunnes Stores Ltd.* Unreported Supreme Court, 20 December 1968.

[69] *Farry* v *G.N. Railway Co. Ltd.* [1898] 2 IR 352; *Phillips* v *G.N. Railway Co. Ltd.* [1903] 4 NIJR 154.

[70] *Burton* v *Davies* [1953] QSR 26.

[71] *Sayers* v *Harlow UDC* [1958] 1 WLR 623.

[72] *Higgins* v *O'Reilly* [194] Ir. Jur. Rep 15.

[73] Restated by the Supreme Court in *McIntyre* v *Attorney General and Another* [1990] 1 IR 121 per Hederman J. at 132.

cution has another element in it and that is invoking a purported authority and abusing it; using it where they have no
right to be using it, abusing the authority of the courts for the
purposes of bringing about a prosecution and the consequences
of that. And that's why that's a completely different element
and the onus is on the plaintiff to show that, if he is to get any
damages under that heading, that in fact the . . . [defendant]
did abuse their position and they brought a prosecution
against him for a completely wrongful motive and in the circumstances in which there was no reasonable cause to bring it
at all. [74]

The plaintiff must show that the defendant was actively instrumental
in putting the prosecution in train,[75] and that the prosecution terminated in his favour if it was capable of termination.[76] The plaintiff
must positively discredit any possible view the defendant might have
had of the situation and if the plaintiff can show that the defendant
did not believe the plaintiff was guilty then he will succeed, irrespective of how reasonable the belief of the defendant might have been.
The defendant must have reasonable and probable cause in the form
of

an honest belief in the guilt of the accused based upon a full
conviction, founded upon reasonable grounds, of the existence
of a state of circumstances which, assuming them to be true,
would lead an ordinary prudent cautious man, placed in the
position of the accuser, to the conclusion that the person
charged was probably guilty of the crime against him.[77]

Malice covers not only spite and ill will but also any motive other
than a desire to bring a criminal to justice. The defendant does not

---

[74] ibid. quoted by Hederman J. at 133.

[75] *Davidson* v *Smyth* 20 LR Ir. 326. The defendant's brother's house was burned
by fire and the defendant was told by the plaintiff's sister that the plaintiff had
been responsible. The defendant reported the matter to the police and actively
encouraged the sister of the plaintiff to act as a witness against the plaintiff. The
plaintiff was acquitted of the charge of arson and sued the defendant for malicious prosecution and had to show that the defendant had been actively instrumental in putting the law into force.

[76] *Basebe* v *Mathews* [1867] LR 2 CP 684.

[77] per Fawsitt J. in *Dullaghen* v *Hillen* [1957] Ir. Jur. 10 at 17, quoting from *Hicks*
v *Faulkener*, 8 QBD 167 at 171, approved by the House of Lords in *Herniman* v
Smith [1938] AC 305.

have to believe the plaintiff is guilty but must at least have a reasonable belief that he is probably guilty.[78]

10.3.4.5 Intentional Infliction of Nervous Shock

The extent and scope of this tort in Ireland is uncertain but the intentional nature of it would take it outside any general form of public liability insurance. The perpetrator of a practical joke which resulted in nervous injury to the defendant was held liable for the consequences of his folly on the basis that he had:

> . . . wilfully done an act calculated to cause harm to the plaintiff, that is to say to infringe her legal right to personal safety, and has in fact thereby caused physical harm to her. That proposition without more appears to me to state a good cause of action, there being no justification alleged for the act. The wilful *injuria* is in law malicious, although no malicious purpose to cause the harm which was caused nor any motive of spite is imputed to the defendant.[79]

10.3.5 TRESPASS TO LAND

10.3.5.1 The tort of trespass to land consists of intentionally or negligently entering on or remaining on or directly causing anything to come into contact with land in the possession of another. There must be actual possession of the land before an action in trespass can be brought,[80] and it makes no difference if possession has been taken by the legal owner forcibly or not.[81] To succeed in an action for trespass to land the plaintiff must show that he had possession of the land at the time of the alleged trespass and that the defendant had no invitation to enter on the land, or that an implied invitation to enter had lapsed or that the defendant had no lawful authority to enter. Entry on to land for a sole purpose extraneous to the terms of an invitation,

---

[78] per Lord Devlin in *Glinski* v *McIver* [1962] AC 726. For a general treatment of malicious prosecution and the misuse of process see chapter 36 of McMahon and Binchy.

[79] *Wilkinson* v *Downton* [1897] 2 QB 57 per Wright J. The defendant had told the plaintiff, as a joke, that her husband had been seriously injured in an accident and she suffered severe shock causing her injury.

[80] *Hegan* v *Carolan* [1916] 2 IR 27.

[81] *Harvey* v *Bridges* 14 M&W 437–442.

expressed or implied, renders the entrant a trespasser.[82] Where a person enters land under authority of law rather than by private invitation and subsequently abuses or exceeds his authority he is deemed to be a trespasser from the time he entered the land.[83] Actual possession rather than title to the land grounds the action.[84] The general public have a right to use the highway for such purposes as it is usual to use the highway.[85] No action in trespass will arise if the user of the highway is ordinary and reasonable but, since 50 per cent of the subsoil under the highway belongs to the property adjoining the highway, the person in possession of that property would have a right of action in trespass against anyone using the highway for an extraneous purpose.[86]

10.3.5.2 Infringement of air space may constitute an actionable trespass up to such height as is necessary for the ordinary use and enjoyment of one's land and the structures on it.[87] Trespass is actionable *per se*, which means that the plaintiff does not have to prove damage to succeed but if he wishes to obtain damages he must of course be in

---

[82] *DPP* v *McMahon* [1987] ILRM 87. Gardai who entered a licensed premises without a search warrant under the Gaming and Lotteries Act, 1956 were held to be trespassers in law in so far as they had no statutory authority and were outside the implied invitation of the owner.

[83] *The Six Carpenters case* [1610] 77 ER 695; *McMullen* v *Bradshaw* [1916] 50 ILTR 205; *Webb* v *Ireland* [1988] ILRM 565. The plaintiffs entered onto land with the implied licence of the owners to visit an ancient church and tomb. They used metal detectors to locate valuable old chalices and then dug them up and removed them. They were held to be trespassers once they began to dig.

[84] *Graham* v *Peat* [1801] 1 East 244.

[85] *Iveagh* v *Martin* [1961] 1 QB 232 at 273 per Paull J:
  On a highway I may stand still for a reasonably short time, but I must not put my bed upon the highway and permanently occupy a portion of it. I may stoop to tie my shoelace, but I may not occupy a pitch and invite people to come upon it and have their hair cut. I may let my van stand still long enough to deliver and load goods but I must not turn my van into a stall.

[86] *Hickman* v *Maisey* [1900] 1 QB 752; *A-G* v *Mayo County Council* [1902] 1 IR 13, see n. 85 above.

[87] *Lord Bernstein* v *Skyviews* [1977] 2 All ER 902. The defendants were involved in aerial photography and the plaintiff claimed trespass of his airspace. The court refused to accept that the proprietorial right to airspace extended indefinitely and that it was necessary to balance the property owner's right to enjoyment of property against the public interest and right to enjoy air travel.

a position to prove some loss.[88] An action in trespass is often brought to resolve disputes between neighbouring properties or to control or restrict development. In *Woolerton & Wilson Ltd.* v *Richard Costain Ltd.*[89] a construction crane swinging fifty feet over adjoining property was held to constitute a trespass. The court gave the injunction sought but in balancing the rights of the parties suspended it until the construction work was completed. In somewhat similar circumstances in *Anchor Brewhouse Developments* v *Berkley House Ltd.*,[90] Scott J. said that:

> if an adjoining owner places a structure on his land that overhangs his neighbour's land he thereby takes into his possession airspace to which his neighbour is entitled. That in my judgment is trespass; it does not depend on any balancing of rights.

The tort of trespass can also be committed by placing any object or substance on the land of another or causing such object or substance to cross the boundary of adjoining property.[91]

10.4 FINANCIAL LOSS

10.4.1 LOSS CONSEQUENT TO DAMAGE

The general public liability policy will provide indemnity in respect of the consequential, financial or economic losses flowing directly from the personal injury or damage to property of a third party occasioned by the negligence of the insured. The negligent insured is not however liable to everyone who suffers damage or loss as a result of his

---

[88] *Tallow* v *Ennis* [1937] IR 549, per Gavan Duffy J. at 552, 553.

[89] *Woollerton & Wilson Ltd.* v *Richard Costain Ltd.* [1970] 1 WLR 411.

[90] *Anchor Brewhouse Developments Ltd.* v *Berkley House (Docklands) Developments Ltd.* [1987] EGLR 173. The defendants' tower cranes were overswinging the plaintiff's land without permission although there had been negotiations for a licence. The cranes had been working for nine months without objection and there was no allegation of damage having been caused. The defendant pleaded that there had been no trespass and no nuisance since damage was an essential ingredient of nuisance. The court granted an injunction but suspended it for 21 days.

[91] *Gibbings* v *Hungerford* [1904] 1 IR 211 (discharge of sewage); *Brannigan* v *Dublin Corporation* [1927] IR 513 (dumping of rubbish).

negligence. The legal maxim, *damnum sine injuria esse potest*, expresses the principle that damage may be inflicted without there being a legal remedy.

10.4.2 ENGLISH LAW

10.4.2.1 In *Electrochrome Ltd.* v *Welsh Plastics Ltd.*,[92] the parties occupied factories on the same industrial estate, approximately five hundred feet apart. During the course of constructional work on the access road to their premises, a van owned by the defendants and driven by their employee struck a fire hydrant which formed part of their factory premises. The mains water supply had to be turned off for several hours to stop the flow of water from the hydrant. The hydrant and the mains were the property of the estate owners. Water was essential to the plaintiff's manufacturing processes and they sued the defendant for the financial losses suffered as a result of the damage to the hydrant. The court held that a person who suffers harm cannot recover compensation on the basis of a wrong done to another and a tortfeasor is not bound to compensate all persons who suffer harm from his wrongdoing. In an earlier case, *Cattle* v *Stockton Water Works Co.*[93] Blackburn J. had said:

> They were, at most common, guilty of a neglect of duty . . . which did not injure any property of the plaintiff. The plaintiff's claim is to recover the damage which he has sustained by his contract . . . becoming less profitable, or it may be, losing a contract . . . we think this does not give him any right of action.

10.4.2.2 That view prevailed also in *Spartan Steel Ltd* v *Martin Ltd.*[94] The defendants' employees were doing road work a quarter of a mile from the plaintiff's factory. In the course of excavating part of the road, they failed to follow the plans they had been given and damaged an electricity cable supplying power to the plaintiff's works which involved the melting of metal in electric furnaces. The plain-

---

[92] [1968] 2 All ER 205; see also *Weller* v *Foot & Mouth Disease Research Institute* [1965] 3 All ER 650, confirming that financial loss suffered by the plaintiffs through the negligence of the defendants whose conduct resulted in the closure of the local cattle mart was not recoverable.

[93] [1875] 10 QB 453.

[94] [1973] 1 QB 27.

tiffs lost production as a result of the power supply being cut off to facilitate repairs. At first instance, the trial judge allowed the plaintiff's claim for direct losses and the loss of profit on the lost production, but on appeal, the court held that mere financial loss was not recoverable. On somewhat similar facts, in *Irish Paper Sacks Ltd.* v *John Sisk & Son (Dublin) Ltd.*[95] O'Keeffe P. felt obliged to apply the principle, which he extracted from the English cases, that a plaintiff suing for damages, suffered as a result of an act or omission of the defendant, cannot recover if that act or omission did not directly injure the plaintiff's person or property, but merely caused consequential loss.

10.4.2.3 That principle was set aside in England, in *Junior Books* v *Veitchi*,[96] when the House of Lords decided that the duty of care does extend to financial loss. The majority were of the view that there was no reason why financial loss of itself should be disallowed while purely pecuniary harm coupled with physical injury was compensated.[97] The facts were that the defendants were specialist floor layers and were sub-contracted to builders who had contracted with the plaintiff to erect a new factory. There was, however, no contract between the plaintiff and the defendant. Two years after completion of the factory the flooring showed defects resulting from bad workmanship or materials, or both, and the plaintiffs sought damages for the cost of remedying the defects and the financial losses due to the temporary removal of equipment and machinery and loss of profit. The House of Lords held that where specialist sub-contractors laid a floor in a factory and it was alleged that the floor had been negligently laid and required replacement, the owners of the factory who were not in a contractual relationship with the sub-contractor were, if the allega-

---

[95] Unreported High Court, 18 May 1972. The defendants' workmen were excavating a trench on the road when they severed a cable supplying power to the plaintiff's factory. The power supply was interrupted for a period of two days causing a suspension of production. The plaintiff claimed they had suffered economic losses in the form of labour, overheads and loss of profit. They had suffered no physical damage and were denied recovery.

[96] *Junior Books* v *Veitchi* [1983] 1 AC 520.

[97] Denning L. J. in *Spartan Steel*, above n. 94, had said: ". . . it seem . . . better to consider the particular relationship in hand, and see whether or not as a matter of policy, economic loss should be recoverable or not". at 37.

tions were made out, entitled to recover the cost of replacing the floor and economic losses consequential on that replacement, despite the fact that it was not alleged that the state of the flooring constituted a danger to any person or to any other part of the factory.

10.4.2.4 This new approach in England was short-lived, however. The *Junior Books* decision was over-ruled in a number of subsequent cases[98] and disposed of in *D&F Estates Ltd.* v *Church Commissioners for England*[99], with Lord Bridge saying:

> The consensus of judicial opinion, with which I concur, seems to be that the decision of the majority [in *Junior Books*] is so far dependent upon the unique, albeit non-contractual, relationship between the pursuer and the defender in that case and the unique scope of the duty of care owed by the defendant to the pursuer arising from that relationship that the decision cannot be regarded as laying down any principle of general application in the law of tort or delict.[100]

In *Simaan General Contracting Co.* v *Pilkington Glass Ltd.*[101] Dillon L. J. added that *Junior Books* had been

> subject to so much analysis and discussion with differing explanations of the basis of the case that the case cannot now be regarded as a useful pointer to any developments of the law. . . . Indeed I find it difficult to see that future citation from *Junior Books* can ever serve any useful purpose.[102]

10.4.3 IRISH LAW

10.4.3.1 This rejection of the *Junior Books* reasoning in England was not carried over to Ireland. Indeed, Costello J., in *Ward* v *McMas-*

---

[98] *Tate & Lyle Ltd.* v *Greater London Council* [1983] 2 AC 509; *Muirhead* v *Industrial Tank Specialities Ltd.* [1985] 3 All ER 705; *Governors of Peabody Donation Fund* v *Sir Lindsay Parkinson & Co. Ltd.* [1985] AC 210; *Leigh & Sullivan Ltd.* v *Alkiamon Shipping Co. Ltd.* [1986] AC 785.

[99] [1988] 2 All ER 992.

[100] ibid. at 1003.

[101] [1988] 1 All ER 791.

[102] ibid. at 805.

ter,[103] appeared to enthusiastically adopt the extension of liability even though some disenchantment was then already evident in England. The Supreme Court has not considered in any great detail whether financial loss, unaccompanied by direct personal injury or damage, is recoverable but Kenny J. in *Dublin Port and Docks Board* v *Bank of Ireland*[104] was of the view that:

> . . . While foreseeability, that one's action or inaction may cause personal injury or damage to property, imposes liability, it does not create any liability for foreseen economic loss unless there is a special relationship between the parties.

10.4.3.2 The High Court, in *Sweeney* v *Duggan*,[105] held that:

> liability, in negligence, extended both to personal injury and to economic loss, and in determining whether the defendant was negligent, the nature of the loss was immaterial.[106]

The plaintiff was an employee of a company of which the defendant was the principal shareholder, and which occupied and operated a quarry where the defendant was quarry manager. The plaintiff was seriously injured at work and obtained judgment against the company which remained unsatisfied because the company was uninsured and had gone into liquidation. The plaintiff then claimed against the defendant for economic loss consequent upon the loss of his judgment against the company. He contended that the defendant, as statutory quarry manager, effective owner and operator of the company's business, owed him a special duty of care and having re-

---

[103] [1985] IR 29 at 44:

There is no doubt that this case [*Junior Books*] has extended the liability . . . for loss sustained by defective workmanship. I find its reasoning persuasive and I have no difficulty in applying it. It follows from it that the concept of reasonable foresight is one to be employed not only in deciding in a given case whether a duty of care exists, but also can be employed in determining its scope. . . . But the duty was not limited to avoiding foreseeable harm to person or property . . . but extended to a duty to avoid causing . . . consequential financial loss . . ."

[104] *Dublin Port & Docks Board* v *Bank of Ireland* [1976] IR 118 at 141.

[105] [1991] 2 IR 274.

[106] ibid. per Barron J. at 283, quoting a passage from the judgment of Henchy J. in *Siney* v *Dublin Corporation* [1980] IR 400 and cited by McCarthy J. in *Ward* v *McMaster* [1988] IR 337 at 349.

gard to the hazardous nature of the plaintiff's employment that the duty extended to taking reasonable steps to ensure that the company would be able to pay compensation to employees injured at work and in particular to arrange an appropriate policy of insurance. In holding against the plaintiff on a number of grounds the court said that the ordinary master and servant relationship did not ordinarily extend to a duty to prevent economic loss to or to protect the economic wellbeing of the other party.

10.4.3.3 In a more recent case, *McShane Wholesale Fruit and Vegetables Ltd.* v *Johnstone Haulage Co. Ltd. & Others*,[107] Flood J. in the High Court, held that where there is such proximity between the parties that, in the reasonable contemplation of one, carelessness on his part may be likely to cause damage to the other, a *prima facie* duty of care arises and, subject to any compelling exemption based on public policy, damages are recoverable for economic loss sustained by the latter as a result of the negligence of the former. The case arose out of a fire on the premises of the defendant which resulted in a power failure at the plaintiff's adjoining premises. The plaintiff alleged that the fire had been caused by the negligence of the defendant and that as a result of the power failure the plaintiff had suffered loss and damage in carrying out its business. In determining a preliminary issue, as to whether damages were recoverable in negligence for economic loss, the court held that, since the decision of the Supreme Court in *Ward* v *McMaster*,[108] an action for negligence lies if there is a sufficient relationship of proximity between the alleged wrongdoer and the person suffering damage such that, in the reasonable contemplation of the former, carelessness on his part may be likely to cause damage to the latter — in which case a *prima facie* duty of care arises — subject to any compelling exemption based on public policy; liability is not excluded by the type of damage suffered whether it be damage to the person, to property or financial or economic damage. The fact that damage is economic is not in itself a bar to recovery.

---

[107] Unreported High Court, 19 January 1996.
[108] [1988] IR 337.

10.4.4 FINANCIAL LOSS INSURANCE

Insurers, generally, are reluctant to provide cover for pure financial loss and the extent of cover provided by a general public liability policy depends entirely on the wording of the policy and the interpretation capable of being put on it. The acceptance by the High Court that the law of negligence in Ireland can impose liability for pure financial loss in the absence of injury or damage to the person or property of the claimant exposes the insured to liability in respect of which a general public liability policy may not provide indemnity.

10.5 GENERAL POLICY EXCLUSIONS

10.5.1 EMPLOYEES

A General Public Liability policy does not cover liability for bodily injury to persons engaged under a contract of service or apprenticeship with the insured where the injury arises out of and in the course of his employment by the insured.[109] Where the injury arises other than in the course of employment by the insured the injured person is regarded as a third party and any liability for the injury would be covered. With the increasing use of sub-contractors, labour-only sub-contractors and self-employed persons, the status of the party at the material time is critical to the determination of whether liability to the injured person is covered under an Employers' Liability policy or a Public Liability policy. The inference that parties under a contract are master and servant or otherwise is a conclusion of law dependent on the rights conferred and the duties imposed by the contract, and if the contractual rights and duties create the relationship of master and servant, a declaration by the parties that the relationship is otherwise is irrelevant.[110] A contract of service exists if: (a) the servant

---

[109] Such liability is the subject of an Employers' Liability policy, dealt with later.

[110] *Ready Mixed Concrete (South East) Ltd.* v *Minister of Pensions & National Insurance* [1968] 2 QB 497. A written contract between the plaintiff company engaged in the marketing and sale of concrete and another party declared to be an independent contractor, provided *inter alia* that for payment at mileage rates the party would carry concrete for the company and make available throughout the contract period a vehicle bought by him from a finance organisation associated with the company. He was to obtain a carrier's licence and was to maintain, repair and insure the vehicle and an attached mixing unit belonging to the company, and to drive the vehicle himself, but might with the company's consent hire

agrees in consideration of a wage or other remuneration to provide his own work and skill in the performance of some service for his master; (b) the servant agrees expressly or implicitly that, in performance of the service he will be subject to the control of the other party sufficiently to make him the master, and (c) the other provisions of the contract are consistent with its being a contract of service.[111] In determining whether a worker is employed pursuant to a contract of service or a contract for services, it is necessary to have regard to the degree of control exercised over him by the employer.[112] Regardless of what the actual contract states or specifies, regard must be had to the realities of the situation, and if it is stated in the contract that it is a contract for services, the entire contract must be looked at in order to decide if it is truly a contract for services.[113] Given the wide range of circumstances which can arise, it is difficult to state any hard and fast rule as to what constitutes a servant and what constitutes an independent contractor. Each case must be determined on its own special facts in the light of the broad guidelines

---

a competent driver if he was unable to drive at any time. He was obliged to paint the vehicle in the company's colours, to wear the company's uniform and to comply with the company's rules. He was prohibited from operating as a carrier of goods except under the contract.

[111] ibid.

[112] *Phelan* v *Coillte Teoranta, Ireland, The Attorney General and the Minister for Fisheries and Forestry* [1993] 1 IR 18. The plaintiff was employed as a heavy machine operator by the first defendant pursuant to a contract of service. He sustained personal injuries at work as a result of the negligence of a person who was a fitter and welder who carried out work for the first defendant on a full time basis. In the course of his work, this person travelled to forests managed by the first defendant on the instruction of its engineers or supervisors for the purposes of carrying out repairs to machinery. He provided his own tools and equipment, but provided no labour other than his own. At the end of each month he submitted an invoice in respect of work carried out and was paid an agreed hourly rate together with a mileage allowance. No tax, PAYE or PRSI contributions were paid by the first defendant and he was not entitled to holiday pay or pension rights. The defendants claimed that the fitter carried out work on behalf of the first defendant pursuant to a contract for services rather than a contract of service, and that they could not therefore be vicariously liable in negligence in respect of his acts or omissions. See also: *Roche* v *Kelly & Co. Ltd.* [1969] IR 100; *Agricultural and Dairy Society Ltd.* v *Gargan* [1939] Ir. Jur. Rep. 77; *O'Coindealbhain* v *Mooney* [1990] 1 IR 422; *Market Investigations Ltd.* v *Minister for Social Security* [1969] 2 QB 173.

[113] *Henry Denny & Sons (Ireland) Ltd. t/a Kerry Foods Ltd.* v *The Minister for Social Welfare*, per Carroll J., Unreported High Court, 15 October 1995.

outlined above, but the High Court in *McAuliffe* v *Minister for Social Welfare*[114] has indicated that the degree of control exercised by the employer over the employed person is the main test of whether a worker is a servant or a contractor.

10.5.2 EXTENSION OF DEFINITION

It is usual for the definition of employee in the policy to be extended to include for the purposes of the policy such persons as: (a) labour masters and persons supplied by them; (b) persons employed by labour-only sub-contractors; (c) self-employed persons; (d) any person hired or borrowed by the insured under an agreement by which the person is deemed to be employed by the insured; (e) persons engaged under work experience programmes. Such persons working for the insured in connection with the insured's business are deemed to be employees for the purpose of the policy and, while liability for personal injury sustained by such persons is excluded, the insured's legal liability for accidents caused by such persons is covered under the policy. However, the fact that such persons are stated in the policy to be employees does not alter their legal status which may not be established until after an accident has occurred. Where the degree of control exercised over a worker by an employer is the same as that exercised by master over a servant, the employer is vicariously liable for the negligence of the worker, irrespective of whether the worker is employed pursuant to a contract of service or a contract for services[115].

---

[114] *McAuliffe* v *Minister for Social Welfare*, Unreported High Court, 19 October 1994. The appellant was a wholesale distributor of newspapers who employed a number of people to deliver papers to retail shops and other outlets. Some of the people engaged by the appellant were engaged for five, six or seven days per week at a daily rate and were paid monthly against invoices submitted to the appellant. The engaged parties owned their own cars and were responsible for all outgoings including tax, insurance, repairs, fuel and depreciation. They had the right to provide substitute drivers acceptable to the appellant when necessary and it was their responsibility to pay those substitute drivers. The appellant was under no obligation to provide the other parties with deliveries or with deliveries on any particular days but they were in fact provided with deliveries on a regular basis. The engaged parties were free to carry goods for any other person both when not engaged on deliveries for the appellant and in conjunction with deliveries made for him, subject only to a restriction on delivering newspapers for another supplier. Some of the engaged parties were registered for VAT and made income tax returns as self-employed persons.

[115] *Phelan* n. 112 above.

10.5.3 MECHANICALLY PROPELLED VEHICLES

The general public liability policy does not cover liability arising out of the ownership, possession or use of any mechanically propelled vehicle in circumstances to which the Road Traffic Acts apply. It is, however, usual for insurers to provide cover under the policy in respect of unlicensed special type vehicles where the use of such vehicles is confined to the insured's own premises or sites which do not constitute a "public place" for the purposes of the compulsory insurance requirements of the Road Traffic Acts.[116] The exclusion does not apply to liability incurred by the insured arising out of the misdirection of third party vehicles as such vehicles would not be in the ownership, possession or use of the insured. Neither would the exclusion apply to non-Road Traffic Act liability arising out of the unauthorised movement of third party vehicles although liability for damage to such vehicles would be excluded by the custody and control exclusion of the policy.

10.5.4 CUSTODY AND CONTROL

Loss of or damage to the insured's own property cannot be covered under a public liability policy as the policy is intended to cover only the insured's legal liability. The policy therefore excludes liability in respect of loss of or damage to property belonging to the insured or in the charge or under the control of the insured. It is standard practice for the policy to provide that the exclusion does not apply to the property of employees, directors or visitors, and special provision can be made in respect of car park liabilities, cloakroom and hotel proprietors' risks. It is usual also for the policy to provide that the exclusion of property in the charge or under the control of the insured shall not apply to premises (including fixtures and fittings thereof) hired or rented to the insured, but the indemnity provided does not apply to liability assumed by the insured under agreement which would not

---

[116] The usual policy wording is on the lines of the following: this policy does not apply to liability in respect of (a) any vehicle licensed for road use, or any trailer, for which compulsory insurance is required by any road traffic legislation if such vehicle is owned leased hired borrowed or used by the Insured or by the person seeking indemnity; (b) the loading or unloading of any such vehicle or trailer; (c) the bringing of a load to such vehicle or trailer for the purpose of loading thereon or the taking away of a load from such vehicle or trailer after unloading therefrom; where indemnity is provided by any motor insurance policy or where compulsory insurance is required by any road traffic legislation.

have attached in the absence of such agreement. The liability of a tenant, or hirer of premises, for damage, particularly fire damage, can be a source of controversy.[117] Whether or not a formal lease or hiring agreement has been completed the tenant or hirer, if negligent, can be liable at common law for the damage caused. The right of the insurers of the damaged property to subrogation against the tenant or hirer may be restricted by the insuring clauses of the lease or agreement. In *Mark Rowlands Ltd. v Berni Inns Ltd.*[118] the plaintiffs owned a building, the basement of which was leased to the defendants. The whole building was substantially damaged as a result of the admitted negligence of the defendant. Insurers of the building, having met the claim in respect of the damage, sought to exercise their rights of subrogation against the defendants. Under the terms of the lease, the landlord was able to insure the building and recover the cost of the insurance from the tenants. The defendant's interest was not noted in the landlord's policy although correspondence on the issue had taken place between the parties and another tenant had succeeded in having its interest noted. The Court of Appeal held that the insurers had no right of recourse against the defendants, despite the fact that they were negligent, on the grounds that the insurance policy effected under the terms of the lease by the plaintiff was intended to benefit both the landlord and the tenant. The landlord had not suffered any financial loss, as the insurers had paid the claim for damage to the property in full, and the defendants, being tenants with a limited interest in the property,[119] could therefore claim the

---

[117] In the past, public liability insurers argued that the risk was a fire risk rather than a liability risk and more correctly insured by a fire policy. The current practice is to provide indemnity in respect of the insured's legal liability under the public liability policy.

[118] *Mark Rowlands v Berni Inns Ltd.* [1986] 1 QB 211.

[119] In *Church & General Insurance Co. v Connolly & McLoughlin*, Unreported High Court, 7 May 1981, the court confirmed that "the law permits a person with a limited interest in a property to insure not only his interest but the interest which others may have in the property" and that a tenant of a property could recover in respect of his interest and also in respect of the damage to the owner's interest.

protection of the policy to the extent of their interest in the property as a whole.[120]

10.5.5 CONTRACTUAL LIABILITY

10.5.5.1 Liability assumed by the insured under agreement, and which would not have attached in the absence of such agreement, is generally excluded by the general public liability policy although insurers will agree to extend the policy provided the conduct and control of all claims is vested in the insurer. Liability for liquidated damages or penalties under contract or agreement is specifically excluded. The intention of the policy is to indemnify the insured in respect of his liability in tort and the cover provided is limited to bodily injury and physical damage to material property. Any extension of cover to include contractual liability is still subject to the policy terms and conditions so that an agreement by an insured to indemnify a principal in respect of "any expense, liability, loss, claim, or proceedings" would be wider and more extensive than the indemnity available to the insured under the policy.[121]

10.5.5.2 In *Rohan* v *Insurance Corporation of Ireland*[122] the courts were required to consider a policy exclusion of indemnity, in respect of "liability assumed by the insured by agreement unless such liability would have attached to the insured notwithstanding such agreement". In the High Court, Keane J. held that the plaintiffs had assumed liability, in respect of any defective workmanship, when they entered into a sub-contract and it was as a result of entering into that sub-contract that they found themselves in a position of potential liability, either as third parties, brought in by the main contractors, or as defendants, in the event of a claim in negligence against them.[123] The fact that a claim against the plaintiffs also lay in tort was not

---

[120] The decision in *Berni Inns* above n. 118 reinforced the principle applied in *Mumford Hotels* v *Wheeler* [1964] CH 117, that where a landlord insured at the tenant's expense it was "an obligation intended to enure for the benefit of both parties".

[121] It would be necessary for the insured to amend the contract wording to restrict the indemnity to liability in negligence to bring it within the scope of the policy.

[122] *Rohan Construction Ltd. & Rohan Group Plc.* v *Insurance Corporation of Ireland Plc.* [1986] ILRM 419, HC and [1988] ILRM 373, SC.

[123] [1986] ILRM 419 at 426, 427.

material. Liability in tort is not any less a "liability assumed by agreement".[124] Where liability arises only because the insured has entered into a contract or agreement, the policy exclusion operates. Where an insured enters into a specific agreement in respect of his potential liability to third parties the exclusion will have no application if the liability exists irrespective of the agreement.[125] The Supreme Court in considering the intention of a Public Liability policy construed the wording as excluding indemnity in respect of any liability the insured might have to the person employing the insured or with whom the insured had a contract.[126] To hold otherwise would be to construe the policy as covering liability for all defective work of the insured and that the policy enured for the benefit of the principal or employer of the insured.

10.5.5.3 It is a basic principle of the common law of contract that the parties to a contract are free to determine for themselves the obligations they accept.[127] In construction contracts, it is usual to impose on the contractor liability for bodily injury and property damage, in specified circumstances and to require the contractor to indemnify the employer.[128] "In contracts between sophisticated parties . . . such exclusions of liability often result from determinations regarding who is in the best position to insure the risk at lowest cost."[129] It is, however, well established that an indemnity clause in a contract does not provide an indemnity in respect of the negligence of the party in whose favour the indemnity is given unless the clause expressly so

---

[124] ibid.

[125] ibid.

[126] [1988] ILRM 373 at 381 per Griffin J.

[127] *Photoproductions Ltd.* v *Securicor Transport Ltd.* [1980] 1 All ER 556.

[128] Standard contract wordings have been agreed by the Construction Industry and the relevant professional bodies and these generally form the basis of most construction contracts, e.g. ICE General Conditions of Contract; RIAI Contract Conditions; ICPA General Conditions for Plant Hire.

[129] *Canadian National Railway Co.* v *Norsk Pacific Steamship Co. Ltd.* [1992] 91 DLR (4th) 289 at 302 per La Forrest J.

provides.[130] In *Smith* v *South Wales Switchgear Ltd.*[131] the House of Lords considered the intention and effect of indemnity clauses and held that the party in receipt of the indemnity was entitled to indemnity in respect of his own negligence or that of his servants or agents only where the indemnity clause contained an express provision to that effect or where the words of the clause in their ordinary meaning were wide enough to cover the negligence of the party in receipt of the indemnity. The word "whatsoever" is no more than a word of emphasis and its inclusion in an indemnity clause cannot be construed as the equivalent to an express reference to negligence.[132]

10.5.6 STANDARD CONTRACT CONDITIONS

The form of building contract most commonly used in Ireland is that issued by the Royal Institute of Architects of Ireland (RIAI) in agreement with the Construction Industry Federation and the Royal Institute of Chartered Surveyors. Clauses 21–27 of the Conditions of Contract deal with liability for and insurance against injury to persons and damage to property.[133] By virtue of Clause 21, the contractor is obliged to indemnify the employer against:

---

[130] *Alderslade* v *Hendon Laundry Ltd.* [1945] 1 All ER 244; *Canada Steamship Lines Ltd.* v *Regem* [1952] 1 All ER 305; *Smith & Others* v *South Wales Switchgear Ltd.* [1978] 1 All ER 18; *White* v *John Warwick & Co.* [1953] 2 All ER 1021; *Caledonia Ltd.* v *Orbit Valve Co.* [1993] 2 Lloyds Rep 418.

[131] [1978] 1 All ER 18. An employee of the appellants, engaged in overhaul work at the respondent's factory, was seriously injured in an accident. The employee brought an action against the respondents alleging negligence and breach of statutory duty. The respondents served a third party notice on the appellants claiming indemnity in respect of the claim under the indemnity clause in the respondent's general conditions of contract. The Court held that the accident was wholly caused by the respondent's negligence and breach of statutory duty. There was no express reference in the clause to negligence.

[132] ibid.

[133] The concepts of Responsibility, Liability and Indemnity in relation to building contracts were first recognised in five rules of construction law incorporated in the Code of Hammurabi in the year 1760 BC. The five rules were: (1) If a builder builds a house for a man and does not make its construction firm and the house which he has built collapses and causes the death of the owner of the house that builder shall be put to death; (2) If it causes the death of the son of the owner of the house, they shall put to death a son of that builder; (3) If it causes the death of a slave of the owner of the house, the builder shall give to the owner of the house a slave of equal value; (4) If it destroys property, the builder shall restore whatever it destroyed, and because he did not make the house which he built firm and it collapsed, he shall re-

a) liability for damage to property, (other than property at the risk of the employer) arising out of the execution of the works, provided the damage is due to the negligence, omission, or default of the contractor or his agents or sub-contractors and even if the damage is partly due to the fault of the employer;

b) liability for bodily injury or disease, unless the injury or disease is due solely to any act or neglect of the employer, or any person for whom the employer is responsible. For the employer to avail of the indemnity, in respect of damage to property, he must prove that the damage was caused by the negligence or default of the contractor, or his servant, sub-contractor or agent.

In the case of bodily injury, the contractor is liable to indemnify the employer unless he can positively prove that the injury was solely due to the negligence of the employer, his servants or agents. In both cases the contractor is made liable, by virtue of the clause, for all compensation for injury or damage, even if such injury or damage is partly, but not if it is solely, due to the fault of the employer or some other party for whom the employer is responsible. This is an extension of the contractor's liability at common law[134] and is a liability assumed by agreement which would not have existed in the absence of the agreement. Sub-section (c) of Clause 21 provides that if the damage or injury is partly caused by the fault of the employer and such damage or injury is covered by the insurances arranged by the contractor in accordance with the terms of the contract, then the contractor shall be fully liable. However, if the damage or injury comes within a permitted exclusion in the contractor's policies or arises otherwise than in connection with an accident, the employer and the contractor share liability for the damage or injury according to fault.

---

build it at his own expense; (5) If a builder builds a house for a man and does not make its construction meet the requirements and a wall falls in, that builder shall strengthen the wall at his own expense.

Quoted in Jacob Feld (1964), *Lessons from Failures of Concrete Structures*, American Concrete Institute and the Iowa State University Press, p. 9. The rules were referred to by Lord Buckmaster in his dissenting judgment in *Donoghue* v *Stevenson* [1932] AC 562.

[134] In the absence of an agreement the contractor and the employer would share liability for compensation in proportion to their responsibility for the occurrence giving rise to a claim. It is therefore necessary to extend a policy or arrange for it to include liability assumed under standard forms of contracts.

10.5.7 DUTY TO INSURE

The duty to insure is placed on the contractor by Clause 21(b) and Clause 23 specifies the exclusions which are permitted. Whilst the duty of the contractor to the employer to insure ends with completion of the contract, the contractor's liability to third parties is not affected by the terms of the contract. If, therefore, some years after completion of the contract, a person is injured or property damaged as a result of a defect in the construction or completion of the works, due to the negligence of the contractor, a claim for compensation may be brought against the contractor by the injured third party.[135] It is therefore necessary for a contractor to maintain a public liability policy which will provide indemnity in respect of occurrences happening during the period of the policy but arising out of work previously completed. Where the contractor requires labour-only sub-contractors to insure liability to the workmen supplied by them, the Supreme Court has held, in *Kelly* v *Michael McNamara & Co.*,[136] that if responsibility for providing insurance was going to be imposed on a sub-contractor, that fact must be made crystal clear to the sub-contractor, and that, not only should it be put in writing, but that it should also be an explicit requirement that the sub-contractor produce written evidence from an insurance company to the effect that the requisite cover is in place.

10.5.8 EXISTING STRUCTURES

10.5.8.1 Clause 26 of the agreement provides that where the contract is for the alteration of or extension to a building, the existing structures, together with the contents thereof, shall be at the sole risk of the employer as regards loss or damage by fire and other specified perils. The contractor remains liable for damage by non-specified perils such as impact, subsidence, theft, and vandalism if the damage arises out of the negligence of the contractor or his servants or agents. While the clause provides that the existing structures shall be "at the sole risk" of the employer, it has been argued that the clause

---

[135] *Cowan* v *Freaghaille, De Spainne, Cumann Luthchleas Gael Teo. and Thos. McInerney & Sons Ltd.*, Unreported High Court, 24 January 1991. A wall, constructed many years previously, collapsed during the 1985 All Ireland Football Final injuring the plaintiff. The builder was found to be 80 per cent liable.

[136] Unreported High Court, 5 June 1996.

does not relieve the contractor of liability for damage by fire or other specified perils caused by his negligence. In *Archdale* v *Comservices Ltd.*[137] the Court of Appeal held that, in the context of the indemnity, liability and insuring clauses of the contract, the natural and proper construction of the clause was that the sole risk of damage by fire, however it was caused, was placed on the employer. However, given the courts' general reluctance to allow parties to a contract exempt themselves from liability for their own negligence[138] there was some doubt whether the decision of the Court of Appeal would be upheld in a similar case. The decision was, however, confirmed by the House of Lords in *Scottish Special Housing Association* v *Wimpey Construction (UK) Ltd.*[139] The defendants had contracted for the modernisation of houses belonging to the plaintiff and in the course of carrying out the work, one of the houses had been damaged by fire, assumed for the purposes of the special case stated to have been caused by the negligence of the defendants. The contract[140] had a clause similar to clause 26 of the RIAI form of contract.

10.5.8.2 The House of Lords was asked to decide, if a contractor, working under a form of contract, which required him to indemnify the employer against damage to property caused by his negligence, or that of his sub-contractors, was liable for damage to the employer's premises, caused by the contractor's negligence, if those premises were said to be "at the sole risk of the employer" as regards loss or damage by fire and other specified perils. Lord Keith of Kinkel said that he considered *Archdale* v *Comservices*[141] to have been correctly decided and to be indistinguishable from the case under considera-

---

[137] [1954] 1 WLR 459. The defendant contractors had entered into a contract to redecorate the plaintiff's factory and offices and through their negligence in carrying out the work caused fire damage to the plaintiff's property. The contract contained a clause placing the existing structures at the sole risk of the plaintiff in respect of fire damage and the defendants successfully relied on it in their defence of the action with the Court of Appeal holding that the sole risk proviso exempted the contractor from liability for fire damage, however caused.

[138] See n. 131 *supra*.

[139] [1986] 2 All ER 957.

[140] JCT Standard form of Building Contract.

[141] [1954] 1 WLR 459.

tion. The wording of the indemnity clause[142] made it clear that the liability of the contractor for damage to property caused by his negligence or that of a sub-contractor was subject to the exception found in the subsequent clause[143] providing that the existing structures and contents owned by the employer were to be at his sole risk as regards damage by fire. No differentiation was to be made between fire damage due to the negligence of the contractor and fire damage due to other causes. The other specified perils included some which could not possibly be caused by the negligence of the contractor, such as earthquake, storm and tempest, but others which might be, such as explosion, flood, and the bursting or overflowing of water pipes. The employer was under an obligation to insure against loss or damage by all of those perils. He found it impossible to resist the conclusion that it was intended that the employer would bear the whole risk of damage by fire, including fire caused by the negligence of the contractor or that of sub-contractors.

10.5.8.3 The rationale for these decisions is one of risk allocation and insurance. Those drafting the model forms of contract conditions believed it more equitable that the employer should arrange for his fire insurers to meet the cost of damage. The existing structures and contents were most likely to be insured against fire and specified perils by the employer and the employer would be in a better position to know the values at risk.

10.5.9 CONSEQUENTIAL LOSS
The contract clauses and the judicial decisions quoted above make it clear that the risk of physical damage to the existing structures and their contents is at the sole risk of the employer in specified circumstances, but the clauses in the contract make no reference to, and there is no legal authority on, liability of the contractor for loss of profits, loss of income or other consequential losses flowing from damage to the existing structures or their contents. While Clause 26 of the RIAI Contract Conditions requires the employer to maintain a "proper policy of insurance" against the risks specified, the clause re-

---

[142] The equivalent to clause 21 of the RIAI Conditions of Contract.

[143] The equivalent to clause 26 of the RIAI Conditions.

fers to loss or damage only and there is no requirement for the employer to arrange a business interruption or consequential loss policy. Clause 21 of the standard RIAI conditions of contract which requires the contractor to indemnify the employer against damage to property, excludes from the indemnity "such loss or damage as is at the sole risk of the employer" under clause 26 and it is arguable that this wording is not sufficiently wide to exclude from the indemnity liability for consequential losses. The issue remains unresolved.[144]

10.5.10 RIGHTS OF SUB-CONTRACTORS

10.5.10.1 One other area of controversy in relation to Clause 26 is the right of a sub-contractor, not party to the contract, to rely on the contract in the event of damage being caused to the existing structures due to his negligence. The sub-contractor is not, generally, a party to the contract between the contractor and the employer, and applying normal legal principles of privity of contract the employer should be able to proceed against the sub-contractor in the event of damage caused by the negligence of the sub-contractor. However, the courts have tended to take into account the role of insurance and the allocation of risk in determining where a loss should fall in such circumstances. In *Norwich City Council* v *Paul Clarke Harvey and Another*[145] the plaintiffs appointed contractors to carry out an extension to a swimming pool complex and the contractors sub-contracted the felt roofing work to the defendants. An employee of the sub-contractors negligently set fire to the extension and the existing complex. The defendants denied they owed a duty of care to the plaintiffs on the grounds that in the overall scheme of the contract the plaintiff accepted the risk of fire damage to the existing property, irrespective of whether the damage was caused by the contractor or any domestic sub-contractor. The Court of Appeal agreed that acceptance of the fire risk by the employer, qualified the duty owed by the sub-contractors. Lord May dismissed the plaintiff's claim to privity of contract, saying:

---

[144] The RIAI conditions are currently under review by the construction industry and the problem of liability for consequential loss is one of a number of issues being addressed.

[145] [1989] 1 All ER 1134.

I do not think that the mere fact that there is no strict privity
between the employer and the sub-contractor should prevent
the latter from relying on the clear basis on which all the parties contracted in relation to damage to the employers building
caused by fire, even due to the negligence of the contractor or
sub-contractors.[146]

10.5.10.2 The point was emphasised in a recent decision of the Court
of Session (Inner House) when, in *British Telecommunications* v
James Thompson & Sons (Engineers),[147] it was held that where an
employer had undertaken to insure against the risk of negligence by
a sub-contractor under a building contract, the sub-contractor was
entitled to assume that he was under no duty of care towards the
employer for loss or damage caused by his actions. Following fire
damage to a building on which the defendants had been working, the
plaintiffs brought an action against the defendant sub-contractors
founded on negligence. The Court held that in deciding whether to
impose a duty of care on the defendants the court should have regard
to the contractual setting derived from the arrangements by which
the parties had regulated their affairs. The plaintiffs, as employers,
had a contractual obligation to insure against the very risk which had
occurred, and the sub-contractor had contracted with the main contractor on that basis. If the sub-contractor was aware that the employer had undertaken to insure against the risk of negligence on the
part of the sub-contractor, then the sub-contractor was entitled to
assume, not only that he need not insure, but that he was under no
duty of care to the employer for any loss or damage caused by him.
Where the contract conditions used are other than the standard form
of contract, liability and indemnity will be determined by the actual
contract provisions. In the absence of any provision to the contrary,
the main contractor will be liable for damage to existing structures

---

[146] Revised contract conditions in the UK (JCT clauses) have overcome the problem by requiring the employer to insure the existing structures in the joint names
of the employer and contractor and sub-contractors are entitled to be named as
co-insureds or to obtain a waiver of subrogation. A similar provision is under
consideration by the Irish construction industry in a review of the Irish conditions.

[147] Unreported, 13 December 1996.

caused by the negligence of specialist sub-contractors engaged by him.[148]

10.5.11 POLLUTION

10.5.11.1 As a result of the adverse effect which claims for environmental damage were having on the financial performance of the insurance industry, all insurers have sought to restrict the cover provided by their general public liability policies in respect of liability for pollution or contamination.[149] General public liability policies now contain an exclusion of indemnity in respect of liability for loss or damage arising out of pollution unless caused by a sudden, unintended and unexpected incident.[150] While insurers are prepared to cover liability for the accidental discharge of a pollutant, under a public liability policy, liability for loss or damage arising out of the gradual build-up or seepage of pollutants can only be covered under a specific Environmental Liability policy. The public liability policy wording is intended to avoid claims for loss or damage arising out of the discharge of toxic fumes or substances or other noxious waste materials which, over a period of time may cause damage to property or bodily injury or financial loss.[151]

10.5.11.2 The restricted nature of the cover provided in respect of "accidental" pollution was confirmed by the Court of Appeal in *Middleton* v *Wiggins*.[152] A factory owner used a landfill site owned by Wiggins to deposit industrial waste, in sealed cells, and covered with earth. It was intended that gas, built up by the method of disposal,

---

[148] *National Trust* v *Haden Young* [1994] Court of Appeal, 26 July.

[149] Insurers were obliged to increase their reserves significantly and in some cases to restructure their companies to protect against the effect of environmental claims under policies issued many years previously. In 1983, the insurance industry attempted to exclude indemnity in respect of pollution liability from public liability policies.

[150] A typical form of wording is as follows:
This policy excludes all liability in respect of pollution or contamination other than caused by a sudden identifiable unintended and unexpected incident which takes place in its entirety at a specific time and place during the period of the policy.

[151] *Hanrahan* v *Merck Sharp & Dohme (Ireland) Ltd.* [1988] ILRM 629.

[152] [1995] *The Independent*, 31 August.

would seep out without causing any damage. The geological nature of the site, however, prevented gradual seepage and instead the gas was forced in the direction of the plaintiff's house, where it became mixed with air drawn into the heating system, causing an explosion which destroyed the house. The factory owner was ultimately held liable and sought an indemnity from insurers of its public liability policy. The policy contained a specific exclusion relieving insurers of:

> liability in respect of injury, illness. disease, loss or damage arising from the disposal of waste materials in the way in which the insured or their servants intended to dispose of them unless such claim arises from an accident in the method of disposal.

The majority of the Court of Appeal held that there had been no accident in the method of disposal. Once the waste material had been buried it had been disposed of by the insured in the manner intended and the accidental explosion had occurred as a consequence of the method of disposal. The Court rejected a suggestion that the "disposal" was a continuing process and included any volatility in the buried waste. It also rejected the argument that the words "in the method of disposal" could be interpreted as meaning "in or arising out of the method of disposal".

CHAPTER ELEVEN

PRODUCT LIABILITY

Prior to the introduction of the Liability for Defective Products Act, 1991, a person who suffered injury or loss due to a defect in a product, used or consumed, had recourse in tort against the manufacturer, or in contract, under the Sale of Goods Acts, 1893 and 1980, against the vendor of the product. The plaintiff in a tort action arising out of a defective product is faced with considerable difficulties in proving negligence against the manufacturer, and privity of contract means that it is only the actual purchaser of the product who has a right of action in contract against the vendor.[1] The Liability for Defective Products Act, 1991 gives effect to the EU Council Directive of 25 July 1985 concerning products liability and introduced strict liability for producers of products in respect of damage or injury due to a defect in the product.[2] Strict liability has existed in the law of contract for centuries and the protection provided to consumers is in fact superior to that afforded by the Act. The Act makes available to manufacturers a number of defences not available to the retailer who is strictly liable in contract. The retailer seldom has a defence to a product liability

---

[1] An exception exists for the user of defective motor vehicles which cause injury or damage to the user of the vehicle, passengers in the vehicle or other users of the public road; Section 13, Sale of Goods and Supply of Services Act, 1980. Under the Married Women's Status Act, 1957, any contract entered into by a mother for the benefit of her children or husband is deemed to be entered into between the particular member of the family sustaining injury and the vendor of the product.

[2] The explanatory memorandum to the Directive describing the necessity for the directive stated that "where the injured person has to prove that the producer was at fault in respect of the defect in the product causing the damage, as is the case under the traditional laws of the majority of Member States, he is in practice without protection. As an individual, he will, in most cases, not succeed in discharging the burden of proof in relation to large manufacturing companies because he has normally no access to the production process."

claim although invariably the retailer is able to pass liability back to the supplier or manufacturer.

11.1 LIABILITY IN TORT

11.1.1 BASIS OF LIABILITY

In *Heaven* v *Pender*[3] in 1883 the courts attempted to enunciate a general principle that a duty to take reasonable care arose when the property of a person was in such proximity to the person or property of another that if such care were not exercised harm might be done by the one to the other.[4] That case played an important part in the historic decision in *Donoghue* v *Stevenson*[5] some fifty years later which established the demand for products liability insurance in the twentieth century. The essence of the tort of negligence is the breach of a legal duty of care which a defendant owes to a plaintiff and which results in unintentional harm to the plaintiff. To establish liability for defective products in tort by using the principles of negligence the plaintiff must prove:

a) that the defendant was careless, and that judged objectively this carelessness amounts to negligence;

b) that the defendant owed the plaintiff a legal duty of care which was breached by the defendant's negligence;

c) that the defendant's negligence caused the plaintiff's injury;

d) that the damage is not too remote.

---

[3] *Heaven* v *Pender* [1883] 11 QBD 503.

[4] per Brett M. R. at p. 509:

> The proposition which these recognised cases suggest, and which is, therefore, to be deduced from them, is that whenever one person is by circumstances placed in such a position with regard to another that everyone of ordinary sense who did think would at once recognise that, if he did not use ordinary care and skill in his own conduct with regard to those circumstances, he would cause danger of injury to the person or property of the other, a duty arises to use ordinary care and skill to avoid such danger. . . . And for a neglect of such ordinary care or skill whereby injury happens a legal liability arises to be enforced by an action for negligence.

[5] *Donoghue* v *Stevenson* [1932] AC 562.

11.1.2 SNAIL IN A BOTTLE

In *Donoghue* v *Stevenson*[6] the court was required to determine whether the manufacturer of goods he sells to a distributor, in circumstances which prevent the distributor or the ultimate purchaser or consumer from discovering a defect by inspection, is under a legal duty to that purchaser or consumer to take reasonable care that the article is free from defect likely to cause harm. In the particular circumstances of the case the plaintiff had drunk half a bottle of ginger beer and when she was refilling her glass the decomposed remains of a snail came out of the bottle. She became ill and sued for damages. The plaintiff had not purchased the bottle of ginger beer. She had entered a café with a friend and it was the friend who had ordered the drink. The plaintiff therefore had no contractual relationship with the cafe proprietor and her claim was made against the manufacturer in negligence. The House of Lords, by a majority of three to two, decided that the manufacturer was liable, with Lord Atkin laying down a general test, based on the neighbour principle, for deciding whether a duty of care exists. He held that a general duty of care was owed to all those (legal neighbours) so closely and directly affected by an act or omission that they ought reasonably to be in contemplation at the time that the tort is committed.[7]

11.1.3 REASONABLE CARE

Donoghue v *Stevenson*[8] decided that a manufacturer owed a duty to consumers to take reasonable care in the manufacture of products but the manufacturer was only liable to a consumer if he had been negligent. The manufacturer did not have to prove that he took every possible precaution to prevent injury or damage but merely that he took all reasonable precautions. In *Daniels* v *R. White & Sons Ltd.*,[9] the

---

[6] ibid.

[7] Per Atkin L. J. at 578:

> . . . You must take reasonable care to avoid acts or omissions which you can reasonably foresee would be likely to injure your neighbour. Who then in law is my neighbour? The answer seems to be — persons who are so closely and directly affected by my act that I ought reasonably to have them in contemplation as being so affected when I am directing my mind to the acts or omissions which are called into question.

[8] [1932] AC 562.

[9] [1938] 4 All ER 258.

defendants escaped liability by showing that they had taken reasonable care. The plaintiff was injured when drinking a bottle of lemonade which contained poison. Despite the obvious inference of negligence, the manufacturer was able to prove that a foolproof system had recently been installed in the bottling plant and that the system was as good as it could be. In deciding that the manufacturer was not liable the judge said:

> I have to remember that the duty owed to the customer . . . by the manufacturer is not to ensure that his goods are perfect. All he has to do is to take reasonable care to see that no injury is done to the customer. . . . It seems to me a little difficult to say that if people supply a foolproof method of cleaning, washing and filling bottles that they have not taken all reasonable care to prevent defects in their commodity. . . . so there is no negligence on the part of the manufacturers.[10]

11.1.4 INTERMEDIATE EXAMINATION

A critical factor in the decision of Lord Atkin, in *Donoghue* v *Stevenson*[11] was the intention of the manufacturer that the goods should reach the ultimate consumer in the form in which they left the manufacturer with no reasonably possibility of intermediate examination. For liability to attach it is not necessary that the product reach the user in the same sealed package in which it left the manufacturer; it is enough that it reached him subject to the same defect. In *Grant* v *Australian Knitting Mills*,[12] the plaintiff developed dermatitis as a result of wearing woollen underwear containing an excess of sulphites. Despite the defendants establishing that their factory was the most modern possible, the Privy Council held against them saying:

> If excess sulphites were left in the garment that could only be because someone was at fault. The appellant is not required to lay his finger on the exact person in the chain who was responsible or to specify what he did wrong. Negligence is found

[10] [1938] 4 All ER 258.

[11] [1932] AC 562.

[12] [1936] AC 95.

as a matter of inference from the existence of the defects, taken in conjunction with all known circumstances.[13]

11.1.5 A FLY IN THE JAM

An Irish case similar to *Donoghue* v *Stevenson* was *Kirby* v *Burke &
Holloway*.[14] The plaintiff's wife bought a pot of jam in a grocer's shop
and gave the jam to the plaintiff and their infant children. The grocer
had bought the jam from the defendant manufacturer. The plaintiff
and three of the children became ill having eaten the jam and the
cause of the problem was established to be bacteria carried by a fly
into the jam during the manufacturing process. Gavan Duffy J. regarded the case as turning on a point of law of "exceptional public
importance, unquestionably fit for the decision of the final tribunal".[15]
Having referred to an 1869 Irish case of *Corry* v *Lucas*,[16] the
"confusion and conflict" in later cases in England, and the "quandary
produced by the baffling inconsistencies among the pre-Treaty judicial pronouncements" he opted for the works of Oliver Wendell Holmes to ground his decision.[17] Of *Donoghue* v *Stevenson*,[18] he had this
to say:

---

[13] Quoted with approval by Kingsmill-Moore J. in *Fleming* v *Henry Denny and
Sons Ltd.* [1955] Unreported Supreme Court, 29 July 1955.

[14] *Kirby* v *Burke & Holloway* [1944] IR 207. John A. Costello K. C. for the defendant, argued that the decision in *Donoghue* v *Stevenson* was unsatisfactory as it
was only decided by a majority of one in a Court of five and that it was not binding on Irish Courts and should not be followed. He submitted that the only obligation on the manufacturer was to take reasonable precautions to ensure the
purity of the goods.

[15] ibid. at 209.

[16] *Corry* v *Lucas* [1869] IR 3 CL 208. The Court held that in the absence of
fraudulent misrepresentation the law could give no redress against the manufacturers to a servant of the purchaser injured by the explosion of a boiler in a steam
engine alleged to be unsafe due to negligence in its construction.

[17] *The Common Law*, by Oliver Wendell Holmes, who subsequently became a
judge of the United States Supreme Court. Gavan Duffy, at [1944] IR 207 at 214,
quoted from the work, published in London in 1887, as follows:
> the foundation of liability at common law for tort is blameworthiness as de-
> termined by the existing average standards of the community; a man fails at
> his peril to conform to those standards. Therefore while loss from accident
> generally lies where it falls, a defendant cannot plead accident if, treated as a
> man of ordinary intelligence and foresight, he ought to have foreseen the dan-
> ger which caused injury to his plaintiff.

The much controverted "Case of the Snail in the Bottle", while leaving subsidiary questions open, has settled the principle of liability on a similar issue finally against the manufacturer in Great Britain. But the House of Lords established that memorable conclusion only . . . by a majority of three Law Lords to two. . . . Where lawyers so learned disagreed, an Irish judge could not assume, as I was invited to assume, as a matter of course, that the view which prevailed must of necessity be the true view of the common law in Ireland. One voice in the House of Lords would have turned the scale; and it is not arguable that blameworthiness according to the actual standards of our people depends on the casting vote in a tribunal exercising no jurisdiction over them. Hence my recourse to the late Mr Justice Holmes. His classic analysis supports the principle of Lord Atkin and the majority. And to that principle I humbly subscribe.[19]

11.1.6 LIABILITY OF REPAIRERS AND OTHERS

The duty of care, breach of which imposes liability for defective products, is not confined to manufacturers. In the Supreme Court, in *Power* v *Bedford Motor Co. Ltd. & Harris Bros.*[20] Lavery J., having considered the views expressed by Lord Atkin,[21] applied the principle established in *Donoghue* v *Stevenson*,[22] saying:

It is clear in principle that the obligation [of manufacturers] is not confined to manufacturers of goods but extends to persons undertaking repairs to articles which will be dangerous to users who should be in contemplation if there is a want of reasonable care in the work. It must also be applied to persons

---

[18] [1932] AC 562.

[19] [1944] 207 at 215.

[20] [1959] IR 391.

[21] [1932] AC 562 at 580, 599.

[22] ibid.

doing work on an article which they foresee would be used by others without examination.[23]

The decision made it clear that the duty of care is not limited to the "ultimate consumer" referred to by Lord Atkin,[24] as the plaintiff was the widow of the owner and driver of a car, which had been purchased by him from the second defendant under a hire purchase agreement, and in which he was killed in an accident caused by a defect in the car. The defendants had undertaken some repair work to the car for the previous owner. The Supreme Court held that the deceased:

> did belong to the class of persons whom [the defendants] should have contemplated as being exposed to the danger if the work were done wrongly. That class of persons included any person who might drive or be a passenger in the car and perhaps others who might be injured if the car went out of control.[25]

The supplier of a motor vehicle with a dangerous defect may be liable for resulting injury or damage, not only to the purchaser, the user, the passengers in the vehicle, but also to other users of the highway or other parties who would foreseeably come into proximity with the vehicle.[26]

A stonemason was held to be under a duty "to every member of the public who might lawfully enter the churchyard and be injured by the

---

[23] [1959] IR 391 at 408. In *Winterbottom* v *Wright* [1842] 152 ER 402, the plaintiff coach driver injured as a result of an accident caused by defective repairs to the vehicle, carried out by the defendant under contract with the driver's employer, failed in an action for compensation in negligence from the defendant on the grounds that there was no legal relationship between the parties to the action. The court did not want to extend the liability of the defendant beyond liability in contract. "If we go one step beyond why should we not go fifty?" The dissenting judgments in *Donoghue* v *Stevenson* felt bound by the decision.

[24] [1932] AC 562 at 599.

[25] [1959] IR 391 at 411.

[26] *O'Sullivan* v *Noonan*, Unreported Supreme Court, 28 July 1972.

fall of a tombstone",[27] and a supplier of amusement equipment for reward owes a duty of care in respect of the safety of those to whom the
equipment is supplied and to any person likely to use it.[28]

11.1.7 DANGEROUS GOODS

A person injured by a defect in goods which he is handling before they
reach the "ultimate consumer" can maintain an action against the
manufacturer,[29] and a person in control of a dangerous substance,
whether as supplier, manufacturer, or vendor has a duty to take reasonable care that anyone acquiring it from him, whether by sale or
otherwise, does not suffer injury or loss.[30] The vendor of a substance
which is dangerous only in the sense that the application of it in excessive doses may be injurious, is under no duty to explain to the purchaser the manner in which the substance could be used safely with
other substances,[31] but a manufacturer of a product which is not dangerous in itself is not absolved from all duty of care to the users of the
product.[32] The extent of the duty of a manufacturer whose product is
alleged to have caused damage or injury is to be determined with regard to what he knew or ought to have known when he released the

---

[27] *Brown* v *Cotterill* [1934] 51 TLR 21. The court applied the principle to impose
liability on a monumental sculptor when a headstone he had erected fell on a
child visiting her grandmother's grave. The sculptor was not allowed escape liability simply because he had contracted to have the stone erected by another
person; per Lawrence J.:

> persons who employ monumental masons to erect tombstones rely on the ma-
> son's skill and not on their own examination, and there is, therefore, nothing
> in their acceptance of the mason's work to exempt him from liability for the de-
> fective work which he has erected in a place to which the public have access.

[28] *Keegan* v *Owens* [1953] IR 267. The plaintiff was an employee of a religious
order, injured by a nail sticking out of a swing boat supplied to the nuns, for reward, in connection with a carnival organised by them to raise funds for charity.
The plaintiff was not acting in the course of his employment at the time but was
helping on a voluntary basis. The defendant suppliers of the swing-boats were
held liable.

[29] *Barnett* v *H.&J. Packer & Co. Ltd.* [1940] 3 All ER 575. The plaintiff, a confec-
tioner, was injured by a piece of confectionery he was placing in a display tray
and was permitted to bring an action against the manufacturer.

[30] *Bolands Ltd.* v *Trouw Ireland Ltd.* Unreported High Court, 1 May 1978. See
also *Purtill* v *Athlone UDC* [1968] IR 205; *Sullivan* v *Creed* [1904] 2 IR 317.

[31] *Bolands supra* at p. 20 per Finlay J.

[32] *Kearney* v *Paul Vincent Ltd.* [1985] Unreported High Court, 30 July per Barron
J. at 20–21.

product on to the market.[33] Where there is a risk of physical injury to the user of a product arising from the material from which it is manufactured, the absence of an appropriate warning constitutes negligence and it is for the defendant to establish that the warning would not have affected the purchase or the conduct of the user of the product.[34] The courts have clearly established the duty of care and the liability in negligence[35] of manufacturers,[36] repairers,[37] installers,[38] and suppliers[39] of defective goods. Where a manufacturer of a product incorporates into the product ingredients obtained from other suppliers, the manufacturer is not obliged to take precautions against every contingency, however remote, but the nature of the precautions he is obliged to take must bear a relationship to the probability or improbability of the risk.[40] A manufacturer discharges his duty to take reasonable care by obtaining ingredients from firms of high repute who have a like responsibility to see that the ingredients are free from any

---

[33] ibid.

[34] *O'Byrne* v *Gloucester* [1988] Unreported Supreme Court, 3 November, per McCarthy J. concurring with the judgment of Finlay C. J., with whose judgment Walsh J. also concurred. The defendant manufacturer of a brushed cotton skirt were found liable for failure to attach to it a warning that it was highly flammable. The plaintiff had been severely burned when the skirt caught fire having come in contact with a gas heater. McCarthy J. concluded that once the trial judge had decided that the absence of a warning constituted negligence on the part of the defendants it was for them to establish that a warning on the garment would not have affected the purchase or the conduct of the wearer of it.

[35] The Sale of Goods Acts provide a remedy in contract.

[36] *Donoghue* v *Stevenson* [1932] AC 562; *Kirby & Burke* v *Holloway* [1944] IR 207.

[37] *Power* v *Bedford Motor Co.* [1959] IR 391.

[38] *Brown* v *Cotterill* [1934] 51 TLR 21.

[39] *Keegan* v *Owens* [1953] IR 267.

[40] *Fleming* v *Henry Denny & Sons Ltd.* Unreported Supreme Court, 29 July 1955, per Kingsmill-Moore J. at pp. 7–8. The court held that the defendant manufacturers of black pudding were entitled to rely on the suppliers of ingredients to take care that what they supplied was free from hidden dangers, such as pieces of metal. The court indicated that the factors to be taken into consideration were:
the nature of the materials purchased, the reputation of the dealer from whom it is purchased, the obligations imposed by law on the vendor, the process through which the materials have already passed in the hands of the manufacturer or dealer, the past experience of the purchaser and the general experience of mankind; all of these have their bearing on the remoteness or otherwise of the contingency.

harmful substance,[41] but if the defect in the ingredient is obvious it may be a failure of reasonable care not to observe it and special circumstances may require special precautions.[42] The liability of the vendor of second-hand goods, particularly second-hand motor vehicles, was recognised by the Supreme Court in *O'Sullivan* v *Noonan*[43] with Walsh J. saying:

> As a motor-car is an object which may become dangerous by reason of the existence of a defect, the person who sells . . . is under a duty to take reasonable care to see it is safe or alternatively to warn the purchaser that he, the vendor, has made no reasonable examination of the vehicle before selling it.[44]

The donor of a gift owes the recipient at least the duty to give warning of any known dangers associated with the gift.[45]

11.2 SALE OF GOODS ACTS

11.2.1 CAVEAT EMPTOR

The doctrine of *Caveat Emptor* placed practically all risks in a sale transaction on the buyer so that if the goods purchased proved to be defective the buyer bore the loss unless the parties had expressly agreed otherwise.[46] Prior to the enactment of the Sale of Goods Act, 1893, the common law had begun to imply into contracts of sale certain undertakings as to title and quality. These implied terms were incorporated into the 1893 Act, but contracting parties were free to

---

[41] ibid. pp. 10–11.

[42] ibid.

[43] Unreported Supreme Court, 28 July 1972. The plaintiff had been a passenger in a car bought second-hand from a car dealer. The car had been supplied with dangerous tyres and the plaintiff had been injured in an accident caused by one of the tyres bursting.

[44] ibid.

[45] *Campbell* v *O'Donnell* [1967] IR 226 at 229, Supreme Court per Walsh J.: "There is now ample authority for the proposition that, independently of any contractual relationship between the parties, the donor owes at least the duty to give warning of any dangers actually known to him."

[46] The leading works on the subject are Benjamin (1992), *Sale of Goods*; Atiyah (1985), *Sale of Goods*; see also Forde (1990), *Commercial Law in Ireland*, Chapter One.

agree otherwise and whatever they agreed governed the transaction. The Act only intervened where there was no agreement and it sought to imply into the transaction terms which it believed typical parties would have agreed upon had they applied their minds to the question. Because the sale of goods or an agreement to sell goods is a contract the Act must be applied within the wider framework of contract law, and because a sale also affects the ownership of property the Act must be applied within the law of personal property.[47] The 1893 Act was adopted primarily for commercial sale transactions where it was reasonable to assume that each party to the transaction was capable of looking after his own interests and the law was intended to facilitate the parties. There were then, and still are, far more private consumer-type sales and consumers generally are not legally or commercially sophisticated. The courts, in an effort to protect the consumer, developed the doctrine of "fundamental breach" and used it to over-ride exemption clauses in contracts of sale which purported to exonerate one party from liability.[48] The Sale of Goods and Supply of Services Act, 1980 was introduced in Ireland in response to the growing demand for consumer protection. The Act defines what is a consumer sale for the purposes of the Acts[49] and revises the implied undertaking by the vendor as to title.[50] Parties to the sale cannot exclude the vendor's liability for breach of that term.[51] The Act revised

---

[47] Section 61(2) of Sale of Goods Act, 1893.

[48] The precise circumstances when the courts will apply the doctrine or the scope of application has not been defined but the doctrine is illustrated in *Clayton Love & Sons (Dublin) Ltd.* v *British and Irish Steam Packet Co. Ltd.* [1970] 104 ILTR 157.

[49] Section 3:

A party to a contract is said to deal as a consumer in relation to another party if (a) he neither makes the contract in the course of a business nor holds himself out as doing so, and (b) the other party does not make the contract in the course of a business, and (c) the goods or services supplied under or in pursuance of the contract are of a type ordinarily supplied for private use or consumption.

The buyer in a sale by competitive tender or, in certain circumstances, a sale by auction will not be regarded as a consumer and it is for those claiming the buyer does not deal as a consumer to prove that he does not.

[50] Section 10 substitutes new wordings for Sections 11, 12, 13, 14 and 15 of the 1893 Act.

[51] Section 11.

the implied terms as to quality or fitness of the goods[52] and in the case of consumer sales the vendor cannot exclude liability for breach of those terms.[53] A new implied term in respect of motor-vehicle sales to consumers has been included,[54] together with provisions in respect of guarantees given with the supply of goods.[55]

11.2.2 STATUTORY PREREQUISITES

Section 4(1) of the 1893 Act provides that a contract for sale of goods valued at £10 or more will not be enforced unless one of four features are present: (1) the buyer must have paid or partly paid for the goods; (2) given something in earnest to bind the contract; (3) he must have accepted or received part of the goods; (4) he must have signed a written memorandum containing the general terms of the contract. The goods must be paid for in money, but part payment in money and part payment by way of trade-in of property may bring the transaction within the Acts, depending on what was agreed.[56]

11.2.3 IMPLIED TERMS

Sections 11 to 15 of the 1893 Act, as amended by the 1980 Act, set out, as regards quality, the terms to be implied into a contract for the sale of goods. Where goods are sold by description there is an implied term that they correspond with that description,[57] and if bought from someone dealing in goods of that description there is an implied term that they be merchantable.[58] Where the buyer discloses the purpose for which the goods are required there is an implied term that they are reasonably fit for such purpose.[59] Similar terms are implied where

---

[52] Section 14.

[53] Section 54(4) of 1893 Act.

[54] Section 13.

[55] Section 15.

[56] *Flynn* v *Mackin* [1974] IR 101. An agreement between the defendants whereby the second defendant accepted the first defendant's car and £250 against anew car to be obtained by the first defendant from a third party was held by the Supreme Court to be an agreement to barter or exchange goods and was not an agreement for the sale of goods within the Sale of Goods Act, 1893.

[57] Section 13(1) of the 1893 Act as amended by Section 10 of the 1980 Act.

[58] Section 14.

[59] Section 14(4).

the goods are sold by sample.[60] The bulk of the goods must correspond with the sample.[61]

11.2.4 MERCHANTABILITY

The concept of merchantabilty is given definition in the 1980 Act,[62] and extensive restrictions are imposed on attempts to exclude obligations under the Acts from the conditions of sale.[63] For the goods to be subject to the Acts they must have been sold in the course of business[64] and where the buyer, expressly or by implication, makes known to the seller any particular purpose for which the goods are being bought, there is an implied condition that the goods are reasonably fit for that purpose, whether or not that is a purpose for which the goods are commonly bought.[65] In *Egan* v *McSweeney*,[66] a coal merchant, with whom the plaintiff had a course of dealing over twenty years, was held liable to the plaintiff, under Section 14(2) of the 1893 Act, although not negligent in supplying coal which exploded when lit. The defendant knew the coal was purchased for domestic use and the plaintiff relied on his skill and judgement. The High Court had no difficulty in finding for a plaintiff poultry breeder when the vaccine, intended for day old chicks, purchased on the recommendation of the vendor, turned out to be a different vaccine suitable only for adult fowl and a large number of chicks died.[67] In *McCullagh Sales Ltd.* v *Chetham Timber Ltd.*,[68] manmade material sold in substitution for timber skirting boards needed special nails for fixing and the nails

---

[60] Section 15(1).

[61] Section 15(2)(a).

[62] Section 10 of the 1980 Act, amending 2(14) by inclusion of Sub-section (3).

[63] Section 11.

[64] Section 14(2) of the 1893 Act as amended by Section 10 of the 1980 Act.

[65] Section 14(4) of the 1893 Act.

[66] [1956] ILTR 40.

[67] *O'Regan & Sons Ltd.* v *Micro-Bio (Ireland) Ltd.* Unreported High Court, 26 February 1980. The court found that the vaccine sold by description did not conform with the description because of greater potency. The goods were described in contract by the trade name (H 52), but the contract was not for the sale of goods under trade name but for the sale of a vaccine which the vendor recommended.

[68] Unreported High Court, 1 February 1983.

were not suitable because of the density of the concrete used in Ireland. It was held that the goods were not reasonably fit for the purpose for which purchased. It is no defence that the vendor could not have reasonably known that the goods were unfit for the purpose because the goods had been manufactured by someone else and contained defects which the vendor could not reasonably have detected before sale. Section 14(4) is

> an assurance that the goods will be reasonably fit for the purpose and that covers not only defects which the seller ought to have detected but also defects which are latent in the sense that even the utmost skill and judgement on the part of the seller would not have detected them.[69]

A vendor found to be in breach of contract may, however, have a claim against his supplier, who in turn may have a claim against the manufacturer who was at fault.[70] The implied term lasts:

> for a reasonable time after delivery, so long as [the goods] remain in the same apparent state as that in which they were delivered, apart from normal wear and tear.[71]

The implied term in respect of fitness for purpose and the merchantability term do not apply to sales where the vendor is not acting in the course of business but selling privately and in those circumstances, the *caveat emptor* doctrine applies. The term "ordinary course of business" has been held to mean an activity being carried on

---

[69] *Henry Kendall & Sons* v *William Lillicoe & Sons Ltd.* [1969] 2 AC 31 at 84.

[70] ibid., and also *Ashington Piggeries Ltd.* v *Christopher Hill Ltd.* [1972] AC 441.

[71] *Lexmead (Basingstoke) Ltd.* v *Lewis* [1983] AC 225 at 276. A farmer bought a towing hitch from a garage and whilst using it to tow a trailer some of it fell out. He continued to use it even though it was only dirt which was holding it together. One day the trailer became detached, killing and injuring the occupants of an oncoming car. The court rejected the farmer's claim that the hitch was unfit for the purpose for which it was bought because he had become aware of the defect and had done nothing to rectify it.

with some degree of regularity.[72] Prior to the 1980 Act, the purchaser had to establish that, as well as disclosing the purpose for which he was purchasing the goods, he had also relied on the skill of the vendor to supply goods fit for that purpose.[73] Now the term will be implied unless the vendor can show that the buyer does not rely, or that it is unreasonable for him to rely, on the seller's skill or judgement.[74]

11.2.5 EXCLUSION CLAUSES

Section 55 of the 1893 Act permitted the vendor to exclude or limit his liability for breach of any or all of the implied terms regarding the quality of the goods, but any such exclusion clause had to be incorporated in the contract of sale and its terms be directly applicable to the defect in respect of which the seller would otherwise be liable.[75] The 1980 Act restricts the right of the vendor to limit or exclude liability. Section 12(3) prohibits the vendor from contracting out of the terms implied in respect of spare parts and Section 13(9) prohibits the contracting out of any of the implied terms in respect of the sale of motor vehicles. An amendment to Section 55 of the 1893 Act provides that none of the implied terms regarding quality or fitness for purpose can be contracted out of in consumer sales contracts, and Section 55(4) of the 1980 Act renders exclusion clauses in non-consumer sales unenforceable unless they are fair and reasonable. In determining, for the purposes of the Act, if a term is fair and reasonable, the test is that it shall be a fair and reasonable one to be included having regard to all the circumstances which were, or ought reasonably to have been, known to or in the contemplation of the parties when the contract

---

[72] *R&B Customs Brokers Co.* v *United Dominions Trust Ltd.* [1988] 1 WLR 321. The plaintiff had bought a car from a garage with the financial assistance of the defendant. The car was used by the company for private and business purposes and the Court of Appeal held that the transaction was a consumer sale on the grounds that the term "ordinary course of business" in the legislation meant an activity carried on with some degree of regularity. The purchase of the car was only incidental to the carrying on of the company's business of ship broking and freight forwarding.

[73] *Draper* v *Rubenstein* [1925] 59 ILTR 119.

[74] Section 14(4).

[75] *Tokn Grass Products Ltd.* v *Sexton & Co. Ltd.* Unreported High Court, 3 October 1983.

was made, having regard to the following which appear to be relevant:

a) the strength of the bargaining positions of the parties relative to each other, taking into account alternative means by which the purchaser's requirements could have been met;

b) whether the customer received an inducement to agree to the term, or in accepting it had an opportunity of entering into a similar contract with other persons, but without having to accept a similar term;

c) whether the customer knew or ought reasonably to have known of the existence and extent of the term (having regard to any custom of the trade and any previous dealings between the parties);

d) where the term excludes or restricts any relevant liability if some condition is not complied with, whether it was reasonable at the time of the contract to expect that compliance with the condition would be practicable;

e) whether any goods involved were manufactured, processed or adapted to the special order of the customer.[76]

The manner in which the Irish courts will interpret these criteria has yet to be determined, but in *George Mitchell* v *Finney Lock Seeds Ltd.*[77] the House of Lords held that, in determining what was "fair and reasonable",

> the court must entertain a whole range of considerations, put them in the scales on one side or the other and decide at the end of the day on which side the balance comes down. There

---

[76] Schedule of the Act of 1980.

[77] [1983] 2 All ER 737. The case is an indication of how the courts are inclined to take into account the existence of or the availability of insurance in respect of legal liabilities. The defendants were undoubtedly liable for breach of contract, but dependent on the court's decision might have been liable for £200 or £92,000. The fact that the defendants could have insured against their liability for the higher amount was an influencing factor.

will sometimes be room for differences of judicial opinion as to what the answer should be.[78]

Lord Bridge added that, in view of this, when such cases come before the appeal courts, they should treat the original decision with the utmost respect, and not interfere unless satisfied that it proceeded on some erroneous principle or was plainly wrong. Applying the criteria set out in the Act to the facts, the House held that it would not be fair or reasonable to allow the defendants to rely on the condition limiting their liability.[79]

11.3 EU DIRECTIVES

The adoption of the EU Directive Concerning Liability for Defective Products was intended to provide greater protection to consumers and to establish a uniform approach across all the member states.[80] The date for implementation was on or before 30 July 1988, but it

---

[78] ibid. per Lord Bridge. The plaintiff farmers ordered a consignment of a particular variety of cabbage seed from the defendant seed merchants at a cost of £201.60. The crop failed completely because the seed supplied was not the seed ordered and was of inferior quality. The plaintiffs claimed the cost incurred in the cultivation of the worthless crop and the anticipated profit. The defendants relied on a condition in the terms of sale which limited their liability to the value of the seeds. The House of Lords held that, at common law, the condition could not be ignored, and that if it stood in isolation the defendants could have relied on it. However, applying the guidance set out in Section 55 of the Sale of Goods Act, 1893 to the facts, their Lordships held that it would not be fair or reasonable to allow the defendants to rely on the condition limiting their liability.

[79] The condition reads:

In the event of any seeds or plants sold or agreed to be sold by us not complying with the express terms of the contract of sale . . . or any seeds or plants proving defective in varietal purity we will, at our option, replace the defective seeds or plants, free of charge to the buyer, or will refund all payments made to us by the buyer in respect of the defective seeds or plants and this shall be the limit of our liability. . . .

[80] It was also felt that the divergences of approach and in the laws of member states might distort competition and restrict the free movement of goods. However, the Directive allowed members a choice of options in respect of the development risk defence, financial limits on liability and derogation from including primary agricultural produce within the ambit of the Act, so that there has been no uniform approach to implementation of the Directive.

was 1991 before the necessary legislation was enacted in Ireland.[81] The Directive imposed strict liability on producers of products for injury or loss occasioned to any person due to a defect in the product, irrespective of the negligence of the producer. The liability imposed is not absolute in so far as certain defences are available to the producer and the liability defined in the directive is intended to provide an additional legal remedy to those existing in tort and under contract law. It was not intended to replace or substitute the existing law of member states but rather to supplement it. Strict liability means that the difficulty of establishing liability is made easier for the plaintiff because fault does not have to be proved and it is much harder for a defendant to defend an action.[82] The notion of strict liability caused insurers some concern when first mooted, but in practice there is no evidence that the incidence or cost of products liability claims have significantly increased. The Directive could justifiably claim credit for the increasingly high standards applied in the manufacture of most products.

In 1989 the EU proposed a Directive on Product Safety which has yet to be implemented in Ireland.[83] The Directive generally requires member states to ensure that only safe products are placed on the market and to take action to minimise the risk if a product presenting an immediate and grave risk appears. Member states are required to introduce legislation for permanent safety monitoring of all features of a product and its presentation which could affect its safety during its life and in its ultimate disposal. It will provide a means of dealing with firms which place unsafe products on the market without incurring the costs of proper quality control. The safety legislation is intended to be complementary to the product liability legislation, but the main difference between the two is that while the product safety legislation, when introduced, will provide criminal sanctions on the

---

[81] Britain introduced the directive in the Consumer Protection Act, 1987, and Germany implemented their Product Liability Act in 1988. Most other countries, like Ireland, failed to meet the deadline.

[82] Strict liability differs from a no-fault regime in that under the latter there are no defences available, while strict liability permits some defences and, in relation to products liability, these are set out in the Act.

[83] EU Directive on Product Safety, Com. (89)-SYN 192.

producer of unsafe products, the product liability legislation imposes civil liability only.[84]

11.4 LIABILITY FOR DEFECTIVE PRODUCTS ACT, 1991

11.4.1 APPLICATION OF THE ACT

The intention of the Act is to give to a person injured by a defective product the ability to bring an action for compensation without having to prove fault against any person involved in the production and distribution process of the product. Section 2(1) of the Act introduces strict liability into this area and provides that: "The producer shall be liable in damages in tort for damage caused wholly or partly by a defect in his product." The Act defines "producer" in such a way as to enable an injured person seeking redress under the Act to name the producer of the finished product, the producer of any raw material, or the manufacturer of a component part in a finished product, any person representing himself as the "producer", and the importer as joint defendants with joint and several liability.[85] "Producer" means the manufacturer of a finished product, the producer of any raw material or the manufacturer of a component part and any person who, by putting his name, trade mark, or other distinguishing features on the

---

[84] The Department of Industry and Commerce issued an explanatory and discussion document in August 1987 in connection with the Directive on Products Liability. In that document it was confirmed that a Product Safety Bill was then being drafted and that the proposed legislation on product safety and product liability was considered as being complementary. That legislation should have been implemented by 1992 but at the time of writing it is understood that a draft Statutory Instrument is "under consideration". In *Frankovich* v *Italy* (C-6/90) and *Bonifaci* v *Italy* (C-9/90), unreported judgments of the European Court of Justice, 19 November 1991, the ECJ decided that a member state could in principle be liable to pay compensation for loss caused by its failure to implement a directive. The failure to implement the safety legislation could therefore have implications for Ireland. See *Coppinger* v *Waterford County Council*, [1996] 2 ILRM 427.

[85] Section 2(2) of the 1980 Act.

product represents himself as the producer.[86] In the case of primary agricultural products which have undergone initial processing, the person who carried out such processing is regarded as the producer for the purposes of the Act.[87] Any person who imports the defective product into a member state, from a place outside the European Union, in order, in the course of any business of his, to supply it to another, is regarded as the producer of the product.[88] In the event that the producer of the defective product cannot be identified, each supplier of the product shall be treated as its producer, unless he informs the injured person, within a reasonable time, of the identity of the producer or of the person who supplied him with the product.[89] Where two or more people are liable by virtue of the Act for the same damage, they will be liable, jointly and severally, as concurrent wrongdoers[90] under the provisions of the Civil Liability Act, 1961. Without prejudice to the right of contribution under that Act, the liability of the producer is not reduced when damage is caused both by a defect in the product and the act or omission of a third party,[91] and the provisions concerning contributory negligence apply where the damage is caused partly by a defect in the product and partly by the fault of the injured person or of any person for whom he is responsible.[92]

11.4.2 DEFINITION OF "DAMAGE"

"Damage" is defined[93] as meaning: (a) death or personal injury, or (b) loss of or damage to, or destruction of, any item of property other than the defective product itself provided that the item of property (i)

---

[86] Section 2(2)(a), (b), (d). The Act imposes liability on the supermarket chains who sell "own brand" products specially manufactured for them by outside manufacturers if the supermarkets hold themselves out as the producer. A declaration on the product that it has been manufactured by a specified manufacturer for the supermarket might possibly relieve the supermarket of liability under the Act but it might still be liable under the Sale of Goods Act if the person injured by the defective product was the purchaser of the product.

[87] Section 2(2)(c).

[88] Section 2(2)(e).

[89] Section 2(3).

[90] Section 8.

[91] Section 9(1).

[92] Section 9(2).

[93] Section 1(1).

is of a type ordinarily intended for private use or consumption, and (ii) was used by the injured person mainly for his own private use or consumption. The Act imposes liability for damage caused to other property by the defective product and does not apply to the defective product itself. A remedy in contract is available to the purchaser of a defective product against the vendor of the product. There does not appear to be anything in the Act which would exclude liability for damage to a finished product caused by a defective component or part. The property damaged must be of a kind ordinarily intended for private use or consumption, and accordingly excludes damage to industrial or commercial property. It is not sufficient for the consumer to prove that the defective product was of a kind ordinarily intended for private use or consumption; it is necessary also to prove that the product was used mainly by the consumer himself. It is unlikely that the definition of damage is sufficiently wide to cover financial loss, even if such loss is a direct consequence of the damage to property. The definition of damage set out in Section 1(a) of the Act differs slightly, but significantly, from Article 9(a) of the Directive. That Article defines "damage" as meaning damage caused by death or personal injury. The definition in the Act could be interpreted as excluding damages for pain and suffering and consequential losses. The Act, however, defines personal injury as "including any disease and any impairment of a person's physical or mental condition" and this could be interpreted as including "pain and suffering". Furthermore, Section 2(1) of the Act provides that the producer shall be liable in "damages in tort" for damage caused and this is probably sufficient to make applicable the domestic Irish rules governing the award of damages for pain and suffering and consequential losses. If the legislature had intended to exclude compensation for pain and suffering from the provisions of the Act it could have so stated in the Act.[94] The

---

[94] In Ireland, damages for pain and suffering form a very large proportion of any award of damages for personal injury. *Rooney* v *Connolly* [1987] ILRM 76. Total damages awarded amounted to £74,383 of which £74,000 related to pain and suffering. The difference in definition was the subject of debate and attempted amendment in the Oireachtas. The Minister of State at the Department of Industry and Commerce, Mr Michael Smith, declined to accept the amendment because, on the advice of the Attorney General, he believed the correct way to translate Article 9(a) into domestic Irish law is by means of the definition of "damage" in Section 2(1) of the Civil Liability Act, 1961, which is the principal statute governing civil liability in this country.

issue has not as yet been tested in the courts but it is likely that damages for pain and suffering are recoverable under the Act.

11.4.3 DEFINITION OF "DEFECTIVE"

The onus is on the injured person concerned to prove the damage, the defect, and the causal relationship between the defect and the damage.[95] It is likely that the established rules on causation and remoteness in the law of tort will apply. A product is defective when it does not provide the safety which a person is entitled to expect, taking all circumstances into account, including:

a) the presentation of the product;

b) the use to which it could reasonably be expected to be put;

c) the time when the product was put into circulation.[96]

A product shall not be considered defective for the sole reason that a better product is subsequently put into circulation.[97] If a product causes damage or injury because it is mis-used it cannot be classified as defective.[98] The requirement that a product be fit for the purpose for which it was purchased is not present in the Act where the sole concept in defining a defective product is "safety".

11.4.4 DEFINITION OF PRODUCT

"Product" means all moveables with the exception of primary agricultural products which have not undergone initial processing, and includes:

a) moveables even though incorporated into another product or into an immovable, whether by virtue of being a component part or raw material or otherwise;

---

[95] See Bird (1992).

[96] Section 4.

[97] Section 5(2).

[98] *Campbell* v *O'Donnell* [1967] IR 226. A ladder is not defective because it does not support the weight of two workmen using it as a horizontal platform between two other ladders.

b) electricity where the damage is caused as a result of a failure in the process of generation of electricity.[99] "Primary Agricultural Products" means the product of the soil or stock farming and of fisheries, excluding products which have undergone initial processing.[100]

11.4.5 LIMITATION OF LIABILITY

The Act does not affect any rights the injured person may have under any other rule of law,[101] and the producer cannot limit or exclude his liability by any term of contract, by any notice or by any other provision.[102] Exemption clauses contained in notices or included with instructions accompanying a product are of no effect, but a producer is obliged to draw attention to the specific risks of his product, particularly for certain users. To discourage small claims, damages of £350 or less are not recoverable nor the first £350 of damages generally. The Directive provided[103] that member states could limit the liability of the producer resulting from a death or injury caused by identical items with the same defect to not less than 70 million ECUs (approx. IR£53 million). In implementing the Directive, Ireland exercised its option to derogate from this provision, which was intended to provide for the type of case where a pharmaceutical product, or component part in a range of products, proved to be defective. The Irish view was that the imposition of such a high limit would not be materially different from unlimited liability and would make no significant difference to the level of insurance premiums and consequently no differ-

---

[99] Section 1.

[100] Section 1. The exclusion of primary agricultural produce is understandable in a country so heavily dependent on agriculture, and most farmers would have objected to the imposition of liability for such products.

[101] Section 11.

[102] Section 10. It does not, however, prevent the various parties in the distribution chain from contracting between themselves on terms which alter their legal rights.

[103] Article 16 of the directive provided that member states may provide for a limit on the total liability of a producer resulting from the death or injury caused by identical items with the same defect but the limit could not be less than 70 million ECUs. Most member states considered the imposition of a limit as being unjust in so far as it could lead to situations whereby early claimants could be compensated in full but later claimants might go uncompensated once the limit was exhausted.

ence to the competitive position of industry. The Act provides that a
limitation period of three years shall apply to proceedings for the recovery of damages under the Act, with the period beginning to run
from the date on which the cause of action accrued or the date (if
later) on which the injured person became aware, or should reasonably have become aware of the damage, the defect and the producer.[104]
However, Section 7(2)(a) of the Act provides that a right of action under the Act shall be extinguished on the expiry of a period of ten
years from the date on which the producer put into circulation the
actual product which caused the damage unless the injured person
has in the meantime instituted proceedings against the producer.
This provision seems to produce an anomalous situation in that a
person injured by a product, purchased nine years after it has been
put into circulation, does not then have three years in which to institute proceedings but only the balance of the period of ten years from
the date it was first put into circulation.[105]

11.4.6 DEFENCES

Under the provisions of the Act, the producer has available to him six
specific defences but he carries the burden of proving any defence
raised.[106] The defences are:

a) That he did not put the product into circulation. If, for instance,
   the product is stolen prior to delivery the producer will not be liable to a person injured by it. The emission of toxic substances
   from a factory would not be regarded as having been put into circulation for the purposes of the Act.

b) That, having regard to the circumstances, it is probable that the
   defect which caused the damage did not exist at the time when the

---

[104] Section 7(1). This limitation period corresponds closely with the provisions of
the Statute of Limitations Acts, 1957 and 1991.

[105] It is obviously advisable for all producers to keep documented records for a
minimum of twelve years, as in Ireland, it is possible for a summons to be issued
the date before the expiry of the limitation period and not be served until the last
day of the following year. Such records should identify the source of raw materials and components to facilitate the involvement of suppliers in the event of a
claim.

[106] Section 6 provides that a producer shall not be liable under the Act if he
proves any one of the specified defences.

product was put into circulation by the producer or that the defect came into being afterwards. A manufacturer would not therefore be liable where goods damaged, in the course of delivery, or following receipt by the distributor or vendor, subsequently caused damage as a result of their defective condition, provided of course that title and risk in the goods had passed from the manufacturer.

c) That the product was neither manufactured for sale, or any form of distribution for an economic purpose nor manufactured or distributed by him in the course of his business. A manufacturer of goods for his own private use does not come within the scope of the Act.

d) That the defect in the product is due to compliance with any requirement imposed by or under any law of the European Community.

e) That the state of scientific and technical knowledge at the time when the product was put into circulation was not such as to enable the existence of the defect to be discovered. In the Directive, member states were given the option of derogating from the Directive by excluding this "development risks" defence. It can be argued that the inclusion of this defence is contrary to the principle of strict liability and can in certain circumstances leave the consumer without recourse for compensation. However, the absence of such a defence could cause problems for manufacturers and stifle innovation. To successfully avail of the defence, the producer would have to prove that because of the state of scientific and technical knowledge at the time the product was put into circulation, the producer could not have been expected to discover the existence of the defect. The defence is dependent on the impossibility of anyone discovering the defect. It is not sufficient to prove that the state of the producer's scientific and technical knowledge did not allow him discover the defect.

f) In the case of a manufacturer of a component or the producer of a raw material, that the defect is attributable to the design of the product in which the component has been fitted or the raw material has been incorporated or to the instructions given by the manufacturer of the product. This defence can be relied upon in circumstances where the defectiveness of a component has been caused by the design of the actual product of which the component forms a part or which has been caused as a result of instructions from the manufacturer. In such cases the manufacturer of the final product would be liable.

11.5 PRODUCT LIABILITY INSURANCE

Strict liability for defective products is of American origin and has been used there extensively as a vehicle for social reform. It has been developed as a means of loss distribution by an American judicial system alert to the economic disparities of that society and applied so as to allocate risk and make those who could pay make financial reparation for the consequences of defects in products. The courts have regarded the purpose of such liability as ensuring that the costs of injuries resulting from defective products are borne by the manufacturers that put such products on the market rather than by the injured persons who are powerless to protect themselves. By insisting on risk allocation rather than fault, the law ensures that the one with the "deepest pocket" will pay for the injury or damage and the existence of product liability insurance has been an influential factor. With the introduction of strict liability into Irish law under the Liability for Defective Products Act, 1991, the growth in consumerism and the development of a litigation culture in Irish society there has never been a greater need for products liability insurance.[107] There is, however, a dearth of case law on the subject.

11.5.1 SCOPE OF COVER

The form of insurance cover available varies enormously but products liability policies generally provide indemnity against:

> all sums which the insured shall become legally liable to pay as compensation for accidental bodily injury or illness to any person or accidental damage to property, occurring during the period of the policy and caused by any defect in goods sold supplied or repaired by the insured.

---

[107] In the early days of product liability insurance the concern was primarily with liability arising out of the sale of food and drink, i.e. food poisoning or ptomaine poisoning as it was referred to.

The definitional problems associated with the word "accidental" referred to previously have been responsible for the omission of the word from the modern form of policy. On the basis of the wording quoted above, the injury or damage would have to be caused by a defect in the goods sold, supplied or repaired by the insured. Some policy wordings omit reference to defect and cover liability arising from goods sold, supplied, delivered, installed, erected, repaired, altered, treated or tested. Such a wording provides a much wider form of cover and it would not be necessary that the goods causing the injury or damage be defective for the cover to operate. The policy would cover liability arising out of the supply of incorrect goods as well as injury or damage caused by goods in perfect condition. Cover would also apply to the containers and packing supplied. Some policy wordings make it clear that cover only applies in respect of goods actually supplied, so that injury or damage arising out of goods still on the premises of the insured would not be covered. The liability is more correctly the subject of a claim under the public liability policy. Liability for injury or damage arising out of the goods being delivered by the insured's own vehicles would be a matter for the motor policy or the general public liability policy as the goods would still be in the possession of the insured.

11.5.2 "LOSS OF OR DAMAGE TO PROPERTY"

"Property" means physical and tangible property and "damage" means physical damage. Neither damage to rights or economic loss without physical damage is covered.[108] The cost of repairing or replacing or recalling the goods would not be covered although cover is available under more specific policies.[109] In *Muirhead* v *Industrial*

---

[108] Some insurers will provide an element of cover for financial loss suffered by any customer or user of goods supplied by the insured where such loss is the direct result of the defective condition of the goods or their failure to perform the function for which they were supplied.

[109] Cover is available from insurers specialising in the products area in respect of the costs incurred in recalling or destroying products believed to be defective. Cover is also available for the costs incurred in replacing products which are defective due to faulty design or manufacture.

Tank Specialities and Others[110] the Court of Appeal held that a manufacturer of defective products will only be liable in negligence for economic losses suffered by the ultimate purchaser of the product if there is a very close proximity of relationship between the manufacturer and the ultimate purchaser, and the ultimate purchaser placed reliance on the manufacturer rather than on the retailer, supplier or distributor of the product. The interpretation to be placed on "loss of or damage to material property" was considered by the Court of Appeal in *F&H Contractors Ltd.* v *Commercial Union Assurance Co.*[111] While the case did not arise out of a defect in a product, but rather the manner in which the product was applied, the comments of Lord Justice Russell are nevertheless relevant. The plaintiffs had been engaged to fertilise seed beds, intended to receive potatoes to be used in crisp production, and which therefore required a degree of uniformity in the resulting crop. The fertiliser was applied unevenly so that as the plants developed their growth varied according to whether the area in which they were planted had received too much or too little fertiliser. Although each individual plant remained healthy, the overall value of the crop was affected by the loss of yield and the difficulty in harvesting. The farmer claimed in contract against the contractor for the loss of anticipated profit and the plaintiff claimed on their insurers contending that the loss came within the policy as "loss of or damage to material property". At first instance, the claim was rejected by Steyn J., as he then was, saying:

----

[110] [1985] 3 All ER 705. The plaintiff was a wholesale fish merchant who wished to expand his business by purchasing lobsters during the summer, storing them in a large tank and then selling them at Christmas when the prices would be significantly higher. The pumps supplied by the company which installed the tank were manufactured in France and unsuitable for use in England. The plaintiff had relied throughout on the advice of the company which installed the tank and the pumps and was not aware of the existence of the pump manufacturers and had no contact with them. The plaintiff lost his entire stock of lobsters due to failure of the pumps. The plaintiff claimed against the manufacturers for damages for the loss of the lobsters and economic losses suffered as a result. The Court of Appeal held that the economic losses were not recoverable, as on the facts the plaintiff had not relied on the manufacturer and there was no proximity between the parties. The court did, however, award damages for the loss of the lobsters as the loss was reasonably foreseeable by the manufacturers.

[111] Unreported, 18 May 1993.

The answer [is] whether a loss of crop due to misapplication of fertiliser can fairly be said to be damage to material property. . . . the policy wording must be approached in a businesslike way giving full effect to the need to avoid emasculating the cover by acute textual analysis. Having said that, it does seem to me that the word "damage" is inapposite to cover the present case which involved the application of fertiliser . . . which resulted in a healthy but reduced crop. It is not easy to see how a mere loss of yield can amount to damage to property.

The Court of Appeal saw no reason to interfere with that decision with Russell L. J. delivering the leading judgment saying:

The point of construction is a short one and in my view is not capable of much elaboration. "Material property" . . . plainly means property in the physical sense. . . . There can be [in this case] but two candidates for the description "material property" — the soil and the potato plants with their potatoes. The soil suffered no damage . . . as for the plants, all produced potatoes of uniform quality. . . . There was no disease in any of the plants or potatoes. There was therefore . . . no damage to material property and consequently no loss within the policy. What was lost was a loss of yield, a purely economic loss capable of being measured in monetary terms but not reflected or mirrored by any material damage to physical or corporeal property. Nor of course was there loss of any material property. . . . before there can be a loss of material property there has to be something physical in existence which is lost.

11.5.3 GEOGRAPHICAL LIMITS

Most product liability policies now provide cover on a world-wide basis, although there may be a restriction on cover in respect of the supply of products to the USA. It is usual for the policy to limit cover to goods supplied from the insured's premises in Ireland, and historically policies required that claims against the insured be brought in Ireland. Products sold or supplied from outside the territorial limits require special consideration. The 1968 Brussels Convention on Jurisdiction and the Enforcement of Judgments was made part of Irish law by the Jurisdiction of Courts and Enforcement of Judgments (European Communities) Act, 1988. Under this convention, a defendant may be sued where he is domiciled, or, in contract, where the obligation was performed or was to be performed, or in tort where the wrong occurred. Co-defendants can be joined where the court has jurisdiction over the first defendant. A consumer may bring an action either in the member state in which the defendant is domiciled or in the member state in which the consumer is domiciled. A judgment obtained in one member state is enforceable in another member state. In consequence of this legislation it is now common to extend policies so that they provide indemnity in respect of claims against the insured brought anywhere within the EU.

11.5.4 CLAIMS MADE BASIS

Many insurers offer products liability insurance on a "claims made" basis only. A "claims made" policy wording is one under which the claim must be made against the insured during the period of the policy or within a specified period after expiry, irrespective of when the act or event which gave rise to the claim happened. An "occurrence" wording on the other hand requires that the event which causes the injury or damage must occur during the currency of the policy, although the actual claim may be made after the period of insurance has expired or even after the policy has lapsed. "Claims made" policy wordings were introduced to deal with a problem of modern industrial society where claims, in respect of personal injury or disease, arising from exposure to harmful products over a long period, are made many years after a policy was effected. There may be a period of many years before the disease or injury manifests itself and before the injured person is aware of his condition. Between the inception of the policy and the making of the claim there may have been significant changes in the law and in the technical and scientific knowledge available within the industry. Insurers are then required to meet current claims out of premiums received years previously and which may be totally inadequate in the light of present day circumstances. These wordings were introduced for the benefit of insurers and reinsurers. The principal disadvantage for the insured arises where there is a change from an "occurrence" type wording to a "claims made" wording, and the new wording does not apply to work done or products sold before a specified date.

11.5.5 INDEMNITY LIMIT

The indemnity limit under the policy is usually an aggregate limit applicable to any one period of insurance and not a limit to any one "accident" or "occurrence". The application of an aggregate limit is intended to limit insurers exposure in circumstances where the supply of a defective or contaminated batch of product could have disastrous consequences, producing numerous claims, and giving rise to a dispute as to whether there was one event or occurrence or a number of them. Insurers generally pay the costs of defending claims against the insured in addition to the compensation awarded but in respect of claims arising out of the supply of products to the USA it is usual to make the limit of indemnity inclusive of costs.

11.5.6 POLICY EXCLUSIONS

The conditions and exclusions in a products liability policy are generally similar to those in a public liability policy. Indemnity is not provided in respect of :

a) property belonging to or in the custody or control of the insured;

b) liability assumed by agreement which would not otherwise attach. Frequently, conditions or contracts of sale extend the liability of the manufacturer or supplier of goods beyond the normal liability and into the area of warranties or guarantees of absolute effectiveness or suitability of the product. The conditions might also provide a total indemnity for injury or damage arising out of the use of the goods as a result of which the insured might be held responsible even where the injury or damage is due to the negligence of the purchaser in the storage or use of the goods;

c) the cost of replacing the defective product, the cost of recall, the cost of replacement, loss of use or remedial work. The intention of the cover is to provide indemnity in respect of liability for injury or damage caused by the goods but not to reimburse the cost of damage to the goods themselves or the costs of repair recall or replacement. Most insurers regard such costs as trade risks and will not provide cover, but some specialist insurers make cover available;

d) liability due to design, plan, drawing, specification, formula or advice. Some insurers apply this exclusion only in respect of manufacturers and are prepared to provide cover for wholesalers retailers or distributors and rely on their subrogation rights against the manufacturer in the event of a claim. It is unusual to provide cover for advisory or design work carried out for a fee, as this is a risk more appropriate to a professional liability policy. Some policies will, for the same reason, exclude liability for instructions, advice or information on the use storage or application of the goods. It is possible to insure, under a Product Guarantee policy, liability arising out of the goods failing to fulfil the purposes for which they were designed.

CHAPTER TWELVE

PROFESSIONAL LIABILITY

*"The only way professional men can save themselves — against
ruinous liability — is by insurance . . ."*[1]

In any examination of the law of negligence — in so far as it relates to
professional people — it is not possible to ignore the relevance of insurance. The availability of Professional Indemnity Insurance has
influenced expansion of negligence principles over the last fifty years
and has been responsible for extension of the liability of a professional, beyond liability to the client, to include liability to third parties to whom they might owe a duty of care.[2] The changeover to a
services based economy has seen a dramatic increase in the incidence
of professional liability litigation to such an extent that, in England
in recent years, the courts have endeavoured to restrict the further
development of professional liability.[3] The huge growth in the number
of medical malpractice claims in Ireland is indicative of the attitude
of society, in general, to look to the professional for redress when anything goes wrong.

12.1 DEFINITION OF "PROFESSIONAL"

The word "profession" used to be confined to the three learned professions, the Church, Medicine and the Law, but it now has a wider
meaning. A professional is accepted as being one engaged in a

> . . . "profession" [which] in the present use of language involves
> the idea of an occupation requiring either purely intellectual

---

[1] Denning M. R., "The Discipline of the Law", at p. 280.

[2] *Hedley Byrne* v *Heller & Partners* [1964] AC 465.

[3] *Caparo Industries* v *Dickman* [1990] 2 AC 605.

skill, or if manual skill, controlled, as in painting and sculp-
ture, or surgery, by the intellectual skill, of the operator, as
distinguished from an occupation which is substantially the
production or sale or arrangements for the production or sale
of commodities. The line of demarcation may vary from time to
time.[4]

In the High Court,[5] Blayney J. believed that these principles were
applicable to mechanics as persons exercising and professing to have
special skill, but in the Supreme Court, in *Kelly* v *St. Laurence's Hospital*,[6] it was held that, in so far as medicine is concerned, the principles were not applicable to nursing staff.

12.2 DUTY OF CARE

The duty of care owed to a client by a professional was set out by Tin-
dal C. J. in 1838:

> Every person who enters into a learned profession undertakes
> to bring to the exercise of it a reasonable degree of care and
> skill. He does not undertake, if he is an attorney, that at all
> events you will gain your case, nor does a surgeon undertake
> that he will perform a cure; nor does he undertake to use the
> highest possible degree of skill. There may be persons who
> have higher education and greater advantages than he has,
> but he undertakes to bring a fair, reasonable and competent
> degree of skill.[7]

In Ireland, the accepted test for the duty of care is that stated in the
Supreme Court by Finlay C. J.:

> The true test . . . is whether [the professional] has proved to be
> guilty of such failure as no practitioner of equal specialist or
> general status and skill would be guilty of in acting with ordi-
> nary care.[8]

Where judgment is called for, the fact that the choice turns out to be a
bad one is not proof of negligence in itself. The duty of care is not a

---

[4] *Commissioners of Inland Revenue* v *Maxsie* [1919] 1 KB 647 at 657.

[5] *Hughes* v *J.J. Power Ltd.* Unreported High Court, 11 May 1988

[6] [1989] ILRM 437.

[7] *Lanphier* v *Phiboss* [1838] ER 581.

[8] *Dunne* v *National Maternity Hospital* [1989] IR 91.

warranty of result. An error of judgment only becomes relevant if it was one that no reasonably well-informed and competent practitioner would have made.

> No matter what profession it may be, the common law does not impose on those who practice it any liability for damage resulting from what turns out to have been errors of judgment, unless the error was such as no reasonably well informed and competent member of that profession could have made.[9]

All professionals must command the corpus of knowledge which forms part of the professional equipment of an ordinary member of the profession and must be alert to the hazards and risks in any professional task undertaken to the extent that other ordinarily competent members of the profession would be alert.[10] A professional must possess such knowledge and skill as conforms to the contemporary standards of their profession and if they are specialist such further and particularised skill as they hold themselves out to possess.[11]

12.3 NEED FOR "SPECIAL RELATIONSHIP"

While *Donoghue* v *Stevenson*[12] established a duty of care in negligence to a previously unimagined range of victims, it did not provide a basis for compensating those who suffered economic loss, unless such loss flowed directly from injury or damage to property, consequent on the negligent act of another. The general principles established, in that case, were not applied to liability for economic loss arising out of negligent advice or information for fear of exposing professionals to "liability in an indeterminate amount for an indeterminate time to an indeterminate class".[13] However, the restriction of compensation for economic loss to those who had suffered injury or damage to physical property was lifted by the House of Lords in *Hedley Byrne* v *Heller &*

---

[9] *Saif Ali* v *Sydney Mitchell & Co.* [1978] 3 All ER 1035, per Lord Diplock at 1041.

[10] *Henderson* v *Merrett Syndicates* [1994] 3 All ER 506.

[11] *Daniels* v *Heskins* [1954] IR 73 per Kingsmill-Moore J. at 86.

[12] [1932] AC 562.

[13] per Cardoza C. J. in *Ultramares Corporate* v *Touche* [1931] 255 NY 170.

Partners.[14] Their Lordships held that a negligent, though honest, misrepresentation, spoken or written, may give rise to an action for damages for financial loss caused thereby, apart from any contract or fiduciary relationship, since the law will imply a duty of care when a
party seeking information from a party possessed of a special skill
trusts him to exercise due care, and that party knew or ought to have
known that reliance was being placed on his skill and judgment. The
Irish High Court, in *Securities Trust Ltd.* v *Hugh Moore & Alexander
Ltd.*[15] accepted the principles of *Hedley Byrne* but could not accept
that the "defendant owed a duty to the world at large".[16] In *Bank of
Ireland* v *Smith,*[17] the defendant auctioneer had been responsible for
publishing an advertisement which incorrectly stated that lands offered for sale were oversown with permanent pasture. The plaintiff
who had purchased the land argued that in purchasing the land he
had relied on the representation in the advertisement. The court, in
refusing to hold that the defendant owed a duty of care to all prospective purchasers who had seen the advertisement, held that such
prospective purchasers did not come within the necessary category of
special relationship. Kenny J. held that liability could be imposed
only where there was a relationship between the parties equivalent to
contract — that is, where there was an assumption of responsibility
in circumstances in which, but for the absence of consideration, there
would be a contract. The need to establish the existence of a special
relationship was subsequently questioned by Gannon J. in *Tulsk Co-
op. Ltd* v *Ulster Bank Ltd.*[18] and by O'Hanlon J. in *Towey* v *Ulster*

---

[14] [1964] AC 465. The plaintiffs wished to check the financial stability of a company with which they intended placing advertising and asked their bank to carry
out the necessary enquiries. The plaintiffs' bank did this by enquiring from the
company's bankers who gave a favourable but negligent response, with a disclaimer of responsibility. The plaintiffs suffered financial loss having relied on
the information given to them and sued the defendants in negligence. They lost
the action in negligence but the House of Lords went into great detail to explain
the circumstances in which a duty of care would have arisen if no disclaimer had
attached to the information provided.

[15] [1964] IR 417.

[16] ibid. per Davitt P. at 421. See McGrath, "Negligence — The Reception of *Hedley
Byrne* into Ireland" (1983) 5 DULJ 296.

[17] *Bank of Ireland* v *Smith* [1966] IR 646. See also *Sweeney* v *Bourke* Unreported
High Court, 24 November 1980.

[18] Unreported High Court, 13 May 1983.

Bank Ltd.[19] In neither case was there difficulty in establishing a special relationship. However, in *Towey*, Gannon J., in expressing the view that liability in negligence for damages is not derived solely from identifiable classifications of relationships, seemed to suggest that the courts were prepared to take a broader approach.

12.4 CONCURRENT LIABILITY

The courts have since tended to take a broader view and it is not now necessary, to establish liability, that a plaintiff should have solicited information or advice from the defendant, provided the defendant ought to have foreseen that the information or advice would be relied upon by the plaintiff.[20] Architects, advising two companies with whom they were not in a contractual relationship were held to owe them a duty of care since advice was given "in circumstances in which responsible men would know that their professional skill and judgment was being relied upon".[21] The Supreme Court, in *Finlay* v *Murtagh*,[22] confirmed that the general duty of care created by the relationship of professional and client entitles the client to sue in negligence if they have suffered damage because of the professional's failure to show due professional care and skill, notwithstanding that the client could sue alternatively in contract. It also confirmed that the professional's liability in tort under the general duty of care extends not only to a client for reward, but to any person for whom the professional undertakes to act professionally without reward, and also to those with whom they have made no arrangement to act but who, as they know, or ought to know, will be relying on their professional care and skill.[23]

---

[19] [1987] ILRM 142.

[20] *Wall* v *Hegarty* [1980] ILRM 124.

[21] *Curley* v *Mulcahy* Unreported High Court, 21 December 1977, per McMahon J. at p. 3. In *Golden Vale Co-Operative Creameries Ltd.* v *Barrett*, Unreported High Court, 16 March 1987, accountants investigating the affairs of a company on behalf of the plaintiffs, who were considering investing in the company, were held negligent, in that they had failed in certain limited respects to protect the plaintiffs from falling into error, even though they had qualified and expressed reservations on their findings.

[22] [1979] IR 249; *Ministry of Housing* v *Sharp* [1970] 2 QB 223; *Lawton* v *BOC Transhield Ltd.* [1987] 2 All ER 608; *Wall* v *Hegarty* [1980] ILRM 124.

[23] *Finlay* v *Murtagh* [1979] IR 249 per Henchy J.

The liability of a professional to a third party was confirmed in the case of *Wall* v *Hegarty*,[24] where a solicitor was held to owe a duty of care to a legatee under a will. Concurrent liability in tort and contract was accepted in *Roche v Peilow*.[25] A more recent House of Lords decision, *Henderson* v *Merrett Syndicates*,[26] confirmed that where a professional or quasi-professional person assumed responsibility to provide services to another who in turn relied on those services, then a duty to exercise reasonable care and skill arose in the carrying out of those duties and even though the parties might have come together under a contractual relationship this did not prevent a concurrent duty in negligence arising. Where the plaintiff has available to them concurrent remedies in contract and in tort they may, unless the contract precludes a tortious remedy, choose which remedy appears the most advantageous. In *Holt* v *Payne Skillington & Others*,[27] the Court of Appeal applied the test in *Henderson* as to when a duty of care in tort may arise and went on to hold that a duty of care in tort may be wider than a concurrent duty in contract.

---

[24] [1980] ILRM 124. The liability of a solicitor to an intended beneficiary was established in England in *Ross* v *Caunters* [1980] 1 Ch. 297. While accepting and approving the judgment of Sir Robert Megarry in that case, Barrington J. was of the view that the Irish Supreme Court had already anticipated the decision in *Finlay* v *Murtagh*, [1979] IR 249. Barrington J. found the reasoning of Megarry V. C. "unanswerable". Megarry V. C. had found that (a) there was no longer any rule that a solicitor could be liable in contract alone, if negligent in his work; (b) the basis of liability was found in either *Hedley Byrne* v *Heller* [1964] AC 465 or *Donoghue* v *Stevenson* [1932] AC 562; (c) a solicitor instructed by a client to carry out a transaction which will confer benefits on an identified third party owes a duty of care towards the third party in carrying out the transaction in that the third party is a person within direct contemplation as someone likely to be so closely and directly affected by his acts or omissions that he can reasonably foresee that the third party is likely to be injured by those acts or omissions; the fact that the loss suffered is purely financial is no bar to a claim; in such circumstances there are no considerations which suffice to negative or limit the scope of the solicitor's duty to the beneficiary. See also: *White* v *Jones* [1993] *The Times*, 9 March and *The Times* 17 February 1995, House of Lords; *Hemmens* v *Wilson Browne* [1993] *The Times*, June 30.

[25] [1986] ILRM 189.

[26] *Henderson* v *Merrett Syndicates* above; *Arbuttnott* v *Feltrim Underwriting Agencies* [1994] 3 All ER 506; the plaintiffs were names at Lloyds and the defendants were underwriting agencies managing the affairs of the plaintiffs.

[27] *Holt* v *Payne Skillington, and DeGroot Collis*, Unreported Court of Appeal, 18 December 1995.

12.5 JUDICIAL RETRENCHMENT

The continued expansion of non-contractual professional liability prompted fears that escalating insurance premiums would force some service providers out of the market and, in England, lead to some retrenchment by the judiciary. In *Caparo Industries* v *Dickman*[28] the House of Lords held that, in establishing liability for negligent statements, the plaintiff must show that there was foreseeability of damage, the proximity of the relationship between the parties was sufficiently close and that it would be fair, just and reasonable in the circumstances to impose liability on the defendant. According to the judgments, tests of proximity, foreseeability and public policy, based upon notions of special relationships and voluntary assumptions of risk, were simply convenient labels used by the courts in deciding cases on their facts, and that these phrases were not susceptible of any such precise definition as would be necessary to give them utility as practical tests.[29] Their Lordships were of the view that the law had moved in the direction of attaching greater significance to the more traditional categorisation of distinct and recognisable situations as guides to the existence, scope and limits of the varied duties of care which the law imposes.[30] The decision suggests that new forms of professional liability should not be imposed on the basis of causation and foreseeability but rather by looking at previous authorities in order to determine the essential characteristics upon which the imposition of liability was based. The need to show that the imposition of a duty of care is "fair, just and reasonable" was confirmed by the House of Lords in *Spring* v *Guardian Assurance plc*.[31] when it held that the defendants owed a duty of care to the subject of an employment reference as well as to the recipient of the reference. The plaintiff, having been dismissed from his employment by the defendants, failed to obtain another position when the prospective employer received a reference from the defendants suggesting that the plaintiff had been guilty of mis-selling life assurance products. A more recent Court of

---

[28] [1990] 1 All ER 568.

[29] ibid. per Lord Bridge at 574.

[30] ibid.

[31] [1994] 3 WLR 354. See Allen, "Liability for References", 58 MLR 553.

Appeal decision, *Rothschild & Co.* v *Berenson*,[32] would suggest that limitation on the duty of care, perceived in *Caparo*[33] may in fact have been illusory. The case arose from the alleged negligence of solicitors acting for a lender engaged in risky lending operations. The solicitors failed to ensure that the lender had proper security for a loan which proved to be irrecoverable. The facts were complex and detailed but what is of interest is that the solicitors were sued, not by their client the lender, nor by the bank to whom they had sent a funds request, but by the syndicate of banks which had funded the lender. The solicitors argued that their duty was owed only to their client and not to the syndicate of banks funding him. The court held that the solicitors were aware in broad terms that other parties were providing funds to the lender and a duty of care was owed to those parties. The decision seems to contradict *Caparo* and suggests that professional advisers are required to bear in mind the interests of third parties involved in transactions with clients whether or not the identity of those third parties is known to the adviser.

12.6 DEFENCE OF GENERAL PRACTICE

One of the features which distinguishes professional negligence from negligence simpliciter is the availability of the defence of general practice. The professional will, usually, be held to have fulfilled the duty of care if they follow a practice common among the members of their profession.[34] Conformity with the widely accepted practice of the profession will normally rebut an allegation of negligence, but if there is a common practice which has inherent defects, which ought to be obvious to any person giving the matter due consideration, the fact that it is shown to have been widely and generally adopted over a period of time does not make the practice any less negligent. Neglect of duty does not cease by repetition to be neglect of duty.[35] A person cannot be said to be acting reasonably if they automatically and mindlessly follow the practice of others when, by taking thought, they

---

[32] Unreported Court of Appeal, February 1996.

[33] [1990] 1 All ER 568.

[34] *Roche* v *Peilow* [1986] ILRM 189, per Henchy J. at 197; *Daniels* v *Heskins* [1954] IR 73.

[35] *O'Donovan* v *Cork County Council* [1967] IR 173 at 193, per Walsh J.

would have realised the practice in question was fraught with peril for their client and was readily avoidable or remediable.[36]

12.7 EXPERT WITNESSES

In professional liability cases, the facility to call expert witnesses is an important exception to the general evidentiary rule precluding the reception of opinion testimony. The duty of expert witnesses is to furnish the judge or jury with the necessary scientific criteria for testing the accuracy of their conclusions, so as to enable the judge or jury to form their own independent judgment by the application of these criteria to the facts proved in evidence. Whilst some degree of consultation between experts and legal advisers is entirely proper, it is necessary that expert evidence to the court should be, and should be seen to be, the independent product of the expert, uninfluenced as to form and content by the exigencies of litigation.[37] The extent of the legal duty in any given situation is a question of law for the court but if there is a practice in a particular profession or some accepted standard of conduct, evidence of that can be given. The courts are however reluctant to accept evidence which amounts to no more than an expression of opinion by a particular professional of what they would have done had they been placed in the position of the defendant. "That is the very question which it is the court's function to decide."[38] The attitude of the Irish courts to expert testimony was expressed by Finlay C. J. in *Best* v *Wellcome Foundation*[39]:

> It is not possible for a trial judge or an Appellate Court to take on the role of a determining scientific authority resolving disputes between distinguished scientists in any particular line of technical expertise. The function which a court can and must perform in the trial of a case in order to acquire a just result is to apply common sense and a careful understanding of the logical and likelihood of events to conflicting opinions and conflicting theories.

---

[36] *Roche* above per Henchy J. at 197.

[37] *Whitehouse* v *Jordan* [1981] 1 WLR 247 per Lord Wilberforce.

[38] *Midland Bank Trust* v *Hett, Stubbs & Kemp* [1978] 3 All ER 571, cited with approval by Barron J. in *McMullen* v *Farrell* Unreported High Court, 18 February 1992.

[39] *Best* v *Wellcome Foundation* [1993] 3 IR 431 at 462.

12.8 PROFESSIONAL INDEMNITY INSURANCE

Claims against professional firms or individuals for professional negligence do not generally arise from accidental injury or damage to
property in circumstances which would bring them within the scope
of the usual form of public liability policy. Public liability policies,
where issued to professionals, generally exclude treatment risks and
liability arising out of advice, design specification or the provision of
services. Professional Indemnity or "Errors and Omissions" policies
have therefore been developed to provide protection to professionals
in respect of their exposure to claims from clients and third parties,
in contract and in tort, arising out of breach of professional duty. As
with most other classes of liability insurance there is no standard
form of wording in general use. The insuring clauses of professional
indemnity policies vary enormously as between insurers and the different professions. Some of the more common wordings are:

> . . . indemnity for any sum which the insured may become le-
> gally liable to pay arising from any claim . . . as a direct result
> of negligence on the part of the insured in the conduct and exe-
> cution of the professional activities and duties specified. . .

> . . . indemnity in respect of legal liability for damages and
> claimants costs and expenses . . . in respect of any claim for
> breach of duty in connection with the business of the insured
> . . . arising from any act, neglect, error or omission. . . .

> Indemnity against liability at law for damages and claimants
> costs and expenses in respect of claims arising out of the con-
> duct of the business . . . for breach of professional duty by rea-
> son of any neglect error or omission occurring or committed in
> good faith by the insured. . . .

In *Wimpey* v *Poole*[40] the court held that a professional indemnity policy did not necessarily only cover negligence; the primary insuring
words were to be given their literal meaning and construed so as to
include any omission or error without negligence but not every loss
caused by an omission or error was recoverable under the policy.[41]

---

[40] [1984] 2 Lloyds Rep 499.

[41] ". . . In the first place . . . it must not be a deliberate error or omission", per
Webster J. at 514.

Whether the act, error or omission giving rise to the claim constitutes negligence, or a breach of contract, it would appear that, irrespective of the form of wording used, the courts will find that the professional indemnity policy should operate so as to provide an indemnity. In *Rohan Construction Ltd.* v *Insurance Corporation of Ireland plc.*[42] the Supreme Court found it difficult to see how the fact that the same act amounted to both a tort and a breach of contract could enable insurers to avoid liability under a Professional Indemnity Policy on the basis that it was a mixed claim:

> . . . if that were the true legal position, such a policy would be of little avail to a professional man . . . as the same act of negligence causing damage to the client is almost invariably a breach of contract also. . . .[43]

12.9 "CLAIMS MADE" BASIS

All professional indemnity policies are issued on a "claims made" basis covering only claims first made against the insured and notified to the insurers during the period of insurance. Provided the claim is made against the insured during the period of the insurance it should not matter when the act of negligence giving rise to the claim occurred. However, most insurers now insert a retroactive date in their policies and indemnity will only be provided in respect of claims notified during the period of insurance and which arise out of incidents arising subsequent to the retroactive date stated in the policy. It is usual for the policy to cover not only the negligence of the insured but also the predecessors in the business or any person at any time employed by the insured or such predecessors. Most professional firms are organised in the form of partnerships and the policy will usually cover the individual partners as well as the firm itself and any new partners appointed during the currency of the policy. The partners in the firm may still have a liability for the negligence of previous partners and the policy will normally provide indemnity to the partner-

---

[42] [1986] ILRM 419 HC; [1988] ILRM 373 SC, per Griffin J. with Finlay C. J. and Hederman J. concurring.

[43] ibid per Griffin J. referring also to *Finlay* v *Murtagh* [1979] IR 249.

ship and the individual partners in respect of negligence which occurred before previous partners retired.[44]

12.10 LIMIT OF INDEMNITY

The limit of indemnity is usually an aggregate limit for any one period of insurance rather than a limit per occurrence or event. Payment of a claim reduces the limit available for the remainder of the
policy period. It is usual for the policy to include claimants' costs and
expenses in the indemnity provided, but the limit of indemnity available is inclusive of such costs. Some insurers cover such costs in addition to the indemnity limit but include a clause limiting their liability for such costs to a proportionate amount where the amount paid
in settlement of the claim exceeds the indemnity limit.

12.11 POLICY EXCLUSIONS

A professional indemnity policy will usually exclude those risks more
properly the subject of other liability policies:

- the ownership, possession or use by or on behalf of the insured of
  any land, buildings, aircraft, watercraft, vessel or mechanically
  propelled vehicle;

- liability arising out of a contract of employment with the insured;

- death of or bodily injury, illness or disease to any person or damage to any property which does not arise out of any advice, design
  service specification, report or research;

- any liability assumed by the insured under any warranty, agreement or guarantee which would otherwise attach;

- the manufacture or supply of any product by or on behalf of the
  insured.

---

[44] In *Jenkins* v *Deane* [1933] 47 Lloyds Rep 342, it was held that the admission of
a new partner could not relieve the insurers of liability to indemnify the original
partners.

12.12 FRAUD AND DISHONESTY

It is not the intention or purpose of a professional indemnity policy to indemnify the insured in respect of liability incurred by them as a result of their own fraud or dishonesty.[45] All policies therefore exclude liability arising out of deliberate acts of the insured. In *Goddard & Smith* v *Frew*,[46] where a client of the insured lost money as a result of embezzlement by an employee of the insured, it was held that the proximate cause of the loss was the fraudulent act of the employee and that the loss was not covered by the professional indemnity policy. The loss was not due to any negligent act, error or omission of the insured. In *West Wake Price & Co.* v *Ching*,[47] it was held that a policy providing indemnity in respect of "any act of neglect, default or error on the part of the insured" covered negligence only and not loss incurred as a result of the dishonesty of an employee of the insured. In *Simon Warrender Ltd.* v *Swain*,[48] where an employee of an insurance broker deliberately failed to arrange cover for a client's property, and then falsely represented that it had been arranged, the court held the employer liable to the client on "some form of neglect" rather than on any vicarious liability for a deliberate default by the employee. Some insurers do provide indemnity in respect of the insured's legal liability arising out of any dishonest or fraudulent act or omission of any employee of the insured, but do not indemnify the person committing or condoning the act. Most insurers will provide the cover on request. Some insurers will also cover, under a professional indemnity policy, loss of money or property of the insured, due to fraud or dishonesty of employees, but the risk is more properly the subject of a fidelity policy.

12.13 POLICY CONDITIONS

The conditions in a professional indemnity policy generally follow the lines of most liability policies, but with one significant exception. All professionals wish to avoid adverse publicity arising out of defence in

---

[45] *Hazeldene* v *Hosken* [1933] 1 KB 822.

[46] *Goddard & Smith* v *Frew* [1939] 4 All ER 358.

[47] *West Wake Price & Co.* v *Ching* [1957] 1 WLR 45.

[48] *Simon Warrender Ltd.* v *Swain* [1960] 2 Lloyds Rep 111.

public of a claim for professional negligence. A conflict of interest can therefore arise where an insurer wishes to defend an action and the insured is anxious to settle with the third party. To avoid such difficulties, professional indemnity policies contain what is known as a Senior Counsel clause which requires that the insured shall, in the event of a claim, give all such assistance as the insurer may require, but shall not be required to contest any legal proceedings unless a Senior Counsel shall advise that such proceedings should be contested with the possibility of success. The clause was referred to by Keane J. in the High Court in *Rohan Construction Ltd.* v *Insurance Corporation of Ireland plc.*[49] and was seen by him as a very strong indication of the kind of liability intended to be covered by the policy. He recognised that:

> ... in the case of persons in positions of individual professional and managerial responsibility, the effect of litigation on their reputations may from their point of view be an extremely important factor in determining whether a particular action should be compromised.

Where insurers do not put the clause into operation they cannot complain if the insured settles a third party claim.[50]

12.14 EXTENSIONS OF COVER

Where the cover is not already provided within the policy, most insurers will extend cover to include:

- breach of warranty of authority committed in faith.

- indemnity in respect of costs and expenses incurred in replacing or restoring documents which are lost destroyed or damaged during the period of insurance.

- libel and slander committed in good faith.

- infringement of copyright, patent, trademark or design rights committed in good faith.

---

[49] *Rohan Construction Ltd.* v *Insurance Corporation of Ireland plc.* [1986] ILRM 419.
[50] *Simon, Haynes, Barlas & Ireland* v *Beer* [1945] 78 Lloyds Rep 337.

CHAPTER THIRTEEN

EMPLOYERS' LIABILITY

13.1 THE DEVELOPMENT OF EMPLOYEE PROTECTION

In 1824, in *Priestly* v *Fowler*,[1] the defence of "common employment"[2] was pleaded to deny the employee plaintiff compensation for the injuries which he sustained at work, and he ended up in a debtors' prison because he could not pay the legal costs incurred by his employer in defending the action. Since then, the law on employers' liability has developed into a system of litigious confrontation between employer and employee, over work-related accidents and industrial disease, which appears to employers to be biased in favour of the protection and compensation of the employee. At common law, an employer has always owed a duty of care to employees to exercise reasonable care for their safety arising out of and in the course of their employment. The industrial revolution brought about an increase in the use of industrial machinery and industrial processes which exposed employees to increased risk of injury and disease. The number of claims by employees against employers increased but the law tended to support the view that, whilst industry was admittedly dangerous, it was socially beneficial. It provided the employer with defences based on concepts of implied contractual terms,[3] absence of a legal duty of care,[4] contributory negligence,[5] common employment[6]

---

[1] [1837] 150 ER 1030.

[2] "The most nefarious judicial ploy for reducing the charge on industry", from Friedman and Ladinskey, "Social Change and the Law of Industrial Accidents", 67 Columbia Law Review, (1967) 50 at 63.

[3] The law was slow to impose liability on the employer for injuries sustained by employees in the course of employment on the basis that the employee could look after his own interests.

[4] *Potts* v *Plunkett* [1859] QB 91 CLR 290.

and voluntary assumption of risk.[7] In addition, the sanction of having to pay costs of an unsuccessful action limited the number of claims brought against employers. Towards the end of the nineteenth century the situation began to change with the growth of the trade union movement. Legislation was introduced to deal with dangerous machinery and provide workers and their dependants with specific rights against employers.[8] A state system of compensation for occupational injuries was introduced in the Workmen's Compensation Act, 1897 and developed in subsequent legislation[9] until finally being absorbed into the Social Welfare system.[10] The Social Welfare legislation does not deprive the injured employee of a right of action in tort against the employer[11] but it was thought that the introduction of a state administered system of compensation would reduce the number of tort actions arising out of industrial injuries.

---

[5] *Guckian* v *Cully*, Unreported Supreme Court, 9 March 1972; *McKeever* v *Dundalk Linen Co.* Unreported Supreme Court, 1966.

[6] *Priestly* v *Fowler* [1837] 150 ER 1030; *Hutchinson* v *York, Newcastle and Berwick Railway Co.* [1950] 155 ER 150

[7] *Flynn* v *Irish Sugar Manufacturing Co.* [1928] IR 525.

[8] Efforts were made to improve industrial safety with the appointment of Factory Inspectors in 1833 to enforce the legislation dealing with dangerous machinery, such as the Threshing Machines Act, 1832. A Factories Act was passed in 1901 giving workers more general protection.

[9] Workmen's Compensation Acts, 1906, 1934, 1953 (Amendment) Act.

[10] Social Welfare (Occupational Injuries) Act, 1966; Social Welfare (Consolidation) Act, 1981. Under this legislation, all employees over sixteen years of age must be covered by pay-related social insurance regardless of their earnings. Contributions are levied on employers and employees and specified benefits are paid out by the state in the event of disability including disability due to injury or disease arising out of occupational accidents or industrial disease. The scheme of compensation operates on a basis which does not require proof of fault but the level of benefits provides partial compensation only.

[11] Section 6(1) of the Workmen's Compensation (Amendment) Act, 1953 provided that an injured workman who had accepted compensation under the Workmen's Compensation legislation could maintain a common-law action in respect of their injury; *O'Brien* v *Manufacturing Engineering Co. Ltd.* [1973] IR 334.

13.2 SAFETY STANDARDS

Legislation has been enacted[12] laying down a common set of safety standards for all places of work in the form of general principles requiring the employer to protect the safety, health and welfare of the people who work for them. A National Authority for Occupational Safety and Health has been established with the power to prosecute an employer, direct improvement in safety standards or close down any workplace where it is considered there is a danger to safety or health.[13] The Single European Act inserted a specific provision on occupational safety and health[14] into the EU Treaty, and since then the Council of Ministers has sought to lay down a comprehensive set of safety rules for all member states.[15] However these attempts at harmonisation of safety standards have done nothing to harmonise the levels of compensation available under the different national legal systems. Damages for personal injuries are higher in Ireland than in most other EU countries[16] and have remained high despite the abolition of juries in personal injury actions in 1988. The Irish workforce is keenly aware of compensation possibilities and this awareness has been furthered by the publicity which surrounds large compensatory

---

[12] Safety, Health and Welfare at Work Act, 1989 and regulations made under it such as Safety, Health and Welfare at Work (General Applications) Regulations, 1993; Safety, Health and Welfare at Work (Construction) Regulations, 1995; Safety, Health and Welfare at Work (Protection from Biological Agents) Regulations, 1995; EC Protection of Workers (Noise) Regulations, 1990; EC Protection of Workers (Exposure to Lead) Regulations, 1993.

[13] Sections 35, 36, 37, of the Safety, Health and Welfare at Work Act, 1989.

[14] Article 118A.

[15] The Council of Ministers attempted to establish a comprehensive set of common rules for all member states as part of the Social Dimension to the Single Market. Directive 89/39/EEC was introduced as a general framework directive, followed by a series of directives dealing with individual aspects of industrial safety. The first six of these Directives were implemented in Ireland by the Safety, Health and Welfare at Work (General Application) Regulations, 1993 (SI No. 44 of 1993).

[16] *Personal Injury Awards in EU and EFTA Countries*, by David McIntosh and Marjorie Holmes of Davies Arnold Cooper and published by Lloyd's of London Press 1994. The report claims that in a comparison of awards for pain and suffering in Ireland and other countries, the damages awarded to a 20-year-old Irish female secretary, single with no dependants, for burns and scarring would be almost four times the EU average and more than twice the amount awarded in England.

awards, the relaxation of the rules governing advertising by solicitors and the increased activity of trade unions in industrial accident and disease claims. In addition, old-fashioned ideas of a job for life and company loyalty, which discouraged workers from claiming in respect of non-serious injury, have been replaced by recession, redundancy and discontent. The average Employers' Liability claims cost rose from £8,953 in 1986 to £13,116 in 1994, when total Employers' Liability claims paid by insurers in Ireland amounted to £60 million.[17]

13.3 COMMON LAW DUTY OF CARE

The common law duty of care which an employer owes to an employee is to take reasonable care for the employee's safety in all the circumstances of the case.[18] The liability of the employer is not however an unlimited one and the duty will be discharged if they do what a reasonable and prudent employer would have done in the circumstances.[19] In formulating that test in *Bradley* v *CIE*[20] Henchy J. had gone on to say that even where certain precautions were obviously required in the interests of safety of the worker, there may be countervailing factors which would justify the employer in not taking those precautions. However, in *Daly* v *Avonmore Creameries Ltd.*,[21] McCarthy J. distanced himself from Henchy J., saying that the statement was "not to be taken as supporting the view that where lives are at stake considerations of expense are any more than vaguely material,"[22] and in *Kennedy* v *Hughes Dairy Ltd.*[23] he encroached further on the Henchy dicta in saying that:

---

[17] *Report on Economic Evaluation of Insurance Costs in Ireland*, by Deloitte & Touche, 1996.

[18] *Paris* v *Stepney Borough Council* [1951] AC 367, applied by the Supreme Court in *Dalton* v *Frendo* Unreported Supreme Court, 15 December 1977; *O'Donnell* v *Hannigan*, Unreported, Supreme Court, 19 July 1960; *Burke* v *John Paul & Co. Ltd.* [1967] IR 277.

[19] *Bradley* v *CIE* [1976] IR 217.

[20] ibid.

[21] [1984] IR 131.

[22] ibid. at 147.

[23] [1989] ILRM 117.

> The essential question in all actions of negligence is whether
> or not the person charged has failed to take reasonable care
> whether by act or omission. . . . In actions resulting from inju-
> ries sustained in what may be termed static conditions —
> those prevailing in a particular employment or a particular
> premises or the like — expert evidence may properly point, as
> a primary matter, to the foreseeable risk of injury and the con-
> sequent requirement of special care. The practice of the trade
> or of the occupiers of similar premises may be powerful rebut-
> ting evidence but, in my view, in a changing world, it should
> seldom, if ever, be conclusive.[24]

Finlay C. J., dissenting, favoured the *Bradley* test and held that the
mere fact that a precaution which could be considered necessary to
prevent a different type of accident, would, by coincidence, have also
ameliorated or prevented injury from the accident which occurred,
was not, in his view, a good ground for reaching a conclusion that it
was a precaution which a reasonable and prudent man would consider obviously necessary to provide against the happening of the accident and the injury.[25]

13.4 VARIABLE DUTY OF CARE

The duty of care may vary according to the circumstances and in
particular may vary with the employee's age, knowledge and experience.[26] Risks inherent in the work[27] and the employer's particular ex-

---

[24] ibid. at 122. The plaintiff was employed as a forklift driver at the defendant's
dairy and his work included the preparation of crates of bottled milk for delivery,
and tidying up broken bottles at the end of loading operations. While carrying a
crate he tripped and fell and sustained a cut to his arm when broken glass fell on
him from the crate. The plaintiff claimed he had not been supplied with proper
protective gloves or gauntlets. In the High Court, Blayney J. held the plaintiff
had failed to prove that employers in the same business followed a practice of
providing the appropriate safety equipment. The Supreme Court, applying *Bradley* v *CIE* [1976] IR 217, held that there had been sufficient evidence to enable a
jury to conclude that the absence of the provision of adequate protective gloves by
the defendants could have exposed the plaintiff to unnecessary risks of injury.

[25] ibid. at 119.

[26] *Dalton* v *Frendo*, Unreported Supreme Court, 15 December 1977; *McKeever* v
Dundalk Linen Co. Ltd., Unreported Supreme Court, 26 May 1966; *Luttrell* v
Gouldings Fertilisers (Cork) Ltd. [1969] 103 IRLT 121; *Byrne* v *Jefferson Smurfit
& Son Ltd.* [1962] Ir. Jur. 49; *Barrett* v *Anglo Irish Beef Producers Ltd.* Unre-
ported High Court, 6 March 1989.

perience[28] may also be taken into account. The employer may not be under an obligation to warn the employee of obvious risks, but in *Phillips* v *Dorgan*[29] the Supreme Court held that, in the particular circumstances of the case, there was an obligation in law on the defendant to warn the plaintiffs of the particular risks and hazards, which could reasonably be foreseen, in the type of work he was asking them to carry out, and to provide them either with a means of carrying out the work which was safe, or to issue them a warning regarding the preparations which might be necessary so that they might carry out the work with safety. The defendant had engaged the plaintiffs to carry out cleaning work in the kitchen of a house belonging to the defendant prior to having it painted and decorated. The kitchen of the house was in an extreme state of dirt and filth consisting of years of accumulated grease. While attempting to clean around the cooker area the first plaintiff slipped due to the greasy condition of the floor and a cloth she was holding caught fire on contact with the cooker. In the resulting fire the first plaintiff suffered extensive burns and the second plaintiff was injured in trying to rescue her. Finlay C. J. held that ". . . the law did not acquit the defendant of negligence . . . by reason of the fact that the plaintiffs could see the condition of the premises. . . ."[30] Where an employer fails to remove an unnecessary risk created by him and relies on giving a detailed warning to an employee he may be liable if the employee is injured.[31] In relation to dangerous machinery, instruction and warning, no matter how explicit, cannot be equated to the presence of a physical

---

[27] *Depuis* v *Haulbowline Industries Ltd.* Unreported Supreme Court, 14 February 1962, per Lavery J. at pp. 5–6:

> In this case the employment is of a sort that admittedly has a certain degree of risk. There is risk in the breaking up of ships . . . for scrap. Particularly the use of an oxy-acetylene burner has risks of an infinite variety. It seems to me the jury must accept the evidence that no one better is able to appreciate and deal with the risks than the plaintiff himself.

See also *O'Sullivan* v *Doyle*, Unreported Supreme Court, 30 July 1962.

[28] *Dalton* v *Frendo*, Unreported Supreme Court, 15 December 1977.

[29] *Phillips* v *Dorgan* [1991] ILRM 321 SC.

[30] ibid. at p. 326.

[31] *Swords* v *St Patrick's Copper Mines Ltd.* Unreported Supreme Court, 30 July 1963.

guard.[32] The employer is not required to foresee every risk of injury and is required to exercise reasonable care only.[33]

13.5 GENERAL DUTY OF CARE

The generalised duty of reasonable care can be broken down into the following component parts:[34]

1) To devise, operate and maintain a safe system of work;

2) To provide adequate and safe plant tools and equipment;

3) To provide competent and suitable fellow workers;

4) To provide a safe place of work and safe means of access and egress.

13.5.1 SAFE SYSTEM OF WORK

An employer must exercise reasonable care in devising and operating a safe system of work, and it must be such as to show that, as a reasonable employer, he has had in mind the problems presented by the work to his employees.[35] It is not sufficient for the employer to devise a safe system; he must also operate a safe system.[36] In *Guckian* v *Cully*,[37] the court had no difficulty in finding an unsafe system in operation in a bakery which prohibited the use of timber to push dough through a machine but permitted operatives to press the dough through with their hands. The plaintiff lost the tops of two fingers when his hand went into the machine as he fell from the stool on which he was standing in order to carry out the procedure. Whether a system of work is safe will depend on the particular circumstances of the job in hand.[38] In *Carey* v *Cork Consumers Gas Co.*[39] the plaintiff

---

[32] ibid.

[33] *Kenneally* v *Waterford County Council* [1959] 97 ILTR; *Kinsella* v *Hammond Lane Industries Ltd.* [1958] 96 ILTR SC.

[34] *O'Donnell* v *Hannigan*, Unreported Supreme Court, 19 July 1960; *Dowling* v *CIE* Unreported Supreme Court, 1 March 1956.

[35] *Wilson & Clyde Coal Co.* v *English* [1937] HL; *Kinsella* v *Hammond Lane Industries Ltd.* [1958] 96 ILTR.

[36] *McDermid* v *Nash Dredging Reclamation Co. Ltd.* [1987] AC 906.

[37] *Guckian* v *Cully* Unreported Supreme Court, 9 March 1972.

[38] *Caulfield* v *George Bell & Co. Ltd.* [1958] IR 326.

failed to establish that an unsafe system of work was responsible for him contracting pneumoconiosis through the inhalation of silica dust over a period of years when he was periodically required to demolish silica bricks. The Supreme Court found there was no evidence that the employers ought to have known of the danger to the employee's health. A plaintiff, suing an employer in negligence, grounded on an unsafe system of work, must prove that the system was unsafe, that the employer could have made the system safe and that the employer's failure to make the system safe was the cause of the accident:

> The expression, "a safe system of work" . . . has to be considered in every case, to which it is appropriate, in relation to the particular circumstances of the job in hand. In the expression, the word "safe" means no more than "as safe as is reasonably possible in the circumstances". The degree of safety would depend on the particular job, and would vary between wide limits.[40]

13.5.2 EQUIPMENT

The employer has to provide whatever equipment is necessary for the work to be carried out, unless by trade custom the employee is responsible for providing his own hand tools. In *Burke* v *John Paul & Co. Ltd.*[41] the Supreme Court held that the employer has a duty to take reasonable care to provide proper appliances and to maintain them in a proper condition, and so to carry on his operations as not to subject those employed by him to unnecessary risks. The employer had supplied a steel cutting machine with blunt blades which required the employee to exert extra pressure with consequent damage to his health. In *Deegan* v *Langan*,[42] the employer supplied the employee carpenter with nails which he knew were liable to disintegrate and was consequently liable for the injury sustained by the plaintiff. The employer may also be liable for failure to provide equipment es-

---

[39] Unreported Supreme Court, 5 March 1958.

[40] per Murnaghan J. in *Caulfield* v *Bell & Co. Ltd.* [1958] IR 326 at p. 333, 334.

[41] [1967] IR 277 at 281 per Budd J. quoting from *Smith* v *Baker & Sons* [1891] AC 325.

[42] [1966] IR 373.

sential to the safety of the employee in carrying out the work[43] and for the failure to maintain equipment in a safe condition.[44] While he has a duty to provide equipment which is safe, he is not at common law strictly liable for defects in the equipment not discoverable by reasonable examination.[45] In *Dowling* v *CIE*,[46] the Supreme Court recognised that the "duty is not a warranty but only a duty to exercise all reasonable care".

13.5.3 FELLOW EMPLOYEES

The employer has a duty to engage employees who are competent, and if he fails to do so, and an employee is injured due to the negligence of another employee, the employer will be liable to the injured employee. The defence of "common employment", established in *Priestly* v *Fowler*[47] and which provided that an employer was not liable for injury caused by one employee to another, was abolished in Ireland by the Law Reform (Personal Injuries) Act, 1958. The distinction between the personal liability of the employer to use due care to select proper and competent fellow employees[48] and the vicarious liability of the employer for the torts of his employees has been eroded by the courts presuming that the employer has control over his employees and is therefore culpable for their misdemeanours. In *Phelan* v *Coillte Teoranta*,[49] the plaintiff was injured by a co-worker repairing forestry machinery. On ordinary principles, the negligent co-worker would be regarded as an independent contractor in as much as he provided his own tools, he was paid by commission, no PAYE returns were made by the defendant and under contract he and the defendant had agreed his status was that of an independent contractor and not an employee. The defendant would not have been liable for the negligence of a non-employee, but Barr J. ignored the

---

[43] *O'Hanlon* v *ESB* [1969] IR 75 SC; *Gahan* v *Engineering Products Ltd.* [1971] IR 30 SC; *McKinney* v *Irish N.W. Railway Co.* [1868] IR 2 CL 600.

[44] *Simpson* v *Pollard* Unreported Supreme Court, 6 April 1967.

[45] *Davey* v *New Merton Board Mills* [1959] AC 604; *Keenan* v *Bergin* [1971] IR 192 SC; *Flynn* v *Irish Sugar Manufacturing Co.* [1928] IR 525.

[46] Unreported Supreme Court, 1 March 1956, per Kingsmill-Moore J. at p. 11.

[47] [1837] 150 ER 1030.

[48] *Skerritt* v *Scallan* [1877] IR 11 CL 389; *Murphy* v *Ross* [1920] 2 IR 199.

[49] [1993] IR 18.

indicia of an independent contractor and recognised that both parties to employment often arrange for a worker to be labelled a non-employee out of economic convenience:

> . . . it seems to me that where an employer and a full-time employee decide to structure their relationship in such a way that it is most cost-effective for both. . . . it would be quite un-real and also unjust for a court to hold in such circumstances that the rights of an injured third party against the employer would be thereby fundamentally altered to such an extent as to render the employer free from vicarious liability which other-wise he would have had for the negligence of his employee.[50]

Where an employer discovers that an employee is incompetent but continues to employ him in work beyond his capabilities he will be liable for any injuries inflicted on fellow employees due to that incompetence.[51]

13.5.4 SAFE PLACE OF WORK

The employer has a duty to take reasonable care that the place where his employees are required to work is safe and he must provide a safe means of access and egress.[52] If there are defects and they are known or ought reasonably to be known to the employer, then he must remedy them. He has a duty to make the premises as safe as reasonable care and skill could make them.[53] In *Christie* v *Odeon (Ireland) Ltd.*[54] Kingsmill-Moore J. suggested that "to make accidents impossible would often be to make work impossible", but if an employer offers without distinction a number of modes of access all of which, except one, are safe, he will not be relieved of liability because a workman

---

[50] ibid.at p. 24. The decision would appear to have been based on the broad stand-point of justice and implies that the plaintiff had a legitimate expectation of having judgment satisfied in extracting compensation from the defendant who could best pay.

[51] *Hudson* v *Ridge Manufacturing Co.* [1957] 2 QB 348.

[52] *Gallagher* v *Mogul Ireland Ltd.* [1975] IR 204 SC.

[53] *Kirwan* v *National Children's Hospital*, Unreported Supreme Court, 10 May 1963, where Walsh J. at p. 3 referred to the duty "to make the premises as safe as reasonable care and skill could make them".

[54] [1956] 91 ILTR 25 at 29.

happens to choose to use the one which is unsafe.[55] His duty is, not to see that some modes of access are safe, but that all of them are safe.[56] Where the employer sends an employee to work on another person's property, the employer would appear to a large extent to be relieved of liability for injuries caused by or arising out of defects in the property unless he has been warned of unusual dangers to which the employee might be exposed. In such circumstances the occupier of the site would appear to be responsible.[57]

13.6 STATUTORY DUTY OF CARE

13.6.1 The relationship between an employer and his employee imposes duties on the employer both at common law and by statute whereby the employee is protected against the negligence or breach of statutory duty of the employer. If such a duty is breached and it causes personal injury to the employee, he has a right to claim damages against the employer. The breach of statutory duty owed to the employee may involve the employer in criminal proceedings under safety legislation, but the converse does not apply unless it can be shown that the particular statute creating the criminal offence, either by virtue of its express provisions or by necessary implication, creates civil liability.

13.6.2 To ground an action for compensation for breach of statutory duty, a plaintiff must establish that the defendant owes him a duty under statute, and if the statute seeks to protect a specific class of person the plaintiff must bring himself within that class. In addition he must prove that the injury sustained was of a kind that the Act seeks to prevent. In *Nicholls* v *Austin (Leyton) Ltd.*[58] the House of Lords held that the defendants were not guilty of any breach of statutory duty, since the obligation to fence machinery imposed by Section 14(1) of the Factories Act, 1937 was an obligation to guard against

---

[55] *Kielthy* v *Ascon Ltd.* [1970] IR 122. On the distinction between the place of work and access to the place of work, see *Cavanagh* v *Ulster Weaving Co. Ltd.* [1959] 2 All ER 745.

[56] ibid. per O'Dalaigh C. J. at 129.

[57] *Cooney* v *Dockerell & Co.* [1965] Ir. Jur. Rep. 31.

[58] [1946] AC 493.

contact with any dangerous part of the machine and not to guard against dangerous materials ejected from it.

13.6.3 In *Young* v *Charles Church (Southern) Ltd. and Another*,[59] a labourer who witnessed the electrocution of a fellow employee working next to him was held to be entitled to recover damages for breach of statutory duty for psychiatric illness, sustained as a result of what he saw. The relevant statutory regulations[60] provided:

> Where any electrically charged overhead cable or apparatus is liable to be a source of danger to persons employed during the course of any operations or works to which these regulations apply . . . all practicable precautions shall be taken to prevent such danger. . . .

The defendant employer admitted breach of the regulation in respect of the employee who was killed, but denied they were in breach in relation to the plaintiff, since he was not injured by electrocution. They argued that the injury he allegedly sustained, i.e. psychiatric injury, was not of a type or inflicted in a manner which the statute was intended to prevent. The Court of Appeal, in reversing the High Court decision, held that the defendants were liable for damages in negligence at common law, and in breach of statutory duty. The court held that the statute was intended to give protection to employees from the kinds of injury which could be foreseen as likely to occur where the electrical cable or equipment was allowed to become a source of danger to employees. That included mental illness caused by the shock of seeing a workmate electrocuted so close to him, in circumstances where the employee had been fortunate to avoid electrocution.

13.6.4 Prior to 1989, the statutory duties owed by an employer to an employee were contained in a maze of legislation and regulations too

---

[59] Unreported Court of Appeal, 24 April 1997.

[60] Regulation 44(2) of the Construction (General Provisions) Regulations (SI 1961/1580).

categorical and technical to be effective.[61] The most important pieces of legislation were the Factories Act, 1955, and the Safety in Industry Act, 1955 as amended by the Safety in Industry Act, 1980. The sanctions contained in these acts were primarily penal but breach of the provisions of the acts gave rise to a civil action for damages for personal injury at the suit of the injured employee. Barron J. in *Dunleavy* v *Glen Abbey Ltd.*[62] accepted that breach of statutory duties imposed by the pre-1989 legislation gave rise to rights of action, provided that the breach of duty was a causative factor in the injury sustained by the employee. A breach of regulations having been established ". . . the question of liability at common law does not have to be determined".[63]

13.7 SAFETY, HEALTH AND WELFARE AT WORK ACT, 1989

13.7.1 SCOPE OF THE ACT

The Barrington Commission established in 1980 produced a unanimous report[64] which formed the blueprint for the Safety, Health and Welfare at Work Act, 1989. The Act represents a comprehensive reform of occupational safety and health law and abandons the excessive reliance on detailed legal regulation, which characterised pre-existing safety legislation, in favour of general framework legislation applicable to all places of work. The aim of the Act is to develop a preventative approach to safety and health at work based on an identification of hazards and the preventive measures necessary. The

---

[61] The Barrington Report (1982) identified 20 statutes and approximately 200 regulations. It estimated that only 20 per cent of the workforce was covered by safety legislation and was of the view that only the most serious infractions were reported to the Department of Labour. The significant volume of pre-1989 legislation is set out in Part 1 of the Second schedule to the Safety, Health and Welfare at Work Act, 1989.

[62] [1992] ILRM 1.

[63] ibid. at 5; confirmed in *Johnson* v *Callow* [1971] AC 335 at 342 per Lord Hailsham: ". . . a breach of the provisions of the code has been held to give rise to a civil action in damages for personal injury at the suit of the injured workman. . . . It is clearly the law now."

[64] Report of the Commission of Inquiry on Health and Welfare at Work (PL 1868). The commission was chaired by Mr Justice Barrington and the report now referred to as the Barrington Report.

Act covers all persons in employment, as well as the self-employed
and persons who may be affected by work activities.[65] Pre-existing
legislation is continued in force but with the intention that it will,
over a period of time, be replaced by Regulations under the 1989 Act
which will apply to all places of work.[66]

13.7.2 "REASONABLY PRACTICABLE"

Part 11 of the Act covers the general duties of employers to employees. Section 6(1) provides that it shall be the duty of every employer
to ensure, so far as is reasonably practicable, the safety, health and
welfare at work of all his employees and Sub-section (2) sets out,
without prejudice to the generality of the employer's duty under 6(1),
the matters to which that duty extends. The extent of the employer's
duty under the Act is qualified by the use of the words "as is reasonably practicable". "Practicable" is accepted as meaning in effect
technologically possible, while "reasonably practicable" is interpreted
to mean a level of precaution which takes account of the balance between the risk involved in a particular situation and the cost of remedying it.[67] This qualification of the statutory duty provides the judiciary with the means to develop the legislation in the light of social and
political necessities. The "reasonably practicable" test is not significantly different to that already established by the courts in determining the employer's common law duty of care based on negligence.[68]

---

[65] For example, members of the public in the immediate vicinity and other workers nearby.

[66] The 1991 Control of Specific Substances and Activities Regulations (SI no. 285
of 1991) repealed 1972 regulations which applied to factories and introduced
measures for all places of work.

[67] An obligation to do something "so far as is reasonably practicable" means that a
precaution must be taken if the cost is relatively low by comparison with the risk
involved but if the cost involved is very high and the risk can be measured as
extremely low an employer on whom the duty is imposed will have committed no
wrong by failing to take the relevant precaution, even though it may be technologically possible; per the Minister for Labour in the Seanad Debate on the 1989
Act, (122 Seanad Debates Col. 809) quoting from *Redgrave's Health and Safety in
Factories*, 2nd edition, Butterworths, 1982.

[68] *Edwards* v *National Coal Board* [1949] 1 KB 704, at 712; *Kirwan* v *Bray UDC*
Unreported Supreme Court, 30 July 1969; *Bradley* v *CIE* [1976] IR 217; *Brady* v
Beckman Instruments Inc. [1986] ILRM 361; *Keane* v *ESB* [1981] IR 44.

13.7.3 DUTY OF CARE UNDER THE ACT

The specific matters described in Section 6 Subsection (2) to which the employer must advert in relation to the general duty of care correspond broadly with the employer's common law duty of care:

a) the design, provision and maintenance of any place of work under the employer's control in a condition that is, so far as is reasonably practicable, safe and without risk to health;

b) the design, provision and maintenance of a safe means of egress and access to any place of work;

c) the design, provision and maintenance of plant and machinery;

d) the provision of systems of work that are planned, organised, performed and maintained so as to be safe and without risk to health;

e) the provision of information, instruction, training and supervision to ensure the safety and health of employees;

f) the provision of and maintenance of such suitable protective clothing or equipment as is necessary;

g) the preparation of adequate emergency plans;

h) to ensure safety and prevention of risk to health at work in connection with the use of any article or substance;

i) the provision and the maintenance of facilities and arrangements for the welfare of the employees at work;

j) obtaining the services of a competent person for the purpose of ensuring the safety and health of employees.

13.7.4 CAUSE OF ACTION

Whereas breach of statutory duty, under the pre-1989 legislation, could ground an action for damages, provided the breach of duty was a causative factor in an injury sustained at work, Section 60 of the 1989 Act excludes breach of the general duties in Section 6 from creating a cause of action.[69] This is not of great import, however, as the general duties reflect common law duties to a great extent and are

---

[69] Section 60 also applies to Sections 7 to 11 of the Act.

unlikely to adversely affect claims in respect of personal injuries. According to Barron J.:

> The whole tenor of the legislation contained in the 1989 Act is to ensure that thought is given to work situations so that dangers from carelessness or from failure to give any thought to a particular danger may be eliminated. Even though the provisions contained in Sections 6 to 11 of Part II of the Act do not by virtue of Section 60 confer any right of action in civil proceedings, an employer cannot escape liability for failure to consider possible dangers merely because the employee can meet the same problem in her ordinary life where she must deal with them herself.[70]

13.7.5 SAFETY STATEMENT

Section 12 of the Act requires the employer to prepare a safety statement identifying the hazards and an assessment of the risks to safety and health at the place of work. The Section does not come within the provisions of Section 60 and failure to comply with the provisions requiring the preparation of a safety statement could be cognisable in criminal proceedings under the Act and also in civil proceedings. Barrington J. was of the opinion that a poorly crafted safety statement might indicate negligence by an employer in the context of a personal injuries claim.[71] In *Mullen* v *Vernal Investments Ltd.*[72] the plaintiff, who was required to buy goods in Dublin for sale in her section of the defendant's business in County Carlow, allegedly sustained injury in carrying the goods to her car. She alleged the goods were too heavy for her to carry and relied on the provisions of Section 12 of the Act to ground her action. It was admitted that there was no safety statement prepared and the court expressed the view that none was required by the circumstances of the case. However, the fact that a statement is not required does not absolve an employer from a common law duty to give consideration to the health and safety of employees who in the course of their employment have to leave their main place of work to carry out their duties elsewhere.[73]

---

[70] *Mullen* v *Vernal Investments Ltd*. Unreported High Court, 15 December 1995.

[71] p. 65 of the Barrington report, n. 64 *supra*.

[72] Unreported High Court, 15 December 1995.

[73] ibid. at pp. 3–4 of the judgment.

13.7.6 DUTY OF EMPLOYEES

Section 9 of the Act deals with the general duties of employees and provides:

1) that it shall be the duty of every employee while at work:

   a) to take reasonable care for his own safety and that of any other person who may be affected by his acts or omissions;

   b) to co-operate with his employer so as to enable him comply with relevant statutory provisions;

   c) to properly use protective clothing and equipment provided;

   d) to report, without delay, any defects in plant, equipment, place of work or system of work, which might endanger safety, of which he becomes aware;

2) No person shall intentionally or recklessly interfere with or mis-use any appliance, protective clothing, convenience, equipment or other means or thing provided for securing the safety, health or welfare of persons arising out of work activities.

The Act repeals a number of provisions in pre-1989 legislation dealing with the statutory duties of employees, which were cognisable in criminal as well as civil proceedings.[74] By reason of Section 60 of the 1989 Act, breach of the duties set out in Section 9 may give rise to criminal proceedings only. It is possible that, in consequence, an employer under a statutory duty cognisable in a civil claim may not be able to plead breach of duty by the employee if it was a duty owed under a provision of the Safety in Industry Acts 1955 and 1980 which have been repealed by the 1989 Act. The employee may, depending on the circumstances, be under a common law duty, breach of which the employer can plead as a factor towards establishing contributory negligence.[75] The employee is obliged to report known defects in

---

[74] Section 4(1)(b) repeals Section 125(1) of the Factories Act, 1955, Section 46 of the Office Premises Act, 1958, Section 65(1) of the Dangerous Substances Act, 1972, and Sections 15(1) and (2) of the Safety Health and Welfare (Offshore Installations) Act, 1987 from the coming into operation of Section 9 of the Act. Section 125(1) of the 1955 Act had already been amended by the Safety in Industry Act, 1980 and the 1987 Act had not been brought into force when the 1989 Act was passed.

[75] For the distinction between Common Law contributory negligence and Statutory negligence, see *Kennedy* v *East Cork Foods Ltd.* [1973] IR 244.

plant, equipment or systems of work but failure to report such defects in breach of the statutory obligation may not, by reason of Section 60(1)(a) be cited as such by the employer in defending a claim for damages brought by the employee. Failure to report a known defect could be cited as disregard for one's own safety, depending on the circumstances, and could be claimed as a contributing factor to the injury sustained.[76]

13.7.7 SCOPE OF STATUTORY DUTY

Implementation of the 1993 Safety, Health and Welfare at Work (General Application) Regulations extended the basis for claiming breach of statutory duty in work-related injury claims. The scope of the Regulations is such that claims for breach of statutory duty are no longer confined to "industrial" accidents but can now arise from accidents in shops, offices, schools, the agricultural arena and the public and private service sectors. The Regulations implemented seven separate EU directives on safety and health at work[77] and introduced new requirements on three other topics.[78] The Regulations do not repeal or revoke any previous acts or regulations but there is provision for the making of a repeal order under the 1989 Act. A feature of the regulations is that they appear to create strict and sometimes absolute duties by the use of phrases such as "there shall be provided" without the statutory limitation of "in so far as is reasonably practicable" or "as far as possible". However, since the regulations are made under the 1989 Act, which makes liberal use of the phrase "so far as is practicable", it is arguable that the Regulations, while creating strict liability, do not impose absolute liability in all cases.[79]

---

[76] *Deegan* v *Langan* [1966] IR 373 is indicative of the difficulty in establishing contributory negligence.

[77] 1989 Framework directive (89/391/EEC); 1991 Directive on Safety and Health of Fixed Duration and Temporary Employees (91/383/EEC); 1989 Directive on the Workplace (89/654/EEC); 1989 Directive on Work Equipment (89/655/EEC); 1990 Directive on Handling of Goods (89/269/EEC); 1989 Directive on Personal Protective Equipment (89/656/EEC); 1990 Directive on Visual Display Screens (90/270/EEC).

[78] New requirements concerning use of electricity at work, the provision of first-aid at work and the notification of accidents.

[79] See "The Extension of the Scope of Breach of Statutory Duty for Accidents at Work", Binchy and Byrne, *Irish Law Times*, Jan/Feb 1995.

The Regulations which deal with safety and health requirements in relation to the workplace, equipment, protective equipment, load handling, display screen equipment, use of electricity, first aid and accident notification are likely to be relied on in work related personal injury claims to a far greater extent than pre-existing safety legislation.

13.8 GENERAL DEFENCES

13.8.1 COMMON EMPLOYMENT

The defence of "common employment", whereby an employer could avoid liability for injuries sustained by an employee due to the negligence of another employee,[80] was abolished in Ireland by the Law Reform Personal Injuries Act, 1958. The law now imposes on an employer liability for the negligent acts or omissions of his employees which arise out of or are within the scope of the employee's employment. This concept of vicarious liability has been used to develop and support the "deep pocket" theory that the person who creates the risk or the enterprise which benefits from the activity causing the damage are generally in the best position to absorb the cost through liability insurance.[81] The employer is presumed to exercise control over his employees and to have the capacity to remedy defects in work practices and equipment. The concept of control is a critical test in determining vicarious liability[82] but in relation to the vicarious liability of an employer, Barr J., in *Phelan* v *Coillte*,[83] said that it was the "control exercisable rather than the control factually exercised" which was critical. For the employer to be liable, it must be shown that the

---

[80] *Priestly* v *Fowler* [1837] 150 ER 1030; *Lancaster* v *LPTB* [1948] 2 All ER 796; *Groves* v *Wimborne* [1898] 2 QB 402; *Doyle* v *Flemings Coal Mines Ltd.* Unreported Supreme Court, 29 July 1955.

[81] *Phelan* v *Coillte Teo.* [1993] 1 IR 18.

[82] *Moynihan* v *Moynihan* [1975] IR 192

[83] *supra* at pp. 22–23 referring to *Roche* v *P. Kelly & Co. Ltd.* [1969] IR 100; *Walshe* v *Bailieboro Co-operative Agricultural & Dairy Society Ltd.* [1939] Ir. Jur. Rep. 77; *O'Coinndealbhain* v *Mooney* [1990] 1 IR 422; *Market Investigations Ltd.* v *Minister of Social Security and Pensions* [1969] 2 QB 173 and *Ready Mixed Concrete* v *Minister of Pensions and National Insurance* [1968] 2 QB 497.

employer had the power to control the way or the method in which the negligent act of the employee was done.[84]

13.8.2 SCOPE OF EMPLOYMENT

An employer will avoid liability if he can show that (a) the negligent person was not an employee for whose negligence he was liable or (b) that the negligence did not arise within the scope of employment. For the purpose of establishing vicarious liability, the term "employee" includes not only the employer's regular workforce but any person doing work for him. The existence of a relationship of employer and employee or master and servant, is a conclusion of law dependent on the rights conferred and the duties imposed on the parties. The method of pay, the right to select or dismiss, the provision of equipment, and the degree of skill possessed are all features to be taken into account but the element of control is the most important, if not the critical, factor in determining the relationship and liability.[85] Where the relationship of employer and employee or master and servant is established the liability of the employer is limited to liability for negligent acts or omissions within the scope of the employee's employment. It is difficult to define what is meant by "scope of employment" as the phrase is interpreted on a case-by-case basis according to the judicial perception of social justice. A car salesman taking two women for a "spin" at 7pm on a Saturday night was held to be acting within the scope of his employment[86] but a commercial traveller, required to use his best endeavours to effect the sale of the goods of the company, was held to be acting outside the scope of his employment when involved in an accident in the company's car, conveying employees of a client company home from a social occasion.[87] A "bouncer" who ignored his employer's commands was not *functus officio*,[88] but a prohibition on a servant from acting in a particular way

---

[84] *Lynch* v *Palgrave Murphy Ltd.* [1964] IR 150; *McCartan* v *Belfast Harbour Commissioners* [1911] 2 IR 143; *Mersey Docks & Harbour Board* v *Coggins & Griffith (Liverpool) Ltd.* [1947] AC 1.

[85] See n. 110, 112, 114 in Chapter 10.

[86] *Boyle* v *Ferguson* [1911] 2 IR 489.

[87] *Kiely* v *McCrea & Sons Ltd.* [1940] Ir. Jur. Rep. 1.

[88] *Daniels* v *Whetstone* [1962] 2 Lloyds Rep 1.

does not automatically relieve the master of liability.[89] Difficulty can arise in determining the scope of employment where the injury is the result of a practical joke or horseplay in the workplace. In *Harrison* v *Michelin Tyre Co. Ltd.*,[90] the employer was held vicariously liable for the act of an employee, employed to push a truck along a passageway, who diverted the truck against a fellow employee for "fun", but in *Hough* v *Irish Base Metals Ltd.*[91] the employer was held not to be liable for serious injuries sustained by a foreman mechanic when other employees engaged in "larking" placed a lighting gas ring under him whilst he was working on a vehicle.[92]

13.8.3 DELEGATION OF DUTY

Although an employer is not, in general, vicariously liable for the negligent acts of an independent contractor engaged by him he can be liable for the selection of an incompetent contractor or the failure to adequately supervise the work. Some duties imposed on employers cannot be delegated to other persons, and an employer will not be relieved of liability by delegating such duties to an independent contractor. Statutory duties, imposing strict liability, can never be delegated and statutory duties requiring an employer to take reasonable care or to fulfil his duties as far as is reasonably practicable, if delegated, become a duty to ensure that reasonable care is taken.[93] Section 57(2) of the Civil Liability Act, 1961 abolishes for all strict statu-

---

[89] *Strong* v *McAuley, McIllroy & Co. Ltd.* [1929] 63 ILTR 39; *Hosford* v *Macken* [1897] 1 IR 292; *Kooragang Investments Pty. Ltd.* v *Richardson and Wrench* [1981] 3 WLR 493. The majority of cases does however indicate that the servant is in such circumstances acting outside the scope of his employment; see: *Byrne* v *Londonderry Tramway* [1902] 2 IR 457; *Cogan* v *Dublin Motor Co.* [1924] 49 ILTR 24; *Rose* v *Plenty and Co-operative Retail Services Ltd.* [1876] 1 All ER 97.

[90] [1985] 1 All ER 918.

[91] Unreported Supreme Court, 8 December 1987.

[92] ibid., per O'Dalaigh C. J.:

The nature of the larking was . . . such as to make it not easily detectable; and in any event it could not reasonably be said that an employer who did not detect it had failed in his duty to provide a safe system of supervision, as the larking in question was of such recent origin and was not of such frequency as must necessarily have been detected in any system of reasonable supervision.

[93] *Wilson* v *Tyneside Window Cleaning* [1958] 2 QB 110; *Groves* v *Wimborne* [1898] 2 QB 402; *Burns* v *Cork and Bandon Railway Co.* 13 Ir. CLR 543; *Ryan* v *Clarkin* [1935] IR 1.

tory forms of liability the defence of delegation of performance of duty or compliance with obligation to another. If the defendant falls within a class to which the statute is addressed he is strictly liable to perform his duty or obligation.

13.8.4 VOLUNTARY ASSUMPTION OF RISK

The Supreme Court accepted, in *Flynn* v *Irish Sugar Manufacturing Co. Ltd.*,[94] that an employer could have a defence to an action for personal injuries if he could show that the injuries were caused by a risk of the employment, known to the employee and voluntarily accepted by him.[95] Section 34(1)(b) of the Civil Liability Act, 1961 now provides that, for such a defence to succeed, the defendant must establish that the plaintiff agreed to waive his legal rights in respect of the act complained of and subsequent decisions of the Supreme Court confirm that only a communicated waiver of right of action will suffice to establish voluntary assumption of risk.[96] In *O'Hanlon* v *ESB*[97] the plaintiff employee was working on a ladder near some live wires. He was equipped with a fuse extractor to neutralise the wires before working on them but did not have it with him when he went up the ladder. He sustained serious personal injuries when he was electrocuted and fell from the ladder. The defendant raised the defence of voluntary assumption of risk and contributory negligence. The Supreme Court held that for the defence of voluntary assumption of risk to succeed, the defendant must show some form of communication by the plaintiff that he had assumed the risk voluntarily. Walsh J. confirmed that "agreement" referred to in Section 34(1)(b) of the 1961 Act:

---

[94] [1928] IR 525.

[95] per Fitzgibbon J. at 536/537. See *Depuis* v *Haulbowline Industries Ltd.* Unreported Supreme Court, 14 February 1962.

[96] *O'Hanlon* v *ESB* [1969] IR 75; In *McComiskey* v *McDermott* [1974] IR 75, per Griffin J.:

> The law on this topic was settled by this Court in *O'Hanlon* v *ESB*. The majority decision . . . was delivered by Mr. Justice Walsh and having set out the terms of . . . the Act he stated at p. 91–92 . . . "the defendants must establish that the plaintiff agreed to waive his legal rights in respect of the act complained of. . . . A one-sided secret determination on the part of the plaintiff to give up his right of action for negligence would not amount to an agreement to do so."

[97] *supra.*

necessarily contemplates some form of . . . communication between the plaintiff and the defendants from which it could be
reasonably inferred that the plaintiff had assured the defendants that he waived any right of action he might have in respect of the negligence of the defendants.

13.8.5 CONTRIBUTORY NEGLIGENCE

A defence of contributory negligence on the part of an employee is
generally treated with suspicion by the courts in the context of statutory liability, and its acceptance regarded as frustrating the policy of
the safety legislation. The paternalistic approach of the courts is expressed in the statements of Walsh J., in the Supreme Court, in
McKenna v *Meighan*[98] that a worker's knowledge of a danger associated with a particular job does not of itself establish contributory
negligence and that a worker, given the alternatives of either doing
the job as he had been instructed to do it or to refuse to do it, could
not be guilty of contributory negligence if he chose to do the job he
was instructed to do.[99] Section 35 of the Civil Liability Act, 1961 provides that breach of statutory duty by the plaintiff should be regarded
as contributory negligence for the purposes of apportioning liability
between the parties, but the case law has sought to restrict the availability of a plea of contributory negligence in employer's liability actions. In *Kennedy* v *East Cork Foods*,[100] O'Dalaigh J. confirmed that
an employee would not be guilty of contributory negligence if what he
did was simple inadvertence, normal forgetfulness or normal inattention. It was necessary that he be, in fact, negligent and careless in
a more positive and definite way.[101] It must be shown that what he did
entered into the realm of downright carelessness as the safety legislation imposing a statutory duty on the employer was passed for the
express purpose of saving workers from their own carelessness and
their own inattention.[102] In an action for breach of statutory duty, con-

---

[98] *McKenna* v *Meighan* [1966] IR 288 at 290 per Walsh J.

[99] *Deegan* v *Langan* [1966] IR 373 at 376.

[100] [1973] IR 244.

[101] ibid. at 249.

[102] per Barron J. in *Dunne* v *Honeywell Control Systems Ltd. and Virginia Milk
Products Ltd.* [1991] ILRM 595 at 602, and referring to *East Cork Foods Ltd.* supra.

tributory negligence has a different meaning to contributory negligence at common law.[103] In *Dunne v Honeywell Control Systems Ltd. and Virginia Milk Products Ltd.*,[104] the plaintiff, an electrical technician employed by Honeywell, sustained serious injuries when he fell from a ladder on Virginia's premises, where in the course of his employment he was engaged in repair work. The ladder was shown to be defective and the plaintiff had carried a case of tools when going up and down the ladder. The plaintiff had requested an over-arm satchel but the employer had insisted on him using a tool case with the employer's logo on it. Barron J. found the plaintiff guilty of contributory negligence of 10 per cent at common law but exonerated him of contributory negligence in his claim for breach of statutory duty. Relying on the principle of law, enunciated by O'Dalaigh J. in *Kennedy v East Cork Foods Ltd.*,[105] he held that the plaintiff was not taking sufficient care for his own safety, not through any positive act on his part, but because the danger did not occur to him.[106]

13.8.6 ABSENCE OF FAULT

Section 43 of the Civil Liability Act, 1961 provides that, in determining contributory negligence under Section 34(1), in an action for breach of statutory duty, the court may take account of the fact that the negligence or wrong of one person consisted only of a breach of strict statutory or common law duty without fault and may hold that it is not just or equitable to cast any part of the damage upon such person. In *O'Sullivan v Dwyer*[107] Walsh J. in the Supreme Court interpreted the Section as meaning that, once the plaintiff is found guilty of contributory negligence, he will fail to recover if the defendant wrongdoer, although guilty of breach of strict statutory or common law duty, can be shown to be without fault. McCarthy J. in *Daly v Avonmore Creameries Ltd.*[108] expressed difficulty with that definition, believing that Section 43 of the Act should be interpreted "as

---

[103] ibid.

[104] [1991] ILRM 595.

[105] n. 100 *supra*.

[106] [1991] ILRM 595 at 602.

[107] [1971] IR 275 at 285.

[108] [1984] IR 131 at 148.

permitting but not compelling absolution from liability in such a case".[109]

13.8.7 CONCURRENT WRONGDOERS

The 1961 Act erodes the distinction between joint and concurrent wrongdoers.[110] Concurrent wrongdoers can be jointly, severally or equally liable, depending on the apportionment of liability determined by the court. The plaintiff can plead breach of both statutory and common law duty, as in *Dunne* v *Honeywell*[111] and liability may be apportioned differently under each heading.[112] There can, however, be no duplication of damages and the plaintiff cannot recover more than the total damages assessed. Under the 1961 Act[113] and Rules of the Supreme Court,[114] the plaintiff has only to establish liability to the minutest degree against any one defendant for him to be liable for 100 per cent of the damages awarded with a right of recovery against the other defendants.

13.8.8 GENERAL PRACTICE

The defence of "general practice" operates in favour of the employer, particularly where the allegation of negligence is based on an omission to do something which might have prevented the injury. In *Caulfield* v *George Bell Ltd.*[115] the court held that the employer could be negligent where his omission was a:

> thing commonly done by other employers in like circumstances, or was so obviously required that it would be folly for

---

[109] "Whilst the judgment does not say so, I cannot so interpret Section 43 . . . unless the word 'may' is to be read as 'shall' . . ." per McCarthy J. at 149.

[110] Section 11(1).

[111] [1991] ILRM 595.

[112] ibid., where the court held there was no contributory negligence in relation to the employer's statutory duty but apportioned liability in respect of breach of the common law duties.

[113] Section 21(1) of the 1961 Act.

[114] Section 12(1) and Rules of the Supreme Court 1986.

[115] [1958] IR 326.

an employer to neglect to provide it; in other words, that no reasonable and prudent employer would have omitted it.[116]

In *Bradley* v *CIE*[117] the plaintiff railway signalman was obliged to service signal lamps at the top of vertical steel posts. The defendants did not provide a surrounding safety cage on the ladders, fixed to the posts, and used by the plaintiff to access the lamps. The plaintiff fell from one of the ladders while descending with a lamp in his hand. Expert evidence on behalf of the plaintiff confirmed that the provision of the safety cage would have prevented the accident to the plaintiff. The defendants produced uncontradicted evidence that the kind of uncaged ladder used by them was in accordance with standard railway practice; that there were over 1,000 of them in use in the railway system; that caged ladders were not in use in railway systems in England or Holland; that, in the ten years prior to the accident, not one person had been injured using the uncaged ladders; that the attachment of the suggested cage would breach the employers' minimum safety clearance between the post and the railway line. The court held that the suggested precaution had not been shown either to have been one which was commonly taken by other railway operators or to have been one which a reasonably prudent employer would think was obviously necessary in the prevailing circumstances. Henchy J. commented that the law does not require an employer to ensure in all circumstances the safety of his workers, and he will have discharged his duty if he does what a reasonable and prudent employer would have done in the circumstances.[118] Where the defence of general practice is raised, the plaintiff, if he is to overcome it, must show that although the defendants were following general practice in not implementing a particular safety feature, the feature was so obviously wanted, for the protection of the plaintiff from injury, that the defendants could be said to have been imprudent or unreasonable in not implementing it.[119] In *Mulligan* v *Holland Dredging Co. (Irl)*

---

[116] per Murnaghan J. at 334.

[117] [1976] IR 217.

[118] ibid. at 223 per Henchy J.

[119] ibid. at 222.

Ltd.[120] O'Flaherty J. accepted that, in relation to the duty of care owed by the employer to an employee, the employee plaintiff is not required to establish that a real or significant danger existed. He said that, in general, in deciding whether the employer has any liability, it is sufficient to ask whether an employer has taken reasonable care for the safety of his employees to prevent injury or damage to them from a foreseeable risk, having regard to all the circumstances of the case.[121]

---

[120] Unreported Supreme Court, 21 November 1996, Hamilton C. J. and Murphy J. concurring.

[121] at p. 10 of judgment.

CHAPTER FOURTEEN

EMPLOYERS' LIABILITY INSURANCE

14.1 INTRODUCTION

In most European countries, the normal mechanism used to compensate persons for work related injury or disease is a workers' compensation scheme sponsored by the state or the private sector. Ireland and the UK provide injured employees with the benefits of a social welfare system[1] and the legal right to lump sum compensation based on the establishment of a breach of common law or statutory duty by the employer. In the UK, it is compulsory for all employers to insure their legal liability.[2] While such insurance is not compulsory in Ireland, the cost and availability of employers' liability insurance is an issue of great concern to Irish industry, insurers and the Government.[3] All business concerns, whether large or small, have seen an

---

[1] In Ireland, the Social Insurance (Consolidation) Act, 1981. Chapter 25 of the Act provides all employees with occupational injury benefits payable to "insured persons who are injured in the course of their employment or who contract prescribed occupational diseases". The injured person does not have to prove fault but the benefits are fixed and provide only partial compensation.

[2] Employers' Liability (Compulsory Insurance) Act, 1969. The legislation was introduced following a number of publicised incidents where employees were killed, including a fire in a Glasgow departmental store, and no compensation was paid because the employers were insolvent, had no insurance or had breached the conditions of their insurance policies. The Act requires all employers to insure for a minimum amount and to display certificates of insurance on their premises. Certain restrictive conditions in policies are prohibited.

[3] In 1996 the Minister of Commerce, Science and Technology commissioned a study on the economic evaluation of insurance costs in Ireland, and a report published by Deloitte & Touche was presented to him in October 1996. The report confirmed that the Irish average claims costs for employers' liability insurance were significantly higher than in the UK, as was the rate of claims per employee.

inexorable rise in the cost of employers' liability insurance and a significant reduction in cover.[4] The increasing cost of employers' liability insurance is, however, only a symptom. The underlying problem is the ever-growing burden on industry, and society generally, of the financial and social costs of occupational accidents and disease.[5] Irish insurers are only just beginning to experience the impact of gradually developing industrial disease claims which have proved to be a catastrophe for UK insurers. Exposure to asbestos, for example, can give rise to both cancer and lung disease which manifest themselves 20, 30, or even 40 years after an employee has left or retired from the employment where they were first exposed to the toxic substance. The limitation period for claims for compensation runs, not from the time the injured plaintiff was first exposed to the risk, but from the date of knowledge of the plaintiff that the injury was significant.[6] An insurer who issued an employers' liability policy to an employer in the 1950s or the 1960s could now be faced with a claim for compensation at 1990s levels, in relation to a policy issued at 1950 premium levels when the potential for such disease claims was not appreciated and which, under the state of the law at that time could not have been brought at such distance in time.

14.2 CHALLENGES FACING EMPLOYERS

Understandably, insurers are now concerned at what the future might hold in terms of new disease problems emerging. Already they are endeavouring to deal with the problems of work-induced stress, repetitive strain injury, passive smoking, asthma, post-traumatic

---

[4] Traditionally and exceptionally, employers' liability policies provided indemnity unlimited by amount but the indemnity is now limited to the amount specified in the policy, which in Ireland is now typically £10 million.

[5] According to the Irish Insurance Federation, insurers made a gross underwriting loss of £56 million in 1996, £29.7 million (1995) and £25.6 million (1994) — on gross premium income of £116 million in 1996 and 1995 and £106 million in 1994.

[6] Section 3 of the Statute of Limitations (Amendment) Act, 1991 amended Section 11 of the 1957 Act so that the three-year limitation period in respect of personal injury actions now runs from the date of the injury or the date of knowledge of the plaintiff, if later. Section 2(1) provides that the date of knowledge is the date when the plaintiff first knows that the injury is significant, that it is attributable in whole or in part to the negligence or breach of statutory duty of the defendants, and the identity of the defendants. The provisions are cumulative and therefore favour the plaintiff.

stress disorder and noise-induced loss of hearing. Latent and gradually developing industrial diseases are not the only factors providing problems for employers and their insurers. The employer's duty of care, as is shown in the previous chapter, has been expanded over the years; social inflation has increased the levels of compensation and new heads of damages have been introduced. The recessionary periods of the 1980s and the early 1990s encouraged workers, made redundant, to bring claims against their previous employers, and trade union organisations have, quite legitimately, been offering their members legal services to pursue such claims. The abolition of juries in personal injury actions, in 1988, may have introduced a greater degree of consistency into the level of awards but it did not bring about the anticipated reduction in damages. There have been calls for alternative systems of compensation and proposals for capping awards, but alternative compensation mechanisms are unlikely to become a serious issue unless the existing system and the availability of insurance protection collapses under the strain of the adverse features mentioned above, or the Government, in response to EU pressures, decides to change the present system. There is no indication that either is likely to happen in the near future. Some large industrial concerns have decided that there is a better way of compensating employees in respect of industrial accidents and diseases, while at the same time reducing the costs of the present adversarial legal system.[7] Such alternative mechanisms cannot, however, fully avoid the need for insurance, the involvement of insurance advisers, or the legal system.

---

[7] Many large companies now retain a substantial portion of the risk for their own account through the mechanisms of large self-insured deductibles, aggregate deductibles, retro-rated insurance arrangements, re-insurance through captive insurance companies or a combination of some if not all such arrangements. They continue to have the need for claims handling services, claims management facilities and catastrophe insurance, utilising the services of risk managers, insurance brokers and adjusters. Some companies, particularly those which self-insure, set up funds to deal with particular disease claims, where there are hundreds of claimants, and the assessment and payment of damages are dealt with under the terms of the scheme once liability has been determined. At least one insurer in the UK — Iron Trades — has developed schemes with the co-operation of trade unions for dealing with noise-induced hearing loss claims and claims in respect of vibration white finger. From the defendant's point of view these schemes are quick and simple, reduce costs, eliminate litigation and generally provide an agreed standard level of compensation.

14.3 INSURANCE POLICY WORDING

14.3.1 INSURING CLAUSE

Of all the different forms of liability policy wording that are used the Employers' Liability Insurance policy is the nearest to a standard form in use throughout the insurance industry. The policy provides that insurers will indemnify the insured:

> against liability at law for damages and claimant's costs and expenses in respect of bodily injury or disease sustained by any employee, while employed in or temporarily outside the Republic of Ireland, caused during the Period of Insurance and arising out of and in the course of his employment by the Insured in the business.

The policy does not cover the insured's moral or social obligations to employees but only his legal liability for bodily injury or disease. Insurers will also pay all costs and expenses recovered by the plaintiff employee against the insured within the limit of the indemnity provided by the policy. In addition, the insurers will pay costs and expenses incurred by the insured with the insurers' consent and fees for representation at proceedings arising out of any alleged breach of statutory duty resulting in bodily injury or disease which may be the subject of indemnity under the policy. Most insurers will now provide indemnity to the insured, or at his request to any director or employee of the insured, against legal costs and expenses incurred in the defence of any criminal proceedings brought for a breach of the Safety (Health and Welfare at Work) Act, 1989 committed or alleged to have been committed during the period of insurance, including legal costs and expenses incurred with the consent of the insurers in an appeal against conviction from such proceedings.

There are three phrases within the insuring clause which require closer examination: "Employee", "caused during the period of insurance", and "arising out of and in the course of employment".

14.3.2 "EMPLOYEE"

For the purpose of the policy, "Employee" is defined as:

a) Any person under a contract of service or apprenticeship with the insured;

b) Any person under any training educational or work experience programme;

c) Any labour master or labour-only sub-contractor or any person supplied by them;

d) Any self-employed person;

e) Any person hired from any Public Authority Company or Firm or individual;

f) Any member of the insured's family or household while engaged in the course of the business.

This expanded definition of "Employee" does not alter the legal status of such persons. Whether a person is an employee or not is a decision ultimately made by the court on the basis of established criteria.[8] It is a matter of administrative convenience for insurers to deal with claims from persons, within the expanded definition, under the employers' liability policy.

14.3.3 CONTRACT OF SERVICE

With the increasing use of independent contractors, sub-contractors, labour-only sub-contractors and self-employed persons, the status of the party at the material time is critical to the determination of whether liability to the injured person is covered under an Employers' Liability policy or a Public Liability policy. Whether the parties contracting are master and servant or otherwise is a conclusion of law dependent on the rights conferred and the duties imposed by the contract, and if the contractual rights and duties create the relationship of master and servant, a declaration by the parties that the relationship is otherwise is irrelevant.[9] A contract of service exists if:

a) the servant agrees in consideration of a wage or other remuneration to provide his own work and skill in the performance of some service for his master;

---

[8] *Walshe* v *Bailieboro Co-Operative Agricultural and Dairy Society Ltd.* [1939] Ir. Jur. Rep. 77; *Ready Mixed Concrete (South East) Ltd.* v *Minister for Pensions and National Insurance* [1968] 2 QB 497; *Market Investigations Ltd.* v *Minister for Social Security and Pensions* [1969] 2 QB 173; *O'Coinndealbhain* v *Mooney* [1990] 1 IR 422; *Phelan* v *Coillte Teo.* [1993] 1 IR 18.

[9] *Phelan supra* per Barr J. at p. 24.

b) the servant agrees expressly or implicitly that, in performance of the service he will be subject to the control of the other party sufficiently to make him the master; and

c) the other provisions of the contract are consistent with its being a contract of service.[10]

In determining whether a worker is employed pursuant to a contract of service or a contract for services, it is necessary to have regard to the degree of control exercised over this worker by the employer,[11] but regardless of what the actual contract states or specifies, regard must be had to the realities of the situation.[12] If it is stated in the contract that it is a contract for services, the entire contract must be looked at in order to decide if it is truly a contract for services.[13] In *Mulligan* v *Holland Dredging Co. (Irl.) Ltd.*,[14] the Supreme Court accepted that the plaintiff was not in an employer/employee relationship with the defendant when working as a deckhand on a vessel operated by a sister company of the defendant. Although his wages were paid by the Irish company, all powers of control over the attendance of the plaintiff for carrying out his duties were exercised by those in charge of the vessel, and no element of control of the workplace, or of the plaintiff's involvement therein, rested with the defendant. While many ingredients may be present in the relationship of master and servant, it is true that the principal one, and almost invariably the determining one, is in fact the master's right to direct the servant not merely as to what is to be done but as to how it is to be done. The fact that the master does not exercise that right, as distinct from possessing it, is of no weight, if he has the right.[15] The decision in *Phelan* v *Coillte Teo.*[16] highlights the predominant thread running through most of the authorities indicating that control of the person by the defendant

---

[10] *Ready Mixed Concrete supra* at p. 515 per McKenna J.

[11] *Phelan* v *Coillte Teo.* [1993] 1 IR 18.

[12] *Denny & Sons (Ireland) Ltd. t/a Kerry Foods* v *Minister for Social Welfare* Unreported High Court, 18 October 1995.

[13] ibid. per Carroll J.

[14] Unreported Supreme Court, 21 November 1996.

[15] *Roche* v *P. Kelly* [1969] IR 100 per Walsh J. at 108.

[16] [1993] 1 IR 18.

employer is critical to determination of an employer/employee relationship. The element of control was identified as crucial 50 years ago by Lord Porter, in the House of Lords, in *Mersey Docks and Harbour Board* v *Coggins & Griffith*[17] when he said:

> Many factors have a bearing on the result. Who is the paymaster, who can dismiss?. . . . The expressions used in any individual case must always be considered in regard to the subject matter under discussion but amongst the many tests suggested, I think that the most satisfactory, by which to ascertain who is the employer at any particular time, is to ask who is entitled to tell the employee the way in which he is to do the work upon which he is engaged. If someone other than his general employer is authorised to do this he will, as a rule, be the person liable for the employee's negligence. But it is not enough that the task to be performed should be under his control; he must also control the method of performing it. It is true that in most cases no orders as to how a job should be done are given or required: the man is left to do his own work in his own way. But the ultimate question is not what specific orders, or whether any specific orders, were given but who is entitled to give the orders as to how the work should be done.

14.3.4 EMPLOYEE OR INDEPENDENT CONTRACTOR

Given the wide range of circumstances which can arise, it is difficult to state any hard-and-fast rule as to what constitutes a servant and what constitutes an independent contractor. Each case must be determined on its own special facts in the light of the broad guidelines outlined above. The High Court in *McAuliffe* v *Minister for Social Welfare*[18] indicated that the degree of control exercised by the employer over the employed person is the main test of whether a worker is a servant or a contractor; but the better view would appear to be that it is the degree of control exercisable rather than control factually exercised which is the main determining factor.[19] In *Lane* v *Shire*

---

[17] *Mersey Docks and Harbour Board* v *Coggins & Griffith (Liverpool) & Others* [1947] AC 1 at 17.

[18] *McAuliffe* v *Minister for Social Welfare,* Unreported High Court, 19 October 1994.

[19] *Dunne* v *Honeywell Control Systems* [1991] ILRM 595 at 600 per Barron J. referring to *Gerard* v *Southby* [1952] 2 QB 174; *Phelan* v *Coillte Teo.* [1993] 1 IR 18.

Roof Co. (Oxford) Ltd.,[20] the Court of Appeal was faced with the problem of establishing if the plaintiff was an employee or independent contractor at the time of the accident. The plaintiff was a one-man builder/roofer/carpenter who enjoyed the tax status of a self-employed person and held the appropriate exemption certificates. The defendants were roofing contractors who hired individuals for specific jobs. They hired the plaintiff to work on a particular site for which he was paid a daily rate. Near the end of the main contract, he was asked to re-roof a porch for which it was agreed he would be paid an all-in price. The defendants provided all the materials and the plaintiff provided his own tools and ladder from which he subsequently fell and was seriously injured. At first instance, the court held that while the defendant would have been in breach of its duty to the plaintiff if the plaintiff was an employee, he was, it held, in fact an independent contractor responsible for his own safety. On appeal, the court noted that there were many reasons why there were now many more people who were technically self-employed than there had been previously, but stated that in the field of health and safety at work it was important to recognise the employer/employee relationship where it existed. It stated that the control test was important but not decisive since skilled workers would often decide how their work should be done and in such circumstances the question would be whose business was it and was the worker carrying out his own business or that of his employers? The court concluded that the plaintiff was more than a labour-only sub-contractor on the "lump"; he was a skilled man, although not a specialist sub-contractor engaged to perform some part of a general building contract. His position lay somewhere between the two. However, applying a test as to control and benefit, the judge was satisfied that the plaintiff's position was closer to the "lump" than a bona fide contractor and held that an employer/employee relationship existed and that the defendants were liable.

14.3.5 LABOUR-ONLY CONTRACTORS

The desirability of having the precise status of the parties agreed before the work commences was illustrated in a recent High Court case,

---

[20] Unreported Court of Appeal, 21 February 1995.

Kelly v *Michael McNamara & Co.*[21] The plaintiff carpenter had been contracted by the defendant for different work over a period of years. In 1991 the defendant asked the plaintiff to carry out some work on a shop in Galway and to bring some other workers with him. There was some discussion about insurance and the plaintiff claimed after the accident that the rate agreed for the job was to include insurance arranged by the defendant. The defendant maintained that the plaintiff was expected to arrange his own insurance. While working on the job, under the charge and supervision of the defendant's general foreman and senior engineer, the plaintiff fell eight feet on to a concrete floor and sustained serious injuries. In response to the claim for damages, the defendant argued that the plaintiff, as an independent contractor and not a direct employee, was not covered by either the 1980 Safety in Industry Act or the 1975 Regulations. The defendant also pleaded contributory negligence to a very high degree as the plaintiff was a very experienced carpenter. Budd J. held that it was reasonable for the plaintiff to be under the impression that the defendant would have insurance in the usual way for those employed by him and who were under their control and management on site and that if responsibility for providing insurance was going to be imposed on the plaintiff, then the court would expect that to be made crystal clear to the plaintiff.[22] The judge accepted that legislation[23] imposed an absolute duty with regard to safety of the workplace and a qualified duty (limited to what is reasonably practicable) with regard to safety of the means of access to and egress from every such place. Having consid-

---

[21] Unreported High Court, 5 June 1996.

[22] per Budd J. at p. 3 of the judgment:

> I am aware that main contractors in Ireland in the past may have built large hotels and even airports without any written agreement between them and the employer; nevertheless, in this day and age I find it incredible that a responsible main contractor would not have insurance cover for labour-only subcontractors. If responsibility for providing such cover was going to be imposed on the sub-contractor, then I would certainly expect this to be made crystal clear to the labour-only sub-contractor and I would expect not only that this would be put in writing to the sub-contractor but that there would also be an explicit requirement that he produce written evidence from an insurance company to the effect that he has the requisite cover in place.

[23] Section 37 of the Factories Act, 1955 as amended by Section 12 of the Safety in Industry Act, 1980.

ered the statutory definition of contractor[24] Budd J. said he understood a contractor to be a person who contracts to furnish supplies, or
to perform any work or service at a certain price or rate or who undertakes work by contract.[25] The defendants claimed that the plaintiff
was a domestic sub-contractor, but in evidence it was conceded that
the defendant had control over the plaintiff and his men. In support
of their claim the defendants relied on the following facts: the plaintiff negotiated a rate for himself and his men; he employed men and
was responsible for their PAYE and PRSI; he made a profit from the
job since he paid the men less than he was paid for their work; he was
paid fortnightly and they were paid weekly; he was employed on the
job on a once-off basis only; he had the right to dismiss his men; books
of account produced were indicative of a person in business on his
own account; he collected and transported his men; he provided his
own tools. The Court, however, had no doubt but that the defendants
were in breach of their statutory duty, that they were responsible for
instituting and maintaining a safe system of work, and had a duty, as
main contractor, of organising the work so as to ensure the safety of
everyone working on site, although the scope of the duty will depend
upon the nature of the work and the experience of the personnel involved.

> Where the sub-contractor is only providing labour and the
> main contractor is organising the work and supplying materi-
> als and equipment, then the main contractor is very much re-
> sponsible for the safety standards on the building site.[26]

14.3.6 "Caused during the Period of Insurance"
In issuing any insurance policy, it is the intention of the insurer to
provide cover for a finite period of time so that he can make provisions for his known and potential liabilities. The operative clause of
the employers' liability policy makes it clear that the insured's liability for bodily injury or disease caused during the period of the policy
is covered. There is generally little or no difficulty in determining

---

[24] Regulation 3 of the Construction (Safety, Health and Welfare) Regulations,
1975.

[25] at p. 17 of the judgment.

[26] at p. 29.

whether bodily injury was or was not caused within the period of insurance, in so far as injury is usually the result of an identifiable incident. The problem lies with industrial diseases and when they can
be said to have been caused in legal terms. The development of employers' liability insurance provided the courts with a mechanism for
spreading risk, on the basis of who best can pay rather than where
does liability rest. A good example of the availability of insurance influencing the judicial approach is the English case of *Firman* v *Ellis
& Others*.[27] Insurers had pleaded that the three-year time limit for
bringing claims for bodily injuries had expired and the claims were
time-barred. The point before the Court of Appeal was whether the
judges had the discretion to extend the three-year period. The Court,
in unanimously holding that the judges did have unfettered discretion to extend the period, were scathing in their remarks on the insurance industry.[28] The insurers involved, in pleading the limitation
period, had maintained that the plaintiff would not lose out in as
much as the plaintiff had rights against the solicitors for failing to
issue proceedings in time. Lord Denning M. R. said that as a matter
of simple justice it was the insurers who should pay as they had received the premium to cover the risk and they should not be allowed
to foist their liability onto the plaintiff's solicitors or their insurers as
if they were playing a game of cards.[29] Ormrod L. J. was equally
forthright:

> If insurance companies through their customers choose to take
> wholly unmeritorious technical points to avoid liability, they
> cannot complain if ultimately their ability to take them is se-
> verely restricted. To retain a wholly formalistic procedure, the
> real effect of which is simply to transfer liability from the
> original tortfeasor's insurers to the plaintiff's solicitor's insur-
> ers, is not very impressive as a piece of public policy.[30]

---

[27] *Firman* v *Ellis & Others* [1978] 2 All ER 851.

[28] Although the case involved a motor accident, the principle is equally applicable
to liability insurance.

[29] [1978] 2 All ER 851 per Denning M. R. at 860.

[30] ibid. per Ormrod L. J. at 863.

14.3.7 TIME LIMITATION OF ACTIONS

Judicial reluctance to acceptance of a time limit in respect of actions in negligence was also apparent in Ireland. In *Morgan* v *Park Developments Ltd.*,[31] Carroll J. was required to decide whether the accrual of a right of action in a negligence case should be the date of discoverability or some earlier date. Having referred to and considered the English authorities and legislation on the matter,[32] she preferred the decision in *Sparham-Souter* v *Town and Country Developments (Essex) Ltd.*[33] that the date of discoverability is the date of accrual of the right of action. Relying on the Irish Constitution for support,[34] she held that despite the provisions of the Statute of Limitations Act,[35] "the date of accrual in an action for negligence, in the building of a house, is the date of discoverability, meaning the date the defect was either discovered or should reasonably have been discovered".[36] It has been suggested that the comments of Carroll J. should be taken as being *obiter* since she had gone on to find that in the instant case the plaintiff's claim was statute-barred, even taking the date of discoverability as the relevant date,[37] but in *Hegarty* v *O'Loughlin*[38] Barron J., in a personal injuries action, held that the relevant section of the Statute of Limitations[39] was capable of one interpretation only and

---

[31] *Morgan* v *Park Developments Ltd.* [1983] ILRM 156.

[32] *Sparham-Souter* v *Town & Country Developments (Essex) Ltd. & Another* [1976] 2 WLR 493; *Anns & Others* v *Merton Borough Council* [1977] 2 WLR 1024; *Pirelli General Cable Works Ltd.* v *Oscar Faber and Partners* [1893] 2 WLR 6; *Cartledge* v *E. Joplin and Sons Ltd.* [1963] AC 758. Neither the English legislation of 1963 nor subsequent legislation in 1975 and 1980 made any special provision for tort actions other than those in respect of personal injuries caused by negligence, nuisance or breach of duty.

[33] *supra.*

[34] Carroll J., having referred to the acknowledgement by the Law Lords in *Cartledge* v *Joplin* (*supra*) and Pirelli's case that the results were unreasonable and unjustifiable in principle and — in the former case — "harsh and absurd", went on as follows: ". . . It seems to me that no law which could be described as harsh and absurd or which the courts could say was unreasonable and unjustifiable in principle . . . could also be constitutional."

[35] Statute of Limitations, 1957, Section 11(2)(b).

[36] [1983] ILRM 156 at 160.

[37] Law Reform Commission Report, p. 7, Chapter Two.

[38] [1987] IR 135.

[39] Section 11(2)(b).

that time began to run from the date of the injury. In doing so he seemed to reprimand Carroll J. for her interpretation of the constitution[40] and suggested that the importation of discoverability into the area was best achieved by legislation.

14.3.8 LAW REFORM

The matter was referred to the Law Reform Commission in 1987, and a report was produced[41] later the same year recommending that legislation should prescribe a "discoverability" test in regard to the limitation of actions relating to personal injuries and that for time to begin to run, it should be necessary to show that the plaintiff is, or ought reasonably to be aware:

1) that he has sustained a personal injury of significant proportions;

2) that the injury is attributable, in at least some degree, to the conduct of another;

3) of the identity of the defendant.

The Commission considered but did not recommend that the legislation should include a "long stop" provision specifying a maximum period of time within which the plaintiff's action must be initiated after the defendant's wrongful conduct. With such a provision, no action initiated after the specified period of time had elapsed would be capable of being sustained, regardless of any question of discoverability of the injury. The Commission recognised that the insurance industry would welcome such a proposal, as it would enable insurers close their books on particular claims, but came to the conclusion that the overriding objectives of its recommendations — the prevention of injustice arising from the absence of a "discoverability" rule — could be frustrated in at least some cases if such a "long stop" provision were to be introduced.[42] The recommendations of the Commission were accepted and implemented by the Statute of Limitations (Amendment)

---

[40] However the constitutionality of the legislation had previously been called into question in *Cahill* v *Sutton* [1980] IR 269 and in *Norris* v *Attorney General* [1984] IR 36.

[41] Law Reform Commission Report 21, 1987, "The Statute of Limitations: Claims in respect of Latent Personal Injuries".

[42] pp. 47, 48.

Act, 1991. Section 2(1) of the Act amends Section 11(2)(b) of the 1957 Act and provides that, for the purposes of any provision of the Act, whereby the time within which an action in respect of an injury may be brought depends on a person's date of knowledge, reference to that person's date of knowledge are references to the date on which he first had knowledge of the following facts:

a) that the person alleged to have been injured had been injured;

b) that the injury in question was significant;

c) that the injury was attributable in whole or in part to the act or omission which is alleged to constitute negligence, nuisance or breach of duty;

d) the identity of the defendant; and

e) if it is alleged that the act or omission was that of a person other than the defendant, the identity of that person and the additional facts supporting the bringing of an action against the defendant.

Knowledge that any acts or omissions did or did not, as a matter of law, involve negligence, nuisance or breach of duty is irrelevant.

14.3.9 JUDICIAL INTERPRETATION

It is likely that, given the policy considerations behind the implementation of the 1991 Amendment Act, the judiciary will, wherever possible, interpret the date of knowledge in favour of the plaintiff. An indication of this is to be found in *Boylan* v *Motor Distributors and Daimler Benz AG*.[43] The plaintiff claimed damages for personal injuries sustained by her on 7 May 1986 and in respect of which the action was commenced on 14 January 1992. The High Court directed a hearing on the preliminary issue of whether the action was statute-barred by virtue of Section 11(2)(b) of the 1957 Act. The plaintiff had lost the top of her right ring finger when attempting to close the door of a van delivering goods to her place of work but she did not know precisely how the injury had occurred. She consulted solicitors on 27 May 1986 and they wrote to the owners of the van holding them responsible for the injuries. A High Court action was commenced against the owners of the van on 22 January 1987. On the advice of

---

[43] Unreported High Court, 9 June 1993.

Senior Counsel, in December 1987, the solicitors requested an engineer's report on the van which was received not earlier than 18 January 1989. The desirability of joining Motor Distributors and Daimler Benz as defendants in the action against the owner was overlooked until after 7 May 1989 and thereafter any cause of action against those parties became absolutely barred by Section 11(2)(b) of the 1957 Act as it then stood. The 1991 Act became law on 10 July 1991 and applied to all causes of action whether accruing before or after its passing and to proceedings pending at its passing. No consideration of the effect of the new Act on the claim against the defendants was undertaken until the end of 1991, when the plaintiff's solicitor and Junior Counsel formed the view that it might be possible to maintain an action against the defendants. As it was not possible to have an application to join the defendants in the action against the owner heard before 18 January 1992, the third anniversary of the date of the engineer's report, a separate action was commenced against the defendants by the issue of plenary summons on 14 January 1992. The court accepted that the plaintiff had no knowledge that her injury was attributable to the defendants nor of the identity of the defendants until the engineer's report was received by her solicitor on or after 18 January 1989. In what can only be described as a generous decision, Lynch J. held that: the plaintiff did not know and could not reasonably be expected to know that her injury was due to a design defect in the van and that the defendants might be blamed for the defect; the plaintiff's solicitor did not have knowledge that the plaintiff's injury might have been so caused from the description of the accident given to him by the plaintiff and could not reasonably be expected to have gleaned such knowledge; the solicitors acquired such knowledge not earlier than 18 January 1989; the plaintiff's date of knowledge for the purposes of the Statute of Limitations was 18 January 1989 and accordingly was not time barred.[44]

14.3.10 PROBLEM FOR INSURERS

The effect on employers' liability insurers of these changes in the law is profound. Insurers are now faced with claims for industrial diseases which originated many years previously, under policies no longer in force and for which records may not readily be found. In-

---

[44] Section 11(2)(b) of 1957 Act as amended by Section 3 of the 1991 Act.

vestigation of such claims is difficult and, because most employers do
not have a complete medical and social history of their employees, it
is difficult to defend a case where an employee, allegedly in good
health at the commencement of employment, presents a case of industrial disease many years later and claims it is due to exposure to
noxious conditions and no other cause is readily apparent. The employers' liability policy covers claims in respect of bodily injury or disease "caused during" the period of the policy and these words present
insurers with considerable difficulty. The relevant time is not, in relation to disease, the time when the disease first manifests itself, but
the time of the first significant damage.[45] Different insurers may have
been on risk at the time and their identity may not be known or ascertainable. It may be difficult to obtain contribution from insurers
who were on risk at different stages of the development of the disease, and the employer may no longer be in existence.[46] Where an
employer believes he may have difficulty establishing proof of insurance in respect of prior years it is possible for him to purchase retroactive cover, either separately or as an extension of his existing policy. Such cover would apply to claims first made against the insured
during the currency of the policy. even though the accident or disease
may have been caused prior to inception, provided the insured was
unable to claim indemnity under any other policy.

14.3.11 "ARISING OUT OF AND IN THE COURSE OF EMPLOYMENT"

A worker's right to benefit under the original worker's compensation
legislative schemes depended essentially on the accident or disease
producing the incapacity for work having "arisen out of or in the
course of employment". The phrase was carried through to employers'
liability insurance policies and has given rise to considerable dispute
between liability insurers over the years. In the ordinary case, when
a worker employed on his employer's premises leaves those premises,
he ceases to be in the course of his employment and conversely, when
he enters the premises for the purpose of taking up his work he is

---

[45] *Cartledge* v *E. Joplin & Sons* [1963] AC 758.

[46] In the UK the Companies Act was amended in 1989 following *Bradley* v *Eagle Star* to permit restoration of a company previously wound up so that injured employees might pursue action for damages in respect of injuries or disease arising out of employment with the company.

usually acting in the course of employment from the time he passes
through the boundary gates to the premises. Difficulties arise, however, in relation to travel to or from the place of work. Two old House
of Lords decisions[47] established that an employee injured on or by a
train provided by the employer for the transport of his employees to
and from their place of employment, could not recover from the employer unless the employee was obliged to travel on the train. That
principle was held to apply also to more modern forms of transport in
Vandyke v *Fender*[48] when the Court of Appeal held that an employee
going to and from work, as a passenger in a motor vehicle provided by
the employer for the purpose of conveying him to and from work, was
not travelling in "the course of employment" unless he was obliged by
the terms of his employment to travel in the vehicle. Denning M. R.
was of the view that some element of compulsion was necessary, and
if that element were missing the employee was not in the course of
employment. Denning's successor as Master of the Rolls, Sir John
Donaldson, cast some doubt on that dictum when, in *Nancollas* v *Insurance Officer* and *Ball* v *Insurance Officer*,[49] he said:

> We cannot over-emphasise the importance of looking at the
> factual picture as a whole and rejecting any approach based on
> the fallacious concept that any one factor is conclusive. The
> addition or subtraction of one factor in a given situation may
> well tip the balance. In another, the addition or subtraction of
> the same factor may well make no difference. We appreciate
> that it would assist if we could lay down rules or even guide-
> lines. However, there are no rules. . . .[50]

He did, however, indicate some guidelines. For example, was the
employee being paid for what he was doing? Was it the employer's
vehicle, and if not was he in receipt of a mileage allowance? Was it of
any concern to the employer that he was where he was? Had he a

---

[47] *St Helen's Colliery Co. Ltd.* v *Hewittson* [1923] All ER 249; *Weaver* v *Tredgar Iron & Coal Co. Ltd.* [1940] 3 All ER 157.

[48] [1970] 2 QB 295.

[49] [1985] 1 All ER 833. Both cases concerned claims for industrial injury benefit in respect of injuries sustained in road accidents. The court held in both cases that in travelling by car and motor-cycle the men were not going to work; travelling was part of their work.

[50] [1985] 1 All ER 833.

fixed place of work and was he going to it? If he had more than one such fixed place, was he travelling between them? He added a caveat that "any such list would mislead, if, as is almost inevitable, it was once thought to be comprehensive".[51] The Supreme Court, in *Buckley's Stores Ltd. v National Employers' Mutual General Insurance Association Ltd. & Others*,[52] endorsed the views expressed by Denning M. R. and confirmed that in determining whether a person is travelling in the course of employment, the question to be asked is whether the person is under an obligation by the terms of his employment to travel in the vehicle in question.

14.3.12 HOUSE OF LORDS GUIDELINES

The House of Lords laid down guidelines when upholding the Court of Appeal decision in *Smith v Stages*[53] that, where an employee was travelling between two places of work, rather than from his home to his place of work, such a journey might well be in the course of his employment, whether or not he was obliged to travel by car. The guidelines are:

- An employee travelling from his ordinary residence to his regular place of work was normally not on duty and was not acting in the course of his employment;

- Travelling in the employer's time between workplaces would normally be in the course of employment;

- Receipt of wages, although not receipt of a travelling allowance, would indicate that the employee was travelling in the course of

---

[51] Sixty years previously Lord Carson had said:
   Ambiguous as the words of the statute are, I doubt if the authorities give any great assistance in elucidating them; nor do I feel certain that any definition can be framed, apart from the particular facts of each case, which will be found helpful to solve the meaning of the statute.
See also *St Helen's Colliery Co. v Hewittson* [1923] All ER 249.

[52] [1978] IR 351. The action arose out of a dispute between three insurers as to which policy should provide indemnity in respect of damages awarded to two employees of the plaintiff in respect of injuries sustained while travelling in a car belonging to the plaintiff and driven by a director of the plaintiff company. The trial judge had held that the women suffered bodily injury arising out of and in the course of their employment but the Supreme Court decided otherwise.

[53] [1989] 1 All ER 833.

his employment, and this was so whether the employee had discretion as to the mode and time of transport;

• An employee travelling in the employer's time from his ordinary
residence to a workplace other than his regular workplace would
normally be in the course of his employment;

• A deviation from or interruption of a journey undertaken in the
course of employment, unless the deviation was merely incidental
to the journey, would for the time being take the employee out of
the course of his employment;

• Return journeys were to be treated on the same footing as outward
journeys.[54]

> All the foregoing propositions are subject to any express ar-
> rangements between the employer and the employee. . . . they
> are not . . . intended to define the position of salaried employ-
> ees with regard to whom the touchstone of payment in the
> employer's time is not generally significant.[55]

The fundamental principle is that an employee is acting in the course
of his employment when he is doing what he is supposed to do or anything which is reasonably incidental to his employment.

14.3.13 ROAD TRAFFIC ACT EXCLUSION

Prior to the coming into force of the Road Traffic (Compulsory Insurance)(Amendment) Regulations, 1992 which implemented the provisions of the Third EC Directive on Motor Insurance,[56] the Road Traffic
Act[57] permitted the exclusion of liability under motor policies in respect of liability to persons claiming in respect of personal injury sustained and caused by or arising out of their employment by the insured. The 1992 Regulations extended compulsory insurance to all
passengers in or on mechanically propelled vehicles, other than motor
cycles and vehicles not generally designed or constructed to carry
passengers. In consequence, all employers' liability policies now carry
an exclusion that "the policy does not apply to liability for which com-

---

[54] per Lord Lowry at p. 851.

[55] ibid.

[56] 90/232/EEC of 10 May 1990 which came into effect on 31 December 1995.

[57] Section 65(1)(f) Road Traffic Act, 1961 as amended.

pulsory insurance is required under any Road Traffic legislation". The Regulations provide that for purposes of Section 65(2) of the Road Traffic Act, 1961, "seating accommodation for passengers" means, in the case of a vehicle, a fixed or folding seat permanently and securely installed in or on the vehicle. Motor insurance policies are now endorsed to the effect that insurers shall not be liable except so far as is necessary to meet the requirements of the Road Traffic Acts in respect of injury to persons in the employment of the insured or of any person claiming to be indemnified under the policy when such injury arises out of and in the course of such employment. As a result of these legislative changes, the position appears to be that where the driver of a motor vehicle is injured in the course of his employment, any claim he might have against his employer will be dealt with under the employers' liability policy since liability to the driver is not a liability which is compulsorily insurable and is not excluded by the policy. Where an employee is injured whilst travelling as a passenger on fixed seating in a motor vehicle, in the course of his employment, any claim against the driver or the employer will be dealt with under the motor policy as a compulsorily insurable liability.[58] A claim for damages from an employee injured in similar circumstances but not seated on fixed seating will fall to be dealt with under the employers' liability policy.

14.4 TERRITORIAL LIMITS

The policy covers employees while employed in or temporarily outside the Republic of Ireland provided that in respect of bodily injury or disease sustained by an employee while temporarily outside the Republic of Ireland the action for damages is brought against the insured in an Irish Court. Where employees are permanently based outside Ireland, it is necessary to effect separate cover either in Ireland or locally in the country where the employees are based.

14.5 INDEMNITY LIMIT

Traditionally, employers' liability policies were issued on a basis providing indemnity unlimited by amount but, following a number of

---

[58] *Sinnott* v *Quinnsworth* [1984] ILRM 522; *Buckley's Stores Ltd.* v *National Employers' Mutual* [1978] IR 351.

major international catastrophes, notably the *Piper Alpha* disaster,[59] insurers introduced a limit to the amount of indemnity provided in respect of any one occurrence. In Ireland, this limit has typically been set at £10 million but many insureds buy additional limits.

14.6 DUTY TO INSURE

Unlike in the UK, employers' liability insurance is not compulsory in Ireland. In *Sweeney* v *Duggan*[60] it was held that the common law could not devise or impose a duty to effect employers' liability insurance which the Oireachtas had not seen fit to impose.[61] The ordinary master and servant relationship, involving a duty of care by one party for the well-being of the other, does not ordinarily extend to a duty to prevent economic loss to, or to protect the economic well-being of the other party, which is a duty of a different kind; such a duty could arise, if at all, only from special circumstances or from a contractual term, whether express or implied on the particular facts, by which the master assumed a duty to his servant in respect of such loss.

14.7 INDEMNITY TO PRINCIPAL

14.7.1 It is usual for an employers' liability policy to provide that, where any contract or agreement, entered into by the insured with any public authority, company, firm or person, so requires, the insurer will indemnify the insured against any liability arising in connection with and assumed by the insured, by virtue of such agreement or contract, or will indemnify the principal, in like manner to the insured, in respect of the principal's liability arising from the performance of such contract or agreement but only so far as concerns liability as described in the policy to an employee of the insured. This extension of cover is subject to the proviso that the insured shall have

---

[59] The *Piper Alpha* oil rig in the North Sea was ripped apart by an explosion in July 1988. Of the 226 people on board, 167 died, and of the 59 survivors many sustained serious burns and all suffered trauma. The total settlement was £120.8 million, split £18.6 million to survivors, £98.7 million to representatives of the deceased and £3.5 million in legal fees. The settlement represented the equivalent of 30 per cent of the total employers' liability premium generated in the UK during 1988.

[60] [1991] 2 IR 274; *Reid* v *Rush & Tomkins Group plc* [1990] 1 WLR 212.

[61] [1991] 2 IR 274 at 281 per Barron J.

arranged with the principal for the conduct and control of all claims to be vested in the insurers and that the principal shall, as though he were the insured, observe, fulfil and be subject to the terms and conditions of the policy in so far as they can apply. A principal will usually require such a clause to be inserted in a contractor's employers' liability policy so that in the event of a claim, in respect of which the contractor would be entitled to indemnity under the policy, being brought or made against the principal, the insurer will indemnify the principal against such claim. A worker who suffers injury is entitled to sue all or any of the persons liable, and if he sues the principal for injury, for which the contractor is liable, the insurers will indemnify the principal under the "indemnity to principals" clause. The principal has direct recourse to the insurers, but the insurers have no greater liability to the principal than they would have had to the insured. Neither do they have a liability to indemnify the principal in respect of his own negligence unless the contract between the insured and the principal specifically obliges the insured to provide such an indemnity.[62]

14.7.2 It is generally accepted as well settled law that, unless an indemnity clause specifically requires one party to the contract to indemnify the other in respect of that other party's negligence, no such undertaking will be implied into the agreement.[63] The Supreme Court confirmed the position recently in *Cuffe v CIE and An Post*,[64] holding that where a party to a contract intends a clause in that contract to be particularly favourable to him (by providing him with an indemnity for his own negligence) it shall be for that party to ensure that the clause has the desired meaning without ambiguity. The plaintiff sustained injuries during the course of his employment as a CIE depot man when he attempted to lift a post bag belonging to An Post. In

---

[62] See for instance Clause 21 of the RIAI Standard Conditions of Contract.

[63] see notes 130 and 131 of Chapter Ten.

It is well settled that indemnity will not lie in respect of loss due to a person's own negligence or that of his servants unless adequate and clear words are used or unless the indemnity could have no reasonable meaning or application unless so applied.

per Sellors L. J. in *Walters v Wessoe Ltd. and Shell Refining Co. Ltd.* Unreported Court of Appeal, 18 November 1960; see also [1968] 2 All ER 811 and 816.

[64] Unreported Supreme Court, 22 October 1996.

the High Court, An Post had been found guilty of negligence in exposing the plaintiff to the risk of lifting a bag which was heavier than its appearance suggested; no appeal was taken against that finding of liability. Under an agreement entered into in 1968, CIE had undertaken to indemnify An Post against

> . . . all actions suits claims or demands arising under the Workmen's Compensation Acts, 1934–1955 or any statutory re-enactment thereof in respect of any personal injury by accident to any guard or servant of CIE while in charge of mails.

Keane J. saw no reason why CIE should have accepted liability for accidents which were due to the negligence of An Post. Although he accepted that the words "actions suits" were more apt to describe common law proceedings than applications under the Workmen's Compensation Code it was for An Post to ensure that the provision had the extended meaning which they sought to attach to it and they could not complain if an ambiguously worded provision inserted for their benefit was read against them.[65]

14.7.3 It is possible, relying on English authorities, to make a case that it is not necessary for the indemnity clause to explicitly cover the negligence of the party in receipt of the indemnity and that such provision may be implied into the clause. In *Walter* v *Wessoe Ltd. and Shell Refining Co. Ltd.*,[66] Devlin L. J. had said that:

> . . . if a person obtains an indemnity against the consequences of certain acts, the indemnity is not to be construed so as to include the consequences of his own negligence unless those consequences are covered expressly or by necessary implication. They are covered by necessary implication if there is no other subject matter on which the indemnity could operate. Like most rules of construction, this one depends upon the presumed intention of the parties.

The principles to be applied in determining whether the indemnity covers the negligence of the recipient of the indemnity by implication

---

[65] Keane J. at p. 6 of judgment quoted Kingsmill-Moore J. in *Roscommon Co. Co.* v *Waldron* [1963] IR 407 at 419: "If the Council desired the clause to have a meaning favourable to it, so onerous to the contractor, and so exceptional in an indemnity, it was the business of the Council to make such meaning clear beyond dubiety."

[66] Unreported Court of Appeal, 18 November 1960; [1968] 2 All ER 811, 816.

were laid down by Morton L. J. in a decision of the Privy Council on an appeal from the Supreme Court of Canada in *Canada Steamship Lines Ltd.* v *Regem*:[67]

> if the words used are wide enough . . . the court must consider whether the head of damage may be based on some ground other than negligence. . . . The "other ground" must not be so fanciful or remote that the *proferens* cannot be supposed to have desired protection against it: but subject to this qualification . . . the existence of a possible head of damage other than that of negligence is fatal to the *proferens* even if the words used are *prima facie* wide enough to cover negligence.[68]

These principles were subsequently applied by the House of Lords in *Smith* v *South Wales Switchgear Ltd.*[69] and confirmed more recently by the Court of Appeal, as correctly stating the law of England, in *E.E. Caledonia Ltd.* v *Orbit Valve plc.*[70] That case arose out of the *Piper Alpha* oil rig disaster in which 165 people died. The plaintiff was the joint owner and operator of the oil rig. The defendant had a contract for the supply, installation and servicing of valves on the rig and one of its employees was killed in an explosion caused by the negligence of an employee of the plaintiff. The contract between the parties contained a clause providing that:

> . . . each party hereto shall indemnify . . . the other, provided that the other party has acted in good faith, from and against any claim . . . arising by reason of any injury to or death of an employee . . . resulting from or in any way connected with the performance of the contract.

---

[67] [1952] AC 192.

[68] ibid at 208. The Crown leased a shed from the plaintiff company under agreement which provided that

> the lessee shall at all times indemnify . . . the lessor from and against all claims . . . by whomsoever made . . . in any manner based upon, occasioned by or attributable to the execution of these presents or any action taken or things done. . . .

Owing to the negligence of the Crown's servants, the shed and its contents were destroyed by fire. The plaintiff and others whose property was destroyed sued the crown for damages but the crown claimed indemnity from the plaintiff, relying on the indemnity clause in the lease. The clause was held not to apply to negligent acts of the crown's servants.

[69] [1978] 1 All ER 18 at 31–33.

[70] [1995] 1 All ER 174; [1994] 2 Lloyds Rep 239.

The dependants of the employee had obtained a judgment for £650,000 against the plaintiff, who sought to obtain indemnity from the defendant under the terms of the indemnity clause. Quoting the principles laid down in *Canada Steamship Lines Ltd* v *Regem*,[71] the Court of Appeal ruled that the words used were potentially wide enough to include negligence but that other grounds of liability, in the form of strict liability for breach of statutory duty, also existed and these were not "fanciful or remote". In the circumstances the court held that the indemnity clause excluded the right to indemnity where the party claiming indemnity had been negligent. In delivering the judgment of the court, Steyn L. J. said that this interpretation matched the reasonable expectations of the parties and that it is inherently improbable, even in a bilateral clause, that a party would be willing to assume a risk of loss caused by the negligence of the other.[72] He suggested that the reason lawyers do not include an express reference to negligence in such clauses is that "they do not want to frighten off one party or the other".

14.7.4 The Supreme Court has not, however, given any indication that it is prepared to imply, into an indemnity clause, indemnity in respect of the negligence of the party in receipt of the indemnity or of that party's servants. In a dissenting judgment, in *Roscommon County Council* v *Waldron*,[73] O'Dalaigh C. J. was prepared to read the indemnity clause as implying a requirement on the defendant to indemnify the plaintiff in respect of all injuries arising out of the engagement of the defendant contractor and his plant, even if such injuries were caused by the plaintiff, its servants or agents. The plaintiff had hired a traxcavator together with its driver from the defendant and in the course of the work the driver was injured, allegedly due to the negligence of the County Council or its employees. The County Council settled the driver's claim and then sought an indemnity from the defendant on the basis of an indemnity clause in the contract which required the contractor to:

---

[71] [1952] AC 192.

[72] [1995] 1 All ER 174 at 185.

[73] [1963] IR 407.

> . . . indemnify and keep indemnified the council against all
> claims at law whether under the common law or statute, in-
> cluding the Workmen's Compensation and Employers' Liability
> in respect of proceedings, actions, demands, costs, charges, ex-
> penses and losses whatsoever which may be made against the
> Council or which the Council may pay or become liable to pay
> or may incur or sustain by reason of the negligence of the Con-
> tractor his agents servants or workmen in the execution of the
> work or in relation to injuries sustained by any of the Council's
> employees, or the Contractor's employees who may be engaged
> in attending on the aforesaid plant and machinery or any com-
> ponent part thereof whether arising from negligence or under
> the Workmen's Compensation or Employers' Liability Acts.[74]

The views of O'Dalaigh C. J. had no support in the Supreme Court.
Lavery J., while recognising that a party to a contract can undertake
to answer for the negligence of the other contracting party, was very
firmly of the opinion[75] that such obligations are not usually undertaken and "if they are to be considered to have been, clear words
would be required. It cannot be a matter of implication." Kingsmill
Moore J., in supporting Lavery J., based his decision primarily on the
ambiguity of the wording used which could be interpreted as covering
negligence in its fullest possible sense or confining it to the negligence
of the Contractor, his servants, and agents. He thought it incredible
"that the parties to the contract intended the indemnity to extend to
the negligence of the plaintiff and its servants".[76] Although referred to
the English authorities,[77] Kingsmill Moore J. was of the view that, in
general, those cases supported the proposition that, where an indemnity is intended to cover liability for the negligent acts of the person indemnified and of his servants, such intention should be made
abundantly clear, and if there is any ambiguity the indemnity will
not be construed so as to cover such liability.

---

[74] ibid at 412.

[75] ibid at 414.

[76] ibid at 418/9.

[77] *Alderslade* v *Hendon Laudry Ltd.* [1945] KB 189; *Canada Steamship Lines Ltd.*
v *Regem* [1952] AC 192.

14.7.5 It is not possible to discern from the latest Supreme Court decision, *Cuffe* v *Coras Iompair Eireann and An Post,*[78] whether the court was asked to consider English case law on the subject, but the court did emphatically refuse to imply into an indemnity clause a requirement that CIE should indemnify An Post in respect of its own negligence. The court was of the view that to imply such a requirement would be to impute to the contracting parties an intention which there was no reason to suppose they had. The Court[79] enthusiastically applied the *contra preferentem* rule and quoted with approval the words of Kingsmill Moore J. in *Roscommon County Council* v *Waldron*:[80]

> If the Council desired the clause to have a meaning so favourable to it, so onerous on the contractor, and so exceptional in an indemnity, it was the business of the Council to make such meaning clear beyond dubiety.

These two Supreme Court decisions give no reason to suppose that any Irish court will in future be prepared to imply into an indemnity clause a requirement that the indemnity should cover the recipient of the indemnity in respect of its negligence or that of its servants, where the wording does not make that requirement absolutely clear.

14.8 POLICY CONDITIONS

The conditions in an employers' liability insurance policy are similar to the general conditions in liability policies already dealt with. They relate to claims notification and co-operation, reasonable precautions, other insurance, cancellation and arbitration. Two are, however, worthy of particular mention.

14.8.1 PREMIUM ADJUSTMENT

The premium adjustment condition requires that the first premium and all renewal premiums are to be regulated by the amount of wages, salaries and other earnings paid to employees during each period of insurance. It further requires that the name of every em-

---

[78] Unreported Supreme Court, 22 October 1996.

[79] Hamilton C. J., Blayney J. and Keane J.

[80] [1963] IR 407 at 419.

ployee and the amounts paid to him be recorded in proper wages books and that the insured shall at all times afford the insurer facilities to inspect such books. Where requested, the insured is obliged to supply an audited account of such wages. If the total wages, salaries and earnings declared exceed the amount on which the original premium was calculated, the insured is required to pay the difference to the insurer, or if the amount declared is less, insurers will refund a proportionate amount to the insured subject to the insurers' right to retain any amount specified as the minimum premium in the policy. Failure by the insured to comply with this condition can have serious repercussions in the event of a claim, if insurers have reason to believe there was any deliberate understatement of wages. In *McMillan & Jervois* v *W. H. Ryan Ltd. and P. Carey*,[81] the plaintiff Lloyds underwriters sought and obtained a declaration that the policy of insurance relied on by Ryan was void because of the fraudulent misstatements made by Ryan as to the amounts of wages and salaries paid or payable by them to their employees, thus distorting the correct amount of the premium to be paid.

14.8.2 SUBROGATION

Incorporated into the claims condition is a provision entitling the insurer to prosecute in the name of the insured for its own benefit any claim for indemnity or damages or otherwise. Whereas in the UK there is an agreement between insurers that they will not subrogate against a fellow employee whose negligence has caused the injury giving rise to the claim against the employer, there is no such agreement between insurers in Ireland. It was the view of Lord Denning M. R. in *Morris* v *Ford Motor Co. Ltd.*,[82] that subrogation is an equitable doctrine which should not be implemented by the courts where implementation would produce results which would be inequitable, but it was a view with which the remainder of the Court of Appeal did not fully concur.[83] In that case the employers' liability insurers of the plaintiff's employer, having indemnified the defendant in respect of an award obtained against them by the plaintiff in respect of injuries

---

[81] Unreported High Court, 20 December 1978.

[82] [1973] QB 792 at 801.

[83] Stamp L. J. at 807 and James L. J. at 812.

sustained as a result of the misconduct of an employee of the defendant, sought to exercise subrogation rights against the employee responsible for the injuries sustained by the plaintiff. The Court of Appeal ruled by a majority that subrogation rights could not be exercised. If the two employees had been employed by the same employer there would not have been any question of the insurer attempting to exercise subrogation rights, as insurers in England had entered into a "gentleman's agreement" not to enforce the strict legal rights accorded to them by the House of Lords ruling in *Lister* v *Romford Ice & Cold Storage Co. Ltd.*[84] The right of an insurer in Ireland to subrogate against an employee, whose negligence has caused an injury or loss in respect of which the insurer has indemnified the employer, was confirmed by the Supreme Court in *Zurich Insurance Co.* v *Shield Insurance Co. Ltd.*[85] Whilst the legal right exists, in practice, however, most employers' liability insurance policies issued in Ireland provide that the insurer will, at the request of the insured, indemnify an employee in respect of liability for injuries sustained by a fellow employee. Whilst the right of an insurer to subrogate is well established in law, it is normal practice to insert into insurance policies of indemnity a subrogation condition which, in addition to affirming the insurer's legal rights, also deals with the conduct required of the insured in the event of a claim under the policy. The effect of the condition is to improve the insurer's legal position by enabling him to take over control of any rights the insured may have against a third party before the insurer actually indemnifies the insured.

14.9 EMPLOYEES' RIGHTS AGAINST INSURERS

In Ireland there is no equivalent statute to the Third Parties (Rights against Insurers) Act, 1930. Section 62 of the Civil Liability Act, 1961, provides that where a person or company insured under a liability insurance policy dies, becomes bankrupt, or is wound up, moneys payable under the policy shall be applied only to discharging in full all valid claims against the insured in respect of which those moneys are payable and the moneys shall not be regarded as assets of the in-

---

[84] [1957] AC 555. "An unfortunate decision" according to Denning M. R. in *Morris* above at 801.

[85] [1988] IR 174.

sured or used for payment of the debts of the insured other than for payment of those claims. In *Dunne v P. J. White Construction Co. Ltd. (in Liquidation) and Michael Payne and Others,*[86] the plaintiff employee had obtained judgment in default of defence against his employer, the first defendant, in respect of an injury sustained by him in the course of his employment. The employer went into liquidation prior to the judgment being obtained and the plaintiff sought to enforce the judgment against the second defendant, who were the insurers of the employer under an employers' liability insurance policy. The insurers maintained that they were entitled to repudiate liability to the insured due to breach of policy conditions. In the High Court, Murphy J. held, as a matter of law, that: the onus was on the plaintiff to establish that a policy of insurance existed; it was issued by the insurers to the first defendants; it covered the risk of an accident such as the accident in respect of which the plaintiff had received damages; and that there was also on the plaintiff the onus of proving as a negative that a right asserted or alleged by the defendants to rescind or repudiate the policy of insurance had not arisen. The High Court decided that the plaintiff had failed to discharge the onus which was on him and the plaintiff appealed the decision to the Supreme Court, relying on Section 62 of the Civil Liability Act, 1961, to ground his action. In the Supreme Court, Finlay C. J. in a judgment with which the other four members all concurred, identified the net issue before the court as being whether the trial judge was correct in his view of the onus which the law placed on the plaintiff.[87] The Court suggested that, in order to properly implement the protection which Section 62 of the Civil Liability Act, 1961 afforded to persons in the precise position of the plaintiff and in accordance with established rules in relation to the onus of proof, it was necessary that the onus of proof should be on the insurance company to prove what it alleged. The Court directed a new trial but the matter was compromised before it came for further hearing. In the course of his judgment, Finlay C. J. had said:

> Section 62 of the Act of 1961 is specifically designed to protect an injured plaintiff in the precise position of Mr Dunne in this

---

[86] [1989] ILRM 803.

[87] ibid. at 804.

> action so as to ensure that moneys payable on a policy of in-
> surance to an insured who is dead, bankrupt, and, in the case
> of a corporate body, who is gone into liquidation, will not be
> eaten up by other creditors, but will go to satisfy his compen-
> sation, and with that purpose in mind the section must, it
> seems to me, give to the plaintiff a right to have that right en-
> forced and protected by the courts, and that means that he has
> got a right to sue as he has sued in this action.[88]

These comments of the Chief Justice were, however, *obiter* and not
part of the decision itself. The judgment was not reserved and was
given *ex tempore*. The case before the Supreme Court was, according
to the Court itself,[89] concerned with establishing the onus of proof and
nothing else. The alleged right of the plaintiff to sue the insurers under the policy was not argued before the High Court or raised in the
pleadings and consequently, because it went unchallenged, the Supreme Court was obliged to assume that such a right existed.[90] However, Finlay C. J. was, as always, careful in his choice of words. In
saying that Section 62 of the 1961 Act gave injured plaintiffs a right
of action against insurers, he qualified the statement by referring to
plaintiffs in the precise position of the plaintiff in that action. That
plaintiff had obtained judgment against the insured employer and
was seeking a declaration that the defendant insurers were, by virtue
of Section 62, obliged to pay the damages and costs awarded to the
plaintiff. There can be no doubt but that a plaintiff who has obtained
judgment against an insured, and that judgment is not met because
of death, bankruptcy, or liquidation, has, by virtue of Section 62, a
right to proceed against insurers for payment of the moneys due under a policy of insurance, covering the insured's liability to the plaintiff. But that is as far as the Act goes. It does not, as does the UK Act,
transfer to the plaintiff the rights of the insured under the policy. It
does not give the plaintiff the right to sue for specific performance of
the contract. It does not give the plaintiff third party the right to arbitrate under the policy if the policy contains an arbitration clause. It
does not in any way attempt to interfere with the privity of contract
rule. Section 62 applies only to moneys "payable" under a policy of

---

[88] ibid. at 805.

[89] at 804.

[90] per Finlay C. J. at 805.

insurance and it must first be established that the moneys are payable before the third party can claim to have them applied to satisfaction of a judgment obtained against the insured. If the insurer had successfully repudiated liability under the policy, Section 62 does not give any rights to the employee to challenge that repudiation. Any such challenge would have to be made by the representatives of the insured or the liquidator of the insured company. The law, as it stands, does not extend direct right of action against insurers to an employee, in respect of injury sustained arising out of or in the course of his employment, unless the employer has gone into liquidation, been wound up or been declared bankrupt, and the employee has obtained a judgment against the employer which remains unsatisfied.

14.10 EMPLOYEES' RIGHTS UNDER THE COMPANIES ACTS

Under the Irish Companies Acts, any amounts due by a company in liquidation in respect of damages payable to an employee injured in an accident in the course of his employment rank as a preferential debt to the extent that the company is not effectively indemnified by insurers.[91] Where an indemnity is being provided by an insurer, Section 62 of the 1961 Civil Liability Act entitles an injured employee to apply to have the moneys due under a policy of insurance paid directly to him as compensation in priority to ordinary creditors provided:

a) he has already established or can establish before winding up of the company that the company is liable to him for the injury sustained and the financial extent of that liability; and

b) the assets of the company are sufficient to meet the liability of the company to all preferential creditors.

Where the assets are insufficient, all preferential creditors' claims are abated in equal proportions.[92] In most liquidations the assets available for distribution are insufficient to meet all creditors' claims and the claims of injured employees against uninsured companies are unlikely to be met in full, if at all. There is no provision in the Irish Companies Acts similar to Section 141 of the English Companies Act

---

[91] Section 285(2)(g), Companies Act, 1963, as amended.

[92] Section 285(7).

of 1989, allowing companies to be brought back to life to enable former employees pursue actions for compensation in respect of injury or disease sustained during the course of employment by the company.[93] This defect in Irish company law may present problems for employees seeking compensation for illness or disease now manifesting itself years after the company has been wound up.

---

[93] Section 310 permits application to the court within two years of dissolution to have the dissolution declared void and proceedings may then be taken as if the company had not been dissolved.

CHAPTER FIFTEEN

MATERIAL DAMAGE INSURANCE

15.1 INTRODUCTION

The insurance of property against material damage was generally effected by means of a "fire" insurance policy, but in recent years such insurance has been more correctly described as material damage insurance. This change was brought about by market competition and the increased sophistication of the insurance buyer in demanding a wider form of cover. The now common "All Risks" material damage policy is the result of natural progression from a fire-only policy, to a fire and specified perils policy, to a policy covering all risks of loss or damage. A product of the North American insurance market, the All Risks Material Damage policy is now almost invariably used to cover property and contents. Competition between insurers for what is generally profitable business has led to a wide variation in the scope of cover provided. Most insurers are prepared to customise the policy wording to the individual requirements of the insured. There is therefore no standard form of policy wording in use in the Irish market but certain conditions, exceptions, perils and principles are common to all.

15.2 INSURING CLAUSE

An All Risks material damage policy will generally provide that:

> . . . if any of the property insured be accidentally lost, destroyed or damaged other than by an excluded cause. . . . the insurers will pay to the insured the value of the property at the time of the happening of its accidental loss, destruction or damage or the insurers, at their option, will reinstate or replace such property or part thereof . . . provided that the liability of the insurers in respect of any one loss shall in no case exceed. . . . the sum expressed in the schedule to be insured thereon or in the whole the total sum insured hereby.

15.3 INDEMNITY

15.3.1 The policy is a policy of indemnity.[1] It is unusual nowadays to issue a valued policy in respect of commercial property but the principle of indemnity[2] has to some extent been diluted by the almost universal application of "reinstatement as new" conditions. Policy provisions do, however, limit the liability of insurers[3] and the insured cannot recover more than their loss. The sum insured specified in the policy is the maximum amount payable by insurers but is not necessarily the amount paid.[4] In the absence of "reinstatement as new" conditions insurers are liable for the value of the property at the time of the loss or destruction or damage. The assessment of that value invariably leads to difficulties but it is necessary, in fulfilment of the

---

[1] "By the law of insurance, though the underwriter directly promises to pay on a certain event, the contract is treated as one of indemnity," per Lord Esher M. R. at p. 61. of *Dane* v *Mortgage Insurance Corporation* [1894] 1 QB 54; "Policies of assurance against fire . . . are . . . properly contracts of indemnity, the insurer agreeing to make good, within certain limited amounts, the losses sustained by the insured," per p. 387 *Dalby* v *India and London Insurance Corporation* [1854] 15 CB 365.

[2] See Chapter Four.

[3] Typical "reinstatement as new" conditions provide that the insurer will pay:
the cost of reinstatement being where the property is destroyed the cost of rebuilding or where the property is damaged the cost of repair to a condition substantially the same as but not better or more extensive than its condition when new. The insurer's liability shall be limited to payment of the value of the property at the time of its destruction or the amount of the damage if the work of reinstatement is not carried out as quickly as is reasonably practicable and until the cost of the reinstatement has actually been incurred.

[4] "You must not run away with the notion that a policy of insurance entitles a man to recover according to the amount represented as insured by the premium paid," per Cockburn C. J. addressing the jury in *Chapman* v *Pole* [1870] 22 Lt 306. From the joint judgment of the High Court of Australia in *British Traders Insurance Co. Ltd.* v *Monson* [1964] 111 Com. LR 86 at p. 92:
It is far too late to doubt that, by common understanding of businessmen and lawyers alike, the nature of such a policy controls its obligation implying conclusively that its statement of the amount the insurer promises to pay merely fixes the maximum amount which in any event he may have to pay and having as its sole purpose and therefore imposing as its only obligation the indemnification of the insured up to the amount of the insurance against loss from the accepted risk.
And in *Vance* v *Forster* [1841] Ir. Cir Rep. 47, per Pennefather B.:
. . . while the insured may name any sum he likes as the sum for which he will pay a premium, he does not, by so proposing that sum, nor does the company by accepting the risk, conclude themselves as to the amount which the plaintiff is to recover in consequence of the loss.

principle of indemnity, to establish a value which will put the insured in the position they would have been in had no loss occurred, in so far as that is possible.

15.3.2 The value established and the amount paid by the insurers must neither impoverish nor enrich the insured.[5] The policy does not define what is meant by value and does not indicate how such value is to be calculated. Insurers will generally, in the absence of reinstatement conditions, attempt to agree the amount payable on the basis of:

a) reinstatement costs less a deduction for betterment,[6] or

b) the cost of equivalent modern replacement,[7] or

c) market value.[8]

15.3.3 The Supreme Court, in *St Albans Investment Co.* v *Sun Alliance & London Insurance Co. Ltd.*[9] held that the insurance contract did not contain terms which entitled the insured to an indemnity, measured by the cost of reinstatement, and, in the absence of a proven intention to reinstate, the estimated market value was the correct basis for measuring the indemnity under the policy. The plaintiffs had purchased property in 1977 for approximately £15,000 which was subsequently insured with the defendants for £300,000.

---

[5] *Murphy* v *Wexford County Council* [1921] 2 IR 230 at 240. The case arose, not under a policy of insurance, but under statute giving compensation to persons whose property had suffered malicious damage.

[6] *Harbutt's Plasticine Ltd.* v *Wayne Tank & Pump Co Ltd.* [1970] 1 QB 447 at 473.

[7] In *Reynolds* v *Phoenix Assurance Co. Ltd.* [1978] 2 Lloyds Rep 440 Forbes J. considered that equivalent modern replacement was not a separate basis of assessment but a valuer's device to arrive at the market value of an old building.

[8] "It all depends on the circumstances of the case. . . . the general rule is that the injured person is to be fairly compensated for the damage he has sustained neither more nor less." per Denning L. J. (as he then was) in *Phillips* v *Ward* [1956] 1 WLR 471 at 473. Henchy J. in *Munnelly* v *Calcon Ltd.* [1978] IR 387 at 399 said:

> In my view, the particular measure of damages allowed should be objectively chosen by the court as being that which is best calculated, in all the circumstances of the case, to put the plaintiff fairly and reasonably in the position in which he was before the damage occurred, so far as pecuniary award can do so.

[9] [1984] ILRM 501.

The property was destroyed by fire three months after purchase. The court had considered the leading English authorities[10] and the possible different methods of valuation which might provide an indemnity.

15.3.4 The insured can only seek to have the cost of reinstatement used as the basis of valuation in calculating the amount payable as indemnity,[11] if he can show that he intends to reinstate the building, that reinstatement is not unreasonable or eccentric in the circumstances,[12] and that the proposed mode of reinstatement is reasonable.[13] The amount recoverable will be subject to a deduction for betterment.[14] The cost of reinstatement is the maximum recoverable by the insured but there is nothing in the policy or by any legitimate inference which provides that the loss to be indemnified is to be the cost of reinstatement when that sum is greater than the actual loss.[15]

15.3.5 A recent Court of Appeal decision held that insurers were not entitled to avoid a household insurance policy where the value insured was significantly less than the actual value, provided the in-

---

[10] *Harbutts v Wayne Tank Co.* [1970] 1 QB 447; *Reynolds v Phoenix Assurance Co. Ltd.* [1978] 2 Lloyds Rep 440; *Hollebone v Midhurst & Fernhurst Builders* [1968] 1 Lloyds Rep 38; *Leppard v Excess Insurance Co. Ltd.* [1979] 1 WLR 512; *Castellain v Preston* [1883] 11 QBD 380; *British Traders Insurance Co. Ltd. v Monson* [1964] 111 CLR 86.

[11] Forbes J. in *Reynolds v Phoenix Assurance Co. Ltd.* [1978] 2 Lloyds Rep 440 at 450:

> I must reject . . . that the parties here contracted on the basis that indemnity was to be measured by the cost of reinstatement. But as the extent of indemnity still remains to be decided, the cost of reinstatement still remains a possible means of measuring it, even though prior agreement to that effect cannot be found in the contract.

[12] *Reynolds* above n. 7 at 453.

[13] The claimant is:

> not bound to accept a shoddy job or put up with an inferior building for the sake of saving the defendant's expense. But I do not consider they are entitled to insist on complete and meticulous restoration when a reasonable building owner would be content with less extensive work . . . and when there is also a vast difference in the cost of such work and the cost of meticulous restoration.

Cantley J. in *Dodd Properties (Kent) Ltd. v Canterbury County Council* [1979] 2 All ER 118 at 124.

[14] *Harbutt's Plasticine Ltd. v Wayne Tank & Pump Co. Ltd.* [1970] 1 QB 447.

[15] *Leppard v Excess Insurance Co. Ltd.* [1979] 1 WLR 512.

sured purported to give the value to the best of their knowledge and belief and were acting honestly and reasonably.[16] The insured plaintiff, on the advice of his father, increased the sum insured under the policy to take account of jewellery and silverware which his parents had brought with them from Cyprus and which they indicated were valued at £3,000–£4,000. Sometime after the premises were burgled and property worth £31,000 stolen — most of it jewellery and valuables belonging to the insured's parents. The total sum insured was £16,000 and the maximum recoverable for valuables was one-third of the sum insured. Insurers repudiated the claim, alleging misrepresentation and non-disclosure of material facts in that the insured had represented the full value of the property as £16,000 whereas at the time of loss, it was £40,000, and that the value of valuables did not exceed one-third (£5,333), whereas it was in fact almost £30,000. The court accepted that the insured honestly believed that £16,000 represented the full value of the property insured.

15.4 REINSTATEMENT AS NEW

15.4.1 Where the policy contains "reinstatement as new" conditions, the amount payable as indemnity is the cost of rebuilding to a condition substantially the same as, but not better or more extensive than, its condition when new. No deduction will be made for betterment or wear and tear.[17] The maximum amount payable is the sum insured in respect of the destroyed property. The policy conditions provide that this basis of valuation will not apply unless the reinstatement is carried out. Where the reinstatement as new conditions apply, the policy provides that:

> . . . in the event of the property insured . . . (ex stock) . . . being destroyed or damaged the basis upon which the amount payable . . . is to be calculated shall be the reinstatement of the property destroyed or damaged subject to the following special provisions and subject also to the policy terms and conditions.

---

[16] *Economides* v *Commercial Union Assurance Co. plc*, Unreported Court of Appeal, 22 May 1997.

[17] In *Harbutt's Plasticine Ltd.* v *Wayne Tank & Pump Co. Ltd.* [1970] 1 QB 447 at 473 Widgery L. J. suggested that a deduction for betterment "would be the equivalent of forcing the plaintiffs to invest in the modernizing of their plant which might be highly inconvenient for them".

... For the purposes of the insurance ... "reinstatement" shall mean (a) where the property is destroyed, the re-building of the property ... or its replacement by similar property, if not a building, in a condition equal to but not better or more extensive than its condition when new, and (b) where property is damaged the repair of the damage and the restoration of the damaged portion of the property to a condition substantially the same as but not better or more extensive than its condition when new.

15.4.2 The main special provisions referred to require that:

a) the work of reinstatement must be commenced and carried out with reasonable dispatch, otherwise the value at the time of the loss is the maximum payable.[18]

b) where there is partial loss only, the maximum amount payable is the sum representing the cost of reinstating the whole of the property if that had been destroyed.

c) Insurers will not pay out more than the pre-loss value until the cost of reinstatement shall have been incurred. In practice, once insurers are satisfied that reinstatement is being undertaken, payments on account will be made with a reasonable retention withheld pending completion.

15.5 AVERAGE

The application of an average clause to the material damage policy has been accepted for may years although it can still be a source of difficulty. The earliest recorded average clause on a fire policy was issued in 1772 and in 1882, standard wordings were agreed between fire insurers.[19] The effect of the average condition is to place the onus on the insured to ensure that the full value of the property is insured under the policy. The standard average clause provides that if the property insured is at the time of the loss of greater value than the sum insured, then the insured shall be considered as being his own

---

[18] See *St. Albans Investment Co.* v *Sun Alliance & London Insurance Ltd.* [1983] IR 363; *Leppard* v *Excess Insurance Co. Ltd.* [1979] 2 Lloyds Rep 91.

[19] "A Study of the general application of Average in the Light of Continuing Inflation", Report of Advanced Study Group No. 184 of Insurance Institute of London [1967].

insurer for the difference and bear a rateable proportion of the loss. A different form of wording is incorporated into the reinstatement as new conditions which provides that:

> . . . if at the time of reinstatement the sum representing eighty-five per cent of the cost which would have been incurred in restatement if the whole of the property covered . . . had been destroyed exceeds the sum insured . . . at the commencement of any destruction or damage . . . then the insured shall be considered as being his own insurer for the difference between the sum insured and the sum representing the cost of reinstatement of the whole of the property and shall bear a rateable proportion of the loss.

15.6 INSURED PERILS

The All Risks material damage policy covers accidental loss, destruction or damage to the insured property without specifying the perils which might give rise to such loss or damage. The policy generally specifies the perils which are not insured; some of these and some of the perils usually insured have been judicially considered.

15.6.1 ACCIDENTAL DAMAGE

The intention is to cover only direct physical loss or damage. In this context, "damage" has been held to mean a change in the property's physical state above and beyond inevitable change due to ordinary wear and tear.[20] "Accidental" means an unintended and unexpected occurrence which produces loss or damage.[21]

15.6.2 FIRE

15.6.2.1 To constitute "fire" under a policy covering loss or damage by fire, there must be ignition of some kind.[22] It has been held that there is loss or damage by fire when there is ignition of the insured property or when the property is damaged, other than by ignition, as a direct consequence of the ignition of other property not intended to

---

[20] *Ranicar* v *Frigmobile pty. Ltd.* [1983] Tas. R. 113.

[21] *Rohan Construction Ltd.* v *Insurance Corporation of Ireland Ltd.* [1988] ILRM 373.

[22] *Everett* v *London Assurance* [1865] 19 CB 126 at 133.

be ignited.[23] There must be a flame or glow. Thermal damage is not sufficient to bring the damage within the definition of "fire". Damage to property by excessive heat will not, as such, be covered by an ordinary fire policy unless there is also ignition of property not intended to be ignited.[24] Damage to the insured property by smoke is covered provided the smoke emanates from the ignition of property not intended to be ignited.[25] The ignition, which is essential to constitute "fire" within the meaning of an insurance policy covering fire, need not be ignition of the property insured. It is sufficient if the damage to the insured property is a direct result of the ignition of other property.

15.6.2.2 The connection between the insured peril and the damage has to be so close that the relation of cause and effect is clearly established. If adjoining property or property in the vicinity of the insured property is ignited and damage is caused to the insured property by falling walls,[26] by water,[27] or otherwise, the insured property is said to be damaged by fire within the meaning of the policy. Warping or thermal damage to the insured property as a result of "fire" in nearby premises is covered, as is water damage from consequential melting of snow and ice, or from rain entering the damaged property, damage by falling masonry and damage which is the consequence of fire-fighting.[28]

---

[23] *Harris* v *Poland* [1941] 1 KB 462. The insured concealed valuables in a fireplace as a precaution against theft and sought to recover under a fire policy when they were destroyed after she lit a fire in the grate.

[24] *Austin* v *Drewe* [1815] 4 Camp. 360.

[25] *"The Diamond"* [1906] 95 LT 550. Smoke damage to furniture or decor from a smoky chimney would not be covered but smoke damage caused by a fire in a chimney would be covered.

[26] *Johnston* v *West of Scotland Insurance Co.* [1828] 7 S 53.

[27] *Stanley* v *Western Insurance Co.* [1868] LR 3 Ex. 71. Followed by the Court of Appeal in *Symington* v *Union Insurance Society of Canton Ltd.* [1928] 97 LJKB 646.

[28] *Re. Hooley Hill Rubber & Chemical Co. and Royal Insurance Co. Ltd.* [1920] 1 KB 257

15.6.2.3 Property damaged when being moved to avoid damage by fire will be treated as being damaged by fire, provided the movement of the property was justified.[29]

> . . . any loss resulting from an apparently necessary and bona fide effort to put out a fire, whether it be by spoiling the goods by water or throwing the article or furniture out a window or even the destroying of a neighbouring house by an explosion for the purpose of checking the progress of the flames, in a word, every loss that clearly and proximately results, whether directly or indirectly from the fire, is within the policy.[30]

To bring a loss within this dictum it would appear that the peril must have begun to operate, the risk of damage to the insured property must be imminent and immediate action necessary to avoid the danger.[31] Although not decided, it would seem that provided the action taken is reasonable in the circumstances, the resulting damage is recoverable, even though no damage would have occurred if no action had been taken.[32] Whether the insured can recover costs incurred in averting or minimising damage by fire or other insured peril has not been judicially decided in the context of property insurance,[33] but it would seem unjust that he could not recover.

15.6.3 LIGHTNING

Loss or damage occasioned by ignition as a result of lightning is a loss by fire,[34] but damage caused by lightning without ignition is loss by lightning.[35]

---

[29] *McPhearson* v *Guardian Insurance Co.* [1893] 7 Nfld. LR 768; *Stanley* v *Western Insurance Co.* [1868] LR 3 Exch. 71.

[30] *"Stanley" supra* per Kelly C. B.

[31] *Symington* v *Union Insurance Society of Canton Ltd.* [1928] 97 LJKB 646.

[32] The majority of American decisions favour this view; See *Harper* v *Pelican Trucking Co.* 176 So. 2d. 767 [1965].

[33] Under Marine insurance law the insured can recover the cost of avoiding or minimizing loss as he has a duty as well as a right to "sue and labour"; *Pyman Steamship Co.* v *Admiralty Commissioners* [1919] 1 KB 49.

[34] *Gordon* v *Rimmington* [1807] 1 Camp. 123.

[35] *Kenniston* v *Merchants County Mutual Insurance Co.* 14. NH 341 [1843].

15.6.4 STORM AND TEMPEST

Storm connotes some sort of violent wind usually accompanied by rain or hail or snow. Storm does not mean persistent bad weather, nor does it mean heavy rain or persistent rain by itself. Tempest means no more than a severe storm and the word storm is therefore the operative word in a policy covering storm and tempest.[36] An isolated gust of wind does not constitute a storm,[37] and whether wind or rain on their own constituted a storm was a question left open in *Anderson v Norwich Union Fire Insurance Society Ltd.*[38] The insured peril of storm or tempest must be the proximate cause of the damage in respect of which the claim is made. Collapse of a building due to the supports being over-stressed was held not to be damage by storm or tempest,[39] and the destruction of a house due to the collapse of a retaining wall was not covered by the insured peril of storm and tempest as the collapse of the wall was shown to be the result of a build-up of water pressure behind the wall rather than a combination of wind and rain at a particular moment in time.[40]

15.6.5 RIOT AND CIVIL COMMOTION

Riot is a technical term of the criminal law and has been interpreted in relation to insurance policies in England.[41] Civil commotion has been defined as "an insurrection of the people for general purposes, not necessarily amounting to a rebellion".[42] The acts constituting the commotion must be done by the rioters together and not merely in concert and simultaneously.[43] While the element of civil disorder is essential, the fact that emergency regulations have been promulgated is not sufficient proof. While it is not necessary to prove that there was commotion at the time and place of the loss, it is necessary to

---

[36] per Veale J. *Oddy v Phoenix Assurance Co. Ltd.* [1966] 1 Lloyds Rep 134 at 138.

[37] *S. & M. Hotels Ltd. v Legal and General Assurance Society Ltd.* [1972] 1 Lloyds Rep 157.

[38] *Anderson v Norwich Union Fire Insurance Society Ltd.* [1977] 1 Lloyds Rep 293.

[39] *Oddy v Phoenix Assurance Co. Ltd.* [1966] 1 Lloyds Rep 134.

[40] *S. & M. Hotels supra.*

[41] *The Andreas Lemos* [1983] QB 647; *Field v Receiver of Metropolitan Police District* [1907] 2 KB 853.

[42] per Lord Mansfield in *Langdale v Mason* [1780] Park, Insurance Vol 2, p. 965.

[43] *London and Manchester Plate Glass Co. v Heath* [1914] 3 KB 411.

show that the loss occurred as a result of the civil commotion. In the Irish case of *Cooper* v *General Accident Fire and Life Assurance Corp. Ltd.*[44] the court held that where the insured vehicle was stolen by men, armed with a stick which the insured mistook for a gun, the loss was caused by civil commotion as it was common knowledge that a state of guerrilla warfare existed in Ireland and the acts of the men could not be said to be those of ordinary thieves. Civil commotion does not include civil war.[45]

15.6.6 SUBSIDENCE

An insured whose property suffers cracking as the result of tree root activity, either by incursion or by the withdrawal of water from the soil has a claim against his insurers, unless subsidence is an excluded peril, on the basis that such loss is an accident.[46] Subsidence has been defined as meaning "primarily sinking in a vertical direction, but may also include settlement i.e. movement in a lateral direction".[47]

15.6.7 THEFT

It is common for material damage policies to refer to theft as an insured peril or as an excluded peril although there is no Irish statutory definition of theft.[48] The parties to an insurance contract are however free to agree a definition of a risk different from that adopted by the criminal law. The 1916 Larceny Act provides that:

> a person steals who, without the consent of the owner, fraudulently and without a claim of right made in good faith, takes and carries away any thing capable of being stolen with intent at the time of such taking, permanently to deprive the owner thereof.[49]

---

[44] *Cooper* v *General Accident Fire and Life Assurance Corp. Ltd.* [1923] 128 LT 481 followed in *Boggan* v *Motor Union Insurance Co.* [1923] 130 LT 588.

[45] *Curtis* v *Mathews* [1919] 1 KB 425; *Johnson & Perrott* v *Holmes* [1925] 21 Lloyds Rep 330.

[46] *Mills* v *Smith* [1964] 1 QB 30.

[47] *David Allen & Sons Bill Posting Ltd.* v *Drysdale* [1939] 4 All ER 113.

[48] Some policies refer to stealing and larceny.

[49] Section 1. The Act defines burglary and housebreaking separately.

In England, the Theft Act 1968 made radical changes in and greatly simplified the law in relation to theft.[50] Section 1(1) of the Act provides that "A person is guilty of theft if he dishonestly appropriates property belonging to another with the intention of permanently depriving the other of it". This new definition of theft covers virtually all the kinds of dishonest conduct which came within the definition of stealing, in all its forms, in the Larceny Act which is still operative in Ireland. Insurers here generally clarify the scope of cover provided by either defining theft as "stealing involving entry to or exit from the premises by forcible and violent means or any attempt thereat" or by excluding theft or any attempt thereat "which does not involve entry to or exit from a building by forcible and violent means or actual or threatened violence". Where property is stolen following a break-in or hold-up at the premises of the insured, there is generally no difficulty in bringing the loss within the insured peril. Where the policy provides cover in respect of theft without qualification there is uncertainty as to whether an insured can recover from insurers where property has been lost as a result of fraud. The issue involves analysis of the criminal law and was considered by the Court of Appeal in *Dobson* v *General Accident Fire and Life Assurance Corp. Ltd.*[51] The insured had offered some jewellery for sale by advertisement and accepted payment by cheque from the purchaser. The cheque proved to be worthless. The policy covered "loss or damage caused by theft" and the Court found in favour of the insured.

15.7 EXCLUDED PERILS

The perils excluded from a material damage All Risks policy are generally either uninsurable, such as corrosion or wear and tear, or are properly the subject of more specific insurance such as engineering insurance. Some of the commonly excluded perils have been the subject of judicial consideration.

---

[50] The Act simplified the law in respect of burglary which had been very complicated. The concept of "breaking" was eliminated entirely.

[51] *The Times* 28th July 1989. See also: *Webster* v *General Accident Fire and Life Assurance Corp.* [1953] 1 QB 520; *Eisinger* v *General Accident Fire and Life Assurance Corp.* [1955] 2 All ER 897; *Lawrence* v *Commissioner of Police for the Metropolis* [1972] AC 626; *R* v *Morris* [1984] AC 320.

15.7.1 WAR

Policies generally now exclude war, invasion, act of foreign enemy, hostilities (whether war be declared or not), civil war, rebellion, revolution, insurrection, or military or usurped power. The word war is not defined in the contract, and whether there is a state of war in existence is a question of fact in each case.[52] If civil war is not specifically mentioned, war is regarded as including civil war.[53] Easter week 1916 was held to be "a week not of mere riot but of civil strife amounting to warfare waged between military and usurped powers and involving bombardment" for purposes of a policy covering loss caused by "war, bombardment, military or usurped power".[54]

15.7.2 EXPLOSION

The policy will not cover loss or damage to the insured property caused by explosion, occasioned by the bursting of a boiler,(not being a boiler used for domestic purposes only) economiser, or other vessel, machine, or apparatus in which internal pressure is due to steam only and belonging to or under the control of the insured, but subsequent damage resulting from an ensuing cause which is not otherwise excluded is covered. "Explosion" has been defined as "an event that is violent, noisy and . . . caused by a very rapid chemical or nuclear reaction, or the bursting out of gas or vapour under pressure".[55]

15.7.3 COLLAPSE

Damage arising from collapse or cracking of buildings is not covered unless resulting from a cause which is not otherwise excluded. In *David Allen & Sons Bill Posting Ltd.* v *Drysdale*[56] it was held that

---

[52] *Kawasaki Kisen Kabushiki of Kobe* v *Bantham SS Co. Ltd.* [1939] 2 KB 544. "War" in an insurance policy is not used in the same sense as in international law.

[53] *Pesquerias y Secaderos de Bacalao de Espana SA* v *Beer* [1949] 82 Lloyds Rep 501.

[54] *Curtis & Sons* v *Mathews* [1918] 2 KB 825, affirmed [1919] 1 KB 425. The revolutionaries were held to be King's enemies in *Secretary of State for War* v *Midland Great Western Railway of Ireland* [1923] 2 IR 102. "*Curtis*" was followed in "*Pesquerias*" supra.

[55] *Commonwealth Smelting Ltd.* v *Guardian Royal Exchange* [1984] 2 Lloyds Rep 608.

[56] [1939] 4 All ER 113.

"collapse" denotes falling, shrinking together, breaking down or giving way through external pressure or loss of rigidity or support but cannot cover intentional demolition.

15.8 POLICY CONDITIONS

The general policy conditions provide that the policy shall be voidable in the event of misrepresentation, misdescription, or non-disclosure in any material particular and require observance of the terms, relating to anything to be done by the insured, as a condition precedent to any liability under the policy.

15.8.1 ALTERATION

15.8.1.1 Most policies prohibit any alteration in the property insured which increases the risk or alternatively require that any such alteration be notified to insurers with failure to so notify rendering the policy void. The policy may specify the alterations which insurers require to be notified or which avoid the policy. Such alterations could include the building becoming unoccupied or vacant. In the absence of specific alterations being mentioned, a condition of this kind would prohibit alterations of a substantial and permanent character.[57] Reconstruction work may constitute an alteration of the risk.[58] The Court of Appeal has held that for the condition to apply there has to be an alteration in the description of the building. In *Exchange Theatre Ltd.* v *Iron Trades Mutual Insurance Co. Ltd.*[59] the introduction of a petrol generator and container into a building described in the policy as a bingo hall did not constitute an alteration within the terms of the particular policy which provided that "this policy shall be avoided with respect to any item thereof in regard to which there be any alteration . . . whereby the risk of destruction or damage is increased".

---

[57] *Shaw* v *Roberts* [1837] 6 AD & E 75.

[58] *Marzouca* v *Atlantic & British Commercial Insurance Co. Ltd.* [1971] 1 Lloyds Rep 449.

[59] [1984] 1 Lloyds Rep 149. For cases where the risk was held to be increased, see: *Reid* v *Gore District Mutual Fire Insurance Co.* [1853] 11 UC QB; *Merrick* v *Provincial Insurance Co.* [1856] 14 UC QB 439; *Farnham* v *Royal Insurance Co. Ltd.* [1976] 2 Lloyds Rep 437; *Linden Alimak Ltd.* v *British Engine Insurance Co. Ltd.* [1984] 1 Lloyds Rep 416; *Guerin* v *Manchester Fire Insurance Co.* [1898] 29 Can. SC 139.

15.8.1.2 In *Hussain* v *Brown* (No. 2)[60] the insured's property had been damaged by fire within four months of cover being effected. The insured had ceased to trade in the premises a number of weeks after effecting cover and at the time of the loss the property had to all intents and purposes been abandoned. The policy contained a condition requiring the insured to give insurers notification of any alteration likely to increase the risk. The court held that:

> wherever there is a contractual requirement for the insured to give the underwriter information which is material, in that it would influence the judgement of a prudent underwriter, in making a decision under the contract, for which the information is required, the continuing duty of good faith requires the insured to make full disclosure of all material facts, whether or not he realises their materiality, and not simply refrain from dishonest, deliberate or culpable concealment.

15.8.1.3 The court accepted that the continuing duty of disclosure could be modified by the terms of the contract between the parties and that, in this particular case, the condition, requiring notification of any alteration likely to increase the risk, represented the extent of the insured's duty. If the insurers wished to make the contract subject to a more extensive and continuing duty of utmost good faith it was necessary that they should do so by clear express terms in the policy. The decision appears to accept that the insured is under a duty of good faith at all times during the period of the policy but that the duty may be modified by the express terms of the contract. The court held the insured in breach of the condition and liable in damages to the insurer. On the basis of the evidence, the court concluded that had they been informed of the alteration, insurers would have insisted on some additional precautions which would have had a 50:50 chance of avoiding the loss. The appropriate level of damages to be awarded to the insurers on their counter-claim was held to be 50 per cent of the loss otherwise payable.

15.8.2 WARRANTIES

15.8.2.1 Where the policy is subject to warranties, the policy usually provides that non-compliance with any such warranty, in so far as it

---

[60] Unreported Court of Appeal, November 1996.

increases the risk of damage, shall be a bar to recovery. A warranty applies and continues in force during the currency of the policy. While the policy wording may not indicate as much, it has been suggested that the effect of a breach of warranty is, not only to defeat a claim, but to discharge the insurance contract on the basis that "the rationale of warranties in insurance law is that the insurer only accepts the risk provided the warranty is fulfilled".[61] However, the wording of a condition in general use provides that a breach of warranty in an earlier period of insurance will not affect a claim in the current period of insurance. If it was the intention that the insurance contract would be discharged by a breach of warranty the condition would specify accordingly. The acknowledgement that an earlier breach of warranty does not affect a claim in the current period of insurance would seem to confirm that the insurance is not discharged by a breach of warranty where such a condition is used.

15.8.2.2 Each case must of course be determined on the basis of the particular policy wording, but the courts are generally against the finding of a continuing warranty. In *Hussain* v *Brown*,[62] the Court of Appeal had to consider the effect of a warranty in the case of a premises damaged by fire. The plaintiff, in completing a proposal form for fire insurance, had confirmed that the premises were protected by an intruder alarm and warranted the truth of the answers on the proposal form. When a fire occurred, five months later, the alarm was not operative and the insurers sought to avoid the policy. The court restated the principle that a continuing warranty was a draconian term, the breach of which produced an automatic cancellation of cover and the fact that the breach was not material to the loss was irrelevant. The court did however suggest that if the insurers wanted protection against a change in the state of affairs, warranted at the inception of the policy, it was for them to so stipulate in clear terms in the policy.

---

[61] *"The Good Luck"* [1992] AC 233 per Lord Goff at 263.

[62] *Hussain* v *Brown* [1996] 1 Lloyds Rep 627.

15.8.2.3 In contrast, in *Transthene Packaging Co. Ltd.* v *Royal Insurance (UK) Ltd.*[63] the court, dealing with an alleged breach of a warranty relating to the storage of oily or greasy rags overnight, saw no reason for restricting the clear words of the warranty and refused to treat it either as one which was a promise as to future intentions or as a "suspensory condition" which merely prevented the insured from recovering if at the time of the loss the warranty was not being complied with. Where insurers have grounds to suspect the validity of the claim, they prefer to plead breach of warranty instead of alleging fraud as the proof of fraud is far more onerous.

15.8.3 FRAUD

15.8.3.1 The policy condition in relation to fraud provides that if a claim is fraudulent in any respect or if fraudulent means are used to obtain benefit under the policy or if the loss destruction or damage is caused by the wilful act of the insured or with his connivance all benefit under the policy shall be forfeited. The requirements for establishing fraud are onerous. The fraud condition generally adopts a wide interpretation of fraud so that the whole benefit of the policy is lost even if only a small part of the claim is fraudulent.[64] In the absence of an express condition in relation to fraud the courts will imply a term into the contract to the effect that if any fraudulent claim is knowingly made by the insured he will not be able to recover.[65]

15.8.3.2 In relying on a defence of fraud to defeat a claim insurers must plead the specific fraud.[66] To prove fraud it is necessary to prove

---

[63] [1996] LRLR 32.

[64] *Lek* v *Mathews* [1927] 29 Lloyds Rep 141. In *Maple Leaf Milling Co.* v *Colonial Assurance Co.* [1917] 2 WWR 1091 it was said that "Fraud in any part of his formal statement of losses taints the whole. Thus corrupted, it should be wholly rejected and the suiter left to repent that he destroyed his actual claim by the poison of his false claim."

[65] *"The Litsion Pride"* [1985] 1 Lloyds Rep 437.

[66] *Superwood Holdings plc. & Others* v *Sun Alliance & London Assurance plc. & Others*, Unreported Supreme Court, 27 June 1995, per Denham J. at p. 26 of her judgment, quoting from *Kerr on Fraud and Mistake*, 7th Edition at p. 644:

When an action is brought for the purpose of impeaching transactions on the ground of fraud, it is essential that the nature of the case should be distinctly and accurately stated. The facts must be so stated as to show distinctly that fraud is charged. Any charge of fraud or misrepresentation must be pleaded

the required intent. The Supreme Court, in *Superwood Holdings plc.*
v *Sun Alliance and London Assurance plc. & Others*,[67] accepted that
the definition of fraud in the dictum of Lord Herschall in *Derry* v
Peek[68] was the foundation of the law of fraud. To establish fraud the
representation has to be made:

1) knowingly; or

2) without belief in its truth; or

3) recklessly careless whether true or false.

15.8.3.3 It is not sufficient that the statement is made inadvertently
or carelessly. The test is whether or not what is said is stated honestly believing it to be true. The fraud must be intended to obtain an
advantage, generally monetary, or to put the other party at a disadvantage. Some licence is however allowed in relation to insurance
claims. Mere exaggeration is not conclusive evidence of fraud.[69]

15.8.3.4 In *Superwood* the trial judge had made a finding of fraud
against the insured on the basis that the amount claimed by the insured was so exaggerated that this, coupled with other findings of
fact, entitled him to draw the inference that the claim was fraudu-

---

with the utmost particularity; it will not be inferred from the circumstances
pleaded, at all events if those circumstances be consistent with innocence. A
general charge of fraud, however strong, without alleging specific facts, is not
sufficient to sustain the action. . . . A charge of fraud must be proved as laid,
and where one kind of fraud has been charged, another kind of fraud cannot be
substituted for it.

[67] at p. 28 of judgment of Denham J.

[68] [1889] 14 App Cas:
First, in order to sustain an action of deceit, there must be proof of fraud, and
nothing short of that will suffice. Secondly, fraud is proved when it is shown
that a false representation has been made (1) knowingly, or (2) without belief
in its truth, or (3) recklessly, careless whether it be true or false. Although I
have treated the second and third as distinct cases, I think the third is but an
instance of the second, for one who makes a statement under such circumstances can have no real belief in the truth of what he states. To prevent a
false statement being fraudulent, there must, I think, always be an honest belief in its truth. And this probably covers the whole ground, for one who
knowingly alleges that which is false, has obviously no such honest belief.
Thirdly, if fraud be proved, the motive of the person guilty of it is immaterial.
It matters not that there was no intention to cheat or injure the person to
whom the statement was made.

[69] *London Assurance* v *Clare* [1937] 57 Lloyds Rep 254 per Goddard J.

lent. The insured premises and contents were destroyed in a fire in 1986 and the insurers paid the material damage claim. Insurers refused to make any interim payments under the consequential loss policy and in 1989 repudiated the policy on the ground of "fraud or a claim exaggerated so excessively as to lead to an inference that it could not have been made honestly". The insured, having refused to refer the matter to arbitration, brought proceedings seeking recovery of the consequential loss arising as a direct result of the fire and damages in respect of breach of contract. The Supreme Court reversed the decision of the trial judge, holding that evidence of exaggeration was not of itself evidence of fraud.[70] The Court refused to allow the original finding to stand on the grounds that the finding of fraud had been against the insured, which were six limited companies, which could only have been guilty of fraud through some individual, who was the directing mind and will of the company, or a servant or agent within the scope of his authority.[71] The onus of proof is on insurers to prove the fraud on the balance of probabilities and where the proof is largely a matter of inference it must not be drawn lightly or without due regard to all the circumstances including the consequences of a finding of fraud.[72] Where the insurer seeks to repudiate the contract on the ground of fraud he cannot subsequently rely on a subordinate term being enforced.[73]

15.8.4 REASONABLE PRECAUTIONS
The policy provides that the insured shall take reasonable precautions to prevent loss, damage or destruction of the property insured. A large percentage of all losses under material damage policies can be

---

[70] per Blayney J. at p. 5 of judgment quoting with approval Goddard J. *supra*: "Mere exaggeration was not conclusive evidence of fraud, for a man might honestly have an exaggerated idea of the value of the stock, or suggest a high figure as a bargaining price."

[71] per Blayney J. at p. 6–7 and Denham J. at p. 29–31.

[72] per Denham J. at p. 32.

[73] *Jureidini* v *National British and Irish Millers Insurance Co. Ltd.* [1915] AC 499. Blayney J. at pp. 11/19 also relied on *Ballasty* v *Army Navy and General Assurance Association Ltd.* [1916] 50 ILTR 114; *Furey* v *Eagle Star and British Dominions Insurance Co. Ltd.* [1922] 56 ILTR 23; *Coen* v *Employers Liability Assurance Corp.* [1962] IR 314. The Supreme Court refused to allow Insurers plead breach of the claims condition having originally pleaded fraud as the ground for repudiation.

directly traced to some act of negligence on the part of the insured or persons for whom the insured is responsible. It is accepted that damage caused by the negligence of the insured or persons employed by him is covered[74] and the courts have interpreted the reasonable precautions condition as meaning that the insured's conduct must be "reckless" before it could be said to be unreasonable in terms of the condition.[75]

15.8.5 SUBROGATION

15.8.5.1 The policy has a subrogation clause providing that the insured shall at the request of the insurer take and permit to be taken all reasonable steps in the name of the insured for enforcing rights against any other party before or after payment of the claim. Where the loss or damage has been caused by the negligence of a third party the insurer is entitled to seek recovery from that party in the name of the insured. In a landmark decision in England, *Capital & Counties* v *Hampshire County Council*,[76] insurers were successful in seeking recovery of a £12 million loss from a local authority fire brigade which was found negligent in fighting the fire. A fire had broken out in the roof of a "state of the art" building in 1990. The building was fitted with an automatic sprinkler system which, if it had been left on during the fire, would have confined the damage to a small area of the roof void. The fire brigade, believing there were no sprinklers in the roof void, ordered the sprinklers to be turned off while the fire was blazing and as a result the fire spread quickly and destroyed much of the building.

15.8.5.2 The right of insurers to subrogation is an equitable right and any moneys recovered by the insured from the third party, in respect of the loss already paid by the insurer, are held subject to an equitable lien by the insured for the insurer.[77] The insurer is the ef-

---

[74] *Shaw* v *Roberts* [1837] 6 AD & E 75; *Cornish* v *Accident Insurance Company* [1889] 23 QBD 453.

[75] *Sofi* v *Prudential Assurance Co. Ltd.* [1993] 2 Lloyds Rep 559; *Fraser* v *Furman (Productions) Ltd.* [1967] 1 WLR 898.

[76] Unreported Court of Appeal, 4 April 1997, on appeal to the House of Lords at time of writing.

[77] *Napier & Ettrick* v *Hunter* [1993] AC 13 HL.

fective beneficial owner of the moneys and has a prior claim over them in the event of the insured becoming insolvent. Where the insurer recovers from the third party more than they have paid out to the insured, the insured, as a matter of general law, is entitled to interest on that amount from the date of receipt of the amount by insurers to the date of payment to the insured and the insured is also entitled to any windfall surplus.[78]

15.9 ADDITIONAL INTERESTS

A person with an interest in property, the insurance of which they do not control, will generally seek to have the interest noted in the policy covering the property. The purpose is twofold, in that the third party wishes to recover under the policy in the event of damage to the property and to be protected against subrogation proceedings in the event of loss or damage caused by him. There are dangers in relying on the insurance arranged by another in the hope that the insurance will benefit all the parties. If the third party wishes to claim under the policy he will have to establish that he is an insured person under the contract. Normally he will only be able to establish that if he is a named insured or he can show that the named insured acted as his agent.

15.9.1 THE "UNNAMED INSURED"

15.9.1.1 The doctrine of the unnamed insured was confirmed in *Mark Rowlands Ltd.* v *Berni Inns Ltd.*[79] A landlord had effected a policy in his own name covering his interests in a building in which the defendants were tenants. The lease obliged the landlord to insure, and to expend any insurance moneys on reinstatement of the property. The property was damaged due to the negligence of the tenant and the insurers, having discharged their liability to the landlord, sought to subrogate against the tenant. The Court of Appeal ruled against the insurers holding that the lease contained an implied term that the landlord would look to the insurers to make good any loss and as the landlord had no right of action against the tenant then

---

[78] *Lonrho Exports Ltd.* v *Export Credits Guarantee Department* [1996] 4 All ER 673.

[79] *Rowlands Ltd.* v *Berni Inns Ltd.* [1985] 3 All ER 473.

neither did the insurers. The decision requires the existence of a common intention between the parties to the effect that the insurance was to be at least in part for the benefit of the tenant or third party.

15.9.1.2 In *Lambert* v *Keywood*,[80] such a common intention could not be proven. The plaintiff was the owner of a building, occupied by the defendant, which was destroyed by the negligence of the defendant in lighting a bonfire close to the building. The landlord had undertaken to insure and had insured the building, but purely in respect of his own interests. Insurers brought proceedings against the tenant in the name of the landlord, and the tenant, by way of defence, pleaded that the landlord had contracted to insure the building for the benefit of the tenant and had failed to do so. The landlord denied that there was an agreement to insure for the benefit of the tenant and even if there had been a claim by the tenant for indemnity, it would not have been covered as the damage had been caused by the tenant's reckless actions. On the evidence, the court could not find a common intention between the parties, concluding that, while there were various oral and written terms whereby the landlord agreed to insure, the agreement was to insure in respect of the landlord's interest only. The decision confirms that not every agreement to insure renders the landlord agent of the tenant so as to make the tenant an insured under the policy or confers an interest in the insurance on the tenant so that he is immune from subrogation proceedings. Even if insurance had been effected for the benefit of the tenant he could not have recovered under it, as his actions in lighting the bonfire so close to the building were "reckless" and therefore in breach of the reasonable precautions condition.

---

[80] [1996] Unreported.

CHAPTER SIXTEEN

BUSINESS INTERRUPTION INSURANCE

16.1 INTRODUCTION

An ordinary property damage policy does not cover loss of profits[1] or loss of market caused by delay arising from damage to property by a peril insured against.[2] Loss of profits and additional costs incurred as a consequence of damage to property can be insured under policies variously referred to as Business Interruption, Consequential Loss or Loss of Profits policies.[3] The first of these descriptions, although imported from the United States, is probably the most apt as the intention of the insurance cover is to indemnify the insured in respect of losses following interruption of the business arising out of damage to property by an insured peril. The use of the word "profits" in the context of this form of insurance can be misleading as the insurance is intended to protect the business from loss of earnings whether those earnings would have realised a profit or merely reduced a potential loss. Business interruption policies are policies of indemnity and the happening of the event insured against does not provide the insured with an automatic right to recover all of his losses or indeed the full sum insured under the policy. As with all policies of indemnity, recovery depends on the terms and conditions of the particular policy. The arrangement of business interruption insurance requires considerable experience and expertise and a detailed analysis of the indi-

---

[1] *Maurice* v *Goldsborough, Mort & Co.* [1939] AC 452; *Theobold* v *Railway Passengers Assurance Co.* [1854] 10 Exch. 45.

[2] *Lewis Emmanuel & Son Ltd.* v *Hepburn* [1960] I Lloyds Rep 304.

[3] Loss of profits and additional expenditure by way of increased costs of working are the items most usually the subject of insurance.

vidual business to ensure protection in the event of a loss. The adjustment of business interruption claims call for insurance and accounting knowledge and an element of commercial awareness to help maintain the insured in business pending reinstatement of the property damage. There is an accepted authoritative work on the subject[4] and the intention of this chapter is to deal only with selected issues and aspects of cover.

16.2 INDEMNITY

The purpose of the insurance is to put the insured in the position they would have been in had there been no interruption of the business due to an insured peril, subject to the limits and conditions of the policy. It follows therefore that any payment under the policy in respect of any loss of profits will be liable to tax.[5] The extent of the loss is generally calculated, in accordance with the terms of the policy, by reference to the performance of the business in the preceding financial year with adjustment for any variations or trends in the business. Where the business may not have been operating for a full year prior to the occurrence of the damage giving rise to the interruption every effort must be made to assess the amount which would have been earned by the business during the period of the interruption.[6] The insurer and the insured have a mutuality of interest in restoring the business to normal trading levels as quickly as possible and the policy terms require the insured to take all reasonable steps to do so. The policy provides that insurers will reimburse the insured the additional expenditure necessarily and reasonably incurred for the sole purpose of avoiding or diminishing the reduction in turnover which but for that expenditure would have taken place during the indemnity period in consequence of the damage, but not exceeding the sum produced by applying the rate of gross profit to the amount of the reduction thereby avoided. In *Henry Booth* v *Commercial Union Assur-*

---

[4] *Riley on Business Interruption Insurance,* 7th edition, Sweet & Maxwell.

[5] *R.* v *Fir and Cedar Lumber Co. Ltd.* [1932] AC 441; *London and Thames Haven Oil Wharves Ltd.* v *Attwood* [1967] Ch. 772.

[6] *Burts & Harvey* v *Vulcan Boiler & General Insurance Co.* [1966] 1 Lloyds Rep 354.

ance Co.[7] it was confirmed that the insured was entitled to both the extra cost of continuing in business and the cost of having to buy partly manufactured goods to replace those destroyed, where the policy covered "such sums as the insured shall necessarily pay for increase in cost of working to continue the business".

16.3 INSURED'S DUTY TO MINIMISE THE LOSS

Apart from any condition in the policy, the insured has a common law duty to minimise his loss.[8] Most policies include an "alternative trading" clause which provides that, if during the indemnity period goods shall be sold or services shall be rendered elsewhere than at the premises specified in the policy for the benefit of the business either by the insured or by others on his behalf, the money paid or payable in respect of such sale or services shall be brought into account in arriving at the turnover during the indemnity period. In the absence of such a clause it could legitimately be claimed by the insured that if he conducts business elsewhere, following damage to the premises insured by the policy, any profits made by him need not be deducted from his claim against insurers. In *City Tailors Ltd.* v *Evans*,[9] the court believed that the policy condition requiring the insured to minimise his loss was relevant only to the business generated at the premises specified in the policy. Atkin L. J. said:

> The clause merely compels the insured to do what they can to diminish the loss at [the premises] by reducing as far as possible the effect of the fire there and producing as much output there after the fire as is reasonably necessary. I do not think that it involves them in the obligation to take any steps to carry on the business elsewhere; nor do I think that if they did carry on the business elsewhere it would import an obligation to account to [insurers] for the profits. I can find no such obligation in the words.[10]

The inclusion of the alternative trading clause makes the position clear and is in accordance with the principle of indemnity.

---

[7] [1923] 14 Lloyds Rep 114.

[8] *City Tailors Ltd.* v *Evans* [1921] 126 ILT 439.

[9] *supra.*

[10] ibid. per Atkin L. J. at p. 445.

16.4 INSURED PERILS

An essential requirement of a business interruption policy is that the interruption to the business should be the result of damage to property and that such damage has been caused by an insured peril. Where cover is provided by an "All Risks" policy the insured, subject to any particular policy exceptions, need only prove that there has been damage to the property which results in the interruption of the business. In this context, damage means a change in the property's physical state above and beyond inevitable change due to ordinary wear and tear.[11] Under a fire and specified perils policy the insured, having established that damage has occurred, must then establish that the damage was caused by an insured peril.[12] The definitions of the normal range of perils covered by a fire and specified perils policy have been dealt with in the previous chapter.

16.5 MATERIAL DAMAGE PROVISO

16.5.1 The standard proviso in a business interruption policy excludes liability where consequential loss arises from damage to property in which the insured has an insurable interest but which he has not insured against damage. The restriction which the proviso imposes on the scope of cover under the policy were considered by the Court of Appeal in *Glengate K.G. Properties Ltd.* v *Norwich Union Fire Insurance Society & Others*.[13] The plaintiffs were property owners and developers and purchased a site in Oxford Street, London, with a view to developing it into a complex of offices and retail outlets. A fire on the site destroyed a large number of architects' drawings and plans and as no copies existed they had to be reproduced at significant cost with consequent delay in completion of the project. The plaintiff claimed against the defendant insurers for the costs involved and loss of revenue due to the delay. The business interruption policy issued to the plaintiff provided cover "if any building used by the insured for the purposes of the business suffered damage other

---

[11] *Ranicar* v *Frigmobile pty Ltd.* [1983] Tas. R. 113.

[12] When considering whether damage has been caused by an insured peril the court will consider whether the damage is occasioned by the direct action of the peril or whether the peril can be said to be the proximate cause of the damage.

[13] [1995] 1 Lloyds Rep 278 at first instance and [1996] 2 All ER 487 CA.

than by an excluded cause, provided at the time there was a material damage insurance in force covering the interest of the insured in the property at the premises". The insurers denied liability on the grounds that (a) the part of the building damaged which contained the plans and drawings was not "used by the insured for the purposes of the business," but rather was being used by the architects; and (b) there was no material damage insurance in force covering the insured's interest in the drawings.

16.5.2 The court held against the defendants in relation to (a) but held that the clear meaning of the clause was that any property in which the plaintiff had an insurable interest and which was not insured against material damage was excluded from the consequential loss cover. The plaintiff then argued that they had no insurable interest in the drawings and had therefore satisfied the policy proviso. The court, having distinguished between insurable interest in the narrow sense of the insured's personal interest and in the wider sense of the insured's ability to insure, held that the plaintiff had an insurable interest in the plans of the building purchased from the original architect but no insurable interest in the plans devised by the architects as sub-contractors to the plaintiff and the copyright of which was owned by the architects.

16.5.3 The policy was construed as providing indemnity in respect of loss of revenue due to delay but not for the cost of redrawing the plans. The decision clearly establishes that if any item of property, in which the insured has an insurable interest, is uninsured and damage to that property materially contributes to an interruption to the business, the proviso is not satisfied and the claim is inadmissible. The definition to be accorded to "insurable interest" in the proviso is crucial. Both at first instance and in the Court of Appeal, in *Glengate*, it was held to apply in the narrow sense of proprietary or possessory interest. At first instance Phillips J. said:

> in my judgment the "interest" referred to is restricted to the insured's own interest in the property in question rather than any wider insurable interest he may have. Thus, only in so far as the loss of value of the property concerned will fall upon the insured does the proviso require the existence of insurance against damage to it. To attempt to give those words a wider

meaning would, in my judgment, produce a result that was unreasonable, if not unworkable.[14]

16.6 LOSS CAUSED BY FAILURE TO INDEMNIFY

16.6.1 The insurer under a business interruption policy undertakes,
subject to the policy terms and conditions, to indemnify the insured
for the loss of profit suffered as a consequence of damage by an insured peril. The insurer's obligation terminates on expiry of the indemnity period or when the business has been returned to a level of
trading which the business would have enjoyed but for the damage
occasioning the interruption, whichever is the sooner. If the period of
the interruption is extended by the failure of the insurer to put the
insured into funds, sufficient to enable him generate previous levels
of turnover, the right to indemnity continues. In practice, insurers
will usually make interim payments, without prejudice to final liability, to maintain cash flow and facilitate the insured's return to pre-
damage trading levels as soon as possible. The insured does not have
a cause of action against insurers for late payment.[15] As soon as an
insured event occurs the insurer is in breach of contract and must
indemnify the insured immediately. Any delay by the insurer is not
an additional breach of contract, and a claim for additional loss
caused by late payment must be recovered under the policy. Delay
may be a ground for awarding interest on the amount of the claim,
but an insured is not entitled as a matter of course to payment of interest on the amount of indemnity due to delay on the part of insurers in paying the agreed loss.[16] Generally interest will only be
awarded if the delay in payment is due to the fault of insurers and a
court has discretion as to the interest it deems fit to award.[17] However, insurers are entitled to a reasonable period of time in which to
decide whether or not to meet the claim, but the insured is not to be

---

[14] at p. 286.

[15] *India* v *Lips Maritime* [1988] AC 395; *Ventouris* v *Mountain (No. 3)* [1992] 2
Lloyds Rep 281.

[16] *Giggens* v *Sargent* [1823] 2 B&C 348; *Webster* v *British Empire Mutual Life
Assurance Co.* [1880] Ch. D 169.

[17] Supreme Court Rules.

prejudiced by any difficulty the insurers may have in determining the amount to be paid by way of indemnity.[18]

16.6.2   In *Sprung* v *Royal Insurance (UK) Ltd.*[19] the plaintiff sought payment of the moneys allegedly due under an insurance policy and damages for late payment, his loss being the failure of his business. The Court of Appeal, confirming previous authority, held that the plaintiff's claim had no foundation in law.[20] The Court did, however, accept that there was an implied term in an insurance contract requiring the insurer to assess the loss and authorise repairs within a reasonable time of the insured peril occurring. The insurers had denied liability in respect of all but one item of damage under the terms of the policy and although the insurers had inspected the damaged property within days, the Court was prepared to assume that the insurers had been in breach of the implied term. On the facts, the Court found that the breach had not caused any loss. The plaintiff's business had failed, not because of the insurer's failure to assess the loss but because of the plaintiff's impecuniosity. The decision recognises that an insurer is obliged to deal with a claim within a reasonable time, but denies that the insurer is liable should the business fail before the claim is settled.

16.7 CLAIMS CONDITION

16.7.1   The policy conditions are generally the same as in the material damage policy but the claims condition deserves mention here as it has been considered in detail by the Supreme Court in *Superwood Holdings plc.* v *Sun Alliance & London Assurance plc.*[21] The insured contended that the condition does not apply until a written claim has been made under the policy, whereas the insurers maintained that the terms of the condition apply either from the date of the fire or event giving rise to the claim or from when there was any claim for loss, even if it was an interim claim. The opening words of the condi-

---

[18] *Burts & Harvey Ltd. and Alchemy Ltd.* v *Vulcan Boiler and General Insurance Co. Ltd.* [1966] 1 Lloyds Rep 354.

[19] Unreported Court of Appeal, June 1996.

[20] see n. 15 *supra*.

[21] Unreported Supreme Court, 27 June 1995.

tion are that: "On the happening of any damage in consequence of which a claim is or may be made under the policy, the insured shall forthwith give notice thereof in writing to insurers". The insured had complied with that part of the condition and there was no argument between the parties on that score. The next part of the condition requires the insured

> with due diligence do and concur in doing and permit to be done all things which may be reasonably practicable to minimise or check any interruption of or interference with the business or to avoid or diminish the loss . . .

The condition continues:

> . . . and in the event of a claim being made under this policy shall not later than thirty days after the expiry of the indemnity period or within such further time as the insurers may in writing allow, at his own expense deliver to the insurers in writing a statement setting forth particulars of his claim together with details of all other insurances covering the damage or any part of it or consequential loss of any kind resulting therefrom.

16.7.2 The Court confirmed that the insured had complied with that section of the condition but identified the next sentence in the condition as critical:

> . . . The insured shall at his own expense also produce and furnish to insurers such books of account and other business books, vouchers, invoices, balance sheets and other documents, proofs, information, explanation and other evidence as may reasonably be required by the insurers for the purpose of investigating the claim together with (if demanded) a statutory declaration of the truth of the claim and of any matters connected therewith.

Denham J. was satisfied that the meaning of that sentence was clear, given its position in the condition and giving to it the ordinary meaning of words.[22] She interpreted the sentence as meaning that the insured must provide books of account and other matters referred to in the condition as well as providing the statement of claim in writ-

---

[22] p. 60 of judgment.

ing, but that such matters being ancillary to the statement of claim could therefore either accompany or follow the claim.[23] The positioning of the word "also" meant that the listed items were to be regarded as an addendum to the claim and could not be required prior to submission of the statement of claim.

16.7.3 She went on to hold that the claim cannot be made by the insured until he knows the damage and assesses it and

> . . . in the instance of a consequential loss claim with an indemnity period of 52 weeks where the [insured] makes the case that the consequential loss runs throughout the 52 weeks they could not . . . make their formal statement of claim until the 52 weeks has run. . . .[24]

16.7.4 The final sentence in the condition reads:

> No claim under this policy shall be payable unless the terms of this condition has been complied with and in the event of non-compliance therewith in any respect any payment on account of the claim already made shall be repaid to the insurers forthwith.

Denham J. interpreted this sentence as contemplating payments on account when the terms of the condition have not yet been met and envisaging interim payments prior to compliance with the claims condition.[25]

16.7.5 In the High Court, the trial judge, in finding against the insured, had made a number of findings of fact including that the insured were

> . . . totally unjustified in not allowing such access to their books and records as was reasonably required . . . for the purpose of assessing the amount which could legitimately be claimed on foot of the consequential loss policy. . . .[26]

---

[23] p. 61 of judgment.

[24] ibid.

[25] p. 62 of judgment.

[26] Unreported High Court, 15 August 1991 and 18 November 1991. Denham J. set out the High Court findings of fact at p. 16 of her judgment.

and that the insured

> ... did their utmost to prevent the Loss Adjusters from uncov-
> ering the weaknesses inherent in the Group management, or-
> ganisation, and accounting systems. . . .[27]

Denham J. held that the trial judge had erred in his interpretation of
the claims condition[28] and that this had an effect on his analysis of
the facts. She believed that, in considering the difficulties experienced by the Loss Adjusters in investigation of the loss rather than
considering the statement of claim submitted after expiry of the period of indemnity, the trial judge's analysis had been clouded. She
held that numerous meetings between the Loss Adjusters and the
insured and the insured's advisers for the purposes of investigation of
the loss and assessment of the likely extent of the claim were "only of
peripheral relevance to the claims condition and the consequential
loss claim as a whole. although these meetings . . . were relevant to
the issue of interim payments and losses".[29]

16.7.6 The insurers had not, prior to the commencement of the trial
of the action, pleaded breach of the claims condition as a basis for repudiation of the contract, and the Supreme Court held that the insured would have succeeded on this pleading ground alone as there
was no application to amend the pleadings.[30] Denham J. also held
that while the contract of insurance does not formally require that
insurers put the insured on notice of a breach of condition prior to
repudiation of the policy it is "a fundamental tenet of constitutional
law and fair procedures that if a person's position is to be detrimen-
tally affected, he should be placed on notice", and the insured would
succeed on this ground alone in the absence of such notice.[31] This
statement would seem to suggest that if insurers, when investigating
a loss or a claim, are of the opinion that the insured is in breach of a
policy condition, they are required to advise the insured and give him

---

[27] ibid.

[28] p. 63 of judgment.

[29] p. 64 of judgment.

[30] p. 56 of judgment.

[31] p. 58 of judgment.

an opportunity to rectify the breach before they seek to repudiate the policy. The decision would also seem to suggest that an insured is not required to comply with the claims condition in the consequential loss policy until he has submitted a statement of claim and that his position under the policy will not be prejudiced by anything done in contravention of the condition during the investigative period.

APPENDICES

The following Appendices are facsimile reproductions of original documents.

Appendix A: Insurance Act, 1989, Part IV

44.—(1) A person shall not act as, or hold himself out to be an Brokers'
qualifications. insurance broker unless—

   (*a*) he is a member of a representative body of insurance brokers Pr.IV S.44 which requires compliance with the provisions of this Act as a condition of membership, and that body is recognised as such by the Minister, and he otherwise complies with the provisions of this Act, or, not being a member of a recognised representative body, he complies with the provisions of this Act, and

   (*b*) he is in a position—

      (i) in the case of non-life insurance, to arrange insurance contracts on behalf of his clients with at least five undertakings, or

      (ii) in the case of life insurance, to arrange insurance contracts on behalf of his clients with at least five undertakings.

(2) A person shall not act as or hold himself out to be an insurance broker unless he holds an appointment in writing from each undertaking for which he is an intermediary.

45.—The Minister may, by regulations, provide that a person shall Intermediaries'
indemnity
insurance. not act as or hold himself out to be an insurance broker or an insurance agent unless he effects a policy of professional indemnity insurance in a specified form, indemnifying him to such sum, in such manner, in respect of such matters and valid for such minimum period as the Minister may prescribe, from time to time, under this section.

46.—(1) An undertaking shall not appoint a person as an Insurance
intermediaries
appointment and
commission
payments. insurance intermediary unless, to the best of the undertaking's knowledge and belief, having caused reasonable enquiry to be made he is either—

   (*a*) a member of a representative body of insurance brokers recognised by the Minister for the purposes of section 44 (1) *(a)*, or

   (*b*) a person who complies with the requirements of this Act but is not a member of a recognised representative body.

(2) An undertaking shall not pay any commission payment other than to an insurance intermediary who, to the best of the undertaking's knowledge and belief, having caused reasonable enquiry to be made, is either—

(*a*) a member of a representative body of insurance brokers
recognised by the Minister for the purposes of section 44
(1) *(a)*, or

(*b*) a person who complies with the provisions of this Act but is
not a member of a recognised representative body.

(3) No insurance intermediary or employee of an undertaking shall
pay any commission payment other than to an insurance intermediary
who complies with this Act, save where a commission payment is
made by an insurance intermediary to a person in connection with a
policy of insurance placed with an undertaking by the said intermediary.

(4) "Commission payment" in subsection (3) has the meaning
given to it in section 2 (3) as if the words "holder of an authorisation"
in that definition referred to an insurance intermediary.

47.—(1) If, at any time in the first accounting year, the aggregate
of moneys lodged by an insurance intermediary to the separate bank
accounts required under section 48 exceeds £25,000, the intermediary
shall effect a bond in a specified form, as respects his insurance
business, to the value of £25,000 in respect of the remainder of the
first accounting year.

(2) Subject to subsection (4), an insurance intermediary shall hold
a bond in a specified form—

(*a*) as respects his non-life insurance business, to the value of
£25,000, and

(*b*) as respects his life assurance business, to the value of £25,000
or 25 per cent. of life assurance turnover, whichever is the
greater, by reference to the previous accounting year.

(3) The requirement in subsection (2) for an insurance intermediary to hold a bond shall be regarded as having been discharged
where the insurance intermediary holds a bond to the value of £25,000
or 25 per cent. of life assurance turnover, whichever is the greater,
by reference to the previous accounting year.

(4) Subsection (2) shall not apply to an insurance intermediary if
his turnover does not exceed £25,000 by reference to the previous
accounting year and does not exceed £25,000 in any subsequent
accounting year.

(5) The bond referred to in this section shall provide that in the

event of the insurance intermediary's inability or failure to meet his   PT.IV S.47
financial obligations in relation to any sums of money received by him
from, or on behalf of, his clients, a sum of money will become
available to a person nominated or approved of by the Minister, to
be applied for the benefit of any client of the intermediary who has
incurred loss or liability because of the inability or failure of the
insurance intermediary to meet such financial obligations.

(6) The person nominated or approved of by the Minister shall,
with the consent of the Minister and up to such sum as may be
specified by the Minister, be indemnified out of the proceeds of the
bond in respect of such reasonable expenses as are incurred in carrying
out the functions provided for in subsection (5).

(7) The person nominated or approved of by the Minister shall keep
all proper and usual accounts, including an income and expenditure
account and a balance sheet, of all moneys received by him on foot
of a bond and of all disbursements made by him from any such moneys
and of any amounts in respect of the expenses referred to in subsection
(6).

(8) The Minister may, by regulations, provide that—

(*a*) arrangements in relation to the bond shall be entered into
only with persons of a class or classes specified in the
regulations,

(*b*) the bond shall be in such form and valid for such minimum
period as may be specified in the regulations,

(*c*) a copy of the bond shall be displayed, for the information of
the public, in a prominent position in all premises occupied
by an insurance intermediary and in which he carries on
business as insurance intermediary, and the bond shall be
mentioned in his sales literature and business note paper.

(9) Any amount or percentage rate in subsections (2), (3) and (4)
may be altered as the Minister may from time to time prescribe and
different amounts and percentages may be prescribed for different
classes of intermediary by reference to turnover or to such other
matters as the Minister may consider appropriate.

(10) For the purposes of this section—

"accounting year" means the year commencing on the date of coming

into force of subsection (1) of this section and subsequent anniversary Pt.IV S.47
accounting years;

"turnover" means the aggregate of all moneys required to be paid by
an intermediary into the separate bank accounts required under
section 48 (1) (*a*) and 48 (1) (*b*);

"life assurance turnover" means the aggregate of all moneys required
to be paid by an intermediary into the separate bank account required
under section 48 (1) (*b*).

48.—(1) An insurance intermediary shall keep a separate bank Keeping of separate
account for each of the following classes of business— bank accounts.

(*a*) an account in connection with premiums payable to insurers
under contracts of non-life insurance, or money paid or
payable to policyholders by undertakings authorised
under the Regulations of 1976;

(*b*) an account in connection with premiums payable to insurers
under contracts of life assurance, or money paid or payable
to policyholders by undertakings authorised under the
Regulations of 1984, and

(i) all moneys, other than commission payments and service charges, received by him in connection with
either such class of business shall be paid into the
appropriate account, and

(ii) neither the State nor any person shall have or obtain
any recourse or right against money standing to the
credit of such account or accounts in respect of a
claim or right against an insurance intermediary until
all proper claims against these moneys have been
satisfied.

(2) The account to be kept—

(*a*) under subsection (1) (*a*) shall be designated in all financial
records maintained by the intermediary as "section
48—Non-life insurance account",

(*b*) under subsection (1) (*b*) shall be designated in all financial
records maintained by the intermediary as "section
48—Life Assurance account".

(3) This section shall not apply as respects a tied insurance agent Pт.IV S.48 insofar as moneys received by him in connection with premiums payable to undertakings under contracts of insurance or moneys payable to policyholders by undertakings, relate to a tied agency agreement or arrangement entered into by the tied insurance agent.

(4) For the purposes of this section—

"service charge" means an amount payable, or payable in certain circumstances, by a client to an intermediary in respect of his services in relation to contracts of insurance but does not include any premium or part thereof payable to an undertaking;

"tied agency agreement or arrangement" has the meaning assigned to it in section 51;

"tied insurance agent" has the meaning assigned to it in section 51.

49.—(1) No person shall act as, or hold himself out to be an Insurance agents' insurance agent unless— qualifications.

(*a*) he holds an appointment in writing from each undertaking for which he is an agent,

(*b*) he states on his letter headings and business forms that he is an insurance agent and the name or names of every undertaking for which he is an agent, and

(*c*) he informs any proposer of an insurance contract that he is an insurance agent and of the name or names of the undertakings for which he is an agent.

(2) Subject to subsection (3), an insurance agent shall hold—

(*a*) in the case of non-life insurance, an appointment in writing from not more than four undertakings authorised under the Regulations of 1976,

(*b*) in the case of life insurance, an appointment in writing from not more than four undertakings authorised under the Regulations of 1984.

(3) The provisions of subsection (2) shall come into force on such

date as the Minister prescribes not being less than two years after the Pᴛ.IV S.49
commencement of this section.

(4) A tied insurance agent shall:

(*a*) state on his letter headings and business forms that he is a
tied insurance agent and the name or names of every
undertaking for which he is a tied insurance agent,

(*b*) inform any proposer of an insurance contract that he is a
tied insurance agent and the name or names of every
undertaking for which he is a tied insurance agent, provided always that the insurance contract in question is of
a type which is subject to a tied agency agreement or
arrangement entered into by the said tied insurance agent.

(5) A tied insurance agent shall not act in relation to contracts of
insurance offered or issued by any other undertaking authorised under
the same Regulations as the undertaking with whom the tied insurance
agent has entered into a tied agency agreement or arrangement.

(6) For the purposes of this section—

"Regulations" means the Regulations of 1976 or the Regulations of
1984, as the case may be;

"tied insurance agent" and "tied insurance agreement or arrangement" have the meanings assigned to them, respectively, in section
51.

50.—Every undertaking shall keep a register of all its appointed Register of
insurance intermediaries at its principal office in the State. The said insurance
register of appointed insurance intermediaries shall be open to public intermediaries.
inspection at reasonable times during normal working hours.

51.—(1) An insurance agent shall be deemed to be acting as the Provisions
agent of the undertaking to whom a proposal for insurance is being regarding scope of
made when, for the purpose of the formation of the insurance con- agency.
tract, he completes in his own hand or helps the proposer of an
insurance policy to complete a proposal for insurance. In such circumstances only, the insurer shall be responsible for any errors or
omissions in the completed proposal.

F

(2) An undertaking shall be responsible for any act or omission of Pt.IV S.51
its tied insurance agent in respect of any matter pertaining to a
contract of insurance offered or issued by that undertaking, as if the
tied insurance agent was an employee of that undertaking.

(3) In this section—

"tied insurance agent" means any person who enters into an agreement or arrangement with an undertaking whereby that person undertakes to refer all proposals of insurance to the undertaking with whom
he has made or entered into the agreement or arrangement, or
any person who enters into an agreement or arrangement with an
undertaking which restricts in any way that person's freedom to refer
proposals of insurance to an undertaking other than the undertaking
with whom the agreement or arrangement has been made or entered
into;

"tied agency agreement or arrangement" means an agreement or
arrangement of the type described in this section.

(4) Nothing in this section shall render an insurance agent or a tied
insurance agent responsible for any false statements supplied to him
by the proposer of an insurance policy or for any information withheld
by the proposer from such agent.

52.—(1) An insurance intermediary shall not accept money from Acceptance by
a client— intermediary of
insurance
proposals.

    (*a*) in respect of a proposal unless it is accompanied by the
        completed proposal or the proposal has been accepted by
        the undertaking, or

    (*b*) in respect of a renewal of a policy of insurance unless it has
        been invited by the undertaking.

(2) The Minister may prescribe any alterations or additions to the
circumstances in which an intermediary may accept money from a
client under subsection (1).

    (3) (*a*) Where an insurance intermediary accepts from a client a
           completed insurance proposal, whether or not
           accompanied by a sum of money, with a view to effecting
           with an undertaking a policy of insurance, or

       (*b*) where an insurance intermediary accepts money from a

client in respect of a renewal of a policy of insurance which Pt.IV S.52
has been invited by the insurer or in respect of a proposal
accepted by an undertaking,

he shall serve on the client a document stating that it is issued in
pursuance of this section and specifying—

> (i) the name and address of the client;

> (ii) the amount of the said sum if any and the date of its
>   receipt by the intermediary;

> (iii) the proposal, renewal or proposal accepted by an
>   undertaking in respect of which such sum was paid;

> (iv) the undertaking with which the policy is to be effected
>   or renewed or by whom the proposal has been
>   accepted.

(4) The document to be issued by intermediaries in a case to which
subsection (3) *(a)* applies shall also specify that such acceptance by
the intermediary does not itself constitute the effecting of a policy of
insurance.

(5) Subsections (3) and (4) shall not apply where the intermediary,
having authority to do so, issues to the client a policy of insurance
with the undertaking.

(6) The Minister may prescribe any alterations or additions to
the matters to be specified in documents required to be issued by
intermediaries under subsections (3) and (4).

(7) A document purporting to be a document to which subsection
(3) or subsection (4) applies shall, without further proof, be evidence
of the matters specified therein unless the contrary is proved.

53.—(1) Where a premium is paid to an insurance intermediary in Treatment of
respect of a renewal of a policy which has been invited by an under- premiums paid to
taking, or in respect of a proposal accepted by an undertaking, the intermediaries.
premium shall be treated as having been paid to the undertaking
when it is paid to the insurance intermediary.

(2) Nothing in this section shall render an undertaking liable for a
premium paid to an intermediary in respect of a proposal accepted
by an undertaking or a renewal of a policy which has been invited by
the undertaking, where the undertaking has given reasonable notice

in writing to the person whose proposal has been accepted or whose Pᴛ.IV S.53
policy is being renewed, that the said intermediary has no authority
to collect such premiums on behalf of the undertaking.

54.—An insurance intermediary who is convicted of an offence Restriction on
arising out of or connected with the performance of his functions as intermediaries
an insurance intermediary shall not, without the permission of the offence.
Court, carry on the business of insurance intermediary in the State
or engage or authorise another insurance intermediary to act as such
on his behalf.

55.—A person shall not, without the permission of the Court, act Disqualification of
as or hold himself out to be an insurance intermediary if— certain persons
from acting as
intermediaries.

    (*a*) he is adjudged bankrupt, or

    (*b*) he makes a composition or arrangement with his creditors,
        or

    (*c*) being an insurance intermediary, he fails to meet his financial
        or legal obligations in relation to any sum of money
        received by him from or on behalf of a client, or

    (*d*) he is convicted of an offence involving fraud or dishonesty,
        whether in connection with insurance or not, or

    (*e*) he is or was a director of any company involved in insurance
        which has been wound up by the Court or by means of a
        creditors' voluntary winding up, or

    (*f*) he is the subject of an order under section 184 of the Com-
        panies Act, 1963.

56.—The Minister may by order prescribe codes of conduct to be Codes of conduct.
observed by insurance brokers or insurance agents in the State. Any
such order may, in particular, specify the practices to be followed by
brokers or agents in their dealings with their clients or undertakings
or with other persons.

57.—(1) This Part shall not apply to— Scope of Part IV.

    (*a*) contracts of reinsurance or to insurance intermediaries engaged solely in relation to the business of effecting Pt.IV S.57 contracts of reinsurance;

(*b*) travel agents and tour operators licensed under the Transport (Tour Operators and Travel Agents) Act, 1982, insofar as they are engaged in the placing of travel insurance or touring assistance contracts as part of, or in conjunction with, an overseas travel contract.

(2) In this section "travel agent", "tour operator" and "overseas travel contract" have the meanings assigned to them respectively under section 2 (1) of the Transport (Tour Operators and Travel Agents) Act, 1982.

Appendix B

Insurance Act, 1989

CODE OF CONDUCT FOR INSURANCE INTERMEDIARIES

Status of Intermediary

An Insurance Intermediary shall:

1. Act with the utmost good faith and to the highest standards of professional integrity in his dealings with clients, insurers, fellow insurance intermediaries and members of the public.

2. Observe all statutory and other legal requirements.

3. Ensure that the interests of the Client are paramount and in particular:

    (a) ensure that the advice given in relation to proposed contracts of insurance is appropriate to the needs and full resources of the client;

    (b) ensure that the client is given promptly information as to the suitability, scope and limitations of any insurance contract under negotiation;

    (c) recognise the privileged nature of the relationship with the client;

    (d) assist the client, where requested, in the completion of insurance proposals drawing his attention to the necessity of full disclosure of all relevant facts and explaining the consequence of non-disclosure;

    (e) ensure that any contract of insurance recommended to a client is in the best interest of the client and disclose any potential conflicts of interest to the client and the insurer;

    (f) furnish the contract of insurance and all documentation relating thereto to the client forthwith on receipt thereof from the insurer;

    (g) shall not impose any charge on the client in addition to the insurance premium without disclosing the amount of such charge **in writing to the client**;

    (h) where notification of a claim is accepted from a client inform the insurer, without delay, thereof and advise the client promptly of the insurer's requirements concerning the claim.

4. In dealing with insurers:

    (a) observe the privileged nature of the relationship between insurer and intermediary;

    (b) remit to the insurer premiums collected from the client in strict accordance with the terms agreed between the insurer and the intermediary.

5. Ensure that all advertisements are legal, honest and truthful and comply with the Advertising Standards Authority of Ireland general code on advertising and the specific codes on advertising and illustrations agreed by the insurance industry.

6. Ensure that the separate client bank accounts required under Section 48 of the Insurance Act, 1989 are properly maintained.

7. Ensure that this Code of Conduct is displayed in a prominent position in the public area of all his business premises and his status or statuses is clearly marked on the code.

Approved by the Department of Enterprise and Employment

SEPT. '94

GUIDELINES TO CODE OF CONDUCT
FOR INSURANCE INTERMEDIARIES
(i.e. INSURANCE BROKERS, INSURANCE AGENTS, TIED INSURANCE AGENTS)

Title (All Intermediaries)

An insurance intermediary should indicate his status in the space provided beneath the title of the Code. By status is meant insurance broker, insurance agent or tied insurance agent (as defined in the Insurance Act, 1989).

Article 3(a) — Advice (All Intermediaries)

An insurance intermediary should give advice only on those matters in which he is knowledgeable and seek or recommend other specialist advice where necessary. It is recognised that an intermediary's ability to give advice may be constrained by the products generally available in the market, products available to the intermediary, the client's ability to pay and the client's disposition to accept advice.

Article 3(e) — Conflicts of Interest (All Intermediaries)

(1) **A broker, an agent or a tied agent** should ensure that at all times the commission received from an insurance company is not an influencing factor in his recommendation as to the most suitable contract for his client.

(2) **A broker or an agent** should advise his client if he has delegated authority from an insurance company to act either as an underwriting or claims settlement agent in respect of the policy of insurance being proposed to the client.

(3) **A broker or an agent** who has a linkage with an insurance company either through a common holding company or the cross holding of its shares, should make it clear to his client both verbally and in writing that such a relationship exists and also satisfy himself that the product recommended is as good as competing products in the marketplace. For the purposes of this paragraph, a "linkage" to be defined as a direct or indirect holding by either an insurance company in a brokerage or agency, or vice versa, in excess of 20% or more of the capital or voting rights.

(4) **A broker, an agent or a tied agent** which has a subsidiary or associated company operating in the same class of business (i.e., life or non-life) under another status (e.g., life broker with subsidiary/associated company operating as a life tied agent) must ensure that the different legal entities operate from separate, different premises, with separate, different staff. The broker/agent/tied agent as aforementioned must also ensure that leads are not passed between the different entities.

Article 3(f) — Documentation to be provided to client (All Intermediaries)

The following is the **minimum** amount of documentation which an intermediary should pass on to his client:-

(1) policy document and supporting schedules;

(2) all endorsements, subsequent amendments to the contract, whether issued separately or as part of renewal documentation;

(3) information contained in renewal notices which insurers are required to provide to policyholders under separate Codes of Conduct approved by the Department of Industry and Commerce.

Article 5 — Advertisements (Insurance Agents and Tied Insurance Agents)

An agent or a tied agent must indicate on any advertisement, in whatever form, that he is an agent or a tied agent and name the insurer(s) for which he is an agent or a tied agent.

Article 6 — Separate Client Accounts (Insurance Brokers and Insurance Agents); Section 52 Receipts (All Intermediaries)

(1) Each Section 48 Bank Account must be clearly designated as such, both in the Intermediary's own records and at the bank(s) in which the Section 48 Account(s) is/are held.

/over . . .

(2)   Where a Section 48 Bank Account for non-life insurance consists of more than one bank account, one of these must be a focal account into which all moneys received which are properly payable to insurers or clients are initially lodged. Similarly, where a Section 48 Bank Account for life assurance consists of more than one bank account, there must be a focal account as outlined in the preceding sentence.

(3)   **A broker or an agent** must ensure that all moneys received which are properly payable to insurers or clients are paid without delay into the appropriate client account(s).

(4)   **A broker or an agent** must ensure that moneys payable out of the client account(s) to either insurers or clients, are paid by cheque drawn specifically on the client account(s); **the faces of the cheques so drawn must be printed by the bank "Section 48 Account — Life" or "Section 48 Account — Non-Life"** as appropriate.

(5)   **A broker or an agent** must ensure that only moneys which are properly due to the intermediary in respect of commission, service fees and, where appropriate, interest are drawn from the client account(s) for the intermediary's own use.

(6)   **A broker or an agent or a tied agent** must maintain adequate records of moneys received (including copies of Section 52 receipts issued); **a broker or an agent** must also maintain adequate records of lodgements to and payments out of each client account and provide an annual report from an **independent** accountant certifying that the accounts have been properly maintained. **An accountant for this purpose is:-**

  — where the intermediary is a limited company, that company's auditor (auditor being a person as so defined in the Companies Acts);

  — where the intermediary is an unincorporated entity, a person who is qualified for appointment as an auditor of a company or as a public auditor (as defined under the Companies Acts)

An independent accountant for this purpose is an accountant as described above who is <u>not</u> —
  — the broker or agent in respect of whose insurance intermediary business the Report is being provided;

  — the employee of the broker or agent in question;

  — a director, secretary, partner or member of the Board of Management of the insurance intermediary business concerned.

The report provided by the independent accountant shall be on his/her own headed paper.

Article 7 — Display of Code and Disclosure of Status

The status of the intermediary (insurance broker/insurance agent/tied insurance agent) must be indicated in the space allocated on the copy/copies of the Code of Conduct displayed in the public areas of his business premises. Where an intermediary holds two statuses (e.g. broker for life business and agent for non-life business) **both** statuses should be indicated on the displayed copy/copies of the Code. In the example given, the insurance intermediary would indicate his status, in the space provided on the Code, as follows:-

INSURANCE BROKER — LIFE   INSURANCE AGENT — NON-LIFE

NOTES

1.   These guidelines do not purport to fully interpret the Code of Conduct but rather to give assistance in interpreting same. Any questions on the Code should be addressed to:

> Insurance Intermediary Compliance Bureau
> 39 Molesworth Street
> Dublin 2
> Phone (01) 676 1850
> Fax: (01) 676 1943

If you are a member of a representative body of insurance brokers, recognised by the Minister for Enterprise and Employment, you should address your questions to that body.

2.   An agent or a tied agent **must** tell the client that he is an agent or a tied agent and must name the companies or company for which he acts as an agent or tied agent.

Appendix C[*]

Text of an Agreement dated 21st December, 1988, between the Minister for the Environment and the Motor Insurers' Bureau of Ireland, extending, with effect from dates specified in the Agreement, the scope of the Bureau's liability, with certain exceptions, for compensation for victims of road accidents involving uninsured or stolen vehicles and unidentified or untraced drivers to the full range of compulsory insurance in respect of injury to person and damage to property under the Road Traffic Act, 1961.

MEMORANDUM OF AGREEMENT made the 21st day of December, 1988 between the **MINISTER FOR THE ENVIRONMENT** (hereinafter referred to as "the Minister") of the one part and **MOTOR INSURERS' BUREAU OF IRELAND** whose registered office is at 3/4 South Frederick Street in the city of Dublin of the other part **SUPPLEMENTAL** to an Agreement (hereinafter called "the Principal Agreement") made the 10th day of March, 1955 between the Minister for Local Government of the one part and Those Insurers Granting Compulsory Motor Vehicle Insurance in Ireland by or on behalf of whom the said Agreement was signed (thereinafter and hereinafter referred to as "the Insurers") of the other part,

WHEREAS in pursuance of the undertaking given by the Insurers in paragraph 1 of the Principal Agreement a Company stands incorporated under the Companies Act, 1963 with the name of Motor Insurers' Bureau of Ireland (being a party to these presents and hereinafter referred to as "M.I.B. of I."):

AND WHEREAS a memorandum of Agreement (hereinafter referred to as "the Agreement of 1955") was made between the Minister and M.I.B. of I. on the 30th day of November, 1955:

AND WHEREAS the Agreement of 1955 was amended by an Addendum thereto made between the Minister and M.I.B. of I. on the 12th day of March 1962:

AND WHEREAS a memorandum of Agreement (hereinafter referred to as "the Agreement of 1964") was made between the Minister and M.I.B. of I. on the 30th day of December, 1964:

AND WHEREAS the Agreement of 1955 was determined by the Agreement of 1964:

NOW THEREFORE IT IS HEREBY AGREED between the parties hereto as follows:-

Determination of Agreement of 1964

1. The Agreement of 1964 is hereby determined but without prejudice to the continued operation of the said Agreement in respect of accidents occurring before the 31st day of December, 1988.

Enforcement of Agreement

2. M.I.B. of I. hereby agrees that a person claiming compensation (hereinafter referred to as "the claimant") may seek to enforce the provisions of this Agreement by-

    (1) making a claim to M.I.B. of I. for compensation which may be settled with or without admission of liability, or
    (2) citing as co-defendants M.I.B. of I. in any proceedings against the owner or user of the vehicle giving rise to the claim except where the owner and user of the vehicle remain unidentified or untraced, or
    (3) citing M.I.B. of I. as sole defendant where the claimant is seeking a court order for the performance of the Agreement by M.I.B. of I. provided the claimant has first applied for compensation to M.I.B. of I. under Sub-clause (1) of this Clause, and has either been refused compensation by M.I.B. of I. or has been offered compensation by M.I.B. of I. which the claimant considers to be inadequate.

Conditions Precedent to M.I.B. of I's Liability

3. The following shall be conditions precedent to M.I.B. of I's liability:

(1) The claimant or the claimant's legal representative shall have given notice in writing, by registered post, of intention to seek compensation:

   (a) in respect of personal injuries or death not later than three years from the date of the accident giving rise to the personal injuries or death;
   (b) in respect of damage to property not later than one year from the date of the accident giving rise to the damage to property.

(2) The claimant shall furnish M.I.B. of I. with all material information reasonably required in relation to the processing of the compensation claim including information relating to the relevant accident, personal injuries or death, medical treatment, funeral expenses, damage to property, and legal, professional or other costs reasonably incurred by or on behalf of the claimant.

(3) The claimant shall furnish M.I.B. of I. with copies of all relevant documentation in relation to the accident and any subsequent legal proceedings relating thereto, including copies of all correspondence, statements and pleadings.

(4) The claimant shall endeavour to establish if an approved policy of insurance covering the use, in a public place, of any vehicle involved in the accident exists by demanding or arranging for the claimant's legal representative to demand, insurance particulars (including policy number if available) of the user or owner of the vehicle in accordance with the provisions of section 73 of the Act.

(5) The claimant shall furnish M.I.B. of I. with details of any claim of which the claimant is aware made in respect of the damage to property arising from the accident under any policy of insurance or otherwise and any report made of which the claimant is aware or notification given to any person in respect of that damage or the use of the vehicle giving rise thereto, as M.I.B. of I. may reasonably require.

(6) Notice of proceedings shall be given by the claimant by registered post before commencement of such proceedings:-

   (i) to the insurer in any case in which there was in force at the time the accident occurred an approved policy of insurance purporting to cover the use of the vehicle and the existence of which is known before the commencement of proceedings to the person bringing same;
   (ii) to M.I.B. of I. in any other case.

(7) If so required by M.I.B. of I. and subject to full indemnity from M.I.B. of I. as to reasonable costs, the person bringing the proceedings (hereinafter called the Plaintiff) shall have taken or shall take all reasonable steps against any person against whom the Plaintiff might have a remedy in respect of or arising out of the injury or death or damage to property provided that any dispute as to the reasonableness of a requirement by M.I.B. of I. that any particular step should be taken to obtain judgment against any such person shall be referred to the Minister whose decision shall be final.

(8) The judgment or judgments (including such judgments as may be obtained under Sub-clause (7) of this Clause) shall be assigned to M.I.B. of I. or its nominee.

(9) The Plaintiff shall give credit to M.I.B. of I. for any amounts paid to him by or on behalf of the defendant in respect of any liability for injury to person or property arising out of the event which occasioned the claim against M.I.B. of I.

Satisfaction of Judgments by M.I.B. of I.

4. (1) Subject to the provisions of Sub-clause (2) of this Clause, if judgment in respect of any liability for injury to person or damage to property which is required to be covered by an approved policy of insurance under Section 56 of the Act is obtained against any person or persons in any court established under the Courts (Establishment and Constitution) Act, 1961 (No. 38 of 1961) whether or not such person or persons be in fact covered by an approved policy of insurance and any such judgment is not satisfied in full within 28 days from the date upon which the person or persons in whose favour such judgment is given become entitled to enforce it then M.I.B. of I. will so far as such judgment relates to injury to person or damage to property and subject to the provisions of these presents pay or cause to be paid to the person or persons in whose favour such judgment was given any sum payable or remaining payable thereunder in respect of the aforesaid liability including taxed costs (or such proportion thereof as is attributable to the relevant liability) or satisfy or cause to be satisfied such judgment whatever may be the cause of the failure of the judgment debtor to satisfy the same.

(2) Where a person has received benefit or compensation from any source in respect of damage to property, M.I.B. of I. may deduct from the sum payable or remaining payable under Sub-clause (1) of this Clause an amount equal to the amount of that benefit or compensation in addition to the deduction of any amounts by virtue of Sub-clauses (4) or (5) of Clause 7.

(3) Where a person applies to the M.I.B. of I. for compensation and no judgment has been obtained or is obtainable, M.I.B. of I. shall, as soon as is reasonably practicable, give a decision on the application and shall give reasons for the decision.

(4) Where M.I.B. of I. and the claimant agree an amount in respect of compensation, M.I.B. of I. shall pay such amount to the claimant within 28 days of such agreement being reached.

Exclusion of certain user and passenger claims

5. (1) Where at the time of an accident, the vehicle had been stolen or obtained by violence or threats of violence or used or taken possession of without the consent of the owner of the vehicle or other lawful authority, the liability of M.I.B. of I. shall not extend to any judgment or claim in respect of injury, death or damage to property sustained while the person injured or killed or the owner of the property damaged was the person or one of the persons who stole or obtained by violence or threats of violence the vehicle or who was in or on such vehicle in collusion with such person or persons, or knew it was stolen, taken by violence or threats of violence or without the consent of the owner.

(2) Where at the time of the accident the person injured or killed or who sustained damage to property knew, or ought reasonably to have known, that there was not in force an approved policy of insurance in respect of the use of the vehicle, the liability of M.I.B. of I. shall not extend to any judgment or claim either in respect of injury or death of such person while the person injured or killed was by his consent in or on such vehicle or in respect of damage to property while the owner of the property was by his consent in or on the vehicle or the property was in or on the vehicle with the consent of the owner of the property.

(3) Where a vehicle, the use of which is not covered by an approved policy of insurance, collides with another vehicle and the use of that other vehicle is also not covered by an approved policy of insurance, the liability of M.I.B. of I. shall not extend to any judgment or claim in respect of injury, death or damage to the property of the user of either vehicle.

Unidentified or untraced vehicle owner or user

6. In the case of an accident occurring on or after the 31st day of December, 1988, the liability of M.I.B. of I. shall extend to the payment of compensation for the personal injury or death of any person caused by the negligent driving of a vehicle in a public place, where the owner or user of the vehicle remains unidentified or untraced.

**Damage to
Property**

7. (1) The provisions of this Agreement extending the liability of M.I.B. of I. to
damage to property shall apply only to an accident occurring on or after the
31st day of December, 1992.

(2) The liability of M.I.B. of I. for damage to property shall not extend to damage
caused by a vehicle the owner or user of which remains unidentified or
untraced.

(3) The liability of M.I.B. of I. for damage to property shall not exceed the
minimum property damage cover required by section 56(2)(a) of the Act
applying at the time of the event giving rise to the claim.

(4) In the case of an accident occurring on or after the 31st day of December, 1992
and before the 31st day of December, 1995, the liability of M.I.B. of I. shall not
extend to the first £1,150 of damage to property suffered by any one property
owner.

(5) In the case of an accident occurring on or after the 31st day of December, 1995,
the liability of M.I.B. of I. shall not extend to:

(a) the first £175 of damage to property suffered by any one property owner
due to the negligent use of a vehicle stolen or obtained by violence or
threats of violence or used or taken possession of without the consent of
the owner of the vehicle or other lawful authority;

(b) subject to the provisions of the foregoing paragraph, the first £350 of
damage to property suffered by any one property owner due to the
negligent use of a vehicle, the use of which is not covered by an approved
policy of insurance.

**Period of
Agreement**

8. This Agreement shall be determinable by the Minister at any time or by M.I.B. of
I. on two years' notice, without prejudice to the continued operation of the
Agreement in respect of accidents occurring before the date of termination.

Recoveries

9. Nothing in this Agreement shall prevent any vehicle insurer from providing by
conditions in its contracts of insurance or by collateral agreements that all sums
paid by it on behalf of M.I.B. of I. or by M.I.B. of I. by virtue of the Principal
Agreement or of these presents in or towards the discharge of the liability of its
policyholders shall be recoverable by it or by M.I.B. of I. from the policyholder or
from any other person.

**Offers in
Satisfaction**

10. When notice of proceedings has been given under Clause 3 it shall be competent for
M.I.B. of I. not later than fourteen days after the closing of the pleadings to offer to
the Plaintiff in full satisfaction of the obligation of M.I.B. of I. such sum as it
considers sufficient in respect of damages together with the equivalent of the taxed
costs to date and if in that action the Plaintiff is awarded in respect of damages a
sum (exclusive of any amounts for which M.I.B. of I. would not be liable under this
Agreement) which is not more than the sum offered under this Clause (exclusive of
the sum for such taxed costs) then in satisfaction of this Agreement M.I.B. of I. shall
not be required to pay more than the total of such damages awarded less any
amounts for which it would not be liable under this Agreement and the sum
offered in respect of costs and shall be entitled to set off any costs incurred by them
after the date of the offer. M.I.B. of I. reserves the right to vary the amount offered
in satisfaction.

**State Vehicles
and Exempted
Persons**

11. (a) M.I.B. of I.'s acceptance of liability in respect of vehicles the use of which is
required to be covered by an approved policy of insurance shall
extend to vehicles owned by or in possession of the State or of an "exempted
person" as defined in section 60 of the Act only so long as there is in force an
approved policy of insurance purporting to cover the use of the vehicle.

(b) For the purpose of this Clause a vehicle which has been unlawfully removed
from the possession of the State or from an "exempted person" shall be taken to
continue in that possession whilst it is so removed.

Domestic Agreement

12. The Agreement entered into between M.I.B. of I. and the insurers of even date with the Agreement of 1955 and referred to in the Agreement of 1955 as "the Domestic Agreement" or any subsequent or amended agreement made in renewal or replacement of the said Domestic Agreement shall not discharge M.I.B. of I. from its liabilities or obligations under these presents.

Operation

13. This Agreement shall come into operation on the 31st day of December, 1988 in respect of claims arising out of the use of a vehicle in a public place on or after that date.

Definitions

14. In this Agreement, "the Act" means the Road Traffic Act, 1961 (No.24 of 1961): "Injury to person" does not include any injury by way of loss of services of the person injured.

IN WITNESS whereof the parties hereto have hereunto set their hands and affixed their seals on the day and year first herein written.

GIVEN under the Official Seal of the Minister for the Environment in the presence of:-

ALICE MULLEN

(L.S.)

MICHAEL J. MURPHY
Civil Servants,
Custom House, Dublin.

PADRAIG FLYNN
Minister for the Environment

Present when the Common Seal of the Motor Insurers' Bureau of Ireland was affixed hereto:-

N.S. MULVIN
Chairman

(L.S.)

J. DOOLIN
Council Member

JAMES V. DOYLE
Council Member

Appendix D: RIAI Form of Building Contract[*]

Liability,   21.   (a) Subject to sub-clause (c) the Contractor shall be liable for and shall indemnify the Employer
Indemnity and   against:-
Insurance for
Damage to Persons   (i)   (except for such loss or damage as is at the risk of the Employer under Clause 26 or 32(b)
and to Property.   where applicable) any liability, loss, claim or proceedings in respect of any injury or damage
                                   whatsoever to any property real or personal insofar as any such injury or damage arises
                                   out of or in the course of or by reason of the execution of the Works and provided that such
                                   injury or damage is due to any negligence, omission or default of the Contractor his
                                   servants or agents or any sub-contractor his servants or agents (whether or not also partly
                                   due to the negligence, omission or default of the Employer or of any person for whom the
                                   Employer is responsible);

                             (ii) any liability, loss, claim or proceedings whatsoever arising under any statute or at Common
                                   Law in respect of personal injury to or disease contracted by or the death of any person
                                   whomsoever arising out of or in the course of or caused by the execution of the Works
                                   unless solely due to any act or neglect of the Employer or of any person for whom the
                                   Employer is responsible.

                   (b) Subject to and in accordance with Clause 23, the Contractor shall take out before commencing
                   the Works and maintain Public Liability insurance and Employers Liability insurance covering any
                   liability, loss, claim or proceedings in respect of the matters referred to in sub-clause (a).

                   (c) Without prejudice to the Contractor's liability at Common Law or by statute sub-clause (a) shall
                   not apply to any liability, loss, claim or proceedings which arise otherwise than in connection with
                   an accident or fall within an exclusion permitted by Clause 23 (e) paragraph (i) or (ii) (as relevant)
                   and which is not covered by an Employers Liability or Public Liability insurance policy of the
                   Contractor.

All Risks   22.   (a) "Ancillary Items" shall in this clause and Clauses 23,24,25, and 30 mean temporary works and
Insurance.   all unfixed materials and goods delivered to and placed on or adjacent to and intended for the
                   Works except temporary buildings, plant, tools or equipment owned or hired by the Contractor or
                   any sub-contractor.

                   (b) Subject to and in accordance with Clause 23, the Contractor shall before commencing the
                   Works take out and shall until practical completion of the Works is certified by the Architect
                   maintain All Risks insurance covering any loss or damage to the Works and Ancillary Items from
                   any cause whatsoever for the full value of the Works and Ancillary Items from time to time plus the
                   "Percentage for Professional Fees" and the "Cost of Site Clearance" stated in the Appendix.

                   (c) The Contractor shall proceed with due diligence to make good any damage to or destruction
                   of the Works by any risk required to be insured by sub-clause (b). The money received under the
                   policy (less the portion included to cover professional fees which shall be paid to the employer)
                   shall be paid into a bank account in the joint names of the Contractor and the Employer. The
                   money shall be paid out with the interest earned to the Contractor by instalments under certificates
                   of the Architect related to the proportion of the work done and materials and goods delivered upon
                   the site for making good the damage or destruction. In respect of such payments Clause 35 (a)
                   and (b) shall apply mutatis mutandis and without deduction of any amount to be retained by the
                   Employer. The Contractor shall not be entitled to any payment in respect of the rebuilding, repair
                   or replacement of the Works or Ancillary Items destroyed or damaged other than the money
                   received under the policy. Where as a result of any variation by the Employer of the Works a
                   balance remains in the said account after completion of making good by the Contractor as required
                   by the Employer the balance shall be paid to the Employer together with the interest earned on
                   that balance.

Contractor's   23.   (a) The Contractor's policies under Clauses 21 and 22 shall be with insurers approved by the
Insurance   Employer, which approval shall not be unreasonably withheld.
Policies.
                   (b) The Contractor's Employers and Public Liability policies under Clause 21(b) shall include
                   provisions by which in the event of any claim in respect of which the Contractor would be entitled
                   to receive indemnity under the policy being brought or made against the Employer the Insurer will
                   indemnify the Employer against such claims and any costs, charges and expenses in respect
                   thereof.

                   (c) The Contractor's All Risks policy under Clause 22 shall be in the joint names of the Contractor
                   and the Employer.

(d) The Contractor shall comply with all conditions in any policy or policies of insurance under Clause 21 or 22.

(e) The Contractor's policies under Clauses 21 and 22 may contain only the exclusions from cover summarised below worded as specified in sub-clause (g):

(i) Employers Liability   "Limited war risk".

(ii) Public Liability...   "Liability in excess of the sum stated in the Appendix to these Conditions of Contract for any one accident".
"War risks".
"Radioactive contamination/nuclear explosion".
"Sonic boom".
"Persons under a contract of service or apprenticeship with the Insured".
"Property belonging to the Insured or in the Insured's custody and control, with exceptions".
"Defective workmanship and materials but not damage resulting therefrom".
"Mechanically propelled vehicles to which the Road Traffic Act applies".
"Loss or damage due to design".

(iii) All Risks...   "War risks, riot and civil commotion".
"Radioactive contamination/nuclear explosion".
"Sonic boom".
"Loss or damage due to design".
"Defective workmanship and materials but not damage resulting therefrom".

"Wear and tear".
"Consequential losses".
"Limited mechanically propelled vehicles".
"Loss or damage due to use, occupation or possession by or on behalf of the Employer".

(f) Without prejudice to Clause 32 if any damage or loss shall occur to the Works or Ancillary Items which is not effectively insured by the policy under Clause 22 (b) by reason of use, occupation or possession of the whole or any part of the Works by or on behalf of the Employer (other than by the Contractor, his servants or agents) which renders the policy void or voidable Clause 24 (a) and (b) shall apply whether or not such use or occupation is permitted by the Contract or with the consent of the Contractor and so that the Employer shall have no claim against the Contractor for such damage or loss whether or not due to any negligence or default of the Contractor, his servants or agents.

NOTE: Before using, occupying or taking possession of any part of the Works for any purpose, however temporary or trivial, the Employer must ensure that full insurance cover will remain in force for any damage to the Works or Ancillary Items and also that he will be covered for any injury or damage caused by such use etc. The Architect should make certain that the necessary cover is provided either through the Contractor's policy, with any necessary adjustment agreed with the Contractor's insurers, or by special policies taken out by the Employer. Refer also to Clause 32.

(g) The Royal Institute of the Architects of Ireland, the Construction Industry Federation and the Society of Chartered Surveyors acting jointly shall publish from time to time permitted wordings of the exclusions from insurance cover permitted by sub-clause (e) and this clause shall take effect as if the permitted wordings of the authorised exclusions at the Designated Date were set out in sub-clause (e).

(h) The Contractor shall before commencing the Works produce to the Employer for inspection any policy or policies of insurance required by Clauses 21 and 22 together with the receipt in respect of premiums paid under such policy or policies and should the Contractor make default in insuring or maintaining insurance the Employer may himself insure against any risk with respect to which the default shall have occurred and may deduct a sum equal to the amount paid in respect of premiums from any money due or to become due to the Contractor.

Damage due to Excluded Risks   **24.**   The following provisions shall apply to any loss or damage to the Works or Ancillary Items from any risk which the Contractor is permitted to exclude by Clause 23 and is excluded from the Contractor's All Risks insurance other than such design risks as are dealt with in Clause 25 (without prejudice to any liability of the Contractor to the Employer for the negligence of the Contractor, his servants or agents):-

(a)   the occurrence of such loss or damage shall be disregarded in computing any amounts payable to the Contractor under this contract;

(b) (i)   if it is just and equitable to do so the employment of the Contractor under this Contract may within twenty working days of the occurrence of such loss or damage be determined at the option of either party by notice sent to the other by registered post or recorded delivery to the principal place of business or last known address of the other party. Within (but not after) five working days of receiving such notice either party may give to the other a written request to concur in the appointment of an arbitrator under Clause 38 of these Conditions in order that it may be determined whether such determination would be just and equitable,

(ii) upon the expiration of five working days of receipt of a notice of determination or, where reference to arbitration is made, upon the arbitrator upholding the notice of determination, the provision of sub-clause (b) except sub-paragraph (v) of Clause 34 of these Conditions shall apply;

(c) if no notice of determination is served or where a reference to arbitration is made, if the arbitrator does not uphold the notice of determination, then

(i) the Contractor with due diligence shall reinstate or make good such loss or damage, and proceed with the carrying out and completion of the Works,

(ii) the reinstatement and making good of such loss or damage to the Works or Ancillary Items and (when required) the removal and disposal of debris shall be deemed to be a variation ordered by the Architect.

Damage due to Design
25. Notwithstanding Clauses 23 (e) (iii) and 24 the Contractor shall proceed with due diligence to repair, rebuild or make good at his own expense any damage to or destruction of the Works or Ancillary Items due to any fault, defect, error or omission in design by the Contractor, his servants or agents (including sub-contractors and suppliers, other than Nominated Sub-Contractors or Nominated Suppliers).

Responsibility for existing Structures.
26. *The existing structures together with the contents thereof shall be at the sole risk of the Employer as regards loss or damage by fire, storm, tempest, flood, bursting or overflowing of water tanks apparatus or pipes or explosion. The Employer shall maintain from the commencement of the Works until the completion by the Contractor of all Works (including the making good of defects) under the Contract a proper policy of insurance against the said risks. The Employer shall before commencement of the Works produce such policy to the Contractor for inspection with the receipt for the last premium paid for its renewal and should the Employer make default in insuring or maintaining insurance the Contractor may himself insure against any risk with respect to which the default shall have occurred and for that purpose shall have such right of entry and inspection as may be required to make a survey and inventory of the existing structures and contents and shall upon production of the receipt for any premium paid by him be entitled to have its amount added to the Contract Sum. If any loss or damage shall be caused to the existing structures by any of the said risks or by war, riot or civil commotion then the terms of Clause 24 (b) shall apply.

War Damage.
27. No liability shall attach to the Contractor under this Contract for any damage to the Works or unfixed materials caused by war, invasion, act of foreign enemy, hostilities (whether war be declared or not), civil war, civil commotion, rebellion, revolution, insurrection or military or usurped power.

BIBLIOGRAPHY

"Injuries Caused by Growing Trees", 25 Ir. Jur. 20 (1959).

"Roots of Trees: Liability for Injury Caused to Neighbour's Premises", 6 Ir. Jur. 20 (1940).

"The Impact of Liability Insurance", 57 Yale L.J. 549 (1948).

Allen (1995), "Liability for References", 58 MLR 553.

Anson (1982), *Law of Contract,* 25th edition, Oxford: Clarendon Press.

Atiyah, P.S. (1993), *Accidents, Compensation and the Law*, 5th Edition, London: Butterworth.

Atiyah, P.S. (1995), *Sale of Goods*, 7th Edition, London: Pitman.

Bacon (1630), *Maxims of the Law*.

Baer (1990), 22 Ottawa Law Review 389, 410.

Barrington, Mr Justice (Chair), "Report of the Commission of Inquiry on Health and Welfare at Work" (PL 1868).

Batten, A.G.M. and W.A. Dinsdale (1960), *Third Party Insurance,* London: Stone and Cox.

Beatson, J. (1992) "Reforming the Law of Contract for the Benefit of Third Parties: A Second Bite at the Cherry," 45 CLP 1.

Benjamin (1992), *Sale of Goods*, 5th Edition, London: Sweet and Maxwell.

Binchy and Byrne (1995), "The Extension of the Scope of Breach of Statutory Duty for Accidents at Work", *Irish Law Times*, Jan/Feb.

Birds, John (1977), "The Statement of Insurance Practice: A Measure of Regulation of the Insurance Contract", 40 MLR 677.

Birds, John (1993), *Modern Insurance Law*, 3rd Edition, London: Sweet and Maxwell.

Burrows, A. (1996), "Reforming Privity of Contract", LMCLQ.

Cheshire Fifoot and Furmston (1986), *Law of Contract*, Eleventh edition, London: Butterworth.

Clarke, M.A. (1994), *The Law of Insurance Contracts,* Second Edition, London: Lloyds of London Press.

Clayton, G. (1971), *British Insurance*, London: Eleck Books.

Coopers and Lybrand (1993), "Costs and Cover: Private Motor Insurance in the Republic of Ireland and the UK", Dublin: Coopers and Lybrand.

Corbin, A. (1930), "Contracts for the Benefit of Third Persons" 46 LQR 12.

Corrigan, M. (1987), "Warranties and the Duty of Disclosure" *Irish Broker*.

Corrigan, Michael (1993), "IIF's Codes of Practice and their Legal Implications", *Irish Broker*, January/February.

Corrigan, Michael and Campbell, John (1995), *Casebook of Irish Insurance Law*, Dublin: Oak Tree Press.

Cross (1990), *Cross on Evidence*, 7th Edition, London: Butterworth.

Deloitte and Touche (1996), "Report on the Economic Evaluation of Insurance Costs in Ireland", October.

Demosthenes, *Private Orations*, Loeb Classics Vol. 1.

Denning (1979), *The Discipline of the Law*, London: Butterworths.

Denning, Alfred Baron (1979), *The Discipline of the Law*, London: Butterworths.

Dickson, P.G.M. (1960), *The Sun Insurance Office 1710–1960*, London: Oxford University Press.

Dover, V. (1962), *A Handbook to Marine Insurance*, 6th Edition, London: Witherby.

Dowrick, F. (1956) "A *Jus Quaesitum Tertio* by Way of Contract in English Law" 19 MLR 374.

Ekelaar (1973), "Nuisance and Strict Liability", 8 Ir. Jur.

Ellis, Henry (1990), "Disclosure and Good Faith in Insurance Contracts" *Irish Law Times*, February.

Ellis, Henry (1990), "Consumer Rights and Insurance Contracts — Some Imminent Reforms", *Dlí*, Autumn.

Emerson (1992), *University of Miami Law Review* 907, 952.

Fleming, John G. (1977), *The Law of Torts,* 5th Edition, Sydney: Law Books.

Forde, M. (1990), *Commercial Law in Ireland*, Dublin: Butterworth.

Forte, A.D.M. (1986), "The Revised Statements of Insurance Practice", MLR Vol. 49.

Fridman (1990), *Law of Agency*, 6th Edition, London: Butterworth.

Friedman and Ladinskey (1967), "Social Change and the Law of Industrial Accidents", 67 Columbia Law Review.

Friedman (1970), "Punitive Damages in Tort", 48 Can. Bar Rev. 373.

Furmston, M. (1960), "Return to *Dunlop* v *Selfridge?*" 23 MLR 373.

Gearty (1989), "The Place of Private Nuisance in a Modern Law of Torts", Camb. LJ 214.

Hardy Ivamy, E.R. (1986), *General Principles of Insurance Law*, 5th Edition, London: Butterworth.

Harnett and Thornton (1948), "Insurable Interest in Property: A Socio-Economic Re-evaluation of a Legal Concept", 48 Col. L. Rev. 1162.

Hasson, R. (1971), "The Basis of the Contract Clause in Insurance Law", 34 MLR 29.

Hasson, R. (1996), "Insurance Contracts: Construction of the Policy and the Policy of Construction", LMCQ.

Hepple and Mathews (1985), *Tort: Cases and Materials*, 3rd Edition, London: Butterworths.

Holmes, O.W. (1881), *The Common Law*, Boston: Little, Brown.

Insurance Institute of London (1967), "A Study of the General Application of Average in the Light of Continuing Inflation", Report of Advanced Study Group No. 184, Insurance Institute of London.

Insurance Institute of London (1994), "Liability Insurance and Compensation", CII Advanced Study Group No. 225, September, Insurance Institute of London.

Insurance Ombudsman in Ireland, 1993 Annual Report.

Insurance Ombudsman in Ireland, 1994 Annual Report.

Insurance Ombudsman in Ireland, 1995 Annual Report.

Irish Insurance Federation (1996), "Insurance Update" No. 43, July.

Jackson and Powell (1987), *Professional Negligence,* London: Sweet and Maxwell.

Jacob Feld (1964), *Lessons from Failures of Concrete Structures*, American Concrete Institute and the Iowa State University Press.

James and Thornton (1950), "Impact of Insurance on the Law of Torts", 15 Law & Cont. Prob. 431.

Keeton, R.E. (1970), "Insurance Law Rights at Variance with Policy Provisions", 83 Harvard Law Review 961, 967.

Keeton, R.E. (1971), *Insurance Law: A Basic Text*, St. Paul, Minn: West Publishing Co.

Kimball, *Insurance and Public Policy*.

Law Commission (1980), "Non-disclosure and Breach of Warranty", Report No. 104.

Law Commission Consultative (1995), "Damages for Personal Injury non-pecuniary Loss",. Paper No. 140.

Law Reform Commission, "Personal Injuries: Period Payments, Structured Settlements".

Law Reform Commission (1987), "The Statute of Limitations: Claims in Respect of Latent Personal Injuries", Report No. 21.

Law Reform Committee (1957), "Report on Conditions and Exceptions in Insurance Policies", Cmnd. 62.

Lewis, Richard (1985), "Insurers' Agreements not to Enforce Strict Legal Rights: Bargaining with Government and in the Shadow of the Law", MLR Vol. 48.

McAleese, Dermot (Chair) (1996), "Growth and Development of the Irish Insurance Industry: Report of the Joint Working Group of the Federation of Irish Insurers and the Department of Enterprise and Employment", March.

McGillivray and Parkington (1988), *Insurance Law*, 8th Edition, London: Sweet and Maxwell.

McGrath (1983), "Negligence — The Reception of *Hedley Byrne* into Ireland" 5 DULJ 296.

McGregor (1965), "Compensation versus Punishment in Damages Awards", 28 Mod. L.Rev. 629.

McGregor (1971), "In Defence of Lord Devlin", 34 Mod. L. Rev. 520.

McIntosh, D. and M. Holmes (1994), *Personal Injury Awards in EU and EFTA Countries*, London: Lloyd's of London Press.

McMahon and Binchy (1990), *Irish Law of Torts*, 2nd edition, Dublin: Butterworth (Ireland) Ltd.

Newark (1949), "The Boundaries of Nuisance", 65 LQ Rev 480.

Park, J.A. (1790), *Law of Marine Insurance*, London: T.W. Rieldon.

Park, J.A. (1842), *System of the Law of Marine Insurance*, London: Butterworth.

Patterson, Edwin W. (1964), "The Interpretation and Construction of Contracts", 64 *Columbia Law Review* 833–835.

Pike, David R. (1991) *Irish Insurance Directory, 1990–1991*, Dublin: Bentos Publications Ltd.

Prosser, W. (1971), *Law of Torts*, 4th Edition, St. Paul, Minn.: West.

Raynes, Harold E. (1964), *History of British Insurance,* 2nd Edition, London: Pitman and Sons Ltd.

Redgrave (1982), *Health and Safety in Factories*, 2nd edition, London: Butterworths.

Reynolds, F.M.B. (1985), *Bowstead on Agency*, 15th edition, London: Sweet and Maxwell.

Riley (1996), *Business Interruption Insurance,* 7th edition, London: Sweet and Maxwell.

Salmond and Heuston (1987), *The Law of Torts*, 19th Edition, London: Sweet and Maxwell.

Santarem, Pedro (1552), "Tractatus de Assecurationibus & Sponsionibus Mercatorum".

Shavell, S. (1987), *Economic Analysis of Tort Law*, Cambridge, Mass.: Harvard U.P.

Sugarman (1985), "Doing away with Tort Law", California Law Review, Vol. 17.

Trenerry, Prof. C.F. (1926), *The Origins and Early History of Insurance*, London: King and Son.

Vance (1909), *Select Essays in Anglo-American Legal History*.

White, John (1987), "Exemplary Damages in Irish Tort Law," 5 ILTR 60.

Wilson, J. (1996) "A Flexible Contract of Carriage — The Third Dimension," LMCLQ 187.

Winfield (1931), "Nuisance as a Tort", 4 Camb LJ 189.

INDEX